TEACHING CIVIC ENGAGEMENT
GLOBALLY

ELIZABETH C. MATTO
ALISON RIOS MILLETT McCARTNEY
ELIZABETH A. BENNION
ALASDAIR BLAIR
TAIYI SUN
DAWN MICHELE WHITEHEAD

AMERICAN POLITICAL SCIENCE ASSOCIATION

Designed by Henry E. Chen

Photo Credits
Cover: Designed by Henry E. Chen. Background image: Chris Gorgio/Getty; Inside the globe from top left to bottom right: Woman presenting (Weedezign/Getty); Black Lives Matter protest (Chris Henry/Unsplash); University students (Nadasaki/Getty); Students (KanchitDon/Getty); Protester (Jacoblund/Getty); Students (Fizkes/Getty); Parkland vigil (Matthew Botha/Getty); Students raising hands (Drazen Zigic/Getty); Smiling student (Wavebreakmedia/Getty); Section I photograph (KanchitDon/Getty); Section II photograph (Drazen Zigic/Getty); Section III photograph (Fizkes/Getty); Section IV photograph: Madeleine Meyer, Taryn Painter, Connor Cameron, and Lewis Laury (Alexander Wright, Towson University).

ISBN (Soft Cover): 978-1-878147-64-6
ISBN (Fixed Layout ePUB): 978-1-878147-65-3

For teacher-scholars in all parts of the world engaged in the important work of teaching democratic citizenship.

Table of Contents

Section I: Global Civic Engagement Education: Ideas, Directions, Collaborations

Section II: Civic Engagement Pedagogy Across the Globe

Section III: Creating Institutions for Civic Engagement Education

Section IV: Civic Engagement Pedagogy Across the Globe

List of Tables and Figures

Chapter 10

Chapter 12

Chapter 13

Chapter 14

Chapter 15

Chapter 17

Preface

Steven Rathgeb Smith

American Political Science Association

In recent years, political polarization has been increasing in many countries around the world. Moreover, threats to democracy and key political institutions are on the rise. Social media has also allowed the spread of misinformation, further undermining the democratic process. Authoritarian political leaders have in turn taken advantage of a chaotic political environment to push through policies that centralize power and reduce the accountability and transparency of government. Given the volatility and unpredictability of different countries' politics, active citizenship becomes increasingly important for the future of democracy and good governance. Citizens participating in their communities through the electoral process and civil society organizations are critical to the building of social capital and effective public policies. This active citizenship requires comprehensive and informed civic education from elementary and secondary schools through higher education institutions. This widespread interest and support for civic education is also reflected in the current legislation in the US Congress entitled *Civics Secures Democracy Act*; if passed, this legislation would authorize the funding for civic education throughout the country.

Civic education is central to the mission of political science as a major social science discipline. Political science courses provide essential instruction on the critical elements of a democracy, the structure of government, the electoral process, and local community organizations. Moreover, political scientists through their teaching promote civic engagement and encourage students to consider participating in their local community and the public sphere more generally. Many political science courses also directly connect students to local public and nonprofit organizations engaged in their local communities. In recent years, political scientists have been increasingly active in supporting the civic engagement of their students and more broadly their local communities. Many political scientists are also very active in conducting research and innovation in civic education.

APSA actively strengthens and supports our members' important work on civic engagement and education. For instance, the APSA RAISE the Vote initiative was launched in 2019 with the specific goal of collecting and developing resources to "amplify and increase student engagement" in the 2020 United States elections. The initiative's resources ranged from teaching guides and activities to blog posts about political science research on voting and political participation. Further, in 2020, the association added a new civic engagement organized section representing over 200 political scientists, which will promote "the teaching of and scholarship in civic engagement" and will recognize scholarship and teaching innovation in that field. Recently, the association has also launched *APSA Educate*, an online resource site for teaching and learning resources including material on teaching civic engagement. The amount of materials continues to grow as does the utilization by members and the broader public. APSA has also increased its ongoing investment in supporting teaching and learning in political science more broadly by offering options such as workshops, webinars and innovative programming at the APSA annual meeting, including an all-day intensive conference on teaching and learning called TLC at APSA.

The publication of this important new book, *Teaching Civic Engagement Globally*, reflects the high priority placed on civic engagement and teaching and learning by the association. In 2013, APSA published *Teaching Civic Engagement: From Student to Active Citizen*, which demonstrated how civic engagement could be taught across all subfields of political science as well as a companion website. This book was then followed by *Teaching Civic Engagement Across the Disciplines* in 2017. These initial two books have been widely used by students and faculty. The latest book reflects the growth of interest by scholars, faculty, students, and policymakers in civic education worldwide. Thus, the chapters include a wide variety of diverse contributions from many different countries reflecting the innovation and creativity that political scientists are bringing to the teaching of civic engagement. The broad span of contributions reflects the increasing importance of civic education in higher education institutions worldwide and the desire to connect students to real-world experiences of civic engagement that will help to spur them to become life-long active citizens. In particular, the teaching of civic engagement has greatly benefited from the upsurge in informed research on best pedagogical practices, as reflected in this book as well as the increase in articles on teaching civic engagement in the key APSA journals, the *Journal of Political Science Education* (JPSE) and *PS: Political Science & Politics*.

The growth and development of the APSA portfolio of programs on teaching civic engagement also reflects changes in higher education, including the professoriate and students. Even prior to the COVID-19 pandemic, higher education was relying much more extensively on online and hybrid instructional methods, offering new methods of course delivery and the ability to reach more students such as the growing number of non-traditional students. Also, more students from many varied backgrounds are attending university. A younger generation of faculty are also more adept at social media and new technology. Consequently, exciting innovation is occurring in the classroom regarding the teaching of political science and civic engagement in particular, as illustrated by the many fine chapters in this new book.

I would like to express my great appreciation for the excellent leadership work of the co-editors, Elizabeth C. Matto, Alison Rios Millett McCartney, Elizabeth A. Bennion, Alasdair Blair, Taiyi Sun, and Dawn Whitehead. This impressive book is truly international in scope and ambition, representing the growing movement on teaching civic engagement and top-notch research underway on effective teaching practices. Terrific support for this project has been provided by Jon Gurstelle, APSA Publishing Director, and Henry Chen, APSA Managing Editor. Our goal is to encourage extensive utilization of this book; consequently, the book is formatted and designed to be easily accessible with separate downloadable chapters. As with the previous books, the companion website will serve as a supplement as well as a dynamic resource for civic engagement scholar-practitioners with links to other APSA programs and services.

This timely book is a great contribution to the literature on civic engagement around the world. Politics is polarized, and democracy is under threat in many countries. Thus, citizens need information and opportunities to be active citizens, including participation in the electoral process and the activities of civil society organizations. *Teaching Civic Engagement Globally* is a very welcome contribution to our understanding of education to promote civic engagement and hence a more robust democracy.

Foreword:

The Urgency of Teaching Civic Engagement Globally

Lynn Pasquerella

Association of American Colleges & Universities

The stunning attack on the US Capitol Building on January 6, 2021, by insurrectionists signaled not only the growing expansiveness of partisan divides and polarization in America but also the fragility of democracy. Amidst a global pandemic and economic crisis that has spurred racist and xenophobic attacks, the violent attempt to disrupt a free and fair election was also emblematic of a worldwide trend toward tyranny and authoritarianism. Indeed, Freedom House's most recent report on political rights and civil liberties, _Freedom in the World 2021_, highlights a long-term democratic decline reflected in a narrative chronicling the 15th consecutive year of waning global freedom.[1]

Characterized by government disinformation campaigns and lack of transparency, censorship, voter suppression, and the use of excessive force in response to protest movements, the burgeoning assault on democracy calls for renewed global leadership and solidarity among democratic states. It also creates a sense of urgency for colleges and universities to respond to the invitation to lead by reaffirming, articulating, and demonstrating the value of civic education in safeguarding democracy and countering authoritarianism.

Championing a liberal education allied to democracy is grounded in an understanding that democracy is not self-sustaining but depends instead on the sustained engagement of free people united in their commitment to the fundamental principles of justice, liberty, human dignity, and the equality of persons. It is an education that empowers all students at every type of institution with both the knowledge and skills and the habits of heart and mind that have the capacity to liberate their thinking, equip them for, and dispose them to the creation of a more just, equitable, and inclusive society through civic involvement.

Liberal education was validated as the form of education most appropriate to advancing democracy in a 2020 report by Anthony Carnevale and his colleagues at Georgetown's Center for Education and the Workforce. "The Role of Education in Taming Authoritarian Attitudes" examines the purpose of colleges and universities in relation to the challenge of rising authoritarianism at the global level and the subsequent threat to democracies.[2] Citing the power of higher education in mitigating against authoritarian tendencies, the study's findings confirm that college graduates at both the bachelor's degree and associate degree levels are less likely to express authoritarian preferences and attitudes than those with less education, particularly when students are exposed to a liberal arts education, with an emphasis of critical analysis and speaking across differences.[3]

According to the study, liberal arts education reduces individuals' sensitivities to potential triggers by providing psychological protection in the form of self-esteem, personal security, and autonomy. It also fosters a level of interpersonal trust associated with lower inclinations toward expressing authoritarian attitudes and preferences. The capacity to deal with complexity and diversity and not be threatened by differences of opinion is significant given that perceptions of threat—to physical safety, economic security, group identity, social norms—often activate authoritarian tendencies. Exposure of liberal arts majors to diverse contexts, histories, ideas, lifestyles, religions, ways of life, and cultures diminishes the likelihood that differing worldviews will trigger authoritarian responses and increases the chances of their being countered with evidence.

In addition, the findings reveal that postsecondary education leads to greater political participation and civic engagement. This, in turn, decreases tendencies toward authoritarianism, regardless of political affiliation. Because democracies with higher levels of education have greater levels of political tolerance and are more likely to survive, the report concludes that "higher education is the cornerstone of successful democracies not easily shaken by authoritarian threats."[4]

Preparing students for success in addressing the complex problems of the future in an interdependent, rapidly changing world necessitates the creation of a critical public culture, the fostering of moral and sympathetic imagination, and a focus on global citizenship. The essays contained in *Teaching Civic Engagement Globally* offer case studies, models of excellence, insights, and global perspectives on how colleges and universities can, and must, play a leadership role in catalyzing institutional transformation that centers civic engagement and democratic participation in the curriculum and co-curriculum. In the process, they remind us of the importance of all institutions of higher education serving as anchor institutions, committed to the idea that the success of colleges and universities is inextricably linked to the economic, social, psychological, physical, and educational well-being of those in the communities in which they are located. Moreover, at this moment of extraordinary opportunity to reimagine higher education, they inspire us to engage in greater collaboration in working toward our shared objectives around teaching civic engagement globally.

Endnotes

1. Freedom House, "Freedom in the World 2021: Democracy Under Siege," (Washington, DC: Freedom House, 2021). https://freedomhouse.org/report/freedom-world/2021/democracy-under-siege.

2. Anthony P. Carnevale, Nicole Smith, Lenka Dražanová, Artem Gulish, and Kathryn Peltier Campbell, "The Role of Education in Taming Authoritarian Attitudes," (Washington, DC: Center on Education and the Workforce, 2020). https://cew.georgetown.edu/cew-reports/authoritarianism.

3. Lynn Pasquerella, "Liberal Education and Threats to Democracy," *Liberal Education* 106, no. 3 (2020). https://www.aacu.org/liberaleducation/2020/fall/president.

4. Ibid.

Acknowledgments

T he call for submissions for *Teaching Civic Engagement Globally* was released in the spring of 2020 as the COVID-19 global health emergency was just taking hold. The months that have followed have been marked by tremendous loss of life, economic devastation, and social turmoil with the impact of this health emergency revealing stark and systemic inequities worldwide. The editors acknowledge all those who have been involved in the publication of this book and thank them for their dedication and perseverance under very difficult circumstances.

We are grateful to Steven Rathgeb Smith, Executive Director of the American Political Science Association (APSA), for his consistent support of this book and the companion website as well as the previous publications on teaching civic engagement. We also thank Tanya Schwarz, the former Director of Teaching and Learning at APSA, for the international partnerships she forged that served as the impetus of this book and for her early support of this text. Jon Gurstelle, APSA's Director of Publishing, and Henry Chen, editorial and publications associate, have been great partners in the preparation and publication of this book. Thank you also Clarissa Noqueira, APSA's Manager of Communications & Web Development, who offered support with the companion website. We thank Lynn Pasquerella, President of the Association of American Colleges and Universities (AAC&U), for not only the foreword she contributed to this text but also her commitment to global learning and engagement. The editors are incredibly grateful to Dick Simpson, professor of political science at the University of Illinois at Chicago, for the advisory role he played in the preparation of this book and for his contribution.

This text is rooted within a broader set of discussions and debates about democratic education and pedagogy, and the editors are grateful to colleagues we've met at various teaching and learning conferences who have contributed to our thinking on teaching civic engagement globally. This publication builds upon *Teaching Civic Engagement: From Student to Active Citizen* and *Teaching Civic Engagement Across the Disciplines* but also marks the start of a new process of bringing global democratic teaching and learning together.

Our students have played a meaningful role in the publication of *Teaching Civic Engagement Globally*. Early on, Cecilia Ritacco of Rutgers University and Cassie Rezac from Towson University prepared a rich database of teacher-scholars of civic engagement education from around the world, an invaluable resource as we disseminated our call for submissions. Kayla Isenbletter and David Hurley from the Indiana University South Bend have offered great support with copyediting draft manuscripts and compiling the bibliography at the end of the book, and Rutgers University's Jackson Snellman has assisted with preparing components of the website and the launch of the book.

The editors also thank the Eagleton Institute of Politics at Rutgers, The State University of New Jersey; the Towson University Office of the Provost and Office of Civic Engagement and Social Responsibility; Indiana University South Bend's Research & Development Committee; the Office of Global Citizenship for Campus, Communities, and Careers at AAC&U; Christopher Newport University's Office of Undergraduate Research and Creative Activity; and De Montfort University's social impact and engagement team.

Finally, we thank our families for their unending patience throughout this effort.

Global Civic Engagement Education: Ideas, Directions, Collaborations

Introduction

Alasdair Blair[1] and Alison Rios Millett McCartney[2]

1. De Montfort University; 2. Towson University

One of the most notable global trends in recent years has been an increasingly held view among the electorate in democratic countries that there is something wrong with their system of government. Although frustration and discontent by the electorate is not a particularly recent phenomenon in relation to specific country studies, the prevalence of this discontent and questioning of the value of democratic institutions and processes is new in the context of global changes. In a recent study based on a dataset from four million people in democracies around the world, Foa et al. found that dissatisfaction with democracy has risen since 1973, hitting an all-time global high in developed democracies in 2019.[1] These numbers are particularly troubling amongst 18–34-year-olds (55%), as this group has the steepest increase in dissatisfaction with democracy and is double the rate of dissatisfaction of the previous generation when they were at the same age. The study's authors posit that this discontent is due to the widespread belief amongst millennials that democracy is not solving common problems like climate change and inequality, while also not creating pathways for their futures.[2] While youth participation in elections has briefly risen in some countries due to highly controversial elections or referendums, the overall global trend has not been positive for many years.[3]

What then are the implications of these developments for the study of civic engagement education, and what might be done to remedy this challenge? In the first instance, we argue that this lack of practicing skills and values of democracy is directly correlated to a decline in civic engagement education. As Dewey told us over a century ago and Butin has reminded us, we have to educate each and every generation about democracy and the skills and values of democracy to maintain democracy because democratic citizens are not just "born."[4] More recently, in his study of the turmoil of US politics, Thomas Carothers has rightly noted that in responding to a decline in the public's trust in democracy, it would be wrong to simply blame the democratic model and to consider that other systems of governance might be better, which would be "misguided thinking."[5] Rather, we need to think about what factors might be leading to this state of affairs and how we might remedy this situation. In addressing this challenge, this book builds upon our two previous works, *Teaching Civic Engagement: From Student to Active Citizen* (2013) and *Teaching Civic Engagement Across the Disciplines* (2017), and seeks to provide pedagogical tools, evidence, and arguments for how colleges and universities can be active players in reversing rising challenges to democracy and trends of low participation across the world. For if we do not, we face backsliding into the authoritarianism and disregard for human rights that was so prevalent in previous centuries and that we spent the last century fighting to eliminate.

How Did We Get Here?

The first 20 years of the 21st century showed that people all around the world want democracy. From the expansion of the European Union (EU) to the Arab Spring, mass movements and major government decisions seemed to bring more democratic principles such as respect for human rights and free and fair elections to more people. This focus on democratic transformation has been a notable feature of world politics since 1945, and particularly so since the end of the Cold War, as technology increasingly connected people around the world via new tools for trade, communication, information, and entertainment. Francis Fukuyama famously considered the end of the Cold War to be "the end of history."[6] For Fukuyama, what this phrase represented was an end to the conflict between the different ideological systems of fascism, communism, and liberal democracies. In essence, for Fukuyama, liberal democracy had become the only "tried, tested and viable form of government,"[7] and it was assumed that the people's preference for democracy would continue on unquestioned.

Some three decades on from the end of the Cold War, we can and should question such a viewpoint. While liberal democracy might be regarded as an optimal form of government,[8] it is also the case that democracies increasingly are under threat, most notably from the rise of populism and corruption. At one extreme, challenges facing democracies might be a reaction to their new status and vulnerability, with newly created democratic structures being less resilient to the cut and thrust of democratic debates. Even though there is an element of truth to such an argument, it is also the case that there is a broader, and in many ways more systemic, change that is occurring in relation to the globalization of the world economy wherein power is being transferred from established democracies to the emerging economies of China and India in particular. This change in turn is impacting societies' confidence levels within established democracies,[9] with electorates expressing a frustration with the decisions that their governments face and sometimes simultaneously having unrealistic expectations that are shaped by an element of lack of understanding of the underlying factors that influence the policies within their countries.

Such a state of affairs has led to a more divisive level of debate among elected politicians, who when faced with challenges from the electorate often fail to tackle the more systemic (and painful) issues that afflict their countries in favor of what are often short-term and populist policies. This anti-democracy threat has been a particular feature of European democracies in recent decades, where a populist tide is being significantly influenced by a sense of insecurity among national electorates in the face of pressures such as economic downturns and migration. In some European countries, these pressures have led to more favorable attitudes towards strongman leadership, most recently in the Baltic states of Latvia and Lithuania.[10] In other countries such as Brazil, the Philippines, and Turkey, democratic systems have been eroded by increasingly authoritarian leaders who use perceived and/or real security threats, in addition to economic issues and migration, to promote the power of an individual leader who is not checked by audit, compliance, and accountability measures. These cases have led to the emergence of what has become known as "illiberal democracies." This seemingly contradictory condition has become a feature of not only fragile states, but also more established democracies.[11] While such developments have often been relatively bloodless, such as with the rise of Victor Orbán in Hungary, it is nevertheless the case that at a global level, from El Salvador to the Democratic Republic of Congo, and from Afghanistan to Ukraine, violence is still used by many leaders as a primary tool to run governments, control others, and violate the people's rights.

Thus, rather than the optimistic and somewhat rose-tinted view of the world that many hoped for after the end of the Cold War, the last three decades have witnessed significant conflict. This violence has ranged from the breakup of Yugoslavia and the genocide in Rwanda in the early 1990s, through to the invasions of Iraq and Afghanistan in the first decade of the twenty-first century, and more recent conflicts in Myanmar and South Sudan. At a global level, the Middle East and North Africa are particularly fragile[12] as being the lowest ranked regions in terms of their democratic status, with war also continuing in Libya, Syria, and Yemen. Populism is rising across the world, with a distinctly authoritarian tilt. In sum, countries with established democracies are facing increasing anti-democratic forces, and many countries that seemed poised for democracy are backsliding into authoritarian tendencies. As we set the stage for our discussion of civic engagement education, we should also note these contexts within which this pedagogy operates because the responsibility for change rests as much with us as educators as it does with anyone. In this sense, it is not just sufficient for political science faculty to write about the political landscape, we also have to influence that landscape for the better, of which teaching (and practicing) civic engagement education at a global level is a critical factor.

Challenges and Changes in the Twenty-First Century

Now in the third decade of the 21st century, a key question that we need to ask is how prepared we are to address existing and new challenges, while also ensuring that we maintain the democratic principles that so many fought for in the previous century. We also need to ask what is our role as educators in this debate. Within democratic governments some advances have been made in areas such as women's rights and LGBTQI rights, yet violence against members of certain racial, ethnic, and gender groups persists and is even growing in these countries.[13] Continuing racism, discrimination, and violence impacts who gets to participate in their communities, how they can participate, and how often they can participate. Moreover, because 'communities' also tend to have often informal, but established 'rules of the game,' this social context can mean that more marginalized communities that engage proactively in civic engagement activities are often not recognized for their efforts and contributions. This additional layer can create further feelings of isolation and establish insider-outsider relationships in society more generally, as members of underrepresented groups may fear speaking up and participating in their communities which can then mean that marginalized communities start out with greater disparities in civic engagement experience and knowledge. Consequently, the lack of their voices can impair society's ability to address their needs and concerns, thus limiting benefits to the majority.[14] This problem and its implications for civic engagement education are explored in the first chapter of this text, and the authors offer solutions which can be adapted to a variety of cultural and political contexts.

At a global level it is critical that faculty represent the students they teach, and the need for a balanced representation is particularly acute in civic engagement education, as students need to see how democracy can work for everyone. Universities are, however, not as diverse as they should be and there is a relative lack of underrepresented faculty to teach and mentor students.[15] To take just one example, at the time of writing in 2021, of 23,000 university full professors in the United Kingdom, less than 1% were Black professors (155 full professors).[16] While the UK is not an exception to this disparity,[17] the figures are nonetheless extremely worrying. It is also the case that women around the world regularly face exclusion from civic engagement opportunities, and "'inhospitable' institutional climates and research norms that discount collaborative work that could nurture women's careers" mean that women face additional barriers and processes of exclusion that make it harder for them to get and keep faculty positions.[18] Indeed, these issues are largely overlooked in the literature on civic engagement education, where there is a relative dearth of discussion with regard to the overall health of the discipline. We see this as a key challenge that we need to address.

Meanwhile, political situations sound alarm bells regarding the long-term implications of the decline of civic education. Multiple challenges, sometimes violent, to free and fair elections and voting rights emerged in the 2020 United States presidential election and its aftermath. On the other side of the Atlantic, the United Kingdom held a highly controversial vote in 2016 which resulted in it leaving the European Union on 31 January 2020. Both situations occurred due in part to leaders' campaigns based on inaccurate and misleading information spread through new technologies and calls to action which in some cases ran contrary to the very foundations of these long-standing democracies. But there is growing evidence that it is this sort of language, what Bartels refers to as "ethnic antagonism," that appeals to pockets of the electorate.[19] Another alarming component of these campaigns included suggestions that democratic processes and rules were too flawed or should be abandoned altogether and that leaders should get "special dispensations" to continue in office. While voter participation increased in both cases and on several demographic measures,[20] the basis upon which some participated—hatred and disinformation—was not conducive to building a future for democracy.[21] Instead, these situations sound alarm bells regarding the long-term implications of the decline of civic education. As civic engagement educators, we need to rise to the challenge of addressing these issues by providing our students with the tools to work effectively within democratic systems, institutions, and processes and to protect their rights. This need is particularly acute given global problems such as advancing climate change that threatens the habitats, jobs, and lives of people everywhere and need global solutions. Meanwhile, the COVID-19 pandemic has shattered illusions that states can ensure the health, prosperity, and security of their people on their own.[22] As civic engagement educators, we need to rise to these challenges by educating students for engagement in local, national, and global realms.

Although it is generally accepted that education and the attainment of basic literacy skills play critical roles in the development and maintenance of healthy democracies,[23] it is nonetheless the case that, at the time of this writing in 2021, one in seven adults across the world is functionally illiterate. Moreover, 66% of illiterate adults are women.[24] Behind these numbers is a broader divide between the wealthy global North and the poorer global South where the majority of illiterate adults reside. The global South is also where the majority of the world's authoritarian regimes exist and where the bloodiest conflicts often occur. Just as it is widely recognized that a lack of education can play an important role in creating the space for authoritarian regimes to take hold in the global South, so too can a lack of importance in instilling the virtues of civic literacy undermine values in more established democracies in the global North.[25] These conditions form a particularly vexing challenge given the role that technology such as the internet can play in popularizing false truths. Consequently, civic engagement educators must keep in mind that just as it is important to establish basic literacy, we must also be concerned about the need to ensure that people have the necessary information skills to navigate a digital world.[26]

Education plays a critical role in enabling people to understand and continually protect their rights, just as education is directly linked to improving the productivity of a country and the life expectancy of its citizens. The United Nations (UN) has focused on the individual person and groups of people rather than just relations between states in recent years. This movement initially took the form of the Millennium Development Goals (MDGs) which were inaugurated in 2000 and committed UN member states to achieve eight key targets by 2015 to combat poverty, hunger, disease, illiteracy, environmental degradation, and discrimination against women.[27] In 2015, these were superseded by agreement on 17 Sustainable Development Goals (SDGs) that are to be achieved by 2030 and focus on issues such as poverty, hunger, health, education, gender equality, clean water , energy, economic growth, inequalities, sustainability, peaceful and just societies, and global partnerships.[28] The latest SDG report in 2020 highlighted that while progress had been made in some areas such as children's health, the underlying changes have been nonetheless slow and worsened by the COVID-19 pandemic, the impact of which has been felt the most in the world's poorest countries and the poorest communities in advanced economies.[29] Achieving these important goals relies on national governments responding to this work in a positive way, and national governments need the support and contributions of their people. Civic engagement education, as explained in chapter three by Taiyi Sun, can help local, state, and national governments work with international institutions to reach these goals and create a better world for all.

The global response to the COVID-19 pandemic has brought to the fore the division between the rich global North whose citizens have benefitted from higher education rates, advanced, research-based industries, and mass vaccination efforts versus the global South, whose citizens have often been left behind as a result of vaccine nationalism in rich countries.[30] While leaders in the global North often refer to global challenges, their efforts have primarily been focused on exclusively solving their own countries' problems. A retrenchment to a national focus illustrated, though not started, by the COVID-19 crisis, is a worrying trend. Somewhat more worrying has been the passive acceptance of this internalism of electorates in these countries. Thus, while civic engagement education emphasizes the importance of leaders seeking and accepting accountability to the people for their actions and decisions, we also see less in the way of challenges by their electorates to what has increasingly become a parochial point of view. Such a state of affairs reflects on the one hand an insular approach of sorting out national problems and on the other hand a lack of knowledge and understanding by many of the inter-relationships and linkages between the local, national, and global levels that are inherent to effectively addressing vital issues such as climate change and global health. Although this is not a new trend, it is one that has been accelerated by COVID-19. Our youth need this global context, and several chapters in this and the previous books explain how civic engagement education can help them make these connections.[31]

In addition, civic engagement education is important because the public often do not really have a comprehensive understanding of the issues that affect them. Research in the US and Europe has highlighted that the decisions taken by electorates are often shaped by their identity and prejudice towards particular issues rather than independent thought.[32] One impact of this information gap is that electorates often misunderstand the issues that they consider to be particularly important. In more recent times, a classic example is the way in which the UK electorate's views were influenced by concerns about immigration. While a study conducted two years before the 2016 EU referendum in the UK revealed that people thought that 24% of the population were immigrants, the figure was actually only 13%.[33]

In these discussions a significant area of concern is a decline in news reporting at a local and global level, partly influenced by a shift to digital news channels and digital advertising. At its most stark, this change has led to a reduction in the sort of detailed reporting of local and overseas events that was once the norm.[34] This decline is especially harmful in the context of civic engagement education as local journalism has a crucial role in the scrutiny of local democracy, which often has the dominant impact on citizens' lives.[35] This state of affairs highlights a potentially worrying trend in knowledge about events at home and abroad and their interconnectedness precisely when the world is at a precarious point in time in relation to its own sustainability. We need news reporting to assist in maintaining an engaged and informed electorate.[36] It is in many ways a perverse state of affairs. While innovations such as the internet mean that the present day is the most interconnected and informed, it is also in many ways a desert of information. With the rise of social media sites that merely serve as "echo chambers" of pre-existing beliefs, this lack of knowledge and exposure to different perspectives is detrimental to a country's civic health. Civic engagement education can help to bridge this information gap and includes use and evaluations of media as an expectation for citizens and an assignment in our courses.[37]

Further, in seeking to bring increased knowledge to students throughout the world, another challenge is that a significant amount of the existing literature on civic engagement relates to case studies of the global North, particularly those in North America. For example, the many articles in journals such as *European Political Science*, the *Journal of Political Science Education*, and *PS: Political Science & Politics*, and the work of teacher-scholars displayed in conferences such as the APSA Teaching and Learning Conference (TLC), the annual APSA conference with the mini-conference of TLC@APSA, the European Consortium of Political Research, and the UK Political Studies Association have fostered considerable progress in the quest to build high-quality civic engagement education in North America and Europe. Where there are obstacles to the organization and running of civic engagement education activities in these regions, they are often based around the time and resources of the university as a provider of civic engagement, the faculty as the developers and leaders of civic engagement education, and the establishment of a campus culture that enables civic engagement to flourish.[38] Yet, for the teaching of civic engagement to operate successfully and become institutionalized in established higher education settings such as North America as well as in new environments such as China, we need to think more widely about the implications of such initiatives. This approach includes more openly questioning whether the teaching of civic engagement has traditionally offered and truly made opportunities available for all students at all types of institutions.

What is Civic Engagement Education?

As we embark upon creating a global platform for civic engagement education, we begin with the definition from McCartney (2013), which proposes that civic engagement education is an evidence-based pedagogy which includes a wide range of activities and co-production actions that develop knowledge about the community, its systems, and its problems, seek constructive solutions to these problems through deliberation and active participation, build skills to enable students to pursue these solutions, foster values of lifelong participation and democracy, and offer opportunities to experience this participation to build a sense of efficacy that one's voice and actions matter. It includes but is not necessarily always the same as political engagement, a sub-set of civic engagement, which "refers to explicitly politically oriented activities that seek a direct impact on political issues, systems, relationships, and structures,"[39] though this is often the case in civic engagement education in political science courses. And civic engagement education is not volunteerism, which, while valuable to the community, can be a one-day or short-term event that is not connected to academic learning, reflection on causes of the situation for which one is volunteering, or finding solutions.[40] Civic engagement education is akin to the term "community engagement education" which is preferred by some who bristle at a political or legal view of the word 'civic." Service-learning can be a pedagogical tool of civic engagement education, though it is not a required component. Some define "critical service-learning" as a separate pedagogy, or perhaps a sub-set of civic engagement education, and it has an explicit social justice orientation and works with the non-profit sector to promote social change.[41]

In sum, civic engagement education includes developing the knowledge, skills, values, and experiences that students can use to work with and within their communities to become leaders and active participants in their political, social, and economic systems. It pursues the goal of helping students to recognize and activate their connection to, roles in, and responsibilities toward their local, national, and global communities. As such, it is a pedagogy that seeks to foster a sense of the "we" in the individual and encourage that individual to bring their talents, viewpoints, and skills to improve the community, while also respecting the same in other community members. Though it is most common in democracies, as democracies guarantee rights such as voting and freedoms of speech, press, assembly, and religion that engender civic engagement, contributors to this book demonstrate how civic engagement education can work in less liberal contexts.

However, as we further develop civic engagement education, we must promote the inclusion of civic engagement education in all students' paths. As stated in *Teaching Civic Engagement Across the Disciplines*, "we need to build our democracy with geographically, demographically, professionally, and politically diverse people who hold a wide variety of viewpoints and experiences and who are educated in how government works, how problems can be peacefully confronted, and how we can work together to find mutually beneficial solutions."[42] We need civically engaged healthcare workers, engineers, scientists, teachers, and business owners to even be able to develop comprehensive approaches to contemporary problems. Thus, our first step to get this breadth of participation is to work within and across our collegiate institutions to infuse our general education structures and our co-curricular programs, as well as our major curricula, with effective civic engagement education. This process includes proper assessment so that we can keep learning what is and is not working and why.[43] It also requires building incentive and rewards systems to support civic engagement education research, teaching, and service within our institutions and to reward and respect each area equally. To not only build but also maintain civic engagement education in higher education, we need ongoing professional development opportunities so that new teacher-scholars can learn this pedagogy and current teacher-scholars can improve their work and contribute to growing the scholarship of teaching and learning (SoTL) literature.

Second, we must develop more work with our local primary and secondary institutions because lifelong civic participation is built on a ladder of learning experiences throughout a person's growth, not on a single platform. Since most people in the world do not attend higher education institutions at this time of writing, we cannot and should not ignore these students if we want more informed people to become civically productive in our communities. As Owen (2013), O'Shaughnessy (2013), Healey (2017) and others have shown, active civic engagement learning experiences in pre-collegiate education can be particularly influential in setting the foundation for lifelong participation, especially when this foundation is built upon the positive perspective of youth as citizens, not citizens-in-training.[44] Political science teacher-scholars once abdicated such a role in the pursuit of the science of research, but hopefully, as Rogers (2017) exhorts,[45] we can reclaim this space and use the knowledge and skills of our discipline to educate students at all levels in all countries. Our role is essential in ensuring that not just the history of our countries is taught, but also the current political systems and contexts that our students are operating in if we are to fully build their futures as competent and confident citizens.

Making Civic Engagement Work for All

Civic engagement education is vital to thwarting authoritarian challenges to democracy and the loss of people's rights, and continued research and idea exchanges on best practices in civic engagement education is crucial to answering these threats. However, we must also recognize that barriers and continuing challenges exist that enable authoritarianism to arise and that hinder teaching civic engagement in authoritarian and less liberal democracies. At another extreme, we face the challenges of enabling all students to benefit from civic engagement education given that the commodity of time is not equal for all students. In addition to time for students and faculty, other factors which we must confront include an increasingly diverse student body, training and retaining high quality faculty dedicated to civic engagement education, the allocation of resources within and between higher education institutions, sources of money to fund higher education, new technology which could enhance civic engagement education, and the launch of a global platform for civic engagement teaching, scholarship, and learning.

Time impacts students, faculty, and staff in different ways. The increasing diversity of the student population brings to the fore broader societal challenges, from family caretaker responsibilities to having to work a modest to substantial number of hours. This situation means that many more students have competing interests which lessen their time to commit to learning, including scheduled class meetings and learning that takes place outside of scheduled classes. These constraints consequently highlight that we need to think about a curriculum that reflects this reality. Students not raised in the dominant culture of the state where a university is located, such as immigrants and students studying abroad, have additional hurdles in encountering civic engagement education norms and expectations. A university curriculum should therefore not just be geared towards the needs of "traditional" 18-year-old students, but should instead recognize the need for a more flexible and supportive learning environment that reflects the myriad challenges that our current student bodies face.

Just as there is a need to create a supportive learning environment for our students, so too do we need to think about how we support and develop our academic faculty and wider staff.[46] The traditional ways of working and developing teaching staff are largely typified by learning on the job with informal mentoring that could at best be viewed as ad hoc, amateurish afterthoughts and at worst as leading to a system of patronage where decisions and processes can lead to assistance given to some individuals over others that can include discrimination on the basis of gender and ethnicity. In some countries, there is also the added challenge of "academic inbreeding," which reflects the tendency for universities (and particularly their faculty) to hire their own graduates.[47] Many of these challenges highlight wider system issues, including low salaries and a pervasive lack of sufficient support for professional development opportunities beyond the wealthiest higher education institutions, and a lack of influence of academic professional associations. Research indicates that this disparity can lead to both a virtuous and vicious circle relating to academic career progression that is shaped by the structural frameworks of working conditions.[48] But they also bring to the fore the challenge of ensuring that there is a sufficient level of academic mobility, networking, respect, and support to enable the sharing of the development of ideas on pedagogical best practices.

Universities cannot solve these issues alone. But, they are often viewed as the key actors in the delivery of civic engagement education, and their missions, coursework, and programs should reflect this need from our societies.[49] While this position partly reflects the historic nature of the role of universities,[50] it is also a reflection of the way in which higher education institutions have become increasingly important as "anchor" industries in their local economies. Universities are more than just educational environments and often take on a service function in their locality, a trend which is often further exacerbated by the decline of local industries and the resulting negative impact on local economic growth and civic life. This trend can place universities in complex situations that straddle moral and ethical roles about the nature of the civic engagement activities that they get engaged in as in some instances what they are committing to is a long-term program of work from which they cannot easily withdraw.

Universities are themselves not immune from financial pressures. Indeed, one of the most notable trends in global higher education is the rising costs attached to running a higher education institution, including such factors as reductions in government funding. In recent years universities in market-focused higher education systems such as Australia, Canada, the US, and the UK have responded to this situation by recruiting more international students to balance their books. The COVID-19 pandemic has, however, cast doubt over this financial model as international students have been unable to travel. While this might just be a short-term development, the impact is likely to be long-term, whether that be through the reduction in research funding, academic restructuring, or the merger (and closure) of institutions.[51] Universities are confronting other financial pressures from increased pension costs because their investment incomes are declining and people are living longer. Resources, in the form of research grants and endowments, are ever more concentrated in the hands of a small elite group of universities at a global level. Meanwhile, for those universities that are more reliant on teaching income, meaning tuition and fees, there is the added challenge of how to balance the books, which can lead to both increased costs and fewer opportunities available for those students who are more likely to be from less privileged backgrounds and may be in more need of civic engagement education even as their institutions have fewer resources.

This is a particularly acute challenge for universities in liberal market economies where the marketization of higher education has created a more competitive environment, with universities acting as businesses that compete with each other for the resources provided by student numbers. At a global level, this competition can also lead to the increasing power and influence of established universities and their elite graduates in the global North which attract full-tuition-paying international students, often from developing countries. Yet, in our thinking about civic engagement education, and in particular the context of less liberal democracies, we also need to be conscious of some of the inherent challenges that a more liberal market economy poses, particularly in relation to the outcomes of competition and the allocation of scarce resources. Looking to the future, we need to think about how some aspects of what we might want to achieve, such as international student recruitment to ensure diversity of thought, sit with other commitments, such as sustainability. In this regard the COVID-19 pandemic has accelerated thinking around technological solutions that aid student mobility, such as virtual learning experiences.

As part of this discussion on resources for civic engagement education, we need to consider the balance between funds for research-oriented higher education institutions versus teaching-oriented higher education institutions. Society needs researchers who can respond to so-called grand challenges that require interdisciplinary and inter-institutional collaboration. Such concerns have largely been the preserve of more research-focused faculty, whom in turn have often been able to benefit from mentoring and support structures to enable them to be ever-more successful. Meanwhile, the less research-focused faculty with larger teaching loads, many of whom teach the classes that focus on civic education, are left to continue the battle for dwindling state resources and the resulting need to raise tuition, fees, and room and board—and thus student loan burdens—on those who can least afford such costs.[52] Yet the numbers show that the majority of students are educated at public institutions and public community colleges. These numbers also reflect a continuing racial dominance and lack of inclusion.[53] In sum, the rich schools, their alumni, and their students keep getting richer, while the rest can only dream about the large endowments that pay for civic engagement programs. If our democracies are going to survive and thrive, we need to think about how to better steer state funding, grants, and private donations to a wider number of higher education institutions, their faculty, and their students. If not, we will just keep educating an elite, and democracy cannot be maintained without the education, participation, and respect of all of its citizens.[54]

Going forward, there is a need to rethink some of these divides and to consider the broader ecosystem of higher education and how we develop and support teaching faculty. As we have already highlighted, there are many pressing and vigorous challenges in terms of the economic, political, and social health of countries across the globe. To handle these challenges, teaching civic engagement education needs to be seen as a priority for universities. As discussed throughout *Teaching Civic Engagement Across the Disciplines* (2017), these challenges go beyond just core political science faculty and require stronger interdisciplinary and inter- and intra-institutional networking.[55]

For civic engagement education to work as a means to preserve and build democracy, we therefore need a "glocal," or global and local, approach. Looking to the future, we need to consider new ways to approach civic engagement education at a global level, as well to consider ways in which higher education over the next decade and beyond will play a part in maintaining and developing healthy democracies. As civic engagement educators, we need to move beyond single national case studies and also reach into more mainstream academic publications. At all levels, civic engagement is more than just the challenge of getting citizens to vote, which has traditionally been regarded as a hallmark of the passive citizen.[56] Civic engagement only works when people are involved in many ways and have the knowledge about how their democratic system works, the skills such as communication and deliberation to work within and improve that system, the values of democracy and regular democratic engagement, and the sense of efficacy that their voices matter. Yet, we cannot just have these debates among the political science community. If civic engagement education is the means to provide this knowledge, skills, value system, and sense of efficacy to help our local, national, and global communities survive and thrive, then as educators we have a responsibility to make the case for this pedagogy within and beyond our professional associations. More importantly, as Simpson proposes in the final chapter, we need to also make this case to our national governments and elected representatives, as well as to international organizations.

The Plan of This Book

This book represents a first attempt to think about the teaching of civic engagement at a global level and in so doing aims to shift the discourse away from traditional case studies that have been largely based on North American situations. Divided into four sections, the book starts by exploring ideas and developments relating to civic engagement education through a number of case studies which include collaborative linkages between local, national, international, and intergovernmental organizations. Section II presents examples of teaching practices around the world that illustrate in a practical way what has and has not worked, as well as charting areas for improvement. Section III looks at the teaching of civic engagement education through the lens of country case studies, including examples of civic engagement centers, study abroad programs, and co-curricular initiatives. Finally, section IV sets out key global issues and challenges in moving civic engagement education forward and identifies necessary pathways for future work.

In this book, several authors explain where their countries are succeeding and failing to provide the educational foundations that people need to navigate through new challenges to democracy across the world. Drawing on a range of global experiences that include case studies from Brazil, China, The Gambia, New Zealand, Romania, Russia, and South Africa, contributors demonstrate where institutions in some countries are making progress and rising to these challenges to develop innovative education models to promote democratic knowledge, skills, values, and experience, whether in democratic, authoritarian, or mixed systems.

These issues are contextualized in section I, which frames the debates regarding the teaching of civic engagement education at a global level. The section begins with a critical stance of the role of civic engagement education as an enabler for a more engaged, inclusive, and democratic environment. Candice Ortbals, J. Cherie Strachan, Lori Poloni-Staudinger, Debora Lopreite, and Celia

Valiente remind us of the implications of and gaps in established approaches to teaching civic engagement education and note the importance of grounding such approaches in transnational feminist activism. By focusing on civic engagement education through such a lens, it is possible to gain a fuller understanding and awareness of globally engaged citizenship and to overcome political hobbyism, which they contend has become the dominant method for teaching civic engagement education. Instead, they propose that a more inclusive framework can advance civic engagement opportunities for all students, regardless of their race, ethnicity, gender, or national identity.

Xaman Minillo and Henrique Zeferino de Mendezes of the Universidade Federal da Paraíba Brazil demonstrate the opportunity for partnerships between local governments and international organizations to tackle global challenges, most notably those relating to the UN's SDGs. Their chapter highlights the significance and importance of government financial resources in bringing about change and the way in which debates and battles at a national level such as shifting funding priorities can remove ladders of opportunity that create links between universities and civil society which have been assisting in transforming society by providing opportunities to a wider range of students.

In chapter three, Taiyi Sun of Christopher Newport University explores the complexity of teaching civic engagement education in authoritarian states through a case study of China. The chapter highlights the work of SEED for Social Innovation, which began as a student organization at Harvard University before becoming established as a non-governmental organization. Through this case study, Sun demonstrates the potential for teaching civic engagement in an authoritarian country and the compromises that sometimes have to be made to ensure acceptance by the state. As such, the chapter brings to the fore the inherent challenge of independence of thought and working in an authoritarian context and the tactics that can be employed to overcome these limitations while still maintaining core principles of civic engagement education, such as deliberation and holding officials accountable.

Catherine Shea Sanger and Wei Lit Yew explore in chapter four the challenge of teaching civic engagement education in less liberal societies through the case study of Singapore. Drawing on their own personal experiences, they discuss the way in which civic engagement education in less liberal societies can be framed in outcomes that are more palatable to government leaders and cultural norms. In so doing, they emphasize both the adaptability of civic engagement education as well as its weaknesses in terms of its pliability

Finally, John Craig of Leeds Beckett University in the UK explores the development of civic engagement education in the UK in chapter five. Through his work, Craig emphasizes the elite-based nature of the UK higher education system and the influence of Oxford University in terms of thinking on civic education and the way in which civic education has only in more recent years become a more strategic priority for the higher education sector.

Overall, the chapters in this book primarily draw on material prior to the COVID-19 pandemic which has had a significant impact on higher education in terms of the delivery of content by highlighting the benefits and the challenges of a digital world, though chapters in section II do incorporate how a number of higher education institutions have dealt with pandemic-era teaching. It is nonetheless apparent that the pandemic has accentuated and exacerbated existing divisions in the experiences of students, faculty, and staff. Many people have struggled to get access to ever-advancing digital technology and the infrastructure to support it. This technology access gap requires us to think about how physical spaces relate to the digital environment and how civic engagement education can operate in a learning environment that combines the best of both worlds.

The overarching goal of this book is to reflect on the improvements made and the challenges which remain for the future of democracy and provide examples of effective civic engagement education around the world which can move civic engagement education forward in various cultural and economic contexts. There is no one perfect democratic or educational system, so we present several pedagogical tools and ideas to build and secure civic engagement education in all types of institutions. By educating our youth and communities on the knowledge, skills, and values of civic engagement, we can give them the means, the power, and the sense of investment in their own countries that will provide a foundation to make the next twenty years a period of democratic growth, peace, and prosperity for all. Given that higher education is now a global enterprise, it is urgent that educators share civic engagement pedagogical tools and ideas and continue to learn from each other by creating a global civic engagement education community of practice that is accessible to all and brings the benefits of civic engagement education to youth around the world. We hope that this book provides encouragement and a useful platform for this global community of practice to flourish.

Endnotes

1. Roberto Stefan Foa, Andrew Klassen, Michael Slade, Alex Rand, and Rosie Collins, *The Global Satisfaction with Democracy Report 2020* (Cambridge, UK: Centre for the Future of Democracy, 2020), https://cam.ac.uk/system/files/report/2020_003.pdf.

2. University of Cambridge, "Democracy: Millennials Are the Most Disillusioned Generation 'in Living Memory'—Global Study," *EurekAlert!* (19 October 2020), https://eurekalert.org/pub/releases/2020-10/uoc-dma101620.php; Roberto Stefan Foa, Andrew Klassen, Daniella Wenger, Alex Rand, and Michael Slade, "Youth and Satisfaction with Democracy: Reversing the Democratic Disconnect?" Centre for the Future of Democracy (2020), https://bennettinstitute.cam.ac.uk/media/uploads/files/Youth_and_Satisfaction_with_Democracy_lite.pdf Note that another study done in 2018 found similar outcomes in 27 countries. See Richard Wike, Laura Silver, and Alexandra Castillo, "Many Across the Globe Are Dissatisfied With How Democracy Is Working," (Washington, DC: Pew Research Center, 2017), https://pewresearch.org/2019/04/29/many-across-the-globe-are-dissatisfied-with-how-democracy-is-working/

3. CIRCLE, "Half of Youth Voted in 2020, An 11-Point Increase From 2016," Center for Information and Research on Civic Learning and Engagement, (29 April 2021), https://circle.tufts.edu/index.php/latest-research/half-youth-voted-2020-11-point-increase-2016/ ; Emily Rainsford, "Young people and Brexit: Not All That we Think," *Political Studies Association*, (20 March 2019) https://psa.ac.uk/psa/news/young-people-and-brexit-not-that-that-we-think.

4. John Dewey, "The Need of an Industrial Education in an Industrial Society," *Manual Training and Vocational Education* 17 (1916); Dan Butin, "Introduction," in *The Engaged Campus: Certificates, Minors, and Majors as the New Community Engagement*, eds. Dan W. Butin and Scott Seider (New York: Palgrave Macmillan, 2012).

5. Thomas Carothers, "Is Democracy the Problem?" *The American Interest*, (16 January 2019), https://www.the-american-interest.com/2019/01/16/is-democracy-the-problem/

6. Francis Fukuyama, *The End of History and the Last Man* (London: Hamish Hamilton, 1992).

7. Alasdair Blair and Steven Curtis, *International Politics: An Introductory Guide* (Edinburgh, UK: Edinburgh University Press, 2009): 305.

8. For example: Daniel Stockemer, "Does Democracy Lead to Good Governance? The Question Applied to Africa and Latin America," *Global Change, Peace & Security* 21, no. 2 (2009): 241–255.

9. Freedom House, *Freedom in the World 2019: Democracy in Retreat*, https://freedomhouse.org/report/freedom-world/2019/democracy-retreat

10. The Economist Intelligence Unit, *Democracy Index 2020: In Sickness and in Health?* (London: The Economist Intelligence Unit, 2020): 34. Available at https://www.eiu.com/n/campaigns/democracy-index-2020/.

11. For example: Boris Vormann and Michael D. Weinman, eds., *The Emergence of Illiberalism: Understanding a Global Phenomenon* (London: Routledge, 2020).

12. World Economic Forum, *These are the World's Most Fragile States in 2019*, https://www.weforum.org/agenda/2019/04/most-fragile-states-in-2019-yemen/

13. Brian Levin and Lisa Nakashima, "Report to the Nation: Illustrated Almanac—Decade Summary: Hate and Extremism with updated 2019 FBI, US City, Canada, & Europe Data," Center for the Study of Hate and Extremism, (San Bernadino, CA: California State University, San Bernardino, 2019), https://csusb.edu/site/default/files/Almanac%2012%202019_0.pdf; Gloria Yang, "Racism Today Versus Racism After 9/11," *Berkeley Political Review*, (30 October 2017), https://bpr.berkeley.edu/2017/10/30/racism-today-versus-racism-after-911/; European Union Agency for Fundamental Rights, "Survey on Minorities and Discrimination in EU (2016), EUAFR, Brussels, (17 April 2017), https://fra.europa.eu/en/publications-and-resources/data-and-maps/ survey-data-explorer-second-eu-minorities-discrimination-survey?mdq1=theme&mdq2=974; Kenneth Roth, "The Dangerous Rise of Populism: Global Attacks on Human Rights values," in *World Report 2017*, Human Rights Watch, n.d. https://hrw.org/world-report/2017/country-chapters/global-4.

14. Joshua Littenberg-Tobias and Alison K. Cohen, "Diverging Paths: Understanding Racial Differences in Civic Engagement Among White, African American, and Latina/o Adolescents Using Structural Equation Modeling," *American Journal of Community Psychology* 57 (2016) 102–117; Joseph Kahne and Ellen Middaugh, "Democracy for Some: The Civic

Opportunity Gap in High School," CIRCLE Working Paper 59, Center for Information and Research on Civic Learning and Engagement (2008), https://files.eric.ed.gov/fulltext/ED503646.pdf; Jessica K. Taft, Sandi Kawecka Nenga, eds., *Youth Engagement: The Civic-Political Lives of Children and Youth* (Bingley, UK: Emerald Group Publishing Limited, 2013); Judith Torney-Purta, Carolyn H. Barber, and Britt Wilkenfeld, "Latino Adolescents' Civic Development in the United States: Research Results from the IEA Civic Education Study," *Journal of Youth and Adolescence* 36, no. 2 (February 2007): 111–125.

15. Horacio Sierra, "Higher Education Lacks Diversity," *Baltimore Sun*, (2 May 2021), https://www.baltimoresun.com/opinion/op-ed/bs-ed-op-0502-academia-ivory-tower-race-20210430-nrzxi3sa75af3bwhyyyxnavvqi-story.html; Aaron Clauset, Samuel Arbesman, and Daniel B. Larremore, "Systemic Inequality and Hierarchy in Faculty Hiring Networks," *Science Advances* 1, no. 1 (2015): doi: 10.1126/sciadv.1400005. See also Chapter 1 by Ortbals et al.

16. Sean Coughlan, "Only 1% of UK University Professors are Black", *BBC News* (19 January 2021), https://www.bbc.co.uk/news/education-55723120

17. In the US in 2018, 40% of all full-time faculty were white males, 35% were white females, 7% were Asian/Pacific Islander males, 5% were Asian/Pacific Islander female, 3% each were Black males, Black females, Hispanic males, and Hispanic females, and the remaining 1% included Native American/Alaskan Native and those who selected two or more races. See National Center for Education Statistics, "Characteristics of Postsecondary Faculty," NCES, (May 2020), https://nces.ed.gov/programs/coe/indicator/csc

18. Fernando Tormos-Aponte and Mayra Velez-Serrano, "Broadening the Pathway for Graduate Students in Political Science," *PS: Political Science & Politics* 53, no. 1 (2020): 145. See also Valeria Sinclair-Chapman, "Leveraging Diversity in Political Science for Institutional and Disciplinary Change," *PS: Political Science & Politics* 48, no. 3 (2015): 454–458; Tiffany Willoughby-Herard, "Conferencing is not a Luxury and Neither is the Scholarly Life of our Future Colleagues," *PS: Political Science & Politics* 53, no. 1 (2020): 146–148; Kesicia A. Dickinson, Jasmine C. Jackson, and Princess H. Williams, "Jackson State University: Challenging Minds and Cultivating the Political Science Pipeline," *PS: Political Science & Politics* 53, no. 1 (2020): 148–151; American Political Science Association, "Political Science in the 21st Century," in *Report of the Taskforce on Political Science in the 21st Century* (Washington, DC: American Political Science Association, 2011).

19. Larry M. Bartels, "Ethnic Antagonism Erodes Republicans' Commitment to Democracy," *Proceedings of the National Academy of Sciences of the United States of America* 117, no. 37 (2020): 22752–22759. https://www.pnas.org/content/pnas/117/37/22752.full.pdf

20. Michael McDonald, "Voter Turnout Demographics 2020," The Election Project (Gainesville, FL: University of Florida, 2020). https://electproject.org/home/voter-turnout/demographics; William H. Frey, "Turnout in 2020 Election Spiked Among Both Democratic and Republican Voting Groups, New Census Data Shows," Brookings Institution (5 May 2021), https://brookings.edu/research/turnout-in-2020-spiked-among-both-democratic-and-republican-voting-groups-new-census-data-shows/; BBC, "EU Referendum: The Result in Maps and Charts," *BBC* (8 June 2021), https://bbc.com/news/uk-politics-36616028.

21. Jemina Kelly, "How Hate Became a Driving Force in Elections," *Financial Times* (15 October 2020), https://www.ft.com/content/018e1286-3641-4921-b7b0-927081ec7fc6

22. Foa et al., 2020b.

23. Amartya Sen, *Development as Freedom* (Oxford:, UK Oxford University Press, 1999).

24. Dan Smith, *The State of the World Atlas* (Oxford, UK: Myriad, 2020).

25. See for example, Joe Westheimer, "Civic Education and the Rise of Populist Nationalism," *Peabody Journal of Education* 94, no. 1 (2019): 4–16.

26. Gianfranco Polizzi, "Information Literacy in the Digital Age: Why Critical Digital Literacy Matters for Democracy," in *Informed Societies: Why Information Literacy Matters for Citizenship, Participation and Democracy,* ed. Stéphanie Goldstein (London: Facet Publishing 2020): 1–23.

27. United Nations, "Millennium Development Goals," Geneva: United Nations (1995), https://www.un.org/millenniumgoals/

28. United Nations, "Sustainable Development Goals," Geneva: United Nations (2015), https://sdgs.un.org/#goal_section

29. United Nations, "The Sustainable Development Goals Report 2020," Geneva: United Nations (2021), https://unstats.un.org/sdgs/report/2020/

30. "Vaccine Nationalism Means that Poor Countries Will Be Left Behind," *The Economist* (28 January 2021). https://www.economist.com/graphic-detail/2021/01/28/vaccine-nationalism-means-that-poor-countries-will-be-left-behind

31. In this book, see Chapters 3, 6, 9, and 14. In other books, see Susan Dicklitch, "Blending Cognitive, Affective, Effective Learning in Civic Engagement Courses: The Case of Human Rights-Human Wrongs," in McCartney et al. 2013: 247–258; Alison Rios Millett McCartney and Sivan Chaban, "Bringing the World Home: Effectively Connecting Civic Engagement and International Relations," in McCartney et al. 2013: 259–278; Michael K. McDonald, "Internships,

Service-Learning, and Study Abroad: Helping Students Integrate Civic Engagement Learning across Multiple Experiences," in McCartney et al. 2013: 369–384.

32. Christopher H. Achen and Larry M. Bartels, *Democracy for Realists* (Princeton, NJ: Princeton University Press, 2016); Ipsos Mori, "Fake News, Filter Bubbles and Post-truth Are Other People's Problems…" (6 September 2018), https://www. ipsos.com/ipsos-mori/en-uk/fake-news-filter-bubbles-and-post-truth-are-other-peoples-problems

33. Ipsos Mori, "Perceptions Are Not Reality: Things the World Gets Wrong," (29 October 2014), https://www.ipsos.com/ ipsos-mori/en-uk/perceptions-are-not-reality-things-world-gets-wrong

34. For example, Janine di Giovanni, "The First Draft of History: Why the Decline of Foreign Reporting Makes for Worse Foreign Policy," *Foreign Policy* (15 January 2021), https://foreignpolicy.com/2021/01/15/history-foreign-correspondents-media-press-journalism-war-reporting-photography/

35. For example, Plum Consulting, *Research into Recent Dynamics of the Press Sector in the UK and Globally*, (May 2020). Report undertaken for the UK Government Department for Digital, Culture, Media and Sport. https://assets.publishing. service.gov.uk/government/uploads/system/uploads/attachment_data/file/924325/Plum_DCMS_press_sector_ dynamics_-_Final_Report_v4.pdf

36. In the UK alone, research into international news reporting in the British press through analysis of news stories published in four newspapers for the first week in March 1979, 1989, 1999, and 2009 demonstrated a decade-on-decade fall in news reports by just under 40% from 502 stories during the week in 1979 to 308 stories during the week in 2009. Martin Moore, *Shrinking World: The Decline of International Reporting in the British Press* (London: Media Standards Trust, 2010): 8. http://mediastandardstrust.org/wp-content/uploads/downloads/2010/10/Shrinking-World-The-decline-of-international-reporting.pdf

37. Alison Rios Millett McCartney, "'Teachnology' and Civic Engagement in the Year of COVID-19 Instruction," Raise the Vote, Washington, DC: American Political Science Association, (17 September 2020) [blog] https://connect.apsanet. org/raisethevote/2020/09/17/technology-and-civic-engagement-in-the-year-of-covid-19-instruction/; Christi Siver and Claire Haeg, "Incorporating and Assessing Methods Across the Political Science Curriculum," in Jeffrey L. Bernstein, ed., *Teaching Research Methods in Political Science* (Cheltenham, UK: Edward Elgar Publishing Limited, 2021): 177–193.

38. Barbara Jacoby and Associates, *Civic Engagement in Higher Education: Concepts and Practices* (San Francisco: Jossey-Bass 2009): 224–5. Nancy Thomas and Margaret Brower, "The Politically Engaged Classroom," in Matto et al., 2017: 21–34; Nancy Thomas and Margaret Brower, "Politics 365: Fostering Campus Climates for Student Political Learning and Engagement, in Matto et al., 2017: 361–374.

39. Alison Rios Millett McCartney, "Teaching Civic Engagement: Debates, Definitions, Benefits, and Challenges," in McCartney et al. 2013: 13–14.

40. Ibid.

41. Sharon Hutchings and Andrea Lyons-Lewis, "Reflections on our Critical Service Learning Provision. Is It Critical or Are We Social Justice Dreamers?" in Eurig Scandrett, ed. *Public Sociology as Educational Practice: Challenges, Dialogues and Counterpublics* (Bristol, UK: Bristol University Press, 2020).

42. Alison Rios Millett McCartney, "Introduction," in Matto et al., 4.

43. For excellent information on building good civic engagement assessment, see Elizabeth A. Bennion, "Assessing Civic and Political Engagement Activities: A Toolkit," in McCartney et al., 2013: 407–422 and Bennion, "Moving Assessment Forward: Teaching Civic Engagement and Beyond," in McCartney et al., 2013: 437–445.

44. Diana Owen, "The Influence of Civic Education on Electoral Engagement and Voting," in McCartney et al., 2013: 313–330; Betty O'Shaughnessy, "High School Students as Election Judges and Campaign Workers: Does the Experience Stick?" in McCartney et al., 2013: 297–312; Diana Owen and Isaac Riddle, "Active Learning and the Acquisition of Political Knowledge in High School," in Matto et al. 2017: 103–122; Shawn Healey, "Essential School Supports for Civic Learning," in Matto et al. 2017, 123–134. See also Lonnie R. Sherrod, Judith Torney-Purta, and Constance A. Flanagan, "Introduction," in Lonnie R. Sherrod, Judith Torney-Purta, and Constance A. Flanagan eds., *Handbook of Research on Civic Engagement in Youth* (Hoboken, NJ: John Wiley and Sons Inc., 2010): 1–20. This handbook was an excellent first endeavor by the editors to connect those interested in youth civic engagement across the world in a single work. It includes many chapters that should be consulted by anyone looking to work with the pre-college population.

45. Rogers 2017.

46. See for example Sarah Surak, Christopher Jensen, Alison Rios Millett McCartney, and Alexander Pope, "Teaching Faculty to Teach Civic Engagement: Interdisciplinary Models to Facilitate Pedagogical Success," in Matto et al. 2017: 231–246; Elizabeth C. Matto and Mary McHugh, "Civic Engagement Centers and Institutes: Promising Routes for Teaching Lessons in Citizenship to Students of All Disciplines," in Matto et al. 2017: 321–346.

47. Philip G. Altbach, Maria Yudkevich and Laura E. Rumbley, "Academic Inbreeding: Local Challenge, Global Problem," *Asia Pacific Education Review* 16, no. 3 (2015): 317–330.

48. Pippa Norris, "What Maximises Productivity and Impact in Political Science Research?," *European Political Science* 20, no. 1 (2021): 34–57.

49. James Simeone, James Sikora, and Deborah Halperin, "Unscripted Learning: Cultivating Engaged Catalysts," in Matto et al. 2017: 273–289. See also Surak et al. 2017; Matto and McHugh 2017.

50. See Craig, Chapter 5; Michael T. Rogers, "The History of Civic Education in Political Science: The Story of a Discipline's Failure to Lead," in Matto et al. 2017: 73–96. See also several chapters in Michael T. Rogers and Donald M. Gooch, eds., *Civic Education in the Twenty-First Century: A Multidimensional Inquiry* (Lanham, MD: Lexington Books, 2015).

51. Andrew Jack and Jamie Smyth, "Coronavirus: Universities Face a Hard Lesson," *Financial Times* (21 April 2020), https://www.ft.com/content/0ae1c300-7fee-11ea-82f6-150830b3b99a

52. Organization for Economic Cooperation, *Benchmarking Higher Education System Performance: Conceptual Framework and Data, Enhancing Higher Education System Performance* (Paris: OECD, 2017), https://www.oecd.org/education/skills-beyond-school/Benchmarking%20Report.pdf; Jon Marcus, "Most Americans Don't Realize State Funding for Higher Ed Fell by Billions," *PBS NewsHour*, (26 February 2019), https://www.pbs.org/newshour/education/most-americans-dont-realize-state-funding-for-higher-ed-fell-by-billions; APM Research Lab Staff, "APM Survey: Americans' Views on Government Funding and Aid for Public Colleges and Universities," *American Public Media*, (25 February 2019) https://www.apmresearchlab.org/highered. According to these reports, American students and their families paid one-third of the cost of higher education, and now they paid one-half of the cost; Richard J. Murphy, Judith Scott-Clayton, and Gillian Wyness, "Lessons from the End of Free College in England," *Evidence Speaks Reports* 2, no. 13. (Washington, DC: Brookings Institute, 2017). https://www.brookings.edu/wp-content/uploads/2017/04/es_20170427_scott-clayton_evidence_speaks.pdf; Denmark, Germany, Norway, and Sweden offer free tuition, though students must pay fees and living expenses. Brian Gerber, "Three Ways R3's Stand Out From the Crowd," *The Evolution*, (15 August 2016), https://evolllution.com/managing-institution/higher_ed_business/three-ways-r3s-stand-out-from-the-crowd/.

53. National Center for Education Statistics, "Annual Report: Undergraduate Enrollment," NCES, (May 2021), https://nces.ed.gov/programs/coe/indicator/cha.

54. Jane Mansbridge, "Why Do We Need Government? The Role of Civic Education in the Face of the Free-Rider Problem," in Matto et al. 2017: 11–20.

55. Caryn McTighe Musil, "Excerpts From A Crucible Moment and Civic Prompts," in Matto et al. 2017: 55–64; McCartney, "Introduction," in Matto et al. 2017: 1–10; Dick Simpson, "Teaching Civic Engagement Today," in Matto et al. 2017: 375–390.

56. Brian M. Harward and Daniel M. Shea, "Higher Education and Multiple Modes of Engagement," in McCartney et al., 21–40.

1 | Stop Training Global Political Hobbyists! Teaching Students How to Be Engaged Global Citizens Through Transnational Women's Activism

Candice D. Ortbals[1], J. Cherie Strachan[2], Lori Poloni-Staudinger[3], Debora Lopreite[4], and Celia Valiente[5]

1. Abilene Christian University; 2. Virginia Commonwealth University;
3. Northern Arizona University; 4. University of Buenos Aires; 5. University Carlos III

This chapter criticizes higher education's "global citizenship" initiatives for prioritizing knowledge about nation-states and familiarity with global communities as a way to prepare students for individual achievement in professions that increasingly require them to work with diverse others in an interconnected world. At best, this approach transforms students into global "political hobbyists" who are willing to debate public issues that cut across national boundaries, but who lack the civic interest or political skills required to resolve them. To cultivate truly engaged global citizens, the authors recommend approaches grounded in transnational feminist epistemology and pedagogy. Such work, which takes seriously women's intersectional identities and variation in their lived experience, underscores the importance of reflexivity and empathy as critical civic skills that students should master before moving on to seek influence over global issues. Specific learning experiences that incorporate transnational feminist practices include listening to and crafting testimonios, addressing local issues that cut across national borders, and preparing for a Fifth World Conference for Women. While higher education in general and political science in particular pose obstacles to transnational feminist activism as civic engagement, the authors argue it is the best way to address the needs and interests of a changing, diverse student body. The learning experiences suggested help to fulfill the civic mission of our institutions and our discipline.

KEYWORDS: Transnational; Feminism; Engagement; Activism; Global.

Hierarchy, Democracy, and Activism

Pedagogy for civic and political engagement, which first emerged in established democracies in the Global North, often begins with the assumption that education can cultivate the skills, knowledge, and identities that will help students to exercise their positive political rights. It assumes citizens can access means of political participation, from voting to lobbying, and can do so vis-à-vis stable, democratic institutions that will respond to their endeavors. In the broader sweep of world history, however, few beyond political elites have had the legal right to influence domestic political decisions in their own countries, let alone international ones. Historically the world was characterized first by patriarchy and then by additional hierarchical structures, including feudalism, slavery, caste systems, and colonialism.[1] The disenfranchised—former peasants, serfs, and slaves; Indigenous people; and women—only gained access to political power through what one scholar of democratization describes as "prolonged and inconclusive political struggles."[2] Moreover, traditional authority figures—patriarchs, monarchs, dictators, and rulers—did not altruistically embrace egalitarian decision-making and establish or expand access and suffrage; rather, the people who traditionally had been denied access to political power organized in the public sphere and engaged in disruptive politics. For instance, some suffragists engaged in hunger strikes and unruly protests to achieve voting rights whereas Indigenous activists in several countries have protested against the privatization of water and for their voices to be heard in decisions regarding natural resources. In short, democratization, political rights, and access to voice transpire when the disenfranchised make it clear that they must be consulted if society is to run smoothly and without disruption. Limited government and positive political rights "are not natural features of the political landscape;" rather "they exist because someone demanded them."[3]

In this chapter, we argue that political engagement pedagogy should teach students these realizations—that the right to participate in decision-making has always been earned through organizing in the public sphere and through collective action. To become engaged citizens in a global world, i.e., to become power-wielding global citizens, students therefore must see social and political change as something that they can demand even when issues of concern cut across national borders. Further, they should be taught to achieve global political influence not by imposing their preferences on those who world history has disenfranchised and subjected to ongoing subordinate status, but by collaborating with people in various locations around the world who also want change. As Poloni-Staudinger and Strachan[4] posit, teaching that stops with knowledge of international political affairs will transform students into political hobbyists who can debate global issues, but who feel no responsibility for resolving them as engaged global citizens. Political hobbyists, or well-educated people who can process political information and make in-depth arguments about political issues, still may have a minimal sense of civic duty and a lack of interest in and/or ability to influence real-world political outcomes.[5]

While gaining knowledge and cultural appreciation is an important first step toward global civic engagement, we argue that teaching must then pivot to explicit political engagement pedagogy. By this we mean that learning experiences must move beyond familiarity with global issues and even voluntarism to practicing the collective action skills required to influence global and/or "glocal" issues, i.e., local issues with global roots or consequences. Most importantly, we contend that traditional political engagement pedagogy be supplemented with approaches grounded in transnational feminist activism, defined here as a grassroots movement but also as an academic perspective with epistemological and pedagogical implications. Transnational feminism underscores awareness of intersectionality and of one's own positionality in relation to others as precursors to collective action strategies.

Note, women and gender studies scholars, despite purposefully teaching students how to influence political outcomes, consciously eschewed the term "civic engagement" in favor of the term "feminist activism."[6] They did so to underscore that feminist activists advocate for radical action to transform a status quo built on patriarchy's hierarchical legacies rather than access to governing institutions as they currently exist. Nevertheless, pedagogy for feminist activism in general and transnational feminist activism in particular overlaps considerably with political engagement pedagogy, as both emphasize not only a "deeper understanding" of issues and those affected by them, but also the collective action and organizing skills required to achieve social and political change.[7]

As this APSA volume and the two that preceded it make clear, applied civic and political learning, focused on influencing outcomes through civic voluntarism and through wielding political power, is increasingly important for students.[8] In the United States (US), embedding civic engagement in the university curriculum is crucial because the quality of US democracy and the role of civil society in promoting citizen participation is declining as evidenced by the erosion of voluntary associations and the rise of professionally staffed public interest groups and think tanks.[9] US citizens show little trust in their political institutions, and the US is considered a "flawed democracy" according to the Democracy Index of the Economist Intelligence Unit.[10] Furthermore, the professionalization of civil society along with the erosion of deliberative voluntary associations in the United States offer limited socializing experiences that previously prepared citizens for civic participation.[11] The US is not alone in its democratic decline; "just 8.4% of the world's population live in a full democracy while more than a third live under authoritarian rule."[12] Although certain countries have seen a robust civil society response to transnational concerns in recent years (see, for example, Argentina below), anti-gender campaigns and increased militarization of the police in other countries signal a fresh wave of hierarchical structures against which ordinary citizens may become mobilized.[13] Learning about active political and civic participation, therefore, might behoove students in various country contexts.

As this chapter explains, a global context of hierarchy is equally challenging for ordinary citizens who desire change. Globalization tests local contexts and actors, and it facilitates the growth of economic inequality at an "unprecedented rate."[14] What is more, activist organizations, namely those that retain a critical, activist role rather than embracing clientelism, service provision, and "deliverables," struggle to attract grant funding.[15] An example drawn from the US might include the success of professionally run public interest groups like the Children's Defense Fund compared to the decline of participatory organizations like Parent Teacher Associations (PTAs).[16] In a world of continued and reemerging hierarchies, we encourage professors to explore new pedagogical practices to prepare students to demand social change.

In the sections below, we contrast our approach of globally engaged citizenship with the one we believe is most common in universities today and tends to produce what we call political hobbyists. After explaining the pedagogical implications of transnational feminism as a way to overcome political hobbyism, we present student engagement activities that teach the skills of reflexivity and empathy as scaffolding for global collective action. We conclude the chapter with a critical discussion of our transnational feminist approach.

Political Hobbyists and Global, Engaged Citizens

In response to globalization, higher education accrediting agencies and professional associations in North America began to emphasize the role of colleges and universities in preparing students for global citizenship.[17] Higher education institutions now celebrate a commitment to global citizenship in their mission statements and highlight efforts to internationalize their curricula through course offerings, "global citizenship" programs, and co-curricular activities such as study abroad.[18] Many institutions' approaches emphasize knowledge about nation-states and global communities as well as students' preparation for individual achievement in professions that increasingly require them to work with diverse others in an interconnected world. The cosmopolitan, neoliberal emphasis underscores "an intellectual and aesthetic sense of openness toward people, places, and experiences with different cultures, especially those from different nations."[19] This approach to education for global citizenship, typical in higher education in the Global North, focuses on transforming students who already happen to be among the most privileged persons in the world into savvy individuals who are more knowledgeable and employable, and at least potentially, more likely to give back to the world community in some way through service.[20] The focus on the student as an individual is key here; rather than changing enduring social structures of discrimination, education changes individual attitudes about the broader world. These attitudes may range from tolerance and openness to a passive sense of "moral and ethical commitments to a global community."[21]

We see this neoliberal, cosmopolitan approach as one that creates political hobbyists. Political hobbyists often acquire substantive knowledge, cross-cultural competency, and appreciation for other cultures, but they do so largely to sustain their own individual growth and/or achievement post-graduation.[22] A political hobbyist is akin to what Parisi and Thornton refer to as a "student as tourist" or a "student as explorer."[23] A student might come to care about global issues and engage in some type of service activity as they study abroad or learn about global issues in courses, but they often do so without a critical understanding of existing power hierarchies and end up reifying them "under the guise of internationalization" and "global citizenship."[24]

We believe that training students to be hobbyists is ill-advised for the individual student as well as for global society writ large. The student as tourist model can be rightly criticized for reinforcing a colonial dynamic of Western (often white), middle-class educators and students in North American and Europe who are charged with producing and spreading knowledge to "others" in the world.[25] The student as a tourist may see people outside their own country as fascinating and perhaps exoticized; when students with privilege try to "help" people, they propagate "binary relations between [the] 'benevolent' West and 'destitute' East" or South as well as the narrative of the "needy Other."[26]

Even today's non-governmental (NGO) sector reflects a colonial dynamic that must be critiqued. Global aid is often provided by countries affiliated with the Organization for Economic Cooperation and Development (OECD). Given successful right-wing political movements in OECD countries along with a global economic crisis, aid criteria increasingly reward efficient, effective service delivery by professionally staffed NGOs over rights-focused, participatory, and grassroots organizing movements.[27] The increasingly hierarchical nature of nonprofit and civic organizations that work to address global issues is problematic on a number of fronts, not least of which is that these organizations often replicate and even exacerbate social hierarchies and inequalities that occur both within, but also between, societies around the globe. Preparing students to work in professionally staffed and hierarchical NGOs is tempting because such programming is often most available and easiest to implement with limited resources; however, such organizations often treat the disenfranchised or formerly disenfranchised like clients in need of services rather than citizens who should play an active role in influencing policy decisions. All too often service-learning and civic engagement projects with global partners reinforce a narrative that positions students from the Global North as "rescuing" those from the Global South who are denied agency, the opportunity to develop their own civic infrastructure, and the opportunity to advance their preferred solutions to public issues of concern.[28] This outcome occurs because universities often choose to partner with professionally staffed and grant-funded NGOs, rather than membership-based civil society organizations committed to structural change.[29] Hence, Parisi and Thornton explain that traditional service-learning models run the risk of focusing on student learning outcomes instead of the goals of the community in which students work.[30] Ultimately, even well-intentioned, top-down, service-oriented approaches that treat people as clients in need instead of equal partners with their own lived experiences and agendas can do more damage than good if they reinforce an oppressive status quo.

If students going abroad are well-intentioned, as they often are, it begs the question of how we can train them to be "helpers" with the goal of "'undoing' colonial legacies that continue to buttress global racial divisions" or other power hierarchies.[31] Furthermore, the many university students around the world who do not have access to study abroad also warrant instruction that helps them to navigate the global world and connects them to others in equitable relationships. In direct contrast to mainstream approaches to global education, therefore, we support critical approaches to global citizenship, and we identify engaged, global citizens as those who seek to wield real-world power in decision-making that affects global issues and transnational affairs.[32] In particular, we highlight those who broker this influence through reciprocal, collaborative, and uncoerced relationships with others through global political organizing, transnational voluntary associations, and local associations responding to global dynamics and/or working with global networks. Thus, the best global citizens recognize that their own "influence" may be best achieved through efforts to facilitate and empower their global partners. As we prepare students to become engaged citizens, it is important that we also teach them not to replicate hierarchal approaches in their own endeavors.

Hence political scientists who aspire to transform students into global citizens through global civic engagement pedagogy should take inspiration from practices embraced by transnational feminists. These scholars have tended to eschew the term civic engagement for the terms "feminist activism" or "feminist pedagogy",[33] and they assert that political engagement education requires preparing students for participation in "struggles for justice" in addition to participation in traditional, transactional political participation.[34] We explain in the section below that the content and skills associated with transnational feminism prepares students to understand themselves within the global world and how their experiences might relate to and intersect with the experiences of activists in local contexts around the world. Our transnational feminist approach suggests that students understand the hierarchical structures that influence their peers around the world and that they listen to and value the knowledge and feelings of ordinary people and activists. It is our hope that students resist the status quo and create social change and that the skills that transnational feminism teaches students—reflexivity and empathy—can be harnessed to change issues of transnational significance beyond those raised by feminism.

Before we elaborate on our pedagogical approach, we first must acknowledge the positionality of the authors. We are privileged in that we live in nation-states that see us as citizens with the right to influence political decisions, but we know not all people (and students) around the world live in open contexts where they can be as politically engaged as we can. Moreover, several of the authors here are from the Global North, and we recognize that the literatures about civic engagement that originally inspired this chapter would not be considered knowledge derived from the Global South. Given awareness of our own positionalities and with a moral imperative for our students, we proceed in this chapter as follows: we explain the usefulness of transnational feminism as a pedagogy, we present engagement activities that educators could use to encourage active global citizens, and we conclude with next steps for educators.

Teaching through the Lens of Transnational Feminism

In addition to being a social movement, transnational feminism is a methodological and pedagogical approach with epistemological implications, and it requires particular skills for scholars and students alike. Transnational feminists aim to "decolonize knowledge production",[35] and they do so through relationships or what could be called active engagements. Some voices are silenced in global (and national and local) arenas; thus, the legitimization of voice creates knowledge that otherwise would not exist. Voices are amplified as people engage one another and are understood in relation to their values, contexts, experiences and political aims.[36]

As with traditional civic engagement pedagogy, we emphasize that *skills* are taught alongside *knowledge* as a way to prepare students for participation in politics and that even simulations or classroom activities that scaffold these civic skills prepare students for engaged citizenship beyond hobbyism.[37] Therefore, using transnational feminism as a lens to teach political engagement requires students to learn about the history and current events of transnational feminism in addition to important skills that prepare them to engage with activists around the world. In the following sections, we present key *knowledge* about transnational feminism that students should comprehend and the necessary *skills* of reflexivity and feminist empathy.

In terms of *knowledge*, we suggest that students should learn about the academic, theoretical basis of transnational feminism, the history of twentieth century, grassroots activism, and, especially, how grassroots activism relates to Black feminism and United Nations' (UN) advocacy. Furthermore, we believe that students must understand how transnational feminism is both local and global in its orientation. Namely, feminist activists across the globe address issues of global significance (e.g., gender violence, land/environmentalism, migration, hyper-militarization and war), but these issues are grounded in local contexts and reflect the political agency and voice of women in those places. Although common issues unite transnational feminists around the world, we do not assume that issues affect women uniformly and thus will draw all women together.[38] For this reason, students must survey transnational feminism in several countries and/or regional contexts in order to have a sufficient knowledge of transnational feminism.

We also argue that the history of global and transnational feminism asks students—and especially students in the Global North—to have the *skills* to critically evaluate their individual identities as well as social structures that maintain and create power differentials. Whereas global feminists may be identified as primarily Western (white) women who seek global sisterhood and universal campaigns for human rights and women's health, transnational feminists historically are women of color, the so-called "subaltern," who critique structures of inequality—such as race, nationalism, and global capital, reject universality, and seek local solutions to enhance social, political, and economic empowerment.[39] We want students to collaborate along the lines of transnational feminism, which demands an interrogation of power, including that of privileged women over women who tend to be "othered." As a result, students need to learn how to question their own privilege through reflexivity and carefully imagine solidarity with women of intersectional identities through feminist empathy before embarking on cross-border collaborations.

Our pedagogy presented below goes beyond the formulation of political hobbyists because students are not encouraged to learn generalities about global struggles facing women (and men) worldwide and discuss them; instead, we ask students to understand their own identities alongside those of persons elsewhere (i.e., the skill of reflexivity) and in relation to local contexts which the students have sought to comprehend (i.e., knowledge); listen to the voices of women and engage and amplify their lived experiences and goals (i.e., the skill of empathy), and, with sufficient knowledge and empathy, act collectively when possible.

Knowledge of Transnational Feminism

In this section, we present academic transnational feminism, grassroots transnational activism, and contemporary examples that stress the parameters of transnational feminism. These examples display the kind of knowledge that a student needs to grasp in order to understand women's agency in the local sphere. Once again, we want students to gain sufficient knowledge of transnational feminism so that they do not assume that all women act with the same goals or within the same contextual constraints and opportunities; with this diverse understanding, students will be more prepared to practice feminist empathy.

The history of transnational feminism is debatable given its multiple forms. One strain of transnational feminism consists of academic scholarship largely situated in United States higher education.[40] Such scholarship can be traced to the 1980s and particularly to the work of Chandra Mohanty, who argued against the imagined universal sisterhood of global feminism and the assumption that patriarchy uniformly oppresses women worldwide.[41] Rather, Mohanty, as well as others,[42] contend that the nation-state and material conditions, influenced by colonial histories, a global liberal economic order, and locally specific variables, oppress women worldwide. These intersections of global and local variables imply attention to intersectionality; as Patil explains, "categories of race, ethnicity, sexuality, culture, nation, and gender not only intersect but are mutually constituted, formed, and transformed within transnational power-laden processes such as European imperialism and colonialism, neoliberal globalization, and so on."[43] This line of scholarship grew exponentially in the 1980s and 1990s, provided a challenge to the nation-state and global capital, and presented a platform for "women's agencies, responses, and resistances to these [intersecting] relationships of power."[44]

A second form of transnational feminism consists of the lived experiences and grassroots activism waged by feminists across borders. *The Oxford Handbook of Transnational Feminist Movements* considers such movements as the "fluid coalescence of organizations, networks, coalitions, campaigns, analysis, and actions that politicize women's rights and gender equality issues beyond the nation-state."[45] A simplistic way to put this is "border-crossing activities and phenomena" by women.[46] This form of transnational feminism increased in the 1990s due to growing globalization and information technologies;[47] however, many sources trace instances of transnational feminism to the early twentieth century and the second wave of feminism. For example, in the interwar period, in the aftermath of British colonialism, British feminists worked alongside Palestinian and

South African women to give voice to their intersectional demands.[48] Moreover, Black feminism from the 1960s and 1970s not only serves as part of the academic genealogy of intersectionality and transnational feminism,[49] but it also was the basis of in-person collaborations between Black women in the US, the United Kingdom, Latin America, and Africa during those decades.[50] The Third World Women's Alliance (TWWA) grew out of the US Civil Rights movement, emphasized the "triple jeopardy" of race, sex, and class, and maintained activism related to anti-imperialism and pan-Africanism.[51]

Additional moments that are essential to the history of transnational feminism pertain to the United Nations' advocacy for women's rights, such as the UN Commission on the Status of Women (CSW), created in 1946, and the four UN World Conferences on Women during the twentieth century (Mexico, 1975; Copenhagen, 1980; Nairobi, 1985; Beijing, 1995). These conferences acted as a "transnational opportunity structure" that allowed women's movements to influence international norms and set goals in local contexts.[52] The successes of the conferences include the 1979 Convention on the Elimination of all Forms of Discrimination Against Women (CEDAW) and the 1995 Beijing Platform for Action. These successes have been marked by conservative backlash, against which feminist activists continue to fight.[53] A fifth UN World Conference on Women arguably is needed in coming years so that the CSW will work more effectively with women's groups to address issues that the activists reportedly care about, such as "land rights, sex trafficking, internet access for women, and the effects of climate change on women."[54]

Additional contemporary examples of transitional feminism conclude our brief overview of *knowledge* about transnational feminism. Recall, transnational activism varies greatly from place to place. Although it is impossible to honor all or even many women's voices in this short space, we have selected key examples of transnational feminism in an attempt to demonstrate the richness of local activisms with which educators and students could engage. It is our argument that students who aspire to influence global issues should be familiar with ongoing local endeavors in countries and regions like the ones below. On the road to becoming active global citizens, students need be knowledgeable in order to avoid acting as an uninformed outsider who rushes in to help others. Instead, students should learn to recognize the ongoing, important work and political agency of women around the world.

Striking contemporary examples that might appeal to many students concern hashtag activism; #MeToo and #NiUnaMenos should be recognized as important examples of online transnational feminism that took on different manifestations in various countries.[55] Because many students will recall #MeToo, professors could also easily draw their attention to #NiUnaMenos, a transnational response to gender violence and femicide in Latin America. The massive Women's March that accompanied the #NiUnaMenos hashtag occurred simultaneously in 80 cities in Argentina on 3 June 2015, with its epicenter in the city of Buenos Aires. The march called for an end to violence against women, and in particular, urged the Argentine federal government to immediately implement its 2009 antiviolence law. The events of 2015 had both local and global ramifications. Coverage by mass media and internet activism found resonance in other countries of the region; first, in Mexico, followed by Chile and Peru. In Mexico, for example, the protests were sparked by the murder of a pregnant, 14-year-old by her boyfriend and were linked to anger over widespread impunity, partially brought on by the country's long-term drug war. Claiming *Vivas nos queremos* (we want us alive), several women's marches called *Ni Una Menos* (Not One Woman Less) were held in Latin America from 2016 onward in countries such as Paraguay, Bolivia, Costa Rica, and Nicaragua. Similar events were then replicated in Canada, the US, France, Italy, and Spain, to name a few.

In 2018 a new feminist movement flooded the streets of Buenos Aires, namely *Marea Verde* (Green Tide). Thousands of women and men took to the streets and claimed the right to free, legal, and safe abortion for all women. Activists wore the green handkerchief of the National Campaign for Free, Legal and Safe Abortion formed by a small group of feminists, legislators, and activists in Argentina in 2007. The Green Tide crossed borders, thus becoming an example of transnational feminism. In Chile, for example, women marched in 2019 wearing the green handkerchief and performing a fight song: *Un Violador en tu Camino* (A rapist in your way). Since 2019 thousands of young women in Argentina, Chile, and Mexico have dressed up in violet and green colors and denounced patriarchal oppression, violence, and abortion restrictions. They sing "*[el patriarcado] se va a caer, se va a caer*", which means "it is going to fall", in reference to the patriarchal system. The green handkerchief continues to appear in Latin American countries but in different ways depending on the country; it was a symbol of celebration in Argentina in late 2020 and early 2021 with the country's legalization of abortion, and it remains a symbol in Mexico as each Mexican state considers abortion legislation. Marea Verde groups in individual Mexican states face distinct legislative paths given Mexico's federal structure. Therefore, Latin America's growing feminist mobilizations during the last decade operate from the local to the global and back again, with feminist activism, through internet networks, becoming essential to growing feminist ideas in the regional context.

While maintaining that women's experiences vary across the African continent, FEMNET (the African Women's Development and Communication Network) works as a pan-African network that focuses on economic development and justice, gender violence, and sexual and reproductive health.[56] The network began in the 1980s as a way for African feminists to collaborate in anticipation of the UN World Conferences on Women, and it continues to work with the CSW to implement the Beijing Platform and monitor the actions of states and regional organizations. Other activities of FEMNET include promoting the participation and empowerment of young women, particularly choosing them to be speakers on panels about women's issues.[57] In 2020, FEMNET "launched the Pan-African Women COVID-19 Online Hub," which is "a one-stop platform containing critical information resources about COVID-19 in Africa from gender and feminist perspectives."[58] Tensions in the network demonstrate the complex nature of transnational collaboration. Some activists in Africa are beset by worries that feminism is too elitist and/or foreign and that the "othering" notion of the "perpetually poor, powerless and pregnant" woman obscures the agency of women from the continent.[59]

Skills of Transnational Feminism

In addition to contextual knowledge of the broad contours of transnational feminism and specific examples of local activisms, a civic engagement pedagogy grounded in transnational feminism requires the skill of reflexivity or "the knowledge of one's own identity and how one is "position[ed] in the social world", i.e., one's positionality.[60] Social scientists constructing ethnographies believe that they must convey their positionality in order to capture the ways in which their identities and views about the social world impact research findings. In a similar way, students' positionalities impact their comprehension of course content and their ability to communicate with others; without awareness of one's own personal identities and experiences, we run the risk of ignoring the complex experiences of others, disregarding intersectional discriminations, and failing to take actions against inequalities. Reflexivity is our pedagogy's means of preventing students from acting like hobbyists who know many facts about the world but are unaware of how their own identities shape what they know and believe and of how much situated knowledge others have and can contribute to conversations and collaborations. Techniques on how to encourage students to become reflexive vary, but scholarship shows that "personal work" through journaling, for example, helps students to "reflect on their personal orientations, behaviors, and attitudes" as they relate to "race and racism" and to act towards social justice.[61]

We consider feminist empathy, an important second skill, to be a process of imagination that builds "sensitivity to injustices suffered in [the] daily" lives of local populations, particularly women, and magnifies people's voices in an attempt to transform structures of inequality.[62] Empathy occurs when a person, through imagination, "enters into the experiential world of another."[63] Our conception of feminist empathy is related to global empathy, defined by Zappile and Beers as "the desire to supportively engage with an "other" who lives outside of one's state";[64] however, we stress that feminist empathy is not passive but active. A person with feminist empathy goes "beyond appreciation" and awareness of another person to listening and amplifying others' voices in cultural and institutional contexts where they lack representation and/or power silences them.[65] The end result of empathy should be to insert women into contexts of power and to provide a check on political and social practices working against women's empowerment.

Two examples of empathy in practice demonstrate how entering the world of another person and seeking to understand her can lead to greater voice for women. The historical example of South African women working with British feminists is instructive. The British journalist Winifred Holtby (1898–1935) worked with labor activists in South Africa as she traveled worldwide to make speeches about labor rights. When she met with South Africans, she listened to them describe racial injustices and went on to write about intersections of class, race, and gender.[66] Though Holtby was a first-wave feminist with an eye to universal human rights and not a transnational feminist of difference, she demonstrates an incipient understanding of intersectionality and the process of listening to the lived experiences of another and voicing them to those in power. In a similar way, the #MeToo movement is an example of listening and empathy. In fact, Tarana "Burke launched the MeToo campaign in 2006 to achieve 'empowerment through empathy' for sexual assault survivors."[67] Burke "defines empathy as that feeling of sharing an experience, of being in one's same shoes."[68] In South Korea, empathy compelled women who did not have #MeToo experiences of assault to share support for friends who did by posting #WithYou on Twitter.[69] Feminist empathy therefore pushes beyond the factual knowledge of hobbyism in that it asks students to feel—to listen, to process the feelings of others, and to support them in some way.

We acknowledge that practicing empathy can be intimidating and tricky. We are asserting a civic engagement pedagogy that asks students to engage emotions related to their own and others' lives and to do so by dialoguing with activists around the world to confront power hierarchies that have caused real life pain and distress. Walking in another's shoes as a way to begin transnational collaborations admittedly can be intimidating because dialogue with people who may or may not be like oneself and about topics that provoke emotions (e.g., sexual violence, war, etc.) is not easy. This is why we suggested that educators first equip students with knowledge about transnational feminist activism and then work on the skills of reflexivity and empathy. Having knowledge about the ills caused by patriarchy, colonialism, and racism and how feminists have responded to them prepares a student to process emotions regarding how these same ills challenge them personally as well as women throughout the world. The skill of empathy gives rise to action, which is not easy (see below) but acts as an empowering salve to inspire activism and motivate change.

Empathy is tricky because too little and too much of it perplexes transnational collaborations.[70] Too little empathy or empathy practiced in a passive way can lead to "sentimental attachment to the other, rather than a genuine engagement with her concerns" or even an exotic gaze reminiscent of colonial oppression.[71] For students, such sentimental attachment might constitute what "Chandra Mohanty has analyzed as the 'feminist-as-tourist' curricular model" in which students become like old-school US and European feminists who see activists in other parts of the world as the "other."[72] Yet too much identification with another woman, or rather trying to embody her or actually be her, can lead to cultural appropriations which are inappropriate.[73] For these reasons, cultivating empathy—whether called global empathy or feminist empathy—is far from automatic. As Gerdes et al. explain, practicing empathy involves both a physiological response and a conscious choice, thus developing empathy requires growing neurological pathways conducive to empathy.[74] These pathways are best built through practice and experiential learning that increases "self/other-awareness and emotion regulation."[75] This is why we suggest that students understand their positionality through reflexivity and practice listening to women from a variety of social positions (through readings, films, art, etc.) before beginning face-to-face or online transnational collaborations (see engagement activities below).

In addition to reflexivity and empathy, we believe that students benefit from cross-cultural and/or civic communication skills. University campuses in the United States, for example, are increasingly likely to offer courses on intergroup dialogue, where similar skills of reflexivity, listening, and empathy are cultivated to facilitate understanding across demographic differences in the United States. Meanwhile Communications departments with concentrations in public engagement may offer courses on deliberative dialogue and/or cross-cultural communication, which teach students a transferrable skill set that could also be used to facilitate transnational activism. Campus programing by diversity and inclusion offices may provide another opportunity for students to hone relevant skills. Therefore, a potential option is to scaffold the skills advocated here by relying on coursework or workshops offered by other units on a university campus.

Engagement Activities: Integrating Knowledge and Skills

The skills of reflexivity and feminist empathy, which prepare students for participation in transnational collective action, may be cultivated through the activities suggested below. We chose engagement activities that our diverse group of authors believe can be done in universities in various countries and that require library resources and/or internet access, but are otherwise low cost and do not require students to travel to collaborate with activists. We did so because we do not want to replicate the "student as tourist" model, and we want the activities to be accessible to students who cannot travel. In describing each activity, we explain how the activity builds on the abovementioned knowledge and skills and how it moves students toward robust, global engagement instead of political hobbyism.

Engagement Activity 1: Testimonio

Testimonios are narratives "told by someone who has had firsthand experience with political repression, violence, or other forms of oppression."[76] Testimonios have a history in Latin American studies and Chicana feminism,[77] and they function as a literary form, methodology, pedagogy, and a political act. An example of a testimonio is Alicia Partnoy's *The Little School*,[78] which is approximately 130 pages in length and tells the story of Partnoy's imprisonment by the military during Argentina's Dirty War.[79] "The Little School" was a concentration camp where prisoners "were to be 'taught a lesson,' mainly through violence, torture, and even murder."[80] Partnoy survived the camp, and she did not remain silent about the state's abuses. She wrote her testimonio—part fictionalized but based on her everyday life in the camp—and it was published soon after the fall of the military regime as a way to bear witness to oppression.

The abatement of the violent, oppressive structures of the 1970s to 1990s that originally propelled testimonio as a form of protest (e.g., military regimes in South America or civil wars in Central America) has led to a decline in testimonio as a practiced literary form. Nevertheless, scholars continue to discuss it as a strategy for uncovering and resisting oppression. Without a doubt, new oppressive structures have (re)emerged in more recent decades (toxic masculinity, anti-feminist populism, anti-gender campaigns, militarized police, etc.), and testimonio is one form of response to them. Testimonio prioritizes voices that are otherwise ignored in academia, particularly the stories of persons from the Global South, and, thus, provides a way to expand the typical epistemology, methodology, and pedagogy of political science. Furthermore, scholars are beginning to track testimonio in regions outside of Latin America. For example, Patricia DeRocher, in *Transnational Testimonios: The Politics of Collective Knowledge Production*, sees women's testimonios around the world as a contemporary "life-writing practice" with the ability "to deliver intersectional, macrolevel social critique."[81] According to DeRocher, when readers "witness" testimonies they are entering into a "reciprocal social pact rooted in epistemic responsibility rather than as a unidirectional form of entertainment."[82] In essence, authors testify to the readers, and the reader becomes responsible for bearing witness. In this way, testimonio is a form of collective action. The author is not writing for the sake of autobiography, but for the purpose of starting larger conversations—conversations that are urgent and pertain to social justice. Thus, a pedagogy based in testimonio satisfied our goals in this chapter to have students gain knowledge of others' experiences and ask them to use the skill of empathy to begin acting for urgent change. The conversations sparked by testimonio should go beyond what we expect of hobbyists (i.e., educated conversations about other parts of the world), because, as we discuss below, we ask students to invoke reflexivity so that they see how social change is necessary to them personally and can be fought for alongside others with different experiences.

Although testimonios have typically been novel or at least novella-length, we suggest that students could write testimonios about their own lives which are much shorter. This is one key way for students to develop reflexivity. How would a student go about writing a short testimonio? To answer this question, we first point out that testimonio is a "flexible" and "outlaw genre" meant "for the people"; thus, it should not be thought of as scholarly or restricted to only certain styles.[83] Second, we point our readers to Ashami, Hernandez, and Flores's article entitled, "Testimonialista Pedagogues: Testimonio Pedagogy in Critical Multicultural Education."[84] These authors suggest a project called "visual testimonio" that begins with students brainstorming their personal stories as these stories relate to their education experiences. For our purposes here, we would ask students to brainstorm their personal story in relation to gender, social, and political empowerment (or lack thereof) and/or leadership experiences (or lack of voice) in social/political organizations. Next, students can be asked to draw, paint, or somehow visually demonstrate "their lived experiences." Drawing, as argued by Ashami, Hernandez, and Flores, makes students "slow down" to think about how experiences of inequality are embedded in institutions, societies, and international/national events, and it literally makes "intersectional oppression visible" to students and their classmates.[85] Whereas the author (i.e., the artist of the visual testimony) hones reflexivity from this activity, the author's classmates practice feminist empathy as they listen and attempt to bear witness to what they have seen/heard.

It is also beneficial for students to read past testimonios published by women around the world, and they could likely employ visual techniques to chart the experiences of these women as well. We can imagine a class presentation scenario in which students present their own visual testimonio and compare it to a woman's testimonio that they have read. Class discussions following such presentations, based on the logic of DeRocher above, are not about summarizing individuals' experiences for the simple sake of learning about them or bemoaning injustice but instead can take on the purpose of collective action. Because the main purpose of testimonio is to start a conversation with others about how to approach or end structural inequalities, we suggest that class discussions include constructing a to-do list, stating how members of the class could act on the necessary political actions implicated by all of the testimonios combined. Here is where empathy should come into play; students and professors must put themselves in another's shoes and think of concrete ways to amplify others' voices. This final step encourages students to move beyond learning content about transnational feminism to participating in civic and political acts intended to influence political outcomes. Designing an activity where students follow through on at least one of the suggestions on the to-do list (e.g., writing a short op-ed in student newspaper or a letter to a public official) begins to move students beyond political hobbyism to more fully engaged global citizenship.

Engagement Activity 2: (G)local actions "at home"

The term "glocal" refers to local activism that is a manifestation of transnational networks and movements.[86] By saying that we should encourage students' participation in glocal actions we are claiming that students might participate most fervently in global engagement in places they know best, i.e., "home." A student does not have to leave her own country and become a global "tourist" to find issues of salience to transnational feminism; rather, "home'… itself is a 'global struggle.'"[87]

We believe that students, particularly in the Global North, likely have the preconceived notion that gross gender inequalities exist "elsewhere," and, in thinking this way, they fall prey to a colonialist sentiment that privileges the Global North over other world regions. To avoid this understanding of global society, we suggest that students learn about migrations taking place in their own country. Essential knowledge for students regarding migration includes the following. First, they should know that more people than ever live outside of their country of birth[88] and that women migrants leave their home countries for a variety of reasons. Some migrant women voluntarily leave in search of economic opportunities and the ability to support their families through remittances, but, when they do, they may face economic and sexual exploitation. Other women involuntarily flee to another country when faced with war, crime, and/or gender violence. Second, given that many women migrants have been "rendered without voice or agency," students should learn about how they can amplify the voices of migrant women through collaboration with local women from various walks of life.[89] We are interested in guiding students to the intersection wherein women "at home" collaborate with migrant women for the purpose of empowerment. For example, grassroots feminism in Argentina is currently self-identified or self-called popular feminism (*feminismo popular*). It mobilizes around poor women, domestic workers (usually migrants from border countries like Paraguay), and transgendered persons, who discuss their aims in terms of localized experiences (*experiencias situadas*), and, in doing so, address intersectionality together. In the United States, students interested in glocal issues could familiarize themselves with issues of the borderlands, and, for instance, the political artwork of Entre NosOtr@s, a collaboration between Chicana, Latina, Indigenous, and gender-nonconforming artists who seek "dialogues about gender, sexuality and culture across borders."[90]

In order to act alongside women in glocal collaborations, we suggest that students develop empathy by conducting online research about women's organizations that are working on issues of migration, gender violence, economic/employment justice for undocumented workers, and/or other intersectional demands. Students could ask themselves the following questions: What major policy issues does the group focus on? How does the group frame its activities, and what are its major strategies for action? Does the group take an intersectional approach to policy? Why, or why not? Another avenue for developing empathy is to create a collage that represents "a day in the life" of a woman in one's own city who is a migrant. Gerdes et al., in teaching social work, ask their students to "create a poster board using material [e.g., business cards, brochures, examples, pictures] found at" a social work site. They do so in order to "expand" their "standpoints" through a type of hands-on role-play.[91] A political science student could do the same kind of project by collecting artifacts (e.g., newspaper headlines, brochures) and photos from stores, restaurants, public transportation, and websites that intersect with the lives of immigrants. A student could follow up the collage experience with journaling or a short class presentation that builds on the concept of reflexivity (i.e., asking themselves how their own daily experiences in same local sphere varies with the experience that they document).

After students have knowledge about the local, lived experiences of women in their home context and have developed reflexivity and empathy, they should consider attending a meeting of a local activist group and/or taking part in activism with the group. We suggest that students write reflexive statements about such engagements, answering the following sorts of questions: did you feel comfortable attending the meeting or speaking up in the group? Why, or why not? What would it take (in terms of personal time, personal growth, etc.) to get you to become involved with this group on a regular basis? How does the activism of this group cause social change, and did/could I contribute to this change? Reflections such as these encourage students to move beyond hobbyism to a posture of active global citizenship, wherein they have developed neural pathways to empathy and will be able to replicate empathetic responses into the future.

Engagement Activity 3: Fifth World Conference on Women and Online Engagements

As of this writing, the last UN World Conference for Women in 1995 took place a quarter of a century ago. As mentioned earlier, an argument can be made that a fifth world conference is needed. The process leading up to past world conferences presented key opportunities to activists; to prepare for the conferences, organizations formed transnational collaborations to "discuss their priorities and knowledge of UN processes," and they received funding from governments, which further increased their organizational capacity.[92] According to Goetz, "this funding supported intellectual work in the Global South to generate feminist critiques of neoliberalism and to insist upon attention to the race and class differences overlooked by Western feminists."[93] Funding opportunities have since diminished, and "only 1 percent" of new government and private foundation funds for global women's rights in the year 2019 went to "strengthening of feminist associations."[94] Although UN Women (United Nations Entity for Gender Equality and the Empowerment of Women), created in 2010, consults with civil society and maintains a Global Advisory Group, transnational feminists have argued that UN institutions related to gender are geared toward government representatives and the ideals of liberal feminism to a greater extent than to transnational feminism.[95] This is concerning because liberal feminists typically work within the status quo provided by government institutions, whereas other feminists, including transnational ones, seek to challenge the very institutions themselves as they present pressing and challenging ideas for social change. What is more, when Rincker et al. surveyed 36 women's NGOs in various world regions, ones which did and did not attend the 2010 CSW meetings, they found that the CSW did not address four of the NGOs' issue priorities: land rights, sex trafficking, internet access for women, and the effects of climate change on women."[96] Because a "key objective of feminist pedagogy is to teach students how to think critically about hegemonic narratives," we believe it is important for students to ask which women have more or less voice at the UN and how and why some issues are not undertaken at conferences.[97] A question, therefore, emerges: how could a fifth conference or an analogous forum assist the efforts of transnational feminists who speak to issues that defy current power hegemonies?

Meg Rincker, professor of political science at Purdue University-Northwest, has designed a pedagogical intervention to answer this question. After students gain knowledge about the history of UN conferences and how they involved local activists, she asks students to choose a country and research one of the four abovementioned issue priorities. For instance, a student could examine land rights activism by women in Bolivia or the effects of climate change in a country in the Sahel. They can utilize secondary sources, websites from local and/or transnational feminist organizations, and the social media content of organizations.[98] We also can imagine a personal interaction (via email or Zoom) with an activist in the student's country of interest, if, of course, the student has practiced the skills of reflexivity and feminist empathy and is prepared to dialogue with transnational activists. The culmination of this activity could be a faux conference where students present their findings to the "international community." This simulation allows students to hone political advocacy skills essential for engaged global citizenship that is focused directly on influencing political outcomes, particularly outcomes that challenge power hegemonies. While one step removed from direct political action, simulations are typically easier for instructors to coordinate, but still offer students an opportunity to practice stepping into the role of an engaged global citizen. Furthermore, we stress that if students hone the skills of reflexivity and empathy before completing such simulations, they will know how to engage feminist voices rather than appropriate and/or misunderstand them.

A few alternative activities include having students host other types of conferences or global gatherings, write policy briefs as if they are advisors to a government administration, and engage in online advocacy. For instance, it is worthwhile to research the World Social Forum, a two decade-old, anti-globalization network, and whether a new meeting of it is likely. Students could investigate what issues women's groups from a variety of countries would elevate at a future meeting of the anti-globalization forum. In a similar vein, students could work in groups and assume the role of bureaucrats in a women's policy agency in a country other than their home country, and they could develop a country report and/or list policy recommendations for a political executive or a particular bureaucratic institution. For instance, a student from Spain or the US could prepare a report from the Minister of Women, Genders, and Diversity in Argentina to be presented to the Argentine President. Or, a student could write a report as if she is a minister who is joining a President on an international diplomatic trip and needs a country report about women, gender policies, and LGBT+ rights in the country to which they are traveling. In this way, students identify opportunities for cooperating with and learning from women, gender activists, and government officials outside their own country. These opportunities take students beyond the realm of hobbyism if students are able to locate the voices of activists elsewhere, listen to them, and brainstorm opportunities and constraints for change *as the activists themselves define change*.

Because many students are familiar with and already participate in digital activism and hashtag feminism, they are likely to be inclined toward pursuing transnational concerns in a digital way.[99] We see online interactions with transnational feminists as a potential accompaniment to a Fifth Conference or as a stand-alone activity. Both students' and professors' increased familiarity with online meeting tools during the COVID-19 pandemic creates another opportunity for in-depth collaboration between students in the Global North and the rest of the world. Average people's ability to consistently influence government requires robust civic infrastructure,[100] and, particularly, the capability to coordinate collective action across geographic distances.[101] Online meeting platforms and internet access, while still out of reach for many, is typically available on college and university campuses and can ignite activism's spread to various global spaces. Hence, in the same way that professors support students' participation in the public sphere by advising on-campus student organizations and campus chapters of national organizations, they may now be able to extend this work to fostering student collaborations with transnational organizations.[102] Through such efforts, higher education institutions, in the tradition of United States land grant institutions that facilitated deliberation and civic engagement in the past[103] could incubate a new, cutting-edge transnational civic infrastructure that must be created before global issues can be routinely addressed.

Obstacles and Call to Action

We believe that our pedagogical approach's largest obstacle is that it challenges the ontological and epistemological norms of many social scientists. Most professors have been trained to teach from a disciplinary canon and to prioritize certain types of data over others. Thus, when transnational feminism seeks to "decolonize knowledge production"[104] by elevating the voices of women outside of the Global North and academia, it tasks professors with shifting to new sources of authority from which to teach. Moreover, transnational feminism asks researchers, professors, and students to reconsider the preeminence of modernist ontology and its dualisms.[105] For example, when debating public policy in class discussions, a professor might give as much significance to sharing emotions, as they relate to testimonios and personal experiences, as to statistical analyses about policy. Feminist relational ontology and epistemology claim that knowing comes from experiences and is "something that is socially constructed by embedded, embodied people who are in relation with each other."[106] The implication for educators is profound. Relationships and the engagement of emotions demand a normative approach which might be undesirable to some professors who do not want to disrupt scientific objectivity and the status quo and/or do not wish to engage their own selves in a reflexive, transparent, and interactive way. Students too, depending on their personalities, identities, experiences, and cultural contexts, might also feel encumbered by the reflexive and relational approach.

Another obstacle presents itself in the form of time limitations on what professors can teach in any given course. We have suggested here that professors teach content and skills related to transnational feminism, as well as introducing opportunities for students to use these skills to participate in global collective action as fully engaged citizens. However, the authors themselves often struggle to teach enough content about global issues to help students become only the most basic of political hobbyists. We want to take students on a journey from political hobbyists to globally engaged citizens, and we admit that the journey is long considering that the goal of obtaining a general knowledge of world politics often comes before mastering specific knowledge about globalization and transnational activism. Skills of reflexivity and empathy might enter the picture even later. Ideally, we see all of the pieces of the prescribed journey coming together over the course of a student's undergraduate career rather than in any one course alone. However, given that our approach challenges status quo knowledge and hierarchies and will not be favored by all academics, we would be remiss to wait for our approach to be scaffolded across a broader curriculum. As such, we advocate including elements of the approach in individual courses (see below).

A final obstacle that we must address is the fact that not all students want to be activists, and some might even seek participation in, for example, anti-gender campaigns that reinscribe hierarchies. Students have free will, and we do not seek to stymie their political agency. We argue, however, that the skill of empathy, whether one embraces the label of feminist or not, is valuable for all citizens as they exist in their own local communities. No matter the students' ideological sympathies, we want them to become sensitive to injustices suffered by members of their local (and global) communities and to care enough about others that they can imagine other people's experiences, with hopes that they will endeavor to find civic and political solutions to the problems which such awareness reveals.

Because we feel it is higher education's moral obligation to prepare students for global citizenship, we conclude this chapter by discussing reasons why our approach can and should work to change power dynamics in our world today. Although we have acknowledged that our approach is bigger than any one course, we feel that our emphasis on "glocal" concerns—and particularly migration—fit in almost any political science class and in any university context. Whether or not a political science course is specifically about international politics, we argue that the transnational sphere and the skills which it requires can be taught. For instance, one author (Strachan) until recently lived in Michigan and considers human trafficking a huge concern given that the state regularly has among the highest rates of human trafficking among all US states across the largely unguarded Canadian border.[107] Human trafficking policy could squarely fit in an American politics course or a state and local government course, even though these courses do not habitually grapple with transnationalism or feminism. Another example from Spain demonstrates how "glocal" issues emerge in a university's physical setting. Spain is a country that in the last decades has received comparatively high numbers of migrants, and many migrant women are household workers who care for children, elderly, or sick individuals. Thus, another co-author (Valiente), believes that her students could benefit from learning from migrant women who live and work close to her university. Similar to human trafficking mentioned above, migration policy in Spain could directly fit in a European (or international) politics course or a state and local government course even though these courses do not usually deal with feminism.

We also believe that the history of violence that inspires testimonios touch more countries than meets the eye. Testimonios grew out of state terrorism in the Global South, but the Global North has significant experience with state violence as well. As former colonial powers, slave states, settler states, and fascist states, the Global North provides a history "close to home" about which students can practice empathy.

What is more, the skills of reflexivity and empathy and our related engagement activities are ones that can be used in a variety of courses whether or not a professor chooses to extensively cover the substance of transnational feminism. For instance, if one was teaching about environmental politics, arguably students would be interested in hearing how global climate change influences local communities around the world. Developing empathy and imagining the experiences of Indigenous activists who defend their land and nations is akin to engaging the work of transnational feminists. Similarly, a professor could flip the engagement activity about the UN World Conference for Women to have students research the local and national perspectives of activists fighting for various kinds of social change.

Students are already engaged in the topics and skills for which we advocate in this chapter, and we must do more so that we do not lose the participation of women and BIPOC (Black, Indigenous and people of color) students in political science. As one author (Lopreite) notes, transnational activism already mobilizes students in Argentina who use social media technology to follow the political issues that motivate them. Another author (Ortbals) knows a student who runs a website and Instagram account to educate peers on "environmentalism, intersectional feminism, anti-neoliberalism, [and] anti-colonialism."[108] If many students are ready to take social action, it only makes sense for professors to educate them on the history and skills of activism that that could enhance their budding activism by embedding civic skills long associated with transnational feminist activism and to prepare students for transnational collective action that addresses issues that cut across national borders into our courses whenever possible. We cannot afford to overlook students in spaces where they are generating activisms or wondering about how to resist hierarchies. Women and people of color have been left out of political conversations for a long time, and they will not be able to boldly insert their voices into political conversations by simply receiving an education that gives them information and casually hopes they can hold their own in political debates.[109] Students deserve an education that cultivates the knowledge, skills, and identities that prepare them to influence political outcomes in an increasingly globalized world. They should be encouraged to do so through reciprocal, collaborative, and uncoerced relationships with their allies around the world and in ways that undermine rather than reify a hierarchical status quo.

Endnotes

1. Gerda Lerner, *The Creation of Patriarchy* (New York: Oxford University Press, 1987); J. Cherie Strachan, Lori M. Poloni-Staudinger, Shannon Jenkins, and Candice D. Ortbals, *Why Don't Women Rule the World?* (Washington, DC: SAGE-CQ Press, 2019).

2. Michael Johnson, *Corruption, Contention and Reform* (New York: Cambridge University Press, 2013): 31.

3. Ibid., 31.

4. Lori M. Poloni-Staudinger and J. Cherie Strachan, "TLC Keynote: Democracy is More Important Than a P-Value: Embracing Political Science's Civic Mission through Intersectional Engaged Learning," *PS: Political Science & Politics* 53, no. 3 (2020): 569–74.

5. Eitan Hersh, *How to Move Beyond Political Hobbyism, Take Action, and Make Real World Change* (2020), https://thehill.com/opinion/campaign/520277-another-political-gender-gap-emerges.

6. Laura Parisi and Lynn Thornton, "Connecting the Local with the Global: Transnational Feminism and Civic Engagement," *Feminist Teacher* 22, no. 3 (2012): 214–32.

7. Ibid., 215.

8. Elizabeth Matto, Alison Rios Millett McCartney, Elizabeth A. Bennion, and Dick Simpson, eds., *Teaching Civic Engagement Across the Disciplines* (Washington, DC: American Political Science Association, 2017); Alison Rios Millet McCartney, Elizabeth A. Bennion, and Dick Simpson, eds., *Teaching Civic Engagement: From Student to Active Citizen* (Washington, DC: American Political Science Association, 2013).

9. Theda Skocpol, *Diminished Democracy, From Membership to Management in American Civic Life* (Cambridge, MA: Harvard University Press, 2003).

10. *The Economist*, "Global Democracy has a Very Bad Year," (February 2 2021), https://www.economist.com/graphic-detail/2021/02/02/global-democracy-has-a-very-bad-year.

11. *Diminished Democracy*; Sydney Verba, Kay Lehman Schlozman, and Henry Brady, *Voice and Equality, Civic Voluntarism in American Politics* (Cambridge, MA: Harvard University Press, 1995).

12. *The Economist*, "Global Democracy has a Very Bad Year," n.p.

13. Gustavo A.Flores-Macías and Jessica Zarkin, "The Militarization of Law Enforcement: Evidence from Latin America," *Perspectives on Politics* 19, no. 2 (2019): 1–20; Anne M. Goetz, "The New Competition in Multilateral Norm-Setting: Transnational Feminists & the Illiberal Backlash," *Daedalus* 149 (Winter 2020): 160–79; Roman Kuhar and David Paternotte, *Anti-Gender Campaigns in Europe: Mobilizing against Equality* (Lanham, MD: Roman and Littlefield, 2017); Edward Lawson, "TRENDS: Police Militarization and the Use of Lethal Force," *Political Research Quarterly* 72, no. 1 (2019): 177–89.

14. Yoonil Auh and Heejung Raina Sim, "Global Justice and Education for Global Citizenship: Considerations for Education Policy-planning Process," *Asian Journal of Political Science* 26, no. 2 (2018): 224.

15. Sonia E. Alvarez, "Advocating Feminism: The Latin American Feminist NGO Boom," *International Feminist Journal of Politics* 1, no. 2 (1999): 181–209; Linda Peake and Karen De Souza, "Feminist Academic and Activist Praxis in Service of the Transnational," in *Critical Transnational Feminist Praxis*, eds. Amanda Lock Swarr and Richa Nagar (Albany, NY: SUNY Press, 2010): 105–23.

16. Skocpol, *Diminished Democracy*.

17. AAC&U, "General Education for a Global Century," (2020), https://www.aacu.org/sites/default/files/files/Global/LuceGlobalLearningProposal.pdf.

18. Fatih Aktas, Kate Pitts, Jessica C. Richards, and Iveta Silova, "Institutionalizing Global Citizenship: A Critical Analysis of Higher Education Programs and Curricula," *Journal of Studies in International Education* 21, no. 1 (2017): 65–80.

19. Julie Matthews and Ravinder Sidu, "Desperately Seeking the Global Subject: International Education, Citizenship, and Cosmopolitanism," *Globalisation, Societies, and Education* 3, no. 1 (2005): 53.

20. Auh and Sim, "Global Justice", 224.

21. Matthews and Sidu, "Desperately Seeking the Global Subject," 53.

22. Hans Schattle, *The Practices of Global Citizenship* (Lanham, MD: Rowman & Littlefield, 2008).

23. Parisi and Thornton, "Connecting the Local with the Global."

24. Parisi and Thornton, "Connecting the Local with the Global," 215; Sam Schulz and Deborah Agnew, "Moving toward Decoloniality in Short-Term Study abroad under New Colombo: Constructing Global Citizenship," *British Journal of Sociology of Education* 41 (2020): 1164–79.

25. Mahnaz Moallem, "The Impact Of Synchronous And Asynchronous Communication Tools On Learner Self-Regulation, Social Presence, Immediacy, Intimacy And Satisfaction In Collaborative Online Learning," *The Online Journal of Distance Education and e-Learning* 3, no. 3 (2015): 332.

26. Schulz and Agnew, "Moving toward Decoloniality."

27. Parisi and Thornton, "Connecting the Local with the Global," 214.

28. Parisi and Thornton, "Connecting the Local with the Global."

29. Nicola Banks, David Hulme, and Michael Edwards, "NGOs, States, and Donors Revisited: Still Too Close for Comfort?" *World Development* 66, no. C (2015): 706–18.

30. Parisi and Thornton, "Connecting the Local with the Global."

31. Schulz and Agnew, "Moving toward Decoloniality," np.

32. Aktas et al., "Institutionalizing Global Citizenship," 65–80.

33. Catherine M. Orr, "Activism," in *Rethinking Women's and Gender Studies*, Catherine M. Orr, Ann Braithwait, and Diane Lichtenstein, eds. (New York: Routledge, 2012).

34. Chandra Talpade Mohanty, *Feminism Without Borders: Decolonizing Theory, Practicing Solidarity* (Durham, NC: Duke University Press, 2003): 243.

35. Sylvanna M. Falcón, "Transnational Feminism as a Paradigm for Decolonizing the Practice of Research: Identifying Feminist Principles and Methodology Criteria for US-Based Scholars," *Frontiers: A Journal of Women Studies* 37, no. 1 (2016): 174–94.

36. Barbara J. Thayer-Bacon, "A Pragmatist and Feminist Relational (E)pistemology," *European Journal of Pragmatism and American Philosophy* 2, no. 1 (2010): 1–22.

37. *Teaching Civic Engagement Across the Disciplines; Teaching Civic Engagement: From Student to Active Citizen.*

38. Patricia Valoy, "Transnational Feminism: Why Feminist Activism Needs to Think Globally," *Everyday Feminism* (January 28, 2015), https://everydayfeminism.com/2015/01/why-we-need-transnational-feminism/.

39. Rosemarie Tong, *Feminist Thought: A More Comprehensive Introduction*, 2nd edition (Boulder, CO: Westview Press, 2009).

40. Janet M. Conway, "Troubling Transnational Feminism(s): Theorising Activist Praxis," *Feminist Theory* 18, no. 2 (2017): 205–27.

41. Leela Fernandes, *Transnational Feminism in the United States: Knowledge, Ethics, Power* (New York: NYU Press, 2013); Chandra Talpade Mohanty, Ann Russo, and Lourdes Torres, eds. *Third World Women and the Politics of Feminism* (Bloomington: Indiana University Press, 1991).

42. For example: M. Jacqui Alexander and Chandra T. Mohanty, *Feminist Genealogies, Colonial Legacies, Democratic Futures* (New York: Routledge, 1997); Caren Kaplan and Inderpal Grewal, "Transnational Feminist Cultural Studies: Beyond the Marxism/Poststructuralism/Feminism Divides," in *Between Women and Nation: Nationalism, Transnational Feminisms, and the State*, eds. Caren Kaplan, Norma Alarcón and Minoo Moallem, 349–63 (Durham, NC and London: Duke University Press, 1999); Maria Mies, *The Lace Makers of Narsapur. Indian Housewives Produce for the World Market* (London: Zed Press, 1982); Aihwa Ong, *Spirits of Resistance and Capitalist Discipline: Factory Women in Malaysia (Suny Series in the Anthropology of Work)* (Albany, NY: State University of New York Press, 1987); Saskia Sassen, *Globalization and Its Discontents* (New York: New Press, 1998).

43. Kaplan and Grewal, "Transnational Feminist Cultural Studies," 848.

44. Fernandes, *Transnational Feminism in the United States.*

45. Rawwida Baksh-Soodeen and Wendy Harcourt, eds. *The Oxford Handbook of Transnational Feminist Movements* (Oxford University Press, USA, 2015): 4.

46. Fernandes, *Transnational Feminism in the United States*, 7.

47. Baksh-Soodeen and Harcourt, *The Oxford Handbook of Transnational Feminist Movements.*

48. Rebecca Cardone, "Empathetic British Feminists at the Crossroads of Colonialism and Self-determination," *International Journal of Sociology and Social Policy* 39 (2019): 84–97.

49. See Vrushali Patil, "From Patriarchy to Intersectionality: A Transnational Feminist Assessment of How Far We've Really Come," *Signs: Journal of Women in Culture and Society* 38, no. 4 (2013): 847–67; Fernandes, *Transnational Feminism in the*

United States.

50. Seidman, "Feminism and Revolution"; Choonib Lee, "Black Panther Women in the Third World," Paper presented at the American Historical Association Session 119 (January 3, 2019), New York, NY, https://aha.confex.com/aha/2015/webprogram/Paper16629.html.

51. Benita Roth, "Second Wave Black Feminism in the African Diaspora: News from New Scholarship," *Agenda: Empowering Women for Gender Equity* 17, no. 58 (2003): 46–58.

52. Myra Marx Ferree and Aili Mari Tripp, eds. *Global Feminism: Transnational Women's Activism, Organizing, and Human Rights* (New York: NYU Press, 2006).

53. Goetz, "The New Competition," 160-79.

54. Meg Rincker, Marisa Henderson, Renato Vidigal, and Daniel Delgado, "Evaluating the Representation and Responsiveness of the United Nations Commission on the Status of Women (CSW) to Diverse Women Populations Worldwide," *Frontiers in Sociology* 4 (2019).

55. For examples of, #MeToo in Korea and India, see Strachan et al., 2019.

56. FEMNET (African Women's Development and Communication Network, 2020), https://femnet.org/; Awino Okech and Dinah Musindarwez, "Building Transnational Feminist Alliances: Reflections on the Post-2015 Development Agenda," *Contexto Internacional* 41, no. 22 (2019): 255–73.

57. Okech and Musindarwez, "Building Transnational Feminist Alliances," 255–73.

58. See FEMNET.

59. Okech and Musindarwezo, "Building Transnational Feminist Alliances," 278.

60. Gouldner (1970) qtd. in Candice D. Ortbals and Meg E. Rincker, "Fieldwork, Identities, and Intersectionality: Negotiating Gender, Race, Class, Religion, Nationality, and Age in the Research Field Abroad: Editors' Introduction," *PS: Political Science & Politics* 42, no. 2 (2009): 287.

61. Thomas F. Nelson Laird and Mark E. Engberg, "Establishing Differences Between Diversity Requirements and Other Courses with Varying Degrees of Diversity Inclusivity," *The Journal of General Education* 60, no. 2 (2011): 117–37; Matthew J. Mayhew and Sonia D. Fernandez, "Pedagogical Practices That Contribute to Social Justice Outcomes," *Review of Higher Education* 31, no. 1 (2007): 58.

62. Cardone, "Empathetic British Feminists," 84–97; Liz Bondi, "Empathy and Identification: Conceptual Resources for Feminist Fieldwork," *ACME: An International Journal for Critical Geographies* 2, no. 1 (2003): 64–76.

63. Bondi, "Empathy and Identification," 71.

64. Tina M. Zappile, Daniel J. Beers, and Chad Raymond, "Promoting Global Empathy and Engagement through Real-Time Problem-Based Simulations," *International Studies Perspectives* 18, no. 2 (2017): 196.

65. Zhou Li, Nancy Regina Gómez Arrieta, and Risa Whitson, "Empathy through Imaginative Reconstruction: Navigating Difference in Feminist Transnational Research in China and Peru," *Gender, Place & Culture* 27, no. 4 (2020): 589; Michelle Rodino-Colocino, "Me Too, #MeToo: Countering Cruelty with Empathy," *Communication and Critical/Cultural Studies* 15, no. 1 (2018): 96–100.

66. Cardone, "Empathetic British Feminists," 84–97.

67. Rodino-Colocino, "Me Too, #MeToo," 97.

68. Ibid.

69. Strachan et al. 2019.

70. Rodino-Colocino, "Me Too, #MeToo," 96–100.

71. Clare Hemmings, "Affective Solidarity: Feminist Reflexivity and Political Transformation," *Feminist Theory* 13, no. 2 (2012): 147–61, 152; Rodino-Colocino, "Me Too, #MeToo," 96–100; bell hooks, *Black Looks: Race and Representation* (New York: Routledge, 1992).

72. Shireen Roshanravan, "Staying Home While Studying Abroad: Anti-Imperial Praxis for Globalizing Feminist Visions," *Journal of Feminist Scholarship* 2 (Spring 2018): 1–23.

73. Li et al., "Empathy through Imaginative Reconstruction," 587–607.

74. Karen E. Gerdes, Elizabeth A. Segal, Kelly F. Jackson, and Jennifer L. Mullins, "Teaching Empathy: A Framework Rooted in Social Cognitive Neuroscience and Social Justice," *Journal of Social Work Education* 47, no. 1 (2011): 109–31.

75. Gerdes et al., "Teaching Empathy," 118.

76. Alejandra C. Elenes, "Nepantla, Spiritual Activism, New Tribalism: Chicana Feminist Transformative Pedagogies and

Social Justice Education," *Journal of Latino- Latin American Studies* (JOLLAS) 5, no. 3 (2013): 137.

77. El Ashmawi, Yvonne Pilar, Ma Eugenia Hernandez Sanchez, and Judith Flores Carmona, "Testimonialista Pedagogues: Testimonio Pedagogy in Critical Multicultural Education," *International Journal of Multicultural Education* 20, no. 1 (2018): 67–85.

78. Alicia, Partnoy and Raquel Partnoy, *The Little School: Tales of Disappearance & Survival*, trans. Lois Edwards Athey and Sandra Braunstein, 2nd edition, (San Francisco, CA: Cleis Press, 1998).

79. Kathryn M. Smith, "Female Voice and Feminist Text: Testimonio as A Form of Resistance in Latin America," *Florida Atlantic Comparative Studies Journal* 12 (2010): 21–37.

80. Ibid., 23.

81. Patricia DeRocher, *Transnational Testimonios: The Politics of Collective Knowledge Production. Decolonizing Feminisms* (Seattle, WA: University of Washington Press, 2018): 8.

82, Ibid., 136.

83. Ibid., 16.

84. El Ashmawi et al., "Testimonialista Pedagogues," 67–85.

85. Ibid., 77.

86. Baksh-Soodeen and Harcourt, *The Oxford Handbook of Transnational Feminist Movements.*

87. Falcón, "Transnational Feminism," 175; Roshanravan, "Staying Home While Studying Abroad," 1–23.

88. Oliva M. Espín and Andrea L. Dottolo, "A Transnational Feminist Perspective on the Psychology of Migration," in *Transnational Psychology of Women: Expanding International and Intersectional Approaches*, eds. L. H. Collins, S. Machizawa, and J. K. Rice (Washington, DC: American Psychological Association, 2019): 121–39.

89. Ibid., 134.

90. Izzy Bartling, "Arizona Professor Talks About Community Activism at US-Mexico Border," *The Daily Orange* (October 1, 2019), http://dailyorange.com/2019/10/arizona-professor-talks-community-activism-u-s-mexico-border/.

91. Gerdes et al., "Teaching Empathy," 121.

92. Rincker et al. 2019; Goetz, 2020.

93. Goetz, "The New Competition," 160–79.

94. Ibid.

95. Rincker et al. 2019.

96. Ibid.

97. Parisi and Thornton, "Connecting the Local with the Global," 217.

98. See List of Transnational Women's Organizations.

99. See Hester Baer, "Redoing Feminism: Digital Activism, Body Politics, and Neoliberalism," *Feminist Media Studies* 16, no. 1 (2016): 17–34.

100. Verba et al., *Voice and Equality, Civic Voluntarism in American Politic.*

101. Skocpol, *Diminished Democracy.*

102. See List of Transnational Women's Organizations.

103. Kathleen Hall Jamieson, "Reconceptualizing Public Engagement by Land-Grant University Scientists," *Proceedings of the National Academy of Sciences* 117, no. 6 (2020): 2734–6; Timothy J. Schaffer, "Supporting the 'Archstone of Democracy': Cooperative Extension's Experiment with Deliberative Group Discussion," *Journal of Extension* 55, no. 5 (2017), https://tigerprints.clemson.edu/joe/vol55/iss5/24.

104. Falcón, "Transnational Feminism," 175.

105. For example: rationality versus emotion, objectivity versus non-objectivity, etc., see Falcón, "Transnational Feminism," 178.

106. Thayer-Bacon, "A Pragmatist and Feminist Relational (E)pistemology," np.

107. World Population Review, *Human Trafficking by State* (2020), https://worldpopulationreview.com/state-rankings/human-trafficking-statistics-by-state.

108. Massiel Valladares, "Beyond the Bubble," (2020), https://massi98v.wixsite.com/beyondthebubble.

109. Hersh, *How to Move Beyond Political Hobbyism.*

2

The University as a Civic Agent: Promoting Civic Engagement and the UN SDGs in Northeastern Brazil

Xaman Minillo[1] & Henrique Zeferino de Menezes[2]

1. Universidade Federal da Paraíba/University of Bristol   2. Universidade Federal da Paraíba

Much civic engagement pedagogy research is conducted in developed countries or with study abroad students from developed countries. Thus, there is less research regarding civic engagement pedagogy in, for, and by institutions in developing countries, which could mean a lack of exploration of civic engagement education on international development initiatives from a developing country's perspective. This chapter demonstrates how universities in developing countries can become civic agents and contribute to the promotion of the United Nations (UN) Sustainable Development Goals (SDGs) by working with civil society, the private sector, and public administrators. It demonstrates how a community outreach project developed by a university in northeastern Brazil contributed to meeting the University's civic responsibilities and implementing the SDGs, indirectly benefiting the citizenry in the region. This was achieved by establishing the crucial connection between the global agenda and local needs and realities through training of key actors and building fertile, institutionalized partnerships between the UN, university, civil society, and public actors.

KEYWORDS: Civil Society and Development; Civic Engagement; Service-Learning; Sustainable Development Goals.

Introduction

While a great deal of civic engagement pedagogy research has been conducted in developed countries, there is less research regarding civic engagement pedagogy in, for, and by institutions in developing countries, which could mean a lack of exploration of civic engagement education on international development initiatives from a developing country's perspective. The discourse on civic engagement pedagogy has largely focused on such issues as service-learning and voter drives, but there is less discussion about global-level initiatives, including the United Nations (UN) Sustainable Development Goals (SDGs). When combined with the fact that civic engagement pedagogy is largely focused on developed countries in the global North, the impact of the UN's Millennium Development Goals (MDGs), which ran from 2000–2015, and their follow-up, the SDGs on civic engagement in developing countries lacks attention in the literature. This gap is surprising, given the potential impact of these initiatives on society in developing countries and how, to be successful in any country, the SDGs require broad public participation and cannot be achieved by governments' sporadic adoption of a set of initiatives. In this chapter, we present a service-learning initiative developed at the Federal University of Paraíba (UFPB) that was based on the recognition of: (1) the importance and richness of the academic debate on development strategies and the roots of underdevelopment in Brazil; (2) the role played by higher education institutions (HEI) in the production and dissemination of qualified scientific and technological knowledge to society; and (3) the need for greater civic engagement in the dissemination and implementation of the SDG agenda.

This case study focuses on a service-learning project which recognized the relevance of civil society's contribution to the implementation of the SDGs and sought to disseminate the SDG agenda's content among civil society organizations, social movements, public managers, and the private sector in the Brazilian northeast. The knowledge dissemination carried out in the initiative was executed by undergraduate students engaged in the project and supervised by academics. This project's immediate goals were to disseminate the SDGs' agenda and encourage its appropriation by key local actors able to influence its adoption in a way which is aligned to the needs and demands of the region. Student participants helped the project to succeed while learning about sustainable development and participatory democracy. It also allowed the establishment of partnerships between our university and some civil society organizations, public agencies, and policymakers, leading to the creation of the Public Policy and Sustainable Development Center, through which further partnerships and civic engagement are developing.

This chapter has three main sections. The first presents the context where the project was developed, the northeastern region of Brazil, and its political and economic conditions. It also reviews the context of the UN's development of the SDGs and examines the connection between the SDGs and citizen participation, highlighting the importance of localizing the UN's 2030 agenda to achieve global and local sustainable development. The second section presents the community engagement project developed by the Department of International Relations at UFPB with the aim of contributing to the implementation of the UN's SDGs through civic engagement. It details the process of structuring the project, the various actions developed as part of it, some of the challenges encountered in this process, and the results achieved.

These explanations are followed by a discussion of how HEIs can act as civic agents and contribute to promoting global-local civic engagement and the SDGs' local implementation, establishing the crucial connection between the global agenda and local needs and realities. Considering the transformative potential of actions developed within the Brazilian higher education environment, it is argued that universities in developing countries can and should play a significant role in promoting civic engagement and sustainable development. This potential is considered in relation to the challenges which emerged during the project's execution and are connected to the limitations faced by a federal HEI in a shifting political context, highlighting the limits which bottom-up civic action may encounter in a federation like Brazil. The chapter demonstrates how all universities can advance their commitments to civic engagement by performing their traditional academic functions grounded in the needs of the communities where they are situated.

Civic Engagement and Development in Northeastern Brazil

While Brazil might be associated with a mix of tropical forests and beautiful beaches with white sand and blue sea, this continental country is complex. Brazil has one of the largest biological reserves in its forests, the largest freshwater reserve in the world, and an Atlantic coastline of almost 7,500 kilometers. However, it is heterogeneous socially and culturally, has considerable geographical, climatic, and environmental diversity, and faces many economic, political, and social challenges. The Brazilian Gross Domestic Product (GDP) per capita income for 2019 was US $8,717. While this level places it among the highest GDP per capita in Latin America, it is far from the average of Organization for Economic Co-Operation and Development (OECD) countries, at US $39,485.90.[1] Brazil faces high rates of inequality, which are reflected in some social indicators, e.g., life expectancy overall in Brazil is 75.9 years,[2] but these numbers vary widely between cities and are lower for rural populations. According to the 2010 census, while the national urban average Human Development Index (HDI) is high (0.75), in rural areas the HDI is medium (0.586).[3]

The Brazilian northeast, the region of Brazil where the project presented in this chapter was carried out, has important characteristics which are relevant for a better understanding of the potential that university community engagement has to foster civic engagement, but also its limitations and challenges. It is a region with more than 50 million inhabitants distributed among nine states and 1,554,000 sq km, which includes biomes ranging from the Atlantic Forest in the coastal region to semi-arid areas inland. The region also faces important socio-economic problems—such as the persistence of pockets of poverty, especially in large cities' agglomerations and in the regions with a more arid climate. The states in this region have high levels of social inequality, infant mortality, and underemployment, and are poorer with a per capita income that is less than half the national average.[4]

Table 1. Human Development Index (HDI) of Brazilian Locations Compared to Other Countries			
Brazilian location	Brazilian location's HDI	Other countries' HDI	Other countries
São Caetano do Sul (SP)	0.862	0.861	Estonia
Águas de São Pedro (SP)	0.854		
Distrito Federal	0.824	0.828	Hungary
São Paulo	0.783	0.782	Bulgaria
Brazil	0.755	0.756	Mexico
		0.754	Georgia
Rio Grande do Norte	0.684	0.684	Indonesia
Ceará	0.682		
Pernambuco	0.673		
Sergipe	0.665		
Bahia	0.660	0.631	Nicaragua
Paraíba	0.658		
Piauí	0.645		
Maranhão	0.639		
Alagoas	0.631		
Fernando Falcão (MA)	0.443	0.442	Ethiopia
Melgaço (PA)	0.418	0.419	Mali
Table created from the 2013 Atlas of Human Development in Brazil, available at: https://www.br.undp.org/content/brazil/pt/home/idho/rankings/idhm-municipios-2010.html			

Table 1 shows the socioeconomic situation of the Brazilian northeastern region contextually, comparing the HDI of the states (in italics) in the region with the Brazilian average, while also highlighting the extremes found in Brazilian municipalities. Including the four tiers of human development found in Brazilian localities, the table illustrates the socio-economic heterogeneity and inequalities found within the country with HDIs comparable to OECD and low-income states.

All states in the northeast have a HDI below the Brazilian average, which is 0.755. The state of *Rio Grande do Norte*, which has the highest HDI in the region, compares with the HDI in Indonesia, while *Alagoas*, the state with the lowest HDI in the northeast, is similar to Nicaragua. The extremes which characterize Brazil are also featured: while *São Caetano do Sul* and *Águas de São Pedro*, two municipalities in the state of *São Paulo*, and the Federal District and the State of *São Paulo* have a very high or high HDI similar to that of European countries, the municipalities of *Melgaço* (in the state of *Pará*) and *Fernando Falcão* (in *Maranhão*) have a low level of development similar to that of less developed countries. The disparities which characterize Brazilian locations indicate the inadequacy of top-down and one-size-fits-all approaches to promoting development. To foster development in lower HDI regions such as the northeast and reduce regional inequalities, the specificities of each region—and even municipalities—must be considered. Also, to acknowledge the connection between social capital and inequality,[5] bottom-up solutions supported by local civic engagement must be at the center of development programs.

An important issue is the role of education. Brazilian education indicators are the lowest score in the country's HDI, and the indicators tend to be lower in the northeast. In 2010, for example, while Brazilian municipal HDI was high (0.727), the life expectancy index was very high (0.816), income was high (0.739), and education was medium (0.637). In the northeast, the municipal HDI was medium (0.663), while the education index was low (0.569).[6] The Brazilian illiteracy rate (for persons aged 15 or older) in 2017 was 7.1% of the national population, while the northeastern average was around 15%. While around 14% of all Brazilians aged 25 or above have completed higher education, the average in the region is less than 10%.[7] The lower education rates and development indicators in northeastern Brazil highlight the importance of focusing on education and on universities as institutions which can promote development.

Brazilian HEIs are usually divided according to their funding and their organization. In terms of academic organization, HEIs can be universities, university centers, or colleges.[8] While colleges are not autonomous, universities enjoy didactic-scientific, administrative, financial, and property management autonomy,[9] even though they are dependent on public resources. In terms of financing, HEIs can be private or public, the latter being funded by governmental resources. Public HEIs can be federal, state, or municipal, depending on which level of public administration provides the resources for their maintenance. In public institutions, the education is completely free, while in private HEIs the funding comes mostly from the payment of tuition fees.[10]

Brazilian HEIs, especially public universities, take on a role which surpasses their educational responsibility. They develop their formative missions by embracing their social commitments to educating citizens and cultivating their civic engagement, reducing inequalities, creating opportunities, and promoting development while constructing and preserving cultural identities.[11] These goals are supported by the constitutionally established principle of inseparability between teaching, research, and community outreach,[12] which underlines the connection between the University and its social, economic, and political context. This principle emphasizes the importance of providing an academic education which prepares students to enter the job market, but also contributes to solving social issues in line with local demands and specificities. It encourages production of high-quality academic and scientific knowledge conducive to overcoming structural socio-economic problems in Brazilian society such as poverty and inequality.

These three dimensions of academic activity—teaching, research, and community outreach—form a tripod which constitutes, according to article 207 of the 1988 Brazilian Constitution, the fundamental basis of Brazilian higher education and a duty of the federal higher education system. They must be understood as complementary but autonomous aspects of a university's mission, necessary to guide a competent, ethical, and socially engaged university which acknowledges its civic responsibilities.[13]

Through their research activities, universities are central to the production of innovative scientific and technological knowledge. Universities can act as catalysts for innovation and knowledge generation, and, as the project presented in this chapter demonstrates, they can develop new approaches, solutions, and technologies in collaboration with local communities through academic outreach. In this context, the accumulation of expertise, structure, equipment, and qualified personnel which universities promote through regular academic activities can contribute in an efficient and multidisciplinary way to deal with contemporary challenges and barriers that currently limit sustainable development.

Just as education has an important role to play, so too has civil society, which has played an increasingly important role in the promotion of development in recent decades.[14] Although this participatory aspect was left out in the formulation of the UN's MDGs in the 1990s,[15] the Millennium Declaration urged governments to partner with civil society. The importance of greater and more effective civic engagement was also noted in the UN's evaluation of the progress made by the MDGs and embraced as a core element in the following 2030 agenda, which highlighted the need to expand the political participatory process and establish more effective mechanisms for civil society involvement as the UN formulated the SDGs.[16]

The 2030 Agenda recognizes the importance of localizing[17] the SDGs for them to be effective, that is, translating the global agenda into policies tailored to meet specific local realities.[18] Localizing involves connecting the international, national, and subnational levels (regional and municipal) so that the global guidelines are seen in the light of national norms and aligned to the specific needs and demands identified at the local level. To achieve a civically engaged bottom-up approach, prioritizing local action is necessary through strengthening the capacities of local communities to engage in civic action, cultivating local governments' material and human resources, mobilizing political will, and developing institutional and legal frameworks at the local, regional, and federal levels.[19]

Brazil has gone through dramatic changes in the last four decades. The year 1985 marked the end of an authoritarian military regime, followed by progress toward an increasingly vibrant democracy. During the first years of the 21st century, especially during Luis Inácio Lula da Silva and Dilma Rousseff's first term, the country experienced a moment of innovative public policies which mitigated extreme poverty and hunger, increased social rights, generated millions of jobs, and contributed to the reduction of social inequalities.[20] These improvements were connected to the decentralized and participatory character of Brazilian re-democratization, which fostered the development of bottom-up socio-political transformations.[21]

The participatory institutions enshrined in Brazilian public governance by the 1988 constitution were empowered two decades later when, during the Lula da Silva administration, the National Policy Councils and National Policy Conferences were reformed. These institutions provide spaces for members of civil society to participate in multi-level deliberative processes to inform drafting of national policies. Thus, these participatory institutions contributed to the definition of government agendas, the enactment of resolutions and recommendations, and the formulation of public policies, plans, strategies, and guidelines to implement them and supervise their application.[22] Participatory budgeting, which had been created in 1989 by the *Partido dos Trabalhadores* (PT), was adopted nationally between 2003-2016. This method was considered a "best practice" among the world's 40 best policy programs by the UN in 1996 and became Brazil's main "democratic export," adopted by more than a thousand cities in almost 50 countries.[23]

In this context of human development, an important policy adopted was the expansion and internalization of the network of Brazilian federal universities, expanding the number of young people in undergraduate and graduate courses and democratizing access to higher education. The expansion and strengthening of this network together with structural political changes increased the possibilities for interaction between universities, local governments, and civil society organizations in the development of collaborative research and community engagement projects.[24]

Due to these advances, there were great expectations for further improvements in Brazilian democratic governance and development in 2014 when the project outlined in this case study was initiated, with the aim of contributing to the advancement of civic engagement and development while relying on the capacity of universities to act as civic agents promoting positive change. Yet, as the chapter highlights, political events since 2016 have shown the frailty of Brazilian institutions and democracy, which has shifted the character of federal governance significantly and led to the project's conclusion. The project's conception, development, and results achieved are addressed in the following section.

Civil Society Participation in the United Nations Sustainable Development Goals Project

The civic engagement project, *Civil Society Participation in the United Nations Sustainable Development Goals,* was developed within the Department of International Relations at UFPB, a small department of 15 scholars based in the Centre of Applied Social Sciences located in the University's João Pessoa Campus.[25] UFPB is a large institution, with four *campi*, 18 centres, and 97 departments.[26] In 2019 it offered 124 undergraduate courses and 112 post-graduate courses and had 30,385 students enrolled in undergraduate studies and 5,937 in post-graduate studies. During that year, the HEI registered 98 patents, published 10,233 scientific articles, and conducted 1,253 community outreach projects.[27]

The project outlined was based on the premise that public engagement and civic participation are critically important for the successful implementation of the SDGs. Considering the importance of localizing the SDG agenda in the northeastern states of Brazil, this initiative aimed to join University and civil society organizations in the region and sought to build bridges between the knowledge produced in the academy and the knowledge of practice from relevant political actors.

From the localizing approach, the coordinators understood from the outset that the global sustainable development agenda cannot thrive based on sporadic top-down actions taken by governments. Instead, this agenda requires a network of actors that internalized and used the SDGs as a language and action tool. To be achieved, the internationally negotiated SDGs must be adopted by a civil society which applies the SDGs in its local communities; by local governments, which make decisions about public policies and resource allocation; and by private initiatives, which define investments and directly affect the natural resources available to society.

In line with this agenda, the project sought to contribute to localizing SDGs in the northeastern region of Brazil, that is, adapting global sustainable development discourses to local realities. To promote sustainable development, the University could disseminate the agenda among relevant local actors, assist in creating a strong, interconnected structure supporting policies aligned with the SDGs and train civil society actors to exert political pressure when necessary. In other words, through an outreach project structured around education and trainings on the theme of the SDGs, the University sought to foster learning and civic engagement among students and local citizens, while strengthening the capacity of local public and civil society actors to promote sustainable development.

Structuring the project

In 2014 the *Political Economy of the United Nations Millennium Development Goals* research project was initiated. This project included three undergraduate students supervised by one member of the faculty from the Department of International Relations. It was developed as part of UFPB's Scientific Initiation program, which aims to provide opportunities for undergraduate students to engage in the practice of developing research. This project[28] provided the conceptual basis for future activities on the SDGs and was developed around two topics: first, the results of the MDGs and their impact on the post-2015 Agenda, and second, the political processes shaping and structuring the SDGs. The project focused on building a comprehensive and in-depth understanding of the political processes for adopting, implementing, and evaluating the United Nations' development agenda and made it possible to develop knowledge about the two specific UN development agendas of the 21st century. It was in the context of this project that partnerships with key actors in the region were examined with the support of the United Nations Development Program (UNDP) special representative for the SDGs for northeast Brazil, marking the beginning of the collaboration with UNDP.

From this organizational and intellectual basis, the *Civil Society Participation in the United Nations Sustainable Development Goals* community engagement project was created the following year. In light of the need to incorporate the SDGs in the logic and practices of municipalities and states, that is localizing the SDGs, the project worked to insert the global goals into local administrations by assisting local adoption of the goals and monitoring of public actions. The coordinators hoped to facilitate these changes by training political and social actors to participate in the implementation of the SDGs while simultaneously identifying the specific demands of these actors related to issues connected to the UN's development agenda.

In order to achieve the project's goals, a team was recruited comprising undergraduate students enrolled in different courses. The participants were not required prior knowledge. The project expected commitment from all team members to the project's goals, as well as a desire to develop an awareness of the importance of civic engagement and an understanding of the particularities of each partner and their contexts.[29] During the initial months of their inclusion in the project, every team member developed the skills necessary to carry out the activities promoted with project partners and to contribute in the preparation of didactic and pedagogical materials and technical reports to support the trainings, presentations, and proposals presented to partners.

Organizationally, this service-learning project was institutionally supported and financed by the Ministry of Education during 2015 and 2016. In each year the project received around R$50,000 (Brazilian Real), a high amount for community outreach projects in social sciences and humanities according to Brazilian standards. The majority of resources were used to fund travel to develop trainings, acquire equipment to develop the training materials, and provide scholarships for participating students.

The project also received institutional support from the UNDP, which, between 2015–2016, maintained a special representative for the SDGs for northeast Brazil based in the city of João Pessoa—where UFPB's International Relations Department is also based. The UNDP supported the production of content for the training activities and facilitated an active dialogue between the University and other institutions throughout the project. Being a well-known, credible organization with access to the spaces needed for initial meetings, the UNDP helped to initiate dialogue with public and private organs.

Civil society organizations were also critical in building bridges between the University and the public administration. The barriers faced by the project in connecting with local and regional actors were mostly related to lack of interest from public administrators. Project leaders felt that many public managers were conducting minimal *box ticking*, i.e., satisfying bureaucratic administrative requirements, instead of seeking innovative ways to improve local conditions. This aforementioned difficulty in connecting to and working together with state agencies was minimized through the contact channels facilitated by civil society organizations which already had established connections and partnerships with the public administration. Throughout the development of the project, some of the participant students linked to NGOs such as "Engajamundo" and "Minha Jampa", which in addition to the organization "Nós Podemos",[30] contributed to establishing the dialogue between the University, NGOs, and local government by intermediating contacts and facilitating the approach to public managers.

The project trained young leaders and civil society organizations, decision makers, and corporate social responsibility organizations. The training sessions and materials were structured based on the team's research about the MDGs and the SDGs, their targets, their goals, their fulfillment, and the identification of priority themes and issues for those being given capacity. The training sought to disseminate knowledge to build technical and organizational capacities so that trainees could contribute to discussions related to socio-economic development and the implementation of public policies.

Developing the project: trainings and their outcomes

Putting these ideas into practice was a major challenge. In addition to difficulties strengthening university-public administration relationships, the immense dimensions of the northeast region (2.5 times greater than France), its relative lack of development, and poorly trained personnel in public administration adversely affected the development of the project. Nevertheless, the project developed varied community activities to disseminate SDGs and to train policymakers and NGO leaders to mediate debate and monitor the implementation of SDGs. Trainings occurred over the 2015–2017 time frame. The tables below detail the training activities carried out, all of which were provided free of charge.

Table 2. Trainings Offered to the Public Sector	
Ceará Mayors' Association (APRECE).	
Venue	Fortaleza/CE:
Target Audience	Representatives from municipalities of the state of Ceará; and state/municipal associations and agencies.
Aims	Training public managers on the SDG agenda and presenting 'best practices' of public policies for the implementation of the SDGs.
Municipal Education Secretary of São Bento do Una/PE	
Venue	São Bento do Una/PE.
Target Audience	Municipal Secretary of Education, São Bento do Una.
Aims	Training for around 600 teachers and public managers from the Municipal Secretary of Education (São Bento do Una/PE). The objective was to reconcile the SDGs with the planning of teaching activities in the municipality.
Municipal Association of Pernambuco (AMUPE)	
Venue	Recife/PE
Target Audience	Representatives from municipalities of the state of Pernambuco, as well as educational institutions and social movements.
Aims	Training public managers on the SDG agenda and presenting 'best practices' of public policies for the implementation of the SDGs.
Paraiba State Secretariat of Planning and Management	
Venue	State Secretariat of Planning and Management, João Pessoa/PB
Target Audience	Public administrators from the State Government
Aims	Presentation and discussion of the SDG Agenda with the managers of the State of Paraíba, in line with the government's demand to bring its planning closer to the goals and targets of the SDGs.
City Hall of Pombal	
Venue	State Secretariat of Planning and Management, João Pessoa/PB
Target Audience	Public administrators from the State Government
Aims	Balance and discussion of activities and actions implemented by the local administration to implement the SDGs, knowledge and experience sharing for the evaluation and improvement of public policies.

Tables 2 and 3 show some of the activities developed by the project. They highlight the broad scope of the project, which managed to reach most of the states of the northeastern region of Brazil. Table 2 displays the agenda of activities which were directed to public institutions with the aim of contributing to the internalization of the SDGs in the process of planning and implementing public policies. Table 3 details the activities targeting civil society institutions which sought to strengthen their capacities to participate in public debates and contribute to their abilities to oversee governmental action. It includes the actions developed with civil society organizations, educational institutions of different levels of training, and business organizations which promote social responsibility activities.

Table 3. Trainings Offered to the Private Sector and Social Responsibility Institutions	
Brazilian Micro and Small Business Support Service (SEBRAE)	
Venue	Natal/RN: Sebrae.
Target Audience	Representatives from municipal and state agencies; associations and institutions and micro and small Business.
Aims	Dissemination of knowledge and good practices on incorporating the SDG agenda into business practices and municipal public management.
Maria Madalena Oliveira Cavalcante Institute (IMMOC).	
Venue	Recife/PE
Target Audience	Around 60 young people, aged between 16 and 21 years, from the communities of the cities of Olinda and Recife/PE.
Aims	Dissemination of knowledge and good practices on incorporating the SDG agenda into corporate social responsibility policies. Training the young people served by the association
Alpargatas Institute	
Venue	João Pessoa/PB
Target Audience	Continuous activities developed in 11 cities, involving all teachers of basic education and municipal education managements.
Aims	Work in partnership with the Alpargatas Institute alongside 11 cities served by the institute to train and qualify teachers and municipal managers on the incorporation of the SDGs in their teaching practices and activities.

The training of members of the public sector, such as the public primary school teachers from São Bento do Una, were developed at the request of the Secretariat of Education of the São Bento do Una municipality, which has been operating since 2014 with a focus on the United Nations' development agendas. Until December 2015, activities revolved around the Millennium Development Goals and, as of 2016, the #MAIS: Morality + Action + Social Integrity Project was initiated, operating under the SDGs framework.

This training focused on preparing and sharing information and materials about the SDGs, helping participants connect the global agenda to their realities, and identifying specific elements which they could relate to and use as the basis for projects in their schools. In this way, the training of 600 teachers offered a conduit to disseminate the contents of the SDGs with the entire public primary school community–teachers from 63 schools attended by 10,129 students. In addition to sharing information on the MDGs and the SDGs, the workshop identified similar projects previously developed by this community, discussed challenges and opportunities in implementing the SDGs and highlighted their roles as local actors relevant to achieving global targets.

The training of civil society multipliers, such as those developed in the state of Ceará, aimed to improve the performance conditions for a network of 280 volunteers trained by UNDP-Brazil to work in their specific states to promote SDGs. The project's contribution focused on the SDGs and took place within a broader event, the Training of ODM/ODS Multipliers. This training took place on 7 August 2015, was sponsored by *Nós Podemos Ceará*, the National Movement for Citizenship and Solidarity and UNDP and also covered the MDGs in Brazil. It touched on the formulation process for SDGs, explained the goals and their targets, and described mechanisms for local mobilization toward their implementation and monitoring.

The training developed in partnership with the Alpargatas Institute—which is the institution responsible for the socio-environmental responsibility agenda of a prominent Brazilian company with global reach—directly impacted the work of the Institute, which supports municipal education secretaries throughout the region. Since the training, the Institute formalized its commitment to the 2030 agenda, aligned its mission to the agenda, emphasized the relevance of social sustainability, and helped to disseminate information about the SDGs. Through this partnership, it was possible to educate teachers and municipal managers on SDGs and help them to align their teaching with the principles of the 2030 Global agenda.

Institutional and educational outcomes

During the development of the project, important partnerships flourished between the University and the institutions involved in it and allowed the institutional and academic maturation of the enterprise engaged in localizing SDGs and multiplying civic engagement activities. Within the University, the Observatory of Sustainable Development Goals initiated its activities during the project's implementation. The observatory is a platform for the dissemination of academic research on the SDGs which monitors activities, actions, publications, and results related to their implementation. The observatory offers analysis of the information it provides and identifies academic projects and activities developed at the Federal University of Paraíba that contribute in some way to the achievement of the Sustainable Development Goals.

Through this initiative it was also possible to establish the Public Policies and Sustainable Development Centre at UFPB (NPDS). NPDS was established as the institutionalization of UFPB's commitment to the SDGs, creating a permanent forum to devise and implement actions designed to internalize the SDGs' goals. The Federal University of Paraíba signed two memoranda of understanding with the UNDP committing to contribute to the achievement of the 2030 Agenda and joined the UN's Sustainable Development Solutions Network (SDSN), an online network which mobilizes scientific and technological knowledge to promote practical solutions for sustainable development and the United Nations' academic impact.[31] The NPDS Centre was created to support the University in implementing the SDGs. It is now a hub that brings together professors, researchers, and students from different areas of knowledge, with a focus on the implementation of sustainable development projects.

Within the NPDS several academic and scientific research, teaching, and community outreach projects which relate to sustainable development and public policies have been or are being developed. It provided a physical space for activities connected to this project and other initiatives which promote the SDGs. The Observatory of Sustainable Development Goals, for instance, whose activities initially had to be developed in the offices of the project's coordinators, can now be housed at the Centre. UFPB also dedicated a few grants to the development of research on the topic.

Another outcome of the project was the launching in August 2020 of the portal *The Federal University of Paraíba and the Sustainable Development Goals*. The portal aims to disseminate scientific and technological knowledge and other service-learning initiatives developed at UFPB that positively impact the implementation of the SDGs. It seeks to encourage future partnerships between the University and actors promoting development in the region. Stimulating the production of knowledge within the University can contribute to sustainable development according to local, regional, and national demands.

The project also prepared participating students to develop trainings, deliver lectures, organize debates, and support the production of projects, didactic, and pedagogical materials. Through the combination of research, production of materials, and practice with training events, they acquired and consolidated their own knowledge about the SDGs and development issues affecting communities in northeastern Brazil. At the same time, they honed their public speaking skills, contributed to debates, worked in groups, and supported development of the project.

In this way, the project strengthened the students' academic knowledge but, most importantly, allowed them to participate in dialogues with actors from outside the University, learn about different social and environmental realities and problems, and develop critical thinking abilities. They mastered the concepts associated with the SDGs, established direct dialogue with civil society and public administrators, learned to prepare project proposals, reacted to problems experienced by people and public administrations, and developed a sense of responsibility toward local development and the public good.

Participating students' sense of accomplishment was nurtured by their ability to directly witness the impact that their actions and the project generated on the partners. The Alpargatas Institute, for example, institutionalized the SDGs as a main element in its social responsibility actions, actively disseminating the sustainable development agenda in its partnership with the eleven municipalities in the region which it supports. The local public administration organs, who were also partners of the University, have been adopting the SDGs as parameters for implementing public policies.

The public and civil society institutions involved in the project benefited from receiving free and personalized trainings on the SDGs according to their social roles and needs. Reaching several public sector bodies in many states of the northeast, a region with lower development levels compared to the Brazilian average, the project contributed to strengthening the capacity of these local and regional institutions in localizing the SDGs and therefore, was conducive to the establishment of conditions where sustainable development can be promoted. Partnering with civil society institutions in the region, the project also helped transmit knowledge about the sustainable development agenda and the role of civic engagement in localizing international goals among organizations which can multiply this knowledge among other civil society actors. This way, this initiative developed within UFPB can indirectly benefit the citizenry in the region through the promotion of sustainable development according to local needs and demands through the channels of both public and civil institutions which received trainings from the project.

Universities as Civic Agents: Bridging the Global SDGs and Local Development Through Community Engagement

The initiative presented in this chapter was developed considering universities as citizen actors[32] which can contribute to progress by developing and disseminating scientific and technological knowledge, and by being committed proponents of civic engagement. Education is important to economic and social development and is essential for disseminating knowledge of sustainable practices to equip new generations to incorporate sustainability as a value and lifestyle.[33] There is a direct relationship between expanding access to basic education, promoting higher education, and increasing investments in science and technology and the improvement of national economic and social indicators. It increases productivity and wages, improves access to health services, increases life expectancy, and contributes to reducing poverty and violence rates, among other indicators.[34]

Traditionally, education and, more specifically, universities can contribute to sustainable development through the production and dissemination of (1) scientific and technological knowledge applicable to technical transformations with social impacts; (2) knowledge that scientifically supports and promotes public policies and development strategies; (3) social technologies to contribute more actively to shaping initiatives that intervene in society; (4) and in the training of human resources. There are, however, limits to these potentials, which are influenced by global and local inequalities. On the international level, there is grave inequality in the distribution of research activities between developed and developing countries, with only 0.5% of researchers being positioned in the developing world, while more than 40% are found in Europe and North America.[35]

The research outputs generated within universities also can be disseminated among social actors through community outreach. Teaching and research facilitates the development of scientific and technological knowledge, while community engagement and service-learning underscore ethical, political, and social dimensions of knowledge and their connections to society. According to article 205 of the 1988 Brazilian Federal Constitution, universities must promote and encourage education as a right of all in collaboration with society. This policy, emanating from the highest norm in Brazilian hierarchy, is complemented by other federal directives, such as the National Plan of University Service-Learning (*Plano Nacional de Extensão Universitária*), which recognizes community engagement as an academic process and ensures that higher education institutions are attuned to social issues.[36] Aligned with top-down federal norms, UFPB fulfills its social role of training professionals with social responsibility and contributing to the scientific, technological, artistic, and cultural development of the country while providing public, free, and high-quality education.[37] According to the University's statute, outreach is an educational, cultural, scientific, and technological process, inseparable from research and teaching. The University explores problems and issues relevant to national, regional and local constituencies and disseminates that knowledge and its benefits to the community. In this way, institutions of higher learning provide a specialized service by establishing an interactive relationship between the university and the community.[38]

Outreach achieved through service-learning and community engagement helps ensure that university research is attuned to society's needs. Developed in parallel to teaching and research, service-learning can be a way to disseminate the technical knowledge generated by scientific research to society. Within the University, service-learning enriches research and teaching by connecting theory and practice, which helps to make academic activities socially relevant. Community outreach activities are developed as a two-way street. On one side, they present opportunities to apply scientific knowledge beyond the ivory tower. On the other, the needs of the community where the university is located can inform socially relevant research and education which is better able to promote sustainable development in a democratic society.[39] This dialogical relationship between the University and society benefits the community in which the University is located and the HEI itself. HEI's engaged with their local communities are renewed by the process, teachers' pedagogies are updated, and research topics are reinvigorated according to their relevance to society, opening the doors to socially committed critical thinking.[40]

The context in which the initiative considered in this chapter was developed was impacted by changes in federal governance, which made the activities of teaching, research, and community outreach more challenging. These changes commenced during Dilma Roussef's second term in the Presidency, when her government was disrupted in August 2016 by a spurious impeachment process. After her departure, Michel Temer, became President. During his administration, from mid-2016 to the end of 2018, the government restricted social expenditures and dismantled the National Councils and Conferences.[41] Under Jair Bolsonaro's government since 2019, Brazil has become increasingly like an authoritarian regime with a massive military presence.[42]

In this context, universities, social organizations, and other political and scientific entities have experienced a financial retraction[43] and faced political and ideological attacks from the federal government.[44] Abrupt curtailment of federal support for the university's community outreach (ProExt) project, has resulted in the conclusion of the service-learning project presented herein, with no prospect of reactivation. The conflict between bottom-up and top-down policies is also present in the area of development. While the federal government adopts an agenda contrary to the SDGs, some states and municipalities in the northeast resist, trying to align public policy planning and implementation with the 2030 development agenda. The result of these disputes is visible in social and economic indicators, which show an increase in inequality in the Brazilian northeast, the resumption of poverty and hunger, rising unemployment, and the risks of a more generalized economic crisis nationally.[45] The negligent federal policies towards the COVID-19 pandemic also highlighted the tensions between the federal government and the federated entities, as the states sought to follow national and international agencies' guidelines to fight the pandemic.[46]

The project reached its limit at the end of 2016, when the Ministry of Education's program, which financed it, was suddenly concluded. This interruption highlights the frailty of small, bottom-up approaches, such as those espoused here, when confronted by opposing, top-down policies. Its impacts, however, continue be felt through activities developed by the trained civil society actors and local public administrators, The project has also left its mark on UFPB, which institutionalized its role as a civic agent by helping to localize SDGs through research, teaching, and outreach projects now centered at the institution's Public Policies and Sustainable Development Centre.

Conclusions

This chapter emphasized the importance of recognizing and encouraging the capacity which universities have to act as civic agents by developing community outreach coupled with its more traditional academic activities. Universities are privileged and important spaces for producing the answers needed to advance towards democracy and development. Through community engagement, the communication between HEIs and public and civil society organizations can be improved, making the outputs of academic endeavors more attuned to society's needs and more visible to other social actors who can benefit from them.

Grounding its traditional academic mission in its social context, through service-learning and community engagement, the Federal University of Paraíba was able to promote civic engagement and contribute to localizing the SDGs in northeastern Brazil. It did so by bridging specific life experiences and needs from the local level with the international sustainable development agenda, which required effective participation of civil society to succeed. Through the three basic activities of Brazilian higher education institutions—namely teaching, developing research, and community engagement—intertwined in a service-learning initiative—this experience demonstrates how universities can act as civic agents and contribute to local development, while increasing student's knowledge and encouraging their civic engagement.

Actively disseminating knowledge about the SDGs and appropriating this global agenda by local actors in Northeastern Brazil, was an effective way for faculty from the Department of International Relations at UFPB to connect the global SDGs framework and the subject matter of International Relations to specific demands of northeastern Brazil. This project contributed to the practices of research and learning within the Department and to the engagement of the University and the participating students with civil society organizations, public managers, and the private sector.

For the students themselves, their contributions included: (1) developing research, (2) preparing material to supplement trainings, (3) delivering trainings involving lectures, (4) promotion of debates, and (5) supporting the development of projects. Contributing to the training of civil society and public sector agents, they promoted local ownership of the global agenda. Acting toward a meaningful goal, such as the promotion of sustainable development, the students reflected on the meaning of democracy and development and kindled their civic commitment by seeing how their agency can promote positive change.

The challenges generated by the shift in Brazilian federal administration and national-level policies which took place in mid-2016 and became more acute since 2019, are immense and point to a direction opposed to that promoted herein. They also highlight, however, the importance of strengthening the commitment of educational institutions, social organizations, and citizens to democracy and the value of bottom-up approaches to civic engagement which connect universities and civil society in positively transforming a society like Brazil.

This project also demonstrates, for other universities invested in developing a similar approach, how local bottom-up initiatives can generate impacts and achieve change even in a shifting context where there are tensions between federated entities. Although parts of the project ended, it managed to institutionalize at UFPB the civic mission of localizing the SDGs, something possible for the Federal University of Paraíba given the didactic and scientific autonomy it enjoys despite its dependence on federal funds, a characteristic of the Brazilian public higher education system.

It is through community outreach that higher education institutions act democratically and in dialogue with the population, qualifying and preparing people for the job market and also for the exercise of citizenship. Through service-learning and community engagement, not only can scientific knowledge be shared with the community beyond the university walls, but higher education institutions can also be updated and have an opportunity to adapt the knowledge which they produce to their social realities. We can only develop solutions to our local problems if we really know them, and socially integrated service-learning has the potential to align the research carried out in Universities to their socio-economic context.

Endnotes

1. World Bank, "GDP per capita (current US$)," https://data.worldbank.org/indicator/NY.GDP.PCAP.CD.

2. UNDP, "The next frontier: Human development and the Anthropocene," *Human Development Report* (2020), http://hdr.undp.org/sites/default/files/hdr2020.pdf,

3. Atlas Brasil, *Atlas do Desenvolvimento Humano no Brasil* (2020), http://www.atlasbrasil.org.br/.

4. Atlas Brasil, *Atlas do Desenvolvimento Humano no Brasil.*

5. Karen Cook, "Social Capital and Inequality: The Significance of Social Connections," in *Handbook of the Social Psychology of Inequality*, eds. J. McLeod, E. Lawler, M. Schwalbe (Dordrecht, Netherlands: Springer, 2014).

6. PNUD, *Desenvolvimento humano nas macrorregiões brasileiras* (Brasília, Brazil: PNUD; IPEA; FJP, 2016), https://1drv.ms/b/s!AuwEBHxVUoYSgbNZGjK6AIgz1ijfmQ?e=VjZxyR.

7. Atlas Brasil, *Atlas do Desenvolvimento Humano no Brasil.*

8. Brazil, "Decree Nº 9.235, of 15 December 2017," *Presidência da República* (2017), http://www.planalto.gov.br/ccivil_03/_Ato2015-2018/2017/Decreto/D9235.htm.

9. Brazil, "Constitution of the Federative Republic of Brazil," *Presidência da República* (1988), http://www.planalto.gov.br/ccivil_03/constituicao/constituicaocompilado.htm.

10. Luciane Stallivieri, "El sistema de educación superior de Brasil: Características, Tendencias y Perspectivas," *Red de Revistas Científicas de América Latina y el Caribe, España y Portugal* (2007).

11. Stallivieri, "El sistema de educación superior de Brasil".

12. Brazil, "Constitution of the Federative Republic of Brazil."

13. Filomena Cordeiro Moita, and Fernando Andrade, "Ensino-pesquisa-extensão: um exercício de indissociabilidade na pós-graduação," *Revista Brasileira de Educação* 14, no. 41 (2009): 269–280; Nancy L. Thomas, "The College and University as Citizen," in *Civic Responsibility and Higher Education,* ed. Thomas Ehrlich (Phoenix, AZ: American Council on Education/Oryx Press, 2000).

14. John Clark (ed.), *Globalizing Civic Engagement: Civil Society and Transnational Action* (London: Earthscan Publications, 2003).

15. Roberto Bissio, "Civil Society and the MDGs," *UNDP Development Policy Journal* 3, no. 1 (2003): 151–160; Maya Fehling, Brett Nelson, Sridhar Venkatapuram, "Limitations of the Millennium Development Goals: a literature review," *Global Public Health: An International Journal for Research, Policy and Practice* 8, no. 10 (2013): 1109–1122.

16. Jan Vandemoortele, "If Not the Millennium Development Goals, Then What?" *Third World Quarterly* 32, no. 1 (2011): 9–25; Sakiko Fukuda-Parr, "From the Millennium Development Goals to the Sustainable Development Goals: Shifts in Purpose, Concept, and Politics of Global Goal Setting for Development," *Gender & Development* 24, no. 1 (2016).

17. The notion of localizing is influenced by the geographical concept of territory and has been evolving in parallel to the implementation and monitoring of the 2030 agenda. It refers to the interventions developed through coordination and dialogue between agents at different levels and in line with local political, economic, social, and cultural dynamics and reflects the recognition of the importance of a multidimensional approach to promoting development. The global 2030 Agenda needs to be translated to national and subnational (regional and municipal) levels, reflecting the specific realities, life experiences and needs of local communities.

18. UCLG, *Turin Communique on Localizing the Post-2015 Development Agenda*, (2014), http://www.uclg.org/sites/default/files/turin_communique_localizing_13_oct.pdf; Thiago G. Galvão, G. Monteiro, "ODS 6: Assegurar a disponibilidade e gestão sustentável da água e saneamento para todas e todos," in *Os objetivos de desenvolvimento sustentável e as relações internacionais*, ed. Henrique Zeferino Menezes, 117–138 (João Pessoa, Brazil: Editora Universidade Federal da Paraíba (EDUFPB), 2019).

19. Thiago G. Galvão, "ODS 11: Tornar as cidades e os assentamentos humanos inclusivos, seguros, resilientes e sustentáveis", in *Os objetivos de desenvolvimento sustentável e as relações internacionais*, 209–234 (João Pessoa, Brazil: Editora

Universidade Federal da Paraíba (EDUFPB), 2019).

20. José Graziano da Silva, Mauro Eduardo Del Grossi, Caio Galvão de França (eds.), *The Fome Zero (Zero Hunger) Program: The Brazilian Experience* (Brasília, Brazil: Ministry of Agrarian Development, 2011), http://www.fao.org/docrep/016/i3023e/i3023e.pdf.

21. Gianpaolo Baiocchi, Patrick Heller, and Marcelo Silva, *Bootstrapping Democracy: Transforming Local Governance and Civil Society in Brazil* (Stanford, CA: Stanford University Press, 2011); John Coonrod, "Participatory Local Democracy: Key to Community-led Rural Development," *Development* 58 (2015): 333–340.

22. Talita Tanscheit and Thamy Pogrebinschi, "Moving Backwards: What Happened to Citizen Participation in Brazil?" *Open Democracy* (2017), https://www.opendemocracy.net/en/democraciaabierta/moving-backwards-what-happened-to-citizen-part/.

23. Tanscheit and Pogrebinschi, "Moving Backwards"; Yves Sintomer, Carsten Herzberg, Giovanni Allegretti and Anja Röcke, *Learning from the South: Participatory Budgeting Worldwide – An Invitation to Global Cooperation* (Bonn, Germany: GIZ, 2010).

24. Historically, Brazilian public universities were concentrated in a few cities, mostly the state capitals. Through the Brazilian Program to Support the Plans for Restructuring and Expansion of the Federal Universities System (REUNI), initiated in 2007, the number of state-funded universities increased and, most importantly, they were interiorized that is, several new *campi* were opened in small towns. The implementation of REUNI strengthened the possibilities of building bridges between civil society and universities in Brazil by bringing local managers and policymakers, urban companies and rural producers and civil society organizations from the vast Brazilian countryside much closer to the Universities and their technical and scientific knowledge.

25. The faculty from UFPB's International Relations Department is responsible for the undergraduate course on International Relations, which in 2020 serviced around 300 active students, and also contributes to two postgraduate programs on Politics and International Relations (41 students in 2020) and Public Management and International Cooperation (50).

26. In 2019, the University had a budget of R$2,069,059,484.00; an infrastructure of 1,196 classrooms, 572 laboratories and 22 libraries; and employed 5,870 regular staff and 1,104 outsourced staff.

27. Elizete Ventura do Monte, *UFPB em números 2012–2019* (João Pessoa, Brazil: EDUFPB, 2020).

28. Just one teacher was involved in this project. The introduction to research program covers the entire university and includes thousands of faculty, each with individual projects supervising the work of undergraduate students.

29. The project's participants included the three students who previously were involved in the Political Economy of the United Nations Millennium Development Goals research project in 2014, as well as other undergraduate students from UFPB who responded to calls publicized by the Department of International Relations to participate in the community outreach project. The applicants were interviewed to identify their interest in the project's goals and if they were able to dedicate 20 hours per week to it. Although this selection did not require prior knowledge about civic engagement or the SDGs, it favored students who were at least on their second year, relatively more mature, and had some knowledge about how the university works. The lack of specific knowledge requirements was handled by immersing every new member of the project in reading and discussing texts on the SDGs and the role of civic engagement in the promotion of development. They were also involved in the project's activities initially as observers, writing reports on the activities developed, and supporting the more senior members in the project's various actions, such as engaging with partners, preparing materials, and carrying out presentations, until they were able to develop these independently.

30. *Engajamundo* roughly translates to English as 'engages the world,' while *Minha Jampa* means 'my João Pessoa', the city where the project was based and capital of the northeastern state of Paraíba. *Nós Podemos* translates to 'we can' in English.

31. Michelly Santos, "UFPB ingressa na elite para desenvolvimento sustentável da ONU," *Ascom/UFPB* (2020), https://www.ufpb.br/ufpb/contents/noticias/ufpb-ingressa-na-elite-para-desenvolvimento-sustentavel-da-onu.

32. Thomas, "The College and University as Citizen."

33. UNGA, "A/RES/57/254 United Nations Decade of Education for Sustainable Development," *United Nations* (2003), https://undocs.org/en/A/RES/57/254.

34. Antonio Caleiro, "Educação e Desenvolvimento: que tipo de relação existe?" in *I Encontro Luso-Angolano em Economia, Sociologia e Desenvolvimento Rural* (Évora, Portugal: 2008).

35. Louise Pakseresht, "What do the Sustainable Development Goals say about... science and Innovation?" *The Royal Society* (2015), http://blogs.royalsociety.org/in-verba/2015/11/19/what-do-the-sustainable-development-goals-say-about-science-and-innovation/.

36. MEC Brasil, "Plano Nacional de Extensão Universitária," *Fórum de Pró-Reitores de Extensão das Universidades Públicas Brasileiras e SESu* (2001), http://www.uemg.br/downloads/plano_nacional_de_extensao_universitaria.pdf.

37. UFPB, "Plano de Desenvolvimento Institucional UFPB: 2019–2023," (2019), http://www.proplan.ufpb.br/proplan/contents/documentos/pdi/pdi_2019-2023_posconsuni-1.pdf.

38. UFPB, "Resolução Nº 07/2002: Aprova o Estatuto da Universidade Federal da Paraíba," *ACI/UFPB* (2002), https://www.ufpb.br/aci/contents/documentos/documentos-ufpb/estatuto-da-ufpb.pdf/view.

39. Boaventura de Sousa Santos, *A universidade no século XXI* (São Paulo, Brazil: Corte, 2004).

40. Cordeiro Moita and Andrade, "Ensino-pesquisa-extensão."

41. Tanscheit and Pogrebinschi, "Moving Backwards."

42. Among the 23 ministries, 10 of the ministers in Bolsonaro's the cabinet are members of the armed forces.

43. Law nº 9.711, established in February 2019 reduced the resources destined to education to the constitutional minimum. The following month, the federal government froze 42% of the budget for the country's science, technology and communications ministry. These measures affected research programs and governmental scholarships, reducing the opportunities for lower-class students to attend universities.

44. In the beginning of 2019, a 30% cut in the budget of Federal Universities was announced, justified by President Bolsonaro's false claim that public universities do not produce research, affirming that most of the research produced in Brazil originated from private and military institutions.In effect, 99% of research produced in Brazil comes from state universities, and according to the Scientific Production Ranking in Brazil 2014–2018, among the 50 institutions that most publish scientific works in the last 5 years, 44 are universities and 43 of those are state funded.

45. When considering inequality, Brazil's position in the UNDP's 2020 HDI ranking fell 20 places, mostly due to lack of advances in the area of education. In 2019 alone, more than 170,000 Brazilians returned to poverty. Currently, the poorest 40% have not yet recovered the income they had in 2014.

46. Débora Prado, Ana Mauad, and Cairo Junqueira, "Covid-19 e os limites da Federação," *O Globo* (2021), https://oglobo.globo.com/opiniao/a-covid-19-os-limites-da-federacao-24854517.

3

Importing Civic Education into Authoritarian China

Taiyi Sun

Christopher Newport University

While teaching civic engagement is intrinsically suitable to democratic regimes and their norms, similar curricula could face tremendous obstacles when taught in authoritarian countries. How could we teach civic engagement in authoritarian states? This chapter discusses the "imported model" by analyzing the experiences of importing civic education pedagogy into mainland China. The case study of SEED for Social Innovation, an NGO the author cofounded in 2012 that first brought Chinese trainees to the US and then subsequently took the curricula to China, is utilized to capture the importing process. Quasi-experimental data comparing the effects of teaching the curriculum in the US and China measuring trust, norms of reciprocity, and willingness for civic engagement are analyzed. This chapter argues that when faced with institutional constraints in authoritarian countries, one could still successfully teach civic engagement by training individuals grounded in their own cultures and who are willing to travel to study civic educations and the pedagogies in democratic cultures. Using these individuals as anchors and turning the trainees into trainers, successful pedagogical models of civic engagement could be grounded even within an authoritarian context. Framing "teaching civic engagement" as academic activities while collaborating with prestigious educational institutions would provide legitimacy and reduce political risk. Collaborating with domestic foundations and philanthropists could make the imported model more sustainable economically. And assembling local civic engagement best practices could further localize the foreign experiences. The experimental data assessing participants' willingness to civically engage also reveal that the interventions impact the workshops conducted in China as much as those in the US.

KEYWORDS: Imported Civic Education; Authoritarianism; Social Capital; Public Narrative; Quasi-Experiment

Introduction

Teaching civic engagement can cultivate informed citizens and strengthen democracies.[1] Civic engagement education pedagogy and research has largely been focused on democratic societies. With the democratic consensus of the post-Cold War order deteriorating and the assertive re-emergence of authoritarianism in the world, teaching and studying civic engagement under authoritarian settings may be more urgent than ever, not only because of the sheer number of people living in non-democracies (about 44.2% of the global population), but also due to the strengthened counter forces that compel people to follow authority and ignore the pursuit of civil and political rights.[2] Major authoritarian countries such as Russia and China continue to consolidate their authoritarian control of their societies, while large democracies like the United States (US), India, and Brazil, infused by waves of nationalism, have faced unprecedented challenges to their people's levels of freedom and democratic values.[3] A notable example of this challenge was the 2020 US presidential election, where some two months after the election one-third of Americans believed that voter fraud led to the victory of President Joe Biden.[4]

While teaching civic engagement is intrinsically suitable to democratic regimes and their norms, similar curricula could face tremendous obstacles when taught in authoritarian countries. Progressive educators, academics, journalists, and community activists have been jailed and removed from their positions in Turkey, non-governmental organizations (NGOs) promoting civic education and democracy have been determined "undesirable" in Russia and were forced to shut down, textbooks and even an entire library that aims to promote civic education have been banned in China, and civic engagement activities face challenges in many countries such as Zimbabwe, Egypt, and Ethiopia.[5] Outside of general education classrooms, a civil society that could serve as fertile soil for civic education may not exist in those authoritarian countries, as the authoritarian state could use NGOs and private entities to channel its control of the society, directly challenging the plural, non-repressive, voluntary, and competitive environment that could foster civic engagement.[6] Even worse, a totalitarian government may penetrate into every corner of the society and private spheres, leaving no room for civic activities.[7] Thus, teaching civic engagement in authoritarian countries may appear to be an oxymoron, even though it is essential for people there to experience such curricula.

In recent decades, we have seen scholars and practitioners putting more emphasis on understanding civic activities of young people globally when teaching and researching civic engagement. The International Association for the Evaluation of Educational Achievement (IEA) conducted a survey in 1994 on fourteen-year-olds' understanding of democratic institutions and processes in 28 countries, and in 2002, a similar survey was conducted in Europe.[8] Such surveys later became routine and the IEA has done its 2009 and 2016 "International Civic and Citizenship Education Study" and plans to do the next round in 2022.[9] Teachers' beliefs regarding the aims of civic education have also been surveyed and studied.[10] However, those surveys do not inform us about the key factors causing the variations in civic activities and beliefs about civic engagement across countries. A few studies have investigated the conditions and causes of increased civic participation and competence. Notable contributions to the field include participating in religious organizations, partaking in educational institutions, increasing migration and the confluence of diverse groups, growing school-to-work linkages, evolving the role of traditional and new media, amplifying family conversations, and adjusting teachers' practices and school characteristics.[11]

Although such literature has laid the groundwork for teaching civic engagement globally, some major shortcomings still exist. First, the majority of work has been focused on developed western democracies, albeit studies occasionally distinguish between old and newer democracies.[12] Second, survey studies mostly reflect just the current state of civic engagement, which can change rapidly, and inferential studies often stop short at reviewing existing literature.[13] Third, for those rare studies that use empirical evidence to capture causal mechanisms and provide major theoretical contributions, the tools used for interventions are typically not made available, thus reducing the replicability of successful practices.[14] There are also problems of endogeneity when using independent variables that are quite similar to the dependent variables. For example, if the independent variable is commonly used as a definition or operationalization of the dependent variable, there is not much value in observed correlation of variables, let alone having meaningful causal relationships.[15] Challenges are even more apparent when studying civic engagement pedagogy in authoritarian countries. Political and logistical risks for educators, practitioners, and students involved have deterred the growth of detailed, in-depth analyses and the systematic collection of evidence for the effectiveness of civic engagement pedagogy in authoritarian countries.[16]

Building on these studies, a new model of importing civic education with a unique pedagogical approach that targets populations living under an authoritarian/autocratic state is introduced. The argument advanced in this chapter is that when faced with institutional constraints in authoritarian countries, it is still possible to successfully teach civic engagement by training individuals grounded in their own cultures and willing to travel to study civic education and participate in pedagogies in democratic cultures. Using these individuals as anchors and turning trainees into trainers, successful pedagogical models of civic engagement could be grounded and localized even within an authoritarian context.

According to Roser, four-fifths of the world's population that live in autocratic regimes are Chinese, so China is an ideal case for this study.[17] Scholars have debated whether there is a "civil society" in China because there is minimal space between the state and the private sphere.[18] Civil society can be assessed in terms of social capital as the two terms are closely related and sometimes used interchangeably. Social capital, defined as the norms, trust, and networks embedded in communities, improves the efficiency of civic lives by facilitating coordinated actions and therefore can be an indicator of civil society.[19] It is thus considered a foundation of civil society and could indicate the quality of a nascent civil society in an authoritarian country like China. Therefore, it is useful to assess experimental data on participants' trust of each other, norms of reciprocity, and willingness to partake in civic engagement activities. The results reveal the increase of social capital within the newly created student networks and suggest that the fabric of a robust civil society and democracy could still be woven under authoritarian settings even when civil society activities are constantly challenged by the state and curricula are tightly controlled. By filling this gap in existing literature, this study not only provides a plausible causal mechanism in promoting civic engagement and civil society activities in an authoritarian country, but also the process and tools can be replicated by other scholars and practitioners hoping to teach civic engagement in authoritarian countries.

In terms of structure, the chapter proceeds as follows. First, it provides a brief discussion on the challenges and opportunities of teaching civic engagement in authoritarian countries in general. Second, the methods and research design are discussed. Third, SEED for social innovation, an NGO originating from civic engagement workshops in the US, and its interactions with the Chinese state are used as a case to demonstrate constraints and challenges which civil societies in such countries face and how an "imported-model" could still achieve partial success in creating social capital and teaching civic engagement. Last, a quasi-experiment is set up to evaluate the effectiveness of teaching civic engagement under such authoritarian constraints in comparison to the same workshop taught in the US, followed by a discussion of the significance and implications of the "imported-model."

The Challenges and Opportunities of Teaching Civic Engagement in Authoritarian States

Due to specific state-society conditions, it is more challenging to promote civic engagement in some countries than others. Strong states with weak mediating institutions prevent systematic inclusion of societal actors, thus making it difficult for citizens to be engaged in politics.[20] History and institutional legacy also sometimes play a key role in shaping a country's civic education. The authoritarian institutional and cultural practices could exclude large sectors of the population from civic education in countries like the Dominican Republic, which is partly due to its colonial heritage and history of political dictatorship and social inequality.[21] Civic engagement in liberal democracies often leads to the subjects' participation in elections and other political activities, yet in non-democracies, it is often not clear where civic engagement education is leading to, given the lack of opportunities for the exercise of civic and political rights.[22] Even in new democracies that had an authoritarian past, the legacy of the authoritarian curriculum could challenge the teaching of civic engagement due to inertia and the slow pace of adapting to change in educational policy, and new spheres like the internet could be found unsuitable for civic activities because they are seen as outside of state parameters and thus perceived as more threatening by the state.[23] Furthermore, empirical evidence has shown that education in authoritarian regimes (including electoral authoritarian regimes) could decrease political participation.[24]

While the challenges to teaching civic engagement in different countries in the world vary, the pressures which Chinese civil society faces from the state are especially dire, and the room for teaching civic engagement is limited. In the period since Xi Jinping took office in 2012, the trend of collective leadership under Jiang Zemin and Hu Jintao during the previous two decades has been reversed. Among his sweeping transformations of Chinese political institutions, the crackdown on grassroots civil society has been well documented. Scholars have paid attention to the impact that this particular crackdown has had on villagers, labor activists, lawyers, feminists, journalists, environmental activists, entrepreneurs, and religious groups.[25] In sum, since Xi Jinping took office in 2012, the space for civil society and social activism in China has been diminishing.[26] Thus, there are high stakes for practitioners who teach civic engagement that does not strictly follow the state's official narrative.

Given the role that university students could play in civic engagement, the Chinese government has targeted students as a key group for authoritarian political control, and the state has deployed structures and measures to nurture political compliance and consolidate its domination of university campuses.[27] Even as China is more and more integrated into the global economy with Chinese individuals having increased access to global cultural and information flows, the government still effectively uses its education system to promote itself relative to global political alternatives.[28] Such an approach is apparent in Hong Kong as a significant politicization of curricula was implemented since a deal was made between London and Beijing for Hong Kong to return to China in 1997.[29] Such moves are not surprising since higher education could create a large pool of potential opposition leaders and generate rivals to the incumbent government who pose an existential threat to authoritarian rule.[30]

In the face of such challenges and constraints, many attempts have been made to promote civic engagement globally, including in authoritarian countries. Some approaches focus on a certain group of people. For example, targeting youth groups and youth-led initiatives when there is a lack of state-led citizenship education could create new civic spaces, and other citizens could be empowered as a result.[31] Similarly, since knowledge "is created through a process of new information interacting with the prior knowledge and experiences of learners," it is beneficial to focus on the learners and generate civic engagement through interactions and constructing new experiences.[32] The learners, of course, could become future trainers, as the "train the trainer" method, which turns trainees into trainers to disseminate information and methodology, has been proven to empower and prepare another specific group—ethnic minorities—to take leadership roles in the future.[33] In non-English speaking communities, implementing a university-affiliated community tutoring program that incorporates service and civic engagement with classroom language learning could be effective.[34]

Despite the major challenges of teaching civic engagement in authoritarian countries, there are occasional opportunities, especially with the rise of the World Wide Web and the increased incidences of disruptions to the political order and activities in the past. The online remix and meme culture, which combines or edits existing materials to produce new creative works or products, could be used by citizens to express and debate sentiments on issues of sensitive social and political relevance in the social commons and thus empower those interested in civic engagement.[35] Internet platforms and applications such as Twitter, when used weekly, could also improve students' political knowledge and political engagement.[36] Even major disruptions such as the COVID-19 pandemic could be windows of opportunities for new interventions to promote global civic engagement because, when organizing activities are forced to be moved online, many students may be more willing to engage in actions to solve global challenges.[37]

Research Design

One potential way to teach civic engagement in authoritarian countries is to import relevant pedagogy from other countries. External factors have played a direct and causal role in constraining some dimensions of autocratic power and enhancing the opposition's power; for example, external ideas and financial resources are crucial to exposing fraud.[38] These external actors can influence democratization, not only through democratic pressures from countries in the West and linkages to democracies, but also by enabling elite agency.[39] Governments promoting democratic practices could use external influences to cultivate civic engagement—although they are often accused of importing values—while International Non-Governmental Organizations (INGOs) could also tackle an acceptable domain such as environmental protection.[40] However, the external actors' influence in civic engagement and democratization could be shaped by geopolitics and could be easily jeopardized due to low levels of freedom domestically, harsh legal environments, and limited domestic support for civil rights movements.[41] Thus, more conscious handling of trade-offs, conceptual precision, and a dynamic conflict analysis could be crucial when imported civic engagement confronts pitfalls.[42]

To capture the process of the "imported civic engagement" model and identify crucial phases, challenges, and the pedagogical interventions of the model discussed, this chapter first utilizes a case study of "SEED for Social Innovation" (referred to as SEED from now on)—an NGO that the author cofounded in 2012—which first brought Chinese trainees to the US and then subsequently took its core curricula to China. To fully reflect on the interactions between different stakeholders such as the Chinese state, other NGOs, and participants of the SEED camps, participant observation and process tracing were used in case analysis to demonstrate the overall approach of "train-the-trainers" and "importing civic engagement" to authoritarian states.

Then, a quasi-experiment was conducted using the "story of self" component, a workshop from the SEED core curriculum as the pedagogical treatment, which was taught in both China (two cities: Shanghai and Zhengzhou) and the US (Newport News, Virginia) by the same instructor at different times to compare the effectiveness of the intervention. For the China workshops, the participants were young adults recruited by partners in China. For the US workshop, participants were undergraduate students of the instructor.[43] Even though the participants' selection process was not completely random, a t-test of gender composition of participants from the US and China reveals that the difference is not statistically significant, providing a basis for the assumption of balanced samples.

A pre-treatment, anonymous survey created by the author was filled out by participants to establish initial conditions. After the workshop was taught and participants told their "stories of self" to their randomly created small groups members (about 3–4 people in each small group), another post-treatment anonymous survey was conducted to assess change in civic engagement attitudes as reflected in replies to three key questions from the surveys to measure trust, norms of reciprocity, and potential participation in a civic discussion on public issues respectively:[44]

- If you have $100 right now, a member of your team wants to borrow money from you (without telling you the purpose), how much would you be willing to lend to your teammate? (Please write down a number between 0-100: _____)

- If it is YOU who hopes to borrow from your teammate, how much do you think your teammate will lend you? (Please write down a number between 0-100: _____)

- If someone from your team asks you to participate in a one-day discussion on public issues (suppose you don't have very important things to do that day), will you participate?

    a) Certainly not b) not that likely c) in between d) maybe will e) will certainly go

The assumption in the first question is that if people trust their small group teammates more, they will be more likely to lend out a larger amount of their money. The second question enquires about the participants' assessments of the team dynamic, particularly if norms of reciprocity are believed to have been established. The third question investigates whether they are willing to give up time (with no schedule conflicts) to take part in civic engagement behavior. The three measurements are annotated as "trust," "reciprocity," and "civic engagement" in the analysis and discussion in this chapter.

The Shanghai workshop had 69 participants while both the Zhengzhou and Newport News workshops had 17 participants each. The Shanghai workshop surveys only included the first two of the three key questions (due to logistical errors, an older version of the survey was printed leaving out the third question) while both the Zhengzhou and Newport News workshop surveys included all three key questions. It is, therefore, logical to assume that the Zhengzhou and Newport News workshops are the most comparable. The workshop in Shanghai, given the larger N, is a robustness test, especially because in all of the actual exercises, participants were randomly divided into small groups of three or four, and the impacts were assessed under the small group settings. All results are presented by cities in this chapter, although state-level comparisons generated similar outcomes.

Case Study: SEED for Social Innovation

The Evolution of SEED

SEED for Social Innovation was founded by a group of Chinese students in the greater Boston area as a student organization at Harvard University in 2012 and later became an NGO in the US with special programs under the ADream Foundation (真爱梦想基金会) in China—due to challenges associated with direct registration. SEED is short for *social responsibility, empathy, empowerment*, and *dedication*—four key values democratically selected by the original founders through a ballot. The founders of SEED had a vision to empower civil society activities in China through teaching civic engagement to practitioners working in the third sector (not the public sector nor the private sector). Even though SEED programs could take place inside or outside of university campuses, the NGO-run workshops are different from traditional university classes.

The core curriculum of SEED is put together based on the availability of educators and practitioners, many of whom are from the greater Boston area and some are directly flown from China. The volunteer organizing committee fundraised both inside and outside of China to pay the workshop faculty members. Those educators and practitioners from China typically have successfully organized campaigns such as girls' empowerment and workers' rights protection and would share their first-hand experiences, tactics, and strategies with participants of the SEED camp. The implications for teaching civic engagement globally from this arrangement are that readily available resources where classes take place (in this case, educational resources in the greater Boston area) as well as resources from countries or communities that are targets of the imported model, can be utilized to combine best practices with the most relevant lessons.

As illustrated in figure 1, in a typical year, the core curriculum could include modules such as "Social Innovations in the US," "Social Innovations in China," "Personnel Management and Leadership," "Project Evaluation," "Design thinking," "Strategic management," "One-on-one coaching and mentoring," "On-site visit of successful NGOs," and "Public Narrative and Leadership." The modules are updated and adjusted yearly based on participants' feedback and internal assessments. The "Public Narrative and Leadership" module by Dr. Marshall Ganz from the Harvard Kennedy School is the only module that has been included every year and remains the highest-rated module throughout the years.

From 2012 to 2019, SEED trained 285 China-based fellows through its workshops and created a community of social entrepreneurs with about 500 people, generating social impact in at least 60 cities in eight countries, mainly in China, the US, and Thailand. Members of the SEED com-

Figure 1. The Relationships Between Different Modules Discussed in This Study

munity reported at least 70,000 hours of community services, and the organization's social media account had more than 100,000 viewers in 2019 alone.[45] SEED is now one of the most influential organizations promoting civic engagement and social innovation in China, winning major awards from the NGO sector including China's "Top 10 Projects" of Action League 2019 Charity Ceremony despite the tightening grip on the society by the authoritarian state.[46] How did SEED achieve such successes?

From the very beginning, SEED aimed to empower everyone involved through practicing what they preach within the organization. Decision-making involved extensive deliberation and voting which engaged the entire organization. The initial core program included a week-long camp at Harvard on civic engagement, bringing young Chinese scholars and civil society practitioners (SEED fellows) to the camp, and then they taught or practiced what they learned back in China. The cofounders were mostly students from the greater Boston area. Given Harvard's reputation, the group decided to register as a student organization at Harvard, even though students from Boston University, Northeastern University, Boston College, and Brandeis University made up most of the team. This intentional decision was rewarding as the Harvard brand was effective in attracting donors, motivating high-quality scholars and practitioners to teach the modules at the SEED camp, and recruiting competent candidates to apply, even during its initial year. When teaching civic engagement globally, it might be beneficial to search for partners and allies from reputable institutions in a city or a country, even if the core team may not directly come from those institutions. Yet, the high-profile activity also drew the attention and scrutiny of the Chinese government, even though the program was conducted completely outside of China. While Harvard is a highly respected academic institution, even by Chinese government officials—President Xi Jinping of China and many other high-level officials sent their children to Harvard—the Chinese government was concerned about the potential for a "color revolution" in China that could challenge the legitimacy of the ruling Chinese Communist Party. Key phrases such as "civic engagement" and "civil society" in SEED's promotional materials made officials in Beijing uneasy. While the first workshop was underway in 2012, a special investigation was set up by the Chinese government to monitor what SEED was doing. The frequency and the intensity of such monitoring of civic engagement activities is unique to authoritarian countries because an active citizenry has the potential to defend democracy against threats to its survival while challenging the rule of authoritarian leaders.[47] What is even more peculiar in this case is the "interdependence sovereignty" which the Chinese state exercised and directly reached outside its borders. Key organizers were contacted and pressured to shut down the program, and individuals associated with SEED were interviewed by Chinese authorities after returning to China. Thus, it is important to keep in mind when importing teaching civic engagement that the target authoritarian country's state apparatus can pose challenges, even outside its boundaries.

The experiences of SEED suggest that authoritarian states not only penetrate through the public sphere and directly interfere in individuals' lives within its given territory, but they also can extend their reach outside their domains. At the core of an authoritarian state, which concentrates political power in an authority not responsible to the people, is the tendency to use strong central power to preserve the political status quo and reject political plurality. Any alternative discourses fostered by its citizens, whether domestic or abroad, could be seen as a threat. This is a manifestation of "interdependence sovereignty"—one of the alternatives to "Westphalian sovereignty"—which deals exclusively with control, especially over trans-border movements.[48] Thus, civic engagement activities that promote or even tolerate the creation of authentic alternative discourses could be assessed as risks and often lead to active suppression from the state. This is a major challenge of teaching civic engagement in authoritarian countries.

Although promoting civic engagement and empowering Chinese citizens with more skills, capacities, and agencies for their rights (through the modules taught) are at the center of SEED's mission, initiating a revolution or overthrowing the government was never part of the goal. On the other hand, the Chinese state is also aware of a common problem faced by authoritarian states wherein too much control of society could contradict its interest of furthering economic development and maintaining regime stability because many civic engagement activities promoted by the third sector (and occasionally the private sector) could facilitate economic growth and contribute to political stability at the local level when the state strategically and deliberately differentiate between regime-challenging and regime-supporting activities.[49] The state could outsource responsibilities for low risk but potentially controversial tasks to civil society organizations (formal or informal) so that it can take the credit when there are no problems and let the civil society organizations take the blame if there were any.

Therefore, when faced with the risks of being terminated while assuming there would be room for maneuver, SEED decided to operate within authoritarian institutional constraints while continuing to teach civic engagement. An essential yet mostly symbolic move was changing the original name of the organization from "SEED for civic and social innovation" to "SEED for social innovation" in 2013 while continuing to teach the same core curriculum. If the state's agents care more about the symbolic aspect of activities and a symbolic action taken by practitioners sends a signal of cooperation, the state's agents may be satisfied with such changes on the surface and the practitioners' mission of teaching civic engagement may be preserved. Practitioners teaching civic engagement in authoritarian countries quite often will need to make compromises such as adjusting curricula for political compliance, but those compromises can be made strategically and partially so that local bureaucrats are satisfied without jeopardizing the whole endeavor.[50]

To reduce political sensitivity, SEED leveraged its successful Harvard camp in 2012 and drew attention from Tsinghua University (equivalent to the Massachusetts Institute of Technology of China) in 2013. SEED ran the curriculum both in Tsinghua and Harvard, each for about a week, teaching the theoretical modules in China and teaching the more practical modules in the US, including the public narrative module studied in this chapter. This move not only reduced tensions with the Chinese government at various levels from the central level to local bureaucrats (the activities are now framed as "academic trainings"), but also allowed SEED, as an organization, to gain an initial foothold inside China and become associated with a reputable university. Even though some of the programs were either openly or clandestinely observed by Chinese government officials, they did not immediately call off the program.

While tensions between the Chinese government and SEED were lowered when trainings were tolerated, the authoritarian state nevertheless continued to pay close attention to its activities to see whether the academic trainings would spill over to anti-government activities. This indicated that the challenges to teaching civic engagement in authoritarian countries not only exist upon entry of the importing organization, but the organization would have to deal with constant pressures and scrutiny from the state. Government agents conducted routine interviews with active members and attended workshops run by SEED. High levels of monitoring could be a threat to civil society organizations operating in authoritarian countries, but also could be utilized as an opportunity since government officials could be targets of civic engagement training. Around 2014, SEED started to organize grassroots demo youth workshops in major cities to provide a shortened version of the full SEED experience. Local authorities in these major cities pressed government officials to monitor the workshops, a common situation for organizing civic engagement activities independently in China. SEED welcomed the suggestion. Thus, it was a common scene when SEED was organizing its camps in a classroom, that some officials were sitting in the back taking notes. At least one official gently spoke to a SEED event organizer after monitoring a grassroots civic engagement event and asked if it was possible to get his son, who was in China, to participate in the upcoming Harvard workshop. His identity as a father was obviously prioritized over his identity as a local government official, and practitioners teaching civic engagement under authoritarian rule could utilize the multi-dimensional nature of officials' identities to sustain their projects.

Importing Western civic education into China was relatively less challenging once the initial challenge from the government was moderated. However, many foreign experiences may not be directly transferable within the Chinese cultural context, especially when individualistic approaches are met with collective, family- and community-oriented social structures. Chinese people at the grassroots level might also be skeptical about civil society organizations which they had never before encountered, due to the lack of legitimacy, resources, and credibility.[51] Thus, SEED started to organize public academic forums to discuss key issues relevant to the third sector as well as organize fieldwork to collect and integrate local successful cases of civic education in 2015. SEED fellows not only taught civic engagement but started to localize the curriculum using Chinese experiences. It was also essential that SEED no longer depended on funding outside of China, as collaborations with philanthropists and charitable foundations inside China were initiated to further SEED's domestic integration with the third sector in 2016. This was also a moment when academic exercises started to transition into practical trainings of civil society practitioners to best achieve SEED's missions and goals. Those pedagogies took root on a larger scale as local partners (especially organizations run by SEED fellows) began to teach civic engagement to their own constituents. It was much less sensitive politically when domestic organizations were teaching the curriculum rather than a foreign organization from Cambridge, Massachusetts, because domestic organizations have typically interacted with local authorities. This meant both building on existing experiences of dealing with potential risks but also that the trust of key government officials had been earned. Quite often, a trusted liaison at the locality could make sure that the local government was not jeopardizing the curriculum. Thus, the collaborations with the third sector actors inside China not only provided financial stability for SEED's operations in China, but also further reduced political risk under an authoritarian state.

Teaching civic engagement in authoritarian countries may face uncertainties and challenges due to a lack of legitimacy, thus having an official status is desirable. However, the Chinese Foreign NGO Law requires any foreign NGO to find a Professional Supervisory Unit (PSU) as a sponsor, usually a government agency in a similar field, and then register with the Ministry of Civil Affairs.[52] This particular stipulation made it impossible for SEED to get registered since no government agency was willing to take the potential risk and serve as SEED's PSU. After consulting with legal experts and allies in the third sector, SEED decided to anchor at the ADream Foundation in Shanghai and officially registered as a special program of the foundation in 2017 to acquire legal status in

China. Even though the institutional environment for teaching civic engagement in authoritarian countries may not be ideal, practitioners could still look for allies within society for help.

Since 2019, SEED has provided training and non-profit consulting for individuals and organizations in China and held training camps in new locations (such as Thailand in 2019) to diversify the sources of best practices in civic engagement. The public narrative module was also taught and exercised by SEED fellows not only in China, but also in the US and Japan, empowering local communities in various countries with their community building, literacy promotion, environmental protection, and poverty alleviation projects.[53] Even during COVID-19, SEED utilized its network and resources in academia, and the third sector, both domestic and foreign, and put together a handbook for diverse social forces to participate and engage in the fight against the negative social and economic impacts and effects of the pandemic. This handbook captured topics ranging from promoting media transparency, to differentiating scientific methods and data from rumors, to self-organizing grassroots civic actions and collaborating with the private sector, and was widely circulated among civil society practitioners in China.[54]

In reflecting on these points, it is important to point out the limitations of this case study and the inherent bias which the author's relationship with SEED could generate.[55] Being able to utilize resources from Harvard and Tsinghua Universities meant that many opportunities were made possible due to elite-level collaborations. Many practitioners who teach civic engagement may not have access to such resources. However, such experiences still point out the importance of using reputable brands and forming alliances when teaching civic engagement in authoritarian states. The brand or ally could be a successful local entrepreneur, a supportive local official, a deep-rooted civil society organization, or whomever possesses sufficient social capital to connect the practitioner to financial, political, and social resources.

Assessment of importing civic engagement by SEED

It was clear that importing the SEED civic education workshops into China would face challenges from multiple dimensions: political, economic, and cultural. The experiences indicate that framing the camp as "academic activity," collaborating with a major Chinese university to further legitimize such academic practices and later seeking opportunities to expand both horizontally (into multiple regions) and vertically (into different age groups), proved to be a sound tactic. The approach to "train the trainers" initially followed by the tactic of partnering with domestic organizations to teach civic engagement also prevented the importing process from being directly targeted as "foreign intervention in Chinese politics and society." Economically, the Harvard brand was able to kick start SEED, successfully encourage domestic philanthropists and foundations to value the curriculum (annual budgets went from about $50,000 initially to about $165,000 in just a few years), and as a result, made the organization more sustainable. The fieldwork that assembled local civic engagement best practices further helped to localize the foreign experiences. Also, SEED was able to evolve and improve after each training in China as feedback from participants was constantly incorporated into the next round of curriculum designs.

There are, of course, problematic actions taken by SEED that merit further discussion in terms of its implications for teaching civic engagement globally. Initial compromises made with the authoritarian state could potentially derail the mission of the organization. To some extent, the outcomes of SEED and SEED fellows' workshops and projects, especially those providing support to minority and poor populations, may have strengthened the regime stability of China, providing authoritarian resilience. However, if the aim is not regime change, the goal of teaching civic engagement effectively and empowering individuals with the resources, mindsets, and emotional capacities necessary to be active and engaging citizens, could still be achieved.

Some specific strategies and tactics from this case are generalizable for teaching civic engagement globally, especially in other authoritarian countries. First, the initial brand building was important. Getting started as a student organization at Harvard effectively attracted high quality collaborators and participants, and fundraising was more effective as a result. Second, framing civic education as academic exercises, as opposed to organizing and mobilizing activities, and forging collaborations between Harvard University and Tsinghua University, a domestically reputable institution in China, reduced tensions between the authoritarian state and SEED. Third, while the suspicion and pressure from the state did not go away, focusing on youth from major cosmopolitan areas as a breakthrough point, and placing more emphasis on promoting social and civil rights (especially minority rights) than political rights, initially created breathing room to localize SEED, with the opportunity to scale up afterward. Fourth, instead of arbitrarily dumping the foreign curricula onto the Chinese participants, SEED organizers conducted their own fieldwork and modified the workshops based on local experiences and cultures, and the workshop modules continue to evolve for best fit with the domestic settings. Fifth, as it matured and was grounded, SEED gradually moved from pure academic exercises to practical programs and overcame legal hurdles by partnering with domestic NGOs for its projects. Such partnerships not only gave SEED more legal and institutional protection, but also created channels for SEED to promote and replicate its pedagogies and norms. SEED, thus, was able to take root inside an authoritarian country and bring its programs to the general public. Lastly, SEED has adhered to the democratic norms, evidence-based thinking, and strong attention to public issues used in its own agenda setting and decision-making process to demonstrate to new participants and observers civic engagement in action. Some of the above takeaways may be valuable for other practitioners and organizations importing civic education into other authoritarian countries.

The "public narrative" pedagogical treatment

As discussed above, the core curriculum involved in the quasi-experiment originates from Dr. Ganz's Harvard Kennedy School class on organizing and civic engagement. This method utilizes storytelling to help individuals find their purposes and shared values and turn those values into purposeful actions by creating agency from emotions.[56] Such an approach cultivates participants' emotional capacities and motivates actions through values realized from their constructed public narratives. Instead of telling people what to do and why they should do it, this approach asks participants to find their own values and motivations through the major choices that they made in their lives when faced with challenges, and thus their actions could be more spontaneous and sustainable. Within the context of authoritarian countries, instructing people to take actions to promote their civil and political rights will not only face pressures from the state, but the individuals could also find the external pressures foreign and arbitrary. Getting individuals to search within, find public issues that they care about, and then equip them with resources and strategies to take action, could be more viable for both the individuals and the political environment. It is worth noting that such a process not only provides a path to civic engagement for the specific issue explored during the workshop, but the methodology could also be replicated by the participants when they encounter future opportunities for civic engagement.

In those workshops, participants are asked to tell a "story of self" to reflect upon the challenges they had faced in their lives and the choices that they made to overcome the challenges, which reflects their values. Then, a second "story of us" is constructed to find the choices that the group as a whole made when faced with challenges to cultivate individual group members' shared values. Finally, the participants are asked to create a "story of now" to clarify their own goals (for example, a better environment or improved minority rights, etc.) and contrast the "dream of action" with the "nightmare of inaction" so urgency is created and collective actions are initiated.[57] For the Harvard Kennedy School classes and the workshops organized by "SEED for Social Innovation," additional tools such as relationship building, strategizing, taking actions, and leadership development are included. For the quasi-experiments in this study, only the "story of self" component from the Ganz' workshop was utilized due to the limited time allowed. The full module could take up to 20–30 hours plus the time that teams spent on accumulating shared experiences while working on a civic engagement project together.

The public narrative approach is significantly different from typical curricula taught in China. In a typical Chinese curriculum, any subjects that have political implications should promote patriotism, collectivism, and the love of socialism, and the proposed 2021 compulsory education curriculum plan and curriculum standard further emphasized the implementation of Chinese president Xi Jinping's thoughts on creating a new era of socialism with Chinese characteristics.[58] Thus, a specific narrative is decided, and alternative narratives and practices are almost impossible to include. In the Ganz approach, the narrative is generated innately and is pluralistic by design without having to adhere to a single political discourse.

Based on a post-training online survey in 2017, SEED participants gave an average of 4.53 points on a 5-point Likert scale for the public narrative module, the highest among nine different modules taught that year. Six months after the camp, the public narrative module was still rated the highest with 4.41 points out of 5, and even three years after the camp, about half of the participants (48.2%) still believed that it was their most impressive memory at Harvard among a list of well-planned activities in the greater Boston area.[59] When asked whether they continue to use the practices learned at the camps, 76% of the 2018 fellows responded that they either always or frequently use the public narrative module, while 24% said they occasionally use it. No one said they never used it.[60] Fellows thought that the module was applicable, practical, and relevant to Chinese civic engagement, for it not only created a community of practitioners that could continue to empower each other, but also provided resources and solutions to members of this community when faced with challenges in the process of civic activities. They often mentioned that the public narrative module experience completely changed their way of thinking, and they consequently became more motivated in civic activities. SEED fellows have used the public narrative practice in vocational training, poverty alleviation, rural education, sex education, LGBTQ empowerment, women and ethnic minority empowerment, environmental protection, and peasant empowerment, among many projects, and continue to teach civic engagement globally, especially in China. Some of those topics may occasionally face resistance from the local society or governments, but SEED fellows have found the skills, capacities, and agencies they acquired from the camps useful in preparing them to overcome these challenges and achieve meaningful results.

Results and Analysis of the Quasi-Experiment

To measure the actual impact of the workshops done in authoritarian China and to compare the effectiveness between countries/regimes, a quasi-experiment was set up. Social capital in terms of trust and norms of reciprocity as well as civic engagement in terms of willingness to participate in public discussions were investigated to assess the effectiveness of the "story of self" component of the public narrative module. The 95% confidence intervals are presented by cities, depicting the changes of trust, norms of reciprocity, and willingness for civic engagement among the participants. Figure 2 shows that on the "trust" question, all three cities had an increased mean, indicating that participants were more willing to lend money to their small group members after just a few hours of intervention—telling their stories of self to each other in a structured way. The changes within

Figure 2. Changes in Trust

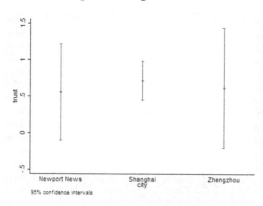

the Shanghai group were statistically significant, indicating that sharing intimate and meaningful personal experiences created new bonding between participants within the same small groups. The graph is collapsed into a 1~5 scale to be comparable across questions, so each unit change represents an additional $20 participants are willing to lend out.

On the question of norms of reciprocity, in which participants were asked how much they expect their teammates would lend them, participants from all three cities also had positive changes

Figure 3. Changes in Norms of Reciprocity

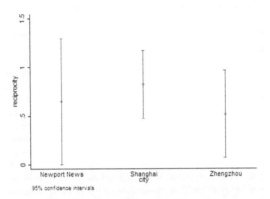

(illustrated in figure 3). The changes in both Chinese cities were statistically significant and the changes in Newport News, had a P value of 0.0502. This indicates that norms of reciprocity were created as participants not only trusted that teammates would return money lent, but also that they expected teammates would be more willing to lend them money.

For the civic engagement question, both students in China and the US had positive changes in their willingness to participate, although the results are not statistically significant as the P-values are both above 0.05. Figure 4 shows the 95% confidence interval of participants' change in their willingness to participate in public discussions. In hindsight, it would be more effective to recruit

Figure 4. Changes in Civic Engagement

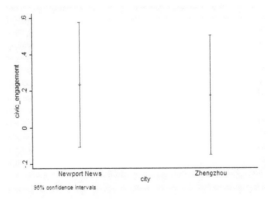

more participants in each of the two cities that answered this question since the question was not asked in Shanghai, which had the most participants. This question could also be framed differently to reflect the number of hours which participants were willing to commit, rather than simply asking them to commit to a one-day event.

The public narrative workshop uses emotional power to motivate individuals to find their own values and their shared values and propel actions and social impacts. It is, therefore, essential to investigate whether the female subgroup would react differently to the interventions as it has been suggested they instill more emotional empathy, which could encourage continued civic engagement.[61]

Figure 5. Changes in Trust for Female Participants

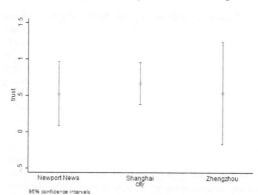

As indicated by figure 5, for the first question on trust, female participants from all cities increased the amount of money they were willing to lend to their teammates. The changes for the students from the Newport News group were statistically significant, while the changes for students from Shanghai remained statistically significant.

For the second question, figure 6 shows that not only did female participants from all three cities increase their norm of reciprocity, the positive changes were statistically significant across cities. Figure 7 indicates that the results for the civic engagement question from the female participants resembled that for the entire group, with positive changes, but not statistically significant.

Overall, trust, norms of reciprocity, and willingness for civic engagement increased after the public narrative intervention in all cities. The impact was more noticeable among female than male participants. In line with Corcoran's research, this could be due to the emotional nature of the "story of self" module. The intervention was less than two hours and only utilized the "story of self" component out of the three stories told in a typical public narrative workshop organized by

Figure 6. Changes in Norms of Reciprocity for Female Participants

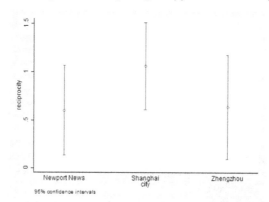

Figure 7. Changes in Civic Engagement for Female Participants

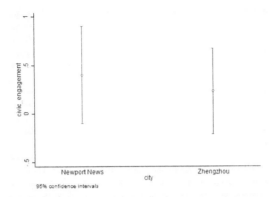

SEED. It is likely that with the whole package, taught repeatedly within Chinese communities for nine years, the impacts could be much larger. The quasi-experimental data assessing participants' social capital creation and willingness of civic engagement also reveal that the interventions have as much impact in the workshops conducted in China as those in the US.

Conclusion

This chapter has used a case study to demonstrate the major challenges that someone teaching civic engagement could encounter in an authoritarian country. The SEED experiences in China revealed that, through using these individuals as anchors and turning trainees into trainers, successful pedagogical models of civic engagement could be grounded even within an authoritarian context—although their effectiveness may be a subject of investigation by future researchers. A further potential constraint—the legitimacy of a foreign entity teaching civic engagement—can be established by collaborating with established domestic partners, especially prestigious academic institutions. In the meantime, foreign experiences could also be localized by incorporating locally-developed best practices. Another tactic worth noting is to start with the most open-minded subgroup of the population and then expand horizontally across different communities while cultivating vertically among different age groups. At the right moment, this tactic proved to be effective so that foreign experiences not only took root but blossomed. Furthermore, the continued diversification of sources of importing civic engagement and the replication of best practices both inside and outside of China made the organization sustainable and adaptive. The imported SEED has now grown into a forest of active participants in Chinese civil society.[62]

Lessons from this Chinese experience could be replicable in attempts to teach civic engagement in other authoritarian societies or even democratic societies. Best practices could be shared in a safe space in a society that is supportive and resourceful for teaching civic engagement. Individuals who are open-minded but well-grounded in their own local societies could be targeted as future trainers and provided with teaching plans and methodologies so that they could absorb the principles of civic engagement and successfully apply them under new conditions, as constraints in different countries may vary. Being able to utilize elite institutions for brand-building greatly increased the chances of success in this case, but the external generalizability is not only limited to practitioners who have access to elite institutions—it is essential to identify resources and allies within a community even when such resources and allies are not initially obvious. It is also worth noting that repression has costs, but not all governments will shut down all civic engagement activities, even in authoritarian countries. Thus, it is important to maintain faith and be strategic when importing civic engagement into authoritarian countries. This study also provided empirical evidence of the successes in creating new social capital and increasing willingness for civic engagement among participants when one specific module from the workshops was tested. It is quite possible that when other modules are tested and taught under different political and institutional environments, additional positive outcomes and challenges could be brought to light. Such explorations are warranted and could be valuable for future researchers as they seek to strengthen civil societies around the world.

Endnotes

1. Ann N. Crigler, Gerald Thomas Goodnight, Stephen Armstrong, and Aditi Ramesh, "Collaborative Civic Engagement: A Multidisciplinary Approach to Teaching Democracy with Elementary and University Students" in *Teaching Civic Engagement Across the Disciplines*, eds. Elizabeth C. Matto, Alison Rios Millett McCartney, Elizabeth A. Bennion, and Dick Simpson (Washington, DC: American Political Science Association, 2013), 261.

2. Zselyke Csaky, "Nations in Transit 2020: Dropping the Democratic Façade," *Freedom House* (2020); Max Roser, "Democracy," *Our World in Data* (2020), https://freedomhouse.org/report/nations-transit/2020/dropping-democratic-facade#Facade.

3. Freedom House, "Freedom in the World 2019: Democracy in Retreat," (2019), https://freedomhouse.org/report/freedom-world/2019/democracy-retreat.

4. NPR/Ipsos 2020

5. Michael W. Apple, *Ideology and Curriculum* (New York: Routledge, 2019); Philanthropy News Digest, "Russia's Crackdown on NGOs Includes Some Unexpected Targets," (2015), https://philanthropynewsdigest.org/news/russia-s-crackdown-on-ngos-includes-some-unexpected-targets; China Development Brief, "Liren Rural Library's Open Letter on the Suspension of Operations," (2014), http://www.chinadevelopmentbrief.org.cn/news-16604.html; Kevin Croke, Guy Grossman, Horacio A. Larreguy, and John Marshal, "Deliberate Disengagement: How Education Decreases Political Participation in Electoral Authoritarian Regimes," *American Political Science Review* 110, no. 3 (2016): 579–600; Saskia Brechenmacher, *Civil Society Under Assault: Repression and Responses in Russia, Egypt, and Ethiopia Vol. 18* (Massachusetts: Carnegie Endowment for International Peace, 2017).

6. Philippe C. Schmitter, "Still the Century of Corporatism?" *The Review of Politics* 36, no. 1 (1974): 85–131.

7. Tang Tsou, *The Cultural Revolution and Post-Mao Reforms: a Historical Perspective* (Chicago: The University of Chicago Press, 1986).

8. Judith Torney-Purta, *Citizenship and Education in Twenty-Eight Countries: Civic Knowledge and Engagement at Age Fourteen* (Amsterdam, The Netherlands: IEA Secreatariat, Herengracht 487, 1017 BT, 2001); Judith Torney-Purta, "Patterns in the Civic Knowledge, Engagement, and Attitudes of European Adolescents: The IEA Civic Education Study," *European Journal of Education* 37, no. 2 (2002): 129–141.

9. International Association for the Evaluation of Educational Achievement, "International Civic and Citizenship Education Study," (2021), https://www.iea.nl/studies/iea/iccs.

10. Frank Reichert and Judith Torney-Purta, "A Cross-National Comparison of Teachers' Beliefs About the Aims of Civic Education in 12 Countries: A Person-Centered Analysis," *Teaching and Teacher Education* 77 (2019): 112–125.

11. Ani Sarkissian, "Religion and Civic Engagement in Muslim Countries," *Journal for the Scientific Study of Religion* 51, no. 4 (2012): 607–622; Joseph Kahne and Joel Westheimer, "In the Service of What? The Politics of Service Learning," *Service Learning for Youth Empowerment and Social Change* (1999): 25–42; James Youniss, Susan Bales, Verona Christmas-Beat, Marcelo Diversi, Millbrey Mclaughlin, and Rainer Silbereisen, "Youth Civic Engagement in the Twenty-First Century," *Journal of Research on Adolescence* 12, no. 1: 121–148; Michael J. Shanahan, Jeylan T. Mortimer, and Helga Kruger, "Adolescence and Adult Work in the Twenty-First Century," *Journal of Research on Adolescence* 12, no. 1 (2002): 99–120; Yinjiao Ye, Ping Xu, and Mingxin Zhang, "Social Media, Public Discourse and Civic Engagement in Modern China," *Telematics and Informatics* 34, no. 3 (2017): 705–714; Hans Oswald, "East German Adolescents' Attitudes Towards West German Democracy," in *Images of Germany: Perceptions and Conceptions,* eds. P.M. Daly, H.W. Frischkopf, T.E. Goldsmith-Reber, and H. Richter (Berlin, Germany: Peter Lang, 2000), 121–134; Ernesto Treviño, Consuelo Béjares, Cristóbal Villalobos, and Eloísa Naranjo, "Influence of Teachers and Schools on Students' Civic Outcomes in Latin America," *The Journal of Educational Research* 110, no. 6 (2017): 604–618.

12. Torney-Purta, "Patterns in the Civic Knowledge," 129–141.

13. Youniss, Bales, Christmas-Beat, Diversi, Mclaughlin, and Silbereisen, "Youth Civic Engagement," 121–148.

14. Sarkissian, "Religion and Civic Engagement," 607–622; Treviño, Béjares, Villalobos, and Naranjo, "Influence of Teachers," 604–618.

15. Brian K. Barber, "Youth Experience in the Palestinian Intifada: A Case Study in Intensity, Complexity, Paradox, and Competence," in *Roots of Civic Identity: International Perspectives on Community Service and Activism in Youth* (1999):

178–204.

16. Xiaojun Yan, "Engineering Stability: Authoritarian Political Control Over University Students in Post-Deng China," *The China Quarterly* (2014), 493–513; Samson Yuen, "Friend or Foe? The Diminishing Space of China's Civil Society," *China Perspectives* no. 3 (2015): 51–56; Ketty Loeb, "A Grim Outlook for China's Civil Society in the Wake of the 9th Party Congress," *Asia Pacific Bulletin* no. 402 (2017).

17. Max Roser, "Democracy."

18. Clemens Ostergaard, "Citizens, Groups, and Nascent Civil Society in China: Towards an Understanding of the 1989 Student Demonstrations," *China Information* 4 (1989): 28–41; Thomas B. Gold, "The Resurgence of Civil Society in China," *Journal of Democracy* 1, no. 1 (1990): 18–31; Mary E. Gallagher, "China: The Limits of Civil Society in a Late Leninist State," in *Civil Society and Political Change in Asia,* ed. Muthiah Alagappa (Stanford: Stanford University Press, 2004); Joseph Fewsmith, *The Logic and Limits of Political Reform in China* (Cambridge, UK: Cambridge University Press, 2013).

19. Robert Putnam, *Making Democracy Work: Civic Traditions in Modern Italy* (Princeton, NJ: Princeton University Press, 1993).

20. Jennifer S. Oh, "Strong State and Strong Civil Society in Contemporary South Korea: Challenges to Democratic Governance," *Asian Survey* 52, no. 3 (2012): 528–549.

21. John Ainley, Wolfram Schulz, and Tim Friedman, "ICCS 2009 Encyclopedia: Approaches to Civic and Citizenship Education Around the World," *The International Civic and Citizenship Education Study* (2013): 125.

22. Alison Rios Millett McCartney, Elizabeth A. Bennion, and Dick Simpson, *Teaching Civic Engagement: From Student to Active Citizen* (Washington DC: American Political Science Association, 2013).

23. Iveta Silova and Elmina Kazimzade, "The Civics Education Applications in Post-Soviet Context," *Academica.edu*, n.d., http://www.academia.edu/download/35812646/Civic_education_in_AZ.doc; Katy E. Pearce, Deen Freelon, and Sarah Kendzior, "The Effect of the Internet on Civic Engagement Under Authoritarianism: The Case of Azerbaijan," *First Monday* (2014).

24. Kevin Croke, Guy Grossman, Horacio A. Larreguy, and John Marshall, "Deliberate Disengagement," 579–600.

25. Kevin J. O'Brien, and Lianjiang Li, *Rightful Resistance in Rural China* (Cambridge, UK: Cambridge University Press, 2006); Anita Chan, *China's Workers Under Assault: The Exploitation of Labor in a Globalizing Economy* (Armonk, NY: Sharpe, 2001); Feng Chen, "Between the State and Labour: The Conflict of Chinese Trade Unions' Double Identity in Market Reform," *China Quarterly* no. 176 (2003): 1006–1028; Kevin J. O'Brien and Lianjiang Li, "Suing the Local State: Administrative Litigation in Rural China," *China Journal* no. 51 (2004): 75–96; Mary Elizabeth Gallagher, *Contagious Capitalism: Globalization and the Politics of Labor in China* (Princeton, NJ: Princeton University Press, 2005); Ching Kwan Lee, *Against the Law: Labor Protests in China's Rustbelt and Sunbelt* (Berkeley: University of California Press, 2007); Mary Elizabeth Gallagher, "China's Workers Movement and the End of the Rapid-Growth Era," *Daedalus* 143, no. 2 (2014): 81–95; Diana Fu and Greg Distelhorst, "Grassroots Participation and Repression under Hu Jintao and Xi Jinping," *The China Journal* no. 69 (2017); Minxin Pei, "Citizens v. Manandarins: Administrative Litigation in China," *The China Quarterly* no. 152 (1997); Kevin J. O'Brien and Rachel E. Stern, "Studying Contention in Contemporary China," in *Popular Protest in China* (Cambridge, MA: Harvard University Press, 2008); Hualing Fu and Richard Cullen, "Weiquan (Rights Protection) Lawyering in an Authoritarian State: Building a Culture of Public-Interest Lawyering," *China Journal* no. 59 (2008): 111–127; Eva Pils, *China's Human Rights Lawyers: Advocacy and Resistance* (New York: Routledge, 2014); Sida Liu, "The Changing Roles of Lawyers in China: State Bureaucrats, Market Brokers, and Political Activists," in *The New Legal Realism: Studying Law Globally,* eds. Heinz Klug and Sally Engle Merry (Cambridge, UK: Cambridge University Press, 2016), 180–198; Susan Greenhalgh, "Fresh Winds in Beijing: Chinese Feminists Speak Out on the One-Child Policy and Women's Lives," *Signs: Journal of Women in Culture and Society* 26, no. 3 (2001): 847–888; Yifei Shen, *Feminism in China: An Analysis of Advocates, Debates, and Strategies,* (Shanghai: Friedrich Eberto Stiftung, 2016); Jonathan Hassid, "China's Contentious Journalists: Reconceptualizing the Media," *Problems of Post-Communism* 55, no. 4 (2008): 52–61; Andrew Mertha, *China's Water Warriors: Citizen Action and Policy Change* (Ithaca, NY: Cornell University Press, 2008); Christoph H. Steinhardt and Fengshi Wu, "In the Name of the Public: Environmental Protest and the Changing Landscape of Popular Contention in China," *China Journal* no. 75 (2016): 61–82; Joseph Fewsmith, *The Logic and Limits*; Carsten T. Vala, "Protestant Christianity and Civil Society in Authoritarian China: The Impact of Official Churches and Unregistered Urban Churches on Civil Society Development in the 2000s," *China Perspectives* 3 (2012): 43; Karrie Koesel, *Religion and Authoritarianism: Cooperation, Conflict, and the Consequences* (Cambridge, UK: Cambridge University Press, 2014).

26. Samson Yuen, "Friend or Foe?" 51–56; Ketty Loeb, "A Grim Outlook."

27. Xiaojun Yan, "Engineering Stability," 493–513.

28. Rene Patnode, *Cosmopolitan Universals and the Chinese University: Authoritarian Education and Its Impact on Global Perspectives* (San Diego: University of California Press, 2017).

29. Paul Morris and Anthony Sweeting, "Education and Politics: The Case of Hong Kong from an Historical Perspective," *Oxford Review of Education* 17, no. 3 (1991): 249–267.

30. Bruce Bueno De Mesquita and George W. Downs, "Development and Democracy," *Foreign Affairs* (2005): 77–86.

31. Aleida Cristina Mendes Borges, "Youth Agency in Civic Education: Contemporary Perspectives from Cabo Verde," *Societies* 32, no. 2 (2020): 53.

32. Joy Du Plessis and Irfan Muzaffar, "Professional Learning Communities in the Teachers' College: A Resource for Teacher Educations," *EQUIP1* 45 (2010): 26; Frances Vavrus, Matthew Thomas, and Lesley Barlett, *Ensuring Quality By Attending to Inquiry: Learner-Centered Pedagogy in Sub-Saharan Africa* (Addis Ababa: UNESCO-IICBA, 2011).

33. Marshalita Sims Peterson, "Public Deliberation and Practical Application of Civic Engagement Through a "Train the Trainer" Process at a Historically Black College," *The Journal of Negro Education* 83, no. 1 (2014): 77–92.

34. Clara Burgo, "Service-Learning For Students of Spanish: Promoting Civic Engagement and Social Justice Through an Exchange Tutoring Service," *Revista de Linguistica y Lenguas Aplicadas* 11 (2016): 11–18.

35. Patrick E. Sharbaugh and Dang Nguyen, "Make Lulz, Not War: How Online Remix and Meme Culture are Empowering Civic Engagement in the Socialist Republic of Vietnam," *Asiascape: Digital Asia* 1, no. 3 (2014): 133–168.

36. Gina Serignese Woodall and Tara M. Lennon, "Using Twitter to Promote Classroom and Civic Engagement," in *Teaching Civic Engagement Across the Disciplines*, eds. Elizabeth C. Matto, Alison Rios Millett McCartney, Elizabeth A. Bennion, and Dick Simpson (Washington, DC: American Political Science Association, 2017): 135–150.

37. Taiyi Sun, "Forced Experimentation: Teaching Civic Engagement Online Amid COVID-19," *PS: Political Science & Politics* (2020).

38. Michael McFaul, "Ukraine Imports Democracy: External Influences on the Orange Revolution," *International Security* 32, no. 2 (2007): 45–83.

39. Steven Levitsky and Lucan A. Way, *Competitive Authoritarianism: Hybrid Regimes After the Cold War* (New York: Cambridge University Press, 2010); Jakob Tolstrup, "When Can External Actors Influence Democratization? Leverage, Linkages, and Gatekeeper Elites," *Democratization* 20, no. 4 (2013): 716–742.

40. Charles N. Quigley and N. Hoar, "Civitas: An International Civic Education Exchange Program," *Spons Agency* 129 (1999); Lynn Staeheli and Caroline R. Nagel, "Whose Awakening Is It? Youth and the Geopolitics of Civic Engagement in the 'Arab Awakening,'" *European Urban and Regional Studies* 20, no. 1 (2013): 115–119; Laura R. Johnson and Julie S. Johnson-Pynn, "Cultivating Compassion and Youth Action Around the Globe: A Preliminary Report on Jane Goodall's Roots & Shoots Program," *Journal of Youth Development* 2, no. 2 (2007): 26–41.

41. Faiz Ahmed Chowdhury, "Geo-Politics, Democratization and External Influence: The Bangladesh Case," *Institute of Governance Studies*, BRAC University, (2013) http://dspace.bracu.ac.bd/xmlui/handle/10361/11662; Ghia Nodia, "External Influence and Democratization: The Revenge of Geopolitics," *Journal of Democracy* 25, no. 4 (2014): 139–150; Karla W. Simon, *Civil Society in China: The Legal Framework from Ancient Times to the New Reform Era*, (Oxford University Press, 2013); Valerie Sperling, "Women's Organizations: Institutionalized Interest Groups or Vulnerable Dissidents?" in *Russian Civil Society: A Critical Assessment,* eds. Alfred Evans, Lisa McIntosh-Sundstrom, and Laura Henry (New York: ME Sharpe, 2006), 161–177.

42. Judith Vorrath, "Post-Conflict Democratization: Pitfalls of External Influence," *CSS Analyses in Security Policy* 79 (2010).

43. IRB approval was received from the author's home institution (IRBNet ID: 1387819-2).

44. Robert Putnam, *Making Democracy Work.*

45. SEED for Social Innovation, "SEED 2019 Annual Report," (2019).

46. Xinhuanet, "'行动者联盟2019公益盛典'举行 ('Action League 2019 Charity Ceremony' was held)," *Xinhua News* (2019) http://www.xinhuanet.com/gongyi/2019-12/09/c_1210388394.htm.

47. Elzbieta Korolczuk, "Explaining Mass Protests Against Abortion Ban in Poland: The Power of Connective Action," *Zoon Politikon* 7 (2016): 91–113; Javier Corrales, "The Authoritarian Resurgence: Autocratic Legalism in Venezuela," *Journal of Democracy* 26, no. 2 (2015): 37–51; Berk Esen and Sebnem Gumuscu, "Rising Competitive Authoritarianism in Turkey," *Third World Quarterly* 37, no. 9 (2016): 1581–1606; Maria Lipman, "At the Turning Pont to Repression: Why There Are More and More 'Undesirable Elements; in Russia," *Russian Politics & Law* 54, no. 4 (2016): 341–350.

48. Stephen D. Krasner, *Sovereignty: Organized Hypocrisy* (Princeton, NJ: Princeton University Press, 1999).

49. Milan W. Svolik, *The Politics of Authoritarian Rule*, (Cambridge University Press, 2012); Taiyi Sun, "Deliberate Differentiation for Outsourcing Responsibilities: The Logic of China's Behavior Toward Civil Society Organizations," *The China Quarterly* 240 (2019): 880–905.

50. Xiaojun Yan, "Engineering Stability," 493–513.

51. Taiyi Sun, "Civic Transformation in the Wake of the Wenchuan Earthquake: State, Society, and the Individual," *Made in China* 3, no. 1 (2018): 66–70.

52. Law Info China, "Law of the People's Republic of China on the Administration of Activities of Overseas Non-

Governmental Organizations within the Territory of China," *Standing Committee of the National People's Congress of China* 44 (2017) http://www.lawinfochina.com/display.aspx?lib=law&id=21963.

53. SEED for Social Innovation, "SEED 2018 Annual Report," (2018).

54. SEED for Social Innovation, "Observations and Analysis of Social Force Participation Under COVID-19, a Research Report," (2020).

55. The author was only heavily involved in the organization during the founding year (2012) and has since taken a seat on the board without being involved in day-to-day operations. Even though the author mostly used publicly available data and tried to objectively document the evolution of the organization and key episodes of importing teaching civic engagement into China, the author's passion and support for this organization could still lead to biases and, as a result, the possibility of overlooking SEED's limitations and negative aspects of its operations.

56. Marshall Ganz, "Leading Change: Leadership, Organization, and Social Movements," *Handbook of Leadership Theory and Practice* 19 (2010): 1–10.

57. Marshall Ganz, "Public Narrative: Self & Us & Now," *Marshallganz usmblogs*, (2013) http://marshallganz.usmblogs.com/files/2012/08/Public-Narrative-Worksheet-Fall-2013-.pdf.

58. MOE (Ministry of Education of the People's Republic of China), "Notice of the Ministry of Education on Printing and Distributing the 'Basic Education Curriculum Reform Outline (Trial)'," (2001) http://www.moe.gov.cn/srcsite/A26/jcj_kcjcgh/200106/t20010608_167343.html; MOE (Ministry of Education of the People's Republic of China), "The New Version of the Compulsory Education Curriculum Plan and Curriculum Standards Will Be Announced Next Year," (2020) https://www.sohu.com/a/428398162_105067.

59. SEED for Social Innovation, "2017 SEED Fellow Revisit Survey Report," (2020).

60. SEED for Social Innovation, "SEED 2018."

61. Katie E. Corcoran, "Emotion, Religion, and Civic Engagement: A Multilevel Analysis of US Congregations," *Sociology of Religion* 81, no. 1 (2020): 20–44.

62. Due to the authoritarian nature of the state, the current positions of these trainees cannot be revealed.

4 Conceptualizing Civic Education and Engagement in Less Liberal Contexts

Catherine Shea Sanger[1] and Wei Lit Yew[2]

1. Yale-NUS College; 2. Hong Kong Baptist University

Civic engagement education has often been associated with promoting and protecting liberal democracy. What does civic engagement education entail in less liberal or illiberal political contexts? In this chapter, we use the lens of "campus climate" to describe ways that broader political-legal contexts (macroclimates), organizational contexts of universities or colleges (mesoclimates), and localized settings within the college, e.g., residential halls and classrooms (microclimates) combine to facilitate or stymie civic engagement education. Using Singapore as an illustration, we describe formal legal restrictions and implicit norms that constitute macroclimatic barriers to certain types of civic engagement. To foster productive microclimates for civic education in this context, we encourage educators to emphasize community engagement in addition to political activism, inquiry and service over confrontational change-making, and communitarian/ collectivist over exclusively liberal/individualized political approaches. To develop these claims, we introduce a short case study of Yale-NUS College in Singapore. Our case study indicates that, through the provision of a facilitative campus climate, there are robust opportunities for civic engagement education in less liberal contexts. A more in-depth case study of civic engagement education at Yale-NUS College is then presented in section III, with findings from focus groups and content analyses.

KEYWORDS: Civic Education; Higher Education; Electoral Authoritarianism; Post-Colonial Politics; Singapore; Campus Climate.

Introduction

Higher education in the liberal arts and sciences has gone global.[1] National liberal arts institutions can be found across the globe, such as Ashesi University in Ghana, Lingnan University in Hong Kong, Ashoka University in India, and US-based small liberal arts colleges like Swarthmore, Williams, Amherst, Kenyon, and Wellesley. Additionally, in recent years transnational institutions and branch campuses such as Duke-Kunshan, NYU-Abu Dhabi, and Yale-NUS College have swelled the ranks of liberal arts colleges and universities throughout the world.

As the liberal arts model spreads, some newer institutions have grappled with fundamental questions of promoting the liberal arts in less liberal countries.[2] High-profile incidents involving these various institutions have caused concerns about their ability to protect academic freedom, expansive education, and critical discussions, which are hallmarks of the liberal arts model. In 2015, for example, an NYU professor who is a fierce critic of the labor policies in the United Arab Emirates was barred from entering the country.[3] The specter of official censorship has continued to haunt branch campuses in China.[4] In fact, the authors' own institution, Yale-NUS College, faced controversy due to a last-minute cancellation of an experiential learning short course on dissent in Singapore because of fears that it was going to involve students violating local laws regarding protest and assembly.[5] Inevitably, these controversies have stoked questions about the viability of implementing liberal education in countries without strong liberal arts traditions, and by extension, of teaching civic engagement in less liberal political contexts.

As educators at Yale-NUS since 2014 and 2018 respectively, we are well-positioned to offer insights into how civic engagement education has developed and can develop within a less liberal polity and how civic engagement might develop in similarly situated institutions. In this chapter, we offer conceptual tools for understanding civic education and sociopolitical engagement in less liberal contexts. While many of these observations will be applicable across a range of political regime types and cultural contexts, we draw heavily from our own experience as non-Singaporeans teaching in Singaporean higher education. Our observations are relevant for all educators who are considering civic education in less liberal settings and those who are working outside their cultural comfort zones, such as educators working at international institutions or branch campuses outside their country of origin.

In this chapter, we deploy the lens of "campus climate" to frame our argument on how the broader political-legal context (the macroclimate), the organizational context (the mesoclimate), and localized settings within the college (microclimates) combine to facilitate and complicate the pedagogy of civic engagement. Campus climate refers to "a complex ecosystem of interconnected structural, cultural, human, and political factors that affect college student learning."[6] Several authors have noted that it is critical for encouraging students' political learning and engagement, because campus climate shapes prevailing attitudes, behaviors, standards, and practices of the members of an institution, which in turn determine the academic experiences of individual students.[7] While existing literature on campus climate has successfully flagged crucial elements facilitating civic engagement among students, it has failed to take into account the specific experiences of universities, particularly liberal arts institutions, in illiberal settings. Our contribution here therefore seeks to build on the recent increase in global liberal arts institutions and correct this regional lacuna.[8]

Furthermore, campus climate tends to be assessed by scholars at the organizational level, understating both the macro (the sociopolitical context) and the micro (everyday sociospatial environments within the campus). Recognizing that there may be diverse experiences based on the students' social group identities (such as race, gender, class, etc.), Vaccaro suggests that the organizational-level environment of an institution is constituted by multiple "microclimates." These micro-sociospatial environments encompass the classroom, dining area, residence hall, and shared sport facilities, essentially "localized, physical settings where daily interpersonal interactions [shape] people's perceptions and experiences."[9] Even though the importance of political context is acknowledged, works on campus climate in the American context tend to characterize the political environment as mere "external forces" or "stakeholders" with whom institutional leaders negotiate.[10] But in less liberal contexts, the blatant intrusion of political forces into the campus is often a plausible scenario. For example, in 2014, a Malaysian university literally locked the gates to prevent the political opposition leader from delivering his scheduled lecture on campus grounds.[11] Similarly, in 2016, democracy activist Joshua Wong was detained and deported by Thai authorities, preventing him from speaking to Chulalongkorn University students.[12]

Thus, to better capture the institutional experiences in less liberal contexts, we (re)center the macro-political environment and microclimates in the discussion below. Because liberal arts education and institutions in less liberal contexts are often not well understood by policymakers and the public, they may be subject to intense political and media scrutiny. Particular liberal principles and politicized forms of engagement may be viewed as "foreign," if not illegal, and therefore undesirable in host societies. For example, in addition to becoming a topic of national parliamentary debate,[13] a former member of Singapore's parliament wrote on the national broadsheet that the Yale-NUS short course on dissent risked fomenting a "color revolution."[14] Thus, free and safe spaces for exploring political ideas and practices on campus—which speak to the microclimates—are a precondition for effective civic learning. This in turn is contingent on how institutional leaders navigate their responsibility in ensuring productive relations with the host government in order to preserve a campus climate that is facilitative of student civic engagement.[15]

The chapter is organized as follows. First, we argue for the importance of taking political context and culture, the macro-climate, into account when designing civic engagement education. Second, we narrow our scope to a particular category of political context: less liberal polities. We contend that to effectively foster civic education under such political climates, the construct of "civic engagement" needs to be reconceptualized and globalized. Specifically, civic education in less liberal contexts tends to emphasize social and community engagement over political activism, inquiry and service over confrontational change-making, and communitarian/collectivist over exclusively liberal/individualized political approaches. Third, we introduce a short case study of Yale-NUS College in Singapore. After describing some key features of the Singaporean political context, we review early criticisms of Yale-NUS. Then, we engage with condemnations that an institution located in Singapore would not be able to foster true civic engagement in part because it could not guarantee total academic freedom. Our case study indicates that, despite these concerns, through the provision of a facilitative campus climate, there are still robust opportunities for civic engagement education in less liberal contexts. This chapter sets the stage for a more in-depth case study of civic engagement education at Yale-NUS College presented in section III. There we share findings from several focus groups and content analyses conducted by the authors in 2020.

Why Context Matters For Civic Education

For educators who strive to teach and encourage civic engagement, attention to context is critical. For those like the authors who are teaching outside their own country of origin, it is especially important to learn the formal and hidden rules of political engagement, speech, and activism in the countries in which they operate. This knowledge is essential not only for risk management, but to identify opportunities for learning and diagnose possible sources of resistance among students to their assignments and pedagogy.

In particular, for educators who were raised or educated in highly liberal democratic political environments, it is important to think critically about what it means to teach civic engagement in less liberal political contexts. First, such educators should start by problematizing overly-simplistic and often xenophobic distinctions of regime types between democratic and authoritarian that may have been part of their upbringing. Most regimes are shades of grey. A more nuanced view helps educators to appreciate new opportunities for civic engagement education in less liberal contexts. Taking a less dichotomous view may also help us to identify novel approaches to political education in self-proclaimed bastions of liberal democracy like the US and France, where growing public and scholarly attention to systemic inequalities and anti-democratic political tactics may signal the need for new approaches to civic engagement education. Second, educators who were trained in Western liberal democracies and are now operating in less liberal contexts need to critically reflect on their goals and approaches to civic engagement education. What works in North America, for example, may not be appropriate or impactful in less liberal environments where there are different rules of the game and cultural norms in terms of political expression and action.

In politically more liberal societies where barriers to political involvement are low and checks on the government are relatively high, the common social obstacles to civic engagement for college students are apathy, ignorance, and lack of incentives and opportunities to get involved. As such, civic education in the American frame has traditionally focused on promoting "civic engagement" through four pathways:[16]

1. Enhancing students' *understanding* of political institutions and processes.
2. Enhancing students' *interest* in social and political issues.
3. Encouraging more active *participation* in the political process.
4. Empowering students with *skills* to take action within those institutions and on those issues they care about.

Less liberal societies have higher institutional and normative barriers to civic participation and fewer constraints on the government. In such a context, the challenge for civic engagement education is not just to promote greater understanding and action. It is to make students feel safe and secure admitting to an interest in politics and societal change in the first place, let alone acquiring deeper knowledge about civic engagement strategies. In more liberal democracies there is an expectation of frequent and peaceful political change. In less liberal states, the status quo is not as likely to be frequently reimagined and challenged in popular discourse.

In less liberal contexts like Singapore, for example, there is no partisan political campaigning on campus.[17] More generally, overtly political civic engagement education can appear and feel subversive, even if the goal of such education is not to destabilize the status quo per se, but instead to understand how to work within the system to achieve positive societal outcomes. This is a very different context than, for example, the United States and many parts of Europe where participating in organized political protest and overt activism is seen as a rite of passage, a "bucket-list" entry in the university experience.[18]

Other than formal political constraints, culture may also have an impact on the public support for democratic institutions and ideas—an issue that remains actively debated by scholars.[19] For instance, while Brunkert, Kruze, and Welzel contend that "emancipative values" or beliefs in universal freedoms especially in the West have helped to anchor democracy,[20] others such as Dalton and Ong have pushed back against claims that Asian orientations toward authority are an impediment to democracy.[21] But insofar as there is a relationship between political institutions and culture, education systems in societies that tend to be more deferential to authority are less likely to encourage students to challenge established norms, institutions, or individuals with power and legitimacy. This context contrasts with the mainstay learning goal of most civic engagement educational models in the Anglo-American tradition: to empower students to challenge conventional wisdom and assert themselves vis-à-vis existing authority structures.

For these reasons alone, context matters, and civic engagement education will take different forms.[22] Civic engagement education in the Singapore context may in some ways look similar to and in other respects be much more limited than in an American or Western European context. Similarities might include assigning research projects and structured debates *within the classroom* on contemporary political issues. However, professors in less liberal contexts are unlikely to encourage students to engage in behaviors which may be illegal like organizing a street protest. Professors may even shy away from encouraging students to write politically-charged opinion articles for the local paper or creating a public course blog if there are risks of government retaliation.

However, civic engagement is not reducible to combative political activism and road-closing protests. Further, conventional Western-informed notions of civic engagement often deliberately and explicitly link civic education to the mission of fostering liberal visions of democracy. Indeed, the introductory chapters of the previous *Teaching Civic Engagement* volumes invoke the call of creating and sustaining democracy within the first two paragraphs.[23] But how should we conduct civic education in a context where "democracy," as well as other adjacent terms such as "civil society," "rule of law" and "political engagement," are deeply contested?

It is worth remembering that civic engagement is also built upon imagination, courage, community-building, and community-tending, which can be taught in many different ways within a less liberal environment. Thus, in order to accommodate various political and cultural considerations, this chapter reframes "civic engagement education" as a more inclusive concept that is focused on the basics and appeals to universal sentiments: *identifying, creating, and maintaining spaces where students can develop knowledge and an interest in social and political issues and engage in genuine conversation, ideation, and disagreement within their local or national contexts.* These are perhaps the most important and foundational elements for civic education that can be useful to reference in less liberal and more authoritarian contexts and, perhaps, may even be instructive in the increasingly untethered and polarized context of the United States as well.[24]

Conceptualizing Civic Engagement Education In Less Liberal Contexts

Before we get to the pertinent question of teaching civic engagement, how should we conceptualize civic engagement in less liberal contexts? After all, barriers to political expression and action vary across time and space, and civic engagement takes on different manifestations accordingly. Some of these constraints are explicit and legal (e.g., whether one is allowed to host representatives of political parties on campus), while often the greatest constraints are implicit and social (e.g., will students or parents complain if teachers discuss socio-economic inequality, electoral politics, racism, heteronormativity, or sexism in the classroom).

To understand and pursue civic education in less liberal contexts, we ought to first globalize the meaning of "civic engagement education" so that we have purchase on that concept when operating in differently-constrained political and cultural environments. In other words, we need to address the meta-context which may well determine the scope and contents of civic engagement education. As we will discuss below, producing change-making agents is not impossible in less liberal settings. But to be relevant in such environments, civic engagement education needs to be more inclusive and imaginative, encompassing 1) social and community engagement in addition to political change; 2) critical inquiry in addition to active change-making; 3) communitarian views in addition to liberal views about state and civil society.[25] In other words, we are not proposing a wholesale redesign of civic education. Rather, we reject the underlying assumptions of an implicit hierarchy that has long informed Anglo-American civic engagement pedagogies, one that sets political engagement apart from service and volunteerism. While sharing Facebook posts, signing petitions, and volunteering may seem "thin" and "shallow" in the Western context,[26] in a less liberal context, these actions may be politically contentious and risk provoking state reprisal. Additionally, despite the foreclosure of many options for political engagement, we point out that deliberation and social engagement can and have plausibly prefigured sustained commitment among students toward more "political" undertakings.

Indeed, low voter turnout among youths in the West has repeatedly been cited as reason for rethinking civic education.[27] Hence, current theorizing on civic engagement activities often pertains to political participation, while civil society is typically seen as *the* natural realm for civic action.[28] Extant scholarship tends to also focus on the liberal West.[29] Put simply, in US-centric or Euro-centric civic engagement literature, this concept has often been treated as synonymous with voting, civil society, and activism. Even within the US-centric literature, there is a lack of consensus as to what counts as civic engagement. A frequently cited definition suggests that it entails an "active citizen" participating "in the life of a community in order to improve conditions for others or to help shape the community's future."[30] This term can describe non-political voluntary service, such as getting involved in community associations and events, which include charities, clubs, religious organizations, and local gatherings. It can also describe political participation and involvement, essentially collective efforts that demand government action, encompassing voting, lobbying, campaigning, and demonstrations. And according to Peterson, active citizenship should ideally be a balance of both political and community participation.[31] To use the categories from Westheimer and Kahne, civic engagement education aims to develop students into "participatory citizens" and "justice-oriented citizens."[32]

In liberal contexts, civic education is imbued with the Putnamian thesis that enhancing civic participation among young citizens consolidates democracy.[33] Fesnic has investigated this phenomena in the context of post-communist countries, showing that while Poland's democratic progress owes partly to its robust civic education, democratic backsliding in Hungary has been partly a result of poor civic education.[34] Civic education has also been refashioned in multicultural nation-states in North America and Western Europe to promote an inclusive citizenship among a diverse population.[35] For example, to ameliorate public concerns over integration and social alienation of minorities, which reached xenophobic levels in the early 21st century due to instances of radicalization and terrorist recruitment among Muslim youths, European governments redoubled civic education efforts to instill so-called "national values" in minorities and immigrant students. While the French civic education model emphasized republican values, the Swedish model took on a more pluralistic approach that centered social democratic principles such equal rights for minorities. Recent iterations of civic education curricula have focused on intercultural dialogue and social responsibility.[36]

In less-liberal countries like Singapore which have regular elections but limits on speech and political activity, civic engagement education is essentially an effort to disseminate engagement, attentiveness, and critical thinking within the parameters of a less liberal state.[37] As Noori elaborates, there are legitimate concerns about the ways in which Western universities and their branch campuses may harbor implicit and explicit political and cultural biases that may be viewed as a form of cultural imperialism.[38] Even in newly democratized Taiwan, authoritarian residues, coupled with conservative cultural restraints, have kept educators from discussing their political agenda and activism with students in the classroom, partly because protests are seen to contradict the Confucian dictum of self-restraint.[39] In these contexts, there are palpable tensions between staying true to the core tenets of liberal education and attending to particular aspects of local politics, culture, and preferences.[40] In any case, tactics for teaching civic engagement must shift to ensure a culturally resonant student experience. For example, in liberal settings, teaching civic engagement using "drive-by" participation—limited and risk-averse forms of engagement—is seen as inferior to more sustained, time-consuming, and transformative forms of civic engagement.[41] However, in less liberal educational contexts, these "drive-by" experiences may necessarily be a best practice and a way to acculturate students who are less comfortable with overt political engagement. After all, in these contexts, these educational institutions are often sites where their once rich history of campus activism has been abruptly—and sometimes violently—discontinued. For example, in post-Tiananmen Chinese universities, Enlightenment values have been rejected in favor of state values, generating "educated acquiescence" among faculty, staff and students.[42] In Malaysia and Singapore, due also to past state control measures, student activism had been effectively contained and is now often discussed in past tense among historians.[43]

To be sure, in many less-liberal contexts in East and Southeast Asia, elements of a more liberal and cosmopolitan conception of civic education have been incorporated into the local educational culture. For example, China's primary and secondary school citizenship curricula have been revised to incorporate "global" perspectives, such as global awareness of interdependence and peaceful development. Similarly, secondary school citizenship education in Indonesia and Malaysia addresses human rights topics and references "global community building." However, such government initiatives to introduce notions of global citizenship into the national curricula are largely responses to economic globalization.[44] Civic education is often unmoored from its liberal principles and transplanted onto a predominantly hierarchical, uncritical framework of knowledge transmission. State-approved civic education is therefore akin to a conveyor belt that produces "well-rounded" students who will be loyal to the state and more productive and competitive in the global market. This general approach regards education mainly as training for the economy, which is historically associated with the region's postcolonial catch-up trajectory.[45]

Further, postcolonial state anxieties about nation-building have rendered civic education an ideal vehicle for fostering national identity.[46] In Singapore, for example, the government's call for Singaporeans to be actively involved in community work is couched in a vision of forging a "Singapore soul."[47] Put simply, while conversations about civic education in the West tend to center on youth apathy to the *political process*, it is apathy to *the nation* that concerns counterparts in many less liberal, post-colonial contexts. Arguably, for the postcolonial state, civic education is a project of political socialization and nation-solidification. In that vein, civic education models in postcolonial states tend to be inflected with "idealized notions of the state,"[48] marginalizing cosmopolitan and social activism discourses that are integral to the Anglo-American praxis of civic engagement.

Also, in less liberal contexts, there are deliberate ambiguities surrounding what constitutes "politics," "civil society," and "active citizenship."[49] In China, for instance, "civil society" was once a widely accepted notion during the 2000s, before becoming politically sensitive in 2011 due to Arab Spring-inspired calls for a "Jasmine revolution."[50] The politically preferred term for "civil society groups" in China now is "social organizations" or "non-profit organizations." In Singapore, the term "civic society," promulgated in 1991 by government minister George Yeo, is preferred to "civil society." In addition to an emphasis on civic responsibilities as opposed to individual rights, "civic society" signals expectations that voluntary organizations ought to work with rather than against the government.[51] The appropriate relationship governing state and society, therefore, revolves around "constructive partnerships." With the "potentially de-stabilizing 'politicking' of civil society" pre-empted, civic society groups, the junior partner of the relationship, are expected to direct their energies toward voluntarism and consultation.[52] As Lee adds, the idea is to "keep citizens occupied in activities that are deemed civic, gracious and kind so that they would keep a safe distance away from real political activities such as political lobbying, protests, campaigning, or even politically induced violence."[53] According to Ho, Sim, and Alviar-Martin, this idea has trickled down to secondary school citizenship education, as students are exhorted to be "gracious" and "law-abiding" and refrain from questioning the wider socio-political structures.[54] These are specific features of civic education in the Singaporean context, but illustrate the importance of understanding the implicit boundaries for political engagement when designing civic engagement education.

Attention to context specifically reveals two important traits of civic engagement in less liberal contexts. First, the distinction between political and apolitical is not a theoretical exercise. It captures the legal and ideological boundaries that the authorities may enforce over active citizenship. In less liberal settings, there is likely to be a more entrenched and consequential delineation between those who are politically engaged and those who are not. The net result is greater attention to service and volunteerism due to their alignment with dominant values and a disinclination toward critical political involvement among educators and students.[55] Deepening and enriching civic education in less liberal contexts requires broadening our imagination for how engagement may look and a better understanding of the kinds of spaces in which it can be enacted. Recognizing these constraints and possibilities across different contexts, educators can be creative in their use of varied media and learning activities to inculcate civic engagement.

Second, instead of diffusing a cosmopolitan, justice-centric viewpoint, nationally mandated civic engagement education in less liberal contexts may be instrumentalized to instill students with a parochial and nationalistic outlook that affirms the official line. Given the bias towards "the safe and the status quo," deference to authority is reinforced rather than questioned.[56] Yet, while civic education in less liberal contexts is expected to act as a socializing force, it is possible for professors to turn it into a site for counter-socialization, "a platform for students to think about the root causes of problems, and challenge existing social, economic, and political norms as a way to strengthen society."[57] Despite pressures to strip the civic engagement concept of its political undertones, teaching civic engagement and seeding "change agents" is still possible in the relatively circumscribed public sphere of less liberal settings. To that end, the pedagogy and praxis of civic engagement should be "culturally relevant" by grounding itself in the students' social opportunities and drawing on discourses from the students' home environment.[58] In other words, civic engagement education can include an interweaving of the familiar and unfamiliar.

To that end, it is useful to call upon the idea of "political space." As Hansson and Weiss argue, "political space," both in its material and discursive manifestations, helps avoid some of the pitfalls of the liberal state-civil society thesis.[59] Specifically, it resists rigid dichotomies (civil versus political, institutional versus non-institutional, physical versus virtual), as well as the impossible ideal of an "independent" space in less liberal contexts. Political space, in that vein, speaks to an existing space that "overlaps state, government and civil society."[60] Moreover, it is congruent with the notions of "free spaces" in social movement theory and "spaces of hope" in urban geography.

These sites are capable of facilitating the constitution of collective actors and identity, as well as the pursuit of alternative politics, thereby generating the cultural challenge that precedes or accompanies progressive social change.[61]

Indeed, political space, or free spaces more broadly, may be a taken-for-granted dimension of teaching civic engagement. And in less liberal settings especially, such free spaces have remarkable salience as 1) sites of socialization; 2) organizing spaces; and 3) spaces of experimentation with and pursuit of alternative ideas. The maintenance of free spaces for civic learning, the microclimates, in turn, relies on the wider campus climate, which is how the university administration understands and promotes student civic engagement.

That there are ever-present free spaces—microclimates—even in unexpected places suggests that civic engagement education in less liberal states—the macroclimates—is far from a mirage in a desert. Civic engagement educators must therefore not only seek out these spaces, but also vigilantly preserve them so that a stable foundation can be laid for collective (re)imagination and community-building. With that in place, educators can then confidently—and safely—articulate an inclusive and culturally relevant civic engagement vocabulary, one that interweaves social *and* political engagement, inquiry *and* change-making, communitarian *and* liberal worldviews—the familiar and the unfamiliar.

Liberal Arts Education In A Less Liberal Context: Highest Hopes Or Worst Fears Realized?

To make this conceptual discussion more concrete, we now introduce a case study of specific efforts to encourage civic engagement in a less liberal context. First, we introduce key features of the Singaporean regime. Next, we describe ways that Yale-NUS College in Singapore has created "free spaces" for civic education and engagement while being attentive to the Singaporean social-political context.

An Illustrative Macroclimate: Singapore Political and Cultural Context

Within Singapore, the country is referred to as a democracy, and it does hold competitive elections. In Singapore, voting is compulsory, and turnout is very high. In fact, in the 2020 general election, the opposition Workers' Party gained more seats than ever before, leading the country's Prime Minister Lee Hsien Loong to formally confer Workers' Party leader Pritam Singh the title of "Leader of the Opposition."[62] As reported by the BBC, this was "the first time any opposition leader in Singapore has been considered relevant enough to hold the post."[63]

Even so, the governing party, People's Action Party (PAP) has won a comfortable majority of seats (89% of the total) as well as a respectable popular vote share of 61%. Since the country's first general election in 1959, the popular vote for PAP has never been below 60% and as such, the PAP has been in government for 62 years. It is therefore on track of matching the record of Mexico's Partido Revolucionario Institucional (PRI) as the world's longest continuously ruling party in an electoral democracy by 2030—an extremely likely event. Clearly, although opposition parties have seized a toehold in the parliamentary system, the PAP still enjoys significant and heavily fortified incumbency advantages. Recent findings suggest that Singaporean voters actually "sincerely" support the PAP because the party has been widely perceived to be credible for ensuring economic growth, social stability, national security, and the efficient delivery of local services.[64] Singapore has one of the world's highest GDP per capita, and according to the Economist Intelligence Unit's Safe Cities Index, it is the second-safest city in the world.[65] More than 80% of the population lives in Singapore's public housing units.

Political scientists, however, have drawn significant attention to the hegemonic control imposed by the government in Singapore, using terms such as "paternalistic,"[66] "patriarchal,"[67] "soft authoritarian,"[68] "electoral autocracy,"[69] and "consultative authoritarianism"[70] to describe Singapore's regime. They have typically located Singapore in the middle of the regime type continuum, neither a liberal democracy nor an archetypal authoritarian regime. For many political scientists and human rights NGOs, free, fair, and regular elections are a baseline for democracy, and "liberal democracy" is used to refer to regimes with relatively high constraints or checks on government actors and independent judiciaries and extensive press and media freedom. Additionally, liberal democracies are those where individual rights and freedoms are more fiercely protected in part to counter majority tyranny. In liberal regimes, there are low barriers to citizens' speech, organizing, and activism.[71] Hence, Freedom House has rated Singapore as "partly free," noting that the political system has permitted "some political pluralism" despite limits on freedoms of expression, assembly and association.[72] Large-scale data-sets like V-Dem, Polity-5, and *The Economist's* Democracy Index also place Singapore roughly in the middle of regimes worldwide in terms of democratic institutions.[73]

Both the media and civil society groups are subjected to close state scrutiny. Major media outlets are owned by companies linked to the government and sometimes headed by former government ministers.[74] In addition, PAP ministers have at times filed defamation suits against opposition politicians and political commentators for slander and libel.[75] Singapore thus ranks a lowly 160th on the 2021 World Press Freedom Index.[76] There are significant limitations on political speech and assembly.[77] Except in a demarcated space in a public park called Hong Lim Park (not unlike the Speaker's Corner in Hyde Park), public acts of protest are illegal. Under the Public Order Act, a police permit is mandatory for any "cause-related" assembly that is held in a public place or in a private venue if members of the general public are invited.[78] Non-citizens, non-Permanent Residents, and non-local entities are barred from sponsoring and participating in public assemblies.[79]

Local activists have in the past been fined or sentenced to prison for organizing peaceful protests and candlelight vigils without proper permits.[80] Most recently, in January 2021 three students were arrested for assembling without a proper permit when they held signs against transphobia on the sidewalk outside the Ministry of Education.[81] In 2019 the government passed the Protection from Online Falsehoods and Manipulation Act (POFMA), which regulates the digital dissemination of "fake news." Advocates say the law will protect the country from adversaries' attempts to erode Singaporean cohesion. Critics say the law was deployed to censor online voices from independent media and opposition politicians ahead of the 2020 general election.[82]

In addition to formal rules which limit protest and political organizing, prevalent social discourse emphasizes the social and economic vulnerability of Singapore because it is a relatively young, very small, multi-racial, and multi-religious country.[83] Domestic tranquility has historically been seen as an essential condition for the economic growth which keeps the relatively new, multi-ethnic and multi-religious nation whole. Additionally, part of the discourse of vulnerability stems from Singapore's status as a "red dot"—a city state of less than six million majority ethnically Chinese residents surrounded by extremely populous (and non-Chinese, majority Muslim) states.[84] Calling attention to potentially divisive issues can be seen as not only counter-cultural but even potentially a threat to national security if it destabilizes the country from within. In other words, Singapore's conservative culture may serve as a potent barrier to particular forms of civic engagement alongside formal restrictions on political organizing and assembly.

Singapore's "civic society" thesis envisions the family, as opposed to individuals, as the basic unit of society, therefore entrenching a communitarian "common sense" that is antithetical to liberalism in the population.[85] To shore up that worldview, families receive preferential treatment over single individuals in the government's public housing allocations.[86] The overarching discursive theme is that a high priority is placed on social stability, the greater good of the collective, and the need to avoid anything that might destabilize the country. As a result, the bar of what constitutes confrontational tactics is lower, and political rhetoric is often treated as uncivil, divisive, and un-Singaporean. Some who embrace overt social and legal change and who are described as activists have been painted as having been corrupted or co-opted by "foreign influence" and "foreign agendas."[87] Moreover, in the past, the government has used local cultural justification to silence criticisms. For example, government ministers had chastised critics with Confucianist idioms for not showing respect for authority and cited "religious sensitivity" as a reason for institutionalizing continued LGBT inequality.[88] This may serve to deter and stymie political opposition.

On the other hand, there are increasing signs of political liberalization. Besides the rise in electoral competition noted above, mildly politically contentious issues that ranged from gender equity, LGBT rights, and migrant labor exploitation to biodiversity and heritage conservation have seen significant public attention and advocacy in recent years.[89] There are a number of very active local non-profit groups advocating for social as well as political change on behalf of women (e.g., AWARE) and transgender/gender queer Singaporeans (e.g., T Project and Oogachaga), migrant workers (e.g., TWC2), and the environment (e.g., SG Climate Rally).

In the chapter thus far, we have identified certain forces that influence civic engagement education in Singapore: formal legal limitations on overtly political action and social norms that encourage deference to authority, consensus, and tradition. Every national, regional, and cultural context will have nuances and complications that need to be thought through in developing effective civic engagement education. To operate productively in this particular political and cultural context, where activism can be painted as dangerous and anti-Singaporean, civic engagement often takes a different set of tactics and distinct rhetoric. The norms we have described are not ubiquitous in Singapore, but they are prevalent features of the local macroclimate and will influence the topics and tactics of civic education at the meso- and micro- level of Singapore universities and classrooms. In the next section of this chapter we move to the mesoclimate of a particular institution, Yale-NUS College.

Yale-NUS College: Liberal Arts and Sciences in Singapore

Having briefly described key features of the Singaporean political and social context, we now discuss how Yale-NUS College has approached civic engagement education in this environment.

Founded in 2011, Yale-NUS College opened to students in 2013. It is a fully residential, undergraduate-serving college with a four-year liberal arts and sciences curriculum. It is a semi-autonomous college within the National University of Singapore (NUS) system, forged in partnership and closely tied to both Yale University and NUS. It is the first college of its kind in Southeast Asia, a regional context where discipline-specific and pre-professional higher education is the norm and fully-residential tertiary education is rare.

From the college's earliest days, concerns emerged regarding two related issues: (1) whether faculty and students would enjoy full academic freedom and (2) whether the college could be a space for civic engagement and genuine social-political education. Upon Yale-NUS' opening, the American Association of University Professors released "An Open Letter to the Yale Community" expressing "growing concern about the character and impact of the university's collaboration with the Singaporean government in establishing Yale-National University of Singapore College," especially its implications for academic freedom and educational standards.[90] Several faculty members at Yale were opposed to and continue to oppose Yale lending its name due to concerns that the College would not be able to protect student and faculty speech, academic freedom, and non-discrimination.[91] Some observers expressed skepticism as to how interrogatory, critical academic freedom could be practiced in the Singapore context.[92]

Yale-NUS might appear caught in a balancing act between fostering engagement among students without encouraging law-breaking. However, for many on "the inside," balance is an appropriate adaptation to the Singaporean context. Yale-NUS' second president and former Singapore parliamentarian Tan Tai Yong reflected on these early criticisms: "we knew we cannot—if we had a liberal arts college here—you cannot have illegal assembly or marches. These are things that are just dictated by Singapore laws but that does not mean that students here cannot discuss topics which the Singapore government may not be comfortable about."[93]

Operating within the law while engaging in free-ranging discussion on all social and political issues is explicitly articulated in college materials. For example, the college's first Student Handbook in 2013 noted that students: "Are encouraged to debate political ideas and those ideas should filter into and out of the classroom. [Students] can and should debate everything from capitalism versus communism... to the benefits and costs of a democracy versus a republic..."[94]

Consistent with local law, partisan political campaigning and fund-raising are not permitted on campus, and attacking or disparaging another race, religion, or ethnicity is illegal. However, the first Student Handbook was clear that students "are encouraged to discuss all aspects of identity—race, religion, sexual orientation, etc... Indeed, it would be disappointing if these were *not* regular discussion topics inside and outside the classroom."[95] This context is echoed in the Faculty Statement on Freedom of Expression: "We are firmly committed to the free expression of ideas in all forms—a central tenet of liberal arts education. There are no questions that cannot be asked, no answers that cannot be discussed and debated. This principle is a cornerstone of our institution."[96]

Champions of the Yale-NUS project argue that there is a certain xenophobia and narrowly "American" view of freedom of speech lurking behind those who doubt the possibilities of a rigorous liberal arts college in Singapore. Some advocates of Yale-NUS take the view that it is engaged in the subtle task of building a new institution, inspired by an American educational model, without cultural imperialism. There is nothing *a priori* wrong, in this view, with taking local context into account in designing curriculum or pedagogy. One scholar notes than the very existence of Yale-NUS College highlights that learning goals like "critical thinking" may take on different meanings. "Instead of [exclusively inculcating] adversarial critical thinking, cooperative critical thinking... allows ample space for diversity of opinions, conciliation and relationship-building" and may be better suited to a Singapore-based institution.[97]

As former Yale-NUS faculty members describe, "In the drama of academic freedom at Yale-NUS as staged in the global media, there has come to be something of a moral impasse between the two main protagonists, the Singapore government (as a spokesperson for postcolonial difference) and [critical faculty from] Yale (as an avatar of universal rights and freedoms)."[98] For its most ardent critics, adaptation to local context makes Yale-NUS a sell-out. For its advocates, so long as core tenets of academic freedom within the College are preserved some adaptation is emblematic of what global education should be all about: learning to bridge diverse cultures and operate effectively across varied contexts. In this complicated milieu, the ability of the institution to promote civic engagement education becomes a critical test of its success, especially because civic engagement has been a core goal of Yale-NUS from its very beginning.

Yale-NUS' Mandate: Civic Engagement from the Start

Years before Yale and NUS decided to partner, the Singapore Ministry of Education (MOE) identified a liberal arts college or pathway as a valuable addition to existing institutions of higher education in Singapore. The 2008 Committee on the Expansion of the University Sector in Singapore wrote of the link between liberal arts education and public service: "Liberal arts education serves to develop independent thinkers, effective communicators and potential leaders... independent and critical thinkers who can go on to become leaders in the economic, social and political fields."[99] The report also acknowledged that "some expressed the view that Singapore was not politically mature enough to accommodate the viewpoints of LAC [liberal arts college] faculty and students, which might sometimes be radical."[100] Nonetheless, the MOE ultimately moved forward, and Yale-NUS came into being.

In terms of its academic vision, from its outset the institution sought to inculcate skills and habits of mind that are building blocks for civic engagement: creative and critical thinking, articulate communication, and collaborative problem solving.[101] A defining feature of Yale-NUS is the Common Curriculum featuring interdisciplinary courses that all students take at the same time and in the same order in their first two years. The inaugural president, Pericles Lewis, described the Common Curriculum as our answer to the question, "'What must a young person learn in order to live a responsible life in this century?'...A Yale-NUS education will create leaders who can adapt to diverse and challenging environments and who are well-placed to embrace the uncertainties of our future as active citizens of the world."[102] In a 2015 address to first-year students, Lewis said, "I hope that the education we provide at Yale-NUS will help you to develop both the intellectual and moral virtues to contribute actively to civic life within your immediate community and beyond... I trust that you will examine your own assumptions about the good life and the best way to live it. I know that you will work together to cultivate a broad ethos of service."[103] These statements reflect a central template underlying the design of the curriculum, with a focus on inculcating knowledge, values, and intellectual skills for civic engagement.

Yale-NUS is hardly unique in its rhetoric about developing global citizens. That has become mainstay brochure-talk across higher education.[104] Part of what sets Yale-NUS apart in addition to its Common Curriculum is its truly global community. Just over half of the student body is Singaporean, and our international students are from over 70 countries worldwide.[105]

Having a heavily international student body and faculty is directly linked to the civic educational goals of the institution. A high percentage of international students promotes civic ties and engagement not just within but across countries.[106] For example, Lewis responded to one vocal opponent of the College, writing in *The New York Times*:

> How does he expect those countries to become more open if their students are denied the benefits of a liberal education and the attendant discussion of political issues on campus? While Mr. Sleeper seems to want to keep a liberal education from any supposed contamination by contact with different political regimes, progress actually depends on encounters with the unfamiliar, which are at the heart of a liberal education.[107]

In this view, the College was anticipated to be a change agent through a liberal arts education that fosters "discussion of political issues" and enables civic engagement and change.

10 Years In: An Early Assessment

The establishment of a service-minded, politically engaged community has been a prime force behind the founding of Yale-NUS. Despite overt commitments to fostering civic engagement, questions have lingered as to whether these lofty aims can be achieved in a conservative, less liberal political context.[108] Cheng Yi'En describes tensions between ideal and constrained action:

> The Yale-NUS brand of the adventurous, risk-taking, and socially engaged liberal arts educated citizen can be seen as a figure that embodies the contradictions between youth governance and autonomy in the city-state of Singapore. On the one hand, Yale-NUS students are encouraged to cultivate a deep sense of social awareness about everyday and global injustices as part of their training in critical thinking but on the other hand, the geographies of action (should students decide to act upon these injustices) are constantly curtailed by what is defined as permissible and what is not.[109]

This delineation suggests that there is a tension between the permissive mesoclimate of the College and the somewhat more restrictive macroclimate of the Singaporean state and cultural landscape for political action.

The authors' own experiences and research conducted on the student experience of the college suggests that Yale-NUS *has* been a site for civic engagement education (for more detail see chapter 13 in section 3). A rich interaction between the curricular, extra-curricular, and residential learning environments promotes different forms of engagement. Students learn habits of mind and communicative and organizational skills for life-long engagement. Moreover, because of its diverse student population, the institution inculcates a facilitative culture for students to learn about and partake in civic engagement.

At the same time, faculty-led and student-led civic engagement does indeed operate within the contours of Singapore's legal system. Much of the student-led civic engagement we have observed is either 1) community building and community service as opposed to overly political involvement, or 2) directed at changing *college policies* rather than *national policies*.

In response to students' change-making and activism directed at the college, current College President Tan Tai Yong stated:

> If you want students to be inquisitive, we train our students that way, always question conventional wisdom, push the boundaries of knowledge, don't take anything for granted, look at things from different perspectives and always be open to people who have different views from you... So if we do that, and then we don't allow [student criticism/ public discourse] to happen then we are being hypocritical.[110]

In this vein, Yale-NUS students have orchestrated Take Back the Night events, Town Halls with senior administrators, and silent gatherings to demand new sexual misconduct policies and administrative transparency.[111] Students have used campus elevators to post provocative ideas and show support for sensitive political causes.[112] This focus on *on*-campus activism has been an important way for students to develop their repertoire for civic engagement.[113] There is a parallel experience here with the American University in Cairo (AUC). Though the AUC president at the time, Lisa Anderson, discouraged students from breaking the law to participate in nationwide protests, maintaining a facilitative climate on campus created a tradition of protest such that students "turned their attention from national politics to rallying against the university's [policies]."[114]

Importantly, on-campus action often prefigures future *off*-campus activism. For instance, Yale-NUS alumnus Tee Zhuo credited his involvement in formulating sexual misconduct policies for the college for showing him "the need for activism in seeking justice and holding people to account."[115] As a national newspaper reporter today, he has helped bring attention to youth activism over climate change and LGBT rights in Singapore through his writings.[116] Yale-NUS students and alumni have pursued vocal and visible change-making beyond campus, writing open letters critical of government officials,[117] organizing the first ever Singapore Climate Rally in response to the Fridays for Future protests,[118] writing and speaking publicly about LGBTQ+ rights,[119] engaging in art-ivism promoting children's and women's rights,[120] openly criticizing entrenched racism, the death penalty, and other forms of inequality and injustice,[121] and organizing events on pressing issues confronting Singapore.[122]

Many of our students have pursued an approach that Dr. Lynette Chua, NUS legal scholar and Residential College Rector at Yale-NUS College describes as "pragmatic resistance," in which "activists adjust their tactics according to changes in formal law and cultural norms and push the limits of those norms while simultaneously adhering to them."[123] For instance, the student group Fossil Free YNC, Singapore's first student fossil fuel divestment movement, learned to adapt its strategy to suit the local context. The group recognized that "while protests, marches or sit-ins are okay in other countries, the available tactics [in Singapore] are more limited—like writing an opinion piece for [newspapers] or asking for meetings with university administrators."[124] Even so, they have been pushing the political envelope, creating notable milestones on the national activist stage. For instance, in the lead up to the 2020 general election, Yale-NUS students played a part in launching the country's first "climate scorecard" that ranked political parties based on their plans on addressing climate change.[125]

At the 2019 graduation, President Tan made clear that civic engagement continues to be a value which the institution proudly celebrates. He exhorted "You are, after all, not only critical but compassionate thinkers—eager to make a meaningful impact on the world around you, and to use what you have been given to change things for the better."[126] Indeed, the experiences and anecdotal reflections of both current and former Yale-NUS College students have often corroborated this achievement. They have attributed their ongoing involvement in various civic engagement projects to a curriculum that, as one student describes, cultivated "the cultural, aesthetic, and rhetorical awareness needed for students to become sensitive and compassionate readers of human experience."[127] These projects have ranged from educational initiatives to teach photography to migrant communities in Latin America, using dance lessons to help young female refugees in Lebanon share their stories, and financial literacy campaigns for Nepali women entrepreneurs. This list speaks to the importance of maintaining context-sensitivity without jeopardizing institutional fidelity to the liberal arts. Purinton and Skaggs note that leadership in the liberal arts requires sending frequent "reminders about their institutions' aims, mission, and methods to faculty, staff, students, parents, employers, and host governments" because their statements and discursive commitments can contribute significantly to having a facilitative campus climate for civic learning.[128] In section III of this volume we present further and more systematic research, which empirically assesses the extent to which these aims have actually been achieved for Yale-NUS students.

Conclusion

This chapter has argued for a context-sensitive approach to civic engagement education, which can help educators teach in a way that cultivates rather than alienates student engagement. Attention to context can empower educators to curate culturally relevant civic engagement education, translating universal vocabularies into locally resonant ideas and praxis.[129] After all, we should not simply be concerned with what and how we teach but also with the meta-concerns over how we can create space to deliver what we envision as part of the civic engagement curriculum in a variety of local contexts.

Rather than dismiss possibilities for civic engagement in a less liberal context, we have found that there are significant forms of civic engagement, though these forms might differ in style and substance from those seen in more liberal polities. For example, community service, inquiry, and deliberation may be emphasized more strongly than overt political mobilization, protest, and confrontational modes of advocacy. Action might be directed at college-level policies rather than national ones. The college serves as an important enclave or mesoclimate for fostering facilitative classrooms, residential spaces, student associations, and other microclimates that encourage student learning about issues, experimentation with repertoire, and networking.

To be sure, paralleling the natural world, macro-climactic political conditions powerfully shape how student civic engagement may be perceived and practiced on the ground, on and off campus. Through firm commitment among institutional leaders, campus climate can be maintained such that there is a buffer against external political pressures. Meso- and micro-climactic conditions, the campus climate, and its constituent free spaces, on the other hand, are equally key to ensuring a vibrant and actively engaged student community.

Endnotes

1. Peter Marber and Daniel Araya, eds. *The Evolution of Liberal Arts in the Global Age* (New York: Routledge, 2017).

2. Ted Purinton and Jennifer Skaggs, "Leadership for the Liberal Arts: Lessons from American Universities Abroad," *Liberal Education* 104, no. 3 (2018): 20–25.

3. Stephanie Saul, "N.Y.U. Professor is Barred by United Arab Emirates," *The New York Times*, (16 March 2015), https://www.nytimes.com/2015/03/17/nyregion/nyu-professor-is-barred-from-the-united-arab-emirates.html.

4. Elizabeth Redden, "China Exerts More Control Over Foreign Universities," *Inside Higher Ed*, (20 November 2017), https://www.insidehighered.com/quicktakes/2017/11/20/china-exerts-more-control-over-foreign-universities.

5. Elizabeth Redden, "Canceled Course Renews Academic Freedom Concerns," *Inside Higher Ed*, (1 October 2019), https://www.insidehighered.com/news/2019/10/01/cancellation-course-dissent-yale-nus-campus-singapore-prompted-academic-freedom.

6. Nancy Thomas and Margaret Brower, "Conceptualizing and Assessing Campus Climates for Political Learning and Engagement in Democracy," *Journal of College and Character* 19, no. 4 (2018): 247.

7. Susan Rankin and Robert Reason, "Transformational Tapestry Model: A Comprehensive Approach to Transforming Campus Climate," *Journal of Diversity in Higher Education* 1, no. 4 (2008): 265.

8. Catherine Shea Sanger and Nancy W. Gleason, eds. *Diversity and Inclusion in Global Higher Education: Lessons from Across*

Asia (Singapore: Springer Singapore, 2020); Ted Purinton and Jennifer Skaggs, eds. *American Universities Abroad: The Leadership of Independent Transnational Higher Education Institutions* (New York; Cairo: American University in Cairo Press, 2017).

9. Annemarie Vaccaro, "Campus Microclimates for LGBT Faculty, Staff, and Students: An Exploration of the Intersections of Social Identity and Campus Roles," *Journal of Student Affairs Research and Practice* 49, no. 4 (2012): 429–446.

10. Thomas and Brower, "Conceptualizing and Assessing Campus Climates".

11. D. Kanyakumari and Priya Kulasagaran, "Crowd Forces Its Way through Locked UM Gates," *The Star*, (27 October 2014), https://www.thestar.com.my/News/Nation/2014/10/27/anwar-ibrahim-talk-universiti-malaya-crowd-build-up.

12. BBC, "Hong Kong Activist Joshua Wong Barred from Entering Thailand," *BBC*, (5 October 2016), https://www.bbc.com/news/world-asia-china-37558908.

13. Hwee Min Ang, "Yale-NUS Course: Schools Should Not be Misused for Partisan Politics, Says Ong Ye Kung," *CNA*, (7 October 2019), https://www.channelnewsasia.com/news/singapore/yale-nus-course-schools-should-not-be-misused-for-partisan-11975994.

14. Choon Kang Goh, "Singapore Does Not Need a 'Colour Revolution'," *The Straits Times*, (21 September 2019), https://www.straitstimes.com/opinion/singapore-does-not-need-a-colour-revolution.

15. Purinton and Skaggs, "Leadership for the Liberal Arts".

16. Elizabeth Beaumont, "Political Learning and Democratic Capacities: Some Challenges and Evidence of Promising Approaches," in *Teaching Civic Engagement: From Student to Active Citizen*, eds. Alison Rios Millett McCartney, Elizabeth A. Bennion, and Dick Simpson (Washington, DC: American Political Science Association, 2013), 41–56; William A. Galston, "Civic Education and Political Participation," *PS: Political Science & Politics* 37, no. 2 (2004): 263–266; Alison Rios Millett McCartney, "Teaching Civic Engagement: Debates, Definitions, Benefits, and Challenges," in *Teaching Civic Engagement: From Student to Active Citizen*, eds. Alison Rios Millett McCartney, Elizabeth A. Bennion, and Dick W. Simpson (Washington, DC: American Political Science Association, 2013), 9–20.

17. Rei Kurohi, "Parliament: Institutions Should Not Expose Students to Risk of Breaking the Law, Says Ong Ye Kung," *The Straits Times*, (8 October 2019), https://www.straitstimes.com/politics/institutions-should-not-expose-students-to-risk-of-breaking-the-law-ong-ye-kung.

18. The American Freshman Survey for example has found that 9% of freshmen plan to participate in protests while in college, and along with other survey findings led researchers to conclude that civic engagement among American college students was at its highest levels in the last 50 years. Jake New, "Get Ready for More Protests" *Inside Higher Ed*, (11 February 2016), https://www.insidehighered.com/news/2016/02/11/survey-finds-nearly-1-10-freshmen-plan-participating-campus-protests. See also: Adrienne Green, "The Re-Politicization of America's Colleges" *The Atlantic*, (12 February 2016), https://www.theatlantic.com/education/archive/2016/02/freshman-survey/462429/. Various "Student Living" online publications continue to include "join a protest" in the university bucket list. For examples, see https://www.studentliving.sodexo.com/student-living/blog/article?tx_news_pi1%5Bnews%5D=89&cHash=6ea9d9e60b18c2c71ead9c8313ea0c63 and https://www.savethestudent.org/freshers/university-bucket-list-36-things-every-student-must-do.html. Reportedly, one in five Americans had taken part in a protest since the beginning of the Trump administration. Commentators have called 2020 the year of student protest, during which college students participated in the Black Lives Matter movement as well as the movement to tear down Confederate symbols in universities. See Michael T. Nietzel, "Five Reasons 2020 will be the Year of the Student Protest," *Forbes*, (10 July 2020), https://www.forbes.com/sites/michaeltnietzel/2020/07/10/five-reasons-2020-is-the-year-of-the-student-protest/?sh=13005ee373ce.

19. For more on the debate over the relationship between political institutions and culture, see: Chin-Lung Chien, "Beyond Authoritarian Personality: The Culture-Inclusive Theory of Chinese Authoritarian Orientation," *Frontiers in Psychology* 7 (2016): 1–14. Rachel Cichowski, "Sustaining Democracy: A Study of Authoritarianism and Personalism in Irish Political Culture," *Center for the Study of Democracy Working Paper Series*, no. 40 (2000): 1–23; Sirianne Dahlum and Carl Henrik Knutsen, "Democracy by Demand? Reinvestigating the Effect of Self-Expression Values on Political Regime Type," *British Journal of Political Science* 47, no. 2 (2017): 437–461; Ben Ahmed Hougua, El Amine Rachid, and Siyouri Hind, "The Authoritarian Spectrum Through the Prism of Individualism/Collectivism: Lessons for Political Socialization in Moroccan Society," *Contemporary Arab Affairs* 11, no. 3 (2018): 47–68; Deyong Ma and Feng Yang, "Authoritarian Orientations and Political Trust in East Asian Societies," *East Asia* 31 (2014): 323–341; Zoran Pavlović and Bojan Todosijević. "Global Cultural Zones the Empirical Way: Value Structure of Cultural Zones and their Relationship with Democracy and the Communist Past," *Quality & Quantity* 54, no. 2 (2020): 603–622; Mitchell A. Seligson and John A. Booth, "Political Culture and Regime Type: Evidence from Nicaragua and Costa Rica," *The Journal of Politics* 55, no. 3 (1993): 777–792; Frederick Solt, "The Social Origins of Authoritarianism," *Political Research Quarterly* 65, no. 4 (2012): 703–713; Wenfang Tang, *Populist Authoritarianism: Chinese Political Culture and Regime Sustainability* (Oxford, UK: Oxford University Press, 2016).

20. Lennart Brunkert, Stefan Kruse, and Christian Welzel, "A Tale of Culture-bound Regime Evolution: the Centennial Democratic Trend and its Recent Reversal," *Democratization* 26, no. 3 (2019): 422–443.

21. Russell J. Dalton and Nhu-Ngoc T. Ong, "Authority Orientations and Democratic Attitudes: A Test of the 'Asian Values' Hypothesis," *Japanese Journal of Political Science* 6, no. 2 (2005): 211–231.

22. Lewis Asimeng-Boahene, "Creating Strategies to Deal with Problems of Teaching Controversial Issues in Social Studies Education in African Schools," *Intercultural Education* 18, no. 3 (2007): 231–242; Li-Ching Ho and Tricia Seow, "Teaching Controversial Issues in Geography: Climate Change Education in Singaporean Schools," *Theory & Research in Social Education* 43, no. 3 (2015): 314–344; Rohit Kumar, "The Importance of Being a Good Political Science Teacher in Modi's India," *The Wire*, (1 December 2019), https://thewire.in/education/the-importance-of-being-a-good-political-science-teacher-in-modis-india; Thomas Misco, "'We Do Not Talk about These Things': the Promises and Challenges of Reflective Thinking and Controversial Issue Discussions in a Chinese High School," *Intercultural Education* 24, no. 5 (2013): 401–416; Jasmine B-Y. Sim and Murray Print, "Citizenship Education in Singapore: Controlling or Empowering Teacher Understanding and Practice?," *Oxford Review of Education* 35, no. 6 (2009): 705–723; Timothy Wai Wa Yuen and Yan Wing Leung, "Political Education: Controversial Issues, Neutrality of Teachers and Merits of Team Teaching," *Citizenship, Social and Economics Education* 8, no. 2–3 (2009): 99–114.

23. Elizabeth C. Matto, Alison Rios Millett McCartney, Elizabeth A. Bennion, and Dick W. Simpson, eds. *Teaching Civic Engagement across the Disciplines* (Washington, DC: American Political Science Association, 2017), 3–10; Alison Rios Millett McCartney, Elizabeth A. Bennion, and Dick Simpson, eds. *Teaching Civic Engagement: From Student to Active Citizen* (Washington, DC: American Political Science Association, 2013).

24. On the relationship between political polarization and education in the United States see Paula McAvoy & Diana Hess, "Classroom Deliberation in an Era of Political Polarization" *Curriculum Inquiry* 43, no. 1 (2013): 14–47; Brett L.M. Levy, Annaly Babb-Guerra, Wolf Owczarek, and Lena M. Batt, "Can Education Reduce Political Polarization?: Fostering Open-Minded Political Engagement during the Legislative Semester" *Educational Theory and Practice* (2019): 29, https://scholarsarchive.library.albany.edu/etap_fac_scholar/29.

25. Chua Beng Huat argues that Singapore's state ideology is communitarian, captured in the mantra of "society above individual" that is anti-liberal. This ideological emphasis on the "collective" has been entrenched, for example, in its public housing and ethnic relations policies. See Beng Huat Chua, *Liberalism Disavowed: Communitarianism and State Capitalism in Singapore* (Singapore: NUS Press, 2017) on communitarian and liberal approaches to governance in Singapore. However, Daniel Bell has challenged the individualism-communitarianism juxtaposition that is often used in Singaporean discourse to encourage people to privilege collective goods over minority or individual wants. See Daniel A. Bell, "A Communitarian Critique of Authoritarianism," *Society* 32, no. 5 (1995): 38–43. While we are not arguing that there are distinctly collectivist or "Asian values" that must be observed in less liberal and/or Asian contexts, we have found as educators that many—though not all—students perceive/believe that there are such distinct values. Some students can find the individualistic approach of liberal "make your voice heard" modes of political engagement to be alienating, even a form of cultural neo-imperialism. Provocation can be an excellent teaching tool when it sparks creativity and new knowledge. At the same time, inclusivity and sensitivity to local context is valuable for gaining students' trust, which is a precondition to impactful teaching. Students from less liberal contexts may be more engaged by educational models that take seriously the impact of individual action on the community, and acknowledgement if not deference to community norms and customs.

26. Brian M. Harward and Daniel M. Shea, "Higher Education and the Multiple Modes of Engagement," in McCartney, Bennion, and Simpson, eds., *Teaching Civic Engagement*, 21–40.

27. Elizabeth A Bennion and Xander E. Laughlin, "Best Practices in Civic Education: Lessons from the Journal of Political Science Education," *Journal of Political Science Education* 14, no. 3 (2018): 287–330; Ana Isabel Pontes, Matt Henn, and Mark D. Griffiths, "Youth Political (Dis) engagement and the Need for Citizenship Education: Encouraging Young People's Civic and Political Participation through the Curriculum," *Education, Citizenship and Social Justice* 14, no. 1 (2019): 3–21.

28. Li-Ching Ho and Keith C. Barton, "Preparation for Civil Society: A Necessary Element of Curriculum for Social Justice," *Theory & Research in Social Education* 48, no. 4 (2020): 471–491; Konstantine Kyriacopoulos, "Research on Civic Engagement and Youth," in *Encyclopedia of Diversity in Education*, ed. James A. Banks (Thousand Oaks, CA: SAGE Publications, 2012), 383–385.

29. Kenneth Paul Tan, "Service Learning Outside the US: Initial Experiences in Singapore's Higher Education," *PS: Political Science & Politics* (2009): 549–557; Soo Jiuan Tan and Siok Kuan Tambyah, "Civic Engagement and Wellbeing in Singapore: The Impact of Generalized Trust, Personal Values, and Religiosity," *Current Politics and Economics of South, Southeastern, and Central Asia* 26, no. 2 (2017): 125–150.

30. Richard P. Adler and Judy Goggin, "What Do We Mean by 'Civic Engagement'?," *Journal of Transformative Education* 3, no. 3 (2005): 241.

31. Andrew Peterson, *Civic Republicanism and Civic Education: The Education of Citizens* (New York: Palgrave Macmillan, 2011).

32. Joel Westheimer and Joseph Kahne, "Educating the 'Good' Citizen: Political Choices and Pedagogical Goals," *PS: Political Science & Politics* 37, no. 2 (2004): 241–247.

33. Robert D. Putnam, "Bowling Alone: America's Declining Social Capital," *Journal of Democracy* 6, no. 1 (1995): 65–78.

34. Florin N. Fesnic, "Can Civic Education Make a Difference for Democracy? Hungary and Poland Compared," *Political Studies* 64, no. 4 (2016): 966–978.

35. James A. Banks, "Failed Citizenship and Transformative Civic Education," *Educational Researcher* 46, no. 7 (2017): 366–377.

36. Per Mouritsen and Astrid Jaeger, *Designing Civic Education for Diverse Societies: Models, Tradeoffs, and Outcomes* (Brussels: Migration Policy Institute Europe, 2018).

37. Leonel Lim, "Critical Thinking and the Anti-liberal State: The Politics of Pedagogic Recontextualization in Singapore," *Discourse: Studies in the Cultural Politics of Education* 35, no. 5 (2014): 692–704.

38. Neema Noori, "Academic Freedom and the Liberal Arts in the Middle East: Can the US Model Be Replicated?," in Marber and Araya, eds., *The Evolution of Liberal Arts,* 141–149.

39. Cheng-Yu Hung, "Educators as Transformative Intellectuals: Taiwanese Teacher Activism during the National Curriculum Controversy," *Curriculum Inquiry* 48, no. 2 (2018): 167–183.

40. Purinton and Skaggs, *American Universities Abroad.*

41. Harward and Shea, "Higher Education".

42. Elizabeth J. Perry, "Educated Acquiescence: How Academia Sustains Authoritarianism in China," *Theory and Society* 49, no. 1 (2020): 1–22.

43. Huang Jianli, "Positioning the Student Political Activism of Singapore: Articulation, Contestation and Omission," *Inter-Asia Cultural Studies* 7, no. 3 (2006): 403–430; Meredith L. Weiss, "Intellectual Containment: The Muting of Students in Semidemocratic Southeast Asia," *Critical Asian Studies* 41, no. 4 (2009): 499–522.

44. Li-Ching Ho, "Conceptions of Global Citizenship Education in East and Southeast Asia," in *The Palgrave Handbook of Global Citizenship and Education*, eds. Ian Davies, Li Ching Ho, Dina Kiwan, Carla L. Peck, Andrew Peterson, Edda Sant and Yusef Waghid (London: Palgrave Macmillan, 2018), 83–95.

45. Tan, "Service Learning Outside the US."

46. Mark Baildon, Jasmine B-Y. Sim and Agnes Paculdar, "A Tale of Two Countries: Comparing Civic Education in the Philippines and Singapore," *Compare: A Journal of Comparative and International Education* 46, no. 1 (2016): 93–115; Tan, "Service Learning Outside the US."

47. Terence Lee, *The Media, Cultural Control and Government in Singapore* (New York; Abingdon, UK: Routledge, 2010), 73.

48. Philip Holden, "A Building with One Side Missing: Liberal Arts and Illiberal Modernities in Singapore," *Sojourn: Journal of Social Issues in Southeast Asia* 33, no. 1 (2018): 4; Wing-Wah Law, "Citizenship, Citizenship Education, and the State in China in a Global Age," *Cambridge Journal of Education* 36, no. 4 (2006): 597–628.

49. Terence Chong, "Civil Society in Singapore: Popular Discourses and Concepts," *Sojourn: Journal of Social Issues in Southeast Asia* 20, no. 2 (2005): 273–301; Lee, *The Media.*

50. Berthold Kuhn, *Civil Society in China: A Snapshot of Discourses, Legislation, and Social Realities* (Berlin: Dialogue of Civilizations Research Institute, 2019).

51. Beng Huat Chua, "The Relative Autonomies of State and Civil Society in Singapore," in *State-Society Relations in Singapore*, ed. Gillian Koh and Giok Ling Ooi (Singapore: Institute of Policy Studies, 2000), 62–76.

52. Tai Ann Koh, "Civil or Civic Society? The Singapore Idea," *The Business Times*, (31 May 1998): 12.

53. Lee, *The Media*, 85.

54. Li-Ching Ho, Jasmine B-Y. Sim, and Theresa Alviar-Martin, "Interrogating Differentiated Citizenship Education: Students' Perceptions of Democracy, Rights and Governance in Two Singapore Schools," *Education, Citizenship and Social Justice* 6, no. 3 (2011): 272.

55. Robert Shumer, Carolina Lam, and Bonnie Laabs, "Ensuring Good Character and Civic Education: Connecting through Service Learning," *Asia Pacific Journal of Education* 32, no. 4 (2012): 430–440; Jasmine B-Y. Sim, Shuyi Chua, and Malathy Krishnasamy, "'Riding the Citizenship Wagon': Citizenship Conceptions of Social Studies Teachers in Singapore," *Teaching and Teacher Education* 63 (2017): 92–102; Tan and Tambyah, "Civic Engagement and Wellbeing."

56. Ho, Sim and Alviar-Martin, "Interrogating Differentiated Citizenship Education."

57. Sim, Chua and Krishnasamy, "'Riding the Citizenship Wagon'," 100.

58. Lim, Tan and Saito, "Culturally Relevant Pedagogy."

59. Eva Hansson and Meredith L. Weiss, eds. *Political Participation in Asia: Defining and Deploying Political Space* (New York: Routledge, 2017).

60. Hansson and Weiss, *Political Participation in Asia,* 6.

61. Jason Luger, "Singaporean 'Spaces of Hope?' Activist Geographies in the City-state," *City* 20, no. 2 (2016): 186–203; Francesca Polletta, "'Free Spaces' in Collective Action," *Theory and Society* 28, no. 1 (1999): 1–38.

62. Sharanjit Leyl, "Singapore Election: Does the Political Shake-up Change Anything?," *BBC*, (22 July 2020), https://www.bbc.com/news/world-asia-53471536.

63. Leyl, "Singapore Election".

64. Steven Oliver and Kai Ostwald, "Explaining Elections in Singapore: Dominant Party Resilience and Valence Politics," *Journal of East Asian Studies* 18, no. 2 (2018): 129–156; Meredith L. Weiss, *The Roots of Resilience: Party Machines and Grassroots Politics in Southeast Asia* (Ithaca, NY: Cornell University Press, 2020).

65. The Economist Intelligence Unit, "Safe Cities Index 2019," *The Economist*, (2020), https://safecities.economist.com/safe-cities-index-2019/.

66. Beng Huat Chua, *Communitarian Ideology and Democracy in Singapore* (London: Routledge, 1997).

67. Kenneth Paul Andrew Sze-Sian Tan, "Civic Society and the New Economy in Patriarchal Singapore: Emasculating the Political, Feminizing the Public," *Crossroads* 15, no. 2 (2001): 95–122.

68. Gordon Paul Means, "Soft Authoritarianism in Malaysia and Singapore," *Journal of Democracy* 7, no. 4 (1996): 103–117.

69. Nazifa Alizada, Rowan Cole, Lisa Gastaldi, Sandra Grahn, Sebastian Hellmeier, Palina Kolvani, Jean Lachapelle, Anna Lührmann, Seraphine F. Maerz, Shreeya Pillai, and Staffan I. Lindberg, *Autocratization Turns Viral. Democracy Report 2021* (University of Gothenburg, Sweden: V-Dem Institute, 2021), 31.

70. Garry Rodan, *Participation without Democracy: Containing Conflict in Southeast Asia* (Ithaca, NY: Cornell University Press, 2018). See also Chong, "Civil Society in Singapore".

71. On the distinction among different types of democracy and our description of Singapore as less liberal, see Alizada et al., *Autocratization Turns Viral*; Bryan Cheang and Donovan Choy, *Liberalism Unveiled: Forging a New Third Way in Singapore* (Singapore: World Scientific Publishing, 2021); Chua, *Liberalism Disavowed*; Coppedge, Michael, John Gerring, Adam Glynn, Carl Henrik Knutsen, Staffan I. Lindberg, Daniel Pemstein, Brigitte Seim, Svend-Erik Skaaning, and Jan Teorell. *Varieties of Democracy: Measuring Two Centuries of Political Change* (Cambridge: Cambridge University Press, 2020); Steven Levitsky and Lucan A. Way, *Competitive Authoritarianism: Hybrid Regimes after the Cold War* (New York: Cambridge University Press, 2010); Lee Morgenbesser, "The Autocratic Mandate: Elections, Legitimacy and Regime Stability in Singapore," *The Pacific Review* 30, no. 2 (2017): 205–231; Kamaludeen Mohamed Nasir and Bryan S. Turner, "Governing as Gardening: Reflections on Soft Authoritarianism in Singapore," *Citizenship Studies* 17, no. 3–4 (2013): 339–352; Neo 2017; Bilveer Singh, *Understanding Singapore Politics* (Hackensack, New Jersey: World Scientific, 2017); Netina Tan, "Singapore: Challenges of 'Good Governance' without Liberal Democracy," in *Governance and Democracy in the Asia-Pacific*, eds. Stephen McCarthy and Mark R. Thompson (London; New York: Routledge, 2020), 48–73.

72. Freedom House, "Freedom on the Net 2020 Country Report," *Freedom House*, (2020), https://freedomhouse.org/country/singapore/freedom-net/2020.

73. Alizada et al., *Autocratization Turns Viral*; Center for Systemic Peace, "Polity5 Regime Narratives 2018," *Center for Systemic Peace* (2020), https://www.systemicpeace.org/p5creports.html; The Economist Intelligence Unit, *Democracy Index 2020: In Sickness and in Health?* (London; Gurgaon; Hong Kong; New York; Dubai: The Economist Intelligence Unit Limited, 2021), https://pages.eiu.com/rs/753-RIQ-438/images/democracy-index-2020.pdf?mkt_tok=NzUzLVJJUS00MzgAAAF9XNoKtC_a1bJCMYF6VDZzBcS0T1FthxFPdtTG1SO54ZuXyCzE-K9WpCkVKhL1QHoXG-tHKUDSyKi5011rwqy3RcVLZS0GaOOYlF-xj8zyQXOQHw.

74. The broadcast media is controlled by MediaCorp which is owned by sovereign wealth fund, Temasek Holdings. Singapore Press Holdings (SPH) holds a virtual print media monopoly. Over the last 15 years, the SPH chairmen have been former cabinet ministers. See Cherian George, *Freedom from the Press: Journalism and State Power in Singapore* (Singapore: NUS Press, 2012); Lee, *The Media*. On recent proposed media reforms by the Singapore government, see Cherian George, "Remaking an Untenable Media System: Why SPH's Proposed Overhaul is Not Enough," *Academia SG*, (7 May 2021), https://www.academia.sg/academic-views/media-system.

75. Lee Morgenbesser, "The Menu of Autocratic Innovation," *Democratization* 27, no. 6 (2020): 1053–1072; Netina Tan, "Manipulating Electoral Laws in Singapore," *Electoral Studies* 32, no. 4 (2013): 632–643; Weiss, *The Roots of Resilience*.

76. Reporters Without Borders, "Singapore: An Alternative Way to Curtail Press Freedom," *Reporters Without Borders*, (2021), https://rsf.org/en/singapore. As legal scholar Lynette Chua writes, "The Singaporean state has no tradition of tolerating open confrontation and protest and uses the law to suppress such actions and cultivate cultural reticence. The rule of law prevails in the Singaporean state, but it takes a specific form. At the helm of the state is the People's Action Party... this same type of rule of law, one of a rule-bound character, is also simultaneously harnessed to quell political differences and engineer social order. The state legitimizes the curtailment of constitutionally guaranteed civil-political liberties, such as speech, assembly, and association, by legislating the restrictions in accordance with existing law; correspondingly, it deploys law to delegitimize dissenting voices through prosecutions and legal sanctions." See Lynette J. Chua, *Mobilizing Gay Singapore: Rights and Resistance in an Authoritarian State* (Singapore: NUS Press, 2014),

4.

77. Human Rights Watch, "'Kill the Chicken to Scare the Monkeys': Suppression of Free Expression and Assembly in Singapore." *Human Rights Watch*, (12 December 2017), https://www.hrw.org/report/2017/12/12/kill-chicken-scare-monkeys/suppression-free-expression-and-assembly-singapore; Morgenbesser, "The Autocratic Mandate".

78. Under the Act, an "'assembly' means a gathering or meeting (whether or not comprising any lecture, talk, address, debate or discussion) of persons the purpose (or one of the purposes) of which is—(a) to demonstrate support for or opposition to the views or actions of any person, group of persons or any government; (b) to publicise a cause or campaign; or (c) to mark or commemorate any event, and includes a demonstration by a person alone for any such purpose referred to in paragraph (a), (b) or (c)." For a full description, it is available at https://sso.agc.gov.sg/Act/POA2009;

79. For example, in February 2021, in the wake of the military coup in Myanmar, the Singapore Police Force released this advisory: "The Police would like to remind the public that organising or participating in a public assembly without a Police permit in Singapore is illegal and constitutes an offence under the Public Order Act. Foreigners visiting, working or living in Singapore are also reminded to abide by our laws. They should not import the politics of their own countries into Singapore. Those who break the law will be dealt with firmly, and this may include termination of visas or work passes." This is available at https://www.police.gov.sg/media-room/news/20210205_police_advisory_police_warn_against_holding_protests_in_relation_to_recent_dev_in_myanmar. As will be discussed in chapter 13, the exclusion of foreigners from certain political activities becomes a significant factor for civic engagement education in a multinational college context.

80. For a few examples of such infractions in the last five years, see Jean Iau, "Louis Ng Public Assembly Investigation: Dos and Don'ts under the Public Order Act." *The Straits Times*, (3 March 2021), https://www.straitstimes.com/singapore/louis-ng-public-assembly-investigation-dos-and-donts-under-the-public-order-act. Activist Jolovan Wham in particular has been charged and sentenced multiple times for his part in organizing candlelight vigils and silent protests. See Human Rights Watch, "'Kill the Chicken'"; Louisa Tang, "Activist Jolovan Wham Chooses 22 days' Jail over Fine for Holding Illegal Public Assembly on MRT Train," *Today*, (15 February 2021), https://www.todayonline.com/singapore/activist-jolovan-wham-chooses-22-days-jail-over-fine-holding-illegal-public-assembly-mrt.

81. Hwee Min Ang, "3 Arrested over Protest against Transphobia outside MOE Building," *CNA*, (26 January 2021), https://www.channelnewsasia.com/news/singapore/moe-transphobia-protest-3-arrested-student-hormone-therapy-14045320.

82. Freedom House, "Freedom on the Net." For a different view, see Ashok Kumar Mirpuri, "Singapore's Ambassador to the US Responds to Criticism of 'Fake News' Law," *The Diplomat*, (16 July 2020), https://thediplomat.com/2020/07/singapores-ambassador-to-the-us-responds-to-criticism-of-fake-news-law/.

83. Martin Perry, Lily Kong, and Brenda S. A. Yeoh, *Singapore: A Developmental City State* (New York: Wiley, 1997).

84. For a description of the relationship between regional politics, internal diversity, and national vulnerability see Lee Hsien Loong, "Choice and Conviction—The Foreign Policy of a Little Red Dot," S Rajaratnam Lecture Series, Ministry of Foreign Affairs Diplomatic Academy, (27 November 2015) https://www.mfa.gov.sg/Newsroom/Press-Statements-Transcripts-and-Photos/2015/11/2015-S-Rajaratnam-Lecture-by-Prime-Minister-Lee-Hsien-Loong-Choice-and-Conviction--The-Foreign-Polic.

85. Koh, "Civil or Civic Society"; Lim, "Critical Thinking".

86. Beng Huat Chua, "Not Depoliticized but Ideologically Successful: the Public Housing Programme in Singapore," *International Journal of Urban and Regional Research* 15, no. 1 (1991): 24–41.

87. Huy Luu Ai and Tulsi Yogesh, "What the Petition against Dr Guruswamy Revealed about 'Foreign Influence' in Singapore," *RICE*, (17 November 2019), https://www.ricemedia.co/current-affairs-commentary-menaka-guruswamy-foreign-influence-377a-singapore/; Kirsten Han, "On Accusations and Gaslighting," *Kirsten Han*, (25 September 2019), https://www.kirstenhan.com/blog/2019/9/26/on-accusations-and-gaslighting; Aqil Haziq Mahmud, "Shanmugam Warns of Foreign Interference in Singapore; Questions Agenda, Funding of The Online Citizen," *CNA*, (20 March 2021), https://www.channelnewsasia.com/news/singapore/the-online-citizen-toc-foreign-interference-singapore-shanmugam-11940004; Sin Yuen, "MHA Says Foreign Sponsors Not Allowed for Pink Dot, or Other Events, at Speakers' Corner," *The Straits Times*, (7 June 2016), https://www.straitstimes.com/singapore/mha-says-foreign-sponsors-not-allowed-for-pink-dot-or-other-events-at-speakers-corner.

88. Chong, "Civil Society in Singapore"; Chua, *Mobilizing Gay Singapore*.

89. Stephan Ortmann, "Political Change and Civil Society Coalitions in Singapore," *Government and Opposition* 50, no. 1 (2015): 119–139.

90. Joan Bertin, Marjorie Heins, Cary Nelson, and Henry Reichman, "An Open Letter from the AAUP to the Yale Community," *American Association of University Professors*, (2012), https://www.aaup.org/news/2012/open-letter-aaup-yale-community.

91. Elizabeth Redden, "Whose Yale College?," *Inside Higher Ed*, (28 March 2012), https://www.insidehighered.com/news/2012/03/28/yale-faculty-raise-governance-questions-about-decision-open-branch-singapore.

92. Holden, "A Building with One Side Missing."

93. Tai Yong Tan, "Oral History Interview with Tan Tai Yong, President of Yale-NUS College," transcript of interview by Jaime Koh, (19 October 2016), *National Archives Singapore*, https://www.nas.gov.sg/archivesonline/oral_history_interviews/interview/E000844.

94. Taken from the *Yale-NUS College Student Handbook* (2013), 71.

95. Emphasis in original.

96. Available at Yale-NUS College official website at https://www.yale-nus.edu.sg/about/policies-and-procedures.

97. Charlene Tan, "Thinking Critically about Liberal Arts Education: Yale-NUS College in Singapore," in Marber and Araya, eds., *The Evolution of Liberal Arts,* 135.

98. Petrus Liu and Colleen Lye, "Liberal Arts for Asians: A Commentary on Yale-NUS," *Interventions* 18, no. 4 (2016): 579.

99. Committee on the Expansion of the University Sector (CEUS), *Report of the Committee on the Expansion of the University Sector: Greater Choice, More Room to Excel Final Report*, Committee Chairman Lui Tuck Yew (Higher Education Division, Ministry of Education, Singapore, 2008), 3–4.

100. CEUS, *Report of the Committee*, 4, 41.

101. The College vision statement reads "A community of learning/ founded by two great universities/ In Asia, for the world." This last stanza speaks to ambitious goals for students, graduates, and staff to shape the world around them. According to the 2014 *Yale-NUS College Faculty Handbook*, the mission statement elaborates, "We educate citizens of the world and uphold the principles of free exchange of ideas, pluralism, and respect for diversity. Our extra-curricular and residential programs support student learning and encourage an ethic of service."

102. Yale-NUS College, *Creating a New Community of Learning: Year in Review 2014* (Singapore: Yale-NUS College, 2014), 5.

103. Yi'En Cheng, "Liberal Arts Educated Citizen: Experimentation, Subjectification and Ambiguous Contours of Youth Citizenship," *Area* 51, no. 4 (2019): 618–626.

104. Cheng, "Liberal Arts Educated Citizen"; Christopher D. Hammond and Avril Keating, "Global Citizens or Global Workers? Comparing University Programmes for Global Citizenship Education in Japan and the UK," *Compare: A Journal of Comparative and International Education* 48, no. 6 (2018): 915–934; Julie Matthews and Ravinder Sidhu, "Desperately Seeking the Global Subject: International Education, Citizenship and Cosmopolitanism," *Globalisation, Societies and Education* 3, no. 1 (2005): 49–66.

105. With few exceptions, small liberal arts institutions in the United States have international student populations less than 20%. In terms of our student body, we have more in common with other new hybrid or partnership universities outside the US, such as Duke Kunshan (30% international) and NYU-Shanghai (50% international).

106. According to Lewis, "the fact is that a very international body is helpful to the government and to Singapore by creating links with people who are going to be leaders in their countries. And for that matter, bringing in people who may stay… may contribute to Singapore economy and society." See Pericles Lewis, "Oral History Interview with Pericles Lewis, President of Yale-NUS College," interviewed by Jaime Koh, The History Workroom, *National Archives Singapore*, (2017): 31, https://www.nas.gov.sg/archivesonline/Flipviewer/publish/a/aa4c0d26-6a78-11ea-a14b-001a4a5ba61b-Yale-NUS_Pericles%20Lewis_001/web/html5/index.html?launchlogo=tablet/OralHistoryInterviews_brandingLogo_.png&pn=31.

107. Pericles Lewis, "US Colleges in Less Open Societies," *The New York Times*, (9 September 2013), https://www.nytimes.com/2013/09/09/opinion/us-colleges-in-less-open-societies.html.

108. Tan, "Thinking Critically."

109. Cheng, "Liberal Arts Educated Citizen", 8.

110. Tan, "Oral History Interview."

111. Jie Ying Yip, "Frustrated at College Administration, Yale-NUS Students Stage Sit-In Protest," *The Octant*, (15 March 2018), https://theoctant.org/edition/ix-6/news/frustrated-college-administration-yale-nus-students-stage-sit-protest/.

112. Jia Qi Yip, "Posters, Town Halls, Angry Opinion Articles: Dissent and Disagreement at Yale-NUS," *The Octant*, (18 March 2019), https://theoctant.org/edition/issue/news/posters-town-halls-angry-opinion-articles-dissent-and-disagreement-at-yale-nus/.

113. See chapter 13 for details on this.

114. Lisa Anderson, "'… To Save Us All': Lessons from the American University in Cairo, a Community of Learning in Revolutionary Times," in Purinton and Skaggs, eds. *American Universities Abroad*, 37.

115. Scholars' Choice, "Scholar's Experiences Details—Mightier than the Sword," *Scholars' Choice*, (12 July 2019), https://www.scholarschoice.com.sg/experience/293/mightier_than_the_sword.

116. See for example: Zhuo Tee, "Millennial Activism: Daryl Yang Fights for LGBT Issues and More," *The Straits Times*, (14 April 2019), https://www.straitstimes.com/lifestyle/millennial-activism-daryl-yang-fights-for-lgbt-issues-and-more; Zhuo Tee, "Millennial Activism: Student Group Calls on NUS to Divest from Fossil Fuels," *The Straits Times*, (14 April 2019), https://www.straitstimes.com/lifestyle/millennial-activism-student-group-calls-on-nus-to-divest-from-fossil-fuels.

117. Janice Heng, "Yale-NUS Rejects Call on Envoy to Quit Post," *The Straits Times*, (6 February 2016), https://www.straitstimes.com/singapore/yale-nus-rejects-call-on-envoy-to-quit-post.

118. Audrey Tan, "Young Activists Planning 'Green Dot' Gathering on Sept 21," *The Straits Times*, (13 August 2019), https://www.straitstimes.com/singapore/environment/young-activists-planning-green-dot-gathering-on-sept-21.

119. Natalie Christian Tan, "Here's How the Conversation around Religion and LGBTQ Needs to Change This Year," *RICE*, (14 January 2019), https://www.ricemedia.co/current-affairs-commentary-singapore-conversation-lgbtq-change-2019/; Tee, "Millennial Activism: Daryl Yang."

120. Robin Spiess, "Female Genital Mutilation: A Cut, Unseen," *Southeast Asia Globe*, (7 June 2019), https://southeastasiaglobe.com/singapore-female-genital-mutilation/.

121. New Naratif, "Subhas Nair, Renaissance Man," *New Naratif*, (5 May 2021), https://newnaratif.com/podcast/subhas-nair-renaissance-man/.

122. See, for example, the information dossiers and events hosted by the student organization Community for Advocacy and Political Education (https://cape.commons.yale-nus.edu.sg) and the student sexuality and gender collective named G-Spot.

123. Chua, *Mobilizing Gay Singapore*, 74.

124. Tee, "Millennial Activism: Student Group".

125. Audrey Tan, "Activists Plan to Compile 'Climate Scorecard' for GE," *The Straits Times*, (15 January 2020), https://www.straitstimes.com/singapore/environment/activists-plan-to-compile-climate-scorecard-for-ge.

126. Tai Yong Tan, "Yale-NUS College Graduation 2019 Speech," Yale-NUS College President's Office, (13 May 2019), https://president.yale-nus.edu.sg/speeches-essays/speech/graduation-2019/.

127. Yihui Xie, "Making Change with the Social Impact Fellowship," *The Octant*, (19 November 2019), https://theoctant.org/edition/issue/allposts/features/making-change-with-the-social-impact-fellowship/.

128. Purinton and Skaggs, "Leadership for the Liberal Arts", 22.

129. Leonel Lim, Michael Tan, and Eisuke Saito, "Culturally Relevant Pedagogy: Developing Principles of Description and Analysis," *Teaching and Teacher Education: An International Journal of Research and Studies* 77, no. 1 (2019): 43–52.

Challenge, Advocacy, and Renewal: The Development of Civic Engagement Education in the United Kingdom

John Craig

Leeds Beckett University

This chapter explores the development of a British model of civic engagement. While much has been written on the development of civic education in the United States, less has been written on other national traditions. The chapter identifies how both political science education and civic engagement developed in the late nineteenth century, influenced by philosophical Idealism and the context of an elitist educational system. This established a dualistic approach combining curricular and extra -curricular elements, which became the model for the expanding sector. However, while this idea remained influential in theory, it receded in practice. The chapter identifies how developments involving political scientists led to the developments in the school sector, which fed back into a renewed interest in civic engagement in universities in the last two decades. This is new approach has led to a range of innovative initiatives and is both more critical and inclusive than what preceded it.

KEYWORDS: Civic Engagement; Leadership; Political Science; Schools; Universities.

Introduction

Politics does not stand still. In all societies, developments continually occur that challenge existing practices and require institutions, communities, and individuals to respond. This chapter explores how political science educators with a commitment to civic engagement education have demonstrated leadership through confronting challenges, advocating for change, and engaging in educational innovation to reinvent practice. The approach is historic, exploring the dynamics of change over a period of more than a hundred years, from the emergence of the discipline in the nineteenth century until the present day. In doing so, it provides a case-study of how approaches to civic engagement education in the United Kingdom (UK) have developed over time as political scientists and civic educators have responded to the challenges arising from the changing social and political contexts in which the university is situated. These have included the development of mass democracy, the rising threat of authoritarianism, and widening participation in the educational system. In this context, the leadership provided by educators as advocates for civic education and innovators, reinventing and renewing pedagogical models, has been significant. The chapter consists of five sections. It begins with a brief comparison between the UK and United States (US) to provide comparative points of reference relating to political and educational contexts and the development of political science as a discipline. The second section analyzes developments at the Universities of Oxford and Cambridge in the late nineteenth century, where a dualistic model of civic engagement emerged. The model was marked by elitist attitudes to both education and wider society and shaped the development of civic engagement education in the university sector over the following century. The following section examines how this model developed across the wider university sector during the twentieth century. In the third section, attention turns to developments in the school sector which became the focus of innovations that were to influence the university sector. In section four, the focus returns to the universities, exploring how the model of civic engagement education has been renewed in the last two decades through a model that is more critical and inclusive. The final section identifies three lessons that arise from this case-study relating to: the ongoing need for civic engagement pedagogies to develop so that they can address the changing political challenges of the times; the importance of a values-based approach; and the key role of political science educators as advocates, innovators, and leaders of change.

The UK in Comparative Context

The context in which civic engagement education has been developed in the UK can be contrasted to that in the US in three key areas.[1] The first relates to changes in the social and political contexts; the second to the structure of the educational system; and the third to the role of actors within the discipline.

In the two-and-a-half centuries since the Declaration of Independence, the UK and the US both developed into mature, if imperfect, liberal democracies through the extension of their electoral franchise and civil and political rights. However, the path that each followed has been different. The US was born a republic, and even if the development of greater democracy required significant political struggles, there was a recognition that active citizens were essential to the governance of the new state.[2] The UK, by contrast, remained a constitutional monarchy, and for much of the period, had a large overseas empire. While there was significant change, such as the development of universal adult suffrage and the emergence of new political forces challenging the social order, the dominant political tradition remained one of "a limited liberal view of representation rooted in the idea of free and fair elections, and a conservative view of responsibility, suggesting that the political elite are best suited to make decisions on behalf of the populace."[3] Thus, while educators in the US could tap into shared references to citizenship within the national popular political discourse to legitimize civic engagement education, this was more difficult in the UK, where citizenship has sometimes been seen as "a foreign concept."[4]

There were also significant differences in the development of the university sector in the UK and the US.[9] Before 1900, the UK had just 10 universities, the majority of which had been founded before 1600.[5] During the next century, the number of universities grew slowly, reaching 20 in 1954 and only exceeding 100 in 2005. Not only were they few in number, they were socially elitist, reaching just one in 885 of the population in the 1930s, compared to one in 215 in the US.[6] As Dorothy Ross has argued, the small, elite-focused university system of the UK was in sharp contrast to the rapidly expanding, decentralized, and diversified system that developed in the US.[7] While the latter facilitated academic innovation aligned to local demands, in the former there were fewer opportunities for change and more deference to established practice. In addition, when expansion did occur in the UK, universities became increasingly reliant on state funding, which remained their major source of income from the mid-twentieth century onward.[8] As the financial influence of the state grew, governments increasingly sought to exert greater influence over the priorities of universities through regulatory and funding regimes. In response, universities and other academic bodies in the UK increasingly aligned their actions to government funding streams and public policy priorities. As a result, the university sector in the UK has been more state-centric than that of the US.

The different structure of each university system also influenced the academic development of politics and other social sciences.[9] 'Political science', or 'political studies' as it is often called in the UK, first appeared in university curriculum in the nineteenth century. While this timing was similar to that in the US, its subsequent development in the UK was slower.[10] Although the teaching of politics at universities grew in the early twentieth century, it was not until the late 1950s that single honors programs in politics were established in the sector.[11] Mirroring this slow pace of development, there was relatively little sense of a shared academic endeavor amongst those who taught politics at different institutions until the second half of the twentieth century. In contrast to the US, academics in the discipline in the UK did not feel the same need for the national coordination and representation of their shared interests. As such, while in the US the American Political Science Association (APSA) was founded in 1903, the UK's Political Studies Association (PSA) was not established until 1950. As a professional association, the PSA has acted to support the academic study of politics at universities through activities such as conferences and publications, but it has not tried to establish 'aims' for the discipline in the way that APSA has. There are no British equivalents to the major APSA publications and initiatives such as the *Report of the Committee of Seven*, *Goals for Political Science*, or the Task Force on Civic Engagement in the 21st Century.[12] It was not until the year 2000 that there was a statement setting out what should be the scope and content of a politics degree in the UK, and this statement was not the result of an initiative within the discipline, but rather a regulatory requirement for the entire UK higher education sector.[13]

The Emergence of the Dualistic Model

Political science became part of the curriculum at the Universities of Oxford and Cambridge in the nineteenth century, and at both institutions it was infused with an ethos that it should equip those who studied it to be active in civic life. At Cambridge, political science was part of the undergraduate curriculum for degrees in Moral Sciences and Modern History, where Professor Sir John Seeley became its leading exponent.[14] Seeley argued that university studies should "prepare the future citizen for his duties" and believed that history was "the school of statesmanship" which would allow students to develop the ideas and opinions required for engaging in political and public life.[15] At Oxford, political science was included in the curriculum for Modern History and Jurisprudence, but its presence was most significant as part of a degree known as *Greats*.[16] While *Greats* was primarily focused on the study of ancient Greek philosophy and Roman history, it also introduced students to elements of social and political theory and came to have "as its principal aim the fostering of a spirit, and preparation for the duties of public office and service."[17] As a result of these origins, political science in this period developed with a strong normative orientation. Students not only explored empirical and analytical questions, but also addressed philosophical and religious issues relating to how society should be ordered and the duties and responsibilities of citizens as ethical beings.

At Oxford, the philosophy of Idealism had a significant impact in shaping how academics and students thought about civic engagement and how it was practiced. Idealism had become prominent at Oxford from the mid-nineteenth century, reflecting intellectual influences including the work of German philosophers such as Kant and Hegel and developments in Christian thought.[18] It was "an intensely moralistic and judgmental philosophy," which developed a strong focus on applied ethics and called on its adherents to put these ideas into action, influencing both political and educational practice.[19] To an extent, the development of Idealism was a reaction against the doctrines of Utilitarianism and *laissez faire* and a response to their perceived inadequacy in the face of social crises.[20] While the UK had become the strongest political, economic, and military power on the globe, there were high levels of poverty and deprivation at home. The expansion of the franchise had brought modern mass electoral politics, but critics asked if those who had now gained the right to vote were able to engage as political actors. While for some the answer lay in eugenics or a social Darwinian survival of the fittest, others argued that an improvement in social conditions could provide a context in which the wider population could play a greater civic role.

It was in this context that Idealists such as T.H. Green worked to develop and advocate for a social ethic based upon a conceptualization of citizenship and educational practice that would encourage students to become active citizens.[21] For the Idealists, citizenship was more than just a legal or political status. As humans are, by their nature, social animals, it was only through an active engagement in the life of the community that a person could develop their potential. There was an imperative, therefore, to remove any obstacles that prevented this, such as ignorance and class prejudice. One type of civic engagement that Idealism inspired was the university settlements, which involved students living for a period of time in poor urban areas with the aim of both undertaking work that benefited the community and learning from their experiences.[22] Activities included educational work, such as courses on citizenship and political science, and political support, including assistance in organizing strikes. In the UK, some of the leading political reformers of the twentieth century were engaged in the settlements and "were duly motivated by its civic idealism and stress in social conscience and duty."[23] The settlement movement also spread overseas and by 1900 was larger in the US than in the UK.[24]

It must be acknowledged that the proportion of students whose education at Oxford or Cambridge inspired civic activism and a commitment to the active pursuit of social justice was limited. The dominant ethos of both institutions encouraged competition and a sense of cultural superiority among their predominantly wealthy, white, and male student body.[25] As such, many of the activities through which students developed skills to engage in civic life were orientated towards their recruitment into elite political leadership. For example, the Oxford Union debating society had procedures modelled on the House of Commons which provided a training ground for those wishing to pursue a career in parliamentary politics.[26] The elite ethos engendered among students also meant that where civic engagement was focused on issues such as poverty, there was a tendency towards paternalism.

Thus, at the start of the twentieth century a dualistic model of civic engagement education had developed at Oxford that combined both curricular and extra-curricular elements to provide students with civic education. Students were introduced to ideas and perspectives that were intended to prepare them for their roles in civic life through their formal studies. However, civic education was developed through engagement in wider university life. It was essentially an elitist model and embodied a paternalistic approach, reflecting the social and educational context in which it had developed. Nevertheless, those who were able to attend as students of these universities were being prepared for active participation and leadership within civic life, and many put this education into action.

The Dualistic Model in Twentieth Century UK Universities

During the twentieth century, UK higher education expanded, and the place of political science grew within it. The growth of universities occurred in three stages, with the emergence of *civic* universities in the first part of the century, followed by a relatively intensive phase of new institutions in the 1950s and 1960s, and thirdly by the incorporation of polytechnics into the university sector in the 1990s. In each of these phases, many questioned the purpose of higher education and the responsibilities of these new universities to prepare their students for engagement in civic life.

At the turn of the nineteenth and twentieth centuries a new type of institution, the *civic university* appeared on the UK higher education landscape. In many ways, these embodied a different view of the university from that represented by Oxford and Cambridge.[27] Based in major cities that had prospered as a result of the UK's commercial and industrial position, they reflected civic pride and local ambitions. They aimed to meet the growing demand for university education from an expanding urban middle class through the provision of courses that were both more affordable and better aligned to local demand for graduates in fields such as science, business, and public service. The London School of Economic and Political Science (LSE) was also established with a more explicitly progressive mission. The LSE's founders, such as Sidney and Beatrice Webb, advocated a gradualist approach to social development led by a technocratic elite and envisaged that the LSE could prepare students to become part of this elite through the study of contemporary social, economic, and political issues.[28]

Although these new institutions offered distinctive models of education that aimed to be more engaged with the social, economic, and political issues of the day, there were also significant elements of continuity with the ideas and practices developed at older institutions. This continuity reflected the social power and prestige attached to these older institutions. However, it also reflected the fact that many of those who administered and taught at the new universities had been educated at Oxford or Cambridge and were "imbued with the Oxbridge ideal."[29]

As such, the conceptualization of education for citizenship that developed in the university sector in the early and mid-twentieth century continued to reflect the dualistic Oxford model that relied on students having the opportunity to engage with moral, social, or political issues through the formal curriculum. The development of the more practical citizenship skills and application of their ideas occurred through extra-curricular activity and participation in the wider life of the university. A typical expression of this formulation can be found in W.H. Hadow's *Citizenship*, based on work undertaken as part of an endowed lectureship in citizenship at the University of Glasgow.[30] In his view, the challenges relating to citizenship education were primarily related to its place in schools. As he explained, in his view, there was no particular problem with what was currently offered in higher education.

> At our universities there is abundant opportunities for historical, political and economic study, all relevant points can be raised in class-rooms and debating societies, and the more freely and exhaustively they are learned and discussed the better for the disputants on both sides.[31]

Similar views could be found in the emerging discipline of political science. Delivering a lecture on citizenship in 1936, one of the UK's leading political scientists, Ernest Barker, opened by declaring that he did not advocate teaching politics in schools and even had doubts about its place in universities.[32] Nevertheless, he saw some scope to address civics, which he identified as "that part of political science which is concerned with the rights and duties of citizenship."[33] Even here he was somewhat cautious, highlighting the dual risks of educating for citizenship, which could take on a statist character and erode individual liberty, and not educating for citizenship, which could leave citizens ill-prepared for their roles in a democracy. What he advocated for was the education of citizens in the UK to "make, inspire, and control the government of our country."[34] This goal was not just confined to formal education, but required that citizens also learn through the experience of engaging in voluntary bodies including trade unions, churches, and community associations. Barker's approach also represented, therefore, the dualistic model of curricular and extra-curricular activity to provide an education for citizenship.

Although the Second World War resulted in many political scientists gaining direct experience of working in government, this experience did not appear to have changed views within the discipline on civic engagement education. In the overview report for an international survey of political science teaching conducted by the United Nations Educational, Scientific, and Cultural Organization (UNESCO), W.A. Robson, Professor of Public Administration at the LSE, rejected the view put forward in the APSA report, *Goals for Political Science*, that citizenship education should be an aim of the discipline. "In the British Universities," Robson argued, "some of the most effective instruments for learning (not teaching) citizenship are the political activities that form part of the student social life," through activities such as visiting speakers and debates, which allow students to "link up their studies with the world outside the classroom, and develop the sense of responsibility that makes men and women good citizens."[35] The same view was expressed by other political scientists such as A.H. Hanson, who stated that he did not believe that the discipline should be taught "with the object of producing 'good citizens' of one kind or another."[36]

Yet, not everyone was as confident in the ability of the university sector to support students' development as citizens, and some leading figures advocated for change. In a lecture delivered in 1917, Sir Henry Jones expressed concern that many students attending Oxford and Cambridge graduated with little preparation for engagement in civic life and called on the universities to implement additional training to prepare students to undertake their duties as citizens.[37] This lack of civic education was particularly problematic, he argued, not only because it limited the students' own development as members of society, but also because in the leadership roles that they would take, they would influence the life of the wider community. As he put it:

> They become land-owners, manufacturers, traders; they come into intimate touch with the lives of men; they have tenants to deal with, workmen to employ and rule, the nation's commerce to sustain and guide, and the civil institutions of the community to maintain in their use and strength.[38]

The conceptualization of a civic education designed for students from a social elite who govern a class-based society is explicit. Jones suggested a remedy to the gap in their civic education was the extension of general and liberal education by the provision of additional lecture series which would cover literature, history, science, economics, and ethics. Jones' advocacy for improved citizenship education in universities was prompted by his reflections on the First World War, and further changes in the social and political context prompted others to advocate for re-inventions of the dualistic model.

Faced with the rising tide of authoritarian political regimes across Europe, the Association for Education in Citizenship (AEC) was founded in 1935 and advocated "training for citizenship in a democratic state."[39] AEC leaders such as Eva Hubback argued that the current practice in school and universities was inadequate. While some students engaged with social and political issues through the formal curriculum, many did not.[40] In addition, she argued, many students did not engage with such questions through extra-curricular activities either and, even when they did, this could "produce a regrettably superficial attitude to serious subjects."[41] As such, practice in both aspects of the dualistic model was failing, and many students who were graduating from university were ill-prepared for their roles as citizens and future leaders in civic life. Hubback advocated that universities expand the teaching of social sciences, ensuring that all students had an opportunity to develop their understanding of social and political issues through either formal or informal education, to prepare them for lives as active citizens.

In the post-war period, concerns that arrangements for civic education were inadequate continued and were voiced by Sir Walter Moberly in his 1948 book *The Crisis in the University*.[42] Moberly was an influential figure as chair of the University Grants Committee, the government body responsible for funding the sector. However, his book was a personal statement, with his Christian beliefs and their relevance to the purpose of education placed center-stage. For Moberly, the modern university had lost a sense of shared moral purpose, leaving it ill-equipped to prepare students for a world in which "bestial cruelty, lust and lawlessness, not only as an occasional morbid aberration, but rampant and in power" had been unleashed and where civilization was threatened by nuclear weapons.[43] While the university's "traditional role was to train students for leadership in a stratified society," this view was no longer widely accepted with the development of a more democratic social order.[44] Although Moberly welcomed some aspects of these changes, he expressed concern that for some students, "that part of his education which look to his life as a responsible citizen has fallen behind."[45] The problem, he suggested, was most acute for students at the *civic universities* who had fewer opportunities to develop as citizens by taking part in university life.

By the 1960s, the dualistic model of civic engagement education that had been developed for students in a small and elitist university sector was proving inadequate to address changing political and social challenges. It had been eroded from both ends. The increasing specialization of courses meant that many students did not have an opportunity to engage with wider questions of social purpose. Indeed, even in political science, the scope of teaching had narrowed, and the second generation of professors to take chairs in the discipline were less committed to an ethos of public engagement than the first.[46] By this time, the impact of behavioralism was beginning to reach Britain, promoting the ideal of scientific objectivity and further eroding the normative element of the discipline. What had once been a key force in animating the dualistic model had dissipated.

Idealism had lost its influence within the university sector, as its emphasis on the realization of the individual within society became associated with authoritarianism.[47] In its place, a more voluntaristic approach emerged, and while students as individuals might be encouraged to engage in civic life, it was without the previous moral imperative.

The second wave of university expansion did little to address this erosion of civic education. Although the expansion of institutions and student numbers was already taking place, the report of the Committee on Higher Education published in 1963 provided an authoritative statement of establishment views on universities at this time.[48] While one of the four aims of higher education was "the transmission of a common culture and a common standard of citizenship," the report did not develop this theme or make recommendations relating to civic engagement education.[49] In addition, new universities of the 1960s were in some ways a step away from the earlier civic model.[50] While they aimed to encourage university life through a stronger residential element, many were developed on greenfield sites and were relatively isolated from their local communities, which reduced the opportunities available for civic engagement. In addition, as the decade progressed, student discontent with university administration and wider political issues grew, resulting in growing activism and protest.[51] In this context, universities were thought to be compromised by their association with industrial and commercial interests. They were seen as institutions to be challenged over their social responsibilities, rather than as capable of providing civic leadership.

The third wave of university expansion in the 1990s entailed the granting of university status to the polytechnic higher education institutions rather than the founding of entirely new institutions. The polytechnics had been established with the aim of strengthening provision of technical and professional higher education. However, many had also developed teaching in the social sciences, and their courses combined academic learning with skills development, often through placement learning.[52] In addition, they tended to serve students from less privileged backgrounds who were more likely to be from the local area. In part, their incorporation into the university sector reflected a shift in government priorities toward the contribution that university education could make to the economy through the development of highly skilled graduates and a de-emphasis on a wider conceptualization of student learning. However, the third wave institutions often had a greater civic orientation than the existing universities, and as argued later in this chapter, this heritage became a source of pedagogic innovation for subsequent developments in civic engagement education.

Civic Engagement in Schools

The place of civic engagement within school-age education had also been discussed during the twentieth century and gave rise to a range of reports, commissions, and working parties that considered how schools might prepare young people for their roles as citizens in adult life. While the particular emphasis of each of these differed, they all tended to share four characteristics identified by Harold Entwistle: macro-orientation, utopianism, quietism, and a theoretical bias.[53] In terms of the first, macro-orientation, an emphasis was placed on the formal functioning of the national institutions of the state. In the British context, this meant a focus on parliament, constitution, and monarchy. These were typically presented in a favorable, utopian light, functioning well within themselves and in relation to one another and the citizen. In many ways, the third characteristic of quietism logically followed. If the institutional arrangements functioned effectively, then why would there be a need for change? As such, Entwistle suggested, the emphasis tended to be on the values of "authority" and "loyalty" in political life, rather than on "participation."[54] Lastly, Entwistle identified the tendency towards a theoretical bias in teaching, which was "largely a matter of teaching *about* the process of government" [emphasis in the original], in which students were only "invited to contemplate political activity as a spectator."[55]

A hierarchical school system also shaped how these characteristics played out in the education experienced by different groups of students. At the private and selective grammar schools that catered to students from more socially privileged backgrounds and from which a higher proportion of students went to university, greater emphasis was placed on developing students to play active leadership roles within social and political institutions. In contrast, at those schools which served the wider population, there was a greater emphasis on citizenship framed in terms of loyalty and duty.[56] While organizations such as the AEC advocated for a greater emphasis on preparing all students for active citizenship, they were not able to overturn this dominant hierarchical approach.

The landscape changed at the end of the 1960s with the emergence of new conceptualizations of what education for citizenship could look like, supported by a sustained body of work and organizational resources to promote it. To explain why change occurred at this time, reference can be made to changes in the political and educational contexts, as well as actions by those in the discipline advocating a different approach. As a state, Britain was transitioning away from its role as an imperial power, having withdrawn from most of its remaining colonies during the 1960s, and was actively exploring new relationships with its European allies. Domestically, the cultural revolution of the 1960s had raised questions about the activism of young people and dissatisfaction with the established political system and cultural norms. Reflecting these changes, the early 1970s saw both the rise in the minimum school leaving age from 14 to 16 and a reduction of the voting age from 21 to 18, significantly narrowing the gap between the completion of compulsory schooling and entry into the formal political system.[57] These changes made the question of how schools prepared young people for citizenship more pertinent and prompted renewed advocacy for civic engagement education among educators. Perhaps the most active and influential individuals providing leadership were Bernard Crick, professor of politics at the University of Sheffield, and Derek Heater, the Head of History at Brighton College of Education.[58] Both Crick and Heater played leading roles in establishing a new organization, the Politics Association, in 1969 which, in contrast to the PSA at that time, was open to politics teachers at all levels of education. For the next four decades, the Politics Association was the main organization championing teaching of politics and civic engagement education in schools.[59]

Writing in a collection of essays edited by Heater and published in 1969, Crick took up the issue of political education in schools, outlining his criticisms of both traditional approaches to civic education and attempts to promote good citizenship. For him, both were inadequate because they attempted to depoliticize politics by making it "dull, safe, and factual" through a focus on the formal roles of state institutions and avoiding the contested issues that drive political conflict and debate.[60] As such, Crick voiced similar concerns to those put forward by Entwistle, that for most students civic education presented the UK political system in an idealized form and at least implicitly encouraged quietism or passivity. Crick was also critical of approaches to political education that focused on preparing students to study for degrees in politics at university, believing this to be unnecessary, and "American style 'teaching of democracy'" which "fabricated democratic situations in the classroom" through "games, debates, mock parliaments and class elections."[61] Yet, he argued, effective political education that supports students to develop as active citizens was needed to address the fact that "our own younger generation is becoming actively alienated or sullenly indifferent to our political institutions."[62]

The task of reforming education for civic engagement was undertaken by the Politics Association which, working with the Hansard Society for Parliamentary Government, developed a Program for Political Education (PPE).[63] This report introduced a broader concept of politics in which traditional central institutions were less prominent and there was more focus on exploring social and political issues. In addition, procedural values, such as fairness, toleration, respect for truth, and reasoned argument were prominent, as was an emphasis on developing students' skills as well as their knowledge. While the work gained some high-level political support, the push to develop political education generated countervailing pressures. Obstacles to implementation included entrenched conservatism, professional interests, and pedagogical barriers such as insufficient training.[64] As a result, the PPE and political literacy failed to make headway.

Changes in the political context in the following decades, however, gave the concept of citizenship new prominence in public policy discourse at the end of the twentieth century and provided new opportunities for advocates of civic engagement education. During the 1980s, the Conservative Government led by Margaret Thatcher pursued policies that aimed to liberalize the economy and extend pro-market and individualistic ideas. These resulted in significant economic and social changes and widespread concerns. Some moderate and traditional conservatives within the government believed that the social fabric of the UK was being damaged. In this context, citizenship was increasingly emphasized by politicians who wanted to chart an alternative course based on values such as social responsibility and cohesion.[65] In an echo of the Idealist reaction to Utilitarianism more than a century before, citizenship was emphasized in political discourse as a potential glue to hold society together and counterbalance what was seen as excessive individualism that risked undermining social cohesion. In addition, citizenship was gaining greater political prominence through the UK's membership in the European Union (EU) and the Council of Europe. For example, the 1993 Maastricht Treaty created the concept of citizenship of the EU which was conferred on the nationals of all member states and included political rights, such as the right to stand and vote in European elections and petition the European Parliament, alongside rights relating to travel, residence, and consular protection.[66]

Citizenship also became a key element of the policies pursued by the Labour Government under Tony Blair which came to power in 1997. The government used the concept of citizenship to frame its attempts to balance rights with responsibilities and empower local communities as an alternative to more top-down approaches to reform.[67] As part of this approach, the government made a commitment to "strengthen education for citizenship and the teaching of democracy in school," appointing an Advisory Group on Citizenship with Crick as chair.[68] The final report of the Advisory Group, *Education for Citizenship and the Teaching of Democracy in Schools* (commonly known as the Crick Report) was published in 1998 and set an ambitious aim for civic engagement education, which was to achieve "a change in the political culture of this country" so that people "think of themselves as active citizens, willing, able and equipped to have an influence in public life."[69] The model of civic engagement education proposed by the Crick Report consisted of three strands: social and moral responsibility; community involvement; and political literacy.[70] To an extent, this approach combined aspects of each of the main approaches that had been championed over the course of the twentieth century, including the older civics curricula, the PPE emphasis on procedural values, and issues-based approaches. Some political scientists criticized the Crick Report for focusing too much on engagement in formal political mechanisms, such as voting in elections, and not addressing structural inequalities in society which created barriers to active citizenship.[71] However, others have identified it as a landmark report, setting out a model of civic engagement education that emphasized that active citizenship entailed the development of both knowledge and behaviors.[72]

The most important recommendation of the Crick report was that there should be a legal requirement for schools to provide citizenship education to their students.[73] The Labour government's backing for this recommendation resulted in an increased emphasis on civic engagement education in schools, with changes to the curriculum that were similar to those occurring in Canada and Australia in the same period.[74] Nevertheless, while the report was a landmark in civic engagement education in the UK and had implications for developments in universities, the reliance on government support also made these advances vulnerable to a further change in political direction which has occurred since 2010.[75] The implications of these developments will be further explored in the next section of this chapter and point to the limitations of models of civic engagement that depend on the support of the government of the time.

Revival within the Universities

A renewed impetus for civic engagement education in schools at the start of the twenty-first century also occurred within the UK university sector and the discipline of political science. It resulted in a significant number of civic education projects and initiatives, some examples of which are listed in table 1. These projects developed pedagogical models based on a more inclusive and critical approach to civic engagement education. Changes in the three areas of political, educational, and disciplinary context were significant in these developments. The greater prominence of citizenship within political discourse at the end of the twentieth century, which was explored in the previous section of the chapter, provides part of the explanation for this change. In addition, both the EU and Council of Europe were active in promoting citizenship education across member states, through the creation of policy and practitioner networks and the publication of reports and competency frameworks.[76] These developments at a European level raised the profile of civic engagement education in the UK and provided policy frameworks which political science educators could use to advocate for action.

There were also changes in the educational and disciplinary contexts which were more specific to higher education. The educational context was influenced by the expansion of the university sector in the 1990s which gave rise to debates on the quality of higher education in the UK and how it might be improved.[77] This debate resulted in a range of policy responses, including the introduction of new systems to regulate universities and national schemes to provide funding and support for educational development projects. Although these did not place civic engagement education as a high priority and instead had a greater focus on issues such as graduate employability, they nevertheless created new opportunities for political science educators to access additional resources to undertake pedagogical development initiatives.[78] Among the strategies used by political scientists were demonstrating how the knowledge and skills that students developed through civic engagement education could contribute to achieving the objectives prioritized by policy makers. Through building on existing educational practices in areas such as work-based learning, educators could reinvent models of civic engagement that built upon the experience of innovation in these areas, adapting existing resources where appropriate. In addition, political science students also engaged in university-wide initiatives such as volunteering programs that were established in many universities, adapting these opportunities toward their ends.[79] These strategies reduced the cost and barriers to innovation, facilitating the re-invention of civic engagement pedagogies.

In terms of the discipline, there was little evidence that civic education was a priority for political science in the UK at the end of the twentieth century. Political scientists developing educational resources to support citizens' education highlighted at the time that no reference was made to this objective in the national curriculum benchmark for the discipline.[80] Neither was there any reference to civic engagement in the report of a major survey of political science departments in UK universities in the 1990s.[81] A number of factors explain this absence. In part, it reflected the continued adherence to the stance taken by Hanson and Robson in the 1950s that it was not the role of political scientists to explicitly teach citizenship. It may have also reflected continuing skepticism in the UK as to whether citizenship could be taught effectively.[82] Other changes in the university sector at the time, including the adoption of information technology in teaching and learning and financial pressures that increased student-to-staff ratios, appeared to many academics to be the most pressing pedagogical concerns.[83] There were political science educators who were committed to civic engagement education and placement learning, which was predominantly found in the former polytechnics, often served as a vehicle for this.[84] However, for the discipline as a whole, it was not the highest priority.

The situation within the discipline began to change, prompted by the higher profile of citizenship as a political issue and the publication of the Crick report in 1998. Although directed to schools, the Crick Report raised the profile of citizenship education as an issue, prompting reflection and discussion within the university sector. It also raised the question of students who had studied citizenship at school and what they might expect from university education and the new opportunities that this experience might present to broaden recruitment to politics courses. However, Crick was not the only source of inspiration for developments in civic engagement education, and political science educators in the UK drew on ideas and practices developed in the US. Influences included Ernest Boyer's concept of different forms of scholarship, John Dewey's work on experiential learning, and the service-learning programs of many universities.[85] This connection reflected both the longer and better developed tradition of civic engagement education in the US and the developing scholarship of teaching and learning that was proving successful in disseminating pedagogical ideas and practices.

Table 1. Examples of Civic Engagement Initiatives at UK Universities
• The Scholarship of Engagement for Politics (Warwick; Coventry; Oxford Brookes). The project developed practice around placement learning, including as a vehicle for civic engagement education.
• Teaching Citizenship in Higher Education (Southampton; Keele; Liverpool John Moores). The project created a range of teaching resources to explore citizenship in the curriculum.
• Case-Based Learning in Politics (Huddersfield). The project produced problem-based learning resources focused on local political issues.
• Making Politics Matter (Canterbury Christ Church University). Students worked with a local television channel to produce a report on local housing problems.
• Policy Commission (De Montfort). Students engaged with the local community through surveys and a pop-up shop to develop policy ideas on how to develop the area for local people.
• Teaching Frameworks for Participation (Manchester Metropolitan). Students participated in community development work with a local not-for-profit football club.
• Teaching applied politics (Birkbeck, London). Aimed to teach students the knowledge and skills needed to take an active role in political activities.
Note: Names of lead universities in brackets. See: Curtis and Blair (2010); Smith et al. (2008); Craig and Hale (2008); Bates (2012); Blair et al. (2018); Kiernan (2012); and Bacon (2018).

The critical focus of current civic engagement education stands in contrast to what preceded it. As discussed earlier, much of the citizenship education that developed in the twentieth century was based on limited views of citizenship which associated it with terms such as "loyalty," "service," and "restraint." To an extent, this conceptualization of citizenship was balanced by currents of thought that focused on the importance of participation in civic activities and the promotion of citizenship education as a defense against totalitarian threats. However, in most of these cases a commitment remained to protecting the established social order. This approach can be contrasted to the more recent work in developing civic engagement education in which there is generally a greater commitment to social change. For example, as Annabel Kiernan identified, her aim in teaching activism was "bringing forward democratic citizenship" and "countering the dominant neoliberal discourse inside and outside the university environment," while Edwin Bacon identified how teaching a model of applied politics can challenge the rationales for higher education based around the enhancement of personal career prospects.[86]

In summary, the current generation of civic engagement work takes a significantly more critical approach than its forerunners. In addition, current initiatives can be distinguished from earlier models in their more inclusive focus. To an extent, the scope of this inclusion is relative. In the UK, although participation rates have risen, still only approximately half of the population have engaged in higher education, and significant inequalities relating to factors such as ethnicity and economic disadvantage remain. Nevertheless, not only is the reach of the sector wider than ever before, but the model of citizenship is also more inclusive. The implicit elitism of Seely's 'school for statesmanship' or the more technocratic variant of the Webbs is far less likely to be found today and has largely been replaced by a conceptualization of citizenship as a relationship of equality, rather than a civic education designed for a world of leaders and followers.

Lessons from Civic Engagement Education in the United Kingdom

This chapter outlined the development of civic engagement education in the UK, charting how it has changed over the course of more than a century. In this extended timeframe, the challenges faced by political science educators committed to preparing students to engage as active citizens have changed as political, educational, and disciplinary contexts have developed. From this discussion, I have drawn three lessons that can inform both the development of civic engagement education in the UK and elsewhere around the globe.

First, models of civic engagement cannot be static and must change to respond to new social and political challenges. In many ways, this responsiveness should be second nature to educators in political science, as it is a distinguishing feature of our discipline that much of what we study changes as the political worlds which we inhabit change. Nevertheless, it bears reiteration, and civic engagement education needs to be in a process of on-going reinvention and renewal to ensure that it meets the needs of both our students and our communities. However effective current practice may be, it cannot stand still, and there will continue to be a need for political science educators who can lead the process of reinventing models of civic engagement education to meet new challenges.

Second, civic engagement education needs to be rooted in ethical values which can sustain a commitment to practice. By contrast, when innovation is driven by incentives such as the pursuit of government funding, it can come to a halt when external priorities change. Such ethical values will change over time, reflecting the preferences of different students and educators. The philosophical Idealism that inspired civic engagement more than a century ago is different than the ideas and values of generation Z today. Nevertheless, whatever the ethical motivation, a normative commitment to a view of how the world should be is essential to sustaining active civic engagement.

Finally, civic engagement education needs advocates. In the UK, citizenship has not always been a priority for political science or for the university sector. At a time when issues of equality, diversity, and social justice have gained a higher profile in the discipline, there is every reason for political scientists to continue to renew our efforts and focus on how we can better support all of our students to engage with the wider world as active citizens who can make a positive impact on our communities.

Endnotes

1. For the development of civic engagement education in the United States, the key points of reference used here are: Iftikhar Ahmad, *Citizenship Education in the United States* (London: Routledge, 2017); and Michael T. Rogers, "The History of Civic Education in Political Science: The Story of a Discipline's Failure to Lead" in *Teaching Civic Engagement Across the Disciplines*, eds. Elizabeth C. Matto, Alison Rios Millet McCartney, Elizabeth A. Bennion, and Dick Simpson, 73-96 (Washington DC: American Political Science Association, 2017).

2. R. Claire Snyder, "Should Political Science Have a Civic Mission? An Overview of the Historical Evidence," *PS: Political Science & Politics* 34, no. 2 (2001): 302.

3. Matthew Hall, David Marsh, and Emma Vines, "A Changing Democracy: Contemporary Challenges to The British Political Tradition," *Policy Studies* 39, no. 4 (2018): 366. See also: Wilfred Carr and Anthony Harnett, "Civic Education, Democracy and the English Political Tradition" in *Beyond Communitarianism: Citizenship, Politics and Education*, eds. Jack Demaine and Harold Entwistle, 64–82 (Basingstoke, Hampshire: Macmillan Press 1996). On debates around the meaning of citizenship in the UK see: Julia Stapleton, "Citizenship versus Patriotism in Twentieth-Century England," *The Historical Journal* 48, no. 1 (2005), 151–178; and Brad Beaven and John Griffiths, "Creating the Exemplary Citizen: The Changing Notion of Citizenship in Britain 1870–1939," *Contemporary British History* 22, no. 2 (2008): 203–225.

4. Elizabeth Fraser, "Citizenship Education: Anti-Political Culture and Political Education in Britain," *Political Studies* 48, no. 1 (2000): 96.

5. Malcolm Tight, "How Many Universities Are There in the United Kingdom? How Many Should There Be?" *Higher Education* 62, no. 5 (2011): 652.

6. W.A.C. Stewart, *Higher Education in Postwar Britain* (Basingstoke, Hampshire: Macmillan, 1989): 23. Although the UK's participation rates had exceeded that of many European countries by 2008, it was still significantly below that of the United States, see Tight, "How Many Universities Are There in the United Kingdom? How Many Should There Be?": 659.

7. Dorothy Ross, *The Origins of American Social Science* (Cambridge, UK): Cambridge University Press, 1991): 160–1.

8. Michael Shattock, *Making Policy in British Higher Education 1945–2011* (Maidenhead, UK: McGraw Hill/Open University Press, 2012).

9. Michael B. Stein, "Major Factors in the Emergence of Political Science as a Discipline in Western Democracies: A Comparative Analysis of the United States, Britain, France, and Germany" in *Regime and Discipline: Democracy and the Development of Political Science,* eds. David Easton, John G. Gunnell, and Michael B. Stein, 169–196 (Ann Arbor, MI: University of Michigan Press, 1995).

10. Wyn Grant, *The Development of a Discipline. The History of the Political Studies Association* (Chichester, UK: Wiley-Blackwell 2010).

11. John Craig, "The Emergence of Politics as a Taught Discipline at Universities in the United Kingdom," *British Journal of Politics and International Relations* 22, no. 2 (2020): 145–163.

12. American Political Science Association, *The Teaching of Government: Report to the American Political Science Association by the Committee on Instruction* (New York: Macmillan, 1916); American Political Science Association, *Goals for Political Science: Report of the Committee for the Advancement of Teaching* (New York: William Sloane Associates, 1951); American Political Science Association, "APSA Task Force on Civic Education in the 21st Century: Expanded Articulation Statement: A Call for Reactions and Contributions" *PS: Political Science & Politics* 31, no. 3 (1998): 636–638.

13. The subject benchmark was first produced in 2000. The current version is: *Quality Assurance Agency, Subject Benchmark Statement: Politics and International Relations*, 4th Edition (Gloucester, UK: Quality Assurance Agency, 2019).

14. Stefan Collini, Donald Winch, and John Burrow, *That Noble Science of Politics: A Study in Nineteenth-Century Intellectual History* (Cambridge, UK: Cambridge University Press, 1983): 345.

15. J.R. Seeley, *Lectures and Essays* (London: Macmillan, 1870): 296, 298.

16. D.G. Ritchie, "The Teaching of Political Science at Oxford," *Annals of the American Academy of Political and Social Science* 2, no. 1 (1891): 85–95.

17. Robert Wokler, "The Professoriate of Political Thought in England Since 1914: A Tale of Three Chairs" in *The History of Political Thought in National Context, eds. Dario Castiglione and Iain Hampsher-Monk*, 134–158 (Cambridge, UK: Cambridge University Press, 2001): 138, 150. As Robert Wokler notes, the first politics professors at the universities of London, Oxford, and Cambridge were all graduates of this degree.

18. See for example: Reba N. Sofer, *Ethics and Society in England: The Revolution in the Social Sciences 1870–1914* (Berkeley, CA: University of California Press, 1978); Andrew Vincent and Raymond Plant, *Philosophy, Politics and Citizenship: The Life and Thought of the British Idealists* (Oxford, UK: Basil Blackwell, 1984); and David Boucher and Andrew Vincent, *British Idealism: A Guide of the Perplexed* (London: Continuum, 2012).

19. Boucher and Vincent, *British Idealism: A Guide of the Perplexed*, 3. See also Vernon Bogdanor, "Oxford and The Mandarin Culture: The Past That Is Gone," *Oxford Review of Education* 32, no. 1 (2006): 147–165.

20. Sofer, *Ethics and Society in England.*

21. Thomas Hill Green (1836–1882). The first lay person to be appointed as a tutor at Balliol College, University of Oxford, and was later appointed Whyte's Professor of Moral Philosophy. See: Melvin Richter, *The Politics of Conscience: T.H. Green and His Age* (London: Weidenfeld and Nicolson, 1964).

22. Vincent and Plant, *Philosophy, Politics and Citizenship*, 132–149.

23. Ibid., 147.

24. Robert C. Reinders, "Toynbee Hall and the American Settlement Movement," *Social Services Review* 56, no. 1 (1982): 39–54.

25. Paul R. Deslandes, *Oxbridge Men: British Masculinity and the Undergraduate Experience, 1850–1920* (Bloomington, IN: Indiana University Press, 2005): 13.

26. Arthur Engel, "Political Education in Oxford 1823–1914," *History of Education Quarterly* 20, no. 3 (1980): 257–280.

27. David R. Jones, *The Origins of Civic Universities: Manchester, Leeds and Liverpool* (London: Routledge, 1988).

28. Ralph Dahrendorf, *A History of the London School of Economics and Political Science 1895–1995* (Oxford, UK: Oxford University Press, 1995): 42. Beatrice Webb (1858–1943) and Sidney Webb (1859–1947) were social scientists and social reformers associated with the Fabian Society and were influential in the Labour Party. Sidney Webb served as a Cabinet Minister and both were involved in the founding of the LSE.

29. Sarah Barnes, "England's Civic Universities and the Triumph of the Oxbridge Ideal," *History of Education Quarterly* 36, no. 3 (1996): 292.

30. W.H. Hadow, *Citizenship* (Oxford, UK: Clarendon Press, 1923). Sir William Henry Haddow (1859–1937) had studied and taught classics at Oxford. Later he became principal of Armstrong College (then part of the University of Durham and later the University of Newcastle) and vice chancellor of the University of Sheffield.

31. Ibid., 194.

32. Ernest Barker, *Education for Citizenship* (London: University of London Institute for Education, 1936). Sir Ernest Barker (1874–1960) studied Literae Humaniores and Modern History at Oxford. He was appointed professor of political science at University of Cambridge in 1927. He was active in the formation of the Political Studies Association in 1950.

33. Ibid., 6.

34. Ibid., 11.

35. W.A. Robson, *The University Teaching of Social Sciences: Political Science* (Paris: UNESCO, 1954): 44. William Robson (1895–1980) was appointed professor of public administration at the LSE in 1947, took part in the founding of the Political Studies Association, and also served as president of the International Political Studies Association.

36. A.H. Hanson, "III. Politics as a University Discipline" *Universities Quarterly* 8, no. 1 (1953): 42. Albert Hanson (1913–1971) was a lecturer at the University of Leeds and later its first professor of politics.

37. Sir Henry Jones, "The Education of the Citizen" in *Essays and Literature and Education*, ed. Sir Henry Jones, 225–281 (London: Hodder and Stoughton, 1947). Jones (1852–1922) was a professor at University of Wales (Bangor), St. Andrews, and University of Glasgow. He was active in reform of education in Wales.

38. Ibid., 271.

39. E.D. Simon, "The Case for Training for Citizenship in Democratic States" in *Training for Citizenship*, eds. Sir Ernest Simon and Eva M. Hubback, 7–16 (Oxford, UK: Oxford University Press, 1935). Sir Ernest Simon had served as a member of Parliament. He was later Chair of Council at Victoria University Manchester and Chair of the Board of Governors of the British Broadcasting Corporation.

40. E.M. Hubback, "Methods of Training for Citizenship" in *Training for Citizenship*, eds. Sir Ernest Simon and Eva M. Hubback, 17–48 (Oxford, UK: Oxford University Press, 1935): 39–4. Eva Hubback (1886–1949) was principal of Morley College and was elected to the London County Council.

41. Ibid., 40.

42. Sir Walter Moberly was a former principal of the University college of South West England (later the University of Exeter) and vice chancellor of Victoria University of Manchester. He was also briefly a lecturer in political science at the University of Aberdeen.

43. Sir Walter Moberly, *The Crisis in the University* (London: SCM Press, 1949): 15.

44. Ibid., 295.

45. Ibid., 170.

46. Wokler, "The Professoriate of Political Thought in England Since 1914," 154.

47. Peter Gordon and John White, *Philosophers as Educational Reformers: The Influence of Idealism on British Educational Though and Practice* (London: Routledge and Keegan Paul, 1979).

48. The committee was chaired by Lord Robbins, a graduate of the History of Political Ideas specialism within the LSE's BSc (Econ) degree in 1923, and then professor of economics at the same institution.

49. Committee on Higher Education, *Report of the Committee appointed by the Prime Minister under the Chairmanship of Lord Robbins* (London: Her Majesty's Stationery Office, 1963): 7.

50. Keith Vernon, "Engagement, Estrangement or Divorce? The New Universities and Their Communities in the 1960s" *Contemporary British History* 31, no. 4 (2017): 501–523.

51. Stewart, *Higher Education in Postwar Britain*, 117–124.

52. Steve Bristow and Vicky Randall, *Politics in the Polytechnics* (London: Political Studies Association and Centre for the Study of Public Policy, University of Strathclyde, 1981). See also: Philip D. Loweand Michael Worboys, "The Teaching of Social Studies of Science and Technology in British Polytechnics," *Social Studies of Science* 5, no. 2 (1975): 177–192; and Harold Silver and John Brennan, *A Liberal Vocationalism* (London: Methuen, 1975).

53. Harold Entwistle, *Political Education in a Democracy* (London: Routledge and Keegan Paul, 1971).

54. Ibid., 28.

55. Ibid., 31.

56. Tom Brennan, *Political Education and Democracy* (Cambridge, UK: Cambridge University Press, 1981): 34. See also Gary McCulloch, *Philosophers and Kings: Education for Leadership in Modern England* (Cambridge, UK: Cambridge University Press, 1991).

57. At around this time, about a third of countries had a voting age of 18, with around half setting the age at 21 years, see Christopher J. Puplick, "Lowering Australia's Voting Age," *Politics* 6, no. 2 (1971): 188–200.

58. Sir Bernard Crick (1929–2008) taught at the LSE, before becoming professor of politics at the University of Sheffield and then at Birkbeck College, University of London. Derek Heater was head of history at Brighton College of Education.

59. When the Politics Association ceased to function in 2008, the Political Studies Association formed a Teachers' Section to meet the needs of politics teachers in schools.

60. Bernard Crick, "The Introducing of Politics" in *The Teaching of Politics*, ed. D.B. Heater, 1–21 (London: Metheun Educational, 1969): 4.

61. Ibid., 18.

62. Ibid., 19.

63. Ian Davies, "What has Happened in the Teaching of Politics in Schools in England in the Last Three Decades, and Why?," *Oxford Review of Education* 25, no. 1/2 (1999): 127; Bernard Crick and Alex Porter, eds., *Political Education and Political Literacy* (London: Longman, 1978).

64. Brennan, *Political Education and Democracy*, 72.

65. Ben Kisby, "New Labour and Citizenship Education" *Parliamentary Affairs* 60, no. 1 (2007): 84–101.

66. Geoff Hoon, "Towards European Citizenship" in *Beyond Communitarianism: Citizenship, Politics and Education*, eds. Jack Demaine and Harold Entwistle, 131–140 (Basingstoke,UK: Macmillan Press, 1996). At the time of writing Hoon was a Labour Member of Parliament and a former Member of the European Parliament. He would later serve as a senior government minister.

67. David Blunkett and Matthew Taylor, "Active Citizenship and Labour" in *Active Citizenship: What Could it Achieve and How?* eds. Bernard Crick and Andrew Lockyer, 26–38 (Edinburgh, UK: University of Edinburgh Press, 2010). For a more critical interpretation see Jonathan S. Davies, "Active Citizenship: Navigating the Conservative Heartlands of The New Labour Project," *Policy & Politics* 40, no. 1 (2012): 3–19.

68. Advisory Committee on Citizenship, *Education for Citizenship and the Teaching of Democracy in Schools* (London: Qualifications and Curriculum Authority, 1998): 4. David Blunkett, the Secretary of State for Education and Employment, appointed Crick as chair. As a student studying for a degree in politics at the University of Sheffield, Crick had taught Blunkett.

69. Advisory Committee on Citizenship, *Education for Citizenship and the Teaching of Democracy in Schools*, 7

70. Ibid., 42.

71. Keith Faulks, "Education of Citizenship in England's Secondary Schools: A Critique of Current Principle and Practice" *Journal of Education Policy* 21, no. 1 (2006): 65.

72. James Weinberg and Matthew Flinders, "Learning for Democracy: The Politics and Practice of Citizenship Education" *British Educational Research Journal* 44, no. 4 (2018): 573–592.

73. Advisory Committee on Citizenship, *Education for Citizenship and the Teaching of Democracy in Schools*, 22. Citizenship education was introduced for students attending schools in England in 2002. The situation for each part of the United Kingdom were different. Notwithstanding their political union, Scotland and England retained distinct education systems and devolved arrangements are in place in Northern Ireland and Wales.

74. Ian Davies and John Issitt, "Reflections on Citizenship Education in Australia, Canada And England" *Comparative Education* 41, no. 4 (2005): 389–410.

75. House of Lords Select Committee on Citizenship and Civic Engagement, *The Ties that Bind: Citizenship and Civic Engagement in the 21st Century*, Report of Session 2017–19, HL Paper 118 (London: House of Lords, 2018).

76. Avril Keating, Debora Hinderliter Ortloff, and Stavroula Philippou, "Citizenship Education Curricula: The Changes and Challenges Presented by Global and European Integration," *Journal of Curriculum Studies* 41, no. 2 (2009): 145–158.

77. David Jary and Martin Parker, "The New Higher Education: Dilemmas and Directions of the Post-Dearing University" in *The New Higher Education: Issues and Directions for the Post-Dearing University*, eds. David Jary and Martin Parker, 3–16 (Stoke-on-Trent, UK: Staffordshire University Press, 1998).

78. David Bates, "'Making Politics Matter': Political Education in a 'Knowledge-Exchange' Context," *European Political Science* 11, no. 2 (2012): 164–174; John Craig and Sarah Hale, "Implementing Problem-Based Learning in Politics," *European Political Science* 7, no. 2 (2008): 165–174; Steven Curtis and Alasdair Blair, "The Scholarship of Engagement for Politics" in *The Scholarship of Engagement for Politics: Placement Learning, Citizenship and Employability*, eds. Steven Curtis and

Alasdair Blair, 3–20 (Birmingham, UK: C-SAP, 2010); Graham Smith, Roger Ottewill, Esther Jubb, Elizabeth Sperling, and Matthew Wyman, "Teaching Citizenship in Higher Education," *European Political Science* 7, no. 2 (2008): 135–143; Tristan McCowan, "Opening Spaces for Citizenship In Higher Education: Three Initiatives In English Universities," *Studies in Higher Education* 37, no. 1 (2012): 51–67. See also David Watson, *Managing Civic and Community Engagement* (Maidenhead, UK: Open University Press, 1987).

79. Georgina Brewis and Clare Holdsworth, "University Support for Student Volunteering in England: Historical Development and Contemporary Value," *Journal of Academic Ethics* 9, no. 2 (2011): 165–176: and Clare Holdsworth and Jocey Quinn, "Student Volunteering in English Higher Education," *Studies in Higher Education* 35, no. 1 (2010): 113–127.

80. Smith et al., "Teaching Citizenship in Higher Education," 137.

81. Neil Stammers, Helga Dittmar, and Janet Henney, "Teaching and Learning Politics: A Survey of Practices and Change in UK Universities" *Political Studies* 47, no. 1 (1999): 114–126.

82. Fraser, "Citizenship and Education," 93. As noted earlier, in 1969, Crick had been unconvinced by approaches developed in the United States.

83. Penny Welch, "Thinking about Teaching Politics," *Politics* 20, no. 2 (2000): 99–104.

84. There is very little literature relating to developments in teaching and learning in politics in the United Kingdom during this period. As such, this reference to isolated development is based on the author's recollections.

85. John Annette, "Character, Civic Renewal and Service Learning for Democratic Citizenship in Higher Education," *British Journal of Educational Studies* 53, no. 3 (2005): 326–340; Michael Bacon and James Sloam, "John Dewey and the Democratic Role of Higher Education in England," *Journal of Political Science Education* 6, no. 4 (2010): 336–352; and Alasdair Blair, "Making and Remaking the Political: Lessons from The US Experience of Civic and Political Engagement In The Teaching Of Political Science" *Politics* 37, no. 4 (2017): 486–499. Steven Curtis and Alasdair Blair, "The Scholarship of Engagement for Politics," 4.

86. Anabelle Kiernan, "Teaching Frameworks for Participation – Can We? Should We?" *European Political Science* 11, no. 2 (2012): 187; and Edwin Bacon, "Teaching Applied Politics: From Employability to Political Imaginary" *Politics* 38, no. 1 (2018): 94–108.

Civic Engagement Pedagogy Across the Globe

Introduction

Elizabeth C. Matto[1] and Taiyi Sun[2]

1. Eagleton Institute of Politics, Rutgers University; 2. Christopher Newport University

The growing body of scholarship on teaching civic engagement underscores the important role higher education plays in preparing students to be participatory democratic citizens. The college campus can serve as a microcosm of democracy with lessons in citizenship coming from a variety of sources including residence life, centers and institutes of civic engagement, and student organizations.[1] Indeed, civic engagement education can be woven into the culture of the campus itself.[2] A key civic learning environment of course is the classroom. What has emerged out of the scholarship of teaching and learning in the United States is a set of evidence-based best practices in how to foster civic knowledge, skills, and dispositions.

In building our body of knowledge on teaching civic engagement, the underlying goal has been to construct a pedagogical "toolbox" of nonpartisan and effective instructional techniques for teaching democratic citizenship. *Teaching Civic Engagement: From Student to Active Citizen* was focused upon surveying and highlighting instructional interventions taking place across sub-fields of political science and on a diversity of campuses throughout the United States. With *Teaching Civic Engagement Across the Disciplines*, the aim was to expand the range of models across disciplines and highlight advances in the study and practice of teaching civic engagement. Efforts to teach democracy must not only extend across disciplines and campuses—they must also extend across the globe. As the study of teaching civic engagement progresses, the subsequent step logically is to turn our attention to the teaching of democratic citizenship taking place in classrooms around the globe.

In Section II, we offer a selection of examples of teaching civic engagement from different regions of the world. The mixture reminds us of the breadth and depth of the research and practice in democratic education globally. Democratic practices can be found in a variety of contexts, and good governance does not only take shape in one form. Studies in this section provide a major contribution in identifying the manner in which teacher-scholars are educating students in democracy and the nature of the scholarship of teaching and learning taking place. These chapters also allow us to consider the diverse set of challenges and opportunities to teaching civic engagement with examples of inventive techniques and models as well as areas of potential growth. From qualitative research on using the arts to connect students with contrasting democratic experiences to experimental research on the effectiveness of extending civic engagement education into high schools, these chapters broaden our lens of teaching civic engagement and expand the range of tools available to teacher-scholars of democracy.

Effective teaching of democratic citizenship and civic engagement involves scaffolding learning or successively building upon students' civic knowledge, skills, and attitudes throughout their schooling.[3] In much the same way, the chapters in this section also examine pedagogical interventions at different stages of civic engagement learning. The section begins with a study by Sharon Feeney and John Hogan from the College of Business at the Technological University in Dublin that evaluates students' perceptions and empowers students to explore concepts of civic engagement. Students enrolled in a similar business program at two different university settings, Ireland and Egypt, create freehand drawings to depict their representation of "civic engagement." Subsequent discussions of the drawings allow students to home in on how they conceptualize civic engagement and envision their role in society. Hogan and Feeney's exercise and the qualitative analysis they employ builds upon research demonstrating the value of weaving civic engagement education into the arts and other disciplines.[4] As Hogan and Feeney show, their freehand drawing exercise facilitates discussions among students whose experiences of democracy vary and offers a route for priming students from different contexts to explore the topic of civic engagement.

In their work, Emily Beausoleil and Claire Timperley from Te Herenga Waka—Victoria University of Wellington focus their teaching on preparing students for civic engagement by fostering their civic agency. In this chapter, the authors share research related to their upper-level undergraduate course in which they offer a unique approach to teaching democratic citizenship—one that places civic agency as the central learning objective. Rather than focus upon the mechanisms of formal politics, the authors focus on issues that are of most concern among their students, including climate change and racism, as methods for enhancing civic agency. Beausoleil and Timperley's course seeks to reconfigure civic education using a structural approach that features systems understanding of key contemporary socio-political issues and extra-institutional forms of civic action. Analysis of summative reflections by students suggests that a pedagogical emphasis on civic action in relation to formal political and civic institutions is a meaningful way to enhance students' civic agency, thus preparing them for future civic and political engagement. This approach aligns with a growing body of scholarship and practice underscoring the need to embed talking about politics in campus life and connecting relevant political issues to civic learning.[5]

Dmitry Lanko, of St. Petersburg State University's School of International Relations, reminds scholars and practitioners that teaching civic engagement in authoritarian countries is possible and necessary and may even result in unexpected outcomes given the setting. By focusing on group-oriented foreign policy analysis, the course combines an introductory lecture with questions-and-answers, a think tank simulation allowing students to formulate recommendations to particular groups seeking influence on foreign policy, and a one-day role-play exercise which allows students to assume different roles and achieve foreign policy goals guided by the lecture and simulation. Using content analysis of reflection and evaluation reports, Lanko demonstrates how simulations and role-play of group-oriented foreign policy analysis can positively impact students' civic engagement. Unlike what political realism typically would suggest, he finds that students pay as much, if not more, attention to economic considerations, humanitarian considerations, soft security considerations, and environmental considerations as geopolitical considerations after participating in group-oriented foreign policy analysis workshops. This research points to the importance of having diverse targeted clients for policy analysis and civic engagement. Instead of having just the government and political leaders' interests in mind, other groups, such as minorities previously excluded from existing discursive practices, could also be placed at the center of policy discussions. Lanko also builds upon work featured in *Teaching Civic Engagement: From Student to Active Citizen* demonstrating that experiential political learning need not just be included in courses focused upon local, state, or national politics but can be integrated into international relations courses effectively.[6]

Actors offering pedagogical interventions aren't always situated within the university setting or even the country itself. In his chapter, Gerardo Berthin from Freedom House shows how workshops offered by universities in partnership with outside agencies, the United Nations in this case, equip students with skills and knowledge for future civic engagement action. In his chapter, Berthin presents how the United Nations Development Program (UNDP) partnering with the University of Belize and USAID-funded Urban Municipal Governance Project in Guatemala resulted in an effective collaboration between international development assistance groups with stakeholders within the targeted country for capacity-building. The "Workshop for Young Leaders" in Belize was designed in the context of the Transparency and Accountability in Local Governments (TRAALOG) regional initiative, a regional technical assistance platform hosted at the UNDP Regional Service Center for Latin America and the Caribbean. The social audit workshops in Guatemala were managed by the USAID Guatemala Democracy and Governance Office, which provides municipal governments with technical assistance to achieve transparent and participatory planning, to improve financial management, and to ensure effective service delivery implementation.

By focusing on the "social audit," a participatory tool and approach, Berthin finds that the pedagogical interventions had relatively positive effects on young participants with regards to improving knowledge, motivation to act, and ideas for future civic engagement. The workshops not only provided opportunities for students to boost their understanding of concepts related to civic engagement, such as governance, public integrity, accountability, and corruption but also allowed students to practice the tools of collecting and accessing public policy evidence and using technology to access information. The result amplifies and broadens our thinking of teaching civic engagement in developing countries with different contexts. Although both Belize and Guatemala are situated in Latin America, Berthin points out that the "country history, context, culture, level of development, and governance systems" are quite different, and therefore, provide unique opportunities to assess and isolate the effects of international development assistance on civic engagement capacity building.

When teaching democracies and civic engagement, scholars and practitioners often immediately point to the United States and Western European countries as models. However, civic engagement scholarship from Greece, the birthplace of democracy, provides a meaningful contribution to our understanding of teaching political participation. Using an experimental design, Theodore Chadjipadelis and Georgia Panagiotidou from Aristotle University Thessaloniki, Greece, demonstrate how a university-based civic engagement course could effectively train students to teach civic education courses on their own to other students in high schools and universities. As the Roman philosopher Seneca said, "While we teach, we learn." Chadjipadelis and Panagiotidou not only present evidence that students could effectively learn while teaching what they have learned, but the act of teaching civic engagement is a form of civic engagement itself. Through hierarchical cluster analysis and multiple correspondence analysis, Chadjipadelis and Panagiotidou investigate the effect of civic engagement intervention on the nature and extent of students' political mobilization and find that participation improved students' scores on almost all political characteristics and enhanced their inclination to choose active modes of civic participation. Building upon the scholarship and practice of active, experiential political learning, the authors find that those students who are taught by their peers also have an opportunity to envision themselves actively engaged in civic education and practices, making the approach more scalable and sustainable.[7]

The chapters featured in Section II offer not only fresh and inventive examples of democratic education around the globe but also advance the scholarship of teaching and learning. From integrating freehand drawings into civic engagement coursework to subjecting students' reactions to content to systematic qualitative analysis to delivering effective experiential civic education online, the authors in this section have expanded and enriched the set of pedagogical tools available to educators in diverse classrooms around the globe.

The collection of work featured also offers opportunities for future research that builds upon previous scholarship of teaching and learning. In both *Teaching Civic Engagement: From Student to Active Citizen* and *Teaching Civic Engagement Across the Disciplines*, Elizabeth Bennion provides guidance on the use of assessment to move us toward a more rigorous scholarship of civic engagement pedagogy. Much of this involves designing assessment plans for civic learning activities with Bennion recommending "backward design" to align desired outcomes with learning activities and assessment measures.[8] Such an approach offers a path to both high quality scholarship and meaningful learning experiences.

Future iterations of the pedagogical interventions highlighted in this section would move the scholarship forward even more by incorporating assessment practices that result in generalizable knowledge about effective democratic instruction. For example, some of the civic learning experiences highlighted in this section when replicated might be enriched by expanding single-instructor studies to multi-course and multi-instructor studies or building pretests and posttests into teacher-scholars' assessment plans. By integrating even more assessment techniques into an expanding range of classrooms, educators of democratic citizenship from all regions of the world can share the collective responsibility of advancing civic engagement scholarship and preparing our students to be informed and engaged democratic participants.

Endnotes

1. John McTague, "Politically Themed Residential Learning Communities as Incubators of Interest in Government and Politics"; Elizabeth C. Matto and Mary McHugh, "Civic Engagement Centers and Institutes: Promising Routes for Teaching Lessons in Citizenship to Students of All Disciplines"; J. Cherie Strachan and Elizabeth A. Bennion, "New Resources for Civic Engagement: The National Survey of Student Leaders, Campus Associational Life, and the Consortium for Inter-Campus SoTL Research," in *Teaching Civic Engagement Across the Disciplines*, eds. Elizabeth C. Matto, Alison Rios Millett McCartney, Elizabeth A. Bennion, and Dick Simpson (Washington, DC: American Political Science Association, 2017).

2. Nancy Thomas and Margaret Brower, "Politics 365: Fostering Campus Climates for Student Political Learning and Engagement," in *Teaching Civic Engagement Across the Disciplines*, eds. Elizabeth C. Matto, Alison Rios Millett McCartney, Elizabeth A. Bennion, and Dick Simpson (Washington, DC: American Political Science Association, 2017).

3. Monica Janzen and Catherine Ford, "Scaffolding Civic Engagement Projects: A Study into the Effectiveness of Supported Small-Scale, Interrelated, Student-Designed Projects," *Transformative Dialogues: Teaching and Learning Journal* 13, no. 3 (Winter 2020): https://journals.kpu.ca/index.php/td/index.

4. Constance DeVereaux, "Fostering Civic Engagement Through the Arts: A Blueprint," in *Teaching Civic Engagement Across the Disciplines*, eds. Elizabeth C. Matto, Alison Rios Millett McCartney, Elizabeth A. Bennion, and Dick Simpson (Washington, DC: American Political Science Association, 2017).

5. Nancy Thomas and Margaret Bower, "The Politically Engaged Classroom," in *Teaching Civic Engagement Across the Disciplines*, eds. Elizabeth C. Matto, Alison Rios Millett McCartney, Elizabeth A. Bennion, and Dick Simpson (Washington, DC: American Political Science Association, 2017).

6. Alison Rios Millett McCartney and Sivan Chaban, "Bringing the World Home: Effectively Connecting Civic Engagement and International Relations," in *Teaching Civic Engagement: From Student to Active Citizen*, eds. Alison Rios Millett McCartney, Elizabeth A. Bennion, and Dick Simpson (Washington, DC: American Political Science Association, 2013).

7. Allison Rios Millett McCartney, "Teaching Civic Engagement: Debates, Definitions, Benefits, and Challenges," in *Teaching Civic Engagement: From Student to Active Citizen*, eds. Alison Rios Millett McCartney, Elizabeth A. Bennion, and Dick Simpson (Washington, DC: American Political Science Association, 2013).

8. Elizabeth A. Bennion, "Moving Assessment Forward: Teaching Civic Engagement and Beyond," in *Teaching Civic Engagement: From Student to Active Citizen*, eds. Alison Rios Millett McCartney, Elizabeth A. Bennion, and Dick Simpson (Washington, DC: American Political Science Association, 2013) and "Moving Forward with Assessment: Important Tips and Resources," in *Teaching Civic Engagement Across the Disciplines*, eds. Elizabeth C. Matto, Alison Rios Millett McCartney, Elizabeth A. Bennion, and Dick Simpson (Washington, DC: American Political Science Association, 2017).

Using Drawings to Understand Undergraduates' Perceptions of Civic Engagement Across Countries – Ireland and Egypt

Sharon Feeney and John Hogan

College of Business, Technological University Dublin

Freehand drawing is a visual representation technique sometimes employed to bypass cognitive verbal processing routes as part of a critical pedagogy. This allows students to produce clear, more critical, and inclusive images of their understanding of a topic regardless of their vocabulary. This chapter presents an interpretation of freehand drawings produced by final year degree students in response to the question: "What is Civic Engagement?" The students were pursuing the same degree, with some studying in an Irish and others in an Egyptian university. Having to explain civic engagement pictorially forced the students to distill the essence of civic engagement's meaning to them and provided insights into how they perceived civic engagement and their roles in their societies. We offer this example as a model for other educators seeking alternative methods for teaching civic engagement and for creating a learning environment where students can develop their own capacity for critical self-reflection.

KEYWORDS: Civic Engagement, Drawing; Freehand; Critical Pedagogy; Learner-Centered.

Introduction

In this chapter, we examine how a sample of Irish and Egyptian students conceived of civic engagement through their generation of freehand drawings. Civic engagement has been defined as a "catch-all term that refers to an individual's activities, alone or as part of a group, that focus on developing knowledge about the community and its political system, identifying or seeking solutions to community problems, pursuing goals to benefit the community, and participating in constructive deliberation among community members about the community's political system and community issues, problems, or solutions."[1]

As educators, we want our students to reflect critically upon society and their place in it. Thus, our aim was to gain an understanding of undergraduates' perceptions of civic engagement in Ireland and Egypt using freehand drawings. We used freehand drawing to create a learning environment in the classroom wherein students could seek to develop meaningful associations with civic engagement. Despite obvious political, cultural, and geographic differences between Ireland and Egypt, all of our participants possess one important factor in common: the same curriculum. Accordingly, we were able to use this exercise, which we will set out in detail in the methods section, to discern the differentiated impact in these two very different settings.

Freehand drawing, as a visual elicitation technique, permits students to grasp the multiple potential ways to understand, analyze, and challenge any issue.[2] Consequently, the drawing exercise central to this research effort serves as a useful aid to facilitate students' conceptualization of their understanding of civic engagement and permits us to examine their reflections. We hypothesize that the drawing exercise, and the subsequent discussion with students of themes and meanings, is a useful approach for enhancing students' individual and collective understanding of civic engagement.[3]

Student-generated drawings are a useful route for comprehending youth observations.[4] This approach is not hindered by the lack of verbal reasoning, vocabulary, language, or inhibitions regarding individual differences of opinion or national identities.[5] The intention in using this approach with students in two very different countries, with very different histories but all undertaking a common curriculum, was to initiate a learner-centered experience that enabled them to utilize a more active, self-managed, and critically reflexive stance, the outputs of which could be discussed, compared and contrasted.[6]

We begin with a discussion on the embedding of civic engagement in the Irish and Egyptian higher education curricula. This is followed by sections on the utility of visual representation and the use of drawings in the context of critical pedagogy. We then describe the research design, encompassing participant selection and the creation and analysis of the drawings. Following this, we report on the themes contained in the drawings, examining four in detail, before finally discussing the pedagogical and policy implications of the approach, highlighting some of the national differences uncovered.

Civic Engagement in Irish and Egyptian Higher Education

Civic engagement and active citizenship emerged as important issues in the European Union (EU) in the past two decades.[7] The catalysts for this were a series of policy initiatives to create a single European Higher Education Area;[8] a European Research Area;[9] and a European Area of Lifelong Learning.[10] This approach has been reinforced by higher education institutions (HEIs) recognizing that their role encompasses a wider responsibility for cultural, social, and civic development.[11] In Ireland in 2007, a "Taskforce on Active Citizenship" was established with the goal of "advising the Government on the steps that [could] be taken to ensure that the wealth of civic spirit and active participation already present in Ireland continue[d] to grow and develop."[12] The National Strategy for Higher Education to 2030 refers to civic and community engagement as one of the "three core roles of higher education."[13] Consequently, in 2014, the leaders of all publicly funded HEIs across Ireland signed a "Campus Engage Charter for Civic and Community Engagement," committing their institutions to further enhance the links between higher education and society. Since then, Irish HEIs continued to expand their provision of community-based modules to increase their links with social and cultural non-governmental organizations (NGOs), as well as state-funded initiatives in the voluntary and community sector.[14]

In Egypt, prior to the Arab Spring, political rights and civil liberties were constrained by the state.[15] Civic engagement occurred outside the formal channels sanctioned by the state, with youth participation ranging from schools and family to the public arena.[16] In 2009, only 5 percent of Egyptians reported volunteering; however, more sought to volunteer in mosques and churches, suggesting a growing influence of religion on volunteer practices.[17] Following the 2011 revolution, the Ministry of Education devoted more attention to the content of citizenship education in schools and universities.[18] 2013 saw the first Egyptian national workshop to launch a community of practice around university community engagement.[19]

For the above reasons, these settings proved conducive to a study of contrasting conceptualizations of civic engagement.

The Utility of Visual Representation

Visual representation occupies a "central role in promoting and facilitating the formation, reflection and inflection of what we "take for granted" about the world."[20] However, despite its ubiquity, the visual is still largely missing from the university classroom.

Employing visual techniques encourages a more vibrant exploration of a phenomenon and challenges conventional wisdom.[21] It functions as "a catalyst, helping them [students] to articulate feelings that had been implicit and were hard to define,"[22] raises participants' voices by allowing them to set the agenda and own the discussion,[23] and creates a "third space" in the room.[24]

Visual methods can help students access information, and sometimes even previously unrecognized insights and embodied and tacit knowledge of their relational and situated experiences.[25] Drawings encourage active participation in the learning process, and the integration of visual with verbal data provides a useful form of data triangulation.[26] Where a professor would prefer not to impose a cognitive framework on students, the use of visual instruments seems ideal.[27]

Gauntlett has used visual and creative methods, including video, drawings, and Lego, to explore identity creation among children and professionals,[28] while others have used plasticine models to explore identities in secondary school and university settings.[29] They serve as a springboard to detailed in-class discussions. More recently, Digital Storytelling (DST) has been used to facilitate critical thinking in youth civic engagement.[30] While it has been customary to use visual data where subjects have lacked verbal or literacy skills, research subjects not lacking in such skills frequently possess more meaningful information than they can convey verbally.[31]

Using Drawings as Critical Pedagogy

Arts-based learning presents a more holistic way of understanding the world than "the traditional tools of logic and rationality."[32] Drawing has been of interest to psychologists for over a century. Most studies on the use of drawings focus on understanding the behavioral patterns of children, and as a way of providing for observations and questions.[33] In recent years, drawings have been used as a method of data collection[34] and as a pedagogic tool.[35] Visual representation "offers a relatively new medium for critical inquiry that accesses modalities of knowing that are sensory, aesthetic, affective, embodied, and that cannot be reduced to the propositional."[36] However, despite its ubiquity, the nexus between politics and visual representation remains insufficiently explored.[37] In fact, Bocken points out that "many political scholars and philosophers remain suspicious of pictures," instead favoring the "precision and depth of language."[38]

Therefore, the visual, hand drawing, can constitute part of a critical pedagogy and in the process, generate critical thinking. Critical pedagogy "formulates a scientific humanist conception that finds its expression in a dialogical praxis in which the teachers and learners together, in the act of analyzing a dehumanized reality, denounce it while announcing its transformation in the name of the liberation of man[kind]."[39] Critical pedagogy is context-specific and descriptive; it critically analyzes the world.[40] For critical pedagogy, the educational institution is where "hegemonic constructions of individual, group, and national identities are buttressed."[41] According to Giroux, critical pedagogy is purposely transformational; it adopts the position that teaching and learning are dedicated to broadening the possibilities for students.[42] Three themes in the critical pedagogy literature help in classroom implementation: displacing faculty as the "expert in knowing"; contesting disciplinary boundaries; and raising issues in a problematizing way.[43] In seeking to gain an understanding of Irish and Egyptian undergraduates' perceptions of civic engagement, we offer these students, through freehand drawing, an educational experience that challenges them to develop their own critical stances and to subsequently express their views in group discussions, which they are invited to lead.[44]

Freehand drawing can encourage a critical approach to a topic, in this case, civic engagement. Thus, for us, freehand drawing constitutes a means of introducing a critical pedagogy, thereby creating an environment for learning wherein critical self-reflection, a rather rare commodity, is actively encouraged among students. The aim, through encouraging critical reflection by means of freehand drawing, is to create a learning space oriented towards helping students construct a more sophisticated understanding of the world.[45]

Research Design

Our objective in this research was to gain an understanding of undergraduates' perceptions of civic engagement in Ireland and Egypt using freehand drawings. Given the potential of freehand drawing as a route for enhancing our understanding of students' conceptualization of civic engagement, we crafted an intervention for students in their final year of study. In this section, we discuss why we chose to use a comparative approach and how our participants in Ireland and Egypt were selected. We then discuss the process by which the participants created their drawings and provided explanations as to what they drew, along with details on how the in-class discussion was conducted. Finally, we explain how the drawings were assessed for both explicit and implicit themes.

Participant selection

By conducting a comparative study, we are seeking to add to the extant literature on civic engagement which is largely made up of single country examinations.[46] We also seek to add to the literature on the use of freehand drawing as a teaching method that can stimulate a critical stance.[47] The students participating in this study were attending universities in Ireland and Egypt. Despite both countries being former colonies, Ireland and Egypt are very different countries economically, socially, politically, and geographically. The population of Ireland is 4.9 million[48] while that of Egypt is just over 100 million.[49] Ireland is a unitary parliamentary republic, whereas Egypt's is a unitary semi-presidential republic. Ireland is a multiparty state and has been a free democratic society for a century, whereas Egypt is not; with Freedom House in 2020 scoring Ireland at 97 and Egypt 21 out of 100 points.[50] Additionally, their economies are very different. Ireland has a highly developed knowledge economy, whereas Egypt's economy is categorized as developing/emerging. Based upon Gross National Income (GNI) per capita, the World Bank in 2021 rated Ireland as a high-income economy and Egypt as a lower-middle income economy.[51] According to the International Monetary Fund (IMF), Ireland's Gross Domestic Product (GDP) stood at $399bn in 2020, slightly larger than Egypt's GDP of $361bn.[52]

The two countries constitute a most different case selection design, as each context is different, other than for the variable under scrutiny—the classroom and the students' interpretation of civic engagement.[53] The Irish university has a student body of almost 30,000 and can trace its origins to the 19th century, while the Egyptian university was established in 2006 and has 10,000 students. The participants were selected for this study as they are directly comparable, being final year students all pursuing the same degree, provided by the same publicly funded Irish university. There has been a partnership agreement between these Irish and Egyptian institutions since 2011.

Creating the drawings

The specific module incorporated in the Business and Management degree, provided by both universities from which we collected the participants' drawings, is entitled Corporate Strategy. Thus, our approach falls outside of the context in which civic engagement is usually taught in universities–namely in political science schools. The learning objectives of the module include developing the learner's awareness and understanding of a range of current ethical and governance issues in relation to business. It is a core module in the final year of the degree, offered in the span of a semester. Whereas previous research using visual techniques examined the creative products of young children in a country,[54] or across countries,[55] we engage with two groups of adult learners from different countries, bound by the same university education. The Irish class consisted of 60 students, and the Egyptian class consisted of 50. Where the Irish class had a slight majority of females, the Egyptian class was overwhelmingly male, giving an overall gender breakdown of 45 females to 65 males. All participants were aged between 21–24, with one Irish exception.

We were curious to establish what each student considered "civic engagement" to mean and how this understanding might be applied in their own lives. We were conscious about the vocabulary we used in order to avoid giving unintended cues to the students during their drawing exercise.

A two-hour guest class session, as a supplement to the course, was dedicated to the drawing exercise in November 2017 in Alexandria, and in January 2018 in Dublin. The guest lecturer for the exercise was independent of the core teaching team in both universities and had no input into the grading or examination of students for any module. Students were typically unsure of how to define civic engagement coherently at the beginning of the session. At the commencement of each class session, we provided the students with A4 (an international standard of paper size used globally measuring 210mm by 297mm) sheets of paper, with instructions on one side stating: "Through a drawing answer the following question: What is civic engagement?" and the other side said: "Now, in your own words, describe/explain what you have drawn." At commencement, students were advised that participation was voluntary and anonymity guaranteed.

Students were given 10 minutes to create their drawings. We then asked them to turn the sheet over and address the instruction on the reverse for 10 minutes. Following this, the students returned their drawings and these formed the central element of the class discussion on civic engagement for the remaining 100, or so, minutes of the class session. As Wittmann tells us, drawing has the advantage of fixing material; not only can that which is graphically preserved be referred to further, but it can also be expanded upon, altered, or reinterpreted by the creator and the observer.[56]

Each drawing was projected on a screen, and the class discussed their collective interpretation of what its creator was saying. We dedicated about one minute per drawing to keep the room energized and to remain within the time allocated for the class, and we affixed flipchart sheets with their insights to the classroom walls after discussing each drawing. The class concluded with a session opening the floor to reflection/discussion, asking what the exercise told us about perspectives and assumptions relating to civic engagement. As interpretive researchers, we ensured that the students were positioned as "co-constructors of knowledge, identity, and culture."[57]

At the end of each class, we discussed the possibility of using the drawings and outputs of the discussion for an academic paper. Participants were asked to indicate if they were happy with their drawings and a summary of the discussion being used. All agreed on the basis of anonymity.[58]

Assessing the drawings

As Barthes points out, in the examination of drawings, it is possible to identify denotation, a picture's literal meaning, and connotation, a picture's suggestive meaning in the mind of the observer. The images were assessed on three levels, as will be seen with the sampled images set out below.[59] They were assessed by the participants themselves, as after they created their drawing they wrote about what they had created; they were assessed by the participants collectively during the in-class discussion; and finally, by the authors of the paper.

Unlike earlier research in this area, the participants here were all adults, and many wrote, on the reverse side of their sheet of paper, about the particular themes present in the images they created.[60] These written explanations were to ensure that the intended message of their drawings could be understood by others as the images were analyzed. These written explanations are an important addition to the data (see below), as it is possible to misinterpret/over-interpret drawings.[61] Our interactions with images are never neutral. As viewers, we bring our own experiences, interests, and prejudices to any interpretation.[62]

The participants, as classes, brought a collective interpretation to each image as they were projected on the classroom screen before them for about one minute. This was the groups' collective understanding of what they were seeing in those images. All of the themes that the classes mentioned as being present in the images are set out in table 1 below.

Finally, borrowing from Gernhardt et al., the images alone were examined by both authors.[63] As with the collective group, we did not seek to distinguish between major and minor themes in the drawings. If we perceived a theme as present, we recorded it. We often perceived more than one theme per drawing. As a result, each drawing possesses both the explicit theme(s) that their creator ascribed to it and the implicit theme(s) that the class collectively and the authors perceived in it.

What the Drawings Tell Us About the Participants' Understanding of Civic Engagement

We followed Barthes's argument in our analysis of the drawings. In determining the themes of the students' drawings (110 in all) we relied upon both denotation and connotation, with the themes emanating from the concrete written content that the creators ascribed to their drawings along with the implicit meanings that were ascribed to those same images by the class and by the authors. In essence, the themes were a result of combining data from all three understandings of the images (creators, class, authors). Using this approach, we identified a total of 14 themes (see table 1). In some ways, the diversity of themes reflects the multifaceted definition of civic engagement offered earlier. Specifically, there are themes that relate to community engagement (such as "charity" or "making a difference") as well as themes that reflect traditional political activities (such as "campaigning" or "voting") and others associated with such skills of civic engagement as "discourse" and "cooperation."

With these themes outlined, we documented the number of times they could be identified in the drawings, with some drawings containing more than one theme. Table 1 documents the frequency with which each of the 14 themes were present in the drawings, disaggregated according to the classroom setting (Ireland or Egypt). As the data in table 1 show, certain themes were more prevalent than others. "Community involvement," "working together," and "communication" were the most prevalent themes overall. Other themes, such as "voting" and "corporate social responsibility," were the least seen. The data also highlight notable differences between responses based on the classroom setting. For example, voting, campaigning, and discourse, themes that would be associated with democracy, appeared 13 times in the Irish drawings while only appearing twice in the Egyptian images.

Table 1. Frequency of Themes Contained in Drawings, by Classroom Setting			
Theme*	Dublin (n=60)	Alexandria (n=50)	Total (n=110)
Campaigning	5	0	5
Charity	3	5	8
Making a difference	7	8	15
Community involvement	23	19	42
Providing employment	2	7	9
Voluntary work	2	3	9
Helping others	7	5	12
Role in society	5	3	8
Working together/ cooperation	12	14	26
Communication	12	9	21
Discourse	5	2	7
Voting	3	0	3
Corporate social responsibility	1	2	3
Social responsibility	10	12	22

* Note: some drawings contained more than one theme, N=110.

While we gathered and analyzed 110 drawings, we present below a sample for illustrative purposes as per Wilson and Wilson,[64] Gernhardt et al.[65] and Hall.[66] This sample, two drawings from each of the classes, is representative of the ideas emanating from the students in Dublin and Alexandria. The drawings show the students' attempts to answer "what is civic engagement?" with what we consider to be primarily a "storytelling approach."[67]

Sampled Student Drawings

Here we present a sample of the drawings by students from each setting. We recognize that using a sample of the participants' drawings, and seeing them as emblematic of the wider pool, raises questions about the generalizability of findings, especially findings from different countries.[68] We have done this in order to allow the reader to get a sense of the nature, variety, and quality of the drawings produced by participants, as well as the factors influencing the analysis of the drawing. Each of the drawings presented is followed by the written narrative provided by the participant on the reverse side of the sheet of paper from their drawing, as an explanation of their illustration; then the collective interpretation of the drawing by the class; and finally the authors' interpretation of the drawing. We have used this approach, to present the students' own stated intention along with the collective interpretation of each drawing, to facilitate a broader appreciation of the knowledge base of each group of students. This approach draws from Gernhardt et al.,[69] Hall,[70] and, Feeney and Hogan.[71]

Irish Student Drawings

Figure 1. Irish Student Drawing Sample 1

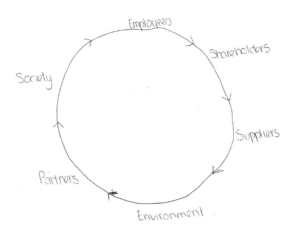

Through a drawing answer the following question: What is Civic Engagement?

When you've drawn your picture, flip over the page and describe/ explain your drawing in your own words.

Student's narrative:

"Civic engagement involves constant interaction between all stakeholders of a particular area."

Collective interpretation:

The students debated whether all 6 of the areas are equally important to the business cycle. Many expressed the belief that "environment" and "society" should not be part of the cycle, where the business cycle would be shown to impact upon both.

Our interpretation:

Figure 1 shows a circle surrounded by six different words and arrows pointing in a clockwise direction. These arrows add a narrative component to the image—a direction of travel. The learner understands that each of these areas of activity (employees, shareholders, suppliers, environment, partners, society) are interlinked and that all provide a cycle of actions that represent civic engagement. In terms of themes, the learner sees corporate social responsibility (CSR) as integral to civic engagement. From table 1, this was the only Irish drawing to touch upon CSR.

Figure 2. Irish Student Drawing Sample 2

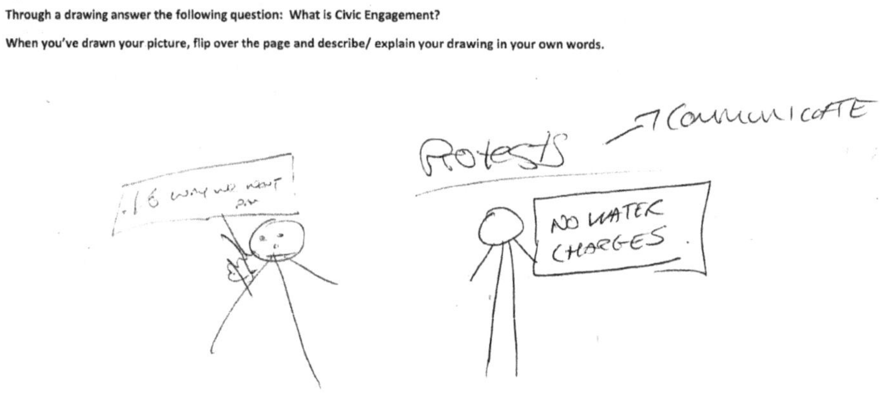

Student's narrative:

"A group of people coming together to share a particular message."

Collective interpretation:

Many students disagreed with the drawing of political protests representing civic engagement. They insisted that political issues did not form part of the civic engagement conversation.

Our interpretation:

Figure 2 depicts two figures protesting water charges and the text above the protesters reads "protests => communicate." The drawing, with its narrative component, possesses a storytelling element.[72] It shows that the learner considers protests to be a kind of communication which constitutes a form of civic engagement. Communication was one of the more represented themes in table 1 (documented in 12 drawings from Irish students and 9 Egyptian students).

Egyptian Student Drawings

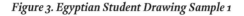

Figure 3. Egyptian Student Drawing Sample 1

Student's narrative:

"1) the first drawing: is about engaging with the community by helping people, being helpful is a good factor in growing the community and become well civilized [sic]. 2) Engaging with the community by giving people advice about how to take care of the community and become the best. 3) Engaging with the community can be by being caring and saving the planet by taking care of trees and streets to become better and live in a better community."

Collective interpretation:

This drawing stimulated lengthy discussion. Many students agreed that helping others is an important aspect of civic engagement. They felt it important that citizens help themselves through advice to affect societal change. Finally, there was consensus that all should take responsibility for the environment.

Our interpretation:

Figure 3, falling within the storytelling approach, depicts three different contexts for the learner's understanding of civic engagement.[73] The drawing starts with two people sharing something. Next, we see a figure talking to others through a screen. Finally, we see a figure watering plants. The themes appear to be discourse, communication and social responsibility. In table 1 this was only one of two Egyptian drawings to touch on the topic of discourse.

Figure 4. Egyptian Student Drawing Sample 2

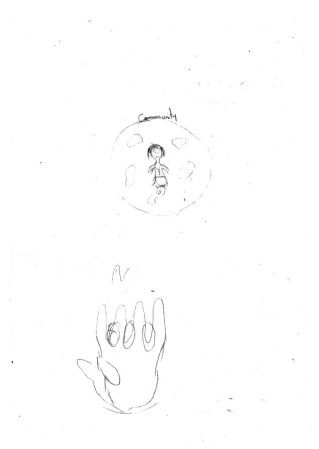

Student's narrative:

"I tried to draw the community which is the whole world and I'm in that world or community I'm a part of this community involved in it [sic]. Another drawing, which is two hands are connected to each other. One is me and the other is the community which shows that we must be connected to each other in every single thing."

Collective interpretation:

There was agreement that the community can be small or global. In this picture, by depicting themselves at the center of the world, many in the class felt that the student shows their role in ensuring engagement is focused on making the world better. Many students felt that the next part of the drawing, depicting joined hands, signifies our connectedness to each other.

Our interpretation:

Figure 4 incorporates significant storytelling detail.[74] The drawing depicts a figure at the center of the world and the word "community" above, with joined hands beneath the globe. It is about joint responsibility at a global level for civic engagement and our connectedness to each other. The themes relate to one's role in society and one's social responsibility, as set out in table 1.

What the Frequency of Themes, Sampled Drawings and In-Class Discussions Tell Us

A variety of themes emerged from the 110 drawings we collected, the most prevalent of which were community involvement, working together/cooperation and social responsibility (see table 1). Voting and campaigning, however, were among the least mentioned themes. It is noteworthy that none of the Egyptian participants mentioned voting and campaigning in their drawings or their written explanations. This finding is not necessarily surprising though, given that Egypt is not a democracy. Our approach, in encouraging students to set out their understanding of a topic visually and to also write about what they had drawn, allows for the unambiguous expression of their feelings; while the guided group discussion permits all viewpoints to be seen and heard. This exercise enhanced our ability to identify and differentiate the views on civic engagement between students' from Ireland and Egypt, two very different countries, regarding democratic tendencies and practices.

In table 1 we see that the theme of community involvement appears in 42 drawings. It is interesting that it appears in 23 of the 60 Irish drawings and 19 of the 50 Egyptian images, which is 38% of the drawings of the students from each country. Thus, despite the differences between the countries, both sets of students equally regarded community involvement as a form of civic engagement.

Given that the research participants are business students, it is not surprising that CSR (figure 1) was mentioned as a form of civic engagement. What was surprising was that it was mentioned so little in table 1, appearing only 3 times. During the in-class discussion CSR drew a lot of attention. Communication between citizens and their government (figure 2) and discourse between citizens (figure 3) were widely seen as forms of civic engagement with communications appearing in 21 drawings while discourse appeared in seven (table 1). The students in the in-class discussion also felt that communications and discourse were central to civic engagement. It is clear from table 1 that while communication was almost equally present in percentage terms in the Irish and Egyptian drawings, discourse was not. However, somewhat contradictorily, there was disagreement among the Irish students as to whether political protests constituted civic engagement. This may have something to do with the historic and deep-rooted conservatism of Irish society, a country created by conservative revolutionaries.[75] Working together/cooperation and helping others (figure 3) was regarded as important aspects of civic engagement and appeared 38 times in the drawings (table 1). As can be seen from table 1, the issue of social responsibility (figures 3 and 4) came up in 22 drawings.

We found that all of the drawings (n=110) were similar in using a narrative approach. Hall refers to drawings, where there is a narrative approach, as storytelling.[76] But, this is to be expected given that we are storytelling animals that like familiar patterns/narratives that we can easily understand.[77] As was mentioned earlier above, an element of national difference was evident under the headings of campaigning, discourse, and voting in table 1. This disparity is possibly due to what Freedom House describes as Egypt's slide back into authoritarian governance since the military coup of 2013.[78] The fruits of its 2011 revolution were short-lived, and it is also not that surprising given the very different democratic histories of both countries. Three of the four sampled drawings, examined in detail above, involved communication and/or a cyclical approach to understanding civic engagement. All of the students understood that civic engagement involves other people and the need to cooperate.

Pedagogical and Policy Implications

There are numerous ways the higher education curriculum in Ireland has provided students with opportunities for their moral and civic development. Service-learning and learning in the community provide some of these opportunities. This is in contrast to Egypt where community links are still in the early stages of development for HEIs. Since 2011, Egypt has experienced a rapid increase in university/community engagement projects.[79]

Freehand drawing encourages students to reflect critically upon what they already know about civic engagement, which is crucial in developing the kind of engaged citizenry vital for a flourishing democracy. The approach also surmounts the long-term bias in instructional pedagogies toward oversimplification[80] and the favoring of propositional knowledge,[81] as it allows students to appreciate that there are many ways to comprehend, contest, and analyze issues. Thus, freehand drawing helps to empower and emancipate students whose unique insights might otherwise be silenced or hidden (see figure 4). Additionally, in allowing participants to also write about what they have drawn, an element of ambiguity present in children's drawings can be avoided here, thus providing us with an additional source of data as to what the image creator was intending (see figure 3). Our approach of image production, followed by guided group discussion, can promote reflexive engagement to produce varied viewpoints (see collective interpretation of figure 2). When we pressed the students in their interpretation of their drawings during the in-class discussion, they began to recognize and query their own and others' conjectures (see collective interpretation of figure 1). There is a narrative journey undertaken in discussing drawings where, according to Wright, drawings constitute a narrative springboard.[82] Thus, the participants recognized that by cooperating in critically examining each other's drawings, they were able to identify aspects of, and nuances in, their understanding.

The principles of best practice for a pedagogy of civic engagement include active learning, learning as a social process, contextual knowledge, reflexive practice, and the ability to represent an idea in a variety of contexts.[83] The traditional approach is classroom-based lectures, and focused upon the development of personally responsible citizens, while the alternative is a service-learning model emphasizing a justice-oriented conception of citizenship.[84] In this respect, the use of images possesses great value, as they have the potential to economically encode significant quantities of complex information.[85] As was seen above in the case of the four sampled images, there was the explicit meaning that the participant assigned to what they had drawn when they wrote about their drawing. However, there was also the implicit meaning that the class as a whole, and the authors also, interpreted into each of the images. Sometimes this interpretation was similar to what the participant said their drawing represented, while at other times it was at variance. In seeking to create a space for nuance and ambiguity in the classroom using drawings, we complicate students' understanding through moving away from certainty towards an acceptance of ambiguity and paradox, complexity rather than simplicity.[86] The realization that the drawings demonstrate more than one definition, or meaning, of civic engagement gives real world examples for students to understand the complexity of ascribing a single, narrow meaning to socially constructed terminology. Our aim in using this approach, with final year degree students from different countries, but pursuing the same degree, was to compare and contrast their understanding of civic engagement.

Conclusion

Employing freehand drawing to promote a dialectical exchange with students about civic engagement—to cultivate their capacity for critical self-reflection—allows them to put into visuals a level of comprehension that is sometimes difficult to articulate verbally. The presentation of information visually can enable students to access unrecognized insights and make sense of complex issues by employing a whole brain approach. Students, employing the higher order thinking integral to visualization, can define their knowledge of a topic that is universally understandable and rich in content.

That the students discussed the drawings as a group, in which every voice was heard, encourages interpretations from multiple perspectives and gives students and professors an opportunity to challenge theories, presumptions, and beliefs. This approach can raise questions about what is being viewed and aids reflection on the wider context. The objective of such critical pedagogies should be to produce citizens capable of self-reflection and willing to question widely held beliefs.

Describing civic engagement pictorially forced participants to think about what the essence of civic engagement was for them. The drawings show that the students possessed a significant amount of knowledge and understanding of civic engagement. With Waltz defining theory as a picture that is mentally formed of a bounded realm, the students were, through their drawings, creating their own theories of civic engagement. The study shows that the students' understanding of civic engagement in both jurisdictions is similar, despite the different political and cultural contexts of each country. By both producing and observing their own drawings, the students were positioned in a way they were unaccustomed to in the classroom—as creators of, and critically reflecting on, knowledge. This study shows how a collaborative learning experience facilitates students readily in demonstrating their level of understanding of, and appreciation for, civic engagement.

For teachers, the use of freehand drawing permits the stimulation of a critical stance, as visual representation allows us to comprehend how we and others "see" the world. Discussing the drawings as a group nurtures a variety of perspectives. Thus, all of the students in a class become involved in the process and not just those assertive students who usually tend to monopolize class discussions. Expression in this non-traditional manner is liberating for the participants. The materials required are minimal—paper and pencil. Thus, this technique could equally be employed with students undertaking any of a range of other types of courses, from the social sciences, to the hard sciences, as well as business courses, and need not be restricted to undergraduates. The value of freehand drawing is that it permits students to examine and reflect upon their understanding of a topic. This conforms to what the objective of universities should be in the 21st century—to develop students not only capable of critical thinking in their future careers, but also as critical beings capable of self-reflection.

Endnotes

1. Alison Rios Millett McCartney, "Teaching Civic Engagement: Debates, Definitions, Benefits, and Challenges," in *Teaching Civic Engagement: From Student to Active Citizen*, eds. Alison Rios Millett McCartney, Elizabeth A. Bennion and Dick Simpson (Washington, DC: American Political Science Association, 2013).

2. Sharon Feeney, John Hogan and Paul F. Donnelly, "What Stick Figures Tell Us about Irish Politics: Creating a Critical and Collaborative Learning Space," *Teaching in Higher Education* 20, no. 3 (2015).

3. Diane Cordell, *Using Images to Teach Critical Thinking Skills* (Santa Barbara, CA: ABC-CLIO, 2016); Paul F. Donnelly and John Hogan, "Engaging Students in the Classroom: 'How Can I Know What I Think Until I See What I Draw?'" *European Political Science* 12, no. 3 (2013); Sharon Feeney and John Hogan, "Using Drawings to Understand Perceptions of Civic Engagement Across Disciplines: "Seeing is Understanding," *Politics* 39, no. 2 (2019).

4. Donnelly and Hogan, "Engaging Students in the Classroom," 2013.

5. Alan. D. Meyer, "Visual Data in Organizational Research," *Organization Science* 2, no. 2 (1991).

6. Gillian Rose, *Visual Methodologies: An Introduction to the Interpretation of Visual Materials* (London: Sage, 2008).

7. Giovanni Moro, *Citizens in Europe: Civic Activism and the Community Democratic Experiment* (New York: Springer, 2012).

8. Sharon Feeney, "Institutional Quality Review in Higher Education in the Republic of Ireland and Northern Ireland: A Comparison of Two Approaches," (PhD diss., University of Sheffield, 2014); Sharon Feeney and Conor Horan, "The Bologna Process and the European Qualifications Framework: A Routines Approach to Understanding the Emergence of Educational Policy Harmonisation – From Abstract Ideas to Policy Implementation," in *Policy Paradigm in Theory and Practice: Discourses, Ideas and Anomalies in Public Policy Dynamics*, eds. John Hogan and Michael Howlett (Basingstoke, UK: Palgrave, 2015).

9. Commission of the European Communities, *Towards a European Research Area. Communication from the Commission to the Council, the European Parliament, the Economic and Social Committee and the Committee of the Regions, COM* (Brussels: Commission of the European Communities, 2000).

10. Prague Communiqué, *Towards the European Higher Education Area* (Communiqué of the meeting of European Ministers in charge of higher education in Prague on May 19th, 2001).

11. European University Association, *Universities as the Motor for the Construction of a Europe of Knowledge. Input to the Barcelona Summit* (Brussels: EUA, 2002); Gert Biesta, "What Kind of Citizenship for European Higher Education? Beyond the Competent Active Citizen," *European Educational Research Journal* 8, no. 2 (2009).

12. Taskforce on Active Citizenship, *Report of the Taskforce on Active Citizenship* (Dublin: 2007).

13. Department of Education and Skills, *National Strategy for Higher Education to 2030* (Dublin: Department of Education and Skills, 2011).

14. Bernie Quillinan, Eileen McEvoy, Ann MacPhail, and Ciara Dempsey, "Lessons Learned from a Community Engagement Initiative Within Irish Higher Education," *Irish Educational Studies* 27, no. 1 (2018).

15. Jason N. Dorio, "The Revolution as a Critical Pedagogical Workshop: Perceptions of University Students Reimagining Participatory Citizenship(s) in Egypt," in *Education during the Time of the Revolution in Egypt: Dialectics of Education in Conflict*, ed. Nagwa Megahed (Rotterdam, Netherlands: Sense Publishers, 2017).

16. Laila Alhamad, "Formal and Informal Venues of Engagement" in *Political Participation in the Middle East*, eds. Ellen Lust-Okar and Saloua Zerhouini (Boulder, CO: Lynne Rienner, 2008).

17. Debbie Haski-Leventhal, Ed Metz, Edward Hogg, Barbara Ibrahim, David H. Smith, and Lili Wang, "Volunteering in Three Life Stages," in *The Palgrave Handbook of Volunteering*, eds. David H. Smith, Robert A. Stebbins and Jurgen Grotz (Basingstoke, UK: Palgrave, 2016).

18. Shereen Aly, "Citizenship Education: A Critical Content Analysis of the Egyptian Citizenship Education Textbooks after the Revolution," in *Education During the Time of the Revolution in Egypt: Dialectics of Education in Conflict*, ed. Nagwa Megahed (Rotterdam, Netherlands: Sense Publishers, 2017).

19. Ruben. S. Garcia, Cita Cook, and Jenice L. View, "Universidad Sin Fronteras: Transgressing Intellectual Borders and Redefining Learning," in *The Cambridge Handbook of Service Learning and Community Engagement*, eds. Corey Dolgon, Tina D. Mitchell, and Timothy K. Eatman (Cambridge, UK: Cambridge University Press, 2017).

20. Natalia Slutskaya, Alex Simpson, and Jason Hughes, "Butchers, Quakers and Bankrupts: Lessons from Photo-elicitation," *Qualitative Research in Organizations and Management* 7, no. 1 (2012).

21. Lee D. Parker, "Photo-elicitation: An Ethno-historical Accounting and Management Research Prospect," *Accounting Auditing & Accountability Journal* 22, no. 8 (2009).

22. Shoshana Zuboff, *In the Age of the Smart Machine: The Future of Work and Power* (New York: Basic Books, 1988).

23. Samantha Warren, "Photography and Voice in Critical Qualitative Management Research," *Accounting, Auditing and Accountability Journal* 18, no. 6 (2009).

24. Parker, "Photo-elicitation: An Ethno-historical Accounting and Management Research Prospect," 2009.

25. Lynn Butler-Kisber and Tiiu Poldma, "The Power of Visual Approaches in Qualitative Inquiry: The Use of Collage Making and Concept Mapping in Experiential Research," *Journal of Research Practice* 6, no. 1 (2010).

26. Uwe Flick, "Triangulation in Data Collection," in *The Sage Handbook of Qualitative Data Collection*, ed. Uwe Flick (London: SAGE, 2018).

27. Alan D. Meyer, "Visual Data in Organizational Research," *Organization Science* 2, no. 2 (1991).

28. David Gauntlett, *Creative Explorations: New Approaches to Identities and Audiences* (London: Routledge, 2007).

29. Nicola Ingram, "Within School and Beyond the Gate: The Complexities of Being Educationally Successful and Working Class," *Sociology* 45, no. 2 (2011); Jessica Abrahams and Nicola Ingram, "The Chameleon Habitus: Exploring Local Students' Negotiations of Multiple Fields," *Sociological Research* 18, no. 4 (2013).

30. Chitat Chan and Melanie Sage, "A Narrative Review of Digital Storytelling for Social Work Practice," *Journal of Social Work Practice* 107, no. 1 (2019).

31. Meyer, "Visual Data in Organizational Research," 1991.

32. Margaret L. Page and Hugo Gaggiotti, "A Visual Enquiry into Ethics and Change," *Qualitative Research in Organizations and Management* 7, no. 1 (2012).

33. Glyn V. Thomas and Richard P. Jolley, "Drawing Conclusions: A Re-examination of Empirical and Conceptual Bases for Psychological Evaluation of Children from their Drawings," *British Journal of Clinical Psychology* 37, no. 2 (1984); Margaret Brooks, "Drawing: The Social Construction of Knowledge," *Australian Journal of Early Childhood* 29, no. 2 (2004).

34. Brooks, "Drawing: The Social Construction of Knowledge," 2004; Brian Merriman and Suzanne Guerin, "Using Children's Drawings as Data in Child-centred Research," *The Irish Journal of Psychology* 27, no. 1 (2006); Ariane Gernhardt, Hartmut Rubeling, and Heidi Keller, "Cultural Perspectives on Children's Tadpole Drawings: At the Interface Between Representation and Production," *Frontiers in Psychology* 6, no. 1 (2015).

35. Donnelly and Hogan, "Engaging Students in the Classroom," 2013.

36. Page and Gaggiotti, "A Visual Enquiry into Ethics and Change," 2012.

37. C. Sylvest, "Interrogating the Subject: Errol Morris's the Fog of War," in *Classics of International Relations: Essays in Criticism and Appreciation*, eds. H. Bliddal, C. Sylvest and P. Wilson (Abingdon, UK: Routledge, 2013).

38. Inigo Bocken, "Learning from Casanus: The Power of Images," *Humboldt Kosmos* 86, no. 1 (2005).

39. Paulo Freire, *The Politics of Education: Culture, Power and Liberation* (Westport, CT: Bergin & Garvey, 1985).

40. Tony Monchinski, *Critical Pedagogy and the Everyday Classroom* (New York: Springer, 2008).

41. Jennifer Leeman and Lisa Rabin, "Critical Perspectives for the Literature Classroom," *Hispania* 90, no. 2 (2007).

42. Henry A. Giroux, *Pedagogy and the Politics of Hope: Theory, Culture, and Schooling* (Boulder, CO: Westview Press, 1997).

43. Gorden M. Dehler, Ann Welsh, and Marianne Lewis, "Critical Pedagogy in the "New Paradigm": Raising Complicated Understanding in Management Learning," in *Essential Readings in Management Learning*, eds. Christopher Grey and Elena Antonacopoulou (London: Sage, 2004).

44. Ronald Barnett, *Higher Education: A Critical Business* (Bristol, PA: The Society for Research into Higher Education and Open University Press, 1997).

45. Dehler, Welsh, and Lewis, "Critical Pedagogy in the "New Paradigm": Raising Complicated Understanding in Management Learning," 2004.

46. Sharon Feeney and John Hogan, "Using Drawings to Understand Perceptions of Civic Engagement Across Disciplines: 'Seeing is Understanding,'" *Politics* 39 no. 2 (2019); Constance Flanagan and Peter Levine, "Civic Engagement and the Transition to Adulthood," *The Future of Children* 20, no. 1 (2010).

47. Donnelly and Hogan, "Engaging Students in the Classroom: 'How Can I Know What I Think Until I See What I Draw?'" 2013.

48. https://www.cso.ie/en/releasesandpublications/er/pme/populationandmigrationestimatesapril2020/

49. https://www.reuters.com/article/us-egypt-population-idUSKBN2051MS

50. https://freedomhouse.org/countries/freedom-world/scores

51. https://datahelpdesk.worldbank.org/knowledgebase/articles/906519-world-bank-country-and-lending-groups

52. https://www.imf.org/en/Publications/WEO/weo-database/2020/October/weo-report

53. John Gerring, *Case Study Research: Principles and Practices* (Cambridge, UK: Cambridge University Press, 2007).

54. Brent Wilson and Marjorie Wilson, "Pictorial Composition and Narrative Structure: Themes and the Creation of Meaning in the Drawings of Egyptian and Japanese Children," *Visual Arts Research* 13, no. 2 (1987).

55. Gernhardt, Rubeling, and Keller, "Cultural Perspectives on Children's Tadpole Drawings: At the Interface Between Representation and Production," 2015.

56. Barbara Wittmann, "Drawing Cure: Children's Drawings as a Psychoanalytic Instrument," *Configurations* 18, no. 3 (2010).

57. Melanie D. Janzen, "Where is the (Postmodern) Child in Early Childhood Education Research?" *Early Years* 28, no. 3 (2008).

58. This use of learner-generated drawings to understand certain concepts is part of a longitudinal study that is being undertaken by the authors. This study received ethical clearance from the universities, subject to participants giving consent for their drawings to be used, that all participants would remain anonymous, and that the main facilitator would have no role in grading students for modules where drawings were collected.

59. Roland Barthes, *Elements of Semiology* (New York: Hill and Wang, 1968).

60. Wilson and Wilson, "Pictorial Composition and Narrative Structure: Themes and the Creation of Meaning in the Drawings of Egyptian and Japanese Children," 1987; Bryan Hawkins, "Children's Drawing, Self-expression, Identity and Imagination," *International Journal of Art & Design Education* 21, no. 3 (2002); Emese Hall, "The Ethics of 'Using' Children's Drawings in Research," in *Visual Methods with Children and Young People. Studies in Childhood and Youth*, eds. Eve Stirling and Dylan Yamada-Rice (London: Palgrave Macmillan, 2015).

61. Ann Lewis and Geoff Lindsay, "Emerging Issues" in *Researching Children's Perspectives*, eds. Ann Lewis and Geoff Lindsay (Buckingham, UK: Open University Press, 2000).

62. Emese Hall, "The Ethics of 'Using' Children's Drawings in Research," in *Visual Methods with Children and Young People. Studies in Childhood and Youth*, eds. Eve Stirling and Dylan Yamada-Rice (London: Palgrave Macmillan, 2015).

63. Gernhardt, Rubeling, and Keller, "Cultural Perspectives on Children's Tadpole Drawings: At the Interface Between Representation and Production," 2015.

64. Wilson and Wilson, "Pictorial Composition and Narrative Structure: Themes and the Creation of Meaning in the Drawings of Egyptian and Japanese Children," 1987.

65. Gernhardt, Rubeling, and Keller, "Cultural Perspectives on Children's Tadpole Drawings: At the Interface Between Representation and Production," 2015.

66. Hall, "The Ethics of 'Using' Children's Drawings in Research," 2015.

67. Emese Hall, ""My Brain Printed it Out!" Drawing, Communication, and Young Children: A Discussion." Paper presented at the British Educational Research Association Annual Conference, Edinburgh, 3–6 September, 2008.

68. Jon Dean, "Drawing what Homelessness Looks Like: Using Creative Visual Methods as a Tool of Critical Pedagogy," *Sociological Research Online* 20, no. 1 (2015).

69. Gernhardt, Rubeling, and Keller, "Cultural Perspectives on Children's Tadpole Drawings: At the Interface Between Representation and Production," 2015.

70. Hall, "The Ethics of 'Using' Children's Drawings in Research," 2015.

71. Feeney and Hogan, "Using Drawings to Understand Perceptions of Civic Engagement Across Disciplines: 'Seeing is Understanding,'" 2019.

72. Hall, ""My Brain Printed it Out!" Drawing, Communication, and Young Children: A Discussion," 2008.

73. Ibid.

74. Ibid.

75. Joseph Lee, *Ireland, 1912–1985* (Cambridge, UK: Cambridge University Press, 1989).

76. Hall, ""My Brain Printed it Out!" Drawing, Communication, and Young Children: A Discussion," 2008.

77. Michael Shermer, *Why People Believe Weird Things: Pseudoscience, Superstition, and Other Confusions of Our Time* (New York: Freeman, 2002).

78. https://freedomhouse.org/country/egypt/freedom-world/2020

79. Ruben S. Garcia, Cita Cook and Jenice L. View, "Universidad Sin Fronteras: Transgressing Intellectual Borders and Redefining Learning," in *The Cambridge Handbook of Service Learning and Community Engagement*, eds. Corey Dolgon, Tina D. Mitchell, and Timothy K. Eatman (Cambridge, UK: Cambridge University Press, 2017.)

80. Gorden M. Dehler, Ann Welsh, and Marianne Lewis, "Critical Pedagogy in the "New Paradigm": Raising Complicated Understanding in Management Learning," in *Essential Readings in Management Learning*, eds. Christopher Grey and Elena Antonacopoulou (London: Sage, 2004).

81. John Heron and Peter Reason, "A Participatory Inquiry Paradigm," *Qualitative Inquiry* 3, no. 3 (1997).

82. Suzanne Wright, "Graphic-narrative Play: Young Children's Authoring through Drawing and Telling," *International Journal of Education and the Arts* 8, no. 8 (2007).

83. Marshall Welch, "Identifying and Teaching Civic Engagement Skills through Service Learning," in *Higher Education and Civic Engagement: International Perspectives*, eds. Iain Mac Labhrainn and Lorraine McIlrath (Hampshire, UK: Ashgate, 2007).

84. Debra L. DeLaet, "A Pedagogy of Civic Engagement for the Undergraduate Political Science Classroom," *Journal of Political Science Education* 12, no. 1 (2010).

85. Pauline Ridley and Angela Rogers, *Drawing to Learn: Arts & Humanities* (Brighton, UK: University of Brighton, 2010).

86. Danah Zohar, *Rewiring the Corporate Brain: Using the New Science to Rethink How We Structure and Lead Organizations* (San Francisco, CA: Berrett-Koehler Publishers, 1997).

7 | Taking a Structural Approach to Civic Education in Aotearoa New Zealand[1]

Emily Beausoleil and Claire Timperley

Te Herenga Waka—Victoria University of Wellington

Conventionally, civic education has sought to enhance students' sense of civic agency by fostering civic literacy and other relevant capacities, with a particular emphasis on civic action in relation to formal political and civic institutions. Yet students' diminished sense of agency has as much to do with the complex, endemic, and seemingly intractable issues that characterize current politics—climate change, settler-colonialism, socioeconomic inequality—as it does with disenchantment or difficulty engaging with formal institutions. This chapter discusses an upper-level undergraduate course from Aotearoa New Zealand that puts this question of agency at its center, and takes a uniquely structural approach to addressing it. We identify two key features of this structural approach to civic education, showing via student testimonies that a strong majority of students observe this course has had significant impact on their sense of civic agency, and that the course's structural approach was a primary contributor to this.

KEYWORDS: Civic Agency, Structural Injustice, Non-Institutional, Civic Action, Efficacy.

Introduction

Civic agency—the ability to act to influence the society in which one lives out of concern for it—is considered a "basic principle of an equitable, democratic society."[2] Yet it hinges on a number of contingencies, including civic literacy, effective channels for voice, structural and personal conditions that determine one's resources, and a sense of agency. This last requirement—a sense of agency, or confidence in one's ability to act—is as key to having agency as these other objective factors, and correlates closely with whether one acts at all.[3] According to the Carnegie Foundation's Political Engagement Project (PEP), the key aim of civic education is to increase students' sense of efficacy, "the necessary attribute of civically engaged citizens."[4] Conventionally, civic education has sought to do this by fostering civic literacy and other relevant capacities, with a particular emphasis on civic action in relation to formal political and civic institutions.[5] Indeed, the existing literature gives little if any attention to non-institutional factors that either impinge upon or contribute to a sense of civic agency. Yet many of the issues that most concern our students, from climate change to racism, are best described as structural issues that are sustained by far more than the mechanisms of formal politics; likewise, with global surges of climate strikes and social movements, our students are witnessing and experiencing a range of extra-institutional civic activities. How might we reconfigure civic education when such features characterize the contexts within which our students as citizens seek to act?

In this chapter, we offer an account of an upper-level undergraduate political science course that sought to foster a sense of agency among its students through a novel approach to civic education: a structural approach. A structural lens on civic education, we argue, both enriches students' analytic capacities regarding many of the sociopolitical issues that they as citizens seek to engage, and enhances their strategic capacities when discerning and designing appropriate forms of civic action to address such issues. Taking a structural approach can thus contribute to developing one of the key aims of civic education: a sense of efficacy. This is certainly what we heard from our 117 students over 2019 and 2020, 90% of whom noted increased awareness of structural injustice in society and a different perception of their own sense of agency as a result of taking this course, and 37% of whom specified particular civic actions they were now taking as a response to what they learned. Moreover, surveyed 6 months and 18 months after the course had ended, 66% of students stated this course had been very relevant or useful to them as a citizen.[6]

In what follows, we first outline the context in which we are teaching this course in a political science department in Aotearoa New Zealand. We then describe what we mean by a structural approach' to civic education, noting that this frame enables both a systems analysis of key contemporary sociopolitical issues and development of a novel repertoire of ten genres of civic action in relation to these systems. A structural approach, we contend, addresses one of the key issues in civic engagement education–how to improve students' sense of their own efficacy. After establishing our theoretical contribution to the scholarship, we then provide a brief synopsis of the course itself before detailing the research design by which we evaluated the course's impacts on students' sense of agency. Our data consists of students' summative reflections on their learning, a final piece of assessment in which we ask them to reflect on their learning experiences across the trimester, as well as their responses to a follow-up survey six months and eighteen months after the course. Using this data, we investigate the extent to which this course: affected students' perspectives on the sociopolitical issues they seek to impact; increased their sense of their own agency; and led to greater or more varied civic action as a result. Without question, our 117 students over 2019 and 2020, both immediately following and after the course, have attested to these impacts. In light of these results, we argue that a structural approach to civic engagement enhances a sense of civic agency, both by developing a sense of the contexts in which they seek, as citizens, to intervene as complex, interdependent, and open at multiple sites to contestation, and by broadening and nuancing their sense of the diverse forms of action available to them within such contexts. We conclude, therefore, that a structural approach to civic education effectively fosters one of the key aims of civic education, that of civic efficacy. We end the chapter with final considerations for such an approach in practice.

Civic Engagement Education in Aotearoa New Zealand

In Aotearoa New Zealand, formal civics education requirements have been conspicuously absent from primary and secondary school curricula.[7] In recent years, movements to support civics education in schools have gained some momentum in the form of specifically designed civics modules, though their elective status means that most students come to post-secondary education with little formal education about their status as citizens, whether in relation to political institutions or as citizens in community.[8] Te Herenga Waka—Victoria University of Wellington, where we teach, is one of eight universities in Aotearoa, all of which are publicly funded. With roughly 850 students enrolled in a political science major or minor, our Political Science and International Relations program is one of the largest in the country. A three-year Bachelor of Arts degree with a political science major requires that students complete at least two introductory, three mid-level, and two upper-level courses in political science. Our course, *POLS353: Contemporary Challenges and Directions for New Zealand Politics*, is one of six 300-level courses offered by our program, and around 60 students take this course each year—some majoring in the subject, and others not.

Located in the nation's capital, our political science program attracts students with a particular interest in studying political science, and after graduation many of our students seek out careers in the civil service, NGOs, and parliament. As instructors in political theory and New Zealand politics, we observed that due to our program's focus on formal politics and institutions, many of our students were graduating with little understanding of politics beyond such terms, or of themselves as civic actors. We designed POLS353 in order to address this perceived gap, to equip our students with a distinctly civic education before they are among the nation's civic and political leaders. With surges of transnational protest in the name of climate action, #MeToo, and Black Lives Matter in mind, and inspired by contemporary political theory, we designed the course to give students an opportunity to explore some of our most pressing sociopolitical issues as well as a suite of non-institutional forms of civic action, each via a structural lens. As such, our key learning objectives for the course are for students to be able to:

> 1. Describe and analyze three defining challenges of the contemporary sociopolitical landscape of Aotearoa NZ using a structural lens;
>
> 2. Critically compare and evaluate multiple forms of civic action in response to these challenges;
>
> 3. Apply this knowledge to critically reflect on the possibilities and challenges of active citizenship in Aotearoa NZ today.[9]

Over the first six weeks of this 12-week course, we introduce students to theories of structural injustice and then explore three major contemporary sociopolitical issues in Aotearoa New Zealand—climate change, socioeconomic inequality, and settler-colonialism—using this structural lens. We then provide an introduction to theories of civic agency and action in week seven, and in the remaining five weeks of the course explore ten genres of civic action in relation to the structural approach introduced at the outset of the course. The particular pedagogical and assessment techniques with which we run and assess learning in the course share much in common with those that civic education scholars find most conducive to fostering a sense of civic agency. Given the importance placed on cultivating an ongoing practice of *structured reflection,* in lieu of conventional essays, our students' main assignment is an ongoing reflective journal in response to weekly prompts, culminating in a summative reflection asking students to connect course learning to their own sense of civic agency.[10] To enable *dialogue and collaboration across difference* and provide *research and action projects,* students also work in small groups to design and facilitate weekly one-hour workshops following lectures, where they present original research on specific case studies that exemplify the structural issue or forms of civic action studied that week, and facilitate civic dialogue about them.[11] Within these two major assignments, we encourage *perspective-taking* by asking workshop groups to present their chosen case studies through consideration of multiple stakeholder vantages, while weekly journal prompts also give opportunities to identify privileged and excluded perspectives in recent Op-Eds regarding course issues, and to interview someone close to them regarding their experiences of civic action. We *connect students to politically active communities* via guest speakers whose civic activities exemplify the ten forms of action we study, and invite them via journal prompts to seek out and reflect upon field experiences of civic action over the term. We are also emphatically *student-led* at every opportunity: from journal prompts to student-run workshops to class activities, we continually invite students to explicitly identify, draw upon, and reflect on their own lived relationships to the issues and activities we study, and to have these perspectives and passions flesh out course content.[12]

And yet, because of the course's distinctly *structural* approach to civic engagement education, what these pedagogical strategies have allowed us to reveal and develop with students is notably different. A structural approach has led us to engage contemporary issues like climate change and economic inequality as complex systems; likewise, it has led us to not only focus on non-institutional forms of action, but to understand and analyze these relationally, as interacting via complex and dynamic relays in diverse ways within the "socio-structural processes" that characterize a given issue.[13] We argue that it is these two distinct accents on what counts as the substance of civic engagement, both made possible by a structural approach, that have been critical in revealing, engaging, and developing a highly distinct set of questions and capacities for our students related to civic engagement. Perhaps most importantly, as a consequence of this approach, students come away with a pronounced sense of both civic responsibility and civic agency, as our data presented below shows.

A Structural Approach to Civic Engagement Education

As noted earlier, most civic education focuses on competencies and literacy regarding institutional and formal politics in order to foster students' sense of efficacy. A structural approach to civic education has led to two notable innovations in this course regarding the substance of civic education. The first is a systems understanding of key contemporary sociopolitical issues, which aims to give students a new evaluative lens through which to understand the key sociopolitical challenges with which they are already familiar. The second, revealed through a systems analysis, is an emphasis on largely extra-institutional forms of civic action.

Structural injustice: A systems approach to civic context

We draw on the work of political theorists Iris Marion Young and Romand Coles to explore how various pressing sociopolitical issues can be understood as *structural* when they cannot be attributed solely to individual actions, policies, or sheer bad luck. For Young and others, 'structural injustice' exists when large-scale processes create predictable patterns of opportunity or constraint for social groups; what is unjust, in such circumstances, is this systemic distribution according to social position. Importantly, Young's account shows that socio-structural injustices are largely the result of unintended consequences by the majority of citizens accepting these socio-structural processes as both legitimate and insignificant as they go about their personal projects.[14]

The commonsense notion of these structures being as monolithic and immutable as "natural laws" is, for Young, one of the key sources of inaction in addressing structural injustice, as it can feed a sense of powerlessness.[15] To counter this sense, we introduce students to Coles' work on complex systems theory, in which he shows that systems are far more open to intervention than we often believe. We explore with students how these systems, despite seeming stable, are constituted and sustained through continual relays and interaction effects, and thus are susceptible to influence throughout. These theories of sociopolitical processes serve as overarching heuristics for the course, examining each of the course's three core issues—climate change, settler-colonialism, and socioeconomic inequality—using a structural lens.

Relational repertoires: A systems approach to civic action

The second substantive innovation involves connecting this structural analysis of key contemporary issues to questions of civic agency and action. Alongside more conventional definitions of civic agency, we explore how agency itself is a structural issue, given that structural conditions greatly impact both one's own capacities and perceptions of agency (*internal efficacy*[16]), as well as how responsive the channels for democratic voice are (*external efficacy*[17]). Influenced by this structural approach, we emphasize that agency is also a collective property, enabled or diminished in continual relation to the ecosystem of relations to other actors, sites, and practices. Finally, just as structural injustice is sustained through the countless daily actions of citizens, to change it "requires," as Young notes, "collective action, and that requires organization."[18] Socio-structural processes are at once the conditions and outcomes of civic agency.

We define civic action, with Adler and Goggin as well as McCartney, as any form of action that citizens take that is at once civic, transformational, and reflective.[19] Understanding structural issues as sustained by the interaction between multiple sites, norms, and practices also highlights how these issues are challenged and changed through a similar diversity of civic actions. We spend the final five weeks of the course exploring ten genres of civic action, each seeking to affect the same sociopolitical issues via a distinct "theory of change." Each week we examine two of these genres, paired to draw out key differences and relationships: (i) Strategic and Prefigurative Action; (ii) Institutional and Direct Action; (iii) Public Spectacle and Everyday Organizing; (iv) Disruption and Education; and (v) Deliberative and Affective Action. These conceptual distinctions help students extend a structural analysis to civic action, as these pairings highlight the distinct means, aims, and impacts of various actions all seeking to change the same sociopolitical issues, as well as how these forms of action interact and impact on one another. As Romand Coles describes, "each system is entangled with others in relationships of symbiosis, parasitism, and conflict, and these relationships are dynamic, phasing in and out of resonance and dissonance according to myriad factors."[20] Taking a structural approach to civic action as much as to injustice, we emphasize that no one form of action can solely make change, and it is through the interaction effects between such diverse forms that structural change occurs. Core questions we explore throughout the course, therefore, are:

> 1. What is the appropriate form of action for a particular context, with a particular group of people, with a particular aim?
>
> 2. How might different forms of action work in relationship to effect change regarding the same issue?

For example, a juxtaposition between "strategic" and "prefigurative" action allows us to explore approaches to change that either strategically find the most expedient means to leverage resources to attain a goal[21] or alternatively, those that align means and ends such that present relations and actions "prefigure" the future we wish for.[22] This conceptual infrastructure allows us to explore how strategic and prefigurative approaches to social transformation can produce highly distinct forms of action that can, at times, be in tension and even conflict—for instance, regarding the use of violence, the value placed on consensus, or focus on cultural as well as material objectives—and yet can also enable, enhance, or shelter the other, as we see in the prefigurative forms of economy and community that the strategic protest actions of Occupy Wall Street made possible.

Research Design

In order to assess the impact of this structural approach to civic education on our students' sense of agency, we use two key sources of data. One of these is the final course assignment, the **summative student reflection**, in which students identify their key learning experiences from the term, including what impact, if any, these have had on how students think about or practice citizenship and civic action.[23] In these reflections, we intentionally pose open-ended questions for the students to use as a guide, so that they are able to reflect on their own learning rather than feel constrained or guided by our objectives as instructors. Because we did not include specific questions eliciting responses focused on our course learning objectives pertaining to either the course's structural approach or civic agency, these reflections serve as a particularly rich data source because they reflect what students independently identified as their key learning from the course. Moreover, this data set captures the responses of all students who completed the course, and thus reflects the full range of experiences.

To evaluate the extent to which students' sense of agency had developed in light of this course, we looked for two indicators: whether they evidenced either (i) an improved sense of agency or (ii) greater civic engagement as a result of the course. We also analyzed these reflections for the extent to which students demonstrated (iii) a structural approach to contemporary issues and civic action. To determine the frequency of students relating these three core objectives, we used this coding scheme in our content analysis:

> 1. We looked for language that explicitly specified a different perception of students' sense of agency as a result of taking the course. In 5 cases we inferred

this sense of agency based on the wider reflection, for example where students noted civic actions they had taken *as a result of* the course.

2. To identify increases in civic engagement, we only counted responses where students named a *specific* action they had taken, and where they explicitly claimed this was a result of this course. We also included instances where students who were already civically active tried new forms of engagement, and attributed this to the course. Though many students said they felt empowered to be more civically engaged after taking this course, or intended to be in the future, we determined that only counting named actions was a stronger measure of engagement, as some students may have indicated a willingness to be more civically engaged in the context of an assessment. Coding only for specific instances, however, means that this figure likely underrepresents those who may have been more civically engaged but did not refer to their specific actions in their reflection, or who had not yet taken action but did do so shortly after completing the course.

3. To identify the use of a structural analysis by students, we looked for language specifically referencing the course's two guiding texts (Young and Coles) regarding structural injustice and complex systems theory, as well as broader analysis that evidenced the applications of such conceptual frameworks.

The second source of data is a **voluntary anonymous follow-up survey**, conducted 18 months after the 2019 course, and 6 months after the 2020 course. This provides a longitudinal lens on the impacts of the course, gauging whether ideas from the course remained significant or useful, or continued to inform students' actions. We attribute this survey's 43% response rate across both cohorts in part to the challenges of conducting a survey during a pandemic, as well as the same factors that contribute to low response rates experienced across the university for online student evaluations. Despite the limitations in this data, responses indicate that the course's impacts regarding its core objectives continued to be felt for a significant number of students even some time after the course ended. We find it particularly notable that the 2019 cohort response rate was higher (51%), when the course was offered in a fully in-person format, compared with the more recent 2020 cohort response (35%), where the course was moved online after 3 weeks due to the pandemic.

In this survey, we measured our objectives more directly, by asking multiple choice questions that focused on each of the three variables, with an additional question asking more broadly about the effect of the course on students' sense of citizenship:

1. Has this course improved your sense of civic agency?

2. Has this course encouraged you to be more civically engaged?

3. Have you taken a structural approach to issues or actions more as a result of this course?

4. Please indicate how relevant or useful this course has been for you as a citizen, whether of Aotearoa or elsewhere.

Students were able to choose from three possible responses that indicated no effect (i.e. "not at all"), some effect (i.e., "somewhat"), or a significant effect (i.e., "a lot"/"very"). In addition to the multiple-choice questions, we also offered open-ended responses to elicit more information about what, in particular, stood out for students, the kinds of civic action they are now engaged in, and whether these ideas or actions are connected to the course.

Findings

Across both data sets, there is clear and substantial evidence that students were influenced on all three measures, indicating across the board: (i) an increased sense of their own agency as citizens, (ii) more civic engagement as a result of the course (both during and after the course), and (iii) a clear understanding of the structural dimensions of sociopolitical issues. Below, we summarize our findings for each data set, showing the extent of these effects. What stands out to us is that, even some time after the course is completed, students continue to recognize and act on this structural account of civic action.

Table 1 summarizes our findings from the summative reflections (the last assessment completed for the course), showing support for the course learning objectives across all three measures, in particular, an *improved sense of civic agency* (90% overall) and *a structural approach* (90% overall). A smaller but sizable percentage of the class indicated that they were *more civically engaged*, with 46% of the 2019 cohort and 27% of the 2020 cohort noting a specific action they had taken as a result of the class.

Table 1. Student Summative Reflections, Submitted as Final Assessment for the Course			
As a result of the course students indicated:	**2019** 57 students	**2020** 60 students	Overall 117 students
Increased sense of civic agency	55 (96%)	51 (85%)	90%
More civically engaged	26 (46%)	16 (27%)	37%
A structural approach	51 (89%)	55 (92%)	90%

As noted in many of the 2020 summative reflections, COVID-19 affected both students' engagement with the course overall (the course was moved online after 3 weeks), as well as opportunities for civic engagement, which is reflected in these lower levels of action. Yet the relatively high percentage of action in the 2019 cohort is cause for optimism, especially given the nature and scope of the activities they had performed in response to this course: some volunteering for the first time for various non-profit organizations or civic events; many making their first Select Committee submission or attending their first protest; several becoming involved in their first advocacy campaign; a number joining political parties or voting in their first local body election; many writing their MPs or particular Ministers, and also encouraging others to do so, which as one student notes, "I would not have done before"; some changing their consumer practices; many becoming increasingly active on social media "to disperse information that relates to the changes I wish to see for my community," with one student starting their own NZ politics webpage; and many noting they now attend more marches and sign more petitions than they did prior to the course. From peace advocacy to revitalization of the Māori language, climate strikes to Black Lives Matter, protesting against plastic use to refugee integration, Indigenous sovereignty to arming the police, students noted that they felt motivated by this course to take actions that "a few months ago, I would have considered a pointless exercise with little impact."

Table 2 summarizes our findings from the post-course survey, showing that *all* students who responded to the survey indicated that the course increased their awareness of structural injustice and improved their sense of civic agency either somewhat or significantly. Notably, a majority of students across both cohorts reported *significant* effects of the course on these two features, with 62% of students reporting increased awareness of structural injustice and 57% reporting an improved sense of civic agency. The great majority of students also indicated the course "somewhat" (63%) or "significantly" (32%) encouraged them to be more civically engaged. Moreover, the final response is particularly encouraging: two-thirds of students (67%) indicated that the course was "very" relevant to them as a citizen of Aotearoa or elsewhere, with the remaining third (32%) reporting that it was "somewhat" relevant to them.

Table 2. Student Responses 18 months (For 2019 Cohort) and 6 Months (For 2020 Cohort) After Completion of Course[24]			
	2019 cohort 29 students	2020 cohort 21 students	Overall 50 students
Have you taken a structural approach to issues or actions more as a result of this course?	Not at all 0 Somewhat 13 A lot 16	Not at all 0 Somewhat 6 A lot 15	0% 38% 62%
Has this course improved your sense of civic agency?	Not at all 0 Somewhat 15 A lot 13	Not at all 0 Somewhat 6 A lot 15	0% 43% 57%
Has this course encouraged you to be more civically engaged?	Not at all 2 Somewhat 18 A lot 8	Not at all 0 Somewhat 13 A lot 8	4% 63% 33%
How relevant or useful has this course been to you as a citizen, whether of Aotearoa or elsewhere?	Not at all 0 Somewhat 11 A lot 17	Not at all 0 Somewhat 5 A lot 16	0% 33% 67%

Despite the passage of time, this course retains relevance and impact for a large number of students. Students shared many ways in which they had "become much more involved in my community as a result of this course" in the months since it finished: volunteering or taking up part-time employment with various community organizations and advocacy groups; becoming involved in climate, nurse, or teacher strikes; door knocking and phone banking during the 2020 general election; changing their consumer choices; attending more protests, making more submissions to local government plans and Select Committees, and writing their local representatives; joining multiple political parties; and, when already politically active prior to taking the course, "using more forms of civic action after the course."

The Impact of a Structural Approach: Student Testimonies

The quantitative data analysis of students' final summative reflections and their responses to open-ended questions on the post-course survey shows the clear effects of the course's structural approach on students' civic engagement. A thematic analysis of these testimonies enables us to identify some key aspects of the course that students link to their increased sense of agency and action. In this section, we highlight five key ways in which students note the structural approach impacted their thinking and action: (i) offering a vocabulary for understanding sociopolitical structures; (ii) revealing points of weakness or possibilities for intervention in these structures; (iii) expanded notions of what constitutes civic action; (iv) discernment regarding appropriate and effective action; (v) galvanizing action.

i. Vocabulary for understanding sociopolitical structures.

Our students' sense of agency was clearly developed via the study of structural injustice. This is not intuitive, perhaps—we might presume that a focus on such complex, diffuse, transnational, and entrenched issues would lead students to feel daunted regarding the potential impact of their actions. Certainly, some students did note that they remain daunted, to a great extent. And yet they noted repeatedly that the heuristic of structural injustice was eye-opening and agency-enhancing, as it gave language and analytic tools to make sense of what until now had remained both opaque and monolithic. We witnessed repeatedly how understanding issues like racism and climate change as complex, dynamic systems produced in students what Coles calls "the Toto effect"—like Dorothy's dog discovering the real Wizard of Oz behind the curtain, it "unveils systems not as totalities but as assemblages of autocatalytic dynamics amid diverse ecologies of other autocatalytic assemblages."[25] The insight that seemingly incalcitrant structural issues are "the outcome of a multitude of actions by many individuals and groups...made [me] realize how much agency I have...to make change." This vocabulary was especially valuable in the context of civic action as these students noted:

- I am genuinely grateful for two key learning experiences... The first is a vocabulary for describing this dilemma I've been struggling with: the idea of structural injustice. In my mind, having such a vocabulary—a shared language—for discussing the issues we see in the world, is the first step in breaking them down, in challenging the idea that systems are "immutable totalities." (Coles 2016, 117)

- One of the significant changes in my thinking was around seeing systems as totalities and how this can prevent change from occurring.

- Despite being very passionate about this issue [climate change], I have often felt hopeless when examining it due to its sheer complexity and the lack of government action in response to it. However, the concept of structural injustice has been a revolutionary lens for me to look at climate change and all sorts of other social issues with...because I can now look at issues as a result of a huge number of norms and practices, rather than just as governmental or corporate failings.

ii. Reveals possibilities for intervention

A structural approach also enables students to identify various multiple sites, registers, actors, and forces related to a given issue, and then to trace specific interaction effects between these nodes in the system. Often, when these systems are what Coles calls "autocatalytic," or self-reinforcing, students can feel overwhelmed—as dynamic as these systems might be, they nonetheless feel insurmountable.[26] Yet, by tarrying with the specifics of these nodes and their interactions, we work to highlight how each is a site of potential intervention. As we begin to study forms of action addressing such issues, this understanding is complemented by a growing awareness of the countless, creative ways citizens like them are in fact intervening and creating various forms of change. Many students noted the value of this vocabulary to both identify the issues and act in relation to them:

- I now think of all change as possible, and no longer as some far-fetched reality... we can start to see this world the same as Toto, that the system is not what we think or this big overlying order. The systems are not fixed... With issues such as gender pay gaps, inequality, racism and settler-colonialism, it makes me realize that we can change the way things work, and it comes down to figuring out how these systems work and using that to voice our concerns and to have a say.

- I found Coles' discussion of complex dynamic systems theory especially empowering and hopeful. Seeing systems as fixed and unchallengeable monoliths was part of why I found resolving my dilemma so difficult.

- A key lesson I have learnt that has given me optimism is that although injustices constrain so many lives, as Coles discusses, structures are dynamic and they are malleable.

- I... began to realise that people can leverage their power to create institutional change. Realising that all these structural injustices are not malevolent but rather the creation of small normative actions.

- By acquiring a deeper understanding of the contributors to New Zealand's structural injustices, I began to appreciate that the system was constructed. I was able to learn about how that construction took place. And as a result, I began to see that it was similarly vulnerable to deconstruction.

iii. Expanded notions of civic action

Prior to our course, students often, as one student phrased it, "had in... mind that politics was essentially just megaphones in the street or suits in debating chambers." It is no surprise, then, how often they reflect that this course expanded their sense of what counts as civic action—that theatre and sharing economies, community-building and museum exhibits are also ways citizens around the world are participating in their communities for the purposes of positive transformation. Students reported, for example:

- Prior to this course, I was ambivalent about the extent to which I could participate in politics, beyond more conventional methods such as voting. However, I now have a better understanding of the various forms of civic action, and the fact that I am able to partake in those that I am either more interested in, or better equipped to do so.

- I have hugely developed my understanding of civic action which has transformed the way I view my role in society. Similar to the public, I had a preconceived idea of what civic action is that consists mainly of disruptive, spectacular actions such as mass protests. I have really enjoyed getting a deeper understanding and exposure to a variety of different forms of civic action that are different from what I previously believed.

- One of the biggest surprises for me in this class is that... things I would not have even viewed as political actions [are political, such as] going to plays, engaging with community, experiencing certain aspects of pop culture...

iv. Discernment regarding appropriate forms of action

In delving into these genres of action via context-specific comparative analysis each week, thereby unpacking the particular strengths, conditions, and impacts of each, students develop capacities for discernment regarding appropriate and effective action. As one student noted, after drawing on this knowledge to determine which forms of action to use in designing a campaign for restarting governmental support for the Syria crisis, "I had more confidence to put this into action since I understood the theory behind it and had knowledge of the systems in place." This was key for students' sense of agency not only because it opens up and develops discernment regarding a wider suite of civic actions to them, but also because its focus on primarily non-institutional forms of action means that, as one student reflected: "While grand institutional change may seem broad and unachievable, small prefigurative environments can be implemented from the ground up with great success in communities... I was surprised to learn how complex civic action was but I also began to appreciate how my role in the community could [contribute as] civic action, especially when institutions remain resolute against the opinions of an individual."

v. Increased civic action

Students repeatedly linked an increase in civic activity to their "understandings of injustice… that I learnt in the course," their "personal growth… in this class," and "being more informed, asking the big questions, [and] questioning the system as opposed to just the actors." They also attributed these activities to the course because it "introduced me to ways that I can take part." Students noted they had been "inspired by this course" to act in these ways because of "the confidence this course gave me"–and this sense of efficacy was consistently attributed to the course's structural approach to both civic action and issues.

We saw this structural approach galvanize students towards action in a number of ways. First, by giving them a language for collective responsibility. Whereas frames of personal liability can lead to either refusal or paralysis, a structural analysis both diffuses these possible reactions by collectivizing responsibility and motivates students for action by highlighting that these issues are largely the unintentional result of countless acts of everyday citizens, and maintained as long as we fail to act to change them.[27, 28] Repeatedly, students note this course has given them a new sense of their own responsibility in relation to these issues, as well as a future-focused and agentic language of collective responsibility when a previous notion of personal guilt held them captive:

- I came into this course feeling relatively disillusioned with the state of political affairs in New Zealand today… I felt paralysed with the immensity of it all and had found myself retreating… This course has taught me that I need to stop considering my reaction to social issues as an individual action… What was a new concept to me, was that because structural injustice is the outcome of collective action and inaction, a collective response would be required to effectively combat it. As a result, I began looking at my relationships with those around me and considered how as a collective, rather than individuals, we can begin to challenge these oppressive structures.

- The course has changed how I think about colonization. As a Pākehā [non-Indigenous] citizen of New Zealand, I had previously felt either defensive or guilty about my role in decolonisation and fighting racism, however this course taught me how I could take responsibility for my actions and history. The course also made me feel like I had more agency and that I could really make a difference.

- This [course] opened my understanding of the role that I can play in society as an individual. Perhaps it is easy to blame the systems for the structural injustice, but I never realized that I was also part of the problem or to some extent, a contributor to the structural injustice by accepting the rules of the system.

Second, this structural approach to both issues and action provided a further source of perceived agency by reinforcing that, just as no one action can cause the change we seek in its entirety, their own actions are working in—albeit unwitting or inadvertent—concert with countless acts of other citizens over time:

- Each action has its unique set of strengths and weaknesses. Structural injustice cannot be solved by one form of action alone… structural injustices [are] complex, interconnected, and dynamic. It is unsurprising then the solutions to them should be equally as intricate.

- Previously, thinking about injustice left me feeling at a loss… but Coles is right to critique this fixed and detached view of structures as something that entrenches a divide between reform and revolution, and undermines our ability to cultivate "radical democratic power and transformation"[29]

- Learning that seemingly conflicting forms of action can function harmoniously through a vectorial relationship was a critical experience.

- In such a globalized world with many modes of civic action, we can mobilize ourselves, exercise our agency, and begin to transform these accepted norms and practices.

This means—and we take care to reinforce this using Coles' own notion of "wormhole hope"—that seemingly ineffective or minor acts can ultimately contribute to broader structural change. As noted above, many students acted on this invigorated sense of their own agency even as the course was unfolding, for the first time making a Select Committee submission, voting in local body elections, attending a protest, or becoming involved in an advocacy campaign, all because, they attested, the course affirmed their own agency. One student, reflecting on her first time volunteering for the Wiki o Te Reo Māori (Māori Language Week) parade in response to our course, invoked Coles' notion of "*wormhole hope*" to consider the impact of this civic action:

> The direct causal consequences might never be known... the school children who I walked with and had conversations with might go on to do activism in relation to Te Reo as a result of our talk, but I will never know. There is something peaceful about that, because it makes me want to go out and be more active in case this plants a seed for another student... Overall, this course has challenged me to consider my own role within society and how I can harness my agency for the better.

In considering the various ways a structural approach shaped our students' views of and engagement with civic action, we see something exciting and altogether rare: in the face of the most vexing, intractable, and pervasive issues that define contemporary politics, at a time when we have record lows in voter turnout, party membership and other standard markers of political engagement, students expressing themselves to be both equipped and motivated to act to meaningfully change the world around them. We see this course as a rare opportunity to affect what these future leaders consider civic action, and to develop the literacies, skills, and sense of agency required to act effectively beyond the terms that formal politics or the occasional protest provide, in their final year with us before they step into and significantly shape the world beyond the classroom:

> - I found this course very life changing as it gave meaning to many of my wonderings as a child who grew up in a small town... [the course] enabled me to understand the role that I assume as a citizen of Aotearoa in the fact that I can partake in civic action as I deem fit. This course made me realise that small actions which at first felt futile can actually contribute to political discourse and even change.

> - I have a deeper understanding... [of] the most pressing challenges that our society is currently facing. I can comprehend the factors that produce injustice, and I know what I can do as a citizen to address these issues. This course has surpassed my expectations and reflecting on the knowledge and wisdom I have gained throughout the semester, I feel empowered to utilize my social advantages to help rethink, reshape and rebuild the systems and structures that create structural injustice and allow it to endure.

Both immediately following and months after the course, the overwhelming majority (over 90%) of students demonstrated pronounced increases in their sense of agency and the use of a structural approach to interpret contemporary issues and civic action to address them as results of this course. They also made continual links between these two impacts, attributing the former to the latter in various ways. In light of these findings, we hold that this structural approach to both civic issues and civic action contributes to students' civic literacy as well as sense of efficacy. It demystifies what can feel monolithic and immutable, revealing multifarious points of potential intervention as well as the contingency of structural conditions on ongoing interactions. At the same time, it provides a wider and more nuanced sense of forms of action available to them and capacities for discernment between them. Finally, it provides a sense of "wormhole hope" borne of a sense that our actions are connected to both countless others that come before us and changes that are to come:

> Every revolutionary event (big or small) is itself made possible by an uncanny connection with a previous time that had a similar revolutionary charge or natal intensity... [This] instills in us a more resilient faith that our own exemplary struggles may themselves reemerge beyond vast stretches of defeat to engage in revitalizing improbable futures long after we are gone.[30]

Challenges and Future Directions

There are, of course, limitations and continual learning ahead in taking this structural approach to civic education. Four in particular stand out to us, in reflecting on our and our students' experiences: the need for better integration with the community, attentiveness to structural issues already present in the classroom, impacts of the global pandemic and online learning, and the need for broader coordination of civic engagement education within our program.

First, in future years we will be focusing our attention on how to be more integrated with politically active communities, so as to give students more opportunities to engage with and contribute to the world outside the classroom. Ideally, we aim for this to take a more structural approach, where student actions are more connected across context and time: in real-time relationship with and guided by local communities, and handed over to the next class for more informed, constellated, and effective actions than "one-off" interventions allow.

Second, we are aware of how the structural issues we study are always-already present in the classroom, most notably in the different social positions of our students and the impacts this has on levels and dynamics of participation. We notice more contributions to class discussion from students who come from more privileged backgrounds, which likely also impact workshop group dynamics. We see structural differences manifest in workshop collaborations, for example when the solitary Indigenous student in a group is looked on as the "representative" voice for Māori. We also contend with the fact that learning about issues like settler-colonialism affects students differently, with some approaching this learning having personally borne the weighty, negative experiences of this structural injustice, while others come to this subject with little recognition of the ways it has offered them protection or enabled their success. This can mean that some learning may come at the expense of others or even put them in harm's way. How we hold the space for radically different positions from which our students come to this joint inquiry is always delicate, complex, and fraught, and we have ongoing questions regarding conditions for safety and discomfort, challenge and advocacy as educators. These questions are, perhaps, more productive as ongoing questions that keep us alert to these ever-present risks–and a structural lens arguably helps to sensitize civic educators to and navigate such concerns and complexities.

Third, it is also worth noting the impact of changing mid-semester to online learning in 2020 due to COVID-19, given the course's focus on collective dialogue, collaboration, and experiential learning. So many of the forms of action that we were studying required being able to physically gather in public, and some of our assessment relied on students seeking field experiences of such actions. We have no doubt this has been a shared challenge among civic educators over this time. Yet the move online also made students more aware of the structural constraints to organizing and preparing for action, and illuminated structural constraints in students' own lives, evidenced in unequal access to the internet, mental health support, and domestic safety. We certainly noticed less engagement with the course than the previous year as students negotiated multiple challenges introduced by this pandemic. Yet, this course was also uniquely positioned to respond to some of the challenges. Students reported feeling a sense of community that was otherwise lacking in their university experiences as a result of the group work and weekly class gathering for the online workshop. Students also reported feeling more urgency to act in the face of structure; though they were overwhelmed in some respects, the pandemic's immense disruption to daily life and witnessing dramatic structural changes by responding governments had the "Toto effect" of exposing the "normal rules and accepted practices" of our society, the exploitation and struggles they cause—for example, of underpaid and vulnerable "essential workers"—and the malleability of these rules, all of which had previously been naturalized and largely invisible.[31] While the pandemic thus forced us to think creatively and perhaps find limits on civic action in the absence of capacities to gather in person, it also provided unexpected resources for sensing agency and possibility in response to structural injustice. As this student noted:

> It seemed fateful that this course occurred at a time when the world is experiencing unprecedented circumstances, coupled with global protests and actions against injustice. During this time I have been able to put into practice some of the key learnings of the course, and I have already found myself engaging more actively in politics, and considering the modes of action available to me. In all, while elements of this class have left me feeling hopeless at times, I have found POLS353 extraordinarily helpful, using what I have learnt to go forth and educate myself and others, and express my own civic agency in the political world.

Finally, there are also limits placed on this course in the absence of complementarity and co-ordination with the broader political science program and institution. Both the structural injustice and civic education scholarship emphasize the importance of multiple sites of experience so as to support learning and change. As McCartney, Rimmerman, McHugh and Mayer, and Coles all agree, "no one course or activity can create a democratically engaged citizen."[32] Students come to this sole course in their third and final year, and it remains the only one in our program that centers the student as a civic actor. Students note that they feel a sense of loss for not having had more opportunities for such thinking earlier in their degree, and we recognize the limited impact of this course given its institutional setting. We hope to leverage the demonstrable impacts of this course on students' sense of agency and responsibility to develop through lines to other courses so that the benefits we see can be deepened and strengthened over the three years we have with these civic actors. This will also enable students' grasp of these wholly new and complex suites of concepts and analytic tools to become more nuanced. Within the 12-week confines of the course, at present this remains more of a survey course, and by the time we finish the course we feel we have only just begun. We look forward to finding modifications that allow us to introduce further nuance in these regards, and developing capacities and sensibilities in further courses so that this course does not seek to carry so much.

By directing our collective attention to those challenges and directions that feel most connected to this diminished sense of civic agency today we have, in this course, sought to respond to the despair, anxiety and uncertainty that feel chronic for our students at this time. We aimed to foster civic efficacy via the development of literacies, skills, and sensibilities necessary for citizens to constructively and reflectively participate in their communities. Yet, because we centered structural injustice and non-institutional forms of action, students developed literacies and skills that are distinct from other civic engagement courses. Their learning entailed, among other things, practical knowledge regarding a repertoire of non-institutional forms of civic action—not simply a vocabulary of genres, but a sense of their respective strengths, conditions, theories of change, and potential impacts—as well as a structural sense of how these different forms of action are interacting across a complex field to produce meaningful change. This picture of both issue and action is admittedly complex—and that, in itself, can prove daunting. Yet, we have seen what a structural, non-institutional approach to civic engagement education can do to grow this sense of agency among our students that is at once most scarce and vital.

Endnotes

1. The indigenous name Aotearoa, or sometimes Aotearoa New Zealand, is increasingly being used to refer to the country. Throughout the chapter we use both versions interchangeably.

2. Adam Fowler, "Civic Agency," in *International Encyclopedia of Civil Society*, eds. Helmut K. Anheier, Stefan Toepler and Regina List (New York: Springer, 2010).

3. Gabriel A. Almond and Sidney Verba, *The Civic Culture: Political Attitudes and Democracy in Five Nations* (Princeton, NJ: Princeton University Press, 1963); Robert Dudley and Alan Gitelson, "Civic Education, Civic Engagement, and Youth Civic Development," *PS: Political Science & Politics* 36, no. 2 (2003): 263–67; Renée Bukovchik VanVechten and Anita Chadha, "How Students Talk to Each Other: An Academic Social Networking Project," in *Teaching Civic Engagement: From Student to Active Citizen*, eds. Alison Rios Millett McCartney, Elizabeth A. Bennion, and Dick Simpson (Washington DC: American Political Science Association, 2013.)

4. McCartney, Bennion, and Simpson 2013, 5.

5. McCartney, Bennion, and Simpson 2013, 5; Joel Westheimer and Joseph Kahne, "Educating the 'Good' Citizen: Political Choices and Pedagogical Tools," *PS: Political Science and Politics* 37, no. 2 (2004): 241–47; Alison Rios Millett McCartney, "Teaching Civic Engagement: Debates, Definitions, Benefits, and Challenges," in *Teaching Civic Engagement: From Student to Active Citizen*, eds. Alison Rios Millett McCartney, Elizabeth A. Bennion, and Dick Simpson, 9–20 (Washington DC: American Political Science Association, 2013).

6. This research was approved by the Victoria University of Wellington Human Ethics Committee [#28622].

7. See 'Our Civic Future', https://nzpsa.com/resources/Documents/Our%20Civic%20Future.pdf.

8. For example, see 'New civics resources for young New Zealanders', https://gazette.education.govt.nz/articles/new-civics-resources-for-young-new-zealanders/; 'Our Civic Future', https://nzpsa.com/resources/Documents/Our%20Civic%20Future.pdf; Make It 16, https://makeit16.org.nz.

9. For more information about the course, please see the course outline available on the companion website.

10. McCartney, Bennion, and Simpson 2013; Michael K. McDonald, "Internships, Service-Learning, and Study Abroad: Helping Students Integrate Civic Engagement Learning across Multiple Experiences," in *Teaching Civic Engagement: From Student to Active Citizen*, eds. Alison Rios Millett McCartney, Elizabeth A. Bennion, and Dick Simpson, 369–83 (Washington DC: American Political Science Association, 2013).

11. Brian M. Harward and Daniel M. Shea, "Higher Education and the Multiple Modes of Engagement," in *Teaching Civic Engagement: From Student to Active Citizen*, eds. Alison Rios Millett McCartney, Elizabeth A. Bennion, and Dick Simpson, 21–40 (Washington DC: American Political Science Association, 2013); Elizabeth Beaumont, "Political Learning and Democratic Capacities: Some Challenges and Evidence of Promising Approaches," in *Teaching Civic Engagement: From Student to Active Citizen*, eds. Alison Rios Millett McCartney, Elizabeth A. Bennion, and Dick Simpson, 41–55 (Washington DC: American Political Science Association, 2013).

12. Many students commented on these pedagogical features of the course, for example noting that: "I found the course's constant emphasis on personal development and personal experience very enriching for my learning. Every topic that we delved into demanded of us personal anecdotes, opinions and experience in order for the material to truly flourish, this in turn has solidified my learning at every week and allowed for a constant standard of analysis of the topics in the way they play out in my own political engagement and activities."

13. Iris Marion Young, *Responsibility for Justice* (Oxford and New York: Oxford University Press, 2011.)

14. Young 2011, 63.

15. Ibid., 154-55.

16. See, for example, Tim Vercelotti and Elizabeth Matto, "The Kitchen-Table Connection: The Effects of Political Discussion on Youth Knowledge and Efficacy," CIRCLE Working Paper #72, 2010; Carole Pateman, "Political Culture, Political Structure and Political Change," *British Journal of Political Science* 1, no. 3 (1971): 298.

17. See, for example, J. Cherie Strachan and Elizabeth Bennion, "New Resources for Civic Engagement: The National Survey of Student Leaders, Campus Associational Life, and the Consortium for Inter-Campus SoTL Research," in *Teaching Civic Engagement Across the Disciplines*, eds. Elizabeth C. Matto, Alison Rios Millett McCartney, Elizabeth A. Bennion, and Dick Simpson 291–307 (Washington DC: American Political Science Association, 2017).

18. Young 2011, 69.

19. Richard P. Adler and Judy Goggin, "What Do We Mean by 'Civic Engagement'?" *Journal of Transformative Education* 3, no. 3 (2005): 236–253; McCartney 2013.

20. Romand Coles, *Visionary Pragmatism: Radical and Ecological Democracy in Neoliberal Times* (Durham, NC: Duke University Press, 2016), 148.

21. Marshall Ganz, "Why David Sometimes Wins: Strategic Capacity in Social Movements," in *The Psychology of Leadership: New Perspectives and Research*, 209–238 (Mahwah, NJ: Lawrence Erlbaum Associates, Publishers, 2005).

22. Benjamin Franks, "The Direct Action Ethic From 59 Upwards," *Anarchist Studies* 11 (2003): 13–41.

23. Our questions were: What stands out to you, from the term, regarding key learning experiences? What impact have these had on how you think about and/or practice citizenship and civic action, and why? What are key lessons and questions that you take with you, and what do you want to do with them going forward?

24. For the 2019 cohort, 29 students responded out of a possible 57 (51%). For the 2020 cohort, 21 students responded out of possible 60 (35%).

25. Coles 2016, 147.

26. Ibid.

27. Avril Bell, "'Cultural Vandalism' and Pākehā Politics of Guilt and Responsibility," In *Tangata Tangata: The Changing Ethnic Contours of New Zealand*, eds. Paul Spoonley, David G. Pearson, and Cluny Macpherson (Southbank, Victoria: Thomson Press, 2004), 89-107.

28. Young 2011.

29. Coles 2016, 117.

30. Coles 2016: 185–7.

31. Young 2011, 48.

32. McCartney 2013, 19; Craig Rimmerman, "Service-Learning Lessons," in *Service-Learning in the Liberal Arts: How and Why It Works,* ed. Craig A. Rimmerman 187–190 (Lanham, MD: Lexington Publishers, 2011); Mary McHugh and Russell Mayer, "The Different Types of Experiential Learning Offered in a Political Science Department: A Comparison of Four Courses," in *Teaching Civic Engagement: From Student to Active Citizen*, eds. Alison Rios Millett McCartney, Elizabeth A. Bennion, and Dick Simpson, 353–67 (Washington, DC: American Political Science Association, 2013); Coles 2016.

8

Teaching Group-Oriented Foreign Policy Analysis for Civic Engagement

Dmitry A. Lanko

St. Petersburg State University

This chapter introduces the concept of group-oriented foreign policy analysis and evaluates the impact that in-class exercises in this area have on students' civic engagement. Group-oriented foreign policy analysis is client-oriented advice relevant to a decision in the field of foreign policy, where the client is not necessarily a governmental institution but any group influenced by particular issues of international affairs. The chapter demonstrates the relevance of in-class exercises in group-oriented foreign policy analysis in countries like Russia, where the authoritarian government encourages the formation of two separate civil societies: those consisting of pro-government non-profits and of "foreign agent" non-profits. It provides a detailed description of such exercises and assesses the impact that taking part in the exercise has on students' civic engagement. Students' feedback collected in multiple forms during the administration of the exercises from 2008–2019 at a Russian university demonstrates that the exercise influences students' civic engagement positively in multiple ways.

KEYWORDS: Civic Engagement, Pedagogy, Higher Education, Public Policy, Foreign Policy, Russia.

Introduction

This chapter focuses upon an in-class exercise in group-oriented foreign policy analysis for graduate-level students majoring in international relations. Research conducted in relation to this course suggests that the exercise positively impacts civic engagement. In this exercise, students participate in two simulations, each designed to promote understanding of foreign policymaking as it appears from the viewpoint of different groups within a nation, not from the national viewpoint. The first portion of the exercise brings the students from the national to the group level of analysis by inviting them to simulate the work of a foreign policy think tank that has to make suggestions to a client concerning its actions. The client can be any group (governmental and non-governmental, private and non-profit) within a nation influenced by international events and foreign policy choices made on the national level. The second portion returns students to the national level by inviting them to discuss the foreign policy choices facing the nation while keeping the interests of individual sub-national groups discussed previously in mind. Students meet this goal by a day-long role-play. During the role-play, the students promote certain favorable policy options from the viewpoint of particular groups, explaining why implementing the options would benefit the nation as a whole.

Previous research demonstrates that such exercises involve either geopolitical and power politics reasoning or economic and humanitarian reasoning. Research conducted in relation to this group-oriented foreign policy analysis exercise demonstrates that the students who have first considered the influence of foreign policy on individual sub-national groups, tend to apply economic and humanitarian reasoning significantly more often compared to geopolitical and power politics reasoning. Moreover, the research demonstrates that the students prefer economic and humanitarian reasoning to geopolitical and power politics reasoning regardless of their gender or country of previous education. The chapter concludes that the exercise discussed is an effective way to encourage students to look at foreign policy as not only the result of "properly understood" national interests, but also of the desire to make the world a more prosperous and better place.

Simulating Foreign Policy Analysis in the Classroom: From Nation-Oriented to Group-Oriented Approach

Most simulation exercises in foreign policy analysis or in foreign policymaking offered to students of public policy graduate programs center around nations and their interests. When assigning students to produce advice relevant to a foreign policy decision, instructors most often assign them to staff members of governmental institutions, for example, parliamentary committees or individual members of parliaments.[1] When assigning students to prepare arguments in support or against a military invasion overseas, instructors most often assign them to find arguments highlighting the positive and negative impact of the intervention for a nation, not for a sub-national or a trans-national group.[2]

National orientation of in-class exercises in foreign policy analysis remains relevant, but at least four tendencies in public policy research and education create the demand to introduce group-oriented foreign policy analysis alongside nation-oriented foreign policy analysis. Group-oriented foreign policy analysis is client-oriented advice that refers to a decision in the field of foreign policy, where the client is not necessarily a governmental institution but any group influenced by particular issues of international affairs. The four tendencies creating the demand for teaching skills relevant to producing such advice are the development of foreign policy analysis as an academic discipline, post-modernization of policy analysis in fields other than foreign policy, globalization of public policy education, and privatization of public policy education.

Foreign policy analysis, the sub-discipline of international studies investigating domestic factors of foreign policy, inspired the introduction of the group-oriented approach. Moravcsik proposed "commercial liberalism" to the scholarly approach that "focuses on incentives created by opportunities for transborder economic transactions"[3] as factors influencing foreign policymaking. Zaller suggested perhaps the most popular approach to the analysis of the role of public opinion in international relations.[4] Feaver and Gelpi investigated the influence of military veterans treated as a non-associated group on foreign policymaking, thus creating the approach used to understand the role of other non-associated groups in the policy area.[5] By having recognized that many other groups, alongside governmental institutions, influence foreign policy, foreign policy analysis created the theoretical background for the group-oriented approach discussed in this chapter.

Policy analysis is "client-oriented advice relevant to public decisions and informed by social values."[6] Thus, the notion of the client is key to understanding the activity. Recently, instructors in policy analysis classrooms attempted to widen the scope of clients by means of post-modernizing the field. They assigned the students to produce recommendations aimed at challenging existing discursive practices instead of producing policy recommendations within these practices. They began considering certain parts of the public previously excluded from public policy by existing discursive practices, such as minorities. Non-associated groups were recognized as potential clients for policy analysis, thus making the latter "more democratic."[7] Although even today "positivism remains the dominant teaching method," "post-positivist methods... did make inroads into the classroom," thus resulting in recognition that not only governmental institutions and political leaders, but any other group associated or not, can be a client.[8] This acknowledgement paved the way for the emergence of group-oriented foreign policy analysis.

Globalization of public policy education has multiple manifestations, from the increase of the share of international students in classrooms to the growing importance of external financial supporters to the public policy graduate programs.[9] On one occasion, that tendency produced the scandal known as the London School of Economics–Gaddafi affair. According to Sim, the case indicates "the difficulties that can arise when universities find themselves pressurized into fund-raising in order to maintain their international profile."[10] That case is, of course, an exception. At the same time, one cannot help noticing that, as a rule, public policy graduate programs face the fact that neither foreign students nor foreign financial supporters are interested in foreign policy analysis being taught as advice oriented to only one client, which is the government of the nation in which the teaching takes place. Instead, they demand group-oriented foreign policy analysis.

Privatization of public policy education is the tendency among an ever-greater number of students who are seeking graduate education in public affairs but are not aiming to join civil service afterwards. *Robertson vs. Princeton*[11] is probably the best example of the tendency, which demonstrated that "throughout much of its history, the [Woodrow Wilson School] put little emphasis on recruiting students who even demonstrated interest in federal service and international affairs."[12] Today, many students of public policy graduate programs do not seek a career in public, foreign, or military service, but in private companies and nonprofits. Those companies and nonprofits are groups whose profits and results depend on public decisions made by the government, including on foreign policy decisions. Thus, they seek influence over public decision-making, including in the foreign policy field. Public policy graduate students seeking careers in such companies and nonprofits demand skills related to such influence, creating the demand for group-oriented foreign policy analysis.

All four of these tendencies are visible in Russia. Foreign policy analysis is gaining prominence among Russian scholars. Policy analysis is taught in public policy graduate programs to make students capable of producing advice relevant to public decisions and informed by social values and interests of various groups. Sadly, many groups are not heard in the course of foreign policymaking in contemporary Russia. A radical approach to Russian politics views Russia as a "subaltern empire," i.e., as an empire, in which all people are deprived of the possibility to make their voices heard.[13] Although a radical approach, it is noteworthy that more Russian voices seek to be heard in the course of public decision-making in the country, including in foreign policymaking.

Globalization and privatization of public policy education also are taking place in Russia. The Russian government motivates universities to attract more foreign students and foreign funds in an effort to boost the country's "educational diplomacy."[14] Professors of public policy in Russia today teach multinational groups of students; foreign students in those groups do not aim to become Russian civil servants because foreigners are not admitted into civil service in Russia. In line with these students' expectations, the professors do not attempt to train future civil servants for Russia in public policy programs. Instead, they formulate other learning outcomes, and teach accordingly. For example, a professor of diplomatic studies in a Russian university teaches students what it takes to be a diplomat of any country, not just a Russian diplomat. The emergence of public policy education in Russia in the 1990s coincided with the times when it was commonly agreed that business-state relations in Russia were one-sided in favor of business and only a handful of studies questioned that one-sidedness.[15] Today, when the situation in business-state relations in Russia is opposite to what it was in the 1990s, many young Russians still enroll in public policy graduate programs with the goal to make careers on the business side of the relationship.

In line with these four tendencies, the exercise in group-oriented foreign policy analysis discussed in this chapter was introduced to students majoring in international relations in a Russian university in 2008 under the name of "analytical practice." The twelve-year experience of supervising and observing students' activities in the administration of the exercise has highlighted its unexpected impact on students' views. Specifically, the exercise has helped many students to understand that foreign policy decisions create consequences not only for the nation as a whole, but for particular groups within a nation. It has helped them to understand that foreign policy is not a result of national interest alone, but also of the interests of those groups. For some of them, this realization has paved the way to civic engagement in foreign policy.

Civic engagement in foreign policy understood in the broadest sense (regarding any individual or group activity addressing issues of foreign policy), is of extreme importance in contemporary Russia. A vital pillar of the legitimacy of the Putin regime is its foreign policy successes, real or imagined. According to Levada Centre, a Russian independent polling company, Defense Minister Sergey Shoigu and Foreign Minister Sergey Lavrov have been among top five trusted politicians in Russia throughout most of the 2010s, despite their popularity (and the popularity of Putin himself) significantly declining since the peak in 2014.[16] The three enjoy the reputation of "wise statesmen" who have "correctly understood" Russia's interests predetermined by the country's place in the international system and its geopolitical position, and who have crafted Russia's foreign policy accordingly. The exercise in group-oriented foreign policy analysis discussed in this chapter provided the students who participated in it with a different perspective on foreign policy. That perspective views foreign policy as an outcome of systematically competing and changing interests of different groups within the nation, not as something constant and predetermined by outside factors.

Course Design

To address the tendencies described above, I proposed a course in group-oriented foreign policy analysis in 2008, and I have taught it since then. Through the decade, the course has changed its official title multiple times. In different versions of the curriculum, it appears as "Group-Oriented Foreign Policy Analysis," as "Foreign Policy Analysis Colloquium" or simply as "Analytical Practice." The name of the course changed thanks to multiple higher education reforms that have taken place in Russia throughout the past decade. At times, those reforms contradicted each other as a result of the "pull between authoritarian tendencies and liberal economic necessities" in Russia, which paralyzed its government's "ability to definitively choose the most appropriate path..."[17] On the level of a particular educational program, those reforms sometimes made no greater impact than just renaming courses without changing their substance.

The course consists of three core parts. The first part involves a one-day introduction including a lecture and questions-and-answers session, which explains the aims and the means of the course, particular assignments that the students are required to complete during the course, and the learning outcomes that the students are expected to achieve as a result. The second and the third parts of the course include the simulation of a think tank, which allows student participants to formulate recommendations to particular groups seeking influence on foreign policy, and a one-day role-play exercise, which allows the students to assume the roles of those groups and try to achieve influence on foreign policy guided by the recommendations created during the think tank simulation. The think tank simulation takes place throughout most of the semester; students meet with the instructor in person or online at least every other week or communicate electronically. The concluding decision-making role-play is organized as a one-day intensive session.

In this chapter, the words "simulation" and "role-play" are used to indicate two different parts of the exercise. In most cases, however, those two words are used as synonyms both in classrooms and in pedagogical literature. In 2005, Asal regretted that although usage of simulations "in the teaching of [international relations was] growing, the pedagogical literature that support[ed] such growth [was] still small."[18] Since then, pedagogical literature on simulations in teaching politics in general[19] and in international relations in particular[20] has significantly expanded. Some of the literature benefitted from analysis of in-class simulations organized in Russian universities.[21] Some of the literature has especially pointed to in-class simulations and role games as inspiring civic action of participants in real life.[22]

When creating the exercise in group-oriented foreign policy analysis, I departed from the assumption that every university is a think tank. Despite Nye's assertion that the gap between academic theorists and foreign policy practitioners is growing, most schools of major universities offering public policy programs are think tanks, and many of them work in the field of foreign policy.[23] The exercise that I have created and administered since 2008 invites students to simulate the activities of a foreign policy think tank working for a particular group as its client. The main educational objective of the exercise is to help students develop their analytical skills in general as well as particular skills useful for those pursuing a career in think tanks, policy planning bureaus of governmental institutions, strategic analysis sections of companies, or situation analysis groups in non-profits.

Case Study Assignment

The course seeks to meet its objective by assigning a group of students with a case study that serves as the focal point of the simulation and role-play. Schodt has noted that "teaching cases are powerful vehicles for helping students..." developing their analytical skills.[24] The exercise assigns students (usually a group of ten to forty students) with a case study in the field of international relations that has attracted public attention. For example, in 2020, students focused upon the series of political demonstrations and protests against the Belarusian Government and President Alexander Lukashenko. In previous years, the cases were around international events, from the Russo-Georgian War of 2008 to Brexit. To find the case that interests students most, I usually encourage a free-topic discussion among students. Students tend to demonstrate better motivation to complete the exercise if the case discussed during the exercise interests them.

Policy Paper

Although students work in groups during the simulation and role-play, each student is expected to submit a policy paper at the conclusion of the exercise. Specifically, each student is assigned to write a policy paper for a different client. Clients are federal, regional and local authorities, political parties, companies and nonprofits, whose everyday operations are influenced by the particular case. It is assumed that the same case influences different groups within the same country in different ways, thus helping each student to write a unique policy paper.

Assigning students with policy paper writing helps achieve another education objective of the exercise—presenting foreign policymaking in a format alternative to traditional lecturing. The policy paper that the students produce by the end of the exercise is expected to contain conclusions clearly explaining what impact the international event being considered could have on the operations of each student's client. It is also expected to contain recommendations for the client concerning possible actions that could be taken in order to maximize the positive and minimize the negative impact of the event on the client's operations. For example, a student writing a policy paper on the influence of the protests in Belarus on Gazprom natural gas company is expected to answer such questions as: How will the protests influence Gazprom's operations? What is the possible harm? What are the possible benefits? How probable are the harm and the benefits? What can Gazprom do to change the situation? What should Gazprom do to minimize the potential harm? What can Gazprom do to utilize the potential benefits in the best possible way?

Stages of the Think Tank Simulation

To help the students adapt these general questions to their particular case and client, as well as to help them find the answers in the most convenient way, I have split the think tank simulation into four stages. Each stage takes approximately a month, during which the students meet with instructor at least twice. The four stages are as follows:

At the first stage, students are required to identify particular activities of their clients that are expected to be influenced most by the international event in question, as well as to assess if those activities are developing in a stable manner, are boosting, or are in crisis. It is important to inform the students at this stage that policy analysis is not exclusively about serving a particular client, that it "is more than simply 'client-oriented advice' but should be rather about democratic dialogue and critique."[25] For example, the students writing a policy paper on the influence of the protests in Belarus on the interests of Gazprom should not simply describe the benefits the company might enjoy from the protests, that is if violence against protesters leads neighboring Lithuania to sanction them, forcing Belarus to buy more natural gas from Gazprom. The student should also consider the deteriorating image of Gazprom among the population of Belarus itself and of other countries, where people sympathize with Belarusian protesters.

At the second stage, students are required to outline a few scenarios of their client's activities most influenced by the case, and to distribute those scenarios on two scales: in terms of their probability and favorability to the client. It is important that students understand at this point that, contrary to conventional wisdom, scenarios are not a forecast of what will be, but "a background for assessing and choosing alternative strategies."[26] The most favorable scenario is the "outcome, which produce[s] a net increase in the [client's] utility, where utility is simply a function of the [client's] preferences over a set of outcomes."[27] Regarding probability, it is important to warn students about the temptation to reify current trends, i.e., to assume that current trends will persist, and to evaluate probabilities of different scenarios accordingly. Rather, students can learn about different models helpful in evaluating scenarios at this stage, for example, the perspectivist scenario building model.[28]

In the third stage, students are required to explore capabilities of their clients, and to produce recommendations to the clients. Different agencies have different capabilities to influence foreign policy decisions. Governmental agencies enjoy institutionalized roles in foreign policymaking. Political parties and associated interest groups can recruit public opinion in their favor. In the case of business associations, it is "the power of money" that makes the difference.[29] Think tanks themselves, though unable to recruit significant resources or large groups of people, are influential to the extent that they are involved in multiple policy networks.[30] When making policy recommendations, students are expected to advise their clients to take responsible actions, which involve measures aimed at not only safeguarding the outcomes of their actions in accordance with their missions, but also safeguarding the security of humans in all countries.[31] The best policy recommendations presented in the students' papers become elements of the foreign policymaking role-play to be described below.

In the fourth stage, students are required to present their work in a coherent policy paper. The ability to write policy papers is a skill often demanded by potential employers of students in public policy programs.[32] As the instructor of this course, I do not assign students with a single format for the policy paper. Students attending this course come from different countries and have different career expectations. Thus, I do my best to work out a special format for each student based on a particular student's personal experience, standards adopted in their home country, in the country where they have studied previously, or even in the country which is the focus of study of a particular group of students. For example, a student majoring in American politics in a Russian university might be interested in applying policy paper standards adopted in the US Department of State.[33] Importantly, students are expected to learn that the correct presentation of the findings is as important as its content from the viewpoint of the effect a paper might have.

One-day role-play

The role-play concluding the course requires students to cooperate. It intentionally organizes students' interactions in several rounds in such a way that students interact with more and more students in subsequent rounds. Vast literature applies game models to international studies.[34] Some professors of international studies have organized role-play simulations based on various game models in classrooms.[35] The role-play discussed in this chapter initially aimed at simply motivating students by means of having fun in the classroom, but the feedback participating students submitted in 2008–2019 provide evidence that the entire exercise in group-oriented foreign policy analysis helps students understand that foreign policy is not only about national interest and geopolitics, but also about human rights, the economy, public health, and protection of the environment, etc.

Making statements are at the core of the role-play, and students have an opportunity to practice this skill at the conclusion of the course by participating in a one-day intensive session. During the role-play, students promote their agendas based on the recommendations they created while simulating think tanks. Groups do not make foreign policy decisions, but states do. At the same time, groups can promote certain options that can become foreign policy decisions. Thus, when simulating think tanks, students often recommend to the groups that are their clients to promote certain foreign policy options. During the role-play, students are given the chance to promote those options themselves. Participants of the role-play promote certain policy options by participating in meetings with each other organized in several rounds. First, they participate in one-on-one meetings. Later, they participate in multilateral meetings.

Organization of students' interactions in multiple rounds is expected to encourage them to cooperate; such expectations are based on Axelrod's conclusion that repetition shifts equilibrium towards cooperation.[36] Asal suggests that students, who struggle with understanding of the neo-liberal institutionalist concept of cooperation, could participate in the Prisoner's Dilemma to the Nth Degree role-play, which is designed by pairing students off in the former rounds of the game, but inviting them into bigger groups during latter rounds of the game.[37] In the beginning of this role-play, each student receives a template of a feedback form to be returned to the instructor after the end of the role-play. In the feedback form, the student writes which students they met and when, which foreign policy option they promoted during that particular meeting, and what arguments they used to convince other students at the meeting that this particular foreign policy option should be accepted.

These feedback forms are important for three reasons. First, they help the students organize their own behavior during the role-play. Second, they assist the instructor in assessing personal performance of each player after the role-play is over: students gain points for actively participating in meetings. Third, my research demonstrating that the exercise in group-oriented foreign policy analysis has an impact on students' views (see results below) is based on the analysis of feedback forms students returned in 2008–2019. In particular, I analyzed the parts of the feedback forms in which the students reported on the arguments that they used to convince other students that a particular foreign policy option should be accepted (or rejected). Below I will refer to such students' explanations as "statements of rationale" or simply "rationale."

Assessment

Assessment of students' performance during the think tank simulation comes at the completion of each stage. At the completion of the first stage, students produce a four-page paper describing the activities of their clients most affected by the case and evaluating those activities as they were before the event constituting the case. At the completion of the second stage, students produce another four-page paper describing possible scenarios, including probability of each scenario (from most probable to least probable) and favorability of each scenario to the client (from very favorable to very unfavorable). At the completion of the third stage, students produce a third four-page paper, which describes the capabilities that their clients possess in order to make the more favorable scenario a more probable one, and a less favorable scenario a less probable one, as well as recommendations to the client. At the completion of the fourth stage, students compile the final policy paper, which presents the conclusions and the recommendations formulated in the preceding three stages in a concise form; the policy paper is usually no longer than 10 pages.

As presented in table 1, each student receives a maximum of 20 points per paper produced during each step of the think tank simulation. Of them, a maximum of seven points are given for accuracy in meeting the deadlines set for each stage at the beginning of the exercise. A maximum of thirteen points are given depending on the extent to which the content of a particular paper corresponds to the expectations described above. Students who have successfully compiled their policy papers are invited to earn additional points by participating in the foreign policymaking simulation role-play.

Table 1. Scoring Students' Performance During the Think Tank Simulation				
Portion of the Exercise		Content	Maximum Scores	
Introduction		Explaining Course Design to the Students	No Points		
Think tank simulation	Maximum number of points given for:		Accuracy in meeting deadline	Content	Total
	First Stage	Explain relationship between the case and the client	7	13	20
	Second Stage	Outline and evaluate scenarios	7	13	20
	Third Stage	Provide recommendations	7	13	20
	Fourth Stage	Compile the final policy paper	7	13	20
Role-play		Find compromise among different groups and make decision for the nation	Up to 20 more points		
Total			Up to 100 points		

Methods

The aim of the course was to help students develop their analytical skills as well as allow them to explore the benefits and shortcomings of a group-oriented approach to foreign policy analysis as contrasted to the nation-oriented approach. Content analysis of the feedback forms completed by the students during the one-day role-plays organized in 2008–2019 offers a way to measure the impact of the course. In particular, these qualitative data offer a way to determine if the students tend to justify their support or opposition to particular foreign policy choices by referring to geopolitical and power politics reasons (which is typical for nation-oriented approach to foreign policy analysis) or for other reasons, primarily of economic, humanitarian and soft security nature (which is typical for group-oriented foreign policy analysis). As such, I analyzed students' statements provided in feedback forms from the role-play in which they explain why they support or oppose particular foreign policy options.

A nation-oriented approach to foreign policy analysis dominates the teaching of international relations in Russia. Accordingly, geopolitics as a discipline is compulsory in many public policy programs taught in Russian universities.[38] Ethnographic research at a Russian major university has shown that geopolitics classes foster discursive practices among students that "fashion the great power discourse with objectivity."[39] One might expect that Russian students invited to participate in the role-play described above would actively employ geopolitical considerations in their statements of rationale. One might expect that Russian students perceive international relations as a game played by great powers driven by geopolitical considerations on the global level and having only minor if any impact on the local level.

The course in group-oriented foreign policy analysis is expected to help students understand that foreign policy is also about other considerations, not only those of the national interest, power or geopolitics. The course is expected to help students understand the "connection between global and local issues," which is critical for civic engagement in international affairs.[40] The course is expected to help students understand that international relations also influence local communities by means of having implications for the economy and soft security, human rights and the environment, etc. Thus, the null hypothesis of this study is that students' statements of rationale will contain few if any reports mentioning geopolitics or national interests as a common rationale for supporting or opposing particular foreign policy options.

H0: students having participated in the course in group-oriented foreign policy analysis rarely justify their choices by geopolitics or national interest.

To test the hypothesis, I have analyzed the feedback forms from the role-play administered in 2008–2019. Through those twelve years, 170 students participated in the role-play. All of them majored in international relations; this course is compulsory to all students majoring in international relations of the particular graduate program where the exercise in group-oriented foreign policy analysis is part of the curriculum. Thus, one cannot say that the only students who registered for the course were those who believed from the outset that foreign policy is more about economics and soft security, human rights and the environment, and less about geopolitics and national interest. Altogether, the 170 students participated in 670 one-to-one and multilateral meetings; feedback forms submitted by the students after completion of the role-play contained 532 unique statements of rationale.

I applied qualitative content analysis to those statements of rationale. Constructivist critique of geopolitics, the scholarship investigating how politicians and political scientists construct ideas about places, and how those ideas influence policy choices among the elite and notions of places and politics among ordinary people provided the method of identifying "geopolitical consider-ations" among the statements of rationale.[41] I coded as "geopolitical considerations" every state-ment of rationale that mentioned the nation as whole and that did not mention particular national, subnational, or transnational groups as beneficiaries of acceptance or rejection of particular for-eign policy options. To be coded as "geopolitical considerations", a statement should include such words as "nation" or "national", "country", or the name of the country expected to make the foreign policy decision in question or to benefit from it.

In a similar manner, statements that included such words as "geopolitics" or "geopolitical," "interests" (unless the statement employs the word "interests" in the meaning of interests of par-ticular national, subnational or transnational group), or "power" were coded as "geopolitical con-siderations". Lastly, statements that included such combinations of words as "international arena," "international system," or "place in the world" were coded as "geopolitical considerations." For ex-ample, I coded the statement of rationale claiming that Russia should lift the ban to sell weapons of a certain type to Iran, because "Iran is Russia's geopolitical ally in the Middle East," as a statement containing "geopolitical considerations".

Besides statements containing "geopolitical considerations," I distinguished seven other types of statements of rationale. First, some statements were coded as "economic considerations." Statements of this type contain such keywords as "profit" and "profitable," "benefit" and "benefi-cial," "economic" and "economy," "revenue" and "loss," "market" and "sector," "trade" and "invest-ment," "producer" and "consumer,", "good" and "service," "spending" and "expenditure," "growth" and "crisis," "demand" and "supply," "price" and "commodity." For example, I coded the statement of rationale claiming that Russia should lift the ban to sell weapons of certain types to Iran, because "it can increase the revenues of enterprises of Russian military industrial complex suffering of Western sanctions" as a statement containing "economic considerations."

Second, some statements were coded as "humanitarian considerations." Statements of this type contained such keywords as "human" and "people," "citizens" and "society," "crime" and "cor-ruption," "right" and "individual," "minority" and "oppressed," "kill" and "murder." For example, I coded the statement of rationale claiming that Russia should not lift the ban to sell weapons of cer-tain type to Iran, because "Iran might use those weapons against its own citizens," as a statement containing "humanitarian considerations."

Third, some statements were coded as "soft security considerations." I included students' con-cerns about terrorism, trafficking, human trafficking, weapons transfer, and illegal migration into statements containing "soft security considerations," because those are the main soft security con-cerns facing Europe in the early 21st century.[42] Statements of this type contained such keywords as "peace" and "peaceful," "security" and "safety," "terrorism" and "proliferation," "trafficking" and "migration," "stability" and "cooperation," "instability" and "destabilization," "cooperative" and "trust," "reliability" and "reliable," "arms" and "weapons." For example, I coded the statement of rationale claiming that Russia should not lift the ban to sell weapons of certain type to Iran, because "it might destabilize the situation in the Middle East" as a statement containing "soft security considerations."

Fourth, some statements were coded "environmental considerations." I included students' concerns about climate change into statements containing "environmental considerations." Statements of this type contain such keywords as "climate" and "warming," "environment" and "environmental," "water" and "air," "endangered" and "extinction," "nature" and "forests." For example, I coded the statement of rationale claiming that Russia should resume cooperation with Iran in the field of nuclear energy, because "thus Iran will burn less coal, and it will be good to the environment" as a statement containing "environmental considerations."

Fifth, some statements were coded "considerations of law and justice." Statements of this type contained such keywords as "law" and "legal," "illegal" and "lawless," "justice" and "just," "fair" and "fairness," as well as mentions of any of the principles of international law recognized in the Charter of the United Nations. For example, I coded the statement of rationale claiming that Russia should not help Belarus President Alexander Lukashenko to remain in power, because "it will be considered interference in domestic affairs of Belarus" as a statement containing "considerations of law and justice."

Sixth, there were statements considering "timing of action considerations." Statements of this type contained such keywords as "time" and "temporal," "early" and "late," For example, I coded the statement of rationale claiming that Russia should not help Belarus President Alexander Lukashenko to remain in power, because "it is not the right time to do so" as a statement containing "timing of action considerations."

Seventh, some statements were categorized as "low expectations considerations." I included statements of rationale claiming that a particular foreign policy option should be rejected for the reason that it might not help in achieving the expected outcome. Statements of this type contain verbs in the future tense and such keywords as "results" and "outcomes," "expectations" and "expected," "achieve" and "achievement." For example, I coded the statement of rationale claiming that Russia should not help Belarus President Alexander Lukashenko to remain in power, because "it will not help achieving expected results" (without indicating what the "expected results" were) as a statement containing "low expectations considerations."

The data allowed me to measure differences between students by country of previous education and by gender. Studies mentioned above identified the tendency to resort to geopolitical reasoning as a characteristic of Russian students in particular. In 2008 through 2019, 41 graduate students, who had graduated from a foreign university, completed the exercise in group-oriented foreign policy analysis alongside 129 students who earned their bachelor's degree from a Russian university. One could expect that students from the latter group would resort to geopolitical reasoning more often than students from the former group, which is the first hypothesis of this study.

H1: students with Russian backgrounds resort to geopolitical reasoning more often than students with foreign backgrounds.

Thirty-three years ago, women were "hidden from international relations" , but since then gender has been considered more seriously in international studies.[43] In the late 20th century, many people considered it "conventional wisdom" that "women [were] more peace-loving or more pacific than men."[44] Reviewing the volume edited by McKelvey, Carpenter noted that it was equally popular among "feminist peace activists and conservatives keen on keeping women out of the military" to believe that "women are naturally less aggressive than men."[45] One might extrapolate from this prejudice that stereotypical men are expected to turn to geopolitical reasoning in foreign policymaking more often in order to justify their natural aggressiveness, while stereotypical women are expected to more often turn to humanitarian reasoning.

The belief is purely anecdotal and needs to be subjected to more rigorous examination. To do so, I hypothesized that male students tend to resort more often to geopolitical reasoning than female students. In 2008–2019, 107 female students participated in the role-play alongside 63 male students. The gender imbalance of participants of the role-play correlates with the general imbalance among students majoring in international relations in Russian universities. At the moment, imbalance in favor of men is characteristic of Russian foreign service. Only one-third of the employees of the Russian Foreign Ministry are women, only two of 130 Russian ambassadors are women, and only two out of 42 heads of departments (sub-divisions of the Russian Foreign Ministry are called "departments"; the "departments" are similar to bureaus in the US Department of State) are women.[46] However, that is expected to change in the long run, because two-thirds of students in Russian universities majoring in international relations are women. This study identified students' gender as it appears in university records; student records in Russian universities allow identifying students as male or female only, no other gender identification applies. Students were not asked to identify their gender at any time before, during, or after having completed the exercise.

H2: male students resort to geopolitical reasoning more often than female students.

Data on the students, who have participated in the role-plays in 2008–2019, is presented in table 2 below.

Table 2. Student Participants in One-Day Role Play, 2008–2019		
	By Gender:	
	Male	63
	Female	107
	By country of previous degree:	
	Russia	129
	Other	41
Total:		170

Data on the meetings that the students held during the role-plays analyzed as explained above, is presented in table 3 (see next page).

Results

Although previous research identified the tendency to resort to geopolitical reasoning as characteristic of Russian students at public policy graduate programs, results of the qualitative content analysis failed to falsify the null-hypothesis outlined above. Students who completed the course in group-oriented foreign policy analysis tended not to resort to geopolitical reasoning. As seen in table 3, only 34 out of 532 unique statements analyzed were coded as "geopolitical reasoning". The majority of the statements of rationale (165 statements) contained "economic considerations." There were almost equal numbers of statements containing "humanitarian considerations" (114 cases) and those containing "soft security considerations" (113 cases).

Sixty-one statements of rationale contained "environmental considerations." The high number of such statements justifies distinguishing them into a separate category instead of including them in "soft security considerations." Only a few statements of rationale fell into the categories of "law and justice considerations," "timing of action considerations," and "low expectations considerations" (44 cases for all the three categories). Thus, one might conclude that participants in the group-oriented foreign policy analysis course tend to resort to geopolitical reasoning far less when discussing international relations than to reason in economic, humanitarian, soft security and environmental terms.

These results do not necessarily indicate that participation in the group-oriented foreign

Table 3. Meetings Held During Role-Plays, 2008–2019									
Statement of rationale contained... / Type of meeting		... economic consider-ations	... human-itarian consider-ations	... soft security consider-ations	... envi-ronmental consider-ations	... geo-po-litical consider-ations	... law and justice con-siderations	... timing of action consider-ations	... low expec-tations consider-ations	Total for each type of meeting
One-on-one meetings, total, of them*:		118 (30.6%)	87 (22.5%)	85 (22%)	43 (11.1%)	25 (6.5%)	11 (2.8%)	10 (2.6%)	7 (1.8%)	386
By gender	2 males	25 (27.5%)	21 (23.1%)	20 (22%)	9 (9.9%)	7 (7.7%)	4 (4.4%)	3 (3.3%)	2 (2.2%)	91
	2 females	55 (31.6%)	41 (23.6%)	39 (22.4%)	18 (10.3%)	7 (4%)	6 (3.4%)	5 (2.9%)	3 (1.7%)	174
	male and female	38 (31.4%)	25 (20.7%)	26 (21.5%)	16 (13.2%)	11 (9.1%)	1 (0.8%)	2 (1.7%)	2 (1.7%)	121
chi-squared=**		.424	.253	.063	.845	2.746	1.200	.833	.000	
By country of previ-ous degree	2 Russian degrees	64 (30.3%)	47 (22.3%)	47 (22.3%)	23 (10.9%)	13 (6.2%)	7 (3.3%)	6 (2.8)	4 (1.9%)	211
	2 foreign degrees	24 (30%)	18 (22.5%)	16 (20%)	10 (12.5%)	7 (8.8%)	3 (3.8%)	1 (1.3%)	1 (1.3%)	80
	Russian and a foreign degree	30 (31.6%)	22 (23.2%)	22 (23.2%)	10 (10.5%)	5 (5.3%)	1 (1.1%)	3 (3.2%)	2 (2.1%)	95
chi-squared=**		.050	.068	.069	.244	1.038	2.000	1.200	.000	
Meetings in larger groups		47 (32.2%)	27 (18.5%)	28 (19.2%)	18 (12.3%)	9 (6.2%)	6 (4.1%)	6 (4.1%)	5 (3.4%)	146
Total		165 (31%)	114 (21.4%)	113 (21.2%)	61 (11.5%)	34 (6.4%)	17 (3.2%)	16 (3%)	12 (2.3%)	532

Total number of statements of rationale returned N=532

* * "2 males" refers to one-on-one meetings between 2 male students. "2 females" refers to one-on-one meetings between 2 female students. "Male and female" refers to one-on-one meetings between 2 students, of whom one is male, and another is female. "2 Russian degrees" refers to one-on-one meetings between 2 students both having degrees from a Russian university in the background. "2 foreign degrees" refers to one-on-one meetings between 2 students both having degrees from a non-Russian university in the background. "Russian and a foreign degree" refers to one-on-one meetings between two students, of whom one has a degree from a Russian university, and another has a degree from a non-Russian university in the background.

** p<0.2 (statistical significance of 80%) when chi-squared>1.061; p<0.1 (statistical significance of 90%) when chi-squared>1.886; p<0.05 (statistical significance of 95%) when chi-squared>2.920.

policy analysis exercise was the decisive factor that discouraged the students from resorting to geopolitical reasoning. The study did not involve a control group, so the generalizability of the results is limited. It is possible that other factors contributed to these results, such as the learning environment of the particular university in which the study was made. Still, it is noteworthy that a majority of students did not provide a geopolitical rationale.

The results of the study did not fully support either hypotheses H1 nor hypothesis H2. None of the results were 95%-significant statistically. Contrary to what one might assume based on the findings discussed in previous literature, students with a degree from a Russian university made statements containing "geopolitical considerations" less often than students with a degree from a foreign university (6.2% to 8.8%). However, statistical significance of that result was less than 80%; thus, it would be wrong to claim that students with a previous degree from a Russian university tend to resort to geopolitical reasoning less often than their peers with a previous degree from a foreign university.

Background education influences students' behavior to a statistically significant extent (over 90% significance) only in relation to their tendency to make statements containing "law and justice considerations." Such statements were made at seven one-one-one meetings between two students with previous degrees from Russian universities and at three one-on-one meetings between two students with previous degrees from foreign universities, which correlates with the overall distribution of such types of one-on-one meetings in the population. However, two students, one of whom held a previous degree from a Russian university, and another that held a previous degree from a foreign university, made a statement containing "law and justice considerations" only once at their one-on-one meeting. Thus, one cannot conclude that these results demonstrate correlation between country of previous degree and propensity to make statements containing "law and justice considerations" due to the insufficient number of cases in this category.

At first glance, results in Table 3 point to correlations between gender and propensity to resort to geopolitical reasoning. Statistical significance of this correlation was the highest among all results, over 90% (although less than 95%). At first glance, male students talk more about geopolitics, while female students talk more about other matters. While 7.7% of one-on-one meetings of two male students produced a statement of rationale containing "geopolitical reasoning," only 4.0% of one-on-one meetings of two female students ended in a similar manner. However, when a male student met with a female student, they made even more statements of rationale containing "geopolitical reasoning" (9.1.%) compared to meetings of two male students. Thus, one may regard this result as coincidence rather than proof that male students are more prone to resort to geopolitical reasoning when contrasted to female students. To conclude, although the students who have participated in the exercise through the 12 years are a very diverse group, the group is coherent in its tendency to rarely resort to geopolitical reasoning.

Discussion

Civic engagement in international relations means caring about processes taking place far from one's home. In its broadest meaning, civic engagement "refers to an individual's activities... that focus on developing knowledge about the community and its political system, identifying or seeking solutions to community problems, pursuing goals to benefit the community, and participating in constructive deliberation among community members about the community's political system and community issues, problems, or solutions."[47] In particular, civic engagement in international relations involves developing knowledge about places far away from one's home, identifying problems arising there and seeking solutions to these problems, pursuing goals to benefit people beyond one's self, one's community and even one's country, and participating in public and private debates on international relations. Thus, teaching civic engagement in international relations involves helping students develop the skill to think beyond oneself, one's community and even one's country. The course in group-oriented foreign policy analysis discussed in this chapter is yet another means to help students develop that skill.

Instructors at public policy programs seeking to teach civic engagement in international relations face multiple challenges. First, it is challenging to encourage students "to learn that politics does not stop at the water's edge."[48] Like many other people, students and alumni of public policy programs are more eager to engage in fixing the wrongs in their local community and in their country, and they are less eager to engage in fixing wrongs in faraway lands. Students attending the course in group-oriented foreign policy analysis are not exceptional in this respect; among their statements of rationale containing economic considerations one can find justifications of opposition to a particular foreign policy option by means of suggesting that the foreign policy option, if taken, would be a "waste of money" that could be "spent at home" instead. This course seeks to overcome such attitudes by assigning students to investigate the relevance of faraway events on local authorities, companies, and nonprofits. Having recognized the relevance of faraway events on their activities, these authorities, companies, and nonprofits transform into interest groups seeking to influence foreign policy of their country.

Second, it is challenging to encourage students to put oneself in someone else's shoes. Foreign policy decisions made in faraway places make an impact on situations in one's home, but decision-makers in faraway places do not necessarily cause the impact intentionally. In most cases, they make those decisions under pressure from domestic groups in their lands. The course in group-oriented foreign policy analysis aims to help students understand that. Globalization of education makes the task easier, because it increases the share of international students in the group. When I assign international students to write policy papers for the purposes of (simulating) foreign policymaking in Russia, they learn to think beyond themselves, their communities and even their countries. By cooperating with international students, Russian students learn that too. The one-day role-play described above, which encourages students to cooperate among themselves and beyond the line between Russian and international students, helps both Russian and international students better understand that the latter are not "added as an isolated group," but that they can achieve the desired outcome only if they work together.[49]

Third, it is power politics and geopolitical considerations that prevent students from actively engaging in foreign policymaking because of fear of harming the balance of power. For example, although historians have no proof that he used the phrase, conservative writers repeatedly have accused US President Franklin D. Roosevelt of having referred to President Anastacio Somoza Garcia of Nicaragua as "our" (i.e., pro-American) bad guy.[50] They claim that the phrase was meant to justify American non-engagement with human rights in Nicaragua in times of Somoza's reign because of power politics and geopolitical considerations. In a similar manner, contemporary Russian students of public policy programs prefer not to engage with human rights in Belarus, not because they have no compassion for the people of Belarus, but because they think that current Belarus President Alexander Lukashenko is "our (i.e., pro-Russian) bad guy." The course in group-oriented foreign policy analysis enhances students' ability to think critically as citizens, including their ability to think critically about geopolitical and power politics considerations.

This chapter finds that although Russian students (and also international students in Russian universities) employ geopolitical considerations, those considerations are not dominant. Previous research has found that it is not only the content of courses, but also the disciplinary practices adopted in some Russian universities that "fashion the great power discourse with objectivity."[51] Thus, if a public policy program wants to encourage its students to actively engage in foreign policymaking instead of justifying non-engagement by geopolitical considerations, the program is expected to change both the content of courses and the learning environment of teaching. The course in group-oriented foreign policy analysis provides an alternative to the traditional way of teaching international relations in Russia both in terms of content and of learning environment. Today, realism–the theory that focuses on the place of a country in the international system as the key factor in its foreign policymaking and that gives only minor considerations to a country's domestic politics–dominates both research and teaching of international relations in Russia.[52]

The course in group-oriented foreign policy analysis invites students to explore other levels of foreign policymaking than just the international level as advised by realism. Thus, it helps students better understand "how examining international phenomena at the systemic, state, or international level of analysis can yield different understandings or perspectives."[53] By inviting the students to formulate recommendations for a particular sub-state group influenced by an international event during the think tank simulation, the exercise encourages them to move from the international to the sub-state level of analysis. By inviting the students to promote the interests of the sub-state group among other such groups during the role-play, the exercise encourages them to move from the sub-state to the state level of analysis. As a result, students develop their knowledge of how events in faraway lands can make an impact on a particular community and of how changes within a particular community can make an impact internationally.

The course helps the students to connect human security issues often regarded as soft security issues by realist scholars to hard security issues. Kaldor and Marcoux advise considering human security issues as concerns of "hard security policy, aimed at protecting individuals from political violence."[54] Following their advice, I distinguished between students' statements of rationale containing "humanitarian considerations" and those containing "soft security considerations" in the study presented above. The results of content-analysis demonstrated that students see the difference between soft security and human security clearly, and that they explain their decisions by humanitarian considerations almost as often as by soft security considerations.

The pedagogical elements of the course, the think tank simulation and one-day role-play in particular, also provide an alternative to traditional teaching of international relations. Shaw noted that in-class simulations and role-plays allow educators to present course materials in an alternative way, to promote student interaction and input, to promote student curiosity and creativity and to simply have fun.[55] At the same time, use of a role-play in the classroom as such does not automatically help students to think critically of geopolitical and power politics considerations. If students simulate bilateral negotiations during the role-play, and especially if Russian students sit across the table from international students, such role-play settings discourage the students from thinking of geopolitics and power politics critically. If, as described in the role-play presented in this chapter, each student regardless of country of previous education has to find the time for a meeting with each other student during a one-day role-play, it creates a learning environment in which geopolitical considerations leave space for economic, humanitarian and other types of considerations.

Conclusions

Globalization and privatization of public policy graduate education have influenced teaching of international relations, including teaching civic engagement in foreign policymaking, in multiple and sometimes contradictory ways. These two tendencies influencing universities all over the world have resulted in the rise of the share of international students at public policy programs, as well as of the share of students, who enroll in such programs without the desire to join civil, foreign or military service upon graduation. As a result, the demand for courses teaching foreign policy from the national perspective declined, and the demand for courses teaching international relations from the perspective of companies, nonprofits and other interest groups increased. To respond to such demand, I introduced the course in group-oriented foreign policy analysis discussed in this chapter. The course introduces a group-oriented approach to foreign policymaking in contrast to a nation-oriented approach, thus developing the students' analytical skills and abilities to think critically of great power relations, national interests and geopolitics.

Research outlined above demonstrates that students of the group-oriented foreign policy analysis course tend to apply power politics and geopolitical reasoning when discussing international affairs significantly less often than previous literature suggested. They tend to perceive foreign policy not as an activity made by and influencing only a bounded circle of chosen ones, but as an activity influencing most people and thus requiring engagement of more people in its making. That fact encourages students themselves to engage in foreign policymaking. It is not the course in group-oriented foreign policy analysis alone that helps the students transcend boundaries preventing their active engagement in foreign policymaking. Privatization and globalization of public policy graduate education also contribute to transcending such boundaries. Privatization helps transcend the boundary between students seeking careers in public, foreign and military service and those seeking careers in private companies and nonprofits. Globalization helps transcend the boundary between Russian and international students, thus allowing the former to better understand the impact that Russian foreign policy makes on faraway lands and communities.

Globalization and privatization of public policy graduate education take place in Russia too. These two tendencies help students at Russian universities transcend boundaries between locals and foreigners, between the public and the private sector, and between foreign policymakers and ordinary people. Transcending those boundaries encourages civic engagement in foreign policymaking. What prevents civic engagement is the widespread belief that there is a "right" foreign policy predetermined by outer factors, such as geopolitics, and that anybody willing to engage in foreign policymaking has to understand which foreign policy course is "right" and to act accordingly. This belief complicates public dialogue on foreign policy issues, because each party in the dialogue tends to perceive its proposed foreign policy option as "right" and the option proposed by the other party as "wrong". Transcending the opposition between "right" and "wrong" foreign policy options will facilitate public dialogue on foreign policy issues and thus civic engagement in foreign policymaking. The course in group-oriented foreign policy analysis discussed in this chapter presents another means to transcend the opposition.

Endnotes

1. B. Welling Hall, "Teaching Students about Congress and Civic Engagement," *PS: Political Science and Politics* 44, no. 4 (2011): 871–81. http://doi.org/10.1017/S1049096511001508.

2. Jeffrey S. Lantis, "Ethics and Foreign Policy: Structured Debates for the International Studies Classroom," *International Studies Perspectives* 5, no. 2 (2004): 117–33. https://doi.org/10.1111/j.1528-3577.2004.00162.x.

3. Andrew Moravcsik, "Taking Preferences Seriously: A Liberal Theory of International Politics," *International Organization* 51, no. 4 (1997): 524. https://doi.org/10.1162/002081897550447

4. John Zaller, *The Nature and Origins of Mass Opinion* (Cambridge, UK: Cambridge University Press, 1992).

5. Peter Feaver and Christopher Gelpi, *Choosing Your Battles: American Civil-Military Relations and the Use of Force* (Princeton, NJ: Princeton University Press, 2004).

6. David L. Weimer and Aidan R. Vining, *Policy Analysis: Concepts and Practice, 6th edition* (New York: Routledge, 2017), 37.

7. Marie Danziger, "Policy Analysis Postmodernized: Some Political and Pedagogical Ramifications," *Policy Studies Journal* 23, no. 3 (1995): 435–450. https://doi.org/10.1111/j.1541-0072.1995.tb00522.x.

8. Randy S. Clemons and Mark K. McBeth, *Public Policy Praxis: A Case Approach to Understanding Policy and Analysis, 4th edition* (New York: Routledge, 2020), 212.

9. Erik A. Devereux and Dan Durning, "Going Global? International Activities by US Schools of Public Policy and Management to Transform Public Affairs Education," *Journal of Public Affairs Education* 7, no. 4 (2001): 241–260. https://doi.org/10.1080/15236803.2001.12023521.

10. Stuart Sim, *Addicted to Profit: Reclaiming Our Lives from the Free Market* (Edinburg, UK: Edinburg University Press, 2012), 129.

11. See: https://www.princeton.edu/news/2008/12/10/understanding-robertson-v-princeton-settlement.

12. Michael Toscano, "Honoring the Past, Securing the Present," *Academic Questions* 28, no. 1 (2015): 106–110. https://doi.org/10.1007/s12129-015-9480-5.

13. Viatcheslav Morozov, *Russia's Postcolonial Identity: A Subaltern Empire in a Eurocentric World* (London: Palgrave Macmillan, 2015).

14. Sirke Mäkinen, "In Search of the Status of an Educational Great Power? Analysis of Russia's Educational Diplomacy Discourse," *Problems of Post-Communism* 63, no. 3 (2016): 183–196. https://doi.org/10.1080/10758216.2016.1172489.

15. Timothy M. Frye, "Capture or Exchange? Business Lobbying in Russia," *Europe-Asia Studies* 54, no. 7 (2002): 1017–1036.

16. See: https://www.levada.ru; Levada Centre, "Doverie politikam i prezidentskoe golosovanie [Trust in Politicians and

Presidential Rating – in Russian]," *Levada Centre's Website*, 3 September 2020. https://www.levada.ru/2020/09/03/doverie-politikam-i-prezidentskoe-golosovanie/

17. Katherine Kuhns, "Globalization of Knowledge and Its Impact on Higher Education Reform in Transitioning States: The Case of Russia," PhD diss., Stanford University, 2011. https://purl.stanford.edu/rc358bn5948.

18. Victor Asal, "Playing Games with International Relations," *International Studies Perspectives* 6, no. 3 (2005): 359–373. https://doi.org/10.1111/j.1528-3577.2005.00213.x.

19. Timothy Wedig, "Getting the Most from Classroom Simulations: Strategies for Maximizing Learning Outcomes," *PS: Political Science & Politics* 43, no. 3 (2010): 547–555. https://doi.org/10.1017/S104909651000079X; Rebecca A. Glazier, "Running Simulations without Ruining Your Life: Simple Ways to Incorporate Active Learning into Your Teaching," *Journal of Political Science Education* 7, no. 4 (2011): 375–393. https://doi.org/10.1080/15512169.2011.615188

20. Stephen M. Shellman and Kürşad Turan, "Do Simulations Enhance Student Learning? An Empirical Evaluation of an IR Simulations," *Journal of Political Science Education* 2, no. 1 (2006): 19–32. https://doi.org/10.1080/15512160500484168; Archie W. Simpson and Bernd Kaussler, "IR Teaching Reloaded: Using Films and Simulations in the Teaching of International Relations," *International Studies Perspectives* 10, no. 4 (2009): 413–427. https://doi.org/10.1111/j.1528-3585.2009.00386.x

21. Tatiana A. Romanova and Nikolay N. Gudalov, "Role-Play Simulation of Negotiations between the EU and the Eurasian Economic Union: Teaching While Enhancing a Transnational Dialogue," *Journal of Contemporary European Research* 15, no. 4 (2019): 410–424. https://doi.org/10.30950/jcer.v15i4.1093

22. Geffrey L. Bernstein, "Cultivating Civic Competence: Simulation and Skill-Building in an Introductory Government Class," *Journal of Political Science Education* 4, no. 1 (2008): 1–20. https://doi.org/10.1080/15512160701815996; Brandon M. Boylan, Mary F. Ehrlander, and Troy J. Bouffard, "A Multimethod and Interdisciplinary Approach to Educating Postsecondary Students on Arctic Challenges and Governance," *Journal of Political Science Education*, published online (2019). https://doi.org/10.1080/15512169.2019.1628766

23. Joseph S. Nye Jr., "Bridging the Gap between Theory and Policy," *Political Psychology* 29, no. 4 (2008): 593–603. https://doi.org/10.1111/j.1467-9221.2008.00651.x.

24. David Schodt, "Using Cases to Teach Analytical Skills," in *The New International Studies Classroom: Active Teaching, Active Learning*, eds. Jeffrey S. Lantis, Lynn M. Luzma, and John Boehrer (Boulder, CO: Lynne Rienner, 2000), 65.

25. Helga Pülzl and Doris Wydra, "The Evaluation of the Implementation of Sustainability Norms: An Expertise for Experts or Citizens?" in *Creating a Sustainable Social Ecology Using Technology-driven Solutions*, ed. Elias. G. Carayannis, 32–45 (Hershey, PA: IGI Global, 2013). https://doi.org/10.4018/978-1-4666-3613-2.ch003

26. Harold S. Becker, "Scenarios: A Tool of Growing Importance to Policy Analysis in Government and Industry," *Technological Forecasting and Social Change* 23, no. 2 (1983): 95–120.

27. Jeffrey Hart, "Three Approaches to the Measurement of Power in International Relations," *International Organization* 30, no. 2 (1976): 289–305. https://doi.org/10.1017/S0020818300018282

28. Iver B. Neumann and Erik F. Øverland, "International Relations and Policy Planning: The Method of Perspectivist Scenario Building," *International Studies Perspectives* 5, no. 3 (2004): 258–77. https://doi.org/10.1111/j.1528-3577.2004.00173.x

29. John Newhouse, "Diplomacy, Inc.: The Influence of Lobbies on US Foreign Policy," *Foreign Affairs* 88, no. 3 (2009): 73–92. https://www.jstor.org/stable/20699564.

30. Diane Stone, "Non-Governmental Policy Transfer: The Strategies of Independent Policy Institutes," *Governance* 13, no. 1 (2000): 45–70. https://doi.org/10.1111/0952-1895.00123

31. Karen Lund Petersen, "Terrorism: When Risk Meets Security," *Alternatives: Global, Local, Political* 33, no. 2 (2008): 173–190. https://doi.org/10.1177%2F030437540803300204

32. Bettina Trueb, "Teaching Students to Write for Real Life: Policy Paper Writing in the Classroom," *PS: Political Science & Politics* 46, no. 1 (2013): 137–141. https://doi.org/10.1017/S1049096512001333

33. Bidisha Biswas and Agnieszka Paczynka, "Teaching Theory, Writing Policy: Integrating Lessons from the Foggy Bottom into the Classroom," *PS: Political Science & Politics* 48, no. 1 (2014): 157–161. https://doi.org/10.1017/S1049096514001707X

34. Classical works include: Glenn H Snyder, "'Prisoner's Dilemma' and 'Chicken' Models in International Politics," *International Studies Quarterly* 15, no. 1 (1971): 66–103. https://doi.org/10.2307/3013593; Robert L. Jervis, "Realism, Game Theory and Cooperation," *World Politics* 40, no. 3 (1988): 317–349. https://doi.org/10.2307/2010216; and William L. Reisinger, "2x2 Games of Commitment in World Politics," *International Studies Quarterly* 33, no. 1 (1989): 111–118. https://doi.org/10.2307/2600496

35. Matthew Mulford and Jeffery Berejikian, "Behavioral Decision Theory and the Gains Debate in International Politics," *Political Studies* 50, no. 2 (2002): 209–229. https://doi.org/10.1111%2F1467-9248.00367

36. Robert Axelrod, *The Evolution of Cooperation* (New York: Basic Books, 1984).

37. Victor Asal, "Playing Games with International Relations."

38. Sirke Mäkinen, "Geopolitics Teaching and Worldviews: Making the Future Generation in Russia," *Geopolitics* 19, no. 1 (2014): 86–108. https://doi.org/10.1080/14650045.2013.847430

39. Martin Müller, "Education and the Formation of Geopolitical Subjects." *International Political Sociology* 5, no. 1 (2011): 1–17. https://doi.org/10.1111/j.1749-5687.2011.00117.x

40. Alison Rios Millet McCartney and Sivan Chaban, "Bringing the World Home: Effectively Connecting Civic Engagement and International Relations," in *Teaching Civic Engagement: From Student to Active Citizen*, eds. Alison Rios Millet McCartney, Elizabeth A. Bennion, and Dick Simpson, 259–277 (Washington: American Political Science Association, 2013).

41. Gearóid ÓTuathail and John Agnew, "Geopolitics and Discourse: Practical Geopolitics Reasoning in American Foreign Policy," *Political Geography* 11, no. 2 (1992): 190–204. https://doi.org/10.1016/0962-6298(92)90048-X

42. Julian Lindley-French, "The Revolution in Security Affairs: Hard and Soft Security Dynamics in the 21st Century," in *Soft Security Threats and Europe*, eds. Anne Aldis and Graeme P. Herd (London and New York: Routledge. 2005), 1–16.

43. Fred Halliday, "Hidden from International Relations: Women and the International Arena," *Millenium: Journal of International Studies* 17, no. 3 (1988): 419–428. https://doi.org/10.1177%2F03058298880170030701

44. Lise Togeby, "The Gender Gap in Foreign Policy Attitudes," *Journal of Peace Research* 31, no. 4 (1994): 375–392. https://doi.org/10.1177%2F0022343394031004002

45. Tara McKelvey, ed., *One of the Guys: Women as Aggressors and Torturers* (New York: Basic Books, 2007); Charli Carpenter, "What to Read on Gender and Foreign Policy," *Foreign Affairs*, 22 December 2009, https://www.foreignaffairs.com/articles/2009-12-22/what-read-gender-and-foreign-policy

46. Kadri Liik, "The Last of the Offended: Russia's First Post-Putin Diplomats," *Policy Brief of the European Council on Foreign Relations*, 19 November 2019, https://ecfr.eu/publication/the_last_of_the_offended_russias_first_post_putin_diplomats/

47. Alison Rios Millet McCartney, "Teaching Civic Engagement: Debates, Definitions, Benefits and Challenges," in *Teaching Civic Engagement: From Student to Active Citizen*, eds. Alison Rios Millet McCartney, Elizabeth A. Bennion, and Dick Simpson, 9–20 (Washington, DC: American Political Science Association, 2013).

48. McCartney and Chaban, "Bringing the World Home: Effectively Connecting Civic Engagement and International Relations."

49. Hans De Wit, "Internationalization of Higher Education: Nine Microconcepts," *International Higher Education* 64 (Summer 2011): 6–7.

50. Charles Krauthammer, "The Immaculate Intervention," *Time*, 26 July 1993, http://content.time.com/time/subscriber/article/0,33009,978947,00.html; Charles Krauthammer, "Dictatorships and Double Standards," *CNN*, 16 September 2002, https://edition.cnn.com/2002/ALLPOLITICS/09/16/time.standards/index.html

51. Martin Müller, "Education and the Formation of Geopolitical Subjects."

52. Olga Krasnyak, *National Styles in Science, Diplomacy, and Science Diplomacy* (Leiden and Boston, MA: Brill, 2019), 23.

53. Victor Asal, Inga Miller, and Charmaine N. Willis, "System, State, or Individual: Gaming Levels of Analysis in International Relations," *International Studies Perspectives* 21, no. 1 (2020): 97–107. https://doi.org/10.1093/isp/ekz018

54. Mary Kaldor and Sonia Marcoux, "La Sécurité Humaine: Un Concept Pertinent?" *Politique Étrangère* 71, no. 4 (2006): 901–914. https://www.jstor.org/stable/42716375

55. Carolyn M. Shaw, "Using Role-Play Scenarios in the IR Classroom: An Examination of Exercises on Peacekeeping Operations and Foreign Policy Decision Making," *International Studies Perspectives* 5, no. 1 (2004): 1–22. https://doi.org/10.1111/j.1528-3577.2004.00151.x

9

Youth Civic Engagement in Developing Countries: Lessons from Belize and Guatemala

Gerardo Berthin

Freedom House

How can youth in developing countries enhance knowledge and capacity for civic engagement? What role can international development assistance play in youth civic learning and capacity development? This chapter weighs in on youth civic engagement from the angle of "social audit," a participatory tool and approach. It does so by examining two specific initiatives designed and implemented by the author in Belize and Guatemala with support from international development organizations and local universities. In addition to describing the social audit approach, including the strategy and methodology, this chapter also provides initial evidence showing that introducing university students in developing countries to civic engagement, even with short and focused workshops that combine a mix of pedagogical approaches, has a potential to lay down a foundation to increase civic engagement and facilitates the development of basic knowledge and skills. Although international development assistance can play a crucial role in supporting youth civic engagement in developing countries, the effort will remain incomplete unless changes on youth attitude and behavior are systematically measured and effort is sustained through continuous civic engagement support by local stakeholders, including universities.

KEYWORDS: Social Audit; Youth Civic Engagement; Accountability; Integrity; Developing Countries.

Introduction

Over the past three decades, many developing countries[1] have transitioned from authoritarian to more democratic and decentralized forms of government. Multilateral and bilateral international development organizations, like the United Nations Development Program (UNDP) and the United States Agency for International Development (USAID), seized the opportunity with this transition and provided support to developing countries. The premise was that such support would help developing countries establish and consolidate more inclusive and accountable democracies. While this support for democratic governance targeted a variety of stakeholders in developing countries, including the governments and civil society organizations, one group received special attention: youth.

Support for youth civic engagement by international development organizations has been a growing component of international cooperation in recent decades, with increasing attention to election participation, political parties' membership and leadership, and skills development in areas such as public integrity and accountability. These efforts are well-guided in that building and strengthening a culture of democratic governance, and such key pillars as integrity and accountability, must start with young people. The theory of change framing this argument is that if young people acquire knowledge and capacity surrounding accountability and integrity, democratic governance would benefit as would civic engagement. Accountability in democratic governance simply means being responsible for decisions made and actions taken on the use of public resources to provide services that meet the needs of constituents.[2] Integrity in governance on the other hand, is associated with consistent and coherent behavior based on ethical principles and values.[3] Both generate trust and strengthen democratic governance.

This chapter seeks to inform our understanding of youth civic engagement in developing countries by exploring two specific initiatives designed and implemented by the author in Belize and Guatemala with support from international development organizations and local universities, and determining how these efforts contributed to the youths' ability to embrace civic life. This chapter will approach civic engagement from the angle of social audit, asking whether youth in Belize and Guatemala enhanced their knowledge and capacity for civic engagement as a result of a social audit workshop, and drawing some initial lessons on the role of international development assistance in support of youth civic learning in emerging democracies.

In addition to describing the social audit approach, including the strategy and methodology, this chapter provides initial evidence showing that introducing university students in developing countries to civic engagement, even with short and focused workshops that combine a mix of pedagogical approaches, has the potential to lay down a foundation to increase civic engagement and facilitate the development of basic knowledge and skills. International development assistance can play a crucial role in supporting youth civic engagement in developing countries, but the effort will remain incomplete unless changes on youth attitude and behavior are systematically measured, and the effort is sustained through broad and continuous civic engagement support by local stakeholders, including universities.

Theoretical Framework for Promoting Youth Civic Engagement through Social Audit

Youth civic engagement is a pivotal issue within global academic and policy debates on democratic governance. As argued elsewhere, elections are an important component of democratic governance, but are not the only measure of it.[4] The existence of effective and accountable public institutions to meet citizen needs and civic engagement are also important components of democratic governance. Longstanding evidence shows the benefits of citizen and youth participation in governance with regards to greater policy effectiveness, accountability, and political legitimacy.[5] Civic engagement refers to the ways in which citizens participate in the life of a community in order to improve conditions for others or to help shape the community's future.[6] As such, civic engagement involves being active and participating in public affairs and focusing on collective interests. Civic engagement is a process that in practice requires knowledge, skills, and motivation. Therefore, civic education and capacity building can be a means to develop knowledge about political processes, governmental institutions, and power relationships, as well as skills for civic engagement.[7]

Young people are an important stakeholder group in developing countries for achieving, strengthening, and sustaining civic engagement. Despite making up more than half of the population in many developing countries, young people (ages 18–30)[8] often find themselves marginalized from mainstream politics and policy decision-making. They struggle to gain the respect of public officials combined with limited educational and economic opportunities. This can leave young people both idle and frustrated with the status quo. As a result, they may be drawn into conflict, crime, and violence, or simply opt to not vote or participate in elections and retreat from civic engagement. This retreat is often reinforced by the lack of civic education.

Multilateral and bilateral international organizations, like the UNDP and USAID, recognize in their respective international development strategies that young people are both individuals transitioning through life's developmental stages and potential actors in the development of their countries and communities.[9] Youth engagement is considered both an end in itself for democratic governance, but also a means to achieve other cross-cutting objectives, like the Sustainable Development Goals (SDGs).[10] While there is no blueprint or single approach to support youth civic engagement, multilateral and bilateral international development organizations focus on integrated approaches that encourage collaboration between government and citizens. General common features of youth civic engagement support and assistance include understanding citizen rights, finding collaborative solutions to problems, and knowing pertinent legislation related to public resources management, access to information and public procurement.

Social audit is one approach to help promote and support civic engagement. A social audit is an accountability mechanism that enables citizens to organize and mobilize to evaluate or audit their government's performance, policy decisions and integrity.[11] There are three main reasons why social audit has the potential to be an important means of civic engagement.[12] First, it can enhance accountability by highlighting integrity risks in democratic governance, including corrupt practices, abuse of power, and fraudulence.[13] Second, social audit can help assess the quality and/or effectiveness of key essential public services, resources management, and the extent to which citizens' demands are being articulated in the public policy and budget cycle processes. Finally, social audit can increase civic participation and engagement by enhancing the ability of citizens to move beyond mere protest and/or apathy, toward an interactive process that helps to engage with bureaucrats and decision-makers in a more informed, organized, constructive, and systematic manner, thus increasing the chances of effective civic engagement.[14]

Social audit, however, is not a magic formula to promote and sustain civic engagement, as evidence shows that not all social audit efforts lead to successful and sustainable outcomes.[15] Nonetheless, conducting a social audit exercise can unlock new opportunities for elected and public officials and their constituencies to have a conversation on public issues of common policy interests. The key element in social audits is the policy dialogue that is established between citizens and decision-makers either by monitoring budget expenses, organizing hearings for participatory policy design, evaluating a policy initiative, and overseeing public works. The ability to engage in a social audit process requires some key prerequisites, such as: knowledge, skills, and motivation to engage policymakers; knowing how to operate within existing normative and policy frameworks; and capacity to develop and implement actions and strategies.[16]

The literature relevant to developing countries suggests that the capacity to conduct effective social audits is affected by three main enabling conditions. First, the political will and responsiveness of public administrations to build an interaction with citizens. Second, having an appropriate normative framework that guarantees the right to public information, citizen participation and accountability. And third, citizens and constituencies who possess the knowledge, skills, and tools to engage with decision-makers.[17]

Young people in developing countries have not been necessarily exposed on a large scale to the potential of social audit to support civic engagement and participation in public policy processes. The social audit workshop described below offers an opportunity to examine how the social audit approach contributes to the promotion of civic engagement among youth university students. In this next section, the social audit approach is explained as well as the method for comparing the impact of their administration in two different settings.

The Method: The Social Audit Approach and Workshops[18]

The social audit "Workshop for Young Leaders" was designed in September 2011 in the context of the Transparency and Accountability in Local Governments (TRAALOG)[19] regional initiative supported by the UNDP and other donors.[20] The TRAALOG was a regional technical assistance platform hosted at the UNDP Regional Service Center for Latin America and the Caribbean.[21]

The workshop was designed to engage youth and youth organizations in emerging democracies to enhance their management, leadership and practical skills for social audit in different areas, including civic education skill sets, and conceptual and technical skills for the design, implementation, communication, and evaluation of social audit processes. The next sections highlight the main goals, content, and components of the social audit workshop.

Goals of the Social Audit Workshop

The strategic goal of the social audit workshop was to influence youth towards civic engagement in their respective communities by exposing them to a method, new knowledge, and collaborative skills. The social audit workshop was conceived as an opportunity for participants to acquire new knowledge into their existing interests and frameworks of understanding.[22] The premise was that as participants became more knowledgeable about social audit and civic issues, all other things being equal, they would more likely participate in civic engagement matters.[23]

For most participants, the workshop would provide the first opportunity to be exposed to issues related to accountability, integrity, and civic engagement. As such, the workshop aimed at strengthening young participants with enhanced knowledge and capacities to understand the context and purpose of civic engagement. Specifically, the workshops were meant to:

- Promote deliberation, consensus building, and collective action;

- Encourage social audit action as a tool to empower youth, promote their participation in the policy-making process, and uphold public integrity; and

- Utilize as a reference and resource *A Practical Guide to Social Audit*.[24]

Key Pedagogical Elements of the Workshop

To accomplish the goals, the social audit workshop:

- Blended theoretical and practical elements by employing an active participatory methodology involving traditional knowledge facilitation, exchange of concepts, tools, exercises, good practices, and experiences;

- Combined and articulated different pedagogical sources, including brief presentations, discussions and debates, the case-study method, group and ludic dynamics, survey analysis and deliberation; and

- Provided a practical opportunity for hands-on experience in identifying community issues that would merit a social audit after the workshop.

Workshop Strategy

The social audit workshop focused on youth not only because of their potential as sources of energy and innovation, but also to bring young people to realize how they could be part of a civic engagement effort and be changemakers. In addition, the workshop was grounded on the larger context of developing countries that were at a stage of consolidating their democratic governance amidst static or declining rates of civic participation among youth, the largest demographic cohort. Like in many other parts of the world, in Latin America and the Caribbean, young people are generally perceived as the source of many policy challenges, such as crime, violence, illegal drugs, high youth unemployment rates, immigration, and early pregnancy among girls. The workshop contextualized these challenges in each country and helped young participants identify how they could be productive, constructive, and contributing members of their communities and their emerging democracies.

Between 2011 and 2018, 17 workshops were conducted with over 350 participants from 20 countries; 15 were national-level workshops, and two were regional workshops.[25] Only three of the 15 national workshops involved local universities, and two are featured in this chapter. Workshop participants were youth between the ages of 18–30, who were selected to participate by the local partners working with UNDP and USAID in democratic governance initiatives. On average, workshops had 40 participants. In general, workshop participants were youth involved in some form of community voluntary activity, who belonged to a local civic organization and were part of advocacy groups or political party affiliates. To ensure the workshop had a diverse and representative group of participants, youth were selected from different communities and localities, racial backgrounds, genders, and academic sectors.

The workshops were designed to be implemented in two to four full days, and according to the length, the agenda could be adjusted accordingly. Typically, the workshops' learning format involved two experienced facilitators with political science background and experience in teaching and training. Facilitators deliver brief presentations to introduce the modules of the workshop, but most importantly, facilitators manage the discussions with and among participants, and promote constructive dialogue. Facilitators need to have the ability to foster workshop engagement, deal with complexity and complex issues, mediate and simplify discussions, and promote high-quality deliberation. The two facilitators are normally assisted by two local assistant facilitators, who help with the logistics and set-up of the various groups and ludic activities that occur throughout the workshop, as well as with providing input on the context where workshops were being held.[26]

Workshop Structure

Although there were some adaptations, nearly every workshop consisted of the following modules.

Module 1

Participants are introduced to the principles of democratic governance which underpin social audit and civic engagement. The main questions addressed in Module 1 include: How is democratic governance defined in the context of your country? What are the main opportunities and challenges of democratic governance in your country? What is the role of government and citizens in your country? Through two exercises, one individual and one in pairs, participants are asked to reflect on "what is" and "what should be" democratic governance. Facilitators encourage and manage a plenary discussion with participants around these questions. By navigating the complexities and nuances of democratic governance systems, participants learn to recognize realities and opportunities in their country's political issues, policies, and systems.

Module 2

Participants learn about the social audit approach and how it can promote civic engagement. The focus is placed on competencies and performance, as well as the roles, rights and obligations of governments and civil society in order to fully promote civic engagement, public integrity and accountability. The main questions addressed in Module 2 include: What is accountability and integrity? What are the consequences of weak accountable governance? What normative frameworks that promote accountability and citizen participation are in place in your country? Participants discuss the role of social audit and civic engagement in promoting accountable governance, the rationale for its application and analyze the types of stakeholders which should be involved in social audit and the requisite skills required by social auditors. Through an exercise in groups of three, participants debate what behaviors of public officials in their country are red flags in terms of accountability, and what role might there be for citizen oversight.

Module 3

Participants are introduced to concepts related to transparent and accountable government management and what is required from both elected authorities and public servants in terms of accountable behavior. It emphasizes public integrity concepts, and tools available to detect, prevent and sanction, acts, practices, and behaviors outside expected accountability and integrity frameworks (e.g., corrupt practices). Participants are divided in groups of seven, and through an outdoor and timed exercise, they are given a map to find eight "treasures," collect them and organize them according to the instructions. The "treasures" are four corrupt practices sanctioned in their country and their respective definitions. Whichever group finds the treasures and matches the corrupt practice and definition first gets a symbolic prize. This occurs typically at the end of a full day and the exercise provides an opportunity to reflect on the competitive nature of the activity, the impact on collaboration and integrity, and lessons for civic engagement.

Module 4

Participants address the issue of civic engagement tools to be applied through social audit. Participants are introduced to actual samples of social audit from their country and other countries across the world such as Kenya, India, and Vietnam, and obtain a better understanding that social audits can occur at any stage of the public policy cycle. The module also equips participants with practical tips about access, veracity, and analysis of public information. Participants are teamed up in groups of six and undertake two exercises; one that promotes discussion on the pros and cons of using social media in a social audit process and as a civic engagement tool; and a second one that exposes participants to the challenges they may face in obtaining access to public information.

Module 5

Participants engage in a discussion of how the results of a social audit can be used and communicated to other community stakeholders as a means of contributing to policy dialogue and change. The module also provides participants with a practical framework for planning a social audit and with an opportunity to prepare a draft action plan for a social audit to be conducted after the workshop.

Measuring the Effectiveness of the Workshop

The workshop is defined by its sequential structure as well as its focus on interactivity among participants and between participants and facilitators. Moreover, the workshop is pedagogically designed in a way that exercises start from individual analysis and gradually evolve into a collective work of two, three, four, and more than five participants, respectively. This helps participants experience the challenges of translating individual into collective work, as well as negotiating and finding consensus in the analysis and debates. The workshop agenda is intensive and designed to be lively and interactive to achieve a careful balance between meeting the learning objectives on the one hand, and engaging the participants to build leadership, management, and teamwork skills through practical exercises, on the other hand. The blended methodology and approach of the workshop involves engaging the participants with short and theory-based presentations to enhance knowledge of key concepts and promote critical thinking, as well as plenary and group discussions and debates (see sample two-day workshop agenda).

The overarching social audit workshop learning goal is for participants to be able to develop and strengthen their knowledge and skills to influence youth towards civic engagement in their respective communities by exposing them to a method (social audit), acquire new knowledge, and collaborative skills. In some cases, the workshop agenda can be tailored to specific requests by the funding international development organization or the partners, such as to include participants as co-facilitators of the workshops, or by administering an anonymous pre-workshop Knowledge, Attitude and Behavior (KAB) survey which requests participants' views on a variety of topics related to civic engagement and democratic governance (see themes of KAB survey).[27]

To measure how well the workshops met their intended goals, we utilized an evaluation that is completed by participants at the end of the workshop. The evaluation is designed with seven structured questions, of which four are qualitative and open-ended in nature, and three require a Likert-type scale response (see sample evaluation). The four qualitative open-ended questions ask participants to: (1) highlight which specific aspects of the workshop best contributed to their understanding of democratic governance, social auditing, and civic engagement; (2) list if they had learned something new or saw something from a new angle, as a result of the workshop; (3) specify what other themes or topics did they think should be incorporated in future workshops; and (4) provide additional specific observations or comments about their experience in the workshop. The three closed-ended questions use a 1-5 scale to rate three areas: (1) whether several aspects of the workshop, such as the objectives were met, the content and themes covered were relevant, the workshop methodology was appropriate, the facilitators' presentations were helpful, materials useful, and if the workshop met their overall expectations; (2) the outcomes, related to whether the workshop improved their knowledge of social audit and civic engagement, had motivated them to act as soon as possible, and had given them ideas of how to apply what they learned; and (3) the logistical aspects of the workshop in terms of the overall organization, facilitators, rooms, materials, and catering. Participants are given as much time as needed to complete the evaluations. All evaluations are anonymous and returned to facilitators through a random collection process managed by co-facilitators. Responses are recorded and coded in an excel datasheet.

In addition to completing the evaluation, participants are encouraged to share their learning expectations about the workshop in plenary at the beginning of the workshop and as part of the introductory portion of the workshop. Moreover, at the end of the workshop, participants are asked to share in plenary their learning takeaways as part of the concluding module at the end of the workshop. If and when the KAB survey is applied as part of the workshop, the data collected can serve as an additional tool to help establish a participant's baseline of knowledge and attitudes, and in the future monitor changes and further influence participants' attitudes towards civic engagement. For this chapter, we will use the qualitative and quantitative data from the evaluations as evidence to measure whether the learning objectives were met, as well as the comments from participants in the evaluations to show evidence of initial impact.

Analysis and Findings from the Belize and Guatemala Social Audit Workshops

To further weigh in on how the social audit approach contributed to the promotion of civic engagement for integrity and accountability, this section will showcase and compare two youth social audit workshop experiences implemented in Belize and Guatemala. We used the most-different method for case selection. Of the 15 national social audit workshops, these two cases were the most different in terms of independent variables, such as country history, context, culture, level of development, and governance systems. Also, the social audit experience in each country had different international development organizations as sponsors and responded to different overall strategies. However, the fidelity of the core social audit workshop methodology remained relatively standard in both cases. These two cases were selected to compare the social audit workshop experience, outcome, and results for participants.[28] For each case, we will offer a brief description of what took place in these workshops, report the evidence of initial impact, and analyze the key findings.

Social Audit Workshop for Young Belizean Leaders

Under the sponsorship of the TRAALOG regional initiative mentioned above, the UNDP Belize Country Office partnered with the University of Belize (UB),[29] a national and the largest higher education system in Belize, to offer a "Workshop on Social Audit for Young Belizean Leaders." The two-day training workshop was held October 25–26, 2013, at the Central Farm Campus of UB in the Cayo District of Belize. Through a memorandum of agreement between UNDP Belize and UB, 34 students from five of the six districts of Belize participated.[30] Participants of the workshops averaged 23.2 years of age, all were first-time university students, and the majority of participants were women. They were selected by the UB under the following criteria: active student at UB; juniors and seniors in bachelors programs across disciplines (education and arts, management and social sciences, nursing and social work, science, environmental and technology); leadership roles in the university (student council) or in social organizations in their communities outside the university; and the same number of male and female participants to ensure parity. Outside their university life, most of the participants had an affiliation to civic and voluntary community organizations. The idea was to ensure participants were influential among their peers and thus had the potential to advance and promote civic engagement through social audit across the country.

Against the background, the workshop sought to: (1) introduce young leaders to the social audit approach as a tool to promote civic engagement; and (2) strengthen knowledge to design and implement a social audit process. At the request of the UB, the KAB survey was not applied to participants in this workshop. One unique feature of the workshop in Belize was the selection, at the request of UB, for nine students to play dual roles as participants and co-facilitators. Their main role was to assist the lead facilitators with the management of group discussions and exercises.

Through participants' interventions during the workshop and evaluations at the end of the workshop, it became clear that they had not been exposed on a large scale and in a systematic way to civic engagement approaches prior to these workshops. The workshop exposed young leaders for the first time to several features of social audit, which could help boost their civic engagement skills. For example: understanding concepts such as governance, public integrity, accountability, and corruption; and collecting and accessing public policy evidence, and the use of technology as a tool to access information.

Although students did not complete the KAB, they did conduct an evaluation at the conclusion. Based on the evaluations, the workshop appears to have acted as a potential catalyst for planning youth civic actions on important policy issues in Belize. The evidence from the evaluation shows that 100% of participants either "strongly agreed" (83%) or "agreed" (17%) that the workshop contributed to improving their knowledge and interest in civic engagement. Moreover, 93% of participants "strongly agreed" (70%) and "agreed" (23%) that the workshop motivated them to act as soon as possible, while 96% of participants felt the workshops gave them new ideas.

Qualitative feedback from the participants in their evaluations indicates that the co-facilitation was valuable to the participants as it afforded the opportunity to strengthen communication and leadership skills, as well as it encouraged a more open, relaxed, and culturally relevant dialogue with the youth participants who responded well to the prompts from their peers. As figure 1 below demonstrates, by the end of the workshop, the participants felt sufficiently empowered to

Figure 1. Selected Comments Made By Participants in the Evaluation

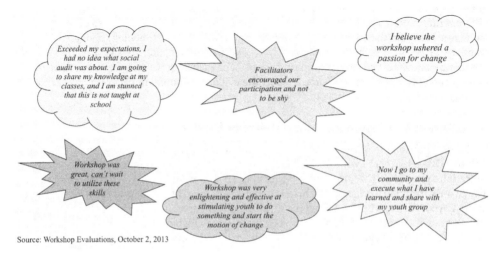

Source: Workshop Evaluations, October 2, 2013

begin taking the first collective steps towards operationalizing youth social audit in Belize. This included the formation of the Belize Youth Social Audit Network (BYSAN) and the establishment of a sub-committee to draft Rules of Engagement for BYSAN; the establishment of a social media (Facebook) presence and a group email list to facilitate communication across the network and to engage other young people across the country. Initial proposals for some potential social audit initiatives included, social audit of university issues (budget), and a social audit of expenditures of community service clubs.[31]

Moreover, prior to the start of the workshop, participants were asked to discuss in plenary their expectations for the workshop. As one participant observed, "the workshop will be a space for skill-building and leadership for civic engagement." Another participant remarked that she was expecting the workshop to "empower her to train others in social auditing." After the workshop, the evaluations highlighted that the workshop was an enabler for future action. One participant noted in the evaluation, "I have increased my knowledge on issues like integrity, accountability, transparency, civic engagement, and social audit planning." Another participant added, the workshop was successful at "giving me a sense of empowerment to bring about change."

Guatemala: University Youth Leadership Workshops for Social Audit

The international development community identified increased citizen participation as a critical element in improving democratic governance and human development in Guatemala.[32] Under the sponsorship of the USAID funded Urban Municipal Governance (UMG) project, five social audit workshops were conducted in 2018, targeting university students. The UMG Project (2017–2022) is managed by the USAID Guatemala Democracy and Governance Office. The project provides municipal governments with technical assistance to achieve transparent and participatory planning, improve financial management, and effective service delivery implementation.

The UMG project also provides technical assistance and capacity building to local civil society groups (youth clubs, citizen's associations, community organizations, and university student organizations) to monitor public policies, service, and expenditure.[33] In that context, five social audit workshops of two days each were conducted targeting students from San Carlos[34] (public) and Rafael Landivar[35] (private) universities. In addition to promoting the development of technical and practical skills for social audit processes, the workshops aimed at encouraging the design of civic engagement strategies through social auditing. Altogether one hundred and ninety-nine (199) mostly undergraduate students from social science careers (social workers, law, public administration, sociology, political science) participated in the workshops, with an average of forty (40) participants per workshop (table 1 shows a summary of the dates and locations of the workshops). The participants were carefully selected by the respective universities and based on guidance and advice from the UMG project's technical personnel. Some workshop participants had previous academic and practical experience on social audit, but the majority were new to the topic of social audit and were selected by the university programs based on their potential to advance a social auditing process in Guatemala, their own individual interest in the subject, and their interest in being part of a civic movement in favor of more youth participation in local and national policy affairs. As can be seen in table 1, participants of the workshops averaged 24.3 years of age. Most of all workshop participants were women.

The workshop had four immediate goals for participants: (1) gain new knowledge, and (2) new skills, (3) develop a draft social audit strategy, and (4) respond anonymously to the KAB survey. According to the pre-workshop KAB survey results and the workshop evaluations at the conclusion, for most of the participants, "social audit" was a new concept and tool. Nonetheless, even for those participants who had previous training and practical experience on social audit, the workshop provided new and expanded knowledge. One key result from the KAB survey revealed that the participants of all five workshops were active in distinct types of community activities, including religious, sports, and university. For example, 25% of respondents indicated that they participated in university activities, another 24% that they were involved in religious activities, and nearly 16%

Table 1. Profile of Social Audit Workshops Participants (by Gender and Average Age)				
Location-University-Date & Participants Home City	Men Numbers & (%)	Women Numbers & (%)	Total (numbers)	Average Age (years)
1. Antigua – Rafael Landivar University (August 24–26, 2018) Participants came from Antigua, Escuintla and Chimaltenango.	9 (19%)	39 (81%)	48	26.6
2. Chiquimula – CUNORI/San Carlos University (August 27–28, 2018) Participants came from Chiquimula, Esquipulas, and Jocotán.	19 (54%)	16 (46%)	35	23.7
3. Zacapa – Rafael Landivar University (August 31–September 1, 2018) Participants came from Colomba, Coatepeque, and Malacatán.	4 (8%)	45 (92%)	49	25.2
4. Quetzaltenango I – CUSAM/San Carlos University (September 4–5, 2018)	21 (54%)	18 (46%)	39	20.8
5. Quetzaltenango II – Rafael Landivar University (September 7–8, 2018) Participants came from Colomba and Coatepeque	2 (7%)	26 (93%)	28	25.2
Grand Total	55 (28%)	144 (72%)	199	24.3
Source: Participants' KAB Survey Results				

volunteered and/or participated in community organizations. An average of 47% of all workshop participants recognized more individualistic motives (e.g., career advancement, professional networking) for getting involved in community activity, while on average, 19% hoped to become activists in order to generate collective benefits for their communities.

The analysis of the KAB survey results detected two dimensions of civic engagement among workshop participants: one linked specifically to the political and policy aspects of participation (political parties and demands for accountability and transparency) and the other linked to a broader platform of community and social activities. The overwhelming majority (82%) of all the workshop participants said they were involved or had been involved in helping their communities and universities collecting money for social causes, and advocating for environmental issues. Only 13% of all workshop participants indicated they participated or had participated in political parties and were or had been involved in advocating for accountability and transparency in public policy processes.

As it was important to identify the motives for civic engagement, it was also of great importance to probe the reasons for which workshop participants did not engage more actively in their respective communities. As shown in figure 2, the majority (40%) of the surveyed participants believed that "there were more opportunities elsewhere to influence change," and 23% reinforced this perception in terms of not believing in civic engagement to attain genuine impact. In part, that response reflected the relatively low level of knowledge on critical issues related to social audit and civic engagement. As shown in figure 3, before the workshop participants were asked to assess themselves on a scale of 1-4 (low to high) with respect to their own level of knowledge in different topics related to civic engagement. The results of the KAB survey point to an overall relatively low (52%) and medium (40%) knowledge ratings. Only 8% of all workshop participants self-evaluated their knowledge as relatively high in all areas. The highest overall areas of knowledge according to the results of the self-evaluation were citizen engagement, public policies and democratic gover-

Figure 2. Why Do You Think That Young People of Your Age Don't Participate in Civic Activities?

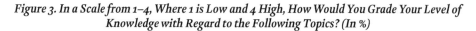

DK/NR
2%

There are other important
things that demand less effort
and give more benefits
14%

I do not believe in civic
engagement as a means to
make impact
23%

Lack of time
6%

Lack of resources
15%

The opportunities to influence
change are elsewhere
40%

N=199

Figure 3. In a Scale from 1–4, Where 1 is Low and 4 High, How Would You Grade Your Level of Knowledge with Regard to the Following Topics? (In %)

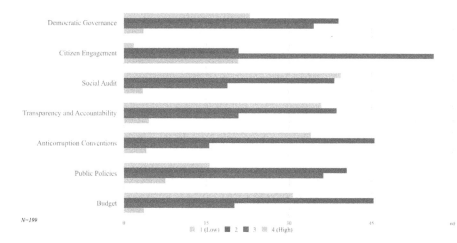

Democratic Governance

Citizen Engagement

Social Audit

Transparency and Accountability

Anticorruption Conventions

Public Policies

Budget

N=199

0   15   30   45   60

1 (Low)   2   3   4 (High)

nance. Workshop participants self-evaluated their level of knowledge in social audit, accountability, anti corruption conventions and budget as relatively low.

The evidence from all the evaluations at the end of the workshops shows that the workshop appears to have had a positive impact on knowledge and motivation for civic engagement. The aggregated evaluation evidence from the five workshops in Guatemala shows that nearly 100% of participants either "strongly agreed" (88%) or "agreed" (11%) that the workshop contributed to improve their knowledge and interest in civic engagement. Moreover, 97% of participants "strongly agreed" (67%) and "agreed" (30%) that the workshop motivated them to act as soon as possible, while 98% of participants felt the workshops gave them new ideas for civic engagement. In that regard, the workshops contributed to the acquisition of new knowledge, it strengthened and expanded existing knowledge, and sought to make connections to broader concepts of democratic governance, public integrity, accountability, and participation.

A recurring theme in the evaluations was that the workshop enabled participants to better understand civic engagement and that they felt empowered to promote change (table 2). The knowledge and skills with which participants were equipped as a result of the workshops enabled them to prepare draft social audit strategies, which were considered initial ideas that needed to be refined before implementation with potential support of the UMG project and/or other similar projects in Guatemala. Altogether 20 draft social audit strategies were produced (4 per workshop). As was the case of Belize, the Guatemala experience also suggests that, exposing youth to approaches, like social audit, and key concepts like accountability and integrity, can enhance knowledge and capacity for civic engagement and youth could be in a better position to positively affect future accountability and integrity efforts.

Table 2. Feedback Provided by Workshop Participants in Their Evaluations

"This workshop has been of utmost importance for my development and to acquire new knowledge, which I was honestly completely unaware." – Antigua Workshop Participant

"I now know what is, how it can be applied and what is the purpose of social audit." – Chiquimula Workshop Participant

"Now I understand better what social audit is, to better manage tools, to work in teams, and to be always observant." – Zacapa Workshop Participant

"I understand the importance of legal frameworks, which complemented my current knowledge, but most importantly I now know how to influence actions for change." – Quetzaltenango Workshop Participant

---

Post Workshop Analysis and Lessons

A key drawback for both cases was not following up with complementary activities, such as a post-workshop survey in the case of Guatemala to better understand and measure the impact the workshop had in increasing participants' knowledge and changed attitudes towards civic participation. Although international development organizations have promoted broad and targeted efforts in support of youth civic engagement in developing countries, comparative evidence of impact on behavior and civic engagement remains limited and mixed. Without data on behavior and attitude change, there is no strong evidence supporting a causal relationship between the workshops and civic engagement.

As the Belize and Guatemala cases highlighted in this chapter suggest though, exposing youth to approaches, like social audit, can enhance knowledge and capacity for civic engagement and youth could be in a better position to positively affect much needed change efforts in emerging democracies. However, translating the knowledge and skills acquired in the workshops into sustainable assets for civic engagement requires additional elements, such as complementary training, mentorship and measuring behavioral change.

Based on the result of the evaluations, the workshops in Belize and Guatemala had a relatively positive effect on young participants with regards to improving knowledge, motivation to act, and ideas for future civic engagement action. However, the efforts were incomplete. Ideally, it would have helped to have additional funding, resources and partnerships from the international development organizations and other local stakeholders, including universities, for a pre- and post KAB survey taken the first and last days of the workshop and to follow up with periodic annual surveys to be able to observe and analyze participants' change in behaviors and attitudes about civic engagement. Similarly, the funding and strategies from international development organizations for the workshops did not consider the need for universities to institutionalize similar workshops as cross-cutting and interdisciplinary initiatives, or the design of a mid to long-term strategy with local stakeholders, such as universities, government and the private sector. Despite the acknowledged limitations, the two selected cases analyzed in this chapter provide initial evidence on the potential impact of social audit workshops on youth civic engagement in developing countries.

The social audit workshop experience in Belize and Guatemala have provided a basis for draw-ing some initial conclusions and key lessons that speak to the larger discussion about the role of international development organizations and universities in promoting youth civic engagement in developing countries, particularly those that are emerging democracies. A few practical lessons from both experiences are worth careful consideration:

The Role of International Development Organizations in Promoting Civic Engagement

Donor-supported civic engagement initiatives in developing countries, like most other initiatives supported by donors, by their nature are "short-term enterprises" with limited resources and timelines (averaging 3-5year projects). Thus, there is a need to connect with larger and more localized initiatives, including supporting universities and engaging the private sector and the government to obtain commitment for scaling-up efforts and multiply the effects beyond a two-day training workshop for youth on civic engagement. Unintended consequences of donor-supported activities like lack of follow-up strategies to monitor youth behavior change, lack of further accompaniment and monitoring, and not measuring civic attitudes before and after the workshop, can be major drawbacks for engaged and enthusiastic youth looking for an outlet or next step in which to apply their newly acquired civic engagement knowledge and skills.

Partnerships

Short-term interventions (projects) can make important and positive differences, especially in reaching and engaging youth, but only if used strategically. Government, the private sector, foundations, and universities are also key stakeholders to promote youth civic engagement. While young people need to play a central role in addressing policy issues that affect them, they cannot tackle the multitude of challenges alone. Youth in developing countries face daunting challenges in an increasingly complex and ever-changing democratic context. Demographic data for young people in developing countries like Belize and Guatemala, indicate a high probability for unemployment, low self-esteem, and risky social behavior, particularly among marginalized groups. Acquiring civic competencies and skills, while critical, is not sufficient to better their lives and build their communities. They also need to be provided with the opportunities to do so. Active partnerships are critical.

Multiplying Effect

Learning civic engagement should have both a theoretical and practical basis. As an initial step, the social audit workshops focused on soft skills. It should be followed-up with complementary efforts to develop additional knowledge about emerging democratic systems. Moreover, universities can systematically incorporate social audit and other civic engagement tools into core academic program components. Expanding the circle of learning by targeting university faculty and staff, can strengthen the enabling environment and reinforce multi-stakeholder initiatives as essential for scaling up and sustaining efforts.

Measuring Change and Impact

Most impact evaluations of efforts to engage and support youth under democratic governance programs funded by international development organizations show mixed results. The focus is on the project or intervention (workshops), not so much on measuring the change of behavior and attitudes among the youth because of interventions. While the evaluations by participants amount to initial evidence that the workshop had an effect on knowledge, motivation and ideas, how youth changed their behavior on civic engagement as a result of the workshop remained unmeasured. A deeper cross-systemic research could provide more evidence of causality. This would be a component that international development organizations and universities should seriously consider in future efforts.

Conclusion

The Belize and Guatemala experiences offer a certain level of optimism about youth civic engagement in emerging democracies. It is vital to acknowledge, however, that every developing country and context is unique and ever-changing. These experiences are not a blue-print or a recipe, but rather a reference to contribute to the ongoing understanding of the complex dynamics of youth civic engagement. Opportunities like the social audit workshops or other approaches that support and promote youth civic engagement cannot take place in a vacuum. Youth issues are cross-cutting and the most successful are often those that work across sectors and interact and are integrated with broader development policies.

While the social audit workshops were an extracurricular initiative for university students, the two cases in this chapter demonstrated their potential effect on youth civic engagement. Young university students in emerging democracies need more spaces where their voice matters, where they have opportunities to have their consciousness raised, and where they can participate in collective learning, engagement, and exchange of information and knowledge. Institutionalizing civic learning and literacy in universities could be a cornerstone for emerging democracies to increase civic, democratic, and political knowledge and engagement among youth. In times of democratic governance backsliding around the world, it is vital for universities in developing countries to strengthen commitment to teaching civics and assume a more proactive, prominent and systematic role in supporting youth civic engagement efforts.

Endnotes

1. The concept of developing country is being used for analytical purposes and using as reference the World Economic Situation and Prospects classification of all countries of the world into three broad categories: developed, in transition, and developing, each one reflecting basic economic country conditions. See, United Nations, *World Economic Situation and Prospects (WESP) 2019* (New York: NY, United Nations, 2019).

2. For more analysis and information on accountability for democratic governance see, Organization for Economic Co-operation and Development (OECD), *Accountability and Democratic Governance: Orientations and Principles for Development* (Paris: OECD, 2014).

3. For more analysis and information on integrity for democratic governance see, L. W. J. C. Huberts, "Integrity: What it is and Why it is Important," Public Integrity 20 (2018): S18–S32.

4. Gerardo Berthin, "Democratic Governance and Corruption in Latin America," in *Latin American Democracy: Emerging Reality or Endangered Species?*, eds. Richard L. Millet, Jennifer S. Holmes, and Orlando J. Perez (New York, NY: Routledge, 2015).

5. See, for example, William Robert Avid, *Increasing Youth Participation in Accountability Mechanisms* (Birmingham, UK: GSDRC, University of Birmingham, 2015); Duncan Green, *Promoting Active Citizenship: What have we learned from 10 Case Studies of Oxfam's Work?* (Oxfam International, 2014); Pedro Dal Bó, Andrew Foster, and Louis Putterman, "Institutions and Behavior: Experimental Evidence on the Effects of Democracy," *American Economic Review* 100, no.5 (2010): 2205–2229; Herwing Cleuren and Patrício Silva, *Widening Democracy: Citizens and Participatory Schemes in Brazil and Chile* (Netherlands: Koninklijke, 2009); Peter Dahlgren, *Young Citizens and New Media: Learning for Democratic Participation* (New York: Routledge, 2007); Yves Zamboni, "Participatory Budgeting and Local Governance: An evidence-based evaluation of participatory budgeting experiences in Brazil," Working Paper, Bristol University, 2007; Brian Wampler, "Expanding Accountability through Participatory Institutions: Mayors, Citizens, and Budgeting in Three Brazilian Municipalities," *Latin American Politics and Society* 46, no. 2 (Summer 2004): 73-99; and Robert Putnam, Robert Leonardi, and Rafaella Nanetti, *Making Democracy Work: Civic Traditions in Modern Italy* (Princeton, NJ: Chichester: Princeton University Press, 1993).

6. Richard P. Adler and Judy Goggin, "What Do We Mean By 'Civic Engagement'?" *Journal of Transformative Education* 3, no. 3 (2005): 236–253.

7. Elizabeth C. Matto, Alison Rios Millett McCartney, Elizabeth A. Bennion, and Dick Simpson, eds., *Teaching Civic Engagement Across the Disciplines* (Washington DC: American Political Science Association, 2017).

8. Definitions of youth and young people vary widely across the world. Internationally accepted definitions include those categorizing people between 0–18 years old as children; those between 14–19 years old as adolescents; those between 15 and 24 years old as youth; and those up to 29 years old as young people. Other regional political and cultural definitions of youth may acknowledge those up to 35 years old as young people.

9. See, United States Agency for International Development (USAID), *Youth in Development Policy: Realizing the Demographic Opportunity* (Washington, DC: USAID, October 2012); and United Nations, *Youth Civic Engagement: World Youth Report* (New York: NY, United Nations/UNDESA, 2016).

10. United Nations, *Youth and the 2030 Agenda for Sustainable Development: World Youth Report* (New York: NY, United Nations/UNDESA, 2018).

11. For the purpose of this chapter, we are using the definition of public integrity sponsored by the Organization for Economic Cooperation and Development (OECD). Public integrity refers to the consistent alignment of, and adherence to, shared ethical values, principles and norms for upholding and prioritizing the public interest over private interests in the public sector. https://www.oecd.org/gov/ethics/recommendation-public-integrity/

12. Gerardo Berthin and Terri-Ann Gilbert-Roberts, "Explaining Youth Policy Participation in Latin America and the Caribbean Through Social Auditing Processes," *Revista Olhares Amazonicos, Boa Vista* 6, no. 2 (2018): 1186–1221; and Gerardo Berthin, *A Practical Guide to Social Audit as a Participatory Tool to Strengthen Democratic Governance, Transparency, and Accountability* (Panama: UNDP Regional Centre for Latin America and the Caribbean, 2011).

13. For a definition of horizontal and vertical accountability see, Derick W. Brinkerhoff and Anna Wetterberg, "Gauging the Effects of Social Accountability on Services, Governance, and Citizen Empowerment," *Public Administration Review* 76, no. 2 (2015): 274–286.

14. For specific cases and examples see, Berthin (2011); Anna Wetterberg, Derick W. Brinkerhoff, and Jana C. Hertz, eds. *Governance and Service Delivery Practical Applications of Social Accountability Across Sectors* (Research Triangle Park, NC: RTI International, 2016); Claudia Baez-Camargo, *Harnessing the Power of Communities against Corruption: A Framework for Contextualizing Social Accountability*, U4 Brief (Bergen, Norway: Michelsen Institute, 2018); and Racheld Nadelman, Ha Le, and Anjali Sah, "How Does the World Bank Build Citizen Engagement Commitments into Project Design? Results from Pilot Assessments in Mozambique, Myanmar, Nigeria, and Pakistan," IDS Working Paper 2019, no. 525 (April 2019).

15. See for example, Berthin (2011); UNICEF, *Making Social Audit work for Viet Nam: Key Findings and Lessons Learned from a Pilot of Four Social Audit Tools* (London: England, ODI, 2011); Kenyatta Mwawashe, "Youth as Drivers of Accountability: Conducting a Youth Social Audit," in *Young Citizens: Youth and Participatory Governance in Africa* (London: International Institute for Environment and Development, 2011); UNDP, "Local Governance and Accountability and Transparency: Exploring Opportunities for a Post 2015 Agenda" in *Report on the Fourth Meeting of the Anti-Corruption Community of Practice in Latin America and the Caribbean* (Panama: UNDP Regional Center, 2014); Jonathan Fox and Brendan Halloran, eds., *Connecting the Dots for Accountability: Civil Society Policy Monitoring and Advocacy Strategies*, report from international workshop, June 18–20, 2015 in Washington, DC (London: Transparency and Accountability Initiative, School of International Service-American University, International Budget Partnership, Government Watch, SIM Lab, 2016); and Jonathan Fox and Joy Aceron, *Doing Accountability Differently: A Proposal for the Vertical Integration of Civil Society Monitoring and Advocacy* (Bergen, Norway: U4 Anti-Corruption Resource Centre/Chr. Michelsen Institute, 2016).

16. Berthin (2011).

17. Berthin & Gilbert-Roberts (2018); Fox & Halloran (2016); and Berthin (2011).

18. The author acquired approval from the participating schools and the UNICEF Representative for this project.

19. The TRAALOG was a regional technical assistance platform hosted at the UNDP Regional Service Center for Latin America and the Caribbean. The regional center served as a hub for over 26 UNDP country offices in the region and was a source of knowledge, technical expertise, and resources provided by a group of international development experts and professionals. The Regional Center was organized around international development practice areas, such as democratic governance, poverty reduction, crisis prevention and recovery and environmental and sustainable development, gender and capacity development. As such, the TRAALOG was a mechanism of the Democratic Governance practice area designed to engage and interact with several UNDP Country Offices and their governmental and non-governmental counterparts in the region and identify and support integrity and accountability entry points and programming opportunities.

20. Both the TRAALOG Project and the Social Audit Workshops, were designed by Gerardo Berthin. The workshops were adapted to each country and/or regional contexts with the assistance of local UNDP program officers. The Caribbean workshops, including for Belize, were adapted and nourished with the assistance of Terri-Ann Gilbert-Roberts.

21. The UNDP Regional Center for Latin America and the Caribbean was located in the City of Knowledge-Panama, a place which once hosted a US Military base. Through Decree Law Nº 6 of 1998, the Government of Panama arranged the transfer of 120 hectares of the former US military base, Fort Clayton, to the City of Knowledge Foundation, the entity that manages the compound. The formal transfer of the base to Panama took place on 30 November 1999. The compound was handed over to the government of Panama and on the same day of the handover ceremony the government passed on to the Foundation the land and facilities that now make up City of Knowledge. In addition to the Latin America and Caribbean Regional Center in Panama, UNDP had similar regional hubs in Bangkok for the Asia and the Pacific region; in Bratislava for Eastern Europe; in Cairo for the Arab States region; in Dakar for West and Central Africa; and Johannesburg for East and Southern Africa.

22. Eric Gorham, "Service Learning and Political Knowledge," *Journal of Political Science Education* 1, no. 3 (2005):345–365; and William A. Galston, "Political Knowledge, Political Engagement and Civic Education," *Annual Review of Political Science* 4, no. 1 (2001): 217–34.

23. Galston (2001); and Kerry Ann Rockquemore and Regan Harwell Schaffer, "Toward a Theory of Engagement: A Cognitive Mapping of Service-Learning Experiences," *Michigan Journal of Community Service Learning* 7, no. 1 (2000): 14–25.

24. Gerardo Berthin, *A Practical Guide to Social Audit as a Participatory Tool to Strengthen Democratic Governance, Transparency, and Accountability* (Panama: UNDP Regional Centre for Latin America and the Caribbean, 2011).

25. Fifteen National workshops (made up of young leaders of the same nationality) were held in Belize, Colombia, Costa Rica, Dominican Republic, El Salvador, Guatemala (5), Jamaica (2), Mexico, Nicaragua, and Peru. The Caribbean regional workshop was held in Jamaica with participants from the following Caribbean countries: Antigua and Barbuda, the Bahamas, Barbados, Belize, Dominica, Grenada, Guyana, Jamaica, Montserrat, St. Kitts and Nevis, St. Lucia, Suriname, and Trinidad and Tobago. The Latin American regional workshop was held in Costa Rica for participants from the following countries: Costa Rica, Mexico, El Salvador, Nicaragua, the Dominican Republic, Colombia, and Peru.

26. On average the total cost of a workshop, including logistics, travel, materials and facilitation oscillated between US $25,000–$30,000, and on average each workshop hosted 40 participants. On that basis, the cost per participant averaged was $750.

27. At the end of the workshop, each participant who completed the full days of learning, is awarded a Certificate of Achievement, and is provided with a Resource Library (on a USB flash drive) with additional materials (including articles, case studies, pertinent legislation and international reports) which will help them to further advance their knowledge and skills.

28. The initial assumption is that the approach and method of the workshop apparently did have a similar initial impact. In an initial observation, the different independent variables did not affect the overall outcome. This might be a correlative evidence that the workshop approach as an independent variable might have some correlation with the dependent variable of contributing to the increase of knowledge to promote civic engagement among youth. We are not implying that this apparent correlation is causality, simply that we might have identified an independent variable as a likely cause of similar initial outcomes. Measuring attitude and behavior change, and deeper cross-systemic research could provide in both cases more causality evidence. For additional information on the theoretical selection approach used, see Adam Przeworski and Henry Teune, *The Logic of Comparative Social Inquiry* (New York: Wiley-Interscience, 1970).

29. On August 1, 2000, the University of Belize (UB) was created from a merger of five institutions: the University College of Belize, the Belize Technical College, the Belize Teachers' Training College, the Belize School of Nursing, and the Belize College of Agriculture. In 2004, the main campus was officially moved to Belmopan City. UB has a student population of over 4,800 and it offers 50 plus degree program offerings, ranging from the associate to master's level.

30. Belize is divided into 6 districts (a territorial division equivalent to a state). For the workshop, representatives from Belize, Cayo, Corozal, Stann Creek, and Toledo districts participated. Representatives from the Orange Walk district were unable to participate.

31. Also, six months after the workshop event, during the first quarter of 2014, the UNDP and UNICEF Belize country offices planned to conduct an assessment to measure the institutional capacity of local government in Belize. An Institutional Capacity Assessment is a tool employed by the United Nations and other international development organizations, to measure the existing ability of institutions to perform key functions and deliver expected results. The results of the assessment serve as inputs to craft an integrated support to strengthen and expand local governments' roles and functions in public policy and development. In the field of international development, the concept of capacity development emerged in the 1980s and became the central purpose of technical assistance to developing countries. For more information, see https://www.undp.org/content/undp/en/home/librarypage/capacity-building/capacity-development-a-undp-primer.html. The assessment generated an opening to involve the BYSAN in the process and put some of the knowledge from the workshop into practice. The assessment team took the decision to involve six BYSAN members in one of the most important steps in conducting institutional capacity assessment – the data collection process. The assessment consisted of various phases and was achieved jointly with senior technical personnel from UNDP, UNICEF and the Belize Ministry of Labor, Local Governance, and Rural Development. The final report was well-received, and it served as a baseline and tool to promote dialogue with the government and to help identify priority capacities to be strengthened. See final report: Belize, Ministry of Labor, Local Government and Rural Development, Rapid Assessment of Belize Local Governments' Capacities (Belize: UNDP and UNICEF, 2014). In retrospect, the involvement of the BYSAN in the institutional capacity assessment process was a win-win for all involved. Inputs from a post-assessment evaluation with BYSAN participants suggested the assessment served to put into practice what they learned in the workshop, further build their confidence, skills and experience, and gave them an opportunity to engage with their local governments.

32. See, UNDP, *Guatemala Independent Country Programme Evaluation (ICPE)* (New York, NY: UNDP/IEO, 2019); USAID, *Guatemala: Country Development Cooperation Strategy (2012–2016)* (2012); and PNUD, *Guatemala: ¿Un país de oportunidades para la juventud? Informe Nacional de Desarrollo Humano 2011/2012* (Guatemala City, Guatemala: 2012).

33. For more information about USAID Guatemala Citizen Security strategy see, https://www.usaid.gov/guatemala/democracy-and-governance

34. The San Carlos University (USAC) is the largest and oldest university in Guatemala. It was founded in 1676 by Royal Decree of the King of Spain Carlos II. USAC is a public university with eight schools, 18 campuses, three institutes, a postgraduate system and over 200,000 students.

35. Rafael Landívar University (URL) is a private, Jesuit university in Guatemala, founded in 1962. The main campus is in Guatemala City. There are satellite campuses in Quetzaltenango, Huehuetenango, Cobán, Zacapa, and other parts of the country. The URL offers undergraduate and graduate degrees and has over 30,000 students

10

Students Teaching Democracy to Other Students: The Effects on Political Engagement

Theodore Chadjipadelis and Georgia Panagiotidou

Aristotle University Thessaloniki

This chapter presents an experiment of teaching "democracy," where political science students at Aristotle University of Thessaloniki are trained and assigned to teach a civic education course to other students in high schools and universities. The research investigates the effect of this civic education intervention on the nature and extent of students' political mobilization. Analysis of survey data from participants indicates that the course in democracy enhances students' political engagement. This chapter offers an example of a university-based civic engagement course that strengthens democracy, allowing students to simulate their role as future citizens in the implemented interactive workshops.

KEYWORDS: Civic Education; Democracy; Political Behavior; Political Engagement; Analysis Methods.

Introduction

Democracy and representation are the foundations on which citizens are expected to become interested and participate in the public sphere. Engagement in public matters and participation in political acts such as elections are vital for a prosperous democratic society. Social scientists, through research, have highlighted the importance of education in cultivating an interest for the commons.[1] In Greece, the educational system has been going through reforms since the 19th century, when it was established. The Greek educational system is based on democracy, participation, freedom, and equality. As mentioned in the constitution of the Hellenic Republic, education is a mission of the State and its purpose is to provide moral, intellectual, professional, and physical training to the Greeks who will develop national and religious consciousness and they will become free and responsible citizens.[2]

Secondary education in Greece is divided in two parts: 1) compulsory three-year gymnasium starting at the age of 12 and 2) non-compulsory three-year lyceum starting at the age of 15. Civic education in Greece has been taught mainly in the final class of compulsory education (Greek Gymnasium) with a course entitled "*Social and Political Education.*" Students come across civic education in high school (Greek Lyceum) with a course entitled "*Citizenship Education.*" It should be noted that weekly hours of civic education are less than other lessons. For example, the courses of religion, history, or ancient Greek are taught more frequently on a weekly basis and for up to nine consecutive years during primary and secondary education. It also is worth noting that since 2020, the number of hours of civic education taught were further decreased by the ministry of education and religious affairs, and "*Sociology*," a course which was compulsory for the entry exams to universities, was abolished.

Civic education is present in compulsory education, even in a limited and inadequate proportion in the current Greek educational system, its approach is limited to the theoretical teaching of basic political terms and institutions. Students are being taught the meaning of democracy, political phenomena, and political institutions and procedures. However, the theoretical transmission of basic concepts is not enough to "understand democracy," which is important in maintaining the social and political status quo with active participation of citizens with high political interest, knowledge, and political engagement.[3] To cultivate a collective or social awareness, individuals must also be aware of their role as citizens, comprehend the democratic procedures, and be aware of the importance of being part of them. To achieve this, civic education must be present in the educational system and cover a greater space in the timetable of all educational levels.[4]

On this basis, the department of political science of Aristotle University of Thessaloniki in Greece designed and introduced into the academic curriculum in 2017 the new module "*Teaching Civic Education*" to provide college students the opportunity to apply the didactic methods they learn in their classrooms in the university by actually teaching "democracy" to high school students as well as a selection of other students in the university. This chapter presents the didactic methodology and the implementation of this innovative academic module and investigates its effects on the political behavior of the high school and university students who attended the civic education workshops taught by the students of the department who administered the "*Teaching Civic Education*" module. Previous research demonstrates causal links between civic education and political knowledge and interest in politics as well as likelihood of participating.[5] Our research furthers this research and lends support to the importance of civic education and its effectiveness at stimulating future political engagement.

Due to the COVID-19 pandemic crisis and extensive quarantine periods, the course most recently was implemented by means of distance learning (e-learning). As a result, the analysis also includes data addressing the impact of the e-learning application of civic education that can be compared with results from the previous in-class courses.

Literature Review

Education is the process by which adult generations influence the formation of the younger ones, as they prepare to enter social life. The educational content is a product of each society and era, thus reflects the social reality. Consequently, education aims to achieve society's continuation, through the successful implementation of the process of "socialization" of the individual.[6] Similarly, in order for democracy to survive, the skills of citizenship must be cultivated through civic education, as a primary content of the educational system of a country.[7]

According to Parsons, "socialization" is the process during which the values of society are integrated in the personality of the individual.[8] Therefore, individuals feel a high degree of commitment towards society's values and feel the need to serve their corresponding roles. Education serves as a catalyst which enhances the process of socialization to future citizens. Moreover, socialization is "political" when the values of society become one with the values of the individual, with the purpose of achieving the stability and legitimacy of the current social and political status quo.[9] As a result, political socialization leads to the construction of the "political self" of the individual.[10] The main carriers or agents of political socialization are family, friends, school, the media, the army, and the working environment. Researchers have demonstrated the gravity of each carrier on the political socialization process. The two most prominent views focus on the importance of school[11] and of family,[12] where school often can function as a corrective factor on the family's influence.

Previous research has shown that a high level of civic education leads to higher levels of active participation in political matters[13] and a higher awareness of the importance of participation.[14] The role of the school in the political socialization process can be accomplished in two ways: teaching democracy directly as part of the curriculum, and indirectly through active participation in the school society with its regulations and procedures,[15] described by Campbell as an open classroom environment civic learning procedure.[16] Therefore, it is vital that education provides sufficient educational opportunities, both direct and indirect, to these future citizens, teaching them citizenship skills such as critical thinking, representation, elections, deliberation, openness to different views, and other important elements which allow the continuance and sustainability of democracy.[17]

Beginning in the 21st century, there has been a general withdrawal from public matters in Greece.[18] Younger people's indifference toward politics and suspicion toward governments and democratic constitutions[19] has resulted in an increase of abstention[20] during the elections.[21] In Greece, the increasing abstention (at 43.4% in 2015) from democratic electoral procedures[22] is explained by the decrease in political interest and political engagement, as well as political knowledge.[23] The important role of civic literacy has been documented in a growing body of literature.[24] When provided through didactic approaches focused on "teaching democracy" in schools and universities, civic instruction cultivates civic and political engagement in individuals, preparing them for their future role as active citizens.[25] Additional research has shown that the inclusion of more participatory activities, which simulate the democratic procedures and the role of the citizen, can enhance the learning process of civic engagement.[26] Similarly, interactive teaching methods[27] with workshop practices like self or group-learning, shared decision-making and team-based project work, which familiarize the students with the democratic principles and the way the state functions, also offer students the opportunity to apply what they learn by interacting with each other and practicing how to integrate into civic society.[28]

Some principles that can be comprehended through team-based learning and workshops are "the electorate," the idea of "representation,"[29] "the Parliament," the "electoral system"[30] and the "party system,"[31] "the government," and "citizenship."[32] Workshops can be very productive for the comprehension of democratic principles, the representative system, and ideal citizenship behavior.[33] Project assignments can be combined with workshops and other possible simulations of representative bodies, into the school communities, by interactive and experiential learning. Furthermore, these combined team-based learning methods have been demonstrated to be more efficient than conventional methods for familiarizing students with the electoral and party system, electoral laws, deliberation, and team coordination for a common purpose. The result of applying the above interactive methods in political science pedagogy is to cultivate self-confidence and teamwork skills in students, two important elements for active future citizens.[34]

The role of civic education remains important to the political socialization of future citizens, and research provides evidence that this can be achieved better through interactive learning.[35] The "teaching democracy" experiment in Greece tries to examine whether the realization of such interactive workshops of civic education can provide significant improvement in the political behavior of young people, raising their interest and active participation in commons, resulting in the facilitation of democracy.

Didactic Approach And Research Design

"*Teaching Civic Education*" is primarily an apprenticeship in democracy. Its purpose is to form a free, responsible, and active citizen, who in a timely and conscious manner will understand the importance and value of democracy, will respect state institutions, and will respect and fight for democracy and the state. The purpose of a successful didactic approach for civic education is to form a citizen with political conscience and critical thinking, in order to actively participate in the local, national, and global social, economic, and political development. Apart from lecturing about consciousness in democracy and civics, election procedures, and the sense of citizenship, the students are required to integrate several teaching methods that could lead to more interactive and well-educated citizens. An example of a proposed method is to utilize workshops to stimulate public discourse about representation issues, the role of representatives to integrate students to electoral procedures and deliberative dialogue, to increase civic knowledge, and to promote participation in commons.

"_Teaching Civic Education_" is a module (an elective course) in our academic curriculum, which was proposed and implemented for the first time in 2017. Since then, it has been repeated for each academic semester in the Department of Political Sciences of Aristotle University of Thessaloniki.[36] This module is under full responsibility of the political sciences department and is taught by its academic staff and equates to four (4) "European Credit Transfer and Accumulation System" credits (ECTS).[37] Its duration is one semester and is offered to students in each semester through the academic year and takes place over thirteen weeks (three hours per week).

This chapter describes the implementation and measured effect of the module during 2019 and 2020.

Twenty-four (24) students chose the course in 2019 and seven (7) students chose it in 2020. These students were familiarized with didactic methods, microteaching, prepared their material, and then went on to teach a civic education class to other students (in high schools and universities). Afterward, the students who attended the class, given by our module's students, participated in a closed-end survey in order to assess the effect on their political behavior.

The module intends to familiarize students with teaching civic education and gives them the opportunity to practice what they have learned in real conditions. The learning objectives of the module are that the students are expected to a) understand the importance of teaching political education in schools, b) connect theory and practice by doing a practical implementation of the teaching process first in the form of "micro-teaching" or a simulation in front of colleagues to prepare for the teaching session in the classrooms to other high school and university students and c) then become familiar with the teaching practice by teaching a civic education class in schools in the area of Thessaloniki.[38]

Course structure

The course is structured into three distinct sections:

1) In the first section, there is an introduction to issues of general and special didactic models and methods. At this stage, the students learn basic civic concepts which they will teach later and teaching methods for interactive learning. The duration of this part is four weeks.

2) The second section deals with micro-teaching, a teaching simulation session during which the students practice teaching lessons by teaching each other.[39] After completing their basic teaching civic education training, the students prepare their teaching material and simulate teaching civic education in front of their co-students and in the presence of their professor. At the end of the simulation, they discuss altogether how to improve the material and their teaching approach. The duration of this part is 4 weeks.

3) Finally, the students who chose the academic module are requested to teach in real conditions to other students in high schools and universities of Thessaloniki (for the academic year 2020 teaching was achieved by means of distance learning). In this last stage of the module, students who will be civic education tutors take part in preparing teaching material, including both lecturing and interactive methods, in order to teach in a secondary education classroom (2nd class of Greek Lyceum) and in a university class (1st year or 2nd year in university). The teaching package they prepare should create conditions for the formation of an active citizen with a strong sense of individual responsibility, social solidarity, and collective action. This last part of the module lasts five weeks.

This last section of the module, which requires the students to teach civic education in the classroom, is structured in two parts. Firstly, the students introduce their audience to basic concepts of democracy and the role of the citizen. When this introductory portion is over, they proceed to the second section which includes the scheduled interactive activities in the form of workshops, which include moderating, deliberation, laboratories, project assignment, group learning, use of posters when necessary, and scenario research with use of questionnaires and evaluation of the results. The interactive activities in the classroom upgrade the educational process, making it more enjoyable for students. The purpose of the didactic approach is to make the students feel closer to what they are being taught through the correlation of the above issues with the school and the student board.[40] The students, after presenting to the class the workshops and with the assistance of the teacher in charge of the classroom, provide answers to the participants' questions, and then they divide them into groups. Alternative didactic approaches have been used per class, sometimes grouping students per workshop or, in other cases, assigning one workshop to the whole class-room. The workshop ends with the participants presenting what they have been assigned during the workshop, which is to discuss altogether and summarize pros and cons of political phenomena they have been taught during the lesson.

Workshop structure

There are three available workshops, and each class of participating high school students is exposed to one of the following three workshops. The content of each workshop includes a set of basic democratic concepts and functions:

Representation and electoral system

Some of the most important concepts for the students to understand are participation and representation. Participation is the basis of modern democracies, as the representatives are elected by the citizens who participate in elections. Students are firstly introduced to the concept of democracy, the differences between direct and indirect democracy, the right to elect, and the right to be elected. Participants are also introduced to the effect of various electoral systems, to the role of parties, the role of candidates, and the procedure of elections. All aforementioned concepts are discussed in class and afterwards, the participants are required to simulate the process of defining the main issues of their school and raise questions about who will be the representative that will be responsible to face these issues, and how will this relationship between the representative and the represented be defined and secured. Participants also have to choose the most appropriate electoral system from their representative body and catalogue the effects of their choice in the possible outcome. The interactive part of the workshop includes a team-based learning project about all the above. The participants are required to coordinate their work within their team, using dialogue and promoting participation of all team members. Following this workshop, the students are expected to understand their role in their school's elected boards and project this role to the future where they, as citizens, will participate in organizing society through the concept of representation. Moreover, they are trained to distinguish between various electoral systems by understanding their effect on their representation in the school board, projecting again the function of various electoral systems on representation in democracy.

Representative's characteristics and electorates criteria

In this workshop, students are acquainted with the four types of representatives (personal, collective, delegates, trustee) and their characteristics.[41] The question raised in this workshop is whose interests the representative does/should satisfy and what are the electorate's various criteria when selecting a candidate or a party. The participants are asked to describe various types of representatives as well as define the ideal one. The workshop ends with a role-playing session during which the participants debate on issues of their school and provide possible solutions. This process raises critical thinking and the sense of common interest which should be the representative's duty. The learning objective of this workshop is to train the students to characterize and identify the appropriate criteria of voting in order to serve the common good.

Deliberation

The last workshop develops a real-time deliberation process about current issues the students face in their school or university. By simulating the deliberation process, meaning the open dialogue with an equal participation share for all citizens, the participants are being familiarized with the concept of deliberative democracy.[42] The learning objective of this workshop is that the students comprehend the way we are led from participation towards deliberation.[43] The outcome of the workshop is a regular think tank for school's or university's issues, which encourages participation of all students and is held on a weekly basis, including an agenda, suggestions, and a record of minutes for every deliberation session.

During the spring semester of 2020, the COVID-19 pandemic changed the daily reality for many countries around the globe. In Greece, the quarantine for the "first wave" of the pandemic lasted three months, beginning in March 2020, leading to the cease of many social and economic functions, including the live-in-classroom education in schools and universities. Education took the form of distance-learning courses, and the "*Teaching Civic Education*" module was continued through means of e-learning. The university students who undertook the module prepared their teaching material for civic education and presented it electronically to other students via the Zoom platform. The participants, as in previous semesters, attended the theoretical part of the course and afterwards participated in the online workshops working in teams, concluding with the presentations of the workshop's results. The spring semester of 2020 provided the opportunity to include in our research a new perspective, to compare results and the effectiveness of the course between the previous participants in live classrooms and the "COVID-19 semester" students in digital classrooms.

Methodology And Data Analysis

The design of the module "*Teaching Civic Education*," as already described, is separated into two basic parts. The first part is the overall completion of the module "*Teaching Civic Education*" for the political sciences students who selected it (24 students in 2019, seven students in 2020): production of the course material by them, their micro-teaching sessions in front of colleagues, and finally their in-classroom and distance learning teaching sessions directly to other students in high schools and universities. In the second part, the impact of the project is assessed, through a closed-end survey to the high school and university students who attended the civic education classes and workshops given by the students who chose the aforementioned academic module.[44] Analyzing the gathered data allows us to measure the effect of the civic education interactive lesson on the high school and university students' political behavior and, more specifically, on their political engagement.

The objective of the research is to investigate whether any significant difference exists between the control group of students and the participants of the civic education workshops in terms of political knowledge, interest, and their preferred way to mobilize on political issues. To achieve this, the survey was conducted on a random sample of students of Aristotle University of Thessaloniki. This sample is used as the "control group" for the research, as it reflects the average political behavior characteristics of the young student population in Thessaloniki. The university and high school students who participated in the civic education workshops, given by the political sciences students of "*Teaching Civic Education*," complete the same survey right after the workshops are completed.

The survey serves as an assessment, where the basic hypothesis is investigated by comparing the participants of the workshops (treatment groups) to the general population (control group), of similar characteristics. More specifically, we explore whether a significant difference is observed between the profiles (as described in table 1) of: a) those who participated in the civic education workshops (groups 2, 3 and 4) and those who did not (group 1) b) in-classroom (group 2 and 4) and distance learning workshop's participants (group 3) and c) high school students (group 4) and the university students who attended the workshops (groups 2 and 3):

Group 1: random sample of university students of Thessaloniki (control group)

Group 2: the university students who attended the course in spring semester 2019 (in-classroom). This group includes the respondents who participated in the workshop implemented in the compulsory course of "*Quantitative methods*" in the political sciences department in the Aristotle University. In this group of university students, all had to participate in the lesson and the workshops.

Group 3: the university students who attended the course during spring semester 2020 (distance-learning). These are the respondents of three compulsory courses of social sciences studies, one from each university (Aristotle university of Thessaloniki. University of Macedonia and International Hellenic university), which was achieved through means of distance learning. All students had to attend the lesson and the workshops.

Group 4: the high-school students who attended the course in spring semester 2019 (in-classroom). The high schools, where "*Teaching Civic Education*" workshop was implemented, were randomly chosen among all high schools of Thessaloniki. In the selected high schools, all the students of the class where the workshops took place had to participate and attend the lesson and the workshops.

It is important to specify that groups 2, 3, and 4 are the subjects of our survey and consist of the high school and university students who were taught civic education by our students who took the course "teaching civic education." Therefore, the subjects of the survey have no option to select or not select to participate. These are randomly chosen classes where our students teach a civic education class. It is these classes who participate in the assessment survey and we compare their results to those of the control group. The students who took the academic course and then taught the civic education classes to groups 2, 3, and 4, do not participate in the survey.

The sample consists of 1618 participants, as shown in table 1. All participating students were aged 17 to 25 years old, 40% were men and 60% women.

Table 1. Demographics of Respondents

Group	Count	Male	Female
1	879	37.83%	62.17%
2	100	38%	62%
3	145	28.47%	71.53%
4	494	52.36%	47.64%
Total	1,618	41.46%	58.54%

The survey instrument is an anonymous questionnaire, including closed ended questions that measure students' political attitudes, mobilization, interest, knowledge, and structure of the political and moral self.[45]

In the questionnaire, the respondents provided answers regarding their level of political interest and how they mobilize when facing an issue. A composite variable for respondents' level of political knowledge was structured based on the synthesis of a set of exploratory questions on knowledge of basic civic facts. The respondents were also asked to position themselves on the left-right ideological axis (0–10) which was later recoded to a five-point scale (1-5). The selection of the questions, during the construction of the questionnaire, was based on similar questions used to measure political characteristics and political behavior, which are used in research projects of the international collaborative research program, Comparative Study of Electoral Systems (CSES), such as the True European Voter (TEV)[46] and the Comparative Candidates Study (CCS) questionnaire.[47] Additionally, the questionnaire included a question about the two most important sources of information about politics. Another section of the questionnaire consisted of 12 pictures presenting various concepts of "democracy" and 12 pictures which represent "constitutive goods"-"personal values". The respondents were asked to choose exactly three of them which represent how they perceive democracy and three pictures which represent their personal values. We base our approach on the theory for the construction of the political and moral self, which is the phenomenological process by which individuals, by analogy and homology, construct symbolic representations of democratic institutions and of their personal moral compass.[48]

<table>
<tr><td colspan="4" align="center">Table 2. Variables</td></tr>
<tr><td>Question</td><td>Variable</td><td>Type</td><td>Values</td></tr>
<tr><td>Gender:</td><td>gender</td><td>binary</td><td>1: male, 2: female</td></tr>
<tr><td>In politics we refer to Left and Right usually using a scale from 0 to 10. Regardless of the content you give to these terms, where would you place yourself on the scale below?</td><td>left-right</td><td>ordinal</td><td>1: left, 2: centre-left, 3: centre, 4: centre-right, 5: right</td></tr>
<tr><td>For a problem that concerns your daily life, which of the following attitudes do you choose (single choice)?</td><td>political mobilization</td><td>categorical</td><td>1: I personally address the authorities, 2: I participate with others in collective mobilizations, 3: I take action through Social Media, 4: I let the authorities do their job, 5: I do not know / I do not answer</td></tr>
<tr><td>How interested are you in politics?</td><td>political interest</td><td>ordinal</td><td>1: very much, 2: quite, 3: a little, 4: not at all</td></tr>
<tr><td>Set of questions to explore level of knowledge on political matters.</td><td>political knowledge</td><td>ordinal</td><td>1: low, 2: moderate, 3: high</td></tr>
<tr><td>How do you mainly acquire information about political issues?</td><td>political info source</td><td>categorical</td><td>1: TV-Radio, 2: Online newspapers-Internet, 3: Social media, 4: Family-relatives, 5: Friends, 6: Newspapers</td></tr>
<tr><td>What does "Democracy" mean to you? Choose three (3) of the following pictures.</td><td>perception of democracy</td><td>categorical</td><td>12 pictures which visualize concepts for how they perceive democracy</td></tr>
<tr><td>Choose three (3) of the following pictures which best represent you</td><td>personal values</td><td>categorical</td><td>12 pictures which visualize concepts of moral values</td></tr>
</table>

The first step of analyzing our data is to present descriptive statistics results for the above variables for all four groups. Proceeding further with the analysis, we compare all groups by pairs in order to detect whether there is any difference between the groups regarding the variables of political mobilization, interest, and knowledge.

Data analysis is based on Hierarchical Cluster Analysis (HCA) and Multiple Correspondence Analysis (MCA) in two steps.[49] In the first step, HCA assigns subjects into distinct groups according to their response patterns. The main output of HCA is a group or cluster membership variable, which reflects the partitioning of the subjects into groups. Furthermore, for each group, the contribution of each question (variable) to the group formation is investigated, in order to reveal a typology of behavioral patterns. To determine the number of clusters, we use the empirical criterion of the change in the ratio of between-cluster inertia to total inertia, when moving from a partition with r clusters to a partition with r-1 clusters.[50] Analysis was conducted with the software M.A.D. (Méthodes de l' Analyse des Données).[51] In the second step, the group membership variable, obtained from the first step, is jointly analyzed with the existing variables via Multiple Correspondence Analysis on the so-called Burt table.[52] Bringing the two analyses together, behavioral patterns and abstract discourses are used to construct a map visualizing the behavioral structure of the variables and the subjects.

Results

In this section, we present the results of the analysis—descriptive statistics for each of the variables of the survey and the relationships among them. Specifically, we analyze the relationship between the civic education intervention and ideological positioning, political interest, knowledge, mobilization, using the appropriate statistical tests to compare the students who attended the intervention and the control group. Finally, we present the results of the multivariate analysis, using HCA and MCA, followed by analysis and interpretation of the findings.

Left-Right Self-Positioning

As indicated, we asked respondents to position themselves on the left-right scale. We found that all groups scored, on average, close to the center. As shown in table 3, a slightly higher score of 3.08 was detected for the high-school in-classroom group (group 4), while groups 2 and 3 for university students in-class and distance learning both scored a value which is closer to center-left (2.79 and 2.74). Respondents from the control group had a slightly higher value, 2.91, closer again to the center. Using one-way ANOVA to test the statistical importance of the differences of the means, we found that there are statistically significant differences.[53] In the post-hoc analysis for each set of pairs, significant difference is found only between the group pairs 1 and 4. We observe small differences in the overall left-right profile of the four groups, with the group of the high-school students positioning themselves slightly more to the right side of the left-right axis. This finding can be attributed to the evolution of ideological identification depending on the changing environments as students mature.[54] These varying relationships within our close environment affect one's ideological affiliation beginning with a tendency in younger children to appear more conservative as they adopt the same political positioning with their families, which later in early adulthood is followed by young adults gravitating towards more liberal or expressivist attitudes.[55]

Table 3. Comparing Groups on Left-Right Scale					
	Mean	Std. Deviation	Std. Error	95% Confidence Interval for Mean	
				Lower Bound	Upper Bound
Group 1	2.91	1.090	.037	2.84	2.98
Group 2	2.79	1.209	.121	2.55	3.03
Group 3	2.74	1.266	.108	2.53	2.96
Group 4	3.08	1.124	.051	2.98	3.18

Political Interest, Knowledge and Mobilization

Next, we present descriptive statistics for the variables of political knowledge, interest, and mobilization per group of respondents. We found that 43.6% of group 1 had "a little" political interest, while groups 2 and 3 scored "very much" or "quite" interested in politics. High school students (group 4) scored mostly "a little" interested in politics with 33.2% indicating they are "quite" interested in politics (see table 4). Groups 1 and 4 have a similar distribution of their answers for political interest, while for groups 2 and 3 political interest is generally higher.

We performed a chi-square test for the group's variable and each one of the political behavior variables. Performing a chi-square test, the Pearson chi-square coefficient proved to be significant (p=0.001), showing that there is a correlation between group category and political interest.[56] We found that groups 2 and 3 exhibit the same level of political interest, while groups 1 and 4 tend to be less interested in politics. We observe that the university students of social sciences departments (groups 2 and 3) appear to respond better in terms of political interest which could derive as an effect of their discipline. Therefore, they are expected to be keener on politics compared to the other groups.

Table 4. Political Interest Frequency Distribution				
Political Interest	Very much	Quite	A little	Not at all
Group 1	10.9%	29%	43.6%	16%
Group 2	33%	45%	22%	0%
Group 3	36.6%	45.5%	16.6%	1.4%
Group 4	7.9%	33.2%	45.3%	12.6%

Regarding political knowledge, we found that more than 50% of the respondents of the control group demonstrated low levels of political knowledge. On the other hand, almost eight out of ten students who participated in the civic education workshops demonstrate an adequate to high level of political knowledge (see table 5). The higher political knowledge measures for group 2 could be explained by their studies in social sciences. Similarly, the high scores for group 4 of high school students could be attributed to the compulsory civic education course which is included in their curriculum at the first and second class of lyceum. The chi-square test indicates a significant relationship between political knowledge and the group categories. More specifically, we see that group 1 demonstrated a significantly lower score in political knowledge, compared to the students of groups 2 and 4 who attended the civic education course. As a result, the civic education intervention seems to have a positive effect on the political knowledge of the young students.

Table 5. Political Knowledge Frequency Distribution				
Political Knowledge	Low	Little	Adequate	High
Group 1	23.2%	35.6%	29%	12.2%
Group 2	4%	13%	45%	38%
Group 4	3%	16.4%	37.5%	43.1%

Political mobilization (table 6) is measured as the action the respondents choose in order to deal with civic issues. In our model, mobilization is summarized in two main forms: active and passive. These two categories are further analyzed into other sub-categories: active on an individual level (address concerns personally to the authorities), active on a collective level (participate in collective mobilizations), active via indirect means (social media) and passive (let others do their job, no answer). From the chi-square test, the Pearson chi-square coefficient proved again to be significant, indicating a strong relationship between the group category and political mobilization. Responses in group 1 reflect that they are in favor of personal mobilization, or appear disengaged choosing "let others do their job" or preferring not to answer. Groups 2 and 3 appear to have a different pattern of answers between them, where group 2 prefers personal and collective mobilization, having a more active profile compared to group 3, whose respondents have higher scores in passive stances such as "let others do their jobs." This can be attributed to the effects of the COVID-19 pandemic, since group 3 participated in the civic education course through distance learning during the lockdown period of spring 2020. Group 4, the high school students, are distributed evenly among the answering options, scoring the highest score among all groups for "social media."

Table 6. Political Mobilization Frequency Distribution					
Political Mobilization	Address Personally	Collective mobilizations	Social Media	Let others to do their job	N/A
Group 1	30.9%	15.0%	13.3%	23.5%	17.2%
Group 2	37.0%	27.0%	14.0%	16.0%	6.0%
Group 3	25.5%	22.8%	13.8%	24.8%	13.1%
Group 4	20.9%	19.8%	19.4%	23.7%	13.6%

To understand the response patterns here, we ran a correspondence analysis test. The first two dimensions explain 96.3% of the phenomenon. Along the first dimension, the main antithesis is between the control group which is linked to a more disengaged stance or active individual mobilization and group 4 which is closer to social media. Along the second dimension, the antithesis is expressed by group 2 which is closer to collective mobilizations which is opposed to passive behavior.

To interpret the results with reference to our research hypothesis, the results suggest that civic education courses impact political mobilization, as the analysis highlights a strong differentiation of group 1 compared to the other groups. Group 1 is connected to a passive stance or individual way of acting, whereas groups 2, 3, and 4 share the opposite behavior (according to the correspondence analysis results) in terms of mobilization, and prefer active, collective, or indirect ways of mobilization and reject the passive stance. The second axis of the analysis is defined by the high level of political mobilization for group 2 and their strong connection to collective mobilizations. These are the university students who attended the civic education in the classroom and are more active. The analysis shows two important effects of the course on the political mobilization of the participants. On the one hand, high school and university students who attended the civic education course appear significantly closer to active forms of participation and more negative to the passive option, compared to the control group who exhibits a tendency not to be mobilized. On the other hand, those who participated in the course are closer to collective forms of participation while the control group is closer to individual mobilization.

Summarizing the above, analysis highlights a strong relationship between political education and active political behavior, since students who participated in the civic education workshops exhibit higher political interest, knowledge, and tend to be mobilized in more active ways when they face an issue. The effect of the course on the political behavior of the participants becomes more prominent when compared to the corresponding results of the control group, formed by a random sample of students in Thessaloniki who resemble the general population's behavior on these political characteristics for young students in Thessaloniki. Analysis of the control group revealed a much lower score on the political knowledge scale and characteristics linked to low political interest, as well as a tendency to be politically inactive and disengaged. In addition to the above findings, chi-square testing shows that a significant difference exists between the four different groups in terms of the aforementioned measured political characteristics. As a result, we conclude that there is a significant difference between those who received civic education through the workshops and those who did not regarding their political activity and positive political attitude towards participation and democracy. Among all participants of the course, the highest effect to political engagement was detected in university students, who actually have a higher degree of freedom as adults. High school students also experienced a positive effect, especially compared to the control group, but to a more limited extent on political knowledge. Overall, the course had a positive effect on the political attitude of the participants whether they were university students or high school students. All three groups who participated in the civic education workshops, in frames of "*Teaching Civic Education*" course, performed better in the assessment survey and exhibited a higher degree of political activity and interest, compared to the random sample of the control group.

Information Source, Perception of Democracy and Moral Values

Proceeding with HCA for the last three variables (information source, perceptions on democracy, and personal values), the respondents are assigned, through hierarchical cluster analysis, in groups of similar behavior. For the variable of information source, HCA revealed eight groups of respondents. Each group is characterized by the respondents' selection of the marked values as shown in table 7. For example, cluster 1 is characterized by those selecting TV-Radio and Family to get informed about politics.

Cluster	Informed preferably from:	Frequency
	Table 7. Eight (8) Clusters of Respondents Based on the Source They Choose to Get Informed About Politics	
1	TV-Radio. Family	11.0%
2	Not informed at all	4.0%
3	Social media and internet	12.3%
4	TV-Radio. Internet	15.1%
5	TV-Radio. Social media	14.6%
6	Newspapers	13.0%
7	Friends	15.9%
8	Family. Social media	13.5%

Following the same procedure with HCA, we observe eight distinct clusters of respondents which are formed according to the way the respondents perceive democracy.[57] In order to understand how they perceive democracy, the survey requested that one chose only three among twelve pictures of different democracy concepts (figure 1). In table 8, we see the eight clusters and their profile regarding the pictures that are chosen by its respondents. For example, cluster 4 comprehends democracy as its electronic form, while cluster 1 identifies democracy as a religious concept.

Cluster	Group of respondents who define democracy as:	Frequency
	Table 8. Eight (8) Clusters of Respondents Regarding the Way They Perceive Democracy	
1	Religion	11.9%
2	e-Democracy. Representative. Corruption. Religion	7.4%
3	Ancient Greece. Representative. Deliberation	14.0%
4	e-Democracy	13.6%
5	Riot. Corruption. Rebellion. Protest	6.0%
6	Movement. Direct. Rebellion. Protest	15.0%
7	Movement. Ancient Greece. Representative. Volunteerism	14.2%
8	Ancient Greece. Direct. Volunteerism. Rebellion	18.1%

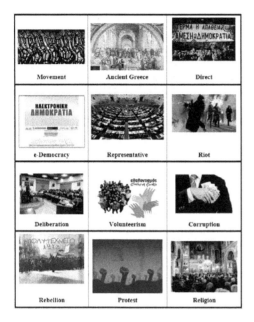

Figure 1. Pictures for Democracy Perception

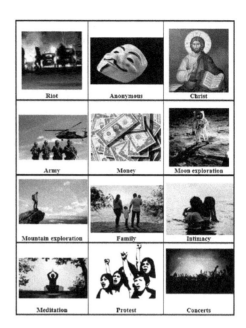

Figure 2. Pictures for Personal Values

Similarly, examining the construction of basic moral rules on a personal level (figure 2), analysis reveals nine groups of respondents. The various combinations of the pictures describe three basic moral attitudes: the expressivist, the naturalist, and the spirituality.[58] In table 9, we can see the nine clusters and their corresponding moral values according to the chosen pictures. For example, the profile of cluster 2 is defined by choosing "anonymous" and "protest" pictures, therefore exhibiting expressivist moral attitudes.

Cluster	Things that express their personal values:	Moral concept	Frequency
1	Riot. Anonymous. Army. Protest	Expressivist	4.2%
2	Anonymous. Protest	Expressivist	7.2%
3	Moon exploration. Mountain exploration. Concerts	Naturalist/Spirituality	9.8%
4	Anonymous. Christ. Army. Money	Expressivist/Naturalist	8.6%
5	Protest	Expressivist	13.4%
6	Mountain exploration. Meditation	Spirituality	15.4%
7	Money. Intimacy	Naturalist	12.4%
8	Christ. Family. Intimacy	Naturalist	13.5%
9	Mountain exploration. Family. Intimacy. Concerts	Naturalist	15.6%

Table 9. Nine (9) Clusters of Respondents Regarding Their Concept of Personal Values

In the last step of our analysis, the three cluster membership variables were jointly analyzed with MCA and HCA with the rest of the variables. The output of the analysis is a Cartesian field (x,y), where all objects (variables values) are projected according to their scores in the two first dimensions of MCA. Each axis (dimension) represents the polarization between the objects (variable categories) which are positioned at its ends. The greater the distance between the categories at its ends, the greater the opposition is between these characteristics.

This can also be described as a map visualizing all dynamics of the phenomenon (figure 3). The most important point of the analysis is that all four groups (i.e. three groups of participants of the civic education course and the control group) are also positioned on the same axis system and appear distinctly in correlation to the rest of the variables and their values. The examination of the map confirms our basic hypothesis that the four groups demonstrate distinct political behavior characteristics, as the group variable categories and the characteristics are clearly positioned on the (x,y) diagram in figure 3.

Figure 3. Map Visualization of the Positions of Variables

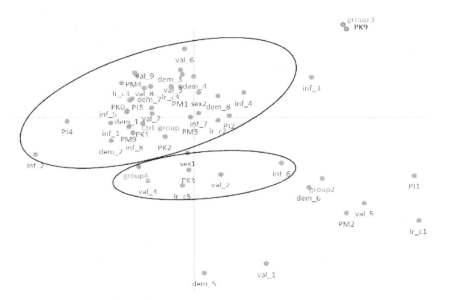

By analyzing their positions on each axis separately, we can detect further differentiation between sets of groups as required by our hypothesis questions. The first axis (horizontal) is created by the differentiation between groups 1–4 (control group and high school students who participated in the intervention) and groups 2–3 (university students participating in-classroom and students participating online). The vertical component of MCA is created by the difference between group 3 (online students) and the rest of the groups altogether. Group 3 is generally positioned a great distance from the others on this axis due to the absence of data for political knowledge, as this group was not measured in the survey for its political knowledge due to the distance learning limitations. In the diagram, we observe that group 3 (online students) is closer to group 2 (university students participating in-classroom), showing similar behavior in the horizontal axis. This result suggests that the distance learning civic education course had no significant difference in its effect on the political behavior of the students.

The analysis proceeds with clustering the coordinates of the axes which were produced in the MCA in the previous step. This time, all four groups are clustered together (HCA) with the variable categories. Table 10 summarizes the profile of each group according to the cluster in which it belongs. In this way, we can see the correspondence between the initial four groups of our respondents (with reference to the intervention) and their behavior regarding all other variables.

Table 10. Groups And Variables Clustered Jointly. Behavioral Patterns Of Each Group Are Distinct						
6 clusters	6a	6b	6c	6d	6e	6f
4 clusters	4a	4a	4b	4b	4c	4d
3 clusters	3a	3a	3b	3b	3b	3c
group	group 3	group 2	group 1		group4	
Left-Right		far left	center-left/ center-right	center-left	far right	
Political Interest		Very	Not very	Somewhat		Not at all
Political Knowledge	No Data		[None/Little] [Adequate]		High	
Political Mobilization		Collective	Let others to do their job	Personal Social Media		N/A
Gender			Female	Male		
Information Source		Social media. Internet/ Newspapers	TV-Radio. Social media/ Friends	[TV-Radio. Internet] [Family. Social media]	TV-Radio. Family	No information
Democracy		Movement. Direct. Rebellion. Protest	[Movement. Ancient Greece. Representative. Volunteerism]	[Ancient Greece. Representative. Deliberation] [Ancient Greece. Direct. Volunteerism. Rebellion]	[Religion] [Representative. Corruption e-Democracy]	Riot. Corruption. Rebellion. Protest
Values		Protest	[Spirituality. Meditation/ Mountain. Family. Intimacy. Concert] [Anonymous. Protest]	Astronaut. Mountain. Concert	[Christ. Family. Intimacy] [Anonymous. Christ. Money. Army/ Money Intimacy]	Riot. Anonymous. Army. Protest

Groups 2 and 3 (university students of e-learning or in-class courses) exhibit similar behavior: high political interest, collective ways of mobilization, they get informed about politics from newspapers, social media, and the internet. They have a more activist and rebellious perception of democracy, and they have expressivist personal values. This is a highly politically mobilized group which ideologically tends to the left and far-left side of the axis. Regarding the initial hypothesis, a comparison between participants in online and in-class groups shows no significant difference on the effect of the course. We conclude that both groups exhibited similar behavior and characteristics, therefore online class had the same effect on students as in-class courses.

Regarding the hypothesis about the difference between participants of the civic education workshops and the control group, we detect that group 1 is distinct and has different characteristics which extend also to the way the respondents perceive democracy and how they construct their moral self. Group 1 (control group) is placed in the center-left or center-right scale. Their level of political knowledge is very low as is their levels of political interest. This group is more likely not to be politically mobilized, and they personally address issues to the authorities. The most prominent characteristic of their perception on democracy is "participation," "ancient Greece," and "e-democracy," and they get informed mostly from TV, family, friends, and social media. Their personal values are mostly naturalistic. The difference between participants of the civic education workshops and respondents of the control group extends to the way the respondents perceive democracy and how they construct their moral self. We observe that while groups 2 and 3 (university students in-class and online) have a more collective and active view on democracy and are characterized as expressivists, respondents of the control group seem to adopt naturalistic values and perceive democracy as "institutional" and "participatory."

The fourth group (high-school students) is positioned to the right side of the axis, having a high level of political knowledge, and they get informed by television and family. They perceive democracy as "representation," "e-democracy" and "corruption," as well as "religion.". In their personal values, we find Christianity in a prominent position, together with naturalistic values of family. Group 4, which consists of the high-school students in secondary education, choose to be closer to the religious, ethnocentric conceptualizations of democracy and adopt mostly naturalistic concepts. This can be attributed to the basic core of the content taught in Greek secondary education, which aims to cultivate the idea of "ethnos" (in terms of ethnicity/ethnic identity) and orthodox Christianity to students, as the core values of Greek society. This group, as expected, is mostly informed about politics by their family, which is the most important political influence on children under 18 years old. As a result, the differentiation of this group is justified by the special characteristics of under aged children and their close connection to family.

Discussion

The teaching experiment in the Aristotle University of Thessaloniki and the overall research derived from it strengthen the general conclusion that the teaching of civic education improves participation in the commons and the perception of young people about democracy and their role as citizens. Comparing the general population, which in Greece has a limited amount of civic education according to the school curriculum, to the students who attended the civic education course given by the political sciences students, uncovered an improved score on almost all political characteristics. Students who participated in these courses also showed an inclination to choose more active modes of participation than the control population. This research highlights the importance of civic education in democratic countries on understanding the role of the citizen and inclination to be actively engaged. Furthermore, the use of interactive methods, such as these workshops, can assist the students in better comprehending the roles and the institutions within democracy. By simulating these roles, they achieve a deeper understanding and adopt a more active stance towards citizenship. The research also shows that civic education can have the same benefits both in classroom courses and distance learning, and it could produce even greater results when applied in younger students—high school students for example, who are influenced to a greater degree by the context of their studies and their environment which formulates their ideas, their democratic and moral self.

There are ways to further enhance this research and examine in greater detail the effects of these interactive civic education workshops on the participants. Additionally, we recognize that the inclusion of social sciences students in the survey may explain some of the higher scores and thereby limit the power of these results. The comparison of the groups is based on their similar backgrounds, but in some cases this is not sufficiently supported. Group 1 (control group) includes university students who are compared with groups 2 and 3 which consist of university students. Even if groups 2 and 3 are students of social sciences and therefore appear more politically motivated, we must note that the Greek educational system provides the same content of education to all university entrant students. As a result, the social sciences students have the same educational background as the rest of the students until the concluding class of Greek Lyceum. On the other hand, group 4 again shares the same civic educational background with university students of group 1, but the difference between these two groups is the age. The same applies for the comparison between groups 2 and 4 where the civic education intervention was applied in the classroom. These differences between the backgrounds of the groups limits the ability to generalize our results in all situations. Future research might examine the differences between sets of groups with almost identical backgrounds by investigating the effects of such an intervention on the same sample comparing its pre-treatment and post-treatment scores. However, this case study supports and extends existing theory regarding political socialization, emphasizing the role of education and, more specifically, civic education in the political socialization process of future citizens.

The research presented in this chapter highlights the important role of civic education and its positive effect in the political behavior and engagement of the students. Analysis from the data shows that the students who were taught in a civic education course by the political science department students who had opted for the "*Teaching Civic Education*" academic module managed to score higher in political behavior characteristics (political interest, knowledge, and mobilization) in comparison to the control group (general student population). In addition to the above, the study shows that the distance learning course (spring semester 2020) had the same effect on the students for political engagement as the in-classroom courses before the COVID-19 pandemic (spring semester 2019). The intervention in the Aristotle University of the Thessaloniki, with students teaching civic education to other students in high schools and universities, shows the importance of teaching democracy, especially when this takes the form of interactive workshops where students can simulate their future role as citizens and be trained on special topics such as representation, deliberation, elections, and understanding the basic democratic institutions and functions. The Aristotle University experiment can serve as an example for other institutions and researchers. Applying the methodology, they can prepare their students to develop and deliver interactive civic education courses to other students, and they can also examine the effect on the political behavior of the young participants. Such intervention could enhance the content of civic education and promote the importance of the inclusion of civic education in the school curriculum, as well as in the university's curriculum, with the aim of strengthening the role of the citizen in contemporary and strong democratic societies.

Endnotes

1. Lawrence Jacobs and Robert Shapiro, *Politicians Don't Pander: Political Manipulation and the Loss of Democratic Responsiveness* (Chicago: University of Chicago, 2000).

2. Syntagma [Constitution] art. 16, para. 2, https://www.hellenicparliament.gr/en/Vouli-ton-Ellinon/To-Politevma/Syntagma/

3. Elizabeth Bennion and Laughlin Xander, "Best Practices in Civic Education: Lessons from Journal of Political Science Education," *Journal of Political Science Education* 14, no. 3 (2018).

4. Jeffrey Bernstein, "Cultivating Civic Competence: Simulations and Skill-Building in an Introductory Government Class," *Journal of Political Science Education* 4, no. 1 (2008).

5. Georgia Panagiotidou and Theodore Chadjipadelis, "First-time Voter in Greece: Views and Attitudes of Youth on Europe and Democracy," in *Data Analysis and Rationality in a Complex World*, eds. Theodore Chadjipadelis et al. (New York: Springer International Publishing, 2019).

6. Emile Durkheim, *Education and Sociology* (New York: Free Press, 1956).

7. John Dewey, *Democracy and Education* (New York: Macmillan, 1916).

8. Talcott Parsons, "An Outline of the Social System," in *Theories of the Society*, eds. Talcott Parsons et al. (Englewood Cliffs, NJ: Prentice-Hall, 1971).

9. Christine Kulke, "Politische Sozialisation und Geschlechterdifferenz," in *Neues Handbuch der Sozialisationsforschung*, eds. Klaus Hurrelmann and Ulich Dieter (Weinheim, Germany: Beltz, 1991)

10. Richard Dawson and Kenneth Prewitt, *Political Socialization* (Boston, MA: Little, Brown & Co, 1969).

11. David Easton and Robert Hess "The Child's Political World," *Midwest Journal of Political Science* 6, no. 3 (1962).

12. Herbert Hyman, *Political Socialization. A Study in the Psychology of Political Behavior* (Glencoe, IL: Free Press, 1959).

13. David Campbell, *Why We Vote: How Schools and Communities Shape Our Civic Life* (Princeton, NJ: Princeton University Press, 2006).

14. Richard Dawson and Kenneth Prewitt, *Political Socialization* (Boston, MA: Little, Brown & Co, 1969).

15. David Hargreaves, *The Challenge for the Comprehensive School: Culture, Curriculum and Community* (London: Routledge, 1982).

16. David Campbell, "Voice in the Classroom: How an Open Classroom Environment Facilitates Adolescents' Civic Development," in *CIRCLE Working Paper* 28 (2005).

17. Alison Rios Millett McCartney, "Teaching Civic Engagement: Debates, Definitions, Benefits, and Challenges," in *Teaching Civic Engagement: From Student to Active Citizen*, eds. Alison Rios Millett McCartney, Elizabeth A. Bennion, and Dick Simpson (Washington, DC: American Political Science Association, 2013).

18. Athanasia Chalari and Serifi Panagiota, "The 'Crisis Generation': The Effect of the Greek Crisis on Youth Identity Formation," *GreeSE Papers* no. 123 (2018).

19. Katherine Barrett and Richard Greene, "Civic Education: A Key to Trust in Government," in *Teaching Civic Engagement Across the Disciplines*, eds. Elizabeth Matto, Alison Rios Millett McCartney, Elizabeth A. Bennion, and Dick Simpson (Washington, DC: American Political Science Association, 2017).

20. See results of voting intention survey in Greece during the period 2010–2020 in https://metronanalysis.gr

21. Jacobs and Shapiro, *Politicians Don't Pander,* 2000.

22. See results of 2015 Greek national election results in http://ekloges-prev.singularlogic.eu/

23. Lies Maurissen, "Political Efficacy and Interest as Mediators of Expected Political Participation Among Belgian Adolescents," *Applied Developmental Science* 24, no. 4 (2020).

24. Henry Milner, *Civic Literacy: How Informed Citizens Make Democracy Work* (Hanover, NH: University Press of New England, 2002).

25. Norman Nie, Jane Junn, and Kenneth Stehlik-Barry, *Education and Democratic Citizenship in America* (Chicago: University of Chicago Press, 1996).

26. Diana Owen, "The Influence of Civic Education on Electoral Engagement and Voting," in *Teaching Civic Engagement: From Student to Active Citizen*, eds. Alison Rios Millett McCartney, Elizabeth A. Bennion, and Dick Simpson (Washington, DC: American Political Science Association, 2013).

27. Gert Biesta and Robert Lawy, "From Teaching Citizenship to Learning Democracy: Overcoming Individualism in Research, Policy and Practice," *Cambridge Journal of Education* 36, no. 1 (2006).

28. Gert Biesta, *Learning Democracy in School and Society, Education, Lifelong Learning and the Politics of Citizenship* (University of Stirling UK: Sense Publishers, 2011).

29. Hanna Pitkin, *The Concept of Representation* (Berkeley: University of California Press, 1967); Arend Lijphart, *Patterns of Democracy* (New Haven, CT: Yale University Press, 1999); Donald Horowitz, "Electoral Systems: A Primer for Decision Makers," *Journal of Democracy* 14, no. 4 (2003); Ioannis Andreadis and Theodore Chadjipadelis, "Differences in Voting Behavior," in *Proceedings of the 20th IPSA World Congress* (Fukuoka, Japan, 2006).

30. Andrew Reynolds, *The Architecture of Democracy* (Oxford, UK: Oxford University Press, 2002); David Farrell, *Electoral Systems: A Comparative Introduction* (London and New York: Palgrave, 2001).

31. Maurice Duverger, *Political Parties: Their Organization and Activity in the Modern State* (New York: John Wiley, 1954).

32. Katherine Nicoll, Andreas Fejes, Maria Olson, Magnus Dahlstedt, and Gert Biesta, "Opening Discourses of Citizenship Education: A Theorization with Foucault," *Journal of Education Policy* 28, no. 6 (2013).

33. Frank Reichert, "Who is the Engaged Citizen? Correlates of Secondary School Students' Concepts of Good Citizenship," *Educational Research and Evaluation* 22, no. 5–6 (2016).

34. Bryan Shelly, "Bonding, Bridging, and Boundary Breaking: The Civic Lessons of High School Activities," *Journal of Political Science Education* 7, no. 3 (2011).

35. Diana Owen and Isaac Riddle, "Active Learning and the Acquisition of Political Knowledge in High School," in *Teaching Civic Engagement across the Disciplines*, eds. Elizabeth Matto, Alison Rios Millett McCartney, Elizabeth A. Bennion, and Dick Simpson (Washington, DC: American Political Science Association, 2017).

36. The module and all its activities are part of the academic curriculum and therefore approved by the board of the Political Science Department, the board of the Aristotle University of Thessaloniki and the Greek Ministry of Education and

Religious Affairs. We should note here that in Greece, University Research activities are free and therefore approved by all parts.

37. Sixty (60) ECTS credits are the equivalent of a full year of study or work

38. Derek Anderson, Don Barr, and Christina Labaj, "Repetitive Microteaching: Learning to Teach Elementary Social Studies," *Journal of Social Studies Education Research* 3, no. 2 (2012).

39. Anderson, Barr, and Labaj, 2012.

40. In Greek educational system, school community, defined as all students attending the particular school, participates in a direct election procedure at the beginning of each year, in order to elect their boards. Each class elects its own five-member board and another fifteen-member board is elected from the total of the students, representing the school' students.

41. Edmund Burke, "Speech to the Electors of Bristol at the Conclusion of the Poll," in *The Works of the Right Honourable Edmund Burke, in Twelve Volumes*, eds. J. C. Nimmo, 2nd ed. (London, 1780).

42. Jon Elster, *Deliberative Democracy* (Cambridge, UK: Cambridge University Press, 1998).

43. Antonio Floridia, *From Participation to Deliberation: A Critical Genealogy of Deliberative Democracy* (ECPR Press, 2007).

44. Elizabeth Bennion, "Assessing Civic and Political Engagement Activities: A Toolkit," in Teaching Civic Engagement: From Student to Active Citizen, eds. Alison Rios Millett McCartney, Elizabeth A. Bennion, and Dick Simpson (Washington, DC: American Political Science Association, 2013).

45. Manusos Maragudakis and Theodore Chadjipadelis, *The Greek Crisis and its Cultural Origins (*New York: Palgrave-Macmillan, 2019).

46. See further at https://www.mzes.uni-mannheim.de/d7/en/projects/the-true-european-voter-a-strategy-for-analysing-the-prospects-of-european-electoral-democracy-that-includes-the-west

47. See further at http://www.comparativecandidates.org/

48. Maragudakis and Chadjipadelis, *The Greek Crisis and its Cultural Origins,* 2019.

49. Theodore Chadjipadelis, "Parties, Candidates, Issues: The Effect of Crisis, Correspondence Analysis and Related Methods," in *CARME* (Napoli, Italy: 2015); Jean Paul Benzécri et al., *L'analyse des données. Tome 1: La taxinomie. Tome 2: Analyse des Correspondances* (Paris: Dunod, 1973).

50. Giannis Papadimitriou and Giannoula Florou, "Contribution of the Euclidean and Chi-square Metrics to Determining the Most Ideal Clustering in Ascending Hierarchy (in Greek)," *Annals in Honor of Professor I. Liakis* (1996).

51. Dimitris Karapistolis, *Software Method of Data Analysis MAD* (2010). See further at http://www.pylimad.gr/

52. Michael Greenacre, *Correspondence Analysis in Practice* (Boca Raton: Chapman and Hall/CRC, 2007).

53. Significance level set at 0.05

54. Annick Percheron, *La Socialisation Politique* (Paris: PFNSP, 1985).

55. Annick Percheron, *L'Univers Politique des Enfants* (Paris: PFNSP, 1974); Annick Percheron, *Les 10–16 Ans et la Politique* (Paris: PFNSP, 1978).

56. Significance level set at 0.05

57. For example, cluster 4 comprehends democracy as its electronic form, while cluster 1 identify democracy as a religious concept.

58. Georgia Panagiotidou and Theodore Chadjipantelis, "First-Time Voter in Greece: Views and Attitudes of Youth on Europe and Democracy" in *Data Analysis and Rationality in a Complex World*, eds. Theodore Chadjipadelis et al. (New York: Springer International Publishing, 2019).

Creating Institutions for Civic Engagement Education

Introduction

Elizabeth A. Bennion[1] and Dawn Michele Whitehead[2]

1. Indiana University, South Bend; 2. Association of American Colleges & Universities

T his section provides diverse examples of interdisciplinary institutional programs that strengthen civic engagement inside and outside of the classroom. The institutions represented are both democratic institutions, which includes the perspective of institutions as constraints and incentives, and higher education institutions, which include programs offered through the organizations at different levels. The examples come in the form of a common curriculum, intentional civic learning for all, education abroad with civic goals, and innovative pedagogies involving theater. The programs promote civic engagement through structures that are not limited to the field of political science, but can be adapted in the political science context.

Two chapters are models of civic engagement that engaged all students. In the American context, Suzanne M. Chod and William Muck, North Central College, and Abraham Goldberg, Dena Pastor, and Carah Ong Whaley, James Madison University, offer a comparative look at how two institutions, a small private liberal arts college in a major metropolitan area and a large comprehensive university in a rural area, embed civic engagement for all students through curricular and co-curricular programs. One institution has integrated civic engagement into general education while the other has developed campus-wide, year-round voter education and engagement initiatives. In the US context, they argue for a sense of urgency in preparing students to participate in a healthy, functional, and inclusive society due to concerns about threats to democracy and widespread inequality in the United States. Catherine Shea Sanger, Yale-NUS College in Singapore, and Wei Lit Yew, Hong Kong Baptist University, offer a model of civic engagement in the less liberal political context of Singapore. Civic engagement is threaded throughout a common curriculum with opportunities for civic learning both inside and outside the classroom. Students confirm that both the institutional culture, common curriculum, active approaches to learning, and residential nature of their globally diverse campus contribute to their preparation for civic and political engagement, despite numerous barriers to engagement for both domestic and international students. Mark Charlton and Alasdair Blair, of De Montfort University in the United Kingdom, explore volunteering to build social capital and create civic engagement opportunities for students of all majors.

Collectively, the authors featured in this section of the book make it clear that innovative and diverse pedagogies should be employed to foster active citizenship that is impactful for students and community partners. Xaman Korai Minillo and Mariana Pimenta Oliveira Baccarini, both of the Federal University of Paraíba in Brazil, offer insight into the power of political theater as a pedagogical approach for a community outreach project in Brazil where state leadership challenges democratic institutions. Students are empowered to practice education as emancipation, a framework inspired by Freire's *Pedagogy of the Oppressed*. They are actively engaged with the community through conversation circles and lectures presented by community members. Students also participate in the theater of the oppressed, identifying topics democratically through communal conversations and suggestions. In the South African context, Laurence Piper, Sondré Bailey, and Robyn Pasensie, all of the University of the Western Cape, explore the connections between Work Integrated Learning (WIL) and the promotion of active citizenship. This pedagogy is most often framed as the integration of theoretical classroom knowledge and practical workplace knowledge. However, the authors of this chapter explain how programs can reimagine and redesign WIL as a form of community-based learning that promotes civic skills and democratic engagement.

Study abroad programs are another space where institutional programs strengthen civic engagement inside and outside the classroom. Two chapters in this section examine programs with US-based students studying abroad in West Africa; each offers a useful model and perspective on civic engagement. Nicole Webster, of Pennsylvania State University, approaches global civic engagement with a critical lens. Her institution's commitment to strategic partnerships facilitated the development of a center with connections to existing partners in Burkina Faso with an emphasis on global challenges. Her work seeks transformation both for students and for communities. There is a clear emphasis on the community's perspectives, histories, and narratives as students seek to learn and engage in their host country. Webster's argument that civic engagement is an ideal pedagogy to develop an informed citizenry comes with the caveat that civic engagement must be inclusive with equitable engagement of the community, guided by a vision of global citizenship that centers social justice and equity. This approach to global civic education requires a decentering of the US or European view.

Amina Sillah and Donn Worgs, of Towson University, also tackle the concept of global citizenship as they lead an experiential learning program for US-based students in The Gambia and Senegal. The program facilitates cross-national interactions between the global North and global South in the context of global citizenship where inequities and issues of justice persist. This chapter offers a model for course design rooted in theories of community development that students test and refine through cultural immersion and critical reflection. The authors examine students' enhanced understandings of global citizenship in light of participation in the program, which includes empathy with community residents, challenges to globalization, and a recognition of the effect of gender roles and religion in shaping individual and community opportunities and outcomes.

The citizenship status of students could impact the way they engage in civic opportunities, and some institutions are careful in crafting student experiences to meet these diverse students. Charlton and Blair explore an institution's efforts to increase political engagement among young people in the UK to combat their low participation. Volunteering is explored as an option to build social capital and create civic engagement. The challenge of engaging in civic activity in a country that is not one's own is explored by Webster and by Sanger and Yew. Webster's emphasis is on the lens that students use when seeking to understand the local community and how to create a better and more equitable understanding of the narratives and lived experiences of community members. Her pedagogical tools encourage students to use an asset framework to facilitate positive interactions and understandings of the host community. Sanger and Yew examine the challenges of navigating political and cultural contexts in a less liberal country where some students are citizens and others are not. While laws constrain political engagement for all students, rules, opportunities, and consequences differ between citizens and non-citizens, requiring instructors and students alike to adapt to the realities of civic engagement in this complex context.

In sum, these chapters offer diverse approaches to institutional civic engagement programs. By offering examples from a variety of countries, disciplines, and institutional types, we seek to spark a conversation about institutional approaches to civic engagement worldwide—approaches that prepare students for diverse and meaningful engagement with their own communities for years to come.

11

Can We Get an Upgrade? How Two College Campuses Are Building the Democracy We Aspire to Be

Suzanne M. Chod[1], Abraham Goldberg[2], William Muck[1], Dena Pastor[2], Carah Ong Whaley[2]

1. North Central College; 2. James Madison University
Authors listed alphabetically

The chapter addresses how a small private liberal arts college in a major metropolitan area and a large comprehensive university in a rural area of the United States advance and assess civic learning and engagement initiatives in a time when democracy is being threatened. Although the approaches differ, common themes and aspirations emerged that could prove instructive. Both institutions commit to reaching all students rather than focusing narrowly on political science majors, recognize civic learning as a public good central to a healthy, functioning, and equitable society, and contend that civic engagement initiatives must embrace politics and pressing public issues regardless of the real or perceived fears their institutions may have of retribution. The authors argue that civic education initiatives should be continually assessed, leverage partnerships across campuses and in the community and aim to create a more inclusive democracy, as opposed to reinforcing privilege.

KEYWORDS: Political Learning; Civic Engagement; Assessment; Democratic Inclusion; Social Justice; Racial Justice.

Introduction

American democracy is in trouble. Fierce partisanship, uncompetitive congressional elections, inequitable party nomination processes, demonization of opposing perspectives, persistent structural and institutional discrimination and racism, and the outsized influence of large campaign donations threaten the core foundation of our political system while countless public problems remain unaddressed and unresolved. Coming of age in the post-9/11 era, young people have witnessed endless wars and military interventions, economic collapse and the costs of greed, the legitimization of hate in the public square, deepening federal debt, voter registration purges, rising costs of education, and now a deadly pandemic gripping our nation. It should come as no surprise that young people are less likely than their older counterparts to view democracy as essential.[1] As presently practiced, democracy seemingly is not working for them. Further, young people are more likely to believe it does not matter which party controls Congress and less likely to believe voting actually gives people a say in what government does.[2] While ambivalence may cause some to avoid engaging in our democracy, we also know barriers to entry can be much higher for young people and especially those from underrepresented, historically marginalized groups.[3] Even those interested in participating are faced with systemic barriers that prevent democratic engagement.[4]

Colleges and universities face the challenge of preparing young people to navigate, and thrive in, an uncertain future, and campus leaders are being called upon to promote nonpartisan, year-round political learning initiatives that are embedded within their institutions' academic infra-structures. The stakes are high. As our colleagues at the Institute for Democracy and Higher Education note "[a]t risk are core ideals of freedom, equality and inclusion, and shared responsibility for protecting democratic principles and practices. Learning for democracy should be a national priority, and our colleges and universities need to lead this charge."[5] Institutions of higher education across the country are answering that call through the development and implementation of curricular and co-curricular initiatives aimed at preparing students to be active and informed participants in civic and political life with a vision of strengthening democracy. This work is simultaneously difficult and necessary.

This chapter addresses how two institutions, a private liberal arts college with 2,800 students in a major metropolitan area, and a public comprehensive university with 22,000 students in a rural region, advance and assess institutional commitments to civic engagement. The approaches are as different as the institutions themselves; however, common themes and aspirations have emerged that could prove instructive for academic leaders tasked with educating for democracy.

First, both institutions are committed to embedding civic engagement in the academic mission of their respective universities with an aim toward reaching **all** students rather than focusing narrowly on political science majors. This is evident below as one institution outlines ways civic learning is deeply embedded within a newly developed general education program and the other through a campus-wide, year-round voter education and engagement initiative that emphasizes learning about public issues and engaging others with different perspectives. Learning for democracy should not be episodic nor decentralized from the core operations of our institutions. Though differently situated, it is an academic initiative at both institutions.

Fortunately, there are resources available to support the monumental challenge of educating all students for democracy. The Association of American Colleges and Universities noted that "[e]ducating students to be socially responsible, informed, and engaged citizens in their workplaces, nation, and the global community should be an expected goal for every major."[6] They followed up with a special issue of *Peer Review* focused on integrating civic learning into disciplines, mini-grants for academic departments to explore ways to develop civic learning within majors, and a series of webinars and regional institutes for departmental teams across 30 different majors. For 20 years, Project Pericles has supported institutional efforts to advance civic engagement through curricular integration, faculty development, dialogue and debate programs, and voter education initiatives.[7] The organization sponsors mini-grant programs such as one used by a school described in this chapter to help journalism students explore hyper-partisanship. They also curate a syllabus bank with civic learning opportunities that are relevant for diverse disciplines such as the arts, biology, chemistry, computer science and business. In several states, Campus Compact offers grants to incentivize and promote community and civic engagement scholarship and curriculum integration.[8] For example, a High-Impact Community Engagement Practices program through Indiana Campus Compact offers funding to advance the development and implementation of both curricular and co-curricular opportunities. The American Political Science Association recently published *Teaching Civic Engagement Across the Disciplines* to support broad undergraduate civic engagement and maintains a corresponding website with course materials, assessments, and access to resources. Both institutions featured here drew heavily on the Thomas and Brower chapter emphasizing the value of campus cultures that foster political learning and engagement throughout one's undergraduate experience. Civic engagement cannot be the purview of a particular discipline. Democracy requires **all** students to develop civic knowledge, skills, and dispositions.[9]

Second, both institutions recognize civic learning as a public good central to a healthy, functioning, and equitable society. Recent social unrest stemming from racially charged incidents of police brutality further demonstrate that systemic anti-Black racism remains a fundamental feature of American society. Both civic engagement initiatives outlined below aim to create a more inclusive, just democracy. This goal requires that racial injustices, xenophobia and social inequities be bluntly confronted. Both campuses featured here do so. One used the experiential power of historic places to teach about civil rights with faculty-led tours to important sites as a central component of a course addressing societal inequities. The other campus created a way for students to engage directly with community members on virtual platforms to discuss racism and discrimination. Additionally, faculty members across all disciplines were offered support and resources to integrate antiracism and social justice education into course work.

There is no silver-bullet to create the equitable and just society we aspire to become, but this chapter provides two models of institutions earnestly trying to improve the situation. And there is help. Accompanying a rush of public pronouncements calling to dismantle racism and white supremacy are a growing number of resources to support this work on campuses. The American Political Science Association curated an impressive collection of scholarship and teaching materials focused on social injustices, protest and politics, activism, and Black Lives Matter along with grants supporting this work in the political science community.[10] The Association of American Colleges and Universities has a long-term commitment to racial healing and inclusion, most notably through its Office of Diversity, Equity, and Student Success.[11] Institutions striving to achieve equity goals can also benefit from the work of the University of Southern California's Race and Equity Center.[12] The Center supports antiracist scholarship and offers research-informed Equity Institutes for 20 leaders to gather for eight weeks on a college campus to have serious conversations about race and racism, how it impacts students and staff on campus, and how to advance racial equity moving forward.

Third, both schools contend that civic engagement on college campuses must embrace politics and pressing public issues regardless of the real or perceived fears their institutions may have of retribution from alumni and donor communities, elected officials, or other advocacy groups. Higher education as well as K-12 have been criticized for deemphasizing civic learning, perhaps at the cost of weakening education's public purpose and graduating students underprepared to address pressing societal issues.[13] Some argue that avoiding political topics may marginalize students and reinforce the status quo.[14] The initiatives featured in this chapter lean into politics and encourage students to engage with public issues, but do so without supporting or endorsing any specific political ideology. The work is nonpartisan, but not apolitical. One campus provides funding on a competitive basis for students to develop projects that respond to social, economic, environmental, or justice issues. The other embeds opportunities for students to engage in dialogue on political questions in prominent public spaces across campus.

Ironically, despite concerns about the state of democracy, youth voter participation levels were higher in the 2018 midterm election than in the previous six midterm elections.[15] Both institutions featured in this chapter recognize that a spike in voting can potentially be leveraged into long-term programs that strengthen the culture of civic engagement on our campuses. The following sections will outline civic engagement initiatives at North Central College and James Madison University, describe student learning assessment strategies, and conclude by outlining lessons learned and future plans.

North Central College: An Innovative Partnership

Founded in 1861, North Central College is a residential, 2,800-student liberal arts college in the Chicago suburb of Naperville, Illinois. With a wide range of majors including pre-professional programs, North Central is firmly grounded in the liberal arts, while offering innovative programs to respond to shifts in both higher education and student needs. While civic education has been important to the college since its founding, there has been a notable cultural shift recently. North Central students are predominantly white, with 40% representing the first generation of their family to attend college. North Central has long dedicated itself to preparing young people to leave campus committed to and equipped for contributing to the overall health of civil society. In a response to an increasingly globalized and complex world fraught with divisions and polarization, North Central has renewed its longstanding emphasis on helping students graduate as better citizens. The Board of Trustees, the college administration, faculty, and staff have all prioritized developing and supporting fully immersive opportunities for civic engagement. To that end, in the last three years, North Central has created a new college mission, redesigned the general education program, overhauled the entire curriculum, and implemented new civic engagement initiatives across campus. While there is not one center or office dedicated to developing and maintaining a culture of civic engagement, there are inventive programmatic pathways where the Political Science Department is central, but success depends on contributions from all corners of the campus.

One of the American Political Science Association's core objectives is "promoting high quality teaching and education about politics and government."[16] This work should not be limited to the political science classroom. If a campus seeks to educate students to understand and participate in an historically exclusionary democracy, it is incumbent upon political science departments to partner with their colleges and universities to work on civic education curricular development, as well as co-curricular and extra-curricular activities. Recent higher education civic engagement research finds that no one class, office, or event will create lifelong, civically engaged adults. Rather, successful civic education requires sustained, wide-reaching, and multi-level partnerships among different parts of a college and university, including the involvement of political scientists.[17] The goal is to create a campus culture of engagement. Campus culture, according to Billings and Terkla, "influences the values and beliefs of faculty, staff, and students and how these values and beliefs impact their behavior" and "are cultivated through public visions, shared expectations, and collective purposes."[18] What follows is a description of how North Central developed and implemented innovative partnerships among faculty, staff, and administrators to create a fully immersive civic developmental experience for students, one that is curricular, co-curricular, extra-curricular—one that ensures students cannot graduate from North Central College without taking courses, working on a community engaged learning project, and attending a talk or workshop directly related to civic education and participation. A fully immersive civic developmental experience is one in which all corners of the campus community understand and are active participants in the effort to develop and assess students' civic engagement. Moreover, it is one that deepens across students' time on campus, creating a journey from introduction, to realization, to action.

The College's Curriculum

North Central College has infused civic education into its curriculum. In the summer of 2017, on the heels of a vote to change the academic calendar from trimesters to semesters, and three credit hour courses to four, a committee of faculty and staff was charged with developing new learning outcomes and suggesting models for an updated general education. The faculty-drafted and adopted learning outcomes are in four categories: Know, Do, Care, and Connect. Each of which reflects the College's newly constructed mission: "We are a diverse community of learners dedicated to preparing students to be curious, engaged, ethical, and purposeful citizens and leaders in local, national and global contexts."[19] The specific outcomes in the Care category focus on students thinking and acting ethically as a citizen of the local, national and global community. They are as follows:

> 1. Student articulates the multiple values they hold as part of their personal worldview.
>
> 2. Student critically evaluates the ethical dimensions of life and work across multiple cultural, philosophic, and/or historical traditions.
>
> 3. Student explains local, national, and global civic identities and commitments with increasing awareness of their environment.

4. Student engages in constructive dialogue in discussing and debating issues of civic importance.

There is an additional learning outcome from the Know category: "Student analyzes power structures that determine hierarchies, inequalities, and opportunities among groups, such as those based on race, ethnicity, gender, or class." Hence, of North Central's 11 general education learning outcomes, five of them speak directly to students' civic mindedness.

The new general education has additional requirements outside of a traditional distribution model to reinforce these outcomes. In the first-year seminar, students are asked to think about their place on campus and in their local, national, and international communities. They also take courses marked with three different designations that relate directly to the college's mission focused on engagement, ethics, and leadership: ethical dimensions, global understanding, and power structures. The heart of North Central's general education is the four courses in a concentrated, themed topic called iCons (interdisciplinary connections).

Students chose one of eight iCons;[20] each one centers on issues of domestic and global citizenship, inequities, and civic participation and consists of courses from a cross-section of departments and programs, providing an interdisciplinary focus. For example, in the spring of 2021, 21 unique courses from 11 different programs are offered in the Engaging Civic Life iCon. Also, in spring 2021, there are 24 unique courses from 11 different programs offered in the Challenging Inequity iCon. Courses in the iCons fulfill other general education requirements, as well as majors and/or minor requirements. POLS 101: The American Political System exemplifies this well. POLS 101 is in both the Challenging Inequity and Engaging Civic Life iCons, fulfills the power structures mission designation (referred to previously), is a community engaged learning course (discussed below), is a social science, and is one of the required gateway courses for the political science major and minor.

The curricular requirements culminate in a senior seminar in which students across majors bring their different experiences to collaborate in the examination of a complex, unstructured issue or problem and develop a constructive response to it. Like the first-year seminar, the class is taught by faculty from across the college and is a stand-alone requirement, separate from students' major courses. Sections are taught by different faculty members, each choosing the "wicked problem" students confront as well as the artifact they produce, yet the plan had been to have public presentations of the students' work. However, as the new general education has only been offered for a year and a half, only a few sections of the senior seminar have been offered, all of them during COVID-19.[21]

In addition to the curricular components, the new North Central general education includes co-curricular requirements such as community-engaged learning (CEL). Community-engaged learning is an educational experience in which students collaborate with community partners to apply academic knowledge and critical thinking skills to meet societal needs. Through critical reflection on their activities, students gain a deeper understanding of course content, a broader appreciation of the discipline, and an enhanced sense of civic efficacy and responsibility. Any CEL course must meet the following requirements: significant engagement with a community with the goal of reciprocal benefits for students and the community; intentional integration of learning outcomes and experience with the community; student preparation, reflection, and analysis; and a minimum of 15 hours devoted to the project. During the 2020–2021 academic year, there are 35 unique CEL courses offered from 15 different departments. COVID-19 has prevented in-community work, so faculty have been creative with how students engage with community partners to ensure reciprocal benefits and interaction with partner organizations. This included virtual engagement and programming with the partner organizations, off-site resource collection and drop off when appropriate, and in-depth interviews with partner organization staff to draft action plans and provide help with web design or social media for virtual community outreach.

Each curricular and co-curricular component mentioned are general education requirements; so, students cannot complete their general education, and thereby graduate, without taking courses and having experiences that focus on issues and complexities of civic life. This process builds from students' first semester to their last, developing and deepening their civic-mindedness along the way. They begin thinking of themselves as local, national, and international citizens in the first-year seminar and in their CEL course. Then, in their iCon courses, they learn about the historically disenfranchising nature of civic life across disciplinary lenses. And finally, they use their knowledge and experiences to collaboratively address a persistent and complex social dilemma, or to identify and act on a new opportunity for civic renewal. By the time a student graduates from North Central, they are armed with the skills required to think and act ethically as citizens of the local, national and global community.

While the faculty spearheaded the drafting of requirements, implementation of both the curricular and co-curricular requirements necessitates partnerships among faculty, staff, and administrators campus-wide. Key players include the College's Center for Global Education and Center for Social Impact, the Office of Engaged Learning, the Center for Faculty Excellence, First Generation Programs, Multicultural Affairs, Student Affairs, and Academic Affairs. Cross-campus partnerships are critical to ensure students have access to, and choices in, their civic developmental journey.

The College's Broader Culture

There are many initiatives and programs that undergird the campus' culture of civic engagement. Four initiatives that exemplify North Central's immersive developmental approach to civic education are highlighted below.

The Sankofa Program

"Sankofa" is an Akan word that means "to go back and get it." To understand the present, we must go back to the past. The Sankofa Program focuses on contemporary civil rights and liberties issues through experiential and retrospective lenses. Each year, faculty members work with the Office of Multicultural Affairs to choose a societal issue. To explore the roots of the issue, students spend spring break with faculty and staff traveling to historical sites, museums, and monuments, as well as libraries and college campuses. Prior to traveling, students participate in three workshops in which faculty guides provide a scholarly and experiential background on issues and the sites to be toured. When students stand on ground where slaves were traded in Birmingham, Alabama, or when they visit Friendship Park on the border of San Diego and Mexico to see separated families briefly reunite through a fence for 30 minutes once a week, or when a Freedom Rider jailed at 13 in Parchman Prison tells them they don't have to do everything, but they must do something, the realities of racial injustice, immigration, and mass incarceration come to life. After spending a week learning from these places, the people who lived these experiences, and academic and policy experts, students write a paper and give a post-trip presentation detailing what they learned about themselves through the experience, and how they can apply these lessons to life beyond college, including how they will contribute to positive social change.

The Changemaker Challenge

In 2016, the college launched the "Changemaker Challenge." It is an extra-curricular, volunteer opportunity for the entire student body. Sponsored by Student Affairs, the Center for Social Impact, one of the Center's student groups (Students for Social Innovation), and the Leadership, Ethics and Values academic program, students pitch innovative projects that respond to social, economic, environmental, or justice issues. Of the 50+ pitches made each year, about four are chosen, and winners are given money to support implementation. These projects range from addressing food deserts to online mental health support for college students. This opportunity allows students to identify a problem and create a solution, thereby channeling their passion into purposeful action. For example, funding for one student's project, The Pad Project, provided increased access to feminine hygiene projects for young women in Kenya. As a Kenyan woman, and a political science and gender and women's studies student, she used her academic knowledge and lived experiences to act and help a community. This is the transition from awareness to engagement.

Model United Nations

Another co-curricular program that fits the broader pattern of engaging and integrating the entire campus community is Model United Nations. While the course is housed within the political science department, it draws students from across the college. Students learn hands-on about civic engagement at the domestic and international level. The experience involves a stand-alone course where students and faculty spend eight weeks researching the history, politics, economics, and culture of the assigned country. That provides the intellectual base for their participation in the annual National Model United Nations Conference in New York City. The national conference brings in thousands of students from all over the world. They learn to see the world through the eyes of a different country and then advocate for policy solutions reflective of their assigned country's interests. Students translate theoretical concepts into tangible policy proposals and learn that progress requires collective and collaborative problem solving. Model UN continues to be a consistent and productive pipeline for students who ultimately work in government or public policy.

Enactus

The Enactus program may be the best model of North Central's fully immersive approach to civic development. Students from all majors get hands-on experience with the challenges and opportunities of socially conscious global trade. Students learn to run North Central's Conscious Bean Coffee business. In doing so they develop cross-border partnerships, traveling to Guatemala twice a year to consult directly with locally sourced coffee farmers. In 2019, the College launched its own on-campus coffee lab enabling students to experience everything from roasting and packaging, to sales of locally sourced coffee. The Enactus Coffee Project has a new initiative this year with the Black Student Association. North Central is now sourcing coffee out of Ethiopia that was grown by Black farmers. One of the leadership classes, Financial Intelligence for Social Entrepreneurship, named the coffee, Black Magic Coffee, set a selling price, identified the market, and began sales. All profits will go to the Black Student Association. This is fully immersive civic development—identifying an issue in civic life and taking action based on the knowledge gained in classes and campus opportunities.

The Centrality of Political Science

Creating a campus culture of civic engagement requires partnerships between academic units and student life. Such partnerships, including diverse disciplinary and interdisciplinary learning opportunities, are critical to promote engagement in civic life. While partnerships are important, and multiple disciplines provide valuable insights into civic life and community problem-solving, it is critical for the political science department to take a leadership role in campus engagement efforts. Without such leadership, it is easy for students and campus leaders to neglect political education and to understate the critical role that politics and public policy play in shaping lives.

The political science department helps shape a culture of engagement. Billings and Terkla find that "students who perceive that the institutional culture is supportive of civic engagement are predicted to hold more civically minded values and beliefs."[22] Curriculum, then, is only one component of building a campus culture of civic engagement. At North Central College, the Department of Political Science has taken the lead in infusing civic education into all aspects of the campus experience. The goal is for students to see and understand how curricular and co-curricular experiences connect to their civic identities. The department does this in class and through a variety of events and experiences. Some raise awareness of, and interest in, pressing political issues. Others take the next step to show students how to transition from awareness to direct civic action.

The department's first learning objective is to train young people to "participate as civically engaged members of a historically exclusionary democratic society." This centers course offerings and course outcomes. More than in-class work though, is what faculty do outside the classroom to foster a campus culture of awareness and engagement. One example of the latter is the Topics in Politics (TIP Talks) lecture series. TIP Talks are held every semester and each event consists of four, 15-minute presentations. They are intentionally not research presentations, but instead structured to highlight important political developments and demonstrate their relevance to the audience. The presenters include faculty from the political science department and other departments (e.g., theatre, history, sociology, communication, health sciences, psychology, math). The series highlights that it is not just political scientists grappling with important political questions. The lectures are given to live audiences, aired on a local TV stations, and uploaded to the Political Science Department's YouTube channel, where they have been viewed thousands of times. This series is a signature event for the department. It raises awareness of our political world while simultaneously encouraging students to use their agency to engage that world. In addition, the department hosts events throughout the year around major political speeches, debates and, of course, election nights. All the events build a culture of civic attentiveness and engagement. This is especially important for minoritized students oppressed by existing political and social systems.

Political Science Department faculty also model to the campus community the importance of broadly applied civic education and engagement. In particular, faculty think creatively about their roles as public intellectuals. Public intellectualism provides an ideal venue for faculty to connect with a broader community and deliver on the core disciplinary responsibility of fostering civic education and engagement. Political science faculty have a unique skill set that sheds light on critical issues and helps the public put those developments in the proper context. Given the current political climate, the ability to provide evidence-based and theoretically grounded analysis is of the utmost importance. Political scientists at North Central have embraced this opportunity and sought a variety of outlets, including media appearances on TV, radio, and podcasts. Most notably, the department has established a relationship with WGN news in Chicago where faculty are regularly invited to offer analysis of political developments. The political science faculty have also embraced podcasting to foster civic engagement. All department members have appeared on a variety of podcasts, and one department member co-hosts their own, *The Politics Lab*, which is a weekly podcast that brings the lens of political science to the major political news stories of the week. A surprise benefit of podcasting has been how many former students listen and report that it gives them a way to stay connected and politically engaged.

How do we know if it is working?

The college rolled out its new curriculum, calendar, and credit hour system in the fall of 2019. Assessment measures matching specific courses and programming to civic learning and behavioral outcomes are pending. This assessment process stretches across all levels and the data will inform institutional adjustments and improvements over time. There is some evidence to suggest that the Political Science Department's own efforts to highlight civic development in its curricular and co-curricular offerings over the last five years has contributed to an increase in both majors and average class size. During that time there has been a 45% increase in majors, and in 2019–2020, the department had the highest number of majors in its history. While there certainly could be a variety of factors contributing to this increase, it can be linked to the placement of political science at the heart of the campus-wide civic culture.

There are other ways in which North Central students and campus partners have become more aware of and committed to civic engagement in the past three years. For example, in 2018, the campus joined the "ALL IN Campus Democracy Challenge" to increase voter registration and turnout. Faculty, staff and students collaborated to create an action plan that outlined specific strategies. To help implement the plan, the campus received a grant from and partnered with the Campus Election Engagement Program (CEEP). With this grant, the Political Science Department funded a student to act as a fellow and lead the campus voter registration initiatives. Some strategies included voter registration via TurboVote publicized at campus events such as the Department's TIP Talks, partnering with the League of Women Voters and other community organizations to promote National Voter Registration Day, and "strolls to the polls" for early election efforts and on Election Day. Data from the National Study of Learning, Voting, and Engagement (NSLVE) show that North Central saw about a 14% increase in registered students and a 23% increase in voting from 2014 to 2018. North Central's increase is greater than the average among campuses compared by NSLVE.

From the mission, to orientation, to every part of the General Education, to experiences on and off campus, North Central College is building a fully immersive civic developmental experience. Now, more than ever, as the world has become more globalized and democracies are fraying across the world, it is imperative to expose college students to civic engagement and use curricular, co-curricular, and extra-curricular opportunities to immerse them in both theory and practice. Understanding the interconnected world and one's responsibility in it is necessary for democracies to not only be stable, but to flourish.

James Madison University

James Madison University created the James Madison Center for Civic Engagement (JMU Civic) in 2017 to advance the institution's strategic plan by supporting civic learning and democratic engagement across the undergraduate experience. The mission is to educate and inspire people to address public issues and cultivate a just and inclusive democracy. As a separate entity from the institution's service-learning office, JMU Civic's work is primarily focused on political learning and engagement in our democracy. The center does its work by developing and supporting curricular and co-curricular opportunities in collaboration with instructional faculty, student affairs professionals, and community organizations. JMU Civic also actively participates in national conversations about leveraging the power of higher education to strengthen democracy and maintains strategic partnerships with nonprofit organizations supporting college student civic engagement initiatives. These efforts have been featured in national outlets such as *Teen Vogue*, *Wall Street Journal*, *Forbes*, *Chronicle of Higher Education*, *Washington Monthly*, *Education Dive*, and *Democracy Counts 2018: Increased Student and Institutional Engagement*.

The Association of American Colleges and Universities' "Crucible Moment" report famously challenged higher education to ensure that the college experience prepares all students for engagement in our democracy.[23] More recently, the Institute for Democracy and Higher Education at Tufts University (IDHE) further encouraged campuses to shift from episodic election-related activities to year-round political learning.[24] JMU Civic developed a significant voter education and engagement program, initiatives to educate students about equity and inclusion, and Census 2020. In each case, the work leans into politics and public issues with a primary focus on learning.

Voting is the front-door for many students to learn about politics and participate in our democracy, and Virginia has elections every year. JMU Civic's efforts are captured in a Voter Engagement Plan with the center's undergraduate democracy fellows as co-creators, co-educators, and co-implementers in collaboration with other students from a diverse array of majors, athletic teams, student organizations, and co-curricular programs across campus. Voter registration is supported by trained undergraduate volunteers visiting classes, conducting programs for new students during orientation, and reaching out to students at campus libraries and the gym. Prior to voter registration deadlines, JMU Civic undergraduate democracy fellows, in collaboration with student political organizations and residence hall advisors, facilitate a traveling town hall to bring political candidates to residence halls to literally meet students where they are.[25] With support from JMU Civic and Political Science Department faculty, students in a political science course interview candidates on pressing public issues and produce a nonpartisan voter education guide that is distributed on campus and in the surrounding community in partnership with local news organizations.

Student engagement extends far beyond JMU's pool of political science majors. On Election Day, with support from the Center for Inclusive Music Engagement, music education students contribute their talents by performing at an on-campus precinct to build a culture that celebrates democracy. Election night features live coverage of returns by the student television station from the JMU Election Night Watch Party. Local media also covered student efforts to register and get-out-the-vote leading up to and on Election Day. Post-election, students and faculty participate in panels to analyze and discuss what the results mean for governance.

Even in the age of COVID-19, JMU Civic has continued election-related programming through virtual means with significant student participation. Town halls were held virtually and on social media, with 55 virtual programs reaching over 260,000 individuals during the 2020 election season. Additionally, JMU Civic faculty partnered with the Office of Residence Life in 2020 to hold virtual training sessions for resident advisors on how to facilitate difficult election conversations with hall residents and offered a new tool to facilitate reflective discussions about how experiences and social identities shape political identities. JMU Civic also partnered with JMU Athletics to host virtual town halls with candidates for over 250 student athletes and an undergraduate democracy fellow registered 100% of JMU student athletes to vote.

Assessment results suggest efforts to promote voter participation in fall 2018 were effective.[26] For instance, 74% of students reported receiving emails about the 2018 midterm election. Almost half of students reported they registered to vote, updated their voter registration, or inquired about voter registration. Slightly less than half reported a visitor registering students to vote in their classes. Over 1 in 4 students reported reading a voter guide prior to the midterm election[27] and 1 in 10 said they heard directly, in-person from candidates.

Like many universities, JMU Civic participates in the National Study of Voting, Learning and Engagement (NSLVE) produced by the Institute for Democracy and Higher Education at Tufts University. JMU's NSLVE reports are the primary means by which JMU Civic faculty and under-graduate democracy fellows assess the Voter Engagement Plan. From 2014 to 2018 (the first year of programming), JMU's voter turnout rate increased by almost 300%. NSLVE is also used to inform improvements and adjustments to voter education and engagement strategy. For example, past reports indicated that JMU's College of Business had exceptionally low participation rates and JMU Civic responded by creating discipline-specific voter education materials in partnership with students.

JMU Civic initiatives not only work to educate and engage students in elections, but also en-courage them to take deliberative action on major issues like racism and social justice, the economy, the public health crisis, the environment, and immigration. Student-led efforts lean into politics through learning-centered, action-oriented dialogues in public spaces. Facilitating opportunities to discuss even the most divisive topics and providing fact-based evidence and multiple viewpoints contribute to a more vibrant learning environment for political engagement.[28] Plus, a recent study on campus indicated a need for such programming. In a 2019 climate study, several students re-ported that they evaded conversations on public issues to avoid being disrespected, attacked, or ridiculed by their peers or professors.[29] To normalize and demystify discourse on public issues, JMU Civic's Tent Talks program was created to focus on current high profile public issues or issues identified as important by students (any student can request us to address an issue to JMU Civic faculty). Such conversations continued virtually during the pandemic, using social media "live" functions and peer-to-peer software programs (such as Zoom). For each Tent Talk, JMU Civic un-dergraduate democracy fellows prepared a primer with facts about the issue and provided prompts for responses from peers who engaged in discussions.

This initiative is especially important as severe political polarization has contributed to the global democratic recession, eroding democratic norms and raising societal anger.[30] Research shows that the United States is exceptional in the nature of its political divide and that there is in-creasingly stark disagreement between Democrats and Republicans on the economy, racial justice, climate change, law enforcement, international engagement and a long list of other issues.[31] While other countries similarly experience the pressures of partisan media, social media, and deeply root-ed racial and ethnic, cultural, historical and regional divides, the rigid two-party electoral system with closely contested elections in the United States has made it difficult to find common cause to address pressing issues. As microcosms of the larger society, college campuses are not immune from these political divides. College faculty and administrators have a heightened responsibility to foster evidence-based discussion on politics and political issues, especially when such topics have been deemed too divisive and therefore off-limits in other areas of students' lives.[32] To promote career readiness and active citizenship in today's world, colleges must equip students with knowledge of which civic skills to use, when to use them, and provide an opportunity to practice those skills. Deliberative dialogue in public spaces fosters a more resilient democracy by developing skills to process evidence, respect differing views, and learn the reasons behind one's own views.[33] But such dialogues must be combined with participatory ideas for taking action to spur change.

JMU Civic's strategic plan emphasizes equity and inclusion as core values. Partnerships with campus and community organizations have been built to address persistent systemic racism and racial gaps in access, voice, and political participation. The salience of systemic racism was heightened in 2020 by police and vigilante shootings of Black Americans and the protests that followed. In response, JMU Civic co-created programming, including online virtual discussions, to uplift the voices, expertise, and experience of Black students, faculty and staff. Workshops led by faculty and staff included opportunities for participants to develop action-oriented plans to integrate antiracism and social justice education into courses, curriculum, and university programming (see companion website).

JMU Civic has also been working at the local, state, and national levels to ensure a complete count in the 2020 Census. Mandated by the US Constitution, the Census presents an opportunity every 10 years to educate and engage students in efforts to build a more just and inclusive democracy. The Census impacts community resources by determining the distribution of billions in federal dollars for programs including Head Start, special education, and public transportation. The Census also determines the number of state representatives to the US House and affects redistricting at the national, state, and local levels. By making historically minoritized, marginalized, and underrepresented communities visible, the Census offers a way to build power for communities who have been traditionally left out of political and decision making processes.

Because federal guidelines require students to be counted where they live most of the year, which is often away from their hometown, colleges and universities have a special responsibility to the communities in which they are situated to ensure a complete count. College students are a hard-to-count population because they are highly mobile, most likely renters, and, as first-time participants, less likely to understand why the Census matters and how to complete it. To counteract past low self-response rates and utilize best practices from scholarship on voter learning and mobilization including class visits, discussions in public spaces, social networking and relational organizing, JMU Civic worked with students enrolled in an interdisciplinary class to learn about the Census and mobilize a "get-out-the-count" initiative.[34] Students developed and implemented a campus-wide educational initiative to assess and increase student knowledge about the Census, how Census data are used, and how to complete the Census. The plan included a partnership with faculty, administrators, state and local government officials, community organizations, and the Census Bureau to pursue joint initiatives to reach several hard-to-count populations in our region. The plan included leveraging the power of trusted individuals and their networks using a range of tactics, including tabling at key events and public spaces at the university, class visits, in-person and virtual town halls with experts, bus ads, door hangers used for canvassing high density off-campus housing complexes, and a social media campaign. Students in the Census course crafted language with key information and direct links to the Census online portal. University administrators and faculty distributed this information campus-wide via email, text message, and a global alert displayed for an entire week in April 2020 in the university's course management system. A global reminder was also sent from the registrar to fill out the 2020 Census when students registered for fall 2020 courses or checked in for May 2020 graduation. Results based on a pre- and post-assessment of exposure to the Census initiative indicate that students have a better understanding of the importance and purpose of the Census. Students also increased their understanding of what information is collected, how it is used, and how to participate; although there was still room for improvement in these areas.[35]

How do we know if it's working?

A solid foundation for quality programming relies on the existence of student learning outcomes and a strong understanding of both the campus climate and the student population. Since its inception in 2017, JMU Civic has partnered with JMU's Center for Assessment and Research Studies (CARS) to establish such a foundation. JMU Civic began by investigating the suitability of JMU's campus climate for civic learning and democratic engagement.[36] JMU's campus climate study, which follows a protocol steered by Thomas and Brower,[37] was part of a larger initiative to improve political learning and engagement in higher education by the Institute for Democracy and Higher Education (IDHE) at Tufts University and AASCU's American Democracy Project (ADP). Between April and September of 2018, 11 two-hour focus groups were conducted consisting of students, faculty, student affairs staff, unit heads, and academic deans. The study revealed that many opportunities exist for political learning and democratic engagement at JMU, but participation is not pervasive and interest in the topic is mixed. It also found that classroom discussions about political issues are challenging for both students and faculty. The study further found that a campus culture of kindness and caring that attracts students and faculty could simultaneously inhibit authentic political engagement. In essence, JMU Civic learned there is potential for substantial and meaningful political learning and engagement on campus, but also found characteristics of the institution that pose challenges.

Knowing that university-level student learning outcomes would promote an institutional culture focused on civic learning and democratic engagement, a team of faculty and staff from across the institution gathered to create JMU-specific learning outcomes. Informed by several resources,[38] our learning outcomes emphasize the acquisition of civic knowledge, the development of civic skills, and the attainment of dispositions to prepare people for informed and meaningful participation in civic and political life. The outcomes also emphasize taking political and civic action to address social and public issues and are used to communicate what is meant by civic engagement on campus and to direct program development, as no single initiative addresses all outcomes.

To better understand the student population and assess the effectiveness of civic engagement programming, JMU Civic and partners at CARS selected and developed a variety of measures that are routinely administered during large-scale data collection opportunities on campus. For example, to understand whether students have the knowledge, skills, and attitudes needed for informed and effective political involvement, the Political Engagement Project Survey (PEPS) has been administered for several years during institution-wide Assessment Days. The PEPS was created by Beaumont et al. for use in the Political Engagement Project, a 2007 multi-institutional study of the effectiveness of 21 higher education programs and courses focused on promoting political understanding and involvement.[39] Random samples of students complete the PEPS upon entry as first-year students and again after having completed 45–70 credit hours. Items were added to the PEPS asking students to indicate their level of exposure to JMU Civic programming, providing opportunities to analyze how our civic engagement initiative affects learning outcomes. The assessment process is continual and provides key insights to inform program development and implementation of JMU's entire civic engagement initiative.

Conclusion: Our Responsibility to our Campuses

Contemporary literature has focused on individual college and university civic engagement initiatives.[40] We hope to add to this literature by outlining the values and strategies characterizing the cultures of civic engagement fostered by two distinct college campus communities. In doing so, we reflect on the opportunities and challenges that arise from such an undertaking, and what is left to do. We see three necessary components for any campus at the beginning stages, in a period of maintenance, or re-evaluating the long-term success of existing programming: equity-focused and inclusive civic education initiatives, ongoing assessment of civic education in general education curricula, and outreach and sustained partnerships across the institution. We discuss the importance of each one, along with suggestions and considerations for implementation.

Equity-focused and inclusive civic education initiatives

On August 18, 2020, the American Political Science Association published a statement titled "The Essential Role of Social Scientific Inquiry in Maintaining a Free, Participatory, Civil, and Law-Governed Society."[41] The statement calls on us to be reflective of the inequities in our discipline, and how they shape it and those participating in it. In the end, those realities affect our students, as well. Specifically, "Our journals, our syllabi, citation patterns and our canons of scholarship—even how we narrate the history of the discipline itself—have been shaped by the prejudices as well as the achievements of past generations."[42] If we are to do better science and be better colleagues and educators, we are compelled to shed conventions. In doing so, we decolonize our syllabi, elevate the experience of minoritized voices, and hopefully create a more inclusive discipline. As we argue that political science departments should be at the center of civic education and engagement on campuses, we need to implement equity-focused and inclusive teaching and research "in house" first. Then, as partnerships across institutions form, the precedent for initiatives and programming has been established.

More than a disciplinary call, though, are the realities of student experiences in higher education. A 2019 report by the American Council on Education finds:

> "Between 1995–96 and 2015–16, the share of students of color among all undergraduate students increased from about 30 percent to approximately 45 percent. This increase was largely driven by the increase in Hispanic undergraduate enrollment."[43]

While college campuses are becoming more racially and ethnically diverse, about 82% of Black college students attend predominantly white institutions and over 73% of faculty members in higher education identify as white.[44] In the past few years, racist incidents on college campuses ranging from microaggressions to violence have increased.[45] The call across higher education to increase diversity, equity, and inclusion initiatives is not just to support minoritized students and teach those with privileged identities to become anti-racist, but it should be an imperative to create a healthier and more equitable society. Therefore, civic education initiatives should aim to create a more inclusive democracy, as opposed to reinforcing privilege. As this is also the task for our discipline, political science can and should be at the forefront. The political science departments at both institutions discussed here have followed this approach.

Ongoing assessment of civic education in general education curricula

We have outlined two institutions whose missions and visions include helping young people find their civic identity and engagement in a complex and historically exclusionary democracy. Not only should this be the goal of colleges and universities grounded in the liberal arts, but across all colleges and universities. Finley notes:

> "Campuses then need to ask: What does success look like in meeting the language of the mission? At a minimum, success should reflect actions, skills, and attitudes for all students—not just the ones who opt into civic experiences."[46]

While JMU Civic has achieved this with partnerships across campus to support curricular and co-curricular initiatives, informed by a rigorous campus climate study and regular assessment, North Central has taken a different approach. With innovative partnerships across all campus units, and baking civic engagement into general education, North Central has set in motion a new campus-wide effort to foster civic engagement organically across campus. It has created a pathway for assessing whether these measures meet both the mission and the moment. A college or university's general education reflects its values; it is what anchors students' learning, growth, and progress. This integration should be both vertical (coherence across the curriculum) and horizontal (examination of multiple disciplines and lenses), and it will only be successful with iterative collaboration among faculty and academic units. Faculty development centers are helpful partners also, as they can support instructors interested in building civic learning into courses.

The civic identity and engagement learning outcomes of the general education should not be limited to first-year seminar and capstone; nor should they exclusively involve disciplines like political science, history, or economics. For vertical and horizontal integration of civic development in general education, there must be courses from a myriad of disciplines and across course levels. During the 2020–2021 academic year at North Central, for example, faculty from over 10 different departments are teaching the first-year seminar, there are 19 disciplines offering power structures courses, and 22 disciplines are represented in the "Thinking Globally" iCon. For institutions looking to create, maintain, or reevaluate its civic campus culture, there must be a mechanism to assess the effects of general education on civic identity and engagement, whether through formal curricular assessment or broader campus climate studies. This is necessary not only to fulfill an institutions' mission, but to heed a call in higher education. Again, as Finley posits, "As the United States enters a new era of reckoning with civil rights and global health, there is no better time to be clear and inclusive about what a civic-minded campus is."[47] Therefore, if assessment and/or campus climate studies show outcomes are not met, then faculty, and other campus stakeholders, need to modify programming and curricula to better align with stated learning objectives.

Outreach and sustained partnerships across the institution

Creating an active civic culture across campus also requires stepping outside of the classroom to nurture connections and partnerships across the institution. To that end, institutions should seek to cultivate a campus climate that embraces political learning and engagement in public spaces that are intentionally not the classroom. This can and should take a variety of forms. The spark for this effort can come from a formal campus center, the political science department, or another program or department on campus. In this chapter, we highlighted how two distinct institutions have taken different paths to achieve the same end goal of developing a more robust and healthy civil society on campus. These case studies suggest that institutions should not shy away from embracing politics or discussing challenging political issues. Being nonpartisan is different from being apolitical. In fact, a holistic and fully immersive civic experience provides students with skills and opportunities required to leave campus better equipped to successfully navigate complex political questions, and to engage in meaningful policy deliberation and political action. This nexus for success requires continuous collaboration among academic and student affairs units and community organizations to ensure that learning is promoted, community needs are addressed, and both agency and campus capacity are considered.

Long-term success is also dependent on leadership and financial support from the top of the institution. A sincere commitment from the board of trustees and administration sends an important signal about institutional priorities and serves to create a ripple effect across campus. This ideally involves embedding civic engagement into the academic mission of colleges and universities. Words matter, a mission statement influences campus priorities, and funding should match this mission and the strategic plan. Institutions need to provide funds for the long-term sustainability of programs focused on civic engagement. Funding allows a campus to support and assess tangible campus-wide outcomes.

According to Foa and Mounk, in 2019, 10 of 29 European and Central Asian countries were classified as democracies, and it was the "14th consecutive year of decline in global freedom."[48] Meanwhile, the United States has seen its freedom score decline by eight points over the past 10 years. In 2020, the world was upended by the pandemic that highlighted and exacerbated existing economic, public health, and racial inequities. The call to educate and engage has never been louder, and as such, should be at the heart of what we do on our campuses.

Endnotes

1. Roberto Stefan Foa and Yascha Mounk, "The Danger of Deconsolidation: The Democratic Disconnect," *Journal of Democracy* 27, no. 3 (2016): 5–17. doi: 10.1353/jod.2016.0049.

2. Carroll Doherty, Jocelyn Kiley, and Bridget Johnson, *Little Partisan Agreement on the Pressing Problems Facing the US* (Washington, DC: Pew Research Center, 2018a); Carroll Doherty, Jocelyn Kiley, and Bridget Johnson, *Elections in America: Concerns over Security, Divisions Over Expanding Access to Voting* (Washington, DC: Pew Research Center, 2018b).

3. Kay L. Schlozman, Henry E. Brady, and Sidney Verba, *Unequal and Unrepresented: Political Inequality and the People's Voice in the New Gilded Age* (Princeton, NJ: Princeton University Press, 2018).

4. John B. Holbein, and D. Sunshine Hillygus, *Making Young Voters: Converting Civic Attitudes Into Civic Action* (Cambridge, England: Cambridge University Press, 2020).

5. Nancy Thomas, Margaret Brower, Ishara Casellas Connors, Adam Gismondi, and Kyle Upchurch, *Election Imperatives Version 2.0: Ten Recommendations to Increase College Student Voting and Improve Political Learning and Engagement* (Medford, MA: Institute for Democracy and Higher Education, 2019), https://idhe.tufts.edu/sites/default/files/ElectionImperatives-v2.pdf.

6. AACU (Association of American Colleges and Universities), "Civic Learning in the Major by Design," (2017), https://www.aacu.org/peerreview/2017/Fall.

7. Project Pericles, "Advocate. Empower. Inspire," (2020), https://www.projectpericles.org/.

8. Campus Compact, "Campus Compact Overview," (2020), https://compact.org/who-we-are/.

9. Nancy Thomas and Margaret Brower, "Politics 365: Fostering Campus Climates for Student Political Learning and Engagement" in *Teaching Civic Engagement Across the Disciplines*, eds. Elizabeth C. Matto, Alison Rios Millett McCartney, Elizabeth A. Bennion, and Dick Simpson, (Washington, DC: American Political Science Association, 2017), 361–374. doi: 10.1017/S1049096517001706.

10. American Political Science Association, "APSA Resources on Systemic Racism & Social Justice," (2020c), https://www.apsanet.org/RESOURCES/APSA-Resources-for-Addressing-Systemic-Racism-Social-Justice.

11. American Association of Colleges and Universities. 2020. "Diversity, Equity, and Student Success." Available at: https://www.aacu.org/diversity-equity-and-student-success.

12. University of Southern California's Race and Equity Center, (2020), https://race.usc.edu/about-us/.

13. The National Task Force on Civic Learning and Democratic Engagement, *A Crucible Moment: College Learning and Democracy's Future* (Washington, DC: Association of American College and Universities, 2012), https://www.aacu.org/sites/default/files/files/crucible/Crucible_508F.pdf

14. Tim Walker, "Education is Political': Neutrality in the Classroom Shortchanges Students," *National Education Association* (11 December 2018), https://www.nea.org/advocating-for-change/new-from-nea/educationpolitical-neutrality-classroom-shortchanges-students

15. CIRCLE (Center for Information and Research on Civic Learning and Engagement), "Election Night 2018: Historically High Youth Turnout, Support for Democrats," (7 November 2018), https://circle.tufts.edu/latest-research/election-night-2018-historically-high-youth-turnout-support-democrats

16. American Political Science Association, "About APSA." (2020a), https://www.apsanet.org/ABOUT/About-APSA.

17. Barbara Jacoby and Elizabeth Hollander, "Securing the Future of Civic Engagement in Higher Education" in *Civic Engagement in Higher Education: Concepts and Practices*, eds. Barbara Jacoby and Associates, 227–248 (San Francisco, CA: Jossey-Bass, 2009); Thomas and Brower, "Politics 365."

18. Meredith S. Billings and Dawn Geronimo Terkla, "The Impact of the Campus Culture on Students' Civic Activities, Values, and Beliefs," *New Directions for Institutional Research* 162 (2014): 43–53. doi: 10.1002/ir.2007.

19. North Central College, "Strategic Plan," (2020), https://www.northcentralcollege.edu/northcentral-college-strategic-plan

20. The iCons are: Being Human, Challenging Inequity, Engaging Civic Life, Examining Health, Experiencing Place, Innovating the World, Sustaining our World, and Thinking Globally.

21. Judith A. Ramaley, "The Changing Role of Higher Education: Learning to Deal with Wicked Problems," *Higher Education* 18, no. 3 (2014): 7–22.

22. Billings and Geronimo Terkla, "The Impact of the Campus Culture."

23. The National Task Force on Civic Learning and Democratic Engagement, *A Crucible Moment: College Learning and Democracy's Future* (Washington, DC: Association of American College and Universities, 2012), https://www.aacu.org/

sites/default/files/files/crucible/Crucible_508F.pdf

24. Nancy Thomas, Margaret Brower, Ishara Casellas Connors, Adam Gismondi, and Kyle Upchurch, *Election Imperatives Version 2.0: Ten Recommendations to Increase College Student Voting and Improve Political Learning and Engagement* (Medford, MA: Institute for Democracy and Higher Education, 2019), https://idhe.tufts.edu/sites/default/files/ElectionImperatives-v2.pdf

25. To understand if the traveling town hall was effective, a survey was used to obtain students' perceptions of how they were affected by the town hall experience, whether they would recommend it to other students, and what they liked (or did not like) about the experience. Because of flaws in our approach to survey dissemination, data were only collected for about 4% of the participants. These students reported increased knowledge about candidates, issues, and elections. They also reported increased interest in political issues and a greater inclination to stay informed and vote. These results, while encouraging, should be considered with extreme caution given the incredibly low number of respondents.

26. Center for Assessment and Research Studies, *The Political Engagement Project Survey Fall 2017 & Spring 2019 Report* (Harrisonburg, VA: James Madison University, 2019).

27. When comparing JMU students who did and did not receive a voter guide, notable differences were found in the extent to which students reported following what is going on in government and public affairs (t(109)= -1.97, p = .05, d = .43). Students who received the guide increased in the extent to which they followed government and public affairs, while those who did not receive a guide decreased (Center for Assessment & Research Studies, 2019).

28. Thomas and Brower, "Politics 365."

29. James Madison Center for Civic Engagement, *Political Learning and Democratic Engagement at JMU: A Campus Climate Study* (Harrisonburg, VA: James Madison University, 2019).

30. Thomas Carothers and Andrew O'Donohue, "Democracies Divided: The Global Challenge of Political Polarization," *Brookings Institution* (24 September 2019), https://www.brookings.edu/book/democracies-divided/

31. Dimock, Michael and Richard Wike. 13 November 2020. "America is Exceptional in the Nature of its Political Divide". Pew Research Center. Available at: https://www.pewresearch.org/fact-tank/2020/11/13/america-is-exceptional-in-the-nature-of-its-political-divide/

32. John Villasenor, "Views Among College Students Regarding the First Amendment: Results from a New Survey," *Brookings Institution* (18 September 2017), https://www.brookings.edu/blog/fixgov/2017/09/18/views-among-college-students-regarding-the-first-amendment-results-from-a-new-survey/

33. Diana C. Mutz, *Hearing the Other Side: Deliberative versus Participatory Democracy* (Cambridge, UK: Cambridge University Press, 2012), doi: 10.1017/CBO9780511617201.

34. Elizabeth A. Bennion and David W. Nickerson, "I Will Register and Vote, If You Teach Me How: A Field Experiment Testing Voter Registration in College Classrooms," *PS: Political Science & Politics* 49, no. 4 (2016): 867–871. doi: 10.1017/S1049096516001360; Holly Teresi and Melissa R. Michelson, "Wired to Mobilize: The Effect of Social Networking Messages on Voter Turnout," *The Social Science Journal* 52, no. 2 (2015): 195–204. doi: 10.1016/j.soscij.2014.09.004; Thomas and Brower, "Politics 365."

35. Abraham Goldberg, Dena A. Pastor, and Carah Ong Whaley, *Assessing the Effectiveness of a Campus-Wide Census 2020 Education Initiative.* (forthcoming).

36. James Madison Center for Civic Engagement, *Political Learning and Democratic Engagement at JMU.*

37. Nancy Thomas and Margaret Brower, "Promising Practices to Facilitate Politically Robust Campus Climates," *Change: The Magazine of Higher Learning* 50, no. 6 (2018): 24–29. doi: 10.1080/00091383.2018.1540818

38. The National Task Force on Civic Learning and Democratic Engagement, *A Crucible Moment: College Learning and Democracy's Future* (Washington, DC: Association of American College and Universities, 2012), https://www.aacu.org/sites/default/files/files/crucible/Crucible_508F.pdf; Judith Torney-Purta, Julio C. Cabrera, Katrina Crotts Roohr, Ou Lydia Liu, and Joseph A. Rios, *Assessing Civic Competency and Engagement in Higher Education: Research Background, Frameworks, and Directions for Next-Generation Assessment. (Research Report No. RR-15-34).* (Princeton, NJ: Educational Testing Service, 2015), doi: 10.1002/ets2.12081.

39. Elizabeth Beaumont, Anne Colby, Thomas Ehrlich, and Judith Torney-Purta, "Promoting Political Competence and Engagement in College Students: An Empirical Study," *Journal of Political Science Education* 2, no. 3 (2006): 249–270. doi: 10.1080/15512160600840467.

40. Jodi Benenson, Barbara Pickering, Andrea M. Weare, and Anthony M. Starke, Jr., "Focused Engagement: Lessons Learned from a Study Assessing Campus Climates for Political Learning and Engagement in Democracy." *Journal of Community Engagement & Higher Education* 11, no. 3 (2019): 58–68; Billings and Geronimo Terkla, "The Impact of the Campus Culture"; Stephanie Martin and Eleanor Weisman, "Aligning Civic Engagement with the Strategic Goals of an Institution: Focus on Allegheny College." *Journal of College and Character* 13, no. 1 (2012): 1–8. doi:10.1515/jcc-2012-1843; Thomas and Brower, "Politics 365."

41. American Political Science Association, "APSA Statement on the Essential Role of Social Scientific Inquiry in Maintaining a Free, Participatory, Civil, and Law-Governed Society," (2020b), https://www.apsanet.org/APSA Statement on the Essential Role of Social Scientific Inquiry in Maintaining a Free, Participatory, Civil, and Law-Governed Society

42. Ibid.

43. Lorelle L. Espinosa, Jonathan M. Turk, Morgan Taylor, and Hollie M. Chessman, *Race and Ethnicity in Higher Education: A Status Report* (Washington, DC: American Council on Education, 2019).

44. NCES, USDE (National Center for Education Statistics, US Department of Education), "Graduation rates," (2019), http://nces.ed.gov/fastfacts/display.asp?id=40; Espinosa et al., *Race and Ethnicity in Higher Education*.

45. Christopher Jones and Richard Anthony Baker, *Report on the Uncivil, Hate and Bias Incidents on Campus Survey*. (Washington, DC: The LEAD Fund, 2019), https://www.aaaed.org/images/aaaed/LEAD_Fund/LEAD-Fund-Report-UHBIOC-Report.pdf

46. Ashley Finley, "Defining and Developing Civic-Minded Institutions," Association of American Colleges & Universities" *Diversity & Democracy* 22, no. 4 (2020), https://www.aacu.org/diversitydemocracy/2020/summer/finley

47. Ibid.

48. Foa and Mounk, "The Danger of Deconsolidation."

12

Re-centering Global Civic Engagement through a Critical Lens: A Collaborative Center Approach

Nicole Webster

Pennsylvania State University

In higher education, global civic engagement (GCE) is often discussed as an educational activity designed to enhance students' educational experiences. Many programs, despite the benefit for students, are developed with minimal inclusion of the perspectives, context, and voices of communities, creating an incomplete context of and limited perspective of the community. In response to the limitations this type of GCE environment creates, the author provides approaches towards developing global civic engagement experiences for college students that are more transformative in nature. Through a university partnership center based in Western Africa, this chapter explores a more inclusive model for GCE focusing on the community's unique perspectives, histories, and narratives to enhance critical teaching and learning. The author constructs a narrative that explains how intentionality in program design builds a framework for teaching and learning that cultivates global civic engagement within the African context and concludes with resources to support teaching from this framework.

KEYWORDS: Global Civic Engagement; West Africa; Burkina Faso; Community-Based Learning; Performative Engagement; Critical Learning; Historical Acknowledgment; Decolonization; Community Voice.

Introduction

Global civic engagement (GCE) in higher education subscribes, for the most part, to a script that follows a Western narrative, one in which the initial development of ideas, the inclusion of students and faculty, and program logistics are developed and framed through a US lens. This is not to say that overseas counterparts have no role in establishing civic engagement programs or that global community partners never co-design such programs. But it can be argued that global civic engagement programs, by and large, are designed to meet students' educational portfolios with little regard to the communities that provide the central landscape for students' learning. Moreover, far too often, these programs operate from a lens of *performative engagement*. Civic actions, conversations, and behaviors are situated in surface layer interactions and feel-good moments, which do little to discomfort students, administrators, and educators to elicit a shift in thinking toward more in-depth learning and living.

This chapter aims to examine approaches towards developing global civic engagement experiences for college students that are more transformative and less situational. Taking an approach of retheorizing civic engagement theory, the author forms a central argument that civic engagement is an ideal teaching instrument to develop a more informed citizenry. Critical theory scholars, and global engagement scholars, and others concerned with the field's limitations, realize that GCE not positioned from a place of inclusivity, respect, and historical acknowledgment leaves a gap in the civic engagement ecosystem. Universities often position civic engagement as a beneficial experience with inadequate consideration of communities' equitable inclusion in the development of these global occurrences. Questions raised by academics critical of GCE tend to focus on the impact on communities whose resources, time, and knowledge are not valued nor incorporated in designing the GCE experience. They explore how this myopic attitude impacts the civic engagement ecosystem. What message does it send to students when community voices are absent from the onset or when the community is portrayed as a passive 'place' with no knowledge or expertise to contribute? Global civic engagement, which includes representation, is critical to creating a more diverse democracy and opportunities for civic participation.

The chapter begins with a discussion of the context of GCE experiences within higher education institutions, and the framework of how these experiences are often developed—the central focus being on the narrow preparation of participants for global service-learning experiences. In particular, the framing of global concepts excludes these international communities' voices, knowledge, and experiences. The author grounds this argument in universities' role in setting the initial tone for civic ideology and the crucial groundwork that is necessary to help students translate a singular experience to civic actions and attitudes that go beyond the global occurrence. To move this narrative forward, the author details a more inclusive civic engagement model that can better capture the community's voices, histories, and narratives through a university partnership in West Africa. She illustrates this through a collaboration between Penn State University and the 2iE Water and Engineering University in Burkina Faso, West Africa. The 2iE-PSU Collaborative Engagement Center, located on the campus of 2iE in Ouagadougou, West Africa, was designed for the 'institution' to move beyond these performative actions and behaviors too often found within the academy. A GCE paradigm centered on community needs and voice was the driver for this engaged scholarship. The Center is designed to exemplify what engagement should look like in order to facilitate change and civic stewardship. Central to this partnership is the university's role in preparing and supporting students to become active and engaged citizens. The paper will highlight the successes, challenges, and overall benefits of this type of community-university partnership between Penn State and 2iE and the impact it has had in developing a more inclusive and engaged approach to civic engagement. Penn State's mission to enhance students' learning experiences by providing them with field experiences with and for the community serves as the impetus for exploring these outcomes. As a note, civic engagement within the University is broadly defined as the actions, behaviors, and attitudes of an individual that enhance or improve a community or institution. This lens has helped to understand students' civic engagement experiences in the global south, specifically within African diaspora communities, and the impact on student learning outcomes. Understanding civic participation through the eyes of students and scholars engaged in communities across the African diaspora can help contribute towards an institutional culture of inclusion through knowledge building. Focusing on student engagement in these particular locales shows how important it is to establish a culture of scholarship for student success that is responsive and inclusive of other ways of knowing. Ultimately, such an approach encourages the development of curriculum and policies that are responsive to the precise needs of communities, as well as helping to prepare critically minded civic stewards.

This chapter provides a deeper examination of GCE's development that helps shift the narrative from Eurocentric university values to the communities in which these experiences occur.[1] A critical feature of this manuscript is the re-centering of civic engagement curriculum to include voices who have been marginalized and unrecognized in these spaces.[2] This recentering acknowledges the importance of viewing community partners as equals rather than a placement site for students. A move such as this requires that educators understand and value the needs of partners, be proactive in the co-construction of activities that speaks to the community's needs, and inclusion of their expertise within these spaces.[3] Communities provide unique perspectives on place-based understandings and knowledge that are often overlooked or undervalued within international contexts.[4] The questions of whose voices are heard and valued within civic engagement experiences matter in the political science field because they contribute to building frameworks that prepare students to be responsible citizens in a more inclusive democracy.

Universities as a Place of Civic Development And Ideologies

In the current socio-cultural context, the university provides an ideal learning space that extends beyond the professional and cultural credentials usually attributed to higher education to include the realm of forming human character. The university plays a vital role in shaping idealistic minds and responding to societal concerns supported through curriculum and research. Essentially, the university's role is to serve as a space for students to examine their surroundings to contribute towards an equitable, moral, and democratic society. Although this is a desired goal, it is not always attained within university settings. Citizenship development generally lacks an inclusive community context and critical examinations of social and political issues that affect global and domestic communities. These subjects are often presented as distinct problems that are only experienced by specific communities or groups of people in either the US or another nation. Only rarely do students gain the perspective of transglobal experiences of communities such as those within the African diaspora within classes or cocurricular activities.

Globalized GCE experiences encourage students to examine their place in an increasingly global and interconnected world.[5] By promoting 'global citizenship,' universities can help students to define their participation in civic life. In essence, global citizenship is a way of living that recognizes the interconnectedness of the environment and people's lives. Most salient to this concept is the social justice, meaning creating equity in the distribution of wealth, opportunities, and privileges within a society. Creating a global citizen mindset such as this has the ability to teach students to appreciate differences and center knowledge beyond a US or Eurocentric view. It encourages individuals to think deeply and critically about policies and systems that impact our social and political environments. Additionally, it makes learners feel more confident regarding ethical issues due to their ability to recognize and assess their own civic actions. A global citizenry curriculum within a university prepares students for the 21st century, developing proactive citizens who are attuned to complex problems, able to think critically, communicate ideas effectively, and work collaboratively in diverse settings. However, this is more difficult to put into practice than it sounds.

A current dilemma for higher education institutions (HEI) is the development of experiences and platforms to prepare students for their civic responsibilities within a highly globalized and interconnected world. Frequently overlooked is how students can recognize that social, physical, and economic shocks exist beyond their immediate community or locale. More responsive GCE education teaches and grounds students with the factors that necessitate significant social action while setting the stage for more impactful relationships within communities. Collectively these goals ensure that students can address challenges within a global context. Because of this, education is at a turning point in preparing students to address global challenges from an engagement point of view, especially now that important issues such as racial inequality, systemic poverty, and sustainability dominate much of the worldwide agenda. These are the types of problems that we must address through public problem-solving in a healthy democracy.[6] According to Rittel and Webber (1973), such problems cannot be defined precisely and are continually changing, requiring adjustments in selecting the appropriate response or solution.[7] Every problem is unique and is often a symptom of a more extensive, more complex set of challenges. For this reason, some academics and universities have responded by creating critical interdisciplinary learning areas to address wicked challenges.[8]

The critical framing and reflection of wicked issues from an international perspective allows students to realize that the dilemmas they see or experience overseas are not unique to that locale but are often encountered in the United States. Students' critical reflection of their GCE experiences sets a tone beyond immersion in an international setting. It offers an opportunity to explore "difficult differences" such as racial, ethnic, or gender inequality and the continuing struggles worldwide for human rights, freedom, and power. A cosmopolitan perspective also frames the global location, providing a backdrop to deconstruct and construct concepts central to the communities and citizens in which students are engaged. Creating a critical-thinking environment for students enhances higher education's role in creating critically thinking global citizens and enables students to draw connections between theory and practice. Developing an active and responsible citizen capable of critically understanding others' development and social wellbeing is fundamental to the university's central purpose.

Moreover, this framework permits students to develop skills that lead to active citizenship, promoting social cohesion, and valuing the diversity of human beings.[9] These ideals are the cornerstones of GCE's global perspective and critical to students' civic development. These values serve as a starting point for defining essential engagement, especially in the African diaspora context.

Critical Global Civic Engagement Within West Africa

At the core of Penn State's strategy for building global citizens is an engaged global network (GEN) of strategic partnerships with peer institutions around the world who share Penn State's commitment to solving the world's most pressing challenges through a multi-layered engagement of research, faculty, and student collaboration. Global Penn State has three distinct, but interwoven, elements in 1) building global competency by sending students, faculty, and staff abroad, 2) internationalizing the university community by bringing international students and scholars to campus, and 3) building a global network of regional partnerships that enable the University to pursue its tripartite mission of teaching, research, and service on the global stage.

This strategic partner network provides access to regional networks of intellectual capital, resources, and funding while capitalizing on the strengths, benefits, and opportunities that arise from a multidisciplinary and multicultural approach to problem-solving. The initiative combines intellectual resources with other major research universities around the world. The program integrates research into Penn State's educational programs, and it provides opportunities for student engagement that build global citizenship and leadership. Furthermore, the strategic partnerships increase opportunities to broaden Penn State students opportunities for studying abroad in diverse contexts. What follows is the discussion of the Global Engagement Network in Africa, located in Ouagadougou, Burkina Faso, and its contribution to developing a new approach towards global civic engagement.

2iE-PSU Engagement Center

Penn State has a longstanding relationship with the International Institute of Water and Environmental Engineering in Ouagadougou due to collaborative partnerships in engineering and STEM in West Africa. The two institutions expanded this collaboration to include pertinent sustainable development other areas, related to the water, food, and energy nexus in Africa. As a result of these programmatic areas and the GEN structure, the 2iE-Penn State Engagement Centre was formed. It is a platform for long-term collaborative multidisciplinary research and educational exchanges in West Africa and improving the wellbeing of people and communities in the African diaspora. Additionally, it illustrates the viewpoints and needs of communities racially, ethnically, and culturally different from Penn State and from the communities in which most Penn State students were born and raised. Partnering with a university in Africa also provides opportunities for academic, governmental, non-government, and private sector entities to work together around specific projects or themes in West Africa that are often critical to other parts of sub-Saharan Africa.

The 2iE-PSU partnership and the Center mainly take advantage of the University's prior and ongoing investments in interdisciplinary research to address community health, education, and sustainability in the global south. The place-based location provides opportunities for student engagement, teamwork, leadership, problem-solving and multicultural skills necessary for student success and promotes academic excellence. The 2iE-PSU Center encourages partners to leverage and steward their resources to tackle complex societal problems at all levels, from local to global. Based on the interdisciplinary framework of the Center, activities are anchored by core principles which foster:

- Partnerships, collaboration, and mutual leveraging of institutional/intellectual capital
- A multidisciplinary/multicultural approach to knowledge creation
- Transformative actions within and across communities

Complementing these core principles are activities designed to set the tone before students depart for Africa while also developing more culturally aware students who will be working and living in communities within Burkina Faso. These activities include:

1. Virtual weekly meetings with the 2iE faculty and staff to assist in situating their work and engagement within their communities.

2. Readings focused on the history, culture, and contemporary issues within Burkina Faso written by Burkinabe authors.[10]

3. Readings on the history of West Africa to help contextualize the history of Burkina Faso within the region written by West African authors.

4. Roundtable discussions with African scholars and students enrolled in the program on issues related to colonization, power, and privilege.

5. Listening sessions with PSU faculty and staff who have worked in the West African region or with particular organizations/communities similar to those of the students.[11]

6. Self-guided reflection journaling (questions provided weekly).[12]

While in country, students engage in a set of activities which include:

1. Weekly meetings with community partners labeled as "learn and share sessions" (sessions meant to help students learn from, and share with community members on contemporary issues) once they arrive in Burkina.

2. Daily debriefings with 2iE scholars and students on cross-cultural issues concerning colonization, power, and privilege within the US and Africa.

3. Weekly journal reflection questions with prompts.

4. Participation and storytelling: In order to hear the stories of community members, the storytelling takes place once a week and is arranged by our staff at the 2iE Center, with the help of community members. The logistics, such as timing and location, can vary depending on the individuals involved.

Learning within the 2iE Center

Combined, these activities aim to foster a more profound experience for Penn State students and center the learning and perspectives about Burkinabe communities and its citizens. The importance of this type of framework is supported by the critical issues impacting communities in Burkina Faso and was seen as an integral to the plan of work of the Center. Since the inception of the Center, the work has largely been driven by two overarching themes: sustainability and community and youth development. In response to a growing youth population and chronic food, energy, and water scarcity, student projects have been designed in consultation with PSU and 2iE faculty and the field-based staff at the Center to offer a network of support to rural and urban communities. Burkinabe staff provide students with the opportunity to connect deeply with communities because of longstanding partnerships and daily interactions. Students used these connections to engage in intensive discussions with local government agencies or non-governmental organizations to understand how their ideas will come to life within Burkinabe districts and communities quite different from their own. For instance, many students find that their viewpoints about the extended family and nuclear family change after they encounter family members from several communities who are vital to the success of each project.

On several occasions, students have remarked that the Center served as an area to critically explore complex themes such as colonization and its effect on African development. Students felt the Center provided a safe space for meaningful and needed reflections and discussions with peers and local staff. Generally speaking, the Center facilitated interdisciplinary collaborations between students and community partners. Students who have worked with the Center had the opportunity to experience information sharing and knowledge building between themselves and local experts and stakeholders, which further enhanced learning and engagement. One example of this was with a solar project that focused on increasing entrepreneurship in Burkina Faso.

Critical efforts to guide entrepreneurs and local communities

Renewable energy entrepreneurs are at the forefront of efforts to extend access to modern energy services in West Africa. Often, their business expertise serves as an excellent way to identify local needs and provide tailored solutions. Some West African entrepreneurs, however, face challenges. In most countries, the business environment is not conducive to private investment, particularly in the power sector. To respond to these issues, governments must work to establish appropriate institutional and regulatory frameworks, implement enabling policies, and advocate for sustainable financing and business models for renewable energy. In spite of such challenges, global and regional institutions, as well as entrepreneurs, are moving to address energy needs in the Economic Community of West African States (ECOWAS). This particular intersection of energy access and equity created an opportunity for Penn State students and scholars to work towards solutions. Penn State students along with a solar professor from Penn State worked with members from the ECOWAS Centre for Renewable Energy and Energy Efficiency (ECREEE) and 2iE on establishing a facility to offer assistance to small and medium-sized renewable energy enterprises, especially those focused on solar photovoltaics (PV). Gradually, students realized that there were hierarchical structures within and between local businesses, NGOs, and other community-based organizations that would impact the integrity of their work. This helped them realize how complexities can arise when working with local businesses to enhance their operations and with entrepreneurs seeking to bring innovative ideas to fruition.

Students found a deeper connection with the local community due to the cultural and political nuances, though this led to frustration. For example, after some conversations with the community, students attended local community meetings organized by youth about current political injustices and how these longstanding issues were connected to colonial histories. Prior to these conversations they noted in their journals they did not understand about the political tensions between community and government and how deep the impact and effects of colonialism still prevailed in the local context. During my observation and discussion with students who were working on the project, I saw some students taking the initiative to work with community organizations they viewed as "out of reach" due to them not understanding how these particular organizations worked to enhance the welfare of the local community. Tensions between community partners and students sometimes arose due to a lack of understanding of cultural norms. In these times of noted tensions caused by students' framing of development from a Western perspective, the professor, who invited me to the discussions to listen and provide context as needed, included more time for open reflection during their group processing time to make deeper meaning of what students felt and observed during their time within the community. Questions or open prompts such as how are the current realities you are seeing supported by what you were taught about or read about prior to traveling? Or who are the actors that have shaped the context of inequities within Africa, particularly within Burkina Faso? The Penn State professor also used dialogues and open discussions with community partners for creating opportunities for deconstructing ways of knowing and being. Their frustration resulted from what they called at times a limited view of the riches and knowledge produced by communities. By virtue of its location and atmosphere, the 2iE-PSU Center enabled the development of a new model for civic awareness in a global setting.

Centering Critical Civic Engagement in Higher Education Discourse

The literature on civic engagement makes it clear that there is a struggle amongst scholars when considering how to define the term "civic engagement." A traditional approach arguably considers the *actions* without regard to structural inequalities, while a critical approach examines the efforts while exploring structural injustices. The term *critical civic engagement* offers an understanding of the distribution of structural and political powers within societies, avoids hierarchies, promotes authentic relationships, and works from a cultural perspective. This definition also influences the role of power systems in understanding inequalities and social injustices.

Critical civic engagement can be seen as an answer to other forms of civic engagement, which may emphasize actions that reinforce misconceptions and stereotypes. Civic engagement activities constructed in an academic setting can unwittingly become an exercise in patronization if not conducted with great care and consciousness. If civic experiences are designed in ways that fail to be cognizant of the university's hierarchical structures or patriarchal philosophies, and do not include the voices or perspectives of locals, then civic engagement activities risk doing more harm than good.

Critical civic engagement allows students to act on social inequalities while also recognizing their privilege as students. As educators, we cannot presume all students are from privileged backgrounds but must be cognizant of how their student status might be perceived by others. For example, in many contexts and communities within the global south, students from universities are considered privileged because of their ability to attend tertiary school, despite their socioeconomic background in the US. The concept of privilege must also be counterpointed by the idea of *othering*, which students must understand in order to engage with others in a critically informed manner. Aram Ziai describes othering as "the construction of a [...] group as" different, "which serves to delimit the identity of a we-group and so on to constitute and thus to justify political claims and exclusions."[13] Students involved in civic engagement activities should reflect not only on their actions but also on the causes of social problems and how to use their privilege to address the social injustices which they are passionate addressing. According to critical race scholars, students will be motivated to take action to affect positive change in their communities once they realize how their actions and behaviors impact others and generate social change.[14]

Civic engagement experiences conducted with a critical lens goes beyond actions such as posting to Facebook or interacting with others on social media. It extends to critically examining systemic problems that lead to public acts and situating this learning beyond the classroom and the walls of the university. A framework of critical civic engagement teaches students how to identify the root causes of systemic problems and learn how to tackle the symptoms and engage with context. This type of learning happens when educators are deliberate with conversations regarding the positioning of issues such as power and privilege to guide student learning and actions. An important benefit of this intentional knowledge building is that it helps students understand the impact of their privilege while also assisting them in understanding the power of privilege when used for the common good. Student learning must focus on the reality that privilege must be acknowledged and used responsibly and in partnership with the community to bring about positive change, and not regarded as a veil for saving individuals. Educators are responsible for ensuring students understand and utilize the role of power and privilege in the communities in which they work. Our positions provide us the space to explore and interrogate concepts like reciprocity, shared visions, and community building with students—all of which are integral to recognizing the strengths and assets that each community brings to their vision of development. By addressing these sometimes delicate topics, we help students realize the importance of critical engagement and re-orient the project's focus towards the partner and not on themselves.

The ultimate solution or glorification of social inequality

Critical civic engagement emphasizes the why of *actions* and reduces reliance on student-centered engagement. Often, civic engagement activities are conducted by students for social change, but are void of language or context which highlights the role and importance of social justice and related actions. Students should be challenged to think about social injustices and how they as students/citizens can contribute to social and civic change after the study abroad experience. The preparation of students should include support and opportunities to ask difficult questions. For example: Why are there significant economic and social differences in our society that contribute to social inequalities? What has led to certain social groups' educational disparities, and how has the public and private sectors of society responded to these inequities? And how do these concepts possibly tie into a global context? (See table 1).

Table 1. A Framework of Understanding Critical Global Service-Learning Experiences			
How learning is framed	How learning is operationalized	How learning is contextualized	Translation to critical service learning in a global context
Develop a program that allows for students to investigate and engage with terms and concepts that can also be explored or discussed in the US context	Terms salient to both the global context and US context are introduced and discussed and are not treated as an *us/them* dichotomy	Strengthens the learning for students to see the connections between terms, occurrences, and histories that impact communities both domestically and internationally	Deeper connection to and understanding of terms such as race, decolonization, historical trauma/legacies that are centrally tied to the formation and resilience of both *global and domestic communities* and stresses the importance of why these terms should be examined through an international and domestic lens
Curriculum inclusive of decolonial/non-Western perspectives	Includes readings, videos, and scholarship developed by individuals from the host country	Emphasizes the importance of non-Western knowledge and ways of being in understanding communities and global spaces	Situates a tone that acknowledges and values the voices, lens, and knowledge of non-US scholars/culture/communities as a source of information crucial to student's learning
Create spaces for self-reflection and group reflection and discussions	During weekly reflections, questions are posed to students to address as an individual (separate from the group), while other questions may be posed for group discussions	Reinforces the role of individuality in students being able to make meaning of their experiences while also allowing for group discussion for greater processing and questioning	Embraces the role and need for multiple spaces of reflection to help students move from "an experience" to critical understanding and consideration of their ability to contribute towards civic change

Table 1. A Framework of Understanding Critical Global Service-Learning Experiences			
Incorporate time for explicit conversations about how learning translates into critical and social justice action	Before departure and in-country conversations reinforce connections between concepts investigated in the global context	Provides structured time for students to discover how they can take action upon return from the host site	Operationalizes the global experience into a learning experience that leads to a critical understanding of civic actions and attitudes in the US and abroad

A critical approach to civic engagement can be more challenging to execute in a global context than in the US because you must acknowledge inequalities both in the US and globally. This requires students to realize their privilege as US citizens and begin to understand and reflect on their privilege. A critical civic engagement experience includes students reflecting on their positionality within society.[15] Along with addressing their positionality, students should critically assess power as a construct within communities and examine its manifestation at the individual and group levels. Additionally, they must examine diversity from the standpoint of advantages, possibilities, and resources, including access to power. Examining these points will help students be better equipped to identify existing inequalities and injustices in society. Because of these meaningful reflections, the student is provided with more in-depth experience and has a better understanding of how to transform simple acts of engagement into meaningful actions linked to critical knowledge.

Universities may struggle to find ways to integrate civic engagement critically even though they seek to engage students in society's civic fabric. The goal of a university is ultimately to put civic engagement principles into practice through activities that promote public involvement in local governance, address pressing issues, and explore public problems. In order for universities to achieve this integration goal, they must design GCE experiences that guide students through critical experiences to transform their thinking, develop creative approaches to problems, and build connections for deeper involvement in society. As a result of the critical approach, students learn how to work with others, designing policies or advocating for equitable reallocation of public resources (see table 1). Critical engagement can help students contribute to communities and advocate for transparency and accountability. Furthermore, it can strengthen the voice of communities to strive toward meaningful community dialogue and actions. For example, the youth development projects in Burkina Faso led to conversations between Penn State students and primary and secondary school principals, as well as NGO's engaged in educating youth about how these challenges could be addressed and sustained once those students returned to the US. In some cases, these initial conversations sparked student-led initiatives to help resist youth recruitment into terrorist groups. In this case, the connection from learning to action was facilitated by conversations held between stakeholders and students, and the willingness for the educator to embrace challenging topics which stimulated more questions than answers among students. During their journaling and informal conversations, students noted that the opportunity to work in the community and learn through dialogues and discussions upended their learned assumptions about African culture, development, and its societies. The conversations helped them to understand development from the standpoint of the community members and institutional partners. Community partners noted the opportunity to speak with students in a conversational manner provided a new norm in two specific ways. The first was them being able to view the students as partners in the process and not just individuals seeking to complete a project. Furthermore, greater respect was shown between community members and students due to the meaningful conversations about their African past which helped contextualize the process and significance of the projects—changing the view of how partnerships can be genuinely beneficial for both the African partner/community and the US institution.

Practical Implications for Educators

Most of the time, GCE in universities seeks to teach students how to effect change in community settings. However, the current reality is that the ability to foster situations that connect historical legacies of racism and injustice with the policies and laws that perpetuate these inequalities gets lost once we move from theory to practice. Critically engaged pedagogies allow educators to move beyond recognizing racial and other historical injustices toward creating inclusionary spaces and sustainable opportunities for action.

A critically engaged global curriculum enables students to initiate meaningful civic actions, which is essential to any service-learning program. However, contextualizing students' learning becomes more important for global programs given that the experience is overseas, and leads to the question of how you situate the overseas experience at home. Educators must help students translate their global experiences to their domestic contexts, resulting in a change in the ways universities develop, orient, and implement programs. In general, a paradigm shift is needed to provide students with a variety of learning opportunities and opportunities for interaction, such as those offered in the 2iE-PSU Engagement Center. Critical lenses give students and educators ways to think about, question, negotiate, and act in order to transform the understanding of knowledge, institutional structures, and relationships. Students often come to appreciate the deeper issues of social-cultural-political nexus when they engage with problem-posing questions and other strategies to analyze, deconstruct, and question what they are experiencing in communities and diverse contexts. The results from these activities range from critical awareness of one's role as a possible change agent to questions about their ability to make change.

The critical lens recognizes the importance of cultural context and the student's ability to challenge oppression and work towards transformational social change even if the learning context is global. When students are encouraged to perceive themselves as part of oppressive systems, they can begin to see their potential roles in challenging and transforming these systems. Additionally, a critical approach calls on educators to conceptualize the contexts within which oppression operates and understand the ways in which social identities shape communities and access to opportunities. A critical lens of engagement requires educators to recognize how context can offer oppressive structures and spaces as well as potential opportunities to raise students' awareness. In other words, a critical perspective of engagement calls for educators to shift from an individualistic point of view to one of citizenship as a communal responsibility.

Educators who engage in meaningful critical engagement should demonstrate an understanding of critical ethics if they expect this type of environment to thrive and be successful. Educators should display a willingness to engage in ongoing critical reflection as part of the collective process of action with students. Additionally, steps need to be taken in order to create a trusting and bi-directional learning environment, where instructors are encouraged to be learners and students are encouraged to be instructors partnering with community leaders. An educational system that utilizes a critical frame of reference for GCE challenges the system of power present in educational institutions—recognizing issues such as power and equity points to the value of a critical approach to civic engagement. A global civic engagement experience, viewed through a critical lens, aids crucial conversations that deepen students' understanding of civic responsibility, including its purpose, value, and significance in a global society.

Endnotes

1. Eve Tuck and Marcia McKenzie, *Place in Research: Theory, Methodology, and Methods* (New York: Routledge, 2015); Kecia Hayes, "Critical Service-Learning and the Black Freedom Movement," in *Critical Service-Learning as Revolutionary Pedagogy: A Project of Student Agency in Action*, 47–70 (Charlotte, NC: Information Age Publishing, 2011).

2. Randy Stoecker, Amy Hilgendorf, and Elizabeth A. Tryon, eds., *The Unheard Voices: Community Organizations and Service Learning* (Philadelphia, PA: Temple University Press, 2009); Kathleen S. Yep, and Tania D. Mitchell, "Decolonizing Community Engagement: Reimagining Service Learning Through an Ethic Studies Lens," in *The Cambridge Handbook of Service Learning and Community Engagement*, 294–303 (Cambridge, UK: Cambridge University Press, 2009).

3. Janice McMillan and Timothy Stanton, "'Learning Service' in International Contexts: Partnership-Based Service-Learning and Research in Cape Town, South Africa," *Michigan Journal of Community Service Learning* 21, no. 1 (2014): 64–78; Viv Clayton et al., "Differentiating and Assessing Relationships in Service-Learning and Civic Engagement: Exploitative,

Transactional, or Transformational," *Michigan Journal of Community Service Learning* 16, no. 2 (2010): 5–21; Begum Verjee, "Critical Race Feminism: A Transformative Vision for Service-Learning Engagement," *Journal of Community Engagement and Scholarship* 5, no. 1 (2018): 7.

4. Noel Habashy, "If I Had More of a Relationship with Them, it Would be Good: Community Members' Perspectives of Community-Engaged Education Abroad Programs in Costa Rica," (PhD diss., Pennsylvania State University, 2019).

5. N.A. García and N.V. Longo, "Going Global: Re-framing Service-Learning in an Interconnected World," *Journal of Higher Education Outreach and Engagement* 17, no. 2 (2013): 111–136.

6. Cheol H. Oh and Robert F. Rich, "Explaining Use of Information in Public Policymaking," *Knowledge and Policy* 9 (1996): 3–35.

7. H.W. Rittel and M. M. Webber, "Dilemmas in a General Theory of Planning," *Policy Sciences* 4, no. 2 (1973): 155–169.

8. Judith A. Ramaley, "Thriving in the 21st Century by Tackling Wicked Problems," *Higher Education* 8, no. 2 (2013): 23–27; Elizabeth C. Matto, Alison R. Millett McCartney, Elizabeth A Bennion, and Dick W. Simpson, eds., *Teaching Civic Engagement Across the Disciplines,* (Washington, DC: American Political Science Association, 2017); Jennifer Schiff and Carol Burton, "'Wicked Problems' in General Education: The Challenges of Diversity, Civic Engagement, and Civil Discourse," *The Journal of General Education* 68, no. 1–2 (2020): 85–103.

9. Fazal Rizvi, "Towards Cosmopolitan Learning," *Discourse: Studies in the Cultural Politics of Education* 30, no. 3 (2009): 253–268.

10. A recommended reading list is available on the companion website for this book.

11. Guides for these listening sessions are posted to the APSA Teaching Civic Engagement website.

12. Journaling prompts are available on APSA's Teaching Civic Engagement website.

13. Aram Ziai, "Postcolonial Perspectives on 'Development,'" in *Peripherie,* 399–426 (Munster, Germany: University of Bonn Center for Development Research, 2010): 404.

14. Richard Delgado and Jean Stefanic, *Critical Race Theory: An Introduction* (Vol. 20) (New York: NYU Press, 2017).

15. Madeline Fox, Kavitha Mediratta, Jessica Ruglis, Brett Stoudt, S. Shah, and Michelle Fine, "Critical Youth Engagement: Participatory Action Research and Organizing," in *Handbook of Research on Civic Engagement in Youth*, eds. Lonnie R. Sherrod, Judith Torney-Purta, and Constance A. Flanagan, 621–649 (Hoboken, NJ: Wiley, 2010).

13

Civic Engagement and the Global Liberal Arts College: Empowering Students through Immersive Curriculum, Interactive Pedagogy, Experiential Learning, and Residential Education

Catherine Shea Sanger[1] and Wei Lit Yew[2]

1. Yale-NUS College; 2. Hong Kong Baptist University

This chapter empirically illustrates how civic engagement education has been fostered and hindered in a less liberal context, with Yale-NUS College in Singapore as the case study. Our findings are informed by focus group interviews, document analysis, and personal observations. Building on the conceptual foundation in Chapter 4, we argue that the liberal arts and sciences common curriculum, active learning pedagogies, intimacy and multinationalism of the college community, support for student initiatives, and can-do culture of Yale-NUS have combined to nourish vibrant spaces for student civic engagement. However, there remain barriers to civic engagement. These include students' workload and major selection, perceived liberal bias in the college, national political regulations, and the intimacy of the college community, which can be a double-edged sword. Additionally, international students have faced distinctive challenges such as Singapore's legal and cultural constraints on political engagement, and the absence of a critical mass of co-nationals for collective action.

KEYWORDS: Civic Education; Study Abroad; Liberal Arts; Active Pedagogy; Core Curricula; Experiential Learning; Residential Education; International Students.

The goal of this chapter is to share insights on curricular, extra-curricular, and pedagogical techniques for fostering civic engagement in less liberal political contexts. Specifically, we reflect on experiences as faculty members and share research conducted on student experiences at Yale-NUS College in Singapore, identifying the structures that have encouraged or hindered civic engagement education. In this study, we are interested in understanding not just what students have done in terms of civic engagement, but whether and how that engagement stems from their educational experience at the College. In other words, we are not only interested in assessing whether there has been civic engagement at Yale-NUS (there clearly has), we are interested in identifying the ways that the campus climate, specifically its curriculum, residential and extra-curricular structures, and pedagogical approach has nourished or inhibited student civic engagement. This chapter is largely empirical, and both builds upon and informs the conceptual arguments presented in Chapter 4 of this volume.[1]

This chapter is organized as follows. First, we briefly discuss the complexities of teaching civic education and engagement in less liberal contexts. We have provided a more detailed discussion of this, and the debate surrounding the creation of Yale-NUS College, in Chapter 4. Next, we present observations gleaned from focus groups, document analysis, and personal reflections to summarize how students' sense of civic engagement has changed over the course of their college experience. Our goal is to identify the specific courses, pedagogical techniques, extracurricular experiences, and institutional features that have had the greatest impact in empowering or obstructing students' civic engagement. We hope that these findings will enable fellow instructors and higher education professionals to benefit from the lessons we have learned as they develop their own curricula, programs, and institutions.

Setting Matters: Civic Education and Engagement in Less Liberal Contexts

In less liberal societies there are different institutional and normative pathways to civic participation than in more liberal societies. While instructors need not actively discourage risky behavior, they must be aware of the political and cultural context in which they are operating and help students develop a different set of tactics and rhetoric that will not be dismissed as dangerous and even seditious.

As we describe in Chapter 4, in Singapore specifically there are significant regulations concerning public assembly and political speech. For example, during an election period "only candidates and their election agents" are allowed to put up election posters.[2] A police permit is mandatory for "cause-related" assemblies that are held in public or hosted in private but open to the public. Local activists have in the past been penalized for organizing peaceful protests without proper permits. Government ministers have been known to file defamation suits against opposition politicians and political commentators for slander and libel.[3] In addition to these legal constraints, there are social pressures which shape how students may respond to and undertake civic engagement. Not only are there concerns over legality and state surveillance, but also reputational costs for behavior which appears too "political" or radical. Students, parents, and teachers may worry about students' employability, for example, if they participate in activities or publicly share views that are overly critical of the sociopolitical status-quo.[4]

In such a context, overtly political civic engagement education can appear and feel subversive. Higher education instructors may need to deliberately create an environment in which students feel safe and secure acquiring knowledge and admitting to an interest in politics and societal change. At the same time that it is important to be sensitive to local legal and cultural structures, we have found that students value having enclaves, micro-climates, or "free spaces" in which to ask challenging questions about social and political issues. Educational spaces create such enclaves. Forms of civic engagement that embrace imagination, empathy, community-building, and community-tending take on special importance in the Singaporean educational context. These skills, so critical in less liberal societies, are also important in "liberal" societies of the 21st century, societies marked by high levels of political polarization and decreasing levels of political deliberation.

Insofar as "civic engagement education" is about creating spaces where students can develop an interest in social and political issues, and engage in genuine conversation and disagreement, we propose a civic engagement pedagogy that is culturally relevant, one that is grounded in the students' sociopolitical opportunities and draws on discourses from the students' home environment.[5] Instructors and students must work together to create spaces where free speech, experimentation, discussion of alternative ideas, and effective strategies for change may take place. In this chapter, we share the results of a preliminary investigation into one college's experience in adapting to the institutional and cultural backdrop of a less liberal society, and explore practices designed to create spaces for civic learning.

Civic Engagement at Yale-NUS College: Bastions and Barriers

In December 2020 we conducted four focus groups with a diverse subset of Yale-NUS students. In addition to the information gleaned from these conversations, we draw upon the authors' personal observations from working at Yale-NUS College since 2014 and 2018 respectively, reflections of our student research assistants, conversations with Yale-NUS students and faculty, and content analysis of student Facebook groups, the student newspaper, and local news outlets.

A total of 24 students took part in 90-minute long focus groups: 13 seniors, 3 juniors, 4 sophomores, and 5 first-years. Focus group findings cannot claim to be representative of the student body as a whole, but we collected valuable and salient information based on a diverse group of subjects; students' backgrounds varied significantly in terms of class year, nationality, major/ primary academic interests, and personal commitment to civic engagement.[6] Thanks to the diverse interests and backgrounds of our participants, several valuable themes emerged across the focus groups which illuminate the ways Yale-NUS structures encourage and discourage civic engagement.

Civic Engagement Means Many Things

The first question we asked in each focus group was "What does 'civic engagement' mean to you? What do you associate with that phrase/idea?" Unsurprisingly, responses reflect the variety of definitions in popular and academic discourse, but also reflect different approaches our students take to civic engagement in our institutional and national context. The definitions students offered ranged along the following spectra:

> *Social v. Political:* Pro-social community engagement <—> Political engagement with the state/law
>
> *Intake v. Output:* Being interested, curious, and paying attention <—> Taking action/change-making
>
> *Intimate v. Public Space:* Speaking about values/opinions only within social/ family circle <—> Publicly taking a stance
>
> *Dialogue v. Action:* Conversations about social/political issues <—> Protest, confrontation, overt activism

Within this non-randomized group, only three students explicitly referenced protest to describe what civic engagement meant to them. Rather than associating the term with a set of observable behaviors, students described the purpose underpinning civic engagement. They were roughly evenly split on some issues. For example, six felt that being attentive and curious about political and social issues—taking information in—was enough to "count" as civic engagement, whereas 10 said that interest without deliberate change-making was insufficient. Students had different opinions about whether community service (e.g., tutoring under-resourced youth, volunteering at elderly homes, beach clean-ups) or Facebook posts "counted" or not. They also had different views on whether action directed at the College administration "counted" or whether civic engagement had to be directed at formal state politics and legal frameworks.

In sum, participants had very different prior beliefs about what constitutes civic engagement. However, as established in Chapter 4, rather than speaking to the need of imposing a uniform ideal of student civic engagement, this speaks to the imperative of broadening the definition of civic engagement such that it is inclusive and culturally resonant across a diverse student body. What matters most is creating the spaces and offering the basic tools and skills for students to keep thinking and rethinking about civic engagement.

Trajectories of Students' Civic Engagement over Time

Prior to the focus groups, the authors identified three categories to describe Yale-NUS students in terms of civic engagement:

> *Politically Engaged:* Those already involved or working towards involvement

in politically-oriented activity, lobbying of political authorities; organizing clubs or events around political issues; citizen journalism/blogging; politically-oriented Instagram accounts; or volunteering for political-minded non-profit organizations.

Socially Engaged: Those who are involved or plan to be involved in charity work, service, or community-building of a less explicitly politically-oriented and more social or cultural nature, e.g., church-based service, reading to the elderly, volunteering at an animal shelter, beach clean-ups.

Unengaged: Those who do not spend time on social or political engagement. Students in this category may intentionally avoid civic engagement because they are skeptical or opposed to such activities or simply be uninterested.

During the focus group sessions, we presented these categories to students and asked them to share which, if any, best described them upon entering Yale-NUS. We then asked how their identification in terms of engagement has changed, or not, over time. A number of students rightly noted that to separate social from political issues reflects a false distinction, since social needs reflect political choices and vice versa. (This observation reflects their training in the social sciences and political philosophy components of our Common Curriculum, described below). Nevertheless, these categories proved useful in revealing the following themes regarding the trajectory of students' engagement over their college career.

First, the focus groups—and our personal experience—suggests that students who identify as "unengaged" often become more engaged. They become, at a minimum, more interested and curious, such that they exhibit "intake" engagement if not "active" engagement. Several shared that, in their families and secondary schools, prior to college they had not been encouraged to engage with sociopolitical issues. Others reported being actively discouraged from engaging. Coming to Yale-NUS College (which students often refer to as "YNC") created not only the opportunity but the expectation to engage with these issues because of the Common Curriculum content and overall sociopolitical appetite of the student body. As one student described, upon arriving to the College they were immediately "intimidated by all these people who were very aware and involved, [whose] main interest in YNC was to become more engaged, because [they] can have [their] voice heard." Or, as another put it, on the first day on campus they concluded "This school is kind of intense–I don't know how to deal with this political engagement. It felt like that was another type of people I didn't know if I was going to become."

Second, we observed that students who entered college "politically engaged" selected Yale-NUS as their college in part to deepen their political engagement within this institutional context. However, among more politically engaged students, the experience of locals and internationals sometimes diverges. While local students of more progressive leanings are more likely to find like-minded change-makers and thereby deepen their engagement at Yale-NUS, many international students reduced their political engagement and/or redirected their energy towards social rather than overtly political causes. This is because they are in a country that is not their own, where they have fewer rights to engage, and where they are less knowledgeable and therefore less confident acting on local issues. Therefore, many of the international students we spoke with have focused their change-making energies on the college itself. We will explore this further below.

In the following section, we develop these insights and highlight the primary institutional, curricular, and normative structures within Yale-NUS that contribute to these trajectories of civic engagement.

Sources of Civic Engagement Education

For students whose interest in social and political issues grew after joining Yale-NUS, four key sources of change emerge from our research.

1. **The Common Curriculum**, which provides a shared language from which to collaborate with peers. We will discuss the curriculum in detail below.

2. **The intimacy of the Yale-NUS community**. The small size and fully residential structure makes it easy to find peers who share interests and to organize into student groups and associations.

3. **The multinationalism of the student body** came up repeatedly as a spark for greater interest in civic engagement. Students reported that meeting peers from other cultural, social, and political contexts made them realize their own views were highly socialized and, therefore, could be open to debate and scrutiny. This generates curiosity and critical reflection of their own upbringing, which encourages greater interest in social and political dynamics in other contexts. Such statements suggest that the multinationalism of the student body is a key instigator of civic engagement.

4. **The creative, can-do culture** of Yale-NUS and administrative support that makes it easy to create new organizations, events, and journals based around shared interests.

Below, following Thomas and Brower, we discuss how these factors have combined to generate social spaces for effective civic engagement education.[7] Specifically, our research surfaced the importance of course design, instructional strategies, campus culture, residential life, and the integration of curricular and extra-curricular activities.

The Common Curriculum: An Immersive Liberal Arts and Sciences Experience

Focus groups suggest that the shared experience and the illuminating content of the Common Curriculum fosters civic engagement—as it was designed to do. All students take the same courses in the same sequence, most of which fall in the first three semesters of their college experience. Each course is team taught, with students assigned to a small seminar for each course. Most seminars—which students typically refer to as "discussion sections"—are capped at 18 students, emphasizing active, team-based, and/or highly dialogic learning.

Features of the Common Curriculum that seem most important for inculcating civic engagement are:

1. Its content, specifically open discussion of cultural differences, sociopolitical systems, and controversial topics. It stokes curiosity, allows students to imagine that change might be possible and desirable, and provides the entire student body with a shared vocabulary and conceptual reference points.

2. The seminar-based, highly interactive mode of instruction, which enlarges students' capacity for active listening, verbal communication, and teamwork.

3. The skill of close-reading and analysis that is developed across several Common Curriculum courses.

Together, the Common Curriculum's content and active learning environment inculcates traits that are building blocks for civic engagement and collective action: openness to new ideas, imagination that things can change, communication, tolerance for disagreement, close reading and analysis, and teamwork.[8] Much of the literature on civic engagement emphasizes teaching students to engage in controversial issues, develop cognitive skills to analyze and understand different perspectives, and locate sources of disagreement and consensus. Learning about and being nudged to take a stand on controversial issues helps prepare students to analyze and find their own mind on many issues they will confront as citizens.[9]

Yale-NUS offers a model of what a classroom should be—interactive, even contentious—that is different from what many students are accustomed to. Dialogue and disagreement over controversial issues is not commonplace in secondary schools around the world. Fostering voice and comfort with constructive disagreement in a conflict-avoidant, more hierarchical educational culture is not easy. Moreover, in contexts where a secondary teacher's primary function is to teach students to achieve high scores in standardized national exams, there is little time or incentive to teach dialogue or disagreement.[10]

For students socialized to absorb and to conform in the classroom, the Common Curriculum marks a departure by asking students to question, probe, and disagree. That the curriculum has this impact is by design. As the first faculty handbook stated, "The freedom of faculty members to explore controversial topics in their teaching and scholarship is critical to the College's educational mission."[11] This chapter now offers some detail into the content and pedagogical techniques that make the Common Curriculum a transformative experience in terms of civic engagement among students.

Common Curriculum Content

During our focus group sessions, when asked whether their academic experience influenced their civic engagement, students most often referenced the Common Curriculum and three courses in particular: Comparative Social Inquiry (CSI), Philosophy and Political Thought (PPT), and Modern Social Thought (MST).

Comparative Social Inquiry, which students take in the first semester of their first year, introduces social institutions, social norms and control, and the socially constructed nature of things. Key topics include intersectionality, power and legitimacy, the psychology of conformity, the nation and state, markets and inequality, gender, race, family structure, social movements and change. Mid-way through the semester students engage in a "Break a Norm" activity where they leave campus and defy a social norm of some kind (without putting themselves in danger or breaking the law). Students conduct these experiments in any variety of ways. For example, some students dress in ways that buck convention, others engage in pro-social behavior like carrying groceries to peoples' cars. In the final assignment students pick a social institution or idea and analyze how it has changed or might change in the future. These are powerful ideas and experiences for first year students, from around the world, to process together.

Students also take a two-semester course on Philosophy and Political Thought, which encourages them to consider the ethics, logic, and consequences of different worldviews and political philosophies. The first semester is designed around several questions, but, perhaps most important, is "How should we live, individually and together?"[12] The second semester again focuses on a set of questions, two of which are: "What is a state and what is its proper purpose? What is the relation between governing and the interests or rights of the governed?"[13] Taken together, the course prompts students to consider how they have lived, and imagine other social systems, encouraging them to see their own state and political context in a comparative light, and to imagine the potential for different political possibilities.

Modern Social Thought, which students take in the first semester of sophomore year, introduces and critiques texts by Max Weber, Emile Durkheim, Karl Marx, Pierre Bourdieu, and Michel Foucault as well as feminist, anti-racist, and decolonial writings of Saba Mahmood, Frederick Douglass, Frantz Fanon, Edward Said, Fei Xiaotong, and others. The course is organized around discussing specific thinkers and themes like gender, race, capitalism and communism, feminism, colonialism and orientalism, repression, bureaucracy, authority, and social solidarity.

These are Common Curriculum courses that students referenced most frequently as sites for controversial and politically salient discussions. Students commented that this Common Curriculum provides "the vocabulary to speak about things" happening in the world and in Singapore, essentially a "shared vocabulary" to explore and discuss social and political issues. CSI and MST were repeatedly credited with, as one student described, "helping make better sense of social realities and drawing attention to the fact that civic engagement is needed" by giving students "the conceptual tools to understand better" and "question various conventions." And, another student explained, by informing a "moral framework and [shaping] the way you view the world," students are able to understand social issues as "stemming from social structures or capitalism which then helped [students] think about how [students] would want to solve them or how [students] would even question them and share that with others."

Perhaps most importantly, the Common Curriculum fosters engagement by acclimating students to openly discussing sensitive issues in diverse groups.[14] Speaking specifically of the philosophy courses, a student noted that these create "safe spaces" for discussion of unconventional issues or ideas: "Philosophy courses can provide a safe space for dissenting opinions, because you get to structure your dissenting opinion around this [text] . . . and your discussion is much more theoretical and conceptual and grounded in some texts that it doesn't become confrontational."

Relatedly, one student noted that the academic environment plays a part in "normalizing" conversations in the "college social sphere." The Common Curriculum offers "a good foundation of exploring" history and philosophy from diverse traditions, while bringing significant political and social "issues to people's minds." Whereas in other environments talking about politics might be seen as too provocative or radical, at Yale-NUS talking about politics and social institutions is required. Engaging with politically charged ideas is effectively homework, and therefore becomes normalized into the fabric of students' intellectual lives. As a result, it becomes socially more safe to engage in politically-relevant discussion and inquiry outside the classroom as well. For students, being exposed to different political and value systems begs the question of, "Okay, what do I do with this information?" This is often the first major step towards greater civic engagement.

Seminar-Based, Active Learning Pedagogy

The curriculum achieves "productive engagement" in part by exposing students to a wide range of authors, worldviews, philosophies, and narrative traditions. But the Common Curriculum also fosters engagement by emphasizing "face-to-face encounters and on the practices of articulate communication" in seminar settings.[15]

Focus group comments reflect the impact of seminar-based, active learning modalities on students' capacity and interest in civic engagement. Not only does the seminar setting give students practice and confidence speaking their own mind, it also acclimates them to being disagreed with, which is helpful for those entering into wider social and political discourse. This finding is exemplified in the following comments:

> My comfort level in talking about [controversial sociopolitical issues] has definitely increased over my college years...because I've also gained a vocabulary for voicing all these concerns... In the past with political issues, I would feel a certain way, but I wouldn't be able to actually verbalize or articulate [my thoughts and feelings] to certain people... The [Yale-NUS] classroom setting... is a very good way to hone those kind of skills:... distilling your thoughts and then sharing it with a wider audience... Talking to my friends, my family about politics...that really alerted me to how much I've grown throughout my college years. And how I'm better able to share, [and] maybe even convince people now.

> I'm better at calling people out... [But] it's a bit of an uphill battle...because people who are not in YNC or have not received the same kind of education do not have the same vocabulary or the same background info as to why I'm saying the things that I'm saying or why I feel strongly about things...YNC has almost

imposed on me some kind of duty to speak up about these things, where I'll feel bad if I don't.

Seminar based [learning]...made it easier for me to...say my opinions, even if people disagree... One reason why I wouldn't participate [prior to college was] because of fear that someone would disagree with what I'm saying, but exposure to seminar style learning has made [me] more comfortable being disagreed with and therefore speaking.

Not all students share this perspective of course. For example, one student stated the Common Curriculum taught them to "articulate my views" but not around politics and social change per se. Identifying as not very politically active, this student claimed, "I'm just someone who prefers to do things on a more individual, on a more small-scale level, which is why I've never identified with any large-scale organization or concerted civic engagement movements." Evidently, this student's enhanced comfort with sharing opinions inside the classroom has not translated to a greater eagerness to be heard outside the classroom or academic context. This sentiment was echoed by others, who suggested that their education had given them *skills* for civic engagement, namely articulate communication, but had not given them an *appetite* for using those skills in explicitly politicized engagement and public discourse.

Emphasis on Close Reading and Analysis

In addition to fostering inquisitiveness and practice in articulate communication, the Common Curriculum also inculcates close, critical reading skills. Although not as prominent or commonly raised, students pointed to this as another way the curriculum encouraged greater civic engagement. For example, with reference to Philosophy and Political Theory, one student described how close reading to "identify sources of disagreements" and "find common ground" among authors are useful skills when engaging in sociopolitical debates. Another student reflected how training in close reading made them a more critical reader, able to distinguish "smoking gun" from "unconfirmed sources." The student noted that even Quantitative Reasoning, a Common Curriculum class that few students explicitly associated with civic engagement, incorporated data visualizations and prompted students to question whether those visualizations provide correct data. This kind of exercise helped develop "a more critical eye."

In sum, the social sciences and explicitly politically charged courses in the Common Curriculum—Comparative Social Inquiry, Modern Social Thought, Philosophy and Political Theory—include content and develop analytical and conversational skills that contribute to engagement with sociopolitical issues. Yet we found that the Humanities and Sciences/Mathematic components of the Common Curriculum also contributed to civic engagement by developing students' close reading skills and data analysis skills, respectively. In this sense, the full liberal arts and sciences nature of the Common Curriculum empowers students to engage more actively and more impactfully in civic affairs.

Complementing this broad curricular context is the residential and extra-curricular experience, to which we now turn.

Residential Life, Student Diversity, and Extra-Curricular Learning

In addition to enjoying small class sizes and active modes of learning, Yale-NUS students experience a fully residential college and, aside from study abroad and leaves of absence, students are expected to live on campus during every semester. This means that students from all over the world get acquainted outside the classroom and have opportunities for iterative discussion and collaboration. As a new college, residential life encourages students to build the college they want to attend, by serving in student government, creating student organizations, authoring student codes and policies, and taking leadership roles in most facets of college life.

We have identified three major ways residential and extra-curricular life fosters civic engagement within the Yale-NUS context: (1) Creating encounters with difference that lead students to problematize their existing norms and worldviews; (2) Fostering intimacy and connection that helps students find like-minded peers; (3) Offering leadership opportunities that prompt students to transition from intake to output modes of civic engagement.

The "Normal" becomes Socially Constructed, The Obvious Becomes Curious

The Yale-NUS student body, in total roughly 1,000 undergraduates, is very diverse in terms of cultures and political systems represented. About 50% of Yale-NUS students are drawn from across Singapore, which is itself a phenomenally diverse country in terms of ethnicity, religion, language, and culture. The international student population represents 70+ different countries. This diversity, combined with the residential requirement and the Common Curriculum, ensures that first year students will have encounters revealing the boundaries and the socially-constructed nature of their belief systems. For Singaporean and international students alike, being on campus creates space to problematize and critically re-assess the values they have been steeped in before college. We heard repeatedly in focus groups that this confluence of factors—the Common Curriculum alongside residential living—makes students curious and able to critically evaluate what they once took for granted. For example, one student reflected that the "diverse backgrounds of my friends" bring out different perspectives so that "what I consider normal, or my political assumptions, are actually not so normal for others, which is very different from the . . . place I grew up. So I think this diverse community . . . provokes my interest in learning more." Statements like this suggest that the residential setting presents opportunities for un-learning pre-existing conceptions to hopefully facilitate self-transformation.[16]

The international composition of the student body shapes the degree of civic discourse that emerges in and out of the classroom. One student observed: "the YNC community is very inclusive of conversation and very encouraging of people to speak up if they have varying opinions [on the College's] Facebook pages... people are encouraged to speak up about something. I think that's really helpful... because we have so many international students and we have so many different backgrounds that there are different people here with varying opinions and so I feel like they take that into consideration."

For internationals, distance from home can create the privacy needed for reflection about and even transgression against the norms of home. Several international students, specifically those from illiberal or less liberal countries in Asia, reported that they had almost no experience talking about politics and contentious social issues before coming to Yale-NUS. In some cases, this was because their families discouraged such talk. In other cases, the students' entire society tended to avoid political talk. Some students are from minority groups within their home countries that are discouraged from being too involved in politics. One international student shared that being "far from home, creates a sense of freedom to speak up... it is safe to be identified as a feminist or activist on campus and college-related social media because my family won't find out."

Some international students deliberately chose Yale-NUS because they foresaw it would serve as an enclave for political awakening and experimentation. Others did not have an interest in politics during secondary school, and that had no impact on their decision to attend Yale-NUS. However, even for international students who entered the College fairly unengaged, the supply of opportunities for involvement in social and political change has enhanced their appetite for engagement. Another student observed that having "a safe space on campus far away from home also meant that I could reflect on political engagement [in my home country]... That distance helped me study those things and those causes and... then be more engaged when I [return home]." But the distance also reduces opportunities for action in home-country politics, leading the same student to conclude that for them time at Yale-NUS "led to more political and civic attentiveness, but not as much action."

Intimacy Creates Community

In addition to generating encounters with difference, the residential setting also facilitates bridge-building, enables students to meet "like-minded people." Several Singaporean participants shared that they chose Yale-NUS because they thought it would be a place they could connect with peers who "share similar interests," and engage with them on issues that might not be as openly discussed elsewhere in Singapore (they provided examples such as reliance on fossil fuels, sexuality, anti-capitalism, and toxic masculinity).

Comparing Yale-NUS to another, larger Singaporean university, one student observed that "the main difference that encourages civic engagement in YNC is the kind of students...there's a greater concentration of students in YNC who already start off caring more about politics or social issues." Given such a critical mass, this student "struggle[d] to find any particular political or social issue that [one] cannot find a community of people to be engaged in together with." This student also pointed to the "many amazing alumni who have done so many great things" to conclude that "it's very easy to latch on and...ride the wave of [organizations and initiatives created by earlier batches of students]...[It is a] conducive environment to develop any kind of interests..." Another student also spoke about how the residential community not only helps you find those with shared interests, it makes students feel safer sharing their true interests because they can have these conversations gradually and in small, close knit spaces. (However, we will see below under "Barriers to Engagement" how the intimacy of the College environment can also stifle civic engagement).

Even students who identified as more socially but less politically engaged shared this observation. One student, for example, said that they have become more interested in mental health issues, and attributes this interest to the interaction of simultaneously taking psychology courses while also living in residence with their peers. For this student, the college environment "opens up a lot more conversations about mental health in dealing with academic stress and the demands of college education, whereas before in [other educational or personal settings] people don't really share these sort of struggles." The student went on to say: "In a residential setting it becomes harder to hide [but] easier to share some of these challenges ... so *both* the [residential setting] and the curriculum definitely teach me about things that are present in society like these [mental health] issues."

Lastly, a theme emerged regarding how the close-knit community helps students not only find like-minded people but also to share responsibility for change-making. One student described themselves as being interested in social change before college and noted that finding a community of people with "parallel journeys and interests" at college "really plays a big part in my continuous engagement" and also in "preventing me from burning out." Students at Yale-NUS can share the strategies and burden of civic action. They also often hand leadership of their student organizations and initiatives over to new students, especially in their senior year when they tend to be busy with academics, job search, and graduate school applications. This tradition creates a sense of continuity and longer-term investment in the causes they care about most.

Many of the comments about campus culture we heard from students are echoed in the reflections of senior administrators. Yale-NUS President Tan Tai Yong worked at the National University of Singapore (NUS)—a very large, competitive university—for decades before joining Yale-NUS. When explaining how Yale-NUS differs from NUS, a much older institution, he points to the campus culture and size:

> Our students are articulate, vocal, they speak up. You see them all the time, in the corridor. They approach you. They're very active as well. So they organize a lot of things themselves, and they're involved in so many things. So they feel that they are part of the community, whereas NUS has 25,000 undergraduates and 10,000 graduates, 35,000 students. Huge. And you had a kind of overlay of bureaucracy that has been in place for the longest time.[17]

According to Tan, unlike the more entrenched, hierarchical culture of NUS, the Yale-NUS community is more inclusive and organic, thereby encouraging a culture of organizing and change-making among its students.[18]

In fact, focus group participants report that the small size and comradery among students helps them strategize on ways to engage without taking undue risks. Since Yale-NUS is a very visible and scrutinized institution, local students feel they must walk a fine line. While many want to use their college years to encourage and mobilize societal change (e.g., advocating for climate policies and socio-economic justice, or the repeal of anti-gay legislation), they worry about job prospects, especially in civil service, if they get tagged as too "activist" or "subversive." Several local students felt that by building a student community interested in politics and change, they can speak more openly with peers and with college staff about strategies for engaging in political activism without dooming career prospects or, worse, courting legal trouble. Some local students felt they would be less comfortable engaging in such open dialogue at other local universities because of their larger size, since it would be harder to find people they could trust.

In sum, the small size and residential nature of the College makes it easier for students to find like-minded peers, to build trust within the community, to organize, and to find emotional and pragmatic support for their civic engagement endeavors.

Leadership Opportunities and a Culture of Student-Led Organizing

Yale-NUS has an extremely active extra-curricular culture, and myriad opportunities for student organizing and self-governance. In this sense, the College provides a physical and institutional site where students practice different forms and repertoires of civic engagement. Three factors contribute to this vibrant extra-curricular culture.

First, when the College opened to students in 2013, it did not yet have extra-curricular infrastructure like a student government, newspaper, debate team, recycling club, or acapella group. To establish this infrastructure quickly, the Dean of Students' office gave students logistical and financial encouragement to build, build, build! This facilitative culture remains. Focus group participants shared that it is easy to get financial and logistical support from the College to organize beach clean-ups, perform concerts, etc. This creates ample opportunity to develop leadership and gain organizing experience, even if taking place outside an explicitly sociopolitical context. Second, Singapore secondary schools heavily promote Co-Curricular Activities (CCAs), and students get formal credit and recognition for participating in them. Many students at Yale-NUS are, therefore, already accustomed to extra-curricular organizing and creating "executive committees" for all manner of student clubs. Third, as a new college, Yale-NUS attracted students who were particularly interested in creating new programs and clubs. This opportunity to build new organizations and initiatives was what drew many of our pioneer batch to the College. This set a tone in our earliest days as an institution that students would be very active—arguably over-committed—when it comes to extra-curricular activities.

Together, these three factors have coalesced into an intense extra-curricular culture where many students are heavily involved in student organizations and various forms of self-governance. Students use the college newspaper, town halls, student government, clubs, policy initiatives, and posters in lifts to spread their ideas.[19] Yale-NUS alumnus Tee Zhuo, now a journalist, stated that his involvement in helping create sexual misconduct policies for the college "shaped [his] ethical beliefs, taught [him] the importance of empathy, and also showed [him] the need for activism in seeking justice and holding people to account."[20] This aligns with the findings of Ho, Sim and Alviar-Martin, that treating students as "full citizens" on campus provides avenues to practice their civic agency.[21]

One of the first student groups formed on campus was CAMPOS—the Committee for Appreciating and Meeting People On Site. CAMPOS created events to involve construction workers on the growing campus, such as community meals and games, as well as literacy workshops. More recently, students founded an Anti-Capitalist Identity Collective, offering a counterpoint to the popular Yale-NUS Consulting Group and the Yale-NUS Student Investment Group. The Debate Society and Model United Nations were also early and prominent groups. Students helped arrange a dialogue session with Hong Kong youth activist Joshua Wong and helped to author a new sexual misconduct policy. When a Yale-NUS board member and Singapore Ambassador at large, Chan Heng Chee, publicly defended a law criminalizing homosexuality, students in the gender and sexuality alliance, G-Spot, demanded she resign and then hosted a dialogue session with her to explain their concerns and hear her perspective. CAPE (Community for Advocacy and Political Education) has become a particularly impactful student organization, dedicated to "raising civic consciousness and building capacity for political literacy in order to make civil participation more accessible." It does so by hosting events and publishing political education resources such as its Advocacy Strategies webpage on how best to conduct advocacy in the Singaporean context.[22]

In the focus groups, students tended to emphasize these student-led initiatives as a foundation for civic engagement. However, the College has also supported formal civic engagement education through extra-curricular programs such as 1) Social Impact Bootcamp,[23] 2) Intergroup Dialogue,[24] and 3) Visiting Speakers Series.[25] These are formal, staff-supported programs to introduce contemporary issues and build student capacity to sustain diverse teams and work towards common purpose. When we asked participants why they did not mention these formal programs in their comments, they shared that while these programs are important for *building capacity* in civic engagement, they do not *create interest* in civic engagement. Students who participate in these events and programs are already quite socially and politically engaged, according to our focus group participants. As such, although they do not inculcate engagement where there previously was little, they likely help build capacity for engagement among those who are already invested.

Across issue areas, Yale-NUS students are encouraged to organize, educate each other, and dialogue. The way students spoke about membership in their clubs and organizations accords with findings on "identity collectives" on campus, as they likewise "provide essential spaces for minority groups to explore their own identities and to find fellowship in similarly-minded people, even if they are not part of the predominant culture or demographic."[26] This culture of student creation and leadership gives students opportunities to hone civic engagement skills such as communication, strategic planning, and teamwork. According to one focus group participant, as "a residential community there's also a large number of avenues for actually actively building the community... I felt like I had a very strong role to play [helping develop orientation and serving as a residential advisor]." Another added, "in developing the kinds of relationships we have within our communities... you create a community that listens to each other and holds space for each other. So I think social engagement can take lots of forms, because we have that space to build the kind of community we want."

Interaction of Curricular and Residential/Extra-Curricular Forces

Repeatedly we heard that the diversity of the student body, the content and format of the Common Curriculum, and the intimacy of residential life *interacted* to foster civic engagement. These forces do not only influence students, they have an immersive and interactive effect which contributes to students' civic engagement education. For example, one student shared how their interest in becoming more proactive in environmental activism stemmed from the interactive effect of 1) extracurricular trips led by student organizations that showed the environmental impact of climate change on ecosystem health, combined with 2) the Common Curriculum module Scientific Inquiry's emphasis on climate change, and 3) interactions in residences with classmates passionate about environmental causes. The abstract classroom learning was important, but the real-world exposure to coral bleaching amplified their commitment. Being in residence with passionate peers helped maintain the momentum and accountability to stay actively engaged.

Rather than being prompted explicitly to act by professors or by peers, students pointed to the immersive nature of the Yale-NUS learning environment and the "confluence of factors" on their interest and intensity of their commitments. "I find it quite difficult to identify a moment where I felt galvanized to act because of something that a professor said... because professors are not always very explicit about it." A few students who had studied abroad in North America for their junior year noted the contrast between their abroad and Yale-NUS experience. In the Singapore context, where protest without a state permit is illegal, professors would not say to students, "there's a protest tomorrow, you can join." Rather, students felt that civic engagement is more often implicit and embedded in classroom discussion so that "the motivation to act comes again from a confluence of factors... you hear certain things in the classroom, you see your friends doing certain things, you go online and you realize that you know people are doing things as well. Then it's just that combination of things that gets you wanting to start."

The interaction between a shared common curricular experience and shared living experience appears to be critical for fostering awareness and self-organization among students. According to one student, specifically referencing Comparative Social Inquiry (CSI), "the conversations I have outside of class with my classmates [about CSI] end up being really interesting... I feel like the courses don't really do anything [to explicitly encourage civic engagement], but they do provide a launch pad to start thinking about it... Because my CSI [class] was right before lunch...we will go out to the dining hall [to have] extended conversations about our classes."

In other words, students have reported something akin to a confluence of multiple free spaces for students to form mini-publics, forming and mobilizing consensus about a plethora of social topics, which in turn may prefigure civic agency.[27]

One student captured what many of their peers had observed during the focus group:

> I think just having both the academic and also social environment of being steeped in these issues makes a very big difference in having people think about them more consciously...[in the] social environment of Yale-NUS people do feel very subtle pressure to...have information and [understanding of local and international sociopolitical issues and] to have an opinion about things. And this is also very much trained by the academic environment that you're in [whereby] you're expected to speak up actively in class, you're expected to have an opinion [about course material], but also to respond and critically build our opinion based on evidence or based on other students' contributions...

The student felt that this expectation of engagement with issues is distinctive within Yale-NUS, and not typical of the Singaporean public. In other words, as the student put it, civic engagement is forged when the "academic and social feed into each other." We have personally observed, and in the focus groups heard testimonials about, how students' exposure to the combination of interdisciplinary curriculum, extra-curricular organizing, and the intimacy of residential life combined to make them more curious and more actively engaged in politics and consequential social issues. For example, one focus group participant shared their personal trajectory from intimidation to empowerment. In their first year, the student shared that "it felt like people who were politically engaged... were another type of people" that they couldn't imagine becoming. Then after reading the popular book, *This Is What Inequality Looks Like*, which was frequently discussed among their peers, this student recognized this "was what it meant to be engaged. It was 'political' just to engage in issues and the things that affect society."

The students in our focus groups described an educational culture that encourages—maybe demands—students to take action to build community and contribute. This culture is also articulated in a student opinion article:

> Having had the good fortune to go through the Common Curriculum at Yale-NUS and thoroughly deconstruct and unlearn all the normative narratives designed to propagate class hierarchies and systemic injustices, [along with] enlightening experiences with inspiring people from diverse backgrounds, sometimes it is difficult to not loathe myself for not doing enough with the immense privilege that I have.[28]

When comments like this surfaced during the focus groups, others would often nod, suggesting this is a widespread view. In this sense, there is implicit peer pressure within the College to seek knowledge, to be opinionated, and to be active on the causes students care about. This might take the form of community service more than explicitly political engagement, but utilizes many of the tools that are also relevant for political engagement such as crafting appealing messaging, consensus-building, and community organizing.

To sum up, the Common Curriculum content, the active modes of pedagogy that are possible due to smaller class size, and students' strong sense of community and self-governance—the curricular and extra-curricular—all come together to cultivate civic engagement among students at the College. However, as the next section shows, there are also palpable obstacles to the scope of such civic engagement.

Barriers to Civic Engagement

As we worked to uncover curricular, extra-curricular, and other structural *drivers* of civic engagement at Yale-NUS, we also sought to identify possible barriers. We generated several hypotheses through structured reflection prior to conducting the focus groups, identifying (1) workload and major selection, (2) perceived liberal bias in the College community, and (3) perceived conservativism in the local political context, as the most likely barriers to engagement. In the focus groups we did hear evidence that these were obstacles to greater civic engagement for many students. However, the focus groups surfaced additional barriers to engagement, namely (4) the intimacy of the College community inhibiting inquiry and honest debate, (5) internationals' being legally prohibited and socially dissuaded from political engagement in Singapore, and (6) student diversity, specifically that international students may lack a critical mass of co-nationals interested in domestic politics of their home countries. In this section we describe these six barriers to civic engagement faced by students.

Workload and Major Selection

Among students who entered the College with relatively low levels of civic engagement, many shared the experience of becoming increasingly socially and politically engaged as they progressed through college. However, for students who entered the College already highly engaged, several reported their engagement actually diminished over their college experience, due primarily to academic workload.

Yale-NUS is an academically demanding environment, with a roughly 5% admit rate over the last several years, the College aims to be on par with Amherst, Williams, Swarthmore, Wellesley, and other highly competitive liberal arts colleges in terms of academic rigor. Students who value good grades and are highly motivated to excel in their courses may not have much time outside class for community engagement or political advocacy. Roughly 20% of students we spoke with named academic workload as a significant barrier to more sustained engagement. Workloads typically grow as students select majors, take more demanding courses, and work on a mandatory two-semester senior thesis (called the Capstone at Yale-NUS).

Workload seems to be a greater inhibitor to engagement for those majoring in fields not as explicitly tied to social and political issues. Students who major in the social sciences and humanities often find their coursework fuels engagement and vice versa. (We heard this specifically with reference to majors/minors in Law and Liberal Arts; Global Affairs; Politics, Philosophy, and Economics; Environmental Studies; Anthropology; and Philosophy). Several students majoring in sciences discussed how the engagement fostered in the Common Curriculum during their first two years dissipated as they transitioned to their major. As one student put it, the engagement "doesn't sustain" and they can only continue it through extra-curricular organizations and volunteering, creating a time trade-off with school work. Some students reported that they desired coursework which integrates science and society, like bioethics and public health courses, so that they could continue to be engaged in social and political issues while also learning science.

Another theme that emerged in our discussion of major selection was the special position of the Environmental Studies (ES) major. Some students majoring in ES and those who had taken courses on environmental politics noted that "the environment" feels "safer" to talk about than some "sensitive" issues in Singapore like criminalization of homosexuality, treatment of foreign workers, racism, and socio-economic inequality. Learning advocacy methods for environmental policy change thus felt less confrontational and divisive than learning advocacy skills in the context of social justice, identity, and class.

Intimacy of Residential Life Cuts Both Ways, Especially Given Perceived Liberal Bias

Although the College's small size and tight-knit nature facilitates engagement by helping students find like-minded peers and learn from those with different views and backgrounds, it may also be a barrier to engagement. Students reported they often hold back from voicing opinions or questions on contentious issues for fear that it would upset people in the community, leading to alienation and social banishment.

The intimacy of the College may especially inhibit international students from more active forms of engagement on campus. For international students, the campus is their only home-base in Singapore, and so there is no way to "lie low" if they make an unintentionally offensive Facebook post or say something controversial in class. We heard several variants of this concern, which is exemplified in this international student's comment:

> My entire life is rooted in this very small campus [where] if you have an opinion about...a political or social issue, you should be ready to defend it...Especially if you have a non-liberal opinion..., you should have very good reasons [to defend that view]. I'm a third year student now, I [am] more selective about what I choose to have an opinion on... I still keep myself informed, but I can't have an opinion about everything, because I'm not ready to defend all of those [views]. And since I live on campus, I don't want to antagonize people and I can't really escape to anywhere else. I can't go back home [for the weekend like local students] or get away from campus to find another space...So I find myself being selectively engaged.

As in campuses worldwide, there is a perception, as illustrated above, among Yale-NUS students that conservative views and causes are more likely to be silenced or ridiculed than liberal ones. This may be more of an issue at Yale-NUS because the term "liberal arts college" is often interpreted in Singapore as referencing political liberalism. Since its founding, champions for more conservative views and those who take a more absolutist view of free speech, have lamented the "intolerance of intolerance" on campus. The authors have talked with students who felt they could not openly ask questions on sensitive topics like the morality of homosexuality, whether transgender identities are healthy, or why hard working "high achievers" should have to pay welfare for poor "low achievers." These themes surfaced in focus groups as well. Some students suggested that while the small scale and free speech commitment of the College makes it easier for progressive students to find each other and organize than they might in other settings, it forces conservative voices underground, making it harder for students with conservative values to find each other. One example pertains to China's crackdown on the Hong Kong protests last year. We heard from several students—in the focus groups and other conversations—who felt uncomfortable publicly defending China's position vis-à-vis Hong Kong protesters.

This view was not unanimous, of course. Several focus group participants shared that, while students might conceal conservative leanings in residence life, different views did get raised in class because the seminars usually entail vibrant debates among different worldviews. However, some reported that both residential life and classroom culture were often a liberal echo chamber. In one student's experience, too often students in seminars will express their more liberal or progressive views openly, while opposing views are not expressed. Therefore, the small seminar-style classrooms and diverse student body can allow students to learn about each other's views and be forced to hone their own arguments accordingly, but only when all students are empowered to share.

This barrier to engagement—perceived liberal bias on campus—is notable for how much it echoes what we hear from the North American higher education context.[29] Of all the barriers to engagement we uncovered, this is the least context-specific. Now we turn to barriers imposed by the Singaporean cultural and legal context, a very different set of forces.

Cultural and Legal Context

Political and legal structures do influence how students weigh the costs and benefits of civic engagement. Some of these cost-benefit calculations are obvious and clear-cut, for example students avoid spontaneously organized, unpermitted protests which are illegal in Singapore, because the consequences would be severe. One student who had studied abroad in North America reflected upon an experience where, immediately following a class on environmental policy, the professor invited students to join him in observing an environmental protest. This is possible because in that country, protests and public assemblies are open to all residents regardless of citizenship. This kind of experience is not likely to be replicated in Singapore where non-citizens are typically not able to attend cause-related public assemblies. In fact, international students are explicitly told not to get involved in formal electoral politics or participate in any speech that could be seen as inciting divisions among races or religions, which is illegal in Singapore.[30]

Some calculations regarding acceptable political engagement activities are more subtle. Students intimated that the general conservativism and controlled political climate in Singapore influenced their choices in how to act on their political and social values. Some international students, for example, were cautioned by parents or friends not to get involved in Singapore politics even in more informal ways, because it could jeopardize their student visa. Local and international students described concerns that a reputation for being too radical or too activist could hurt job prospects upon graduation. Some students, for example, take pause before championing very liberal or activist positions on social media. This was an especially pressing concern for those looking to work for the public and business sectors.

Concerns about reputational damage surface not only in students' reflections about their own actions, but also in how they react to their peers' actions. One student recalled a situation where students organized a gathering in the college courtyard to demand the school administration adopt new sexual misconduct policies and event registration policies, among other issues.[31] Such public gatherings regarding contentious issues are uncommon in Singapore, and in some cases may be considered illegal. Students who joined the gathering were aggrieved that more of their peers did not participate. However, some who did not join felt that the students staging it were putting the larger student body at risk. In addition to worries about legal trouble, they felt that if even a small number of students are too vocal and too activist, it will give the College a bad reputation in the local job market. Some local students that the authors spoke to at the time felt that international students who contributed to the gathering were insensitive to the risks for local students planning to anchor their career in Singapore. Specifically, they worried that government ministries and conservative firms may be hesitant to hire Yale-NUS graduates if they are seen as too antagonistic to local order. They did not want their Yale-NUS degree to connote rabble-rousing and liberal "external influence."[32] After this gathering, a heated debate ensued within the tight-knit student community. As one focus group participant put it, the situation "fractured a lot of relationships."

Beyond concerns regarding legality and economic prospects, students also spoke of cultural and intellectual challenges to extending engagement beyond Yale-NUS. It was a common theme that attempts to bring such conversations *beyond* Yale-NUS are often stymied by a lack of shared vocabulary with those outside the College. Some students reported they worried that they came across as arrogant or obnoxious when discussing politics outside the College because they wanted to reference theoretical frameworks or authors who their non-Yale-NUS acquaintances did not know.

In this sense, the very exceptional nature of the Yale-NUS enclave has created limits on how far within-College engagement can travel beyond the campus. To be sure, residential, cultural, and intellectual life within the College has formed a vibrant space that enables students to inquire, organize, and lobby for causes they are passionate about. But there remain barriers to bringing that vitality beyond the College gates.

Complexities for International Students

The focus groups revealed three interrelated barriers to civic engagement education for international students at Yale-NUS. These factors are likely to shape international students' experience in similar institutions located in politically constrained environments.

Lack of Formal Rights

International students face additional legal constraints, because as non-citizens, they are denied some opportunities to voice, organize, or access spaces for political assembly. The Parliamentary Elections and Presidential Elections Acts restrict foreigners from participating in "election activities."[33] Non-citizens are also barred from attending or hosting gatherings at Hong Lim Park (Singapore's Speaker's Corner where pre-approved, government-sanctioned assemblies are permissible). In this sense, foreign students' ability to have anything like a "front row" seat to local politics is limited.

Not Wanting to Undermine a Cause by Championing It

International students we spoke to were pragmatic and understood they could endanger causes they cared about by being too visibly involved. A prevalent discourse in Singapore often blames "foreign influence" for more progressive, social justice-oriented activism.[34] This assertion serves to dismiss certain perspectives and causes as not coming from Singaporean concerns or interests, and thus not warranting sympathetic attention.

Many international students felt it was important to take a "back seat" to their Singaporean peers for on-campus but especially off-campus organizing around sensitive issues. Some came to this view independently, others reported that they had been explicitly told by their Singaporean peers to keep a low profile in politically-oriented student groups, lest that group, or the causes it supports, be falsely portrayed as a trojan horse for foreign values. One student recalled being "firmly told" they could join a politically-oriented group, but was discouraged from taking any high profile leadership roles. Others intuited these limitations, as one politically engaged international student shared: "No one told me explicitly, neither my parents [nor peers], that I shouldn't be engaged politically, but I refrain from doing so because of the impression...I get from media and news sources."

In general, international students were sympathetic to the public relations imperative that social-political causes needed to be fronted by Singaporean student leaders, as exemplified in the following comments by two different focus group participants:

> The primary stakeholders...are first and foremost Singapore citizens themselves... I'm still an international student who's just here to study... I can stand in solidarity and agree or disagree with the policy and the opinions of my fellow students, but ultimately, they're the ones... facing the brunt of decision-making by the government... Their voice should be the one that should be heard...

> Being an international student in Singapore does feel like a constraining scenario...when it comes to political engagement ... You're...feeling like this is not my place to be doing activism, and as much as I would like to extend solidarity with work that is already happening, I was never able to find a space in which I could directly engage, or.. feel comfortable doing so.

With these constraints on involvement, international students we spoke to tend to funnel their energy in two ways: (1) to community/social services rather than policy change and (2) to change-making within the College itself. They may not be citizens of Singapore, but each one is 1/1000th of the Yale-NUS student body, and therefore more empowered to use their voice and organize for change vis-à-vis campus politics.

Lack of Critical Mass for Home-Country Engagement

Another way international students can maintain civic engagement during college in Singapore is to focus on dynamics in their home country. However, the diversity of the student body and faculty makes it challenging to find a sufficient number of co-nationals to collaborate with. There are 70+ nationalities represented among the roughly 450 strong international student population (just under half the student body). Students from some major feeder countries like China, India, and South Korea may have an easier time finding partners. But those from less represented countries and regions such as Eastern Europe, Africa, and South America described struggling to find peers or professors engaged with politics in their home countries. As one said, "some of the loudest voices are more interested in the American and to some extent European contexts." Even students from countries neighboring Singapore have faced this dilemma.

We suspect that we would hear similar reports if we were to interview international students at small liberal arts colleges in North America. Overcoming barriers to engagement for international students, regardless political context, warrants further attention.

Summary and Conclusion

This chapter, building on the conceptual groundwork laid in Chapter 4, reports on our research into sources and impediments to civic engagement within Yale-NUS College in Singapore. Our findings reflect focus groups, personal reflection, document analysis, and many conversations with students over many years working at the institution.

Our findings are not necessarily representative of the College as a whole and are inherently incomplete due to the modest size of our focus groups and the limits of our own experience. Nonetheless, we believe that this chapter presents **important findings regarding the bastions and barriers to civic engagement in two more generalizable contexts.**

1) Highly multinational colleges and universities: those with high percentages of international undergraduate students such as Yale-NUS. This category includes similarly transnational institutions or branch campuses that have emerged in recent years such as NYU-Abu Dhabi, NYU-Shanghai, Duke-Kunshan, and the Minerva Colleges. This category also includes older institutions with large international undergraduate populations such as Franklin University Switzerland, University of Hong Kong, ETH Zurich, Imperial College London, and several others. These institutions have opportunities to foster political curiosity, imagination, and ambition by bringing together students from such varied social-political contexts. These institutions also need to think through the barriers to engagement faced by international students that are discussed above. Some of those barriers may include legal rights to engage in local politics. Other barriers may be more subtle, such as lack of a critical mass of students from one's home country with whom to organize. One strategy is to create opportunities for students to engage in change-making directed at the college itself.

2) Colleges and universities in less liberal contexts: this study has found that the less liberal sociopolitical context in Singapore does create both formal and informal barriers to civic engagement for students. However, this does not preclude civic engagement education. Specifically, we identify ways in which the broad-based curriculum, active learning pedagogies, residential requirement, small class size, and administrative support for student extra-curricular pursuits combine to equip students with interest in and skills for civic engagement. Regardless of context, students who wish to make a difference in their communities need to be thoughtful about the nature of those contexts. Learning tools for civic engagement within a less liberal context may even be a more

Table 1: Summary of Findings	
Drivers of Civic Engagement	Barriers to Civic Engagement
Liberal Arts and Sciences Common Curriculum: Learning about different social-political systems, recognizing socially constructed nature of own value systems and behaviors, close reading and analytical skills, normalizes discussion about political and social change.	**Academic Workload:** Not enough time for civic engagement, especially for those in majors that are not directly related to societal and political issues.
Active Learning Pedagogies: Students find their voice, learn to develop own opinions rather than learning 'right answers,' communication skills, increases comfort with disagreement and genuine dialogue.	**Perceived Liberal Bias:** Conservative students may not voice their views as freely, therefore not find like-minded students as easily with which to engage.
Size, Residential Requirement, and Intimacy of Student Body: Facilitates finding like-minded students, organizing, deepening knowledge and interest in social-political issues, feeling of safety to explore new ideas and identities being on campus and away from family/ cultural origins.	**Size, Residential Requirement, and Intimacy of Student Body:** Students do not want to be lambasted or ostracized for unpopular or ignorant comments. Will keep some questions or views to themselves because there is no anonymity within such an intimate campus community.
Multinationalism of College Community: Creates encounters with difference which spark imagination, interest in scrutinizing rather than accepting students' norms and practices of own cultural context/country of origin.	**Political Limitations and Perceptions of Conservative Local Culture:** Local students do not want to risk legal trouble. International students do not want to risk deportation. Concerns that provocative action could be seen as too antagonistic for local culture and would jeopardize job prospects.
Creative, Can-Do Culture: Administrative encouragement of students who want to organize new clubs and initiatives. Gives students hands-on practice in mobilizing, organizing, messaging.	**Constraints on Political Participation and Lack of Critical Mass of Co-Nationals among International Students:** Foreign students are not permitted to participate in many forms of political engagement in Singapore. Concerns that foreign students will undermine the causes they care about if they are too vocal, making those causes seem like "imported" rather than real Singaporean issues. Inability of foreign students from less well represented nationalities to find collaborators from their home countries with which to engage.

challenging endeavor, as students develop site-specific forms of change-making.

To situate civic education in diverse contexts, it is important to highlight that engagement is not limited to physical demonstrations or confrontational tactics. In less liberal settings, fear for reputation, future employment, and family legal security present real barriers to inculcating civic engagement. As such, methods for civic mobilization need to take these barriers into account. Learning about your students, their prior interests/activities, and perceived vulnerabilities is an important starting point for educators who want to foster civic engagement. In contexts with more constrained voice opportunities, it is helpful to expose students to multiple forms of engagement and various spaces for engagement (online activism, petitions, op-eds, art-ivism, activist documentaries, academic interrogation, service learning, dialogue, etc.). In fact, social media and the Internet have increasingly been used in less liberal contexts to champion and discuss various social causes.[35] Yale-NUS students have likewise harnessed social media to promote key issues, such as sustainable living.[36]

Effective teaching strategies may vary for different populations and locations. The means to empower groups to become more politically engaged will vary from liberal to illiberal contexts. Students have funnelled energies into educating peers and the public about politics, history, and sensitive sociopolitical issues. For example, the student-run Community for Advocacy and Political

Education (CAPE) has a very instructive website providing information and analysis on "big ideas" and tracking important features of local politics. It offers information and context not readily available elsewhere and has, therefore, become a resource cited in local media.

At the same time, limits on political action beyond the college's gates shape student's goals and strategies. It is easy to form spaces for discussion and to find peers and get college support to start identity collectives, debates, and discussion groups. As one student described, at Yale-NUS "there are lots of opportunities to talk about issues, no matter how radical. But at times it feels very difficult to translate that to action." In a political context where students cannot freely howl at the moon, they must be quite strategic and nuanced in their approach. In particular, students use the college administration as a target for mobilization efforts, a sort of practice-round with more permissive norms around speech and activism.

Many of the students we spoke to who experienced barriers to political engagement either because of constraints on political advocacy in Singapore, lack of a critical mass of co-nationals (in the case of international students), or other barriers, chose to direct advocacy efforts towards Yale-NUS as an institution. One example is the student divestment campaign, Fossil Free Yale-NUS. Students also contribute to policy development at the College, through curriculum reviews, student government initiatives, and through representation on high-level committees. As one student shared: "Another barrier for international students is just the lack of knowledge and living experience of this place [Singapore]... How could I stand up and speak for this group or defend freedom of speech in Singapore, when I just came here for college? So for me, most of my engagements or concerns are more targeted at the College." The implication here is that if highly multinational educational institutions want students to develop the communicative and organizational skills that underpin civic engagement, they need to let the college or university itself serve as the canvas (and even the target) of student organizing.

Within the College, interaction between classes, extra-curricular programs, and the residential life system offers students opportunities to hone their goals in terms of social and political change and determine how to pursue those goals across different political climates. To that end, while operating within a less liberal political climate, Yale-NUS maintains a facilitative campus climate, providing students with ample opportunities to develop their interests and space for experimentation, allowing them to develop repertoires that work at Yale-NUS and in their home countries. Civic engagement education can thrive in less liberal contexts if educators and administrators create culturally responsive, socially supportive, and intellectually immersive campus and classroom climates.[37]

Endnotes

1. Gratitude and Acknowledgements: As with all the contributors, we conducted this research during the COVID-19 pandemic, which made it even more meaningful to study students' experience and goals in terms of civic engagement and community service. In this challenging time, we were extremely fortunate to have assistance executing this project. We had terrific editors who reviewed multiple drafts and helped us to sharpen the work. We wish to thank our research assistants Hanna Wdzieczak, Nahian Chowdhury, and Yuen En Ning Grace. Grace worked with us throughout the project and was tremendously helpful and efficient under tight time pressures. Our thanks also to colleagues at and beyond Yale-NUS who provided feedback on earlier drafts, especially Lynette Chua, Trisha Craig, Fiona Soh, and Claire Timperley. Above all we are grateful to students who participated in our research and generously shared their experiences, insights, and aspirations.

2. More electoral regulations in Singapore can be found at https://www.eld.gov.sg/faq_candidates.html.

3. Lee Morgenbesser, "The Autocratic Mandate: Elections, Legitimacy and Regime Stability in Singapore," *The Pacific Review* 30, no. 2 (2017): 205–231; Netina Tan, "Singapore: Challenges of 'Good Governance' without Liberal Democracy," in *Governance and Democracy in the Asia-Pacific*, ed. Stephen McCarthy and Mark R. Thompson, 48–73 (London/New York: Routledge, 2020); Meredith L. Weiss, *The Roots of Resilience: Party Machines and Grassroots Politics in Southeast Asia* (Ithaca, NY: Cornell University Press, 2020); Human Rights Watch, "'Kill the Chicken to Scare the Monkeys': Suppression of Free Expression and Assembly in Singapore," *Human Rights Watch* (December 12, 2017), Accessed June 8, 2021. https://www.hrw.org/report/2017/12/12/kill-chicken-scare-monkeys/suppression-free-expression-and-assembly-singapore; Louisa Tang, "Activist Jolovan Wham Chooses 22 days' Jail Over Fine for Holding Illegal Public Assembly

on MRT Train," *Today* (February 15, 2021), Accessed June 8, 2021. https://www.todayonline.com/singapore/activist-jolovan-wham-chooses-22-days-jail-over-fine-holding-illegal-public-assembly-mrt.

4. This may be why during the most recent Singapore General Election, a prestigious junior college (secondary education serving mostly 17- and 18-year-olds) sent an advisory asking all students to avoid posting anything related to the election on social media. According to the school's spokesperson, "it is the school's position that social media is not a suitable platform for students to be discussing their views on national issues, especially during an election period...We certainly do not want our students to be apathetic regarding national issues. But because of their youth, we also do not want them to be inadvertently embroiled in agendas beyond their control." See Rei Kurohi, "Singapore GE2020: Hwa Chong Defends Advice to Students to Not Discuss Election on Social Media," *The Straits Times* (July 4, 2020), https://www.straitstimes.com/politics/singapore-ge2020-hwa-chong-defends-advice-to-students-to-not-discuss-election-on-social.

5. Leonel Lim, Michael Tan, and Eisuke Saito, "Culturally Relevant Pedagogy: Developing Principles of Description and Analysis," *Teaching and Teacher Education: An International Journal of Research and Studies* 77, no. 1 (2019): 43–52.

6. Participants were nearly equally divided between international (11) and local (14) students, a category that includes Singapore citizens and permanent residents. The international student participants hailed from Southeast Asia, South Asia, East Asia, Central Asia, West Asia, North America, and South America. Participants represented the following majors: Politics, Philosophy and Economics; Environmental Studies; Law and Liberal Arts; Life Sciences; Economics; Anthropology; Philosophy; and Mathematical, Computational and Statistical Science (MCS). First year and second year participants are undeclared, as Yale-NUS students only select a major at the end of their second year. Due to space constraints, we were not able to share all salient comments and excerpts from our focus groups or textual analysis. We have endeavoured to select the most illuminating and representative data.

7. Nancy Thomas and Margaret Brower, "Conceptualizing and Assessing Campus Climates for Political Learning and Engagement in Democracy," *Journal of College and Character* 19, no. 4 (2018): 247–263.

8. Anne Colby, Elizabeth Beaumont, Thomas Ehrlich, and John Corngold, *Educating for Democracy Preparing Undergraduates for Responsible Political Engagement* (San Francisco, CA: Jossey-Bass, 2007).

9. Ronald W. Evans and David W. Saxe, eds., *Handbook On Teaching Social Issues* (Washington, DC: National Council for the Social Studies 1996).

10. Lewis Asimeng-Boahene, "Creating Strategies to Deal with Problems of Teaching Controversial Issues in Social Studies Education in African Schools," *Intercultural Education* 18, no. 3 (2007): 231–242.

11. Taken from the Yale-NUS College, *Creating a New Community of Learning: Year in Review 2014* (Singapore: Yale-NUS College, 2014)

12. Excerpt from the syllabus document of academic year 2020–2021.

13. Excerpt from the syllabus document of academic year 2019–2020.

14. The internal 2013 report on the Common Curriculum submitted by the inaugural Curriculum Committee of the College states this as a clear objective: "[T]he particular context of Singapore is one in which a certain amount of cosmopolitanism is a necessary part of responsible citizenship... many of our students will find themselves facing new opportunities for participation in civil society and politics. Given the conjunction of civilizations and cultures in the city and the region, responsible citizenship will require increasingly resilient habits of productive engagement across traditional civilizational boundaries." See Curriculum Committee of Yale-NUS College, *Yale-NUS College: A New Community of Learning* (Singapore: Yale-NUS College, 2013).

15. Ibid, 25.

16. Stephanie L. Curley, Jeong-eun Rhee, Binava Subhedi, and Sharon Subreenduth, "Activism as/in/for Global Citizenship: Putting Un-Learning to Work towards Educating the Future," in *The Palgrave Handbook of Global Citizenship and Education* eds. Ian Davies, Li-Ching Ho, Dina Kiwan, Carla L. Peck, Andrew Peterson, Edda Sant and Yusef Waghid, 589–606 (London: Palgrave Macmillan 2018).

17. Tai Yong Tan, "Oral History Interview with Tan Tai Yong, President of Yale-NUS College," Transcript of interview by Jaime Koh, *National Archives Singapore* (October 19, 2016) https://www.nas.gov.sg/archivesonline/oral_history_interviews/interview/E000844.

18. In describing his transition from working at NUS to becoming Executive Vice President (Provost) of Yale-NUS College, Tan noted the cultural difference: "In NUS, things were a lot more settled... [There], the hierarchy is very established, and the culture of the place also. Because if I had a view and I go to the Provost, the Provost disagrees, I have to accept that he's a Provost, he has the final say. Over here [at Yale-NUS], people may not treat you the same way. They say that if I don't agree with you, you have to persuade me to agree with you. It's not that just because you are EVP everything you say, goes. That's the culture of this place." See Tan 2016, 19.

19. Lucy Davis and Qi Siang Ng, "Why Yale-NUS Must Divest," *The Octant* (April 7, 2017), Accessed June 8, 2021. https://theoctant.org/edition/issue/opinion/yale-nus-must-divest; Jia Qi Yip, "Posters, Town Halls, Angry Opinion Articles:

Dissent and Disagreement at Yale-NUS," *The Octant* (March 18, 2019), Accessed June 8, 2021. https://theoctant.org/edition/issue/news/posters-town-halls-angry-opinion-articles-dissent-and-disagreement-at-yale-nus/; Minh Soon, "Dissent And Sensibility: Yale-NUS and Anti Establishmentarianism," *The Octant* (2020), Accessed June 8, 2021. https://theoctant.org/edition/issue/news/dissent-and-sensibility-yale-nus-and-anti-establishmentarianism/.

20. Scholars' Choice, "Scholar's Experiences Details - Mightier than the Sword," *Scholars' Choice* (July 12, 2019), Accessed June 8, 2021. https://www.scholarschoice.com.sg/experience/293/mightier_than_the_sword.

21. Li-Ching Ho, Jasmine B-Y. Sim, and Theresa Alviar-Martin, "Interrogating Differentiated Citizenship Education: Students' Perceptions of Democracy, Rights and Governance in Two Singapore Schools," *Education, Citizenship and Social Justice* 6, no. 3 (2011): 265–276.

22. CAPE, "Issue 1: Importance of Context," *Community for Advocacy and Political Education (CAPE)* (March 20, 2019), Accessed June 8, 2021. https://cape.commons.yale-nus.edu.sg/2019/03/18/issue-1-importance-of-context/.

23. Daryl Yang, "How to Make a Difference to the World: Yale-NUS Students Learn All about Social Impact Work," *Yale-NUS College Newsroom* (July 10, 2018), Accessed June 8, 2021. https://www.yale-nus.edu.sg/newsroom/10-july-2018-how-to-make-a-difference-to-the-world-yale-nus-students-learn-all-about-social-impact-work/.

24. Yale-NUS College, "Intergroup Dialogue," *Yale-NUS College Student Life*, Accessed June 8, 2021. https://studentlife.yale-nus.edu.sg/intercultural-engagement/intergroup-dialogue/.

25. For example, see Prisca Ang, "Yale-NUS Talk by Lawyer Who Helped Strike down India's Gay Sex Law Carries Low Risk of Contempt of Court Here: Shanmugam," *The Straits Times* (November 11, 2019), Accessed June 8, 2021. https://www.straitstimes.com/singapore/no-significant-risk-of-sub-judice-with-yale-nus-talk-on-indias-section-377-law-despite.

26. Shaun Lee and Zachary Loh, "Breaking Out of Capitalist Realism: Minority Political Perspectives in Yale-NUS," *The Octant* (September 24, 2020), Accessed June 8, 2021. https://theoctant.org/edition/issue/allposts/opinion/breaking-out-of-capitalist-realism-minority-political-perspectives-in-yale-nus/.

27. Wei Lit Yew, "Matrix of Free Spaces in China: Mobilizing Citizens and the Law through Digital and Organizational Spaces," *International Journal of Communication* 13 (2019): 3341–3360.

28. Shikhar Agarwal, "Coping: With Reality, With Myself, With the End of the World," *The Octant* (February 14, 2020), Accessed June 8, 2021. https://theoctant.org/edition/issue/opinion/coping-with-reality-with-myself-with-the-end-of-the-world/.

29. Delaney Vetter, "'They Don't Let Me Finish My Sentences:' Conservative Students Share Their Experiences on a Liberal Campus," *The Beacon* (April 17, 2019), Accessed June 8, 2021. https://www.upbeacon.com/article/2019/04/conservatives-on-campus.

30. Only Singapore citizens can engage in "Internet Election Advertising," defined as "any material that can reasonably be regarded as intended to promote or procure the electoral success at any election for one or more identifiable political parties, candidates or groups of candidates... This includes election advertising published on websites, social media platforms, chat rooms or discussion forums, content sharing services, or published using email, instant messaging services, SMS services or MMS services." This includes unpaid "advertising." The list of prohibitions can be found at https://www.eld.gov.sg/faq_candidates.html.

31. For coverage of the event, see Jewel Stolarchuk, "Yale-NUS Students Protest School's Decision-making Methods; Demand More Student Representation," *The Independent* (March 11, 2018), Accessed June 8, 2021. https://theindependent.sg/yale-nus-students-protest-schools-decision-making-methods-demand-more-student-representation/; Jie Ying Yip, "Frustrated At College Administration, Yale-NUS Students Stage Sit-In Protest," *The Octant* (March 15, 2018), Accessed June 8, 2021. https://theoctant.org/edition/ix-6/news/frustrated-college-administration-yale-nus-students-stage-sit-protest/.

32. For an example of how Yale-NUS is sometimes described as a threat to Singapore by posing "the risks of infiltration by external influences," see an opinion piece by former Singaporean parliamentarian Goh Choon Kang. Choon Kang Goh, "Singapore Does Not Need a 'Colour Revolution'," *The Straits Times* (September 21, 2019), Accessed June 8, 2021. https://www.straitstimes.com/opinion/singapore-does-not-need-a-colour-revolution.

33. Sin Yuen, "S'pore GE: Candidates Must Guard against Foreign Interference, Stay Clear of Negative Campaigning," *The Straits Times*, (18 June 2020), https://www.straitstimes.com/politics/spore-ge-candidates-must-guard-against-foreign-interference-stay-clear-of-negative.

34. Huy Luu Ai and Tulsi Yogesh, "What the Petition Against Dr Guruswamy Revealed About 'Foreign Influence' in Singapore," *RICE* (November 17, 2019), Accessed June 8, 2021. https://www.ricemedia.co/current-affairs-commentary-menaka-guruswamy-foreign-influence-377a-singapore/; For how the Education Minister implicitly drew linkages between foreign sponsorship and local activism, see Rei Kurohi, "Parliament: Institutions Should Not Expose Students to Risk of Breaking the Law, Says Ong Ye Kung," *The Straits Times* (October 8, 2019), Accessed June 8, 2021. https://www.straitstimes.com/politics/institutions-should-not-expose-students-to-risk-of-breaking-the-law-ong-ye-kung; The Minister stated that educational institutions "should not work with speakers and instructors who have been convicted

of public order-related offences, or who are working with political advocacy groups funded by foreigners, or who openly show disloyalty to Singapore."

35. Kai Khiun Liew, Natalie Pang, and Brenda Chan, "New Media and New Politics with Old Cemeteries and Disused Railways: Advocacy Goes Digital in Singapore," *Asian Journal of Communication* 23, no. 6 (2013): 605–619.

36. Asher Mak, "How 4 Millennial Greenfluencers Advocate Sustainable Living Using Social Media," *Zula* (January 15, 2020), Accessed June 8, 2021. https://zula.sg/millennial-greenfluencers/.

37. The National University of Singapore Institutional Review Board approved this research.

14

Studying Community and Development in The Gambia and Senegal: A Case Study of the Initial Offering of a Unique Course

Aminata Sillah and Donn Worgs

Towson University

This case study describes the development and initial offering of a unique study abroad course centered on community-driven development in The Gambia and Senegal. The objectives for the course were to enhance students' understanding of the roles and impacts of civil society, social capital, and community-driven development, while fostering an ethic of global citizenship, as they studied theories of community development and nongovernmental organizations. Students were exposed to a range of experiences, including site visits to development projects, cultural events, visits with local families, lectures, reflective sessions, guest speakers and service projects. Key lessons learned from this initial offering of the course centered on the impact and importance of: local partners, a clear organizing theme (in this case community-driven development), interpersonal connections, service projects, and frequent opportunities for student reflection. We end with a set of recommendations for others planning to offer similar courses.

KEYWORDS: Civic Engagement; Study Abroad; Community Development; Reflections; Development.

Introduction

As discussions of civic engagement and civic education have evolved in recent years, some have pushed the conversation beyond a notion of active citizenship within one's country, toward calls for promoting values of global citizenship.[1] As if cultivating civic engagement were not hard enough, the idea of cultivating and promoting a sense of global citizenship (or a sense of connection to and responsibility for the well-being of others beyond one's own country) is an even larger mountain to climb. And yet, it is essential. A broader sense of global citizenship is more necessary as transnational interactions are normalized, the global economy and global interactions increasingly shape fates of communities, and the well-being of individuals around the world increasingly depend on developments, trends, and decisions made outside of their own country. Thus, in our role as educators, we are called upon to craft learning experiences to push students toward an ethic of global citizenship.

Of course, this task is complicated by the current nature of cross-national interactions—especially between those of the global North and the global South. The history of colonization, neo-colonialism, paternalism, racism, and ethnocentrism challenges the prospect of cultivating notions of global citizenship characterized by transnational standards of justice and equity that recognize and respect the full humanity of all individuals and empathizes without romanticization or paternalism. Yet, this is the task that the authors of this chapter set out to accomplish. We attempted to craft a course that would enhance our students' understanding of the role of locally controlled civic organizations in developing their own communities while also enhancing our students' sense of global citizenship.[2]

This chapter is a description of how through effective course design, ideal partners, and good fortune—we developed and implemented a new study abroad course that facilitated student learning about theories of community and development and, at least in the short term, increased students' understanding of global interdependence, fostered greater empathy with others outside the US, and enhanced students' sense of responsibility for fellow global citizens and their sense of efficacy relating to improving conditions of under-developed communities.

Study Abroad as a Vehicle to Promote Civic Engagement and Global Citizenship

Many college students find study abroad inaccessible regardless of ethnicity or race. They tend to look at cost and self-segregate. Cost has been cited as the main obstacle to participation especially among minority and first-generation students.[3] Universities and government institutions have been deliberate in their quest to diversify study abroad programs.

In recent years, there has been increasing interest in, and support for, study abroad programs. Once on the margins of the university curriculum, these programs have gained a more central location. No longer is international study abroad relegated only to specific departments. There has been an awakening within various academic departments about the value in international education and a push to meaningfully engage students to provide a more holistic college experience. The Institute of International Education (IIE) indicated that during the 2017/18 academic year, study abroad participation increased by 11% to 341,751 students.[4] This increase continued the next year as well.[5] This includes a noticeable rise in students of color and from lower-resourced backgrounds.[6] Increasing involvement in these programs has been supported by federal funding of programs such as the Gilman and Boren scholarships. This government support has strengthened and expanded various study abroad programs.[7] The COVID-19 pandemic halted study abroad during the 2020/21 academic year, so long-term impacts remain to be seen.

Empirical research shows that students who participate in study abroad programs report being positively transformed by it and often bring ideas, knowledge and resources back home.[8] Yet, while these experiences are beneficial to students, little attention is given to how unique courses are developed and to the impact such experiences have on outcomes related to civic orientation, a sense of global citizenship, or cultural understandings that transcend the specifics of the setting for a particular class.

Extant research on study abroad programs tends to focus on learning outcomes and assessment.[9] Program design, such as level of integration with local student population, housing situation, and level of interaction with host culture, is also a focus.[10] We set out to develop a course to do what we believed was essential, despite the limited literature and the paucity of models using a similar approach focused on the array of outcomes we were seeking: to help students understand the roles and impacts of civil society, social capital, and community driven development and enhance their sense of global citizenship. For us, enhancing notions of global citizenship means developing students' understanding of other people (including an appreciation of their challenges as well as their capacities) and increasing their sense of responsibility for others beyond their own country.

Based on these learning objectives, a key element of the course design was student engagement in "service" projects, and thus we had to be intentional about staying away from the "charity mode" typical of other short-term study abroad programs. Asghar and Rowe (2017) have described the exploitative nature of short-term programs that fail to provide appropriate appreciation of power struggles and inequities entrenched in working with poor, disenfranchised, and marginalized communities.[11] We consciously sought to avoid cultivating the "white savior" mentality which Nordmeyer et al. (2016) describe as being less about justice, than about the students having an emotional experience that "validates privilege."[12] We did not want our students to help those in the communities we visited just to feel good about themselves. Thus, we consciously designed experiences to help them to understand their privilege yet enable them to engage and interact with residents in ways to avoid this privilege being a defining or dominant dynamic of these interactions.

This chapter contributes to the broader literature on civic engagement and study abroad experiences by describing and analyzing a unique study abroad experience that straddled and connected multiple perspectives and voices from local communities, community organizations, international nongovernmental organizations, and academia. Important questions are raised and answered regarding our understanding of community development, civic engagement, and what it means to cultivate a sense of global citizenship. We believe our reflections and experiences will be useful to educators who seek to design study abroad courses and other community-based learning experiences that foster a sense of global responsibility, interdependence, and citizenship.

Developing the Course

Faculty leaders began to seriously consider the idea for a course on nongovernmental organizations, civic engagement and community at the international level in 2017. Conversations centered on the potential value of a course that examined theories of community development (including theories of development and theories of community) along with practical real-world examples of community-driven development in a setting outside of the United States.

By the spring of 2018, the authors decided to pursue such a course in The Gambia. We selected The Gambia because Dr. Sillah is from there and has intimate knowledge of the country. We later added Senegal given its proximity and the opportunity for exposure to a different political context and different civic initiatives. Dakar is one of the largest and most dynamic cities in Africa and offers a striking contrast to the rural communities and small urban areas of The Gambia. Furthermore, Senegal offers cultural and historical sites to enhance participants' awareness of the context for their civic engagement activities. We proposed a course to Towson University's study-abroad office to explore community development and local NGO's efforts to address community needs in The Gambia and Senegal.

The authors relied on past experiences to craft a vision for the course. While we had not previously taught a study abroad course, we each had taught service learning/civic engagement courses in Baltimore City. In both of our cases, the courses highlighted community-led efforts envisioned by residents themselves. The projects in these courses invited students to engage community-led initiatives. These courses included lectures by the faculty leaders and guests along with readings and site visits where students learned about development projects while working closely with local residents and activists.

We wanted to take the same approach with the study abroad course. Thus, the new course would center site visits and conversations with leaders engaged in community driven development initiatives, and the students would participate in projects contributing to these organizations' existing work.

By centering these experiences, we hoped to prevent students falling into "tourist mode." We also sought to avoid the colonizer/colonized view - students giving their "service" and the community receiving the "service." Importantly, the purpose of the course was not "charity," "service," or even "giving back." The service or engagement projects would be designed for students to learn more about community-driven development with the intent to help students identify as contributors and collaborators in ongoing development efforts.

Given the differences between the previous civic engagement courses we taught and the planned study abroad course, we anticipated the need to deviate from our previous approach. Thus, we added cultural and historical site visits to further student understanding of the context of their experience. We also limited readings given the limited time and the expectation that days would be filled with varied activities. We focused on a few targeted readings that exposed students to the cultures of The Gambia and Senegal. Readings focused mostly on The Gambia for several reasons. First, Gambia was our base and the foundation for the course. Second, most community partners were Gambian based. Finally, cultural immersion and student placement with host families and host institutions were done there. In Senegal, we met with community partners who were activists, and visited some cultural sites. The readings for Senegal were limited to history and geography of the country since the two countries shared the same dialects, culture, and customs. Our goal was to allow the students to forge interpersonal connections through experiential learning and decolonizing the concept of community development. This meant that theoretical content would primarily come from formal lectures and informal discussions.

A majority of the two weeks abroad would be spent in The Gambia (10 to 12 days) with the balance in Senegal (three to four days). The student experience would include formal lectures from faculty leaders, guest lectures from local activists, visits to local cultural and historical sites, site visits to community driven projects for a hands-on service project, and readings including a short novel by a Gambian author. Service projects were key to the experience to help students feel like contributors rather than mere observers or tourists. We included a range of service experiences, including a half-day spent in one community, student placements with local organizations, as well as other activities arranged by a local partner.

Given that vision, the most important task in developing the course was locating local partners that fit the model we used in Baltimore. Since what we envisioned was not a traditional study abroad course, we did not want to partner with a traditional study abroad organization. We needed partners who had expertise in the country, understood our approach to development, and would be able to offer the kinds of service/engagement projects consistent with our vision. That was a tall order. As fortune would have it, we found an ideal lead partner in Global Hands Inc., who—along with a number of other well-suited local organizations—agreed to work with us.

Global Hands is an international NGO based in England with direct connections to The Gambia. Its leader and co-founder Dr. Momodou Sallah of De Montfort University, is Gambian, and The Gambia is their primary focus. The organization addresses issues of "local and global inequality by raising consciousness about local and global issues through community engagement."[13] Global Hands help individuals and communities build capacity to transform lives. The organization's mission was aligned with our vision. To say Global Hands was ideal is an understatement. In shaping the course, they pushed the experience beyond what we had initially envisioned. Thus, the outcome of the course was a product of the Towson faculty leaders' collaboration with the leaders of Global Hands.

We initially sought to work with Global Hands to house our students in their facility– The Manduar Development Hub. As we learned more about them, we learned they had run what they called the "Gambian Development School" for both college students and others. They had extensive experience doing what we sought to do from a perspective that aligned with our vision of development. Thus, after settling on Global Hands as primary partner for lodging and logistics, the relationship expanded to include core content.

In finalizing the course, we adjusted plans to fit with Global Hands' mission, vision, and expertise. Collectively we crafted the students' experience. During the course, we regularly met with Global Hands staff to make adjustments and reach consensus on actions. In that regard, our approach was consistent with the insights and recommendations of Tinkler et al. (2014), that faculty should pay attention to community partner's mission, vision, and resources throughout service-learning experiences. This is easier when the partner's vision and mission align with the vision of the faculty leaders and course objectives.[14]

Global Hands' relationships with organizations engaged in the work we sought to explore complemented Dr. Sillah's knowledge of and connections to the area. Our combined efforts facilitated partnerships with local organizations that helped develop interesting experiences for our students. In particular, Global Hands pushed us to expand the scope of the immersive cultural experiences we incorporated into the program plan. Those experiences proved to be invaluable additions to the course design.

The Course Design

Our final vision was rather ambitious. We designed a course for students to learn about theories of community development and nongovernmental organizations in the context of two predominantly Muslim African countries. It is important to note that our understanding of the term "community development" is rather broad. We agree with Ferguson and Dickens' notion that conceives community development in broad terms, including a wide range of activities to enhance the "quality of life" for residents in a particular area.[15] Given this concept of community development, we wanted students to take note of how local residents defined "development" and how they conceived their "development" priorities. Thus, the course is centered on direct exposure to community-driven development projects.

The primary objectives for the course are to enhance students' understanding of the roles and impacts of civil society, social capital, and community-driven development while forming an ethic of global citizenship. By the end of the course, we hoped our students would demonstrate an understanding of, (1) The history of The Gambia and Senegal, (2) contemporary attributes of each country and, (3) community development as a strategy to address current issues and challenges (for details see table 1).

Each outcome was aligned with specific planned experiences. To understand whether students gain the knowledge, skills, and values connected to the course, we required them to make daily, reflective journal entries in response to specific prompts. These journals were collected at the end of the trip. Students were also required to write a final essay upon return to the US (See table 1)

Planned experiences ranged from site visits to development projects, cultural events, visits with local families, lectures, reflective sessions, guest speakers, and service projects. We purposefully went beyond contemporary development projects to present students with content related to the countries' history (e.g., the transatlantic slave trade, colonization, neocolonialism and independence), as well as contemporary challenges facing each nation (e.g., the construction of democratic institutions and practices in the aftermath of authoritarian rule). We felt that understanding the historical and contemporary context was essential to understanding community development strategies and the visions guiding development work of the organizations studied.

We planned to spend most time in The Gambia travelling to both urban and rural areas. We would reside in Manduar, a village outside the urban center of Brikama. This was key to give students a sense of life in a rural community (limited access to infrastructure and key services) with vibrant civic organizations and a strong sense of community. We would also spend three days in Senegal staying in Dakar, one of the most dynamic cities in West Africa. We anticipated the contrast would be insightful.

Implementation: The Actual Experience

The course was initially offered during the minimester of January 2020. Students departed on January 2nd and returned on January 20th. Ultimately, 11 students took the course, including one freshman, two seniors and eight juniors. Of this eleven, six majored in political science or a related field. One student was from another campus and did not take the course for formal credit. Below we describe some key experiences—both highlights and lowlights—followed by a description of student outcomes and key lessons gained from the course development and the initial offering. We begin with a brief description of the two countries followed by a discussion of our experiences.

The Gambia and Senegal

The Gambia is small with a population of about 2.2 million. It achieved independence from

Table 1. Learning Outcomes	
After completing this course, students will have an enhanced understanding of:	**These outcomes will be achieved through the following activities:**

The history and culture of The Gambia and Senegal, including:
 	
    • The history of the area prior to contact with Europeans
 	
    • The role of this region in the Transatlantic slave trade, and the impact of the transatlantic slave trade on the region.
 	
    • The process and European colonization and the impact of colonization on the people of the region
 	
    • The process of decolonization and movements for independence.
	• The Hub activities
	• Lecture from Minister of Culture
	Visits to:
	• Senegal Monument
	• Museums (Katchikally)
	• *Senegal museum*
	• Historical sites
	• Fort Bullen
	• Kunta Kente Island
	• Goree Island

Contemporary attributes of each country including:
 	
    • Cultural practices,
 	
    • Recent economic, social, and political developments
 	
    • Current issues and challenges facing each country
 	
    • *Natural and Ecological attributes*
	• Community Visits
	• Market visit
	• Kerr Omar Farm visit
	• Hub exercise and discussion
	• Reading "The Magic Calabash"
	• Family visit
	• Community partner—activities
	• Logic of the System Conference
	• Guest lectures

Community development as a strategy to address current issues and challenges, including:
 	
    • The concept of community development
 	
    • The range of actors who participate in community development and their impacts
 	
    • Local visions of development
 	
    • Key examples of community-driven initiatives seeking to address: education and youth development; gender equity and women's rights; environmental justice and sustainability; economic development and poverty alleviation; health and wellness.
	• Lecture: Theory of Comm Dev
	• Lecture: status of women
	• Lecture: local issues, groups
	• Talk on Female Circumcision (FGM)
	• Visits to Starfish, Kafuto, Komforo
	• Community Placements
	• Community Projects
	• Hub Activities
	• School visits
	• Guest lectures

The use of the arts as a vehicle for community development	• Senegal rap group • Senegal mural tours

Britain in 1965. From independence until 1994, it had a long record of democratic practice and tolerance. Under its first president, Sir Dawda Jawara, the country's status as a stable democracy and promoter of human rights led to the establishment of headquarters for the first permanent Secretariat of the African Commission on Human and People's Rights in The Gambia. Jawara was a renowned peace promoter and internationally acclaimed for his commitment to the rule of law and multiparty democracy.[16] Jawara's successor, Yahya Jammeh, undermined the democratic process and turned toward authoritarianism—with a broad record of repression and human rights violations that included the silencing of political opposition.[17] Jammeh's rule ended in 2016 when he lost the presidential election and was pressured by Economic Community of West African States' (ECOWAS's) military forces to accept the election outcome and leave office.[18] Under Jammeh's successor, Adama Barrow, civil society organizations have re-emerged and re-opened democratic space. The government has strengthened civic participation through policies that engage young people and increase volunteerism.

Senegal borders The Gambia on three sides and is much larger, with 16 million people. The countries have a common cultural heritage and religious make-up despite the fact that The Gambia is English-speaking, and Senegal is French speaking. Senegal achieved independence from France in 1960. It too has a record of democratic governance. However, while its government is democratically elected and politically stable, authorities have been known to arrest members of opposition movements to suppress dissent. Yet, there is space for dissent, and opposition movements have had successes in recent years. It too has a vibrant civil society.[19]

We arrived in The Gambia on January 3 after 20 hours of travel. We were picked up by representatives of Global Hands who brought us to the Manduar Development Hub, where we would reside while in The Gambia. This location was important to give students a sense of security and see firsthand what development meant to people who lacked a direct voice in national policies. We were embedded within the community. While we had consistent access to running water (cold) and electricity, and even sporadic WiFi access, our neighbors' access to these essential services varied. Yet, the community had a visible drive toward their own notion of development. The origin of the Hub exhibited this drive. It was the product of a partnership between Global Hands and the village of Manduar and was the site for various development projects. Global Hands staff (some who lived in Manduar) explained that the *Alkalo* (the village head) played a key role in establishing the Hub. The village provided the land and community members worked at the site. There appeared to be a real sense of partnership. The facility is a valuable asset as a space where residents can access running water, electricity, and the internet. Through conversations with staff and neighbors, we came to understand we were not merely guests of Global Hands—we were in fact guests of the Manduar community. Much of what we learned about the village and the origins of the Hub came through informal conversations—highlighting the potential for civic learning that comes with being embedded within the community.

Throughout our time abroad, we engaged in a range of activities—planned and unplanned—that immersed and intimately engaged students (and faculty) into local culture and development efforts geared to building capacity among local communities. The course can be divided into five sets of activities: cultural immersion, historical sites, community development site visits and guest lectures, engagement activities, and the journey to and from Senegal. Most of the cultural and historical activities occurred during the first few days of the trip, while community development and engagement activities occurred in the latter days. The trip to Senegal occurred from day eight through day ten and stood out as the most challenging portion of the course, deserving of its own category.

Cultural Immersion

The first few days were dedicated to immersion into the local culture while familiarizing ourselves with the country's languages, religious practices, clothing, food, etc. The highlights of this phase were the visit to the *Alkalo* on our second night and the students' visit with local families on the third day. When visiting the *Alkalo*, we brought kola nuts (a traditional offering and sign of respect used in traditional ceremonies like marriages and naming ceremonies) and other gifts. When we later learned the *Alkalo's* role in establishing the Hub, we all better understood the importance of paying our respects as guests of the village. The family visits had a special impact. Students spent the entire day with local families who had been pre-selected by Global Hands. Students later said these visits with individual families were among the most valuable experiences of the course. They observed gender roles, as well as the day-to-day challenges of maintaining a household when preparing meals required hours of work. Students participated in these activities but almost all reported they were not very efficient in their tasks.

During a reflective discussion the next day, students were excited to share their experiences, practically "bragging" about their host families. One student excitedly told others the mother in her host family was the leader of the guild of tailors in the village and another exclaimed that their host mother coordinated the guild that produced the soap used for washing clothes in the area.

The students were particularly struck by their conversations with residents. Two students, for example, described a conversation they had with a host (a young man) who had studied in Libya. His experience gave them perspective on the roots of African migration—the seeking of opportunities in other countries—as well as the difficulty obtaining an education.

It is important to note that while English is the official language in the Gambia, not everyone speaks English. Since families tended to live in compounds, usually someone who lives there speaks English because they have attended primary, high school, or even university. Most host mothers did not speak English yet communicated with our students because of the diversity found in the family compounds. While communication between the students and their host families was not easy, it was possible and ultimately impactful.

Immersion into the culture included other activities–some small, like drinking tea with villagers, and others more extensive—such as visiting the Brikama market and attending a community festival. Visiting the Brikama market was cited by several students as eye opening. Brikama, the closest city to Manduar, is one of the largest and fastest growing urban areas in The Gambia and contains an extensive market where locals sell every product one might need—from food to clothing to various consumer goods. The market was busy, bright, bustling, with a blend of traditional and western items. Students were tasked with exploring the market to look for visible impacts of globalization. Students later presented their observations of how products and services available at the market (imported consumer products, financial exchanges, local produced goods, etc.), revealed ways globalization impacted the Gambian economy, politics, technology, environment, and culture. The students articulated the interconnectedness of various facets of globalization and how an isolated community in a small West African country is part of, and impacted by, globalization in both negative and positive ways.

Two final experiences that offered insight into Gambian life and culture included a guest lecture from Nana Grey-Johnson, author of *The Magic Calabash*, a Gambian novel students had read, and a community festival hosted by the Hub. The novel and discussions with the author gave a glimpse into Gambian folklore as well as aspects of Gambian religious and political history. The festival included drummers, dancers, a DJ, and other performers, and was well attended by local residents–many of whom performed. The event was fun and gave another glimpse into the local culture and the nature of community. Perhaps most notable were interactions between students and the families they had stayed with earlier. They were excited to see one another and expressed a sense of connection and pride. The students were overjoyed when some of the host mothers drummed and danced during the festival.

Overall, the value of interpersonal connections and extended immersion in the community gave students a deeper understanding of the needs and nature of development in the community. They witnessed a vibrant cultural life. A number of students later noted how that perspective shaped their understanding of what development ought to look like.

Historical Sites

Notwithstanding our focus on community development, it was key to learn the region's history. This was achieved through visits to historical sites, museums, and a conference call with the Gambian Minister of Culture. Highlights were visits to Kunta Kente Island (formerly James Island) and Fort Bullen in The Gambia, and Goree Island and the African Renaissance Monument in Senegal.

Kunta Kinte Island contained ruins of a fort that held enslaved captives awaiting transport to the Americas. It was renamed for Kunta Kinteh—author Alex Haley's ancestor described in *Roots*—who had been captive there. Fort Bullen was built as a British outpost to suppress the slave trade on the River Gambia—after the British banned the trade.[20] Visits to slave forts in both countries were emotionally moving as testaments to the horrors of the Transatlantic Slave trade and they symbolized the region's role in a global economy since at least the 1700s. Such global linkages were also manifested in the African Renaissance Monument which is said to point back to a still standing slave fort on Goree Island, and toward the Statue of Liberty across the Atlantic. This monument houses exhibits articulating the Pan-African movement and the African Diaspora.[21]

Community Development: Lectures, Site Visits and Engagement Projects

At the outset of the experience, we presented students with a general definition of community development to help frame our experiences. Our definition borrowed heavily from Ferguson and Dickens describing community development as a process that "produces assets that enhance the quality of life of residents" in a targeted community.[22] We emphasized this process may produce enhanced assets such as physical capital, social capital, intellectual or human capital, financial capital and political capital among residents (or within the community) or increase access to basic services and needs (e.g., food security, access to water, electricity, healthcare and transportation).

We wanted students to understand that this broad definition allowed a wide variety of initiatives to come within our purview. We also hoped students would observe how local residents defined community development for themselves and what kinds of initiatives they felt should be prioritized. Lastly, we wanted the students to develop their own sense of what development means, and whose vision of development ought to guide efforts for particular communities.

The core experiences of the course centered on guest lectures, site visits with organizations engaged in development activities, and service projects at the Hub and with other partners. Among all these experiences, three are particularly noteworthy: the visit with Starfish International, our visit to the Kafuta community, and the Logic of the System conference held at The Hub.

Starfish International is a youth development NGO focused on the education and development of girls. Our entire group visited the site, and a smaller group spent an additional day of service. Starfish stood out due to their comprehensive vision and the impact it had on youth. Students were struck by the mission and the work—given challenges related to girls' education and gender roles. Students cited the independence of the organization as well as the indigenous nature of the group—it was founded by a woman from the community who returned home after studying in the US. It was one of many examples of community-driven initiatives not dependent on an international development agenda. Rather, Starfish crafted its own agenda and garnered its own resources to support itself. This organization combined programing around the arts, entrepreneurship, academic training, and workshops on independent living. We were all impressed by the dynamic of the girls in the program and the young women who staffed it. As a community-led and community-driven initiative, Starfish embodied the core focus of the course: programs designed by the community, for the community, to promote sustainable economic and cultural growth.

The visit to the Kufuta community provided our first opportunity to do hands-on "service." We went there only knowing our role was to help community members clean out and paint a building. As we worked, we learned more about the project. The Kufuta Community Development Association (KCDA) sponsors a number of initiatives in the Kufuta community. The building we worked on was to house a community library. The previous site had been damaged by termites. We learned about the important role the local library played and about other initiatives of the organization such as micro-enterprise programs and computer coding classes for girls. This project was locally led and largely financed by Gambian supporters. Students worked alongside community members contributing their effort and time to the project. Next, the leader of the KCDA took us to meet his mentor in the neighboring community of Komforro. We met the gentleman in a deceptively humble building on the side of the road. He spoke to the vast range of development projects he was working on. These included environmental projects to protect wildlife and technological projects to prevent deforestation. He also described micro-enterprise programs, such as one to train local residents in bee-keeping both as an economic project (for their finances) and as an environmental project to preserve the local bee population. We were surprised to learn they had planted some 5,000 trees in the area and were currently battling Chinese logging companies nearby. The extent and range of activities in Kufuta and Komforro demonstrated both local capacity as well as the local vision of development.

A third experience was less exciting, but impactful. Global Hands organized a conference that coincided with our visit. The theme of the conference was "Constructing Counter Narratives," and featured scholars and activists from The Gambia and elsewhere. The recurring theme of the presentations was the need for Gambians to chart their own path of development and what that might look like. There was a constant critique of development agendas being thrust upon communities, and a desire for greater appreciation of local people's capacity to know what they want and to define for themselves what development means and should look like in their community. This had a strong effect on the students. More than half noted in their final essays how their experiences presented them with "counter narratives."

Building capacity for self-sufficiency was a recurring theme. We saw this in Kufuta, Komforro, Starfish International, as well as in the Hub. We heard this discussed at the conference. It was key for our students to appreciate the centrality of this sentiment. One final story illustrates this notion of building capacity for self-sufficiency. As our time to depart The Gambia approached, we decided to make a contribution to the Hub. We discussed working on their library—building shelves, fixing furniture, sorting and shelving books, etc. When we approached the Global Hands staff, they suggested we speak with some local residents. We learned that they liked the idea of fixing up the library, but really wanted a chicken coop. They explained a chicken coop would be a source of food and income for village residents. While we lacked the capacity to build a chicken coop – we did help get the project started. We bought tools and worked alongside residents to clear the field where they would build a coop. As educators, of course we love libraries, but it was important to model the theme of the course, which was letting communities chart their own course for development.

Senegal

The journey to and from Dakar was easily the lowlight of the course. We chartered a bus to drive from Manduar to Dakar. The journey entailed crossing the River Gambia by ferry, a border crossing, and driving through Senegal to Dakar. A trip estimated to take six hours took more than 12—each way! Delays were caused by crossings at the ferry and border, but the main obstacles were the frustratingly frequent stops by Senegalese police. We were stopped no less than twenty times on the way to Dakar. We later learned this was common for commercial vehicles with Gambian license plates such as ours.

While in Dakar, frequent police stops and ubiquitous traffic congestion made for a difficult experience. Though miserable, there were valuable lessons. The congestion spoke to the city's rapid growth. Physical development was evident in new construction projects, a light rail system, and other signs of growth in a vibrant city. In addition to cultural sites mentioned above, the highlight of our time in Dakar was a visit with local activists. Ya No Marre is a movement led by one of Africa's premiere rap groups and a group of young journalists that challenges the nation's political leadership amid demands for reform. They offered the clearest example we witnessed of the intersection between arts and civic activism. The students were struck by their commitment and approach to activism–using music to promote social change–despite contending with repressive responses from political leaders. Both activists we met with had been imprisoned for their activity.

Even though accommodations in Dakar were more familiar—hot water, mirrors, WiFi, restaurants, etc.—the difficulties in Senegal made our return to Manduar feel like coming "home." Students were happy to be back to our modest lifestyle. Cold showers, no mirrors and limited WiFi etc., were barely noticeable inconveniences. As one student noted in her final essay, she considered Manduar "more like home" than Dakar, which "looked more like home." This revealed an appreciation for living in the community that may not have been apparent without the contrast to our experience in Dakar. Of course, the nature of the trip was different. We were there a shorter time and were not embedded within a community. We experienced the country and city as outsiders. That may have ultimately been the biggest difference. Navigating the city was difficult—we were more like tourists—which contrasted with the interpersonal experiences we had in The Gambia.

Student Outcomes

The array of experiences apparently led to many desired outcomes—at least in the short term. We have already listed an extensive menu of intended learning outcomes, here we will discuss outcomes related to community development and global citizenship as revealed in the students' final essays and their responses to a post experience survey. We also describe outcomes we observed from our vantage point.

Students were required to submit a final reflective essay upon return to the US. The prompt for the essay required students to describe insights gained from three key experiences and to discuss the overall experience of the course, including what if any impact it had on their understanding of development and plans for the future. We examined student essays looking for evidence of the following outcomes:

1. Enhanced understanding of global citizenship—the impact of global dynamics on the local experiences of residents.

2. Enhanced understanding, recognition, and appreciation of local visions of development and/or a recognition and appreciation of local culture and community dynamics.

3. Plans to expand engagement around global issues.

Of the 10 students who completed the assignment, nine demonstrated an understanding of the global impact on local communities, all demonstrated a recognition and appreciation of local visions of development and/or local culture and community dynamics, and nine expressed an intention to expand their engagement activities around global issues.

We were struck by the extent to which all students expressed an appreciation of the importance of local communities crafting their own visions of development—and the legitimacy of these visions. The following quotes from three student essays reflect this perspective:

"One major takeaway that will always remain in the forefront of my mind is to always assess the wants and needs of the people. It does not matter what an outsider of a community may think the people need, it only matters what the people of that community express that they need."

"Development is the actualization of whatever community vision emerges, completely divorced from outside agenda or restrictive institutions."

"They are able to assert their own agendas and impact change in the way they deem most important without having to listen to an outside source."

Overall, the students' essays revealed that they now see the world differently. Upon their return, students saw the world from a different perspective and recognized the limits of their previous perspectives. The following quotes are indicative:

"There came a point where I became emotional because I was never taught about the world in a Non-American context."

"With these experiences I was able to slowly build a more accurate vision about Africa instead of the one portrayed in the media."

Responses to the post-experience survey also suggest that students were positively impacted by the experience. When asked if they could "provide an example of how your education or applied experiences have helped you see communities that might otherwise remain unseen," seven students gave examples. Two responses are typical:

"The harsh reality is that many of our most in need communities—domestically and internationally—are hidden and unseen by most everyone. Engaging with and living alongside such communities allows for a greater understanding of how to better acknowledge these groups."

It made me realize that when we talk about Third World countries, we ignore the people living there. We put too much focus on organizations, governments, institutions.

Survey responses also indicated students believe the experience will impact their future engagement. They claimed to feel an increased sense of efficacy. When asked if the study abroad experiences influenced their "personal sense of [their] ability to make a difference, locally or globally," eight students said yes. As their responses reflect, this seems due to their belief they participated in or observed activities that made a difference.

"Yes, the hub showed a way to have a community center that created tangible change and programming."

"I feel much more motivated to impact my local community and to improve the lives of others. I viewed institutional barriers or government negligence as insurmountable previously, but the trip really transformed how I quantify and identity tangible change."

"I now feel more empowered to make a difference on each level because I was able to participate in events that made a difference."

But there was some nuance, as indicated by one student's claim, "Yes, I feel more power in a local sense, less power on a global sense."

Lastly, eight students said they will "engage in advocacy" more than they did before the experience. Interestingly, some noted how they planned to target their advocacy—with some saying they would focus on local issues (e.g., education in Baltimore) and others claiming they will focus on global issues.

We recognize that these responses were made in the days after their experience, and it is likely not all will actually expand their engagement in civic and global issues. However, the significance in these responses is that the experience disrupted their normal thinking and, for a little while at least, helped them see the world and their role in it differently. It remains to be seen if this impact will be sustained over time.

Faculty Observations

Beyond what was evident in the students' papers and survey responses, we observed some important outcomes worth noting. In particular, the reflective sessions and informal conversations allowed us to see how they were processing their experiences. In this regard, four observations were especially significant.

Their identification and empathy with community members: We noticed that students exhibited a level of empathy with residents. For the most part, this was not overly paternalistic (although there was a bit of that). Their empathy primarily took the form of appreciation for the lived experiences and the challenges facing people they grew to care about and respect. They also expressed respect for local knowledge and local visions as reflected in their writings above.

Recognition of the impact and challenges posed by globalization: We began to see this from the first visit to Brikama Market, but it was a theme throughout the course. There was an underlying consciousness of the impact global dynamics had on local conditions we saw in The Gambia. Perhaps the most telling observation came during a reflective session following one of the student service days. The student working with the Brikama Development Corporation described their project producing innovative wood burning stoves that allowed locals to cook with less wood than typical stoves. The organization considered this a community-based solution to the challenge of deforestation by giving residents a tool to limit their consumption of wood. The student was impressed with this local solution to a key ecological challenge. The student's enthusiasm was dampened, however, after we visited the Komforro Organization and learned of their ongoing battles to prevent deforestation. A specific focus of their efforts was to curb the activities of Chinese lumber companies. Our student recognized the limited impact of more efficient stoves if the real culprits of deforestation were global economic actors. For our purposes, it was significant that the student told this story during a reflective session—thus all the students were able to process that understanding.

Recognition of gender roles: Much informal discussion and some formal reflections centered on gender roles. The students were at times frustrated with limitations on women and girls and were especially upset by the cultural practice of female circumcision. This was a factor in the level of impact of the FGM discussion and the visit with Starfish. That visit was emotional as students were inspired by the girls they met, so much so that two were planning to return to the Gambia to serve as interns for Starfish. Overall, they were moved that local efforts were addressing these concerns, not outsiders coming in to condemn local customs.

Religion: This was more an absence of concern. This was the first time any of them had spent time in a predominantly Muslim country, yet there was no discernable discomfort. We were all conscious we were in a Muslim country, by the mosques, signs celebrating religious leaders, the attire of some women and girls, the prayer calls, and occasional observations of residents pausing to pray. We did not detect much discomfort among students—nor did they comment on it much. With all the students had to say, their lack of comments on religion was noticeable. We took this as a positive indication of students moving beyond religion as an obstacle or impediment to connecting with the people or empathizing with their life experiences.

Lessons Learned

As we reflected on this experience—from course development through the initial offering—we identified some key lessons. The first lesson relates to the *importance of partners*. As mentioned above, Global Hands provided significant input to the final design of the course. It was key that their experiences and vision aligned with our own. Other local partners, like Starfish and Kufuta, also shared our understanding of development and our perspective on the contributions our students could make. On the other hand, we would have benefitted significantly from an on-the-ground partner in Dakar. A local partner could have helped navigate that experience, travelled with us, and provided context, making our time spent in traffic more productive—and less painful.

Overall, our interaction with the partners was consistent with previous research and recommendations around faculty managing of community partnerships.[23] Faculty leaders were engaged throughout and consciously "managed" the student interactions with Global Hands and the other partner organizations. We maintained constant communication with the partners (e.g. regular meetings with Global Hands leadership) and sought to manage both the student and partner expectations. Managing the relationship at times meant trusting the judgment of the partners (as with the home visits which ended up being invaluable) or deferring to the partners' desires (as with the decision to work on a chicken coop, rather than a library). But, again, this was possible because our vision was well aligned with the partners.

A second key lesson is the value of establishing a clear theme to provide a lens through which we would process our experiences. The guiding theme—community-driven development efforts—helped us to view our experiences through the lens of a community focus. This lens also served the objective to enhance notions of global citizenship as it highlighted local agency and local visions, rather than viewing residents as people needing to be saved. That frame helped us avoid the savior dynamic as well as tendencies to otherize people from different circumstances. We believe highlighting the expertise and vision of our partners shaped students' responses to them. We suspect the effectiveness of this approach may lie in how we (the instructors) prepare and contextualize the experiences. Given that we view the organization's objectives and approaches as legitimate and even innovative, this may have shaped the students' response to these organizations both in the US and during our time abroad.

A third lesson is to reiterate the *potential impact of service/engagement projects* for a course on community development. In total, each student engaged in approximately 12 to 18 hours of service (four hours in Kufuta, four to six hours in placements with local organizations, three to five hours on a community action day for youth in Manduar, and two to three hours clearing land for the chicken coop). It is clear that students' mindsets change when they are "contributors" versus "recipients" of information. Whether they were working on the library in Kufuta or at the Hub, students were no longer passively absorbing information. They were investing their energy, committed to the ultimate success of the project. This shift in student mindsets seemed to affect their perspective, even on projects they did not contribute to.

The fourth key lesson is that interpersonal *connections were critical.* Cultural immersion was critical to understanding the community and the development strategies it pursued. While we underappreciated that in our initial vision for the course, we came to understand that such experiences are essential to course objectives. These experiences, however, have to be planned carefully. Home visits, for example, were organized by Global Hands which had found those experiences to be valuable in the past. The value of these interactions was probably maximized by the fact that Global Hands had worked with the families before, and they understood the dynamic of working with foreign visitors.

A final lesson was that the *importance of reflective sessions* cannot be overstated. The formal and informal reflective sessions were used to explore theoretical concepts and to provide broader context. We consciously led these sessions to resist dwelling on feelings (or worse—gripes) and endeavored to direct conversations fruitfully. Thus, we found they served as effective vehicles for theoretical discourse propelled by students' observations. They also presented opportunities to draw connections to student experiences in the US. In all, our experience affirms earlier findings that critical reflection helps one comprehend complex social issues and that more extensive reflection leads to preferable student outcomes in service-learning courses.[24]

Given these lessons, we offer some recommendations to faculty who wish to develop a course with similar objectives. As they develop courses, they should:

- Have a clear organizing theme for the experiences and a clear perspective or lens through which experiences can be processed.

- In designing the course, prioritize the types of "outside the classroom" experiences that bring about the desired outcomes.

- Prioritize selecting the right partners. While others are unlikely to find a partner like we did—with a facility embedded in the community and deep relationships and compatible experiences—the key is partners with comparable understandings of key objectives of the course.

- If possible, include service/engagement opportunities. This was key to avoiding a tourist orientation and promoted an orientation of contribution and collaboration. While service can be problematic, appropriately designed experiences model civic engagement, respect for others, and a willingness to contribute to the public good, as defined by the local community that collaborative work is designed to benefit.

- Prioritize inter-personal connections: This has implications for where you stay and the types of experiences planned.

- Prioritize formal and informal reflective sessions. Most of our theoretical insights came in the reflective sessions. These need to be led by faculty in order to keep the focus on the theoretical insights rather than gripe fests or what students like or don't like. There may be a place for sharing frustrations, but for courses such as ours, the reflection was more about the process to mine ways that uncover and inspire theoretical insights.

- Lastly, learn from previous experiences. Students are the same, although the context is different. Thus, lessons and understandings from typical courses and engagement experiences are relevant.

These recommendations may not apply to all such efforts, but we suspect they may help in many cases. Our experience with this course has laid a foundation for future study abroad courses focused on community development and will help in traditional on-campus courses. Overall, we crafted an effective course design that led to an unforgettable experience. By prioritizing inter-personal connections, active onsite learning, and structured reflection, we deepened students' understanding of themselves, of the importance of local agency and autonomy in fostering community and economic development, and of their role as global citizens in an interconnected world.

Endnotes

1. Pat Crawford and Brett Burquist, eds., *Community Engagement Abroad: Perspectives and Practices on Service, Engagement, and Learning Overseas* (East Lansing, MI: State University Press, 2020).

2. Students were informed that their comments might be used anonymously for this study and were given the option to not have their comments included in the publication. All students gave informed consent, and this research is classified as exempt under the Towson University Institutional Review Board guidelines.

3. Jacqueline M. Brux and Blake Fry, "Multicultural Students in Study Abroad: Their Interests, Their Issues, and Their Constraints," *Journal of Studies in International Education* 14, no. 5 (2010): 508–527.

4. Institute for International Education, *Open Doors, 2019* (2019).

5. Institute for International Education, *Open Doors, 2020* (2020).

6. *Open Doors, 2020.*

7. R. Gutiérrez, J. Auerbach, and R. Bhandar, "Expanding U.S. Study Abroad Capacity: Findings From an IEE-forum Survey," in *Institute of International Education Study Abroad White Paper Series 6* (New York: Institute of International Education, 2009).

8. Michael Tarrant, "The Added Value of Study Abroad Fostering a Global Citizenry," *Journal of Studies in International Education* 18, no. 2 (2010): 141–161; Roger Martin and Sally Osberg, *Getting Beyond Better: How Social Entrepreneurship*

Works (Boston, MA: Harvard Business Review Press, 2015).

9. Mell Bolen, ed., *A Guide to Outcomes Assessment in Education Abroad* (Carlisle, PA: Forum on Education Abroad, 2007); Holly Emert and Diane Pearson, "Expanding the Vision of International Education: Collaboration, Assessment, and Intercultural Development," *New Directions for Community Colleges* 13 (2007): 67–75; George Kuh, *High-Impact Educational Practices: What They Are, Who has Access to Them, and Why They Matter.* (Washington, DC: Association of American Colleges and Universities, 2008).

10. Elizabeth Redden, "The Middlemen of Study Abroad," *Inside Higher Ed* 20 (2007); Michael Vande Berg, R. Michael Paige, and Kris Hemming Lou, *Student Learning Abroad: What Our Students are Learning, What They're Not, and What We Can Do About It* (Sterling, VA: Stylus Publishing, 2012).

11. Mandy Asghar and Nick Rowe, "Reciprocity and Critical Reflection as the Key to Social Justice in Service Learning: A Case Study," *Innovations in Education and Teaching International* 54, no. 2 (2017): 117–125.

12. Kristjane Nordmeyer, Nicole Bedera, and Trisha Teig, "Ending White Saviorism in Study Abroad," *Contexts* 15, no. 4 (2016): 78–79.

13. See http://www.global-hands.co.uk/gambia.html

14. Rona Karasik, "Community Partners' Perspectives and the Faculty Role in Community-Based Learning," *Journal of Experiential Education* 43, no. 2 (2020): 113–135; Alan Tinkler, Barri Tinkler, Ethan Hausman, and Gabe Tufo-Strouse, "Key Elements of Effective Service-Learning Partnerships from the Perspective of Community Partners," *Partnerships: A Journal of Service-Learning and Civic Engagement* 5, no. 2 (2014): 137–152.

15. Ronald Ferguson and William Dickens, eds., *Urban Problems and Community Development* (Washington, DC: Brookings, 1999).

16. Abdoulaye Saine, "The Military and Human Rights in The Gambia 1994–1999," *Journal of Third World Studies* 19, no. 2 (2002): 167–187.

17. Ibid.

18. Christof Hartmann, "ECOWAS and the Restoration of Democracy ion the Gambia," *Africa Spectrum* 52, no. 1 (2017): 85–99.

19. For a good timeline of events in Senegal since 1960, see the timeline construction hosted by the faculty of the University of Central Arkansas at https://uca.edu/politicalscience/dadm-project/sub-saharan-africa-region/senegal-1960-present/.

20. Stephen Golub and Ahmadou Mbaye, "National Trade Policies and Smuggling in Africa: The Case of Gambia and Senegal," *World Development* 37, no. 3 (2009): 595–606.

21. Stanley Talbert, "Connecting to Africa," *Union News* (Union Theological Seminary: New York, 2019) available at https://utsnyc.edu/connecting-to-africa/.

22. Ferguson and Dickens, 4.

23. Karasik, 113–135.

24. Martha Atwood Sanders, Tracy Van Oss, and Signian McGeary, "Analyzing Reflections in Service Learning to Promote Personal Growth and Community Self-Efficacy," *Journal of Experiential Education* 39, no. 1 (2016): 73–88; David L. Painter and Courtney Howell, "Community Engagement in the Liberal Arts: How Service Hours and Reflections Influence Course Value," *Journal of Experiential Education* 43, no. 4 (2020): 416–430.

15

In a Democracy We Must Act! Theatre as a Tool for Developing Civic Engagement

Xaman Minillo[1] & Mariana Pimenta Oliveira Baccarini[2]

1. Universidade Federal da Paraíba/University of Bristol   2. Universidade Federal da Paraíba

The development of civic values and skills is particularly critical in societies like Brazil in which political change has historically had little connection to popular action, and far-right leaders promote authoritarianism in ways that challenge the nation's commitment to minority rights and democratic institutions. This chapter explains how political theater can foster deep engagement with political issues and active citizenship among college students in Brazil. It presents our pedagogical approach, inspired by Freire's program of education as a promoter of emancipation, as well as Boal's theatre of the oppressed, both of which guided the development of a community outreach project. We also detail the development of the Interna-só-na-mente *Political Theater Group and, through its assessment, demonstrate how art, including theatre, can promote civic values, knowledge, and engagement in a student-led community outreach initiative.*

KEYWORDS: Civic Engagement; Education as Emancipation; Art In Education; Theater of the Oppressed; Brazilian Democracy.

Introduction

Civic engagement is not widespread in Brazil. It is a hierarchical society stratified by race, gender, and class, with limited opportunities for young people to actively participate in politics. In this context, we believe higher education can and must help students gain the knowledge, skills, values, and experiences required to make a meaningful difference through politics and community leadership.[1]

Entering the University is, for most students, the gateway to adult life. In humanities courses, especially in political science and international relations, they are exposed to theories and critical views that prompt them to question reality and critically reflect on their experiences. However, these courses often are focused on content transmission and fail to develop the skills and competencies needed to put this knowledge into practice. Students cannot automatically convert theory to practice without an active learning environment that encourages them to practice and to develop active political participation skills. This chapter presents a community engagement initiative established by the Department of International Relations at the Federal University of Paraiba (UFPB). This project, a Political Theatre inspired by the work of Augusto Boal, succeeded in promoting civic values and skills among enrolled students.

The chapter starts with a contextualization section, which presents the political and civic engagement scenario in Brazil. We then present our pedagogical approach inspired by Freire's pedagogy of emancipation[2] and Boal's theater of the oppressed[3] which, through a student led active learning methodology, promoted political discussions of social and political issues through theater. The project's stages are then detailed, followed by its assessment which was done through interviews with some of the participants. This case study reveals how participating in a theater group can engage university students in discussions of relevant social and political issues with their community, allow them to experience being part of a politically active group, and develop confidence in their agency, their civic knowledge, values and competences.

Democracy and Civic Engagement in Brazil

According to Putnam,[4] communities with a high standard of civic participation and social solidarity, constitute fertile ground for democratic institutions. Civic engagement involves active participation in community life and seeking to influence it for the better. It demands work toward making a difference in one's community by promoting quality of life through processes and activities of public and personal interest. Civic engagement education cultivates a combination of knowledge, skills, values, attitudes and motivations to make such differences in society.[5] Developed individually, or as part of a group, civic engagement activities help students develop knowledge about the community and its political system. Such engagement teaches students to identify problems the community faces and to seek solutions. It encourages students to benefit the community by using the political system to participate in constructive deliberations on community issues, problems, and solutions.[6]

Civic engagement and political participation in a democratic system require active citizenship. Since democracy does not flourish as a spectator sport, participants who only watch political events and processes unfold are incompatible with an engaged citizenry.[7] Unfortunately, in Latin America, and in Brazil in particular, social capital has not blossomed. Latin America is the most suspicious region on earth, and Brazil stands out from its neighbors for the lack of interpersonal trust.[8] This phenomenon is attributed to Brazil's history of colonization and the legacy of its path to independence. That legacy was characterized by the Portuguese colonial empire transferring power to an embedded Portuguese elite and had little connection to popular action. The history of authoritarian governments also influenced Brazil, such that a tradition emerged that political change comes from the top down. Thus, the 'traditional political culture' that has prevailed in Brazil is characterized by authoritarianism, elitism, statism, anti-liberalism, patrimonialism, corporatism, personalism, populism, and anti-institutionalism.[9]

In 1964, a military coup was followed by more than two decades of a military authoritarian regime. The transition to a democracy in 1985 came about through an agreement between elites and an indirect election, which continued this tradition of political change detached from popular actions. This culture, marked by a mixture of democratic and authoritarian attitudes, still permeates social and political relations in the country. It manifests in political apathy, detachment from and distrust of political institutions, resignation regarding their inefficiency, and a general low regard for the institutions of representative democracy.[10]

Data from Latino Barómetro[11] shows that among Latin American countries, Brazilians are the least supportive of democracy and have the lowest confidence in institutions, political parties, and their elected representatives. In 2018, 41% of Brazilian respondents were indifferent to the political regime, while only 34% pointed to democracy as their preferred form of government. Citizens share a strong distrust and criticism of the democratic regime. Almost two thirds (65%) of Brazilians identify problems in their democracy while 17% say that there is no democracy in the country and 90% assert that the government only represents a few.

These attitudes are reflected in the country's 2018 presidential and 2020 municipal elections. Although voting is compulsory in Brazil, more than 21% of registered voters did not vote in 2018 and more than 45 million people (30.6% of the voters) abstained in 2020.[12] The campaign period was polarized and marked by the aggressive use of fake news, social networks, and online messaging services and the President-elect Jair Bolsonaro waged a campaign marred by contempt for democratic principles. Threats of violence were made and, in some cases, carried out, against candidates, political supporters, journalists, and members of the judiciary.[13]

Brazil is still recognized as a democracy, though flawed, according to The Economist Intelligence Unit's Democracy Index 2019. Freedom House (an NGO that monitors regimes based on democratic principles) still ranks Brazil as free, though its score has fallen in the last couple of years. The country holds competitive elections, yet citizens are disillusioned with political parties due to corruption. Economic, racial, sexual, and gender minorities face violence and discrimination and are underrepresented in the government.[14] The assassination of Rio de Janeiro councilwoman and black lesbian activist Marielle Franco in 2018 is indicative of the social discrimination and violence against minorities which grows in the country, as well as the challenges that political activists face.[15]

Artists have also been threatened and several artistic works have been censored in the name of preserving Christian values.[16] Despite Brazil being a secular state, the connection between the government and Christianity has been linked to the repression of sexual and gender rights, as well as Afro-Brazilian religions. This is especially notable in the policies of the evangelical pastor and Minister of Women, Family and Human Rights, Damares Alves.

The area of education has had specific challenges. In the last couple of years, a series of five Ministers for Education have been appointed, with questionable credentials and limited experience in the field of education.[17] There have been dramatic budget cuts which affect governmental scholarships and reduce opportunities for lower-class students to attend universities.[18] The education sector has also been targeted ideologically. When a 30% budget cut of Federal Universities was announced, it was justified by confusing, vague, and unfounded claims of containing the "racket in these institutions," and false accusations that public universities do not produce research.[19] These initiatives indicate a strategy of delegitimizing and scrapping state-funded universities.

These challenges are also compounded by parallel attempts to curtail academic freedom, many of them connected to the Nonpartisan School (Escola sem Partido) project, which, since 2014, has promoted traditionalist norms and the exclusion of minority and vulnerable groups such as the LGBTQ community, women, and people of color, citing a need for political and ideological neutrality and the rights of the parents to control the moral and religious education of their children.[20]

Even though this project was counteracted by civil initiatives such as the Association of Mothers and Fathers for Democracy, and was rejected by the Supreme Court in July 2020, it succeeded in fostering a climate of suspicion and vigilance in classrooms.[21] These challenges, together with the curtailment of religious, artistic and academic freedoms, and governmental tolerance of violence and harassment against journalists and activists—discourage trust in the government. Cumulatively, this atmosphere fosters self-censorship and dissuades civic and political participation. In this context, it is more important than ever to promote civic engagement through education.

The *Interna-só-na-mente* Political Theater Project

This section presents the *Interna-só-na-mente* Political Theater Group community outreach project. It is divided into three parts. The first presents the theoretical references which inspired the project and its methodology, followed by a description of the project's goals. This is followed by a section on the implementation of the project. It details the institutional context in which the project was developed and the activities developed within its scope, outlining the different phases the participants went through on each thematic cycle to prepare for external engagements with the community. Specific outputs in the form of presentations and events the group organized are provided. Finally, the third subsection assesses the outcomes of the project in relation to student's learning and community engagement.

An emancipatory educational approach applied in a university community outreach project inspired by the Theater of the Oppressed

Although many students want to contribute to democracy, they often do not know how to do so.[22] The democratic system is complex, and courses in politics can help students prepare for it. To do this, instead of relying on knowledge transmission, it is useful to create learning opportunities in which students take responsibility for their own development by engaging with their own community using their own political system.[23] Recognizing the potential of education to uncover ways to participate in the transformation of the world and to deal with reality critically, we structured a community outreach project inspired by Paulo Freire's vision of education as political and emancipatory.[24] Following Freire's lead, we use art and theater to foster civic engagement among the undergraduate students at the Federal University of Paraíba, in Northeastern Brazil.

Education for civic engagement can contribute to the democratic formation of students, by cultivating their interest in politics, helping them to be more informed and developing their abilities to become actively involved in political action whatever their ideological inclination.[25] It also builds a sense of responsibility and effectiveness, which contribute to the development of informed citizens who regularly and productively participate in their communities.[26]

Freire's education as emancipation approach is a way through which civic engagement can be fostered while educating. Freire highlights the intimate connection between the students' perspectives and their contexts and histories, which are valued through dialogue and the relationships between the students and teachers. Rejecting more traditional, top-down, educational methods as an instrument of oppression which encourages authoritarianism, passivity, and a certain dependence and naivety, Freire emphasizes the value of dialogue, which presupposes mutual respect and reciprocity, as well as the awareness that everyone—including the teacher—is learning. His methodology instigates curiosity, experimentation, proactivity and critical analysis of reality, which is problematized and questioned, while respecting diversity and discouraging discrimination. By stimulating critical awareness of reality and the taking of action by students and teachers, who are recognized as political agents and citizens, it encourages responsibility and the development of autonomy through individual effort and maturing in the context of human interactions.[27]

Interna-só-na-mente Political Theater Group Project Goals

Inspired by Freire's pedagogy, the *Interna-só-na-mente* Political Theater Group was established at the UFPB's International Relations Department in 2016. As a community engagement project, the main goal of the group was to promote discussions of relevant socio-political problems, using art as a way to foster the interest of students and members of the community in contributing to the debates. It was hoped that through theater the students would be able to learn about relevant political and social issues and engage with these issues at a deeper level, develop critical reflections, and take action to develop the project and produce plays which involved the community members in the audience in debates and even in the plays themselves, turning them into *spect-actors*.

A Student-Led Learning Approach

The project's goal in relation to the students was to, through the practice of art, and more specifically theatre, educate and cultivate civic engagement among the participants by: (1) building the participant's knowledge about issues which were relevant to the community and the importance of civic and political engagement, (2) consolidating democratic values such as autonomy, responsibility and interest in contributing to the common good, (3) promoting a critical stance, (4) developing their confidence in expressing their opinion and defending their points of view, as well as their disposition to listen to others, and (5) enhancing their skills such as communicating and expressing their ideas and opinions in debates.

With the aim of changing the traditional and hierarchical dynamics of the classroom and developing an emancipatory education that promoted civic engagement, an active learning approach was adopted. Active learning creates a more conducive environment for learning by basing its practices on the active posture of students who develop their leadership whilst performing activities, while the teacher adopts a supportive role that resembles tutoring.[28] By associating learning with the students' experiences, new knowledge is integrated in a way that makes sense to the pupil according to their individual experience. By valuing the student's previous experiences in the knowledge building process, educators can also reduce the influence of their own perspective, using their authority without authoritarianism.[29]

Seeking to provide a political and artistic emancipatory education experience, a non-hierarchical, student led approach was adopted. That is, the students took on the main responsibilities involved in participating in the Political Theater Group and counted on the guidance of the supervising teacher playing the role of tutor. Even the initial idea of formulating the project was motivated by conversations with the students, where many indicated a desire to expand their knowledge on relevant political issues and express themselves artistically.

The topic to be worked on during each academic year would be chosen democratically within the group, and not unilaterally appointed by the tutor. The same logic applied to selecting the texts which would be read and presented within the meetings, and to deciding the format of the discussions–with the support of the tutor. The students were also expected to organize lectures, raise funds and develop publicization strategies. The aim was to make them responsible for different areas of the project based on the different ways they could contribute according to their individual potential, and in this way, encourage them to take responsibility for seeking and developing their knowledge.

Augusto Boal's Theater of the Oppressed and Community Engagement

As a community outreach project, the Political Theater Group sought to engage the community in two ways. The first was to, within the creative process of studying a topic which guided the project within an academic year, invite people from the community to conversation circles and to lectures by specialists from the community. This way, members of the community shared their lived experiences and expertise, contributing to the formulation of knowledge about the topic being studied and having some of their experiences being (anonymously) incorporated in the plays. The second, and more ambitious way that the community would be engaged, was through the development of a Theater of the Oppressed. For Augusto Boal, oppression is operationalized by words, images, and sound. He highlighted the importance of art and aesthetics in the process of constructing a democratic society, since it allows developing awareness of oppression, and the desire to stop it, improving society. He proposes that a play's spectators should not be content with their "role of non-intervening witnesses."[30] To overcome oppression and acquire confidence, self-knowledge, and self-esteem all citizens should create art and culture, transmuting democratic ideas into concrete and continuous social acts.[31]

His Theater of the Oppressed—developed in the 1970s, during the Brazilian military dictatorship—is not intended to entertain. It encompasses different exercises, techniques and dramatic practices with the goal of serving as a political and social instrument to encourage the transformation of the oppressive reality. For example, through the Newspaper Theater, the artists identified social and political issues and denounced them in plays. In the Invisible Theater, scenes of oppression were staged on the streets, in places where the injustice being staged usually takes place, without the audience knowing that the act had the aim of emotionally touching passers-by and motivating them to intervene. The Legislative Theater, created when Boal became a municipal councilor in Rio de Janeiro, encouraged audiences to understand the mechanisms of law-making, and to develop their citizenship by demanding the creation of laws which challenged oppression.[32]

The Forum Theater breaks the invisible fourth wall of the theater, inviting the audience to intervene directly in the plays, taking the actors' places, determining the protagonist's actions in the face of the oppressions enacted and presenting solutions to the social issues the play represents based on their own experiences and thoughts.[33] The goal is that, expressing their opinions, needs and desires and acting in the face of oppressions, the spectators become *spect-actors* and rehearse social action, and are empowered to engage in civic and political action.[34]

Implementing the Project

The group was formalized as a community engagement project at the university under the Continuous Flow of Community Engagement Program (FLUEX) in 2017 and, since 2018, was institutionalized as an option under the Community Engagement Scholarship Program (PROBEX). Currently community outreach projects can be formalized in a Brazilian Federal Universities such as UFPB in two main ways. One is the PROBEX, which signifies institutional recognition; implies that the project will be closely evaluated by the institution through periodic reports; guarantees that all participating students receive, at the end of the academic year, a certificate stating the hours dedicated to the project; and grants one scholarship (less than $100 US dollars per month) to be allocated to one of the students in the project, regardless of the total number of participants.[35] The FLUEX program is more flexible and also grants certificates for the participants, but offers no resources other than access to university facilities.[36]

Faculty in state-funded universities are expected to develop activities of teaching, research and community engagement, according to the constitutionally established principle of inseparability between them.[37] For students, at least 10% of their undergraduate course work must correspond to community engagement activities.[38] With these institutional demands and scarce resource allocations, most community outreach projects constitute small initiatives which are developed with few resources and depend heavily on the creativity and voluntary dedication of teachers and students to obtain funds.

The Political Theater project is open to any student, teacher, or staff from the university, as well as to those who are not part of the academic community and want to participate. However, to maintain the group's cohesion (as well as its identity and internal trust), participants for acting and supportive roles were selected from those who were genuinely committed to the project—not due to artistic or creative (in)capacity.

In the project's first meeting, 30 students showed up. Of these, 12 participated assiduously and became formal members of the group. Since the beginning, heterogeneity has been an important characteristic of the group, whose members reflect the composition of the UFPB student body, consisting mostly of women, many LGBTQ persons and black people, students originating from the Northeast, as well as more economically vulnerable students. The initial conversations within the group confirmed the students' interest in a student-led experience, and during the first year of activities, the actions focused on nurturing the group itself, with the aim of establishing a democratic and safe space where the students could develop their initiative and responsibility in building their own knowledge. During this period, through the weekly meetings and the theatrical exercises, the group's identity was strengthened, as were the ties of trust between the participants. It was also possible, through the exercises, to identify the areas of the project (i.e. artistic, staging, costumes, makeup, writing short plays with the aim of promoting discussions) where each student could best contribute based on their previous experiences and personal inclinations. This way, the students embraced the responsibility for seeking and developing their knowledge.

Depression and Mental Illness as a Theme

After this first year, with a more cohesive group and a more mature project, it was possible to advance to a new phase, which would be divided into five stages and repeated the following three academic years. The first stage was deciding on the main topic which would guide the group's endeavors. This selection was done democratically within the group. All participants suggested issues they considered relevant for the community, justified their position, and then voted.

The first topic selected was *Depression*, an issue which is extremely relevant for Brazilian society which, according to the World Health Organization, had the fifth highest rates of depression in the world, as well as the highest incidence of anxiety disorders.[39] This disease was also experienced by several university students, including members of the group. The Theater Group discussions on this theme focused on how oppressions inherent in contemporary capitalist society, and pressures to be productive, happy, and fully satisfied in all aspects of life, can impact mental health. Students agreed the Theater Group should be a space of reflection, unburdening and joint reconstruction.

The second stage was the academic and theatrical study. On the academic side, during this phase, the members of the group read books and articles on the chosen topic, developed conversation circles with people who experienced this issue and organized public lectures by specialists to guide the group's approach to the issue. In the *Depression* cycle, the participating students organized a lecture by a professor from UFPB, which was open to the community, on "Melancholy, Depression and the Changes of Capitalism." They also set up conversation circles for students living with depression and psychologists. These circles were restricted in access to provide a safe space for those who were sharing their experiences.

At the same time, the participants also improved their artistic skills, studying theatrical techniques and focusing specifically on Augusto Boal's methodology, which involves exercises and theatrical performances which will later serve as the basis for writing a play. Collectively, from the exercises, the group assembles ideas on how to stage the chosen theme in the most persuasive, emotional, and comprehensive way possible. The goal is not to teach moral lessons or point to possible oppressors, but to facilitate listening and dialogue and to prompt questions about oppressions experienced by the spectators.

The third stage was the development of skits. The students opted for writing three skits with different styles (dramatic, comical and philosophical) to provide unity and dynamism to the piece. The writing reflects all the previous work developed within the group on the topic of the year. It is inspired by the texts read, the lectures organized and attended, and the conversations, debates and exercises developed. At this stage, the transformation is developed within the group, among the students. The community participates in the previous events and in the moment of the play's presentation as well as the debate which takes place after it.

In 2018, the result of the writing was the play *Depression*, which consisted of three skits. With the aim of drawing the viewers' attention, *Tobias' War*, the play's featured production, describes the internal struggle of the main character, Tobias, with his various emotions, which are personified and fight each other, causing chaos in Tobias' mind while he lies inert in a chair, until, exhausted, he screams silencing them. The second sketch, *Disguises*, focuses on the relationship between the individual and society, and how the latter can be exclusionary, while individuals follow social conventions seeking acceptance. Finally, to finish on a more relaxed note before the discussion, *From Sofia to Sofia*, is a comical skit which addresses the character's daily relationship with her depression, personified in a parody of herself. During the transitions between the skits, while the actors and scenery change, other characters disclosed information about the group and about how to access psychological assistance.

The fourth stage is the play's debut within the university. After the play is elaborated and rehearsed, the Political Theater Group presents it to the university community. On September 20, 2018, the group made its first formal presentation, with two sets of *Depression*. After the presentation, the group initiated a discussion inviting feedback from the audience on how to improve the piece and contribute to the creative process and how the audience felt about the topic. There were few suggestions for changes, the viewers mostly contributed with more personal insights such as reporting experiences with the disease. These first presentations were important for the group because they demonstrated that the group had effectively used artistic expression to promote a deep and respectful discussion, unveiling prejudices and obstacles that viewers may have held around this sensitive topic.

The fifth and final stage entails performing in the community, presenting the play at cultural events, schools, unions, and other interested institutions. After the presentations, the group holds a conversation with the audience, seeking to establish a dialogue between students and community. Typically, this stage has proven very successful. Viewers offer their interpretations of the play and sometimes share personal and family experiences relating to the theme presented.

After initial feedback at the Professor Maria Jacy Costa School presentation, some in the audience requested to talk to the theater group in a more private place. In the privacy of the school library, a group of 10 high-school students joined the members of the theater group for a more intimate conversation on personal experiences of mental health issues. Spectators from the presentations at the school and at UFPB exchanged confidences, emotions, and anxieties around their experiences with depression. Ultimately the theater group emphasized the importance of seeking psychological assistance and shared contact information for institutions that offered such assistance free of charge.[40]

In this first cycle, three lessons were learned: (1) the group should keep costs low by avoiding elaborate scenarios and costumes due to scarce funding and the need to adapt the play/skit for presentations in different locations; (2) the importance of preparing varied skits so as to adapt the presentation according to the target audience; and (3) elect a skit to be the flagship, considering that in some events it is not possible to present the complete play. In 2018 we were able to present the *Tobias' War* skit on four other occasions, two of them before the full play even premiered.

Table 1. The Activities with the Community in the 2018 Cycle			
Activity developed	Event	Location	Date
Visits to hospital patients	Taking humor to hospital patients	UFPB University Hospital	26 April 2018
Workshop Art as a social project: Society acting through theater	VII International Relations Academic Week (VII SARI UFPB)	Federal University of Paraiba	27 and 28 August 2018
Tobias' War presentation	Yellow September	Regional Council of Accounting	19 September 2018
Tobias' War presentation	II Brazilian Meeting of Peace Studies (II EBEP)	Federal University of Paraiba	21 September 2018
Depression play presentation	Presentation for public schools	Professor Maria Jacy Costa School	28 November 2018
Tobias' War presentation	Cultural Turn	José Lins do Rego Cultural Venue	30 September 2018

Religious Intolerance as a Theme

The second theme, developed in 2019, was *Religious Intolerance*. After researching about several religions, we focused on those which are more prevalent in Brazil: Umbanda, Candomblé, Catholicism, Protestantism, Islam, the Spiritist doctrine, as well as Wicca, representing new religions and faiths which emerged in the 21st century.

There was a noticeable difference in students' engagement and positioning in the organization of the first to the second cycle. While in 2018 the students sought leadership and direction from the teacher, in the preparations for *Religious Intolerance*, in the third year of the project, and with the presence of several veterans who had participated in the previous creation, the students assumed the lead in the project. Divided in groups headed by the veterans, students studied different religions, attended lectures on the topic and even organized visits to religious institutions.

During the academic and theatrical study, the students organized an event on Cultural and Political Roots of Religious Intolerance where specialists from UFPB's Department of Science of Religions gave talks to the community. Circles of conversation were also held with members of the community of different religions and representatives of Paraíba's Religious Diversity Forum with the aim of getting to know specificities of each religion and understand how their members experienced intolerance. This way the group identified that (1) people face religious intolerance from society, their families and the state; (2) prejudice can manifest in multiple ways such as physical violence and verbal abuse disguised as jokes; and (3) in Brazil there is a strong connection between religious intolerance and racism with African-based religions being the most common target of discrimination.

Three skits were developed to constitute the *Religious Intolerance* play. *Religions* uses characters to portray what each religion preaches. Due to the use of similar garments and the preaching of similar precepts (love, faith in God, and respect), it is not easy to identify which religion each character represents. Toward the end, the use of recognizable symbols reveals which religion is represented by each character. The second and featured skit, *Between Heaven and Earth* illustrates how intolerance can result in physical violence using a fictitious religion, to avoid stereotypes and facilitate discussions with all viewers, regardless of their religion. Finally, *Faith Elevator* comically demonstrates the intolerance present in everyday conversations through interactions between members of different religions trapped in an elevator. The conclusion highlights how, regardless of differences, all are equal and respect is necessary.

The play *Religious Intolerance* was first launched within UFPB through two sessions presented on September 29, 2019. Once again, the debate provided an open environment for spectators to narrate personal experiences and exchange ideas between themselves and the members of the group, becoming *spect-actors*. Also, based on audience feedback, students decided to alter the order of the skits so that the more impactful *Between Heaven and Earth* would close the show. Students felt that concluding the show this way would impel the audience to question the discrimination previously presented in *Faith Elevator* and review their own prejudices. Another incorporated suggestion was adding, during the play's transitions, the disclosure of the possibility of calling the number 100, to reach a reporting hotline run by the government to denounce episodes of human rights abuses such as religious intolerance. The reformulated play was presented again to the university's community in two sessions on the 31st of October, as part of a larger event on Human Rights and Religious Diversity in Brazil, and on the 20th of November as part of a Black Consciousness and the Public Policies Followed at UFPB event.

Table 2. The Activities with the Community in the 2019 Cycle			
Activity developed	Event	Location	Date
Religious Intolerance play presentation	Presentation for high school students from the João Goulart School	Educator Training Center	25 November 2019
Religious Intolerance play presentation	Presentation for high school students	José Lins do Rego School	26 November 2019
Religious Intolerance play presentation	Presentation for the staff	Brazilian Urban Trains Company (CBTU)	29 November 2019

Among the presentations made to the community, it was notable that most students from the João Goulart School came from Christian families, both Protestant and Catholic. They were very curious about other religions and actively participated in the debate, reporting personal experiences and discussing the issues raised in the play. The debate after the play at CBTU, with a smaller and older audience, was very productive. The *spect-actors* noted the nuances of the play and were very engaged, reporting personal experiences of intolerance.

Hunger and Food Insecurity as a Theme

The group began the activities of 2020 with the aim of further implementing Boal's Theater of the Oppressed through the Forum Theater and extending the audience participation from the discussions after the plays to the performances themselves. This way, as well as participating in dialogues, the *spect-actors* would experience acting and intervening in the show. To do this, it was necessary to (1) train some member students as jokers, who mediate the connection between the audience and the show; and (2) to make this experience possible in presentations made to large groups.

A short skit with the expectation of direct audience intervention was produced through Forum Theater exercises on the topic of violence against women and was prepared to be presented on March 20, 2020, at Unipê college in connection to International Women's Day celebrations. However, due to the COVID-19 pandemic it was cancelled and the project of developing the Forum Theater was postponed.

The pandemic dramatically changed the circumstances: UFPB switched to online activities and the group had to reinvent itself and adapt its methodology. Members continued to work remotely, demonstrating students' proactive attitude despite the challenging circumstances impacting their routines.[41]

To motivate the students, the coordinator proposed displaying the group's digital performances on social networks.[42] They focused on Instagram, formulating an aesthetic content capable of reaching a greater audience with three types of posts: (1) curiosities about theater; (2) information on the new chosen theme; and (3) the EnCena project, posting digitally staged scenes from classic plays which were played, recorded and edited by members of the group.

The chosen theme for 2020 was *Hunger*, a relevant topic in Brazilian society, where more than 10 million persons are undernourished according to data collected by the Brazilian Institute of Geography and Statistics (IBGE) in 2018. The participating students took the lead in organizing several online lectures given by experts focusing on nutritional, political and cultural aspects of food and the consequences of hunger. In the process, students formalized a partnership with the research group FOMERI (Hunger and International Relations).

Table 3. Online Lectures Organized by the Participating Students in the 2020 Cycle	
Date	Title
10 June 2020	Nutrition: Superfoods and Industrialization
23 June 2020	Hunger in Brazil and the North-eastern region
07 July 2020	The programs to Fight Hunger Nowadays
21 July 2020	Monitoring and Evaluating Hunger and Food Security: experiences beyond academia
06 August 2020	Intestine Connections: we want Food, Fun and Art

Next, the students wrote the first version of the play *Hunger* with three sketches. The first, *The Dispute*, presents a contest between the characters Hunger and Death to see who can take more souls, showing that death by starvation should not be naturalized. The scene includes the owner of a supermarket, his employees and a starving person, revealing a situation of squalor caused by the policies adopted by the Owner of Brazil (a character who is further developed in the second skit) and the neglect of the elite, portrayed in the supermarket owner. The second sketch, *Speak the Truth or Die Lying* depicts a television program where the interviewee—the Owner of Brazil—agrees to participate in the condition of dying if he lies, which is what ends up happening. The third skit follows the character after his death, where Death and Hunger duel and confront him to face his faults.

After writing the play, the group staged the second skit, considered the best to be digitally performed. On December 3, 2020, *Speak the Truth or Die Lying* was staged and broadcast live on YouTube to an audience of around a hundred persons. The experience was challenging and there were technical difficulties. Two of the actors had connectivity problems during the play and one had to be replaced in a hurry by the project's coordinator and the General Director (the scholarship holder) until they managed to solve the issue. Regardless, the play was a success, highlighting the professionalism and dedication of the group.

Due to the difficulties in the pandemic context, the group was not able to fully implement the Forum Theater at this stage. However, it was possible to include audience participation in the play, through encouraging the interaction of the actors—especially the presenter of the television program–with the audience of the online presentation through the YouTube live chat feature. In this period, despite the difficulties, it was also possible to publish an e-book authored by the coordinator and six participating students on the theater group and social change.

Assessing the Project

The project was assessed through interviews developed in December 2020 with nine current and former members of the Political Theater Group. The informants participated in at least one live performance of the plays and are either still part of the project or graduated at the end of the 2020 academic year.

Methodology and Teaching Civic Principles

To assess if participating in the group enhanced their civic knowledge, we asked the informants about their understanding of the concepts of political participation and civic engagement. They connected political participation to partaking in political decision making through exercising the right to vote, which is mandatory in Brazil. They also mentioned being aware of the political situation of their region and country, participating in demonstrations and demanding accountability of political representatives. They related civic engagement to taking action toward something you believe is right while being aware of what is going on in society around you, to being connected to the collectivity through a common cause, and promoting change through everyday politics.

The group selection was open to all interested in voluntary participation in a community outreach project to discuss social and political issues through theater. To detect if the project changed the student's attitudes and interest in political participation and civic engagement, we inquired if they participated in any social movement or political association before joining the group. All of the interviewees but one—who was a member of a Christian group—did not participate in political and/or social associations or movements. Most stated they had entered the group due to their interest in art. Other motivators, less mentioned, were the connection between art and politics, friendship with other participants and a desire to lose their inhibitions.

The majority of the participants entered the project at the beginning of their undergraduate studies and felt that the theater group was a turning point, changing them. One of the informants noted, "I see colleagues entering one way and leaving another." Most mentioned it increased their awareness of political and social issues and heightened their interest in engaging in social action due to their identity or religion, but also because of the empathy they felt for other minority groups.

All respondents acknowledged that the methodology enhanced their awareness of socio-political issues. Some mentioned the project was an "eye opener." The participants recognized a growth in their awareness of social and political issues that are relevant for the nation but about which they previously had little knowledge. They highlighted how engaging with persons from the community helped them understand how others are affected by social and political issues and enabled them to put themselves in other people's shoes. They also experienced a desire to learn more about social issues and were emboldened to act in the face of oppression. One respondent mentioned that during the project they started thinking about how to be an agent of positive change and fight oppression through social intervention. Another revealed going through an experience of religious intolerance and being able to act in this situation, believing "if it weren't for the theater experience I wouldn't react, I would be in shock."

Asked about the project's student-led methodology, which included readings, organizing lectures, conversation circles, visits outside the university, producing plays, and participating in debates, all respondents evaluated it positively. They mentioned that it was different from all their other experiences in the university. One stated that "many (of the exercises) take me out of my comfort zone, but in a welcoming environment." They highlighted the discomfort that emerged from feeling touched by the themes they explored; from hearing people's testimonies after the plays that were inspired by what had been represented; from participating in exercises such as interpreting someone professing a religion different from their own; from being shown their mistakes and becoming aware of their privileges.

There is pedagogical value in situations which take students out of their comfort zone and engage them in ideas and their consequences, contributing to the development of an emancipatory education that encourages and prepares students for civic and political engagement.[43] Learning can be a painful, scary and uncomfortable process. Renowned author, professor, and feminist social activist bell hooks distinguishes a safe space from a controlled space.[44] For her, disrupting the serious atmosphere of the university classroom with stimulating discussions can increase students' interest and commitment, stimulate their serious intellectual engagement with political ideas and values, promote critical thinking and catalyze the processes of finding their own voices. To create an environment of freedom and intellectual rigor, she proposes building classroom communities that share an appreciation for goals of learning and listening, thereby making higher education an exercise in recognition and democracy where everyone's presence is valued and recognized. We were happy to have achieved this within the theater group. The participants of the project described it as a place of "personal growth" and "empowerment," a "real healing space" where they reduced their fears and "shame" and developed their "self-knowledge" and "critical sense," widening their horizons and generating personal growth and self-discovery. Learning permeates the group in the sense that the participants recognize the oppressions experienced not only at the individual level, but by all members of the group who, despite being part of an intellectual elite which has access to higher education, identify as minorities because they are women, LGBTQ, black and/or Northeastern.[45] They learn from the experience of the other.

Teaching Interpersonal Skills and Perceptions of Competency

A few mentioned they used to feel very shy and insecure and were a bit uncomfortable in the beginning. The project's methodology was key in helping them to gradually increase their confidence and lessen fears of being judged, making it easier for them to express their opinions in other environments. They see the group as a safe space, receptive to different expressions where they developed respect for the others and were able to gain confidence to participate in discussions and to contribute to reaching consensus in debates. One student emphasized the project helped them feel part of a group and made them more comfortable expressing their opinions and participating in discussions. These learnings carried over to other situations and made the student feel like a different person from before joining. For many, the group provided a space where they could play a leadership role and assume responsibilities which built their "self-confidence," while recognizing the impact of their actions. Through the exercises and the coexistence, they "let go of the idea of ridicule" and, according to one of the interviewees "you lose your shame, and create trust, security, intimacy, with an absurd sense of respect for the other, with the body, talk, attitude of the other."

Asked about skills and competencies, the respondents mentioned that they understood they had become citizens more capable of putting themselves in the other's place. "Empathy" is a term that appears several times in the responses. They also highlighted that the theater methodology helped them learn to think "outside the box," to propose innovative solutions. They feel that they are better able to express themselves, both improving their communication skills but also feeling more comfortable expressing their views. The project helped students confront their fears, especially of other people's judgement. After participating, many felt better prepared to interact with others who think differently from them and to take on responsibilities and leadership roles, having lost the fear of taking action and speaking out.

All participants feel the group helped them to believe in themselves and their capacity, being more confident and feeling comfortable in themselves. They developed skills which they see as valuable for their undergraduate studies and applicable to their professional careers. They anticipated increased involvement in politics because they feel they are better equipped to participate in group activities and achieve consensus, to deal with differences and novelties, being more empathetic and sensitive to the issues around them and having developed a political consciousness, seeing how they are connected to society.

They evaluated the project's methodology favorably in comparison to other teaching-learning experiences of their undergraduate coursework. They found it more practical, enabling them to better see how the theoretical aspects they read about were connected to their reality. The methodology increased their ability to share their knowledge with others while helping them better understand other people's perspectives. They mentioned other higher educational learning experiences felt dissociated from their reality and were, therefore, more difficult to grasp. Some students observed that the project's methodology is more humane and fostered a less competitive environment than they experienced in other university activities. One pointed out, "While in the undergraduate program some are successful, because they have a more solid background or adapt well to the traditional teaching model, others do not adapt so well. Higher education feels more like a natural selection… There is no such competition in the theater."

All participants consider the project life-changing, altering how they see themselves, allowing them to feel comfortable being themselves, generating personal growth and allowing them to feel useful, having achieved something in the moments they were engaged with the community. According to respondents it was "one of the best things which happened in my life." Another highlighted, "There is (name) before and (name) after the political theater… It defined where I am from… It kind of gave me a purpose in the (undergraduate) course, of wanting to work with art in the International Relations. It is my north, the center of where I want to go, what I want to do. It has had a huge impact on my life." They also mentioned that it is a place where they were happy, were able to make friends and a source of stability in the context of the COVID-19 pandemic.

Conclusions: The Possibilities and Limitations of the Political Theater

This chapter demonstrates how education and art can be joined to promote engagement with socio-political issues in a small university community engagement project which can be replicated at a low cost. Through it, learning and civic engagement were promoted by using theater with an active, student-led approach. The stages of the project illustrate the involvement of the students in different activities which allowed them to be part of a politically active group engaging in political discussions in a welcoming, collaborative and respectful environment. Participating in the theater group engaged students in the study of social and political issues which are relevant to them and Brazilian society. Participants also developed their active citizenship skills by devising creative ways to engage with the community in deep discussions on these topics.

Members of the community were included in the project by accessing the lectures the group organized and sharing their lived experiences in conversation circles which were anonymously incorporated in the plays. After the plays, the audience was invited to participate, contributing with their impressions, opinions and ideas in open discussions of the scenes of oppression the plays conveyed. In the last play performed online, viewers were invited to interact with the actors during the play. Through these engagements, the audience participated, raising their voices and becoming *spect-actors*.

The student-led methodology took the students out of their comfort zone while keeping them in a safe space while they took over the role of agents responsible for building their own knowledge through exchanges with the community while keeping the project viable despite the scarcity of resources. This gave the participants encouragement and space to develop their agency toward the advancement of the project, allowing them to learn how to navigate difficulties and solve problems and, by achieving their goals, to gain confidence and understand the importance of taking action. This project enhanced the students' awareness of their connection to the community and of their responsibilities toward it. They came to understand the relevance of their agency and how they can promote reflections on and discussions of relevant political issues among their community—an important contribution considering the scenario of increasing apathy of the Brazilian population in relation to political participation. This helped students appreciate the importance of civic and political engagement while addressing issues relevant to their community, all while acquiring valuable competencies such as critical thinking, autonomy, and a sense of civic responsibility.

The project will continue developing new plays on new topics while working toward better incorporating audience participation in the plays themselves and in post-play discussions of the scenes of oppression. To this end, the group members should be trained to become 'jokers' by a Theater of the Oppressed official member. This requires a substantial investment, and to that end the participants are seeking grants.

The project has faced some challenges, such as the limited financial support available (one scholarship), which is common for most community outreach projects developed in UFPB. Limited resources made it difficult for the program to grow and access other communities, but such obstacles encouraged the students to proactively and creatively seek ways to raise resources to bear costs such as transportation to present the plays, makeup to improve production quality and to make the project more sustainable.

Another goal is to improve the assessment tools used to measure the project's efficacy. Given the project's limited capacity, interviews with the students post-participation has been the only method by which results are measured. These evaluative tools can be unreliable in assessing changes in attitudes or quantifying differences in their levels of civic interest and engagement from before they entered the project. Assessing the program's impact will be strengthened by using pre-project and post-project surveys. Such surveys can also be administered to a diverse group of students who are not involved in the project in order to provide a control group. Improving assessment methods may also strengthen the case needed to raise funds for the program by demonstrating the real impact this project has on improving citizenship among Brazil's future leaders.

Even in the face of challenges due to financial and material limitations in the Brazilian public education system and the insecurity that federal policies have been generating in the pandemic setting, the *Interna-só-na-mente* Political Theater Group continues empowering students and members of society to actively contribute to deconstruct prejudices. The growth that the project allowed through student-led learning using art and the interactions between the students and the community strengthens our certainty that with empathetic civic engagement we can build a more democratic future.[46]

Endnotes

1. Robert Putnam, *Comunidade e Democracia* (Rio de Janeiro: FGV, 1993).

2. Paulo Freire, *Pedagogia do Oprimido* (Rio de Janeiro: Editora Paz e Terra, 1987).

3. Augusto Boal, *A Estética do Oprimido* (Rio de Janeiro: Editora Garamond, 2009).

4. Putnam, *Comunidade e Democracia*.

5. Anne Colby, Elizabeth Beaumont, Thomas Ehrlich, and Josh Corngold, *Educating for Democracy: Preparing Undergraduates for Responsible Political Engagement* (San Francisco: Jossey-Bass, 2007), https://files.eric.ed.gov/fulltext/ED498989.pdf; Robert D. Reason and Kevin Hemer, "Civic Learning and Engagement: A Review of the Literature on Civic Learning, Assessment, and Instruments", *Research Institute for Studies in Education (RISE) Iowa State University* (2015), https://www.aacu.org/sites/default/files/files/qc/CivicLearningLiteratureReviewRev1-26-15.pdf, 4.

6. Alison Rios Millett McCartney, "Teaching Civic Engagement: Debates, Definitions, Benefits, and Challenges" in *Teaching Civic Engagement: From Student to Active Citizen*, eds. Alison Rios Millett McCartney, Elizabeth A. Bennion, and Dick Simpson, (Washington, DC: American Political Science Association, 2013), 14.

7. Ibid., 15.

8. Latinobarómetro, "Análisis de datos," (2018), https://www.latinobarometro.org/latOnline.jsp.

9. Marcello Baquero "Cultura política participativa e desconsolidação democrática: reflexões sobre o Brasil contemporâneo," *São Paulo em Perspectiva* 15, no. 4 (2001): 98–104; Raymundo Faoro, *Os donos do poder* (Rio de Janeiro, Globo, 1975); Paulo Freire, *Pedagogia da Esperança: um reencontro com a Pedagogia do Oprimido* (São Paulo: Paz e Terra, 1992); Gilberto Freyre, *Casa-grande & senzala* (25th ed. Rio de Janeiro: José Olympio, 1986); Sérgio Buarque de Holanda, *Raízes do Brasil* (Rio de Janeiro: José Olympio, 1969); Lilia Moritz Schwarcz, *Sobre O Autoritarismo Brasileiro* (São Paulo: Companhia Das Letras, 2019).

10. Baquero "Cultura política participativa e desconsolidação democrática"; Marcello Baquero, *Cultura(s) Política(s) e Democracia no Século XXI na América Latina* (Porto Alegre: Editora UFRGS, 2011); Schwarcz, *Sobre O Autoritarismo*

Brasileiro.

11. Latinobarómetro, "Análisis de datos."

12. Globo, *Eleições 2018*, (2018), https://g1.globo.com/politica/eleicoes/2018/apuracao/presidente.ghtml; Walacy Ferrari "Brasil tem recorde de ausências, votos brancos e nulos em eleições municipais em 2020", *UOL* (2020), https://aventurasnahistoria.uol.com.br/noticias/historia-hoje/brasil-tem-recorde-de-ausencias-votos-brancos-e-nulos-em-eleicoes-municipais-em-2020.phtml.

13. Freedom House "Brazil", *Freedom in the World* (2020), https://freedomhouse.org/country/brazil/freedom-world/2020.

14. Women, for example, hold only 15% of the seats in the Chamber of Deputies and 16% in the Senate, while of Bolsonaro's 23 ministers, only two are women. Also, all of the ministers in his administration are white.

15. The investigations of Marielle's murder are still ongoing, and they have revealed the increasing power of militia groups which involve police forces, and whose interests, together with corruption, undermine the development of a government for the people.

16. Ricardo Della Coletta and Danielle Brant, "Bolsonaro nega praticar censura, mas defende valores cristãos na cultura," *Folha de São Paulo* (2019), https://www1.folha.uol.com.br/ilustrada/2019/10/bolsonaro-nega-praticar-censura-mas-defende-valores-cristaos-na-cultura.shtml.

17. Independente, "Deputada questiona despreparo de Ricardo Velez, ministro da Educação, em comissão na Câmara" (2019), https://www.youtube.com/watch?v=ngFoaSWUegg&fbclid=IwAR3iK8bvIPCPFeeJeJ_lLQ8uM1BJEb7mnotGZ4cqmJGdquIbaPJkOERgTqs; Paulo Saldaña, "Weintraub escolhe gestores não ligados à educação para secretarias do MEC" (2019), https://www1.folha.uol.com.br/educacao/2019/04/weintraub-escolhe-gestores-nao-ligados-a-educacao-para-secretarias-do-mec.shtml?fbclid=IwAR3LBLWME5CHZThOzlfC66XfQZvaXnh-nuTveKHGUvB_CSbpKfEwQnEhzo8.

18. Law nº 9.711, February 15, 2019 reduced the resources destined to education to the constitutional minimum. The following month, the federal government froze 42% of the budget for the country's science, technology and communications ministry seriously affecting the development of research programs. Claudio Angelo, "Brazil's government freezes nearly half of its science spending," *Nature* 568 (2019): 155–156; ABC, "Corte orçamentário atinge desenvolvimento e soberania nacionais" (2019), http://www.abc.org.br/2019/04/01/corte-orcamentario-atinge-desenvolvimento-e-soberania-nacionais/; ANDIFES, "Entidades científicas e acadêmicas publicam nota sobre severo corte do orçamento" (2019), https://www.andifes.org.br/?p=62862.

19. The bias against state funded higher education institutions is clear by Bolsonaro's statement denying public universities produced research and affirming that most of the research was being produced by private and military institutions, while effectively more than 95% of research produced in Brazil comes from state universities and according to the Scientific Production Ranking in Brazil 2014–2018, among the 50 institutions that most published scientific works in the last 5 years, 44 are universities and 43 of those are state funded. Investe São Paulo, "99% das pesquisas são feitas pelas universidades públicas", (2019) https://www.investe.sp.gov.br/noticia/99-das-pesquisas-sao-feitas-pelas-universidades-publicas/; Mariluce Moura, "Universidades públicas respondem por mais de 95% da produção científica do brasil" *Cência na Rua* (2019), https://ciencianarua.net/universidades-publicas-respondem-por-mais-de-95-da-producao-cientifica-do-brasil/; Igor Carvalho, "Confusão em dados sobre corte nas universidades federais é proposital, diz professor," *Brasil de Fato* (2019), https://www.brasildefato.com.br/2019/05/14/confusao-em-dados-sobre-corte-nas-universidades-federais-e-propositaldiz-professor/.

20. For a comprehensive mapping of the law projects inspired by the Nonpartisan School Project, see: Fernanda Moura and Diogo da Costa Salles, "O Escola sem Partido e o ódio aos professores que formam crianças (des)viadas," *Revista Periódicus* 9, no. 1 (2018): 136–160.

21. Itamar Melo, "O que é a Associação Mães & Pais pela Democracia, que se contrapõe ao Escola Sem Partido," *GZH* (2019), https://gauchazh.clicrbs.com.br/educacao-e-emprego/noticia/2019/08/o-que-e-a-associacao-maes-pais-pela-democracia-que-se-contrapoe-ao-escola-sem-partido-cjz2ruu36ooipo1qm2fhyx4vb.html; Salomão Ximenes and Fernanda Vick, "A extinção judicial do Escola sem Partido," *Le Monde Diplomatique Brasil* (2020), https://diplomatique.org.br/a-extincao-judicial-do-escola-sem-partido/.

22. Alison Rios Millett McCartney "Introduction", in *Teaching Civic Engagement Across the Disciplines*, eds. Elizabeth C. Matto, Alison Rios Millett McCartney, Elizabeth A. Bennion, and Dick Simpson (Washington, DC: American Political Science Association, 2017).

23. Brian M. Harward and Daniel M. Shea, "Higher Education and the Multiple Modes of Engagement," in *Teaching Civic Engagement*, eds. McCartney et al., 21–40; Veriene Melo, "Emancipatory education and youth engagement in Brazil: A case study bridging the theory and practice of education for social transformation," *Education Sciences* 9, no. 1 (2019): 1–14.

24. Freire, *Pedagogia do Oprimido*.

25. Elizabeth Beaumont, "Higher Education and the Multiple Modes of Engagement," in *Teaching Civic Engagement*, eds.

McCartney et al., 41–55.

26. Christine M. Cress, Cathy Burack, Dwight E. Giles, Julie Elkins, and Margaret C. Stevens, *A Promising Connection: Increasing College Access and Success through Civic Engagement* (Boston, MA: Campus Compact, 2010), https://docs. google.com/viewerng/viewer?url=https://compact.org/wp-content/uploads/large/2015/04/A-Promising-Connection-corrected.pdf&hl=en; McCartney "Introduction", 4–5.

27. Freire, *Pedagogia do Oprimido.*

28. Andrew L. Oros, "Let's Debate: Active Learning Encourages Student Participation and Critical Thinking," *Journal of Political Science Education* 3, no. 3 (2007): 293–311.

29. Freire, *Pedagogia do Oprimido*; bell hooks, *Teaching to Transgress: Education as the Practice of Freedom* (New York: Routledge, 1994).

30. Boal, *A Estética do Oprimido*, 107.

31. Ibid., 18.

32. Boal, *A Estética do Oprimido*; Augusto Boal, *STOP: C'est Magique!* (Rio de Janeiro: Civilização Brasileira, 1980).

33. Boal, *A Estética do Oprimido*; Flavio Sanctum, "Estética do Oprimido de Augusto Boal Uma Odisseia pelos Sentidos," Master's thesis, Federal Fluminense University (2011).

34. Boal, *A Estética do Oprimido*, 189.

35. The grant the Political Theater project has access to under PROBEX is allocated to a student who takes on the role of 'General Director', coordinates the group activities and elaborates activity reports.

36. Until 2016 Brazilian Federal Universities could apply for the University Community Outreach Program (ProExt), which allowed more ample resources to be accessed. However, in 2016 ProEXT was suddenly withdrawn with no explanations from the Federal government, and no perspectives of being reactivated.

37. Brazil, "Constitution of the Federative Republic of Brazil" (1988), http://www.planalto.gov.br/ccivil_03/constituicao/constituicaocompilado.htm.

38. Brasil, "Resolução nº 7, de 18 de dezembro de 2018" (2018), https://www.in.gov.br/materia/-/asset_publisher/KujrwoTZC2Mb/content/id/55877808; Brasil, "Plano Nacional de Educação (PNE) 2014–2024" (2014), http://pne.mec.gov.br/18-planos-subnacionais-de-educacao/543-plano-nacional-de-educacao-lei-n-13-005-2014.

39. WHO, *Depression and Other Common Mental Disorders Global Health Estimates* (2017), https://apps.who.int/iris/bitstream/handle/10665/254610/WHO-MSD-MER-2017.2-eng.pdf;jsessionid=EB34AFA4AF067816FE69C784A4A75D85?sequence=1.

40. This moment is still remembered by the former members of the theater as one of the most moving during their time in the group.

41. Some of the members missed some online meetings or lectures due to problems in their internet connections and technological devices, as well as medical issues. This is understandable since, according to a survey conducted jointly by UFPB's International Relations Undergraduate Course Coordination and the Academic Center on October 2020, showed that only 53.7% of the students had a favorable environment for continuing education online and 31.7% reported that they had been diagnosed with mental illness before of the pandemic.

42. Instagram: @internasonamente; Youtube: https://m.youtube.com/channel/UC2vVKUrr5ywU6WSeJGivw3w.

43. Brian M. Harward and Daniel M. Shea, "Higher Education and the Multiple Modes of Engagement," 40.

44. bell hooks, *Teaching to Transgress: Education as the Practice of Freedom*, 30.

45. The North-eastern region of Brazil, where UFPB is located, is the least developed in the country, having the lowest Human Development Index. Within the national setting, Northeasterners are discriminated against because of their geographical origin, which became associated with a type of racial differentiation, as their identities as people from a less developed region became understood as backwards. UNDP, *Desenvolvimento humano nas macrorregiões brasileiras* (Brasília: PNUD; IPEA; FJP, 2016), https://1drv.ms/b/s!AuwEBHxVUoYSgbNZGjK6AIgz1ijfmQ?e=VjZxyR; Jose R. M Batista, "Os estereótipos e o efeito do contato virtual no preconceito contra negros e nordestinos," *Tese de Doutorado UFPB/CCHLA* (2014), https://repositorio.ufpb.br/jspui/bitstream/tede/7561/2/arquivototal.pdf; Stanley E. Blake, *The Vigorous Core of Our Nationality: Race and Regional Identity in Northeastern Brazil* (University of Pittsburgh Press, 2011).

46. The Federal University of Paraiba approved this research.

16

Civic Engagement through Work-Integrated Learning: Reflections from Community-Based Research on Social Grants in South Africa

Laurence Piper, Sondré Bailey, and Robyn Pasensie

University of the Western Cape

This chapter will advance the argument that Work Integrated Learning (WIL) can reinforce active citizenship as illustrated with an example from the South African context. WIL is an approach that holds that students will learn better in a program that integrates theoretical knowledge in the classroom with practical knowledge in the workplace. While WIL is not inherently orientated towards building active citizenship, the strategic use of WIL can result in learning outcomes very similar to civic engagement pedagogy, particularly when conceptualized as a collaborative and participatory form of community-based research. This claim is demonstrated through reflection on a research project conducted by master's candidates at the University of the Western Cape in Cape Town, South Africa, in conjunction with a human rights NGO, the Black Sash. The research required students, supported by Black Sash fieldworkers, to run participatory workshops in various poor communities to explore the impact of the privatization of the social grant payment system in South Africa. We show how the project reinforced the ideas and practices of active citizenship for the students involved and for the fieldworkers from Black Sash with whom they worked. Thus, while not intrinsic to WIL, active citizenship can be built through the strategic use of WIL programs to conduct community-based research or community engagement activities.

KEYWORDS: Work-Integrated Learning; Active Citizenship; Postgraduate Students; Participatory Methods; Community-Based Research.

Introduction

A key theme in the deepening democracy literature is the idea that healthy democracies require citizens who are politically active. When citizens and residents vote and get broadly and actively involved in their communities, various democracy-enhancing benefits follow. These include a sense of civic-mindedness and civic duty, a greater awareness of the power of citizenship, stronger horizontal relations of trust and shared values, and a greater willingness to hold elected representatives accountable. In this spirit, the democracy education literature advocates for civic engagement, understood as actively participating in community decision-making activities,[1] as an effective way to cultivate active citizenship among students at universities, as well as the organizations and communities in which they work.

While the civic engagement literature emerges from a North American context, in this chapter we explore a very similar idea: the notion that a Work-Integrated Learning (WIL) program in South Africa can cultivate active citizenship among university students through partnerships with community-engaged nonprofit, nongovernmental organizations. While Work-Integrated Learning historically has been focused on undergraduate training for the working life through workplace internships alongside theoretical training in the classroom, we reflect on a new initiative at the University of the Western Cape for postgraduate students to conduct applied research for host organizations under the WIL banner. We argue that WIL provides an opportunity for forms of work-based learning that, when designed appropriately and orientated around community-based research, can enhance active citizenship, defined as active engagement in community decision-making, for all involved.

There is no inherent relationship between WIL and civic engagement. WIL is broadly conceived as a form of learning for students that integrates theoretical knowledge in the classroom with practical knowledge in the workplace, while civic engagement is understood as actively participating in community decision-making activities. While not all WIL experiences involve civic engagement or promote active citizenship, we argue that WIL programs can (and should) be used to promote both workplace preparedness and active citizenship skills.

In what follows, we reflect on a pilot WIL program implemented by the Department of Political Studies at the University of the Western Cape (UWC) in South Africa. The program was created and administered in partnership with the non-governmental organization (NGO), The Black Sash, and funded through the Participedia research network.[2] It will show how this partnership can provide both NGOs with valuable research at low or no cost and simultaneously empower students with professional skills, while also producing greater forms of active citizenship for all participants. Of course, no one program is a panacea, and we reflect too on the limitations or drawbacks of the program. Nevertheless, considered as a whole, the case supports the idea that civic engagement can be pursued under a WIL banner, albeit with a very specific awareness of the objective of affirming active citizenship for all involved.

In making this case, we begin by outlining the relevant civic engagement and WIL literatures before reflecting theoretically on active citizenship to operationalize it for our analysis. Following Gaventa and Barrett,[3] we define active citizenship as some combination of (i) building consciousness about citizenship and rights; (ii) learning new ways of engaging the state and claiming recognition and rights; (iii) demanding more accountability and responsiveness from the state; and (iv) building new relations of solidarity among participants. Then we apply this framework to two sets of data from the students who drove the applied research, and the fieldworkers from Black Sash.

From Civic Engagement to Work-Integrated Learning

Where the civic engagement movement in higher education is concerned with cultivating students who will become socially and politically engaged participants in a democracy, Work-Integrated Learning, as used in the South African context, is aimed at educating students for the workplace through internships. Where the former is more overtly political, the latter is geared toward preparation for the world of work.

Civic engagement in North America

The existing literature around civic engagement is well established in North American academia, and as Rios et al. (2013) point out, has evolved over 30 years through many forms, from notions of community service in the 1980s, through service-learning in the 1990s, to civic engagement in the 2000s.[4] Notably, while all three iterations involve students engaging in the community in some way, community service was intended to make students more community-aware, and service-learning tended to involve forms of volunteering, with fewer students participating in politics.[5] Thus, despite the significant growth of service learning in the 1990s, it appeared not to have a positive impact on active citizenship, particularly when examining political forms of engagement such as voting, protesting, petitioning, and participating in political campaigns.[6] There was a gap between community work and politics that prompted the development of the idea of "civic engagement". Here, the focus was "to use service-learning and other community-based experiences to strengthen the civic learning of students and the public problem-solving capacities of institutions of higher education."[7]

Whether civic engagement programs are achieving this larger political goal of creating active citizens is still an open question, but at least the goal of civic engagement is clearer.[8] It involves creating active citizens who will vote and join political parties,[9] but also encourages citizens to engage in deliberative practices[10] or forms of activism.[11] This clearer goal also helps differentiate civic engagement programs and objectives from forms of community service and volunteering that may not necessarily link to academic training nor build active citizenship.

Work Integrated Learning in South Africa

Historically, the South African post-secondary landscape was made up of two different types of institutions, namely the Technikon (similar to a US technical college) and the traditional university. The distinguishing feature was that Technikons would prepare students for practical trades or skills together with a theoretical underpinning while the university was the place for advanced research. However, the clear distinction between these types of tertiary institutions and their functions shifted following a merger in the higher education sector in South Africa that took place between 2002 and 2005.[12] During this merger, some Technikons merged with other Technikons; while in other instances, traditional universities merged with Technikons to become comprehensive universities.[13] This merger set the groundwork for WIL in previously traditional South African universities. This also meant that universities now had to find ways in which they could integrate Technikon processes, such as job placements, into their usual study schedule. One reason for this shift, as Maseko notes,[14] is that all South African universities have started to recognize the increased need for WIL programs to become globally competitive.

Following the merger of Technikons and research-based universities in the early 2000s, work on the policy framework continued to incorporate skills-based learning into tertiary institutions' curricula.[15] One of the seminal pieces of policy in this regard is the White Paper for Post-School Education and Training published in 2013.[16] Simply put, this includes all forms of education for adults older than 18 (i.e. the school leaving age), including universities, Technical and Vocational Education and Training (TVET) colleges, private and adult education institutions, amongst others. The White Paper is important because its objective is not only the creation of a single coordinated post-secondary education system that includes higher education, but it also aims to create a system that can assist in creating a fair and democratic South Africa.

Just as this chapter recognizes the value of WIL as a potential form of civic engagement pedagogy, the White Paper also recognized the importance of integrated learning for deepening democracy by building civic skills and commitments among participants. It goes further to mention that a post-secondary school education and training system is needed that is "responsive to the needs of individual citizens, employers in both public and private sectors, as well as broader societal and developmental objectives."[17] The White Paper specifically mentions "work-integrated learning" and sets a groundwork for introducing WIL on a larger scale in South Africa.

However, it is not only the White Paper for Post-School Education and Training that has helped shape a policy framework around WIL in South Africa. The first mention of work-integrated learning came in 2007 when the South African Higher Education Qualifications Framework (HEQF) published a set of revised qualifications that required the re-evaluation and redesign of programs to align with the new framework and, for the first time, used the term "Work-Integrated

Learning."[18] Following this, the HEQF established some of the parameters of WIL in other policy documents. These emphasized WIL in public skills development programs such as the National Skills Development Strategy for 2011–2016, the National Development Plan and the National Skills Accord. All these documents describe WIL as essential to high-quality vocational and occupational education and training.[19]

In respect of higher education specifically, the Council for Higher Education published the *Work-Integrated Learning: Good Practice Guide* in 2011 that recommends approaches for curriculum design, teaching, assessment, partnership and management of WIL programs.[20] It defines WIL as follows:

> WIL is used as an umbrella term to describe curricular, pedagogic and assessment practices, across a range of academic disciplines that integrate formal learning and workplace concerns. The integration of theory and practice in student learning can occur through a range of WIL approaches, apart from formal or informal work placements.[21]

The focus is thus on the integration of different kinds of knowledge, which opens up WIL to a much larger range of innovative practices. In this framing, WIL approaches Billett's bridging model rather than a deficit model, in that both theoretical and practical knowledge are seen as key to student success, rather than just one or the other.[22] Thus, against the deficit views that theoretical knowledge is of no use, or practical knowledge is too limited, the bridging view affirms both as important to learning.

This bridging conception of learning is evident in the official WIL good practice guide of the Centre for Higher Education (CHE). In the section on student "professional development and employability," the advantages of a WIL approach are listed as fourfold:[23]

- Academic benefits, such as improved general academic performance, enhancement of interdisciplinary thinking, increased motivation to learn
- Personal benefits, such as increased communication skills, teamwork, leadership and co-operation
- Career benefits such as career clarification, professional identity, increased employment opportunities and salaries, development of positive work values and ethics
- Skills development, including increased competence and increased technical knowledge and skills.

The succession of these policy documents has shown that there is a shift in the way that higher education is presented in South Africa, with increasing emphasis on preparing students for work post-university but also to align these work-based skills with university curricula. Additionally, the guide notes that WIL programs could be used to create more socially engaged students who ultimately become better equipped to participate in a democracy. Hence it states:

> Programmes offered by traditional universities that do not take into account graduates' career trajectories need to consider issues of citizenship, graduateness and employability (without succumbing to "vocational drift").[24]

Work-integrated learning in Political Studies at UWC

Building on the momentum that WIL has gained in South Africa's higher education landscape and building on a local tradition of engaged research with nongovernmental organizations (NGOs), the Department of Political Studies at UWC is establishing a work-integrated learning master's program. The program is currently undergoing national accreditation, but we have piloted several WIL projects with host organizations in the City of Cape Town as proof of concept for the accreditation process. The UWC-Black Sash study outlined below is one of these pilot cases.

The proposed master's degree is a two-year program, where the first year is taught in the classroom and the second is a placement with a host organization to do applied research for the organization. The data collected is also used towards the students' thesis. This relationship is all framed by a Memorandum of Understanding between the student, supervisor, and host organization, set up in year one of the master's. Cooperation between the university and the community partner, and the integration of theoretical and practical knowledge, are at the heart of this research design.

This model of WIL is uncommon in South Africa in that it is situated at the postgraduate level, and unique in that it is based around an applied research project defined in conjunction with a nonprofit, nongovernmental, or governmental host agency. This applied research could take a multiplicity of forms including a desk-top study reviewing South Africa's international agreements in relation to refugee rights for the parliamentary research office; a survey of popular attitudes towards immigrants for a refugee rights NGO; or a participatory action research project in gender-based violence in a poor area of Cape Town conducted with a gender rights NGO.

A key reason for introducing this innovation at the postgraduate level is that political studies is not a vocational discipline and has multiple potential career outlets including academia, research, the media, the nonprofit sector, political parties, and government employment. For this reason, a narrowly framed "professional learning" model of WIL will not work for students in the Political Studies graduate program. Political Studies trains students to make arguments informed by research, and it is at the master's level that students have research skills developed enough to be of use to a host organization. The ambition, in addition to conducting applied research, is to further the development of our students across the four dimensions identified above in the CHE WIL Good Practice Guide: academic, personal, career, and skills. Thus, the model is a bridging rather than a deficit model and orientated towards partnership rather than service.

It is critical to note that, in its formal conception, the WIL master's program is not explicitly a civic engagement program intended to develop active citizens. WIL is broadly conceived as a form of learning for students that integrates theoretical knowledge in the classroom with practical knowledge in the workplace. It is intended to enhance student learning by exposing them to practical knowledge in the workplace, in addition to theoretical knowledge, which in our case is applied research. However, as we shall demonstrate through the case-study below, the WIL program does contain the potential to develop active citizenship through the right kind of research project with the right host organization. But first, we must define what is meant by active citizenship.

Operationalizing Active Citizenship

At the heart of the argument so far is the claim that universities can both educate students as knowers and as active citizens through programs that involve student work in the wider community, broadly framed. Volunteering, community service, and service learning do not necessarily translate into active citizenship.

In this regard, the work of Gaventa & Barrett is informative.[25] Synthesizing the findings of the Development Research Centre on Citizenship, Participation and Accountability, of the Institute for Development Studies at the University of Sussex in the United Kingdom, a project that conducted hundreds of case-studies from all over the globe over a 10-year period,[26] they conclude that participation in civil society, defined as engaging in community political processes with organizations outside the market and for-profit sector, can contribute to four democratic outcomes. These are, (i) building consciousness about citizenship and rights; (ii) learning new practices of participation, that is new ways of engaging the state and claiming recognition and rights; (iii) demanding more accountability and responsiveness from the state; and (iv) building new relations of solidarity among participants.

Because these four outcomes amount to an emergent theory on what participation in political life can bring about, they also provide a basis to define the active citizen. Hence, when evaluating whether a program like the WIL master's produces active citizens, we can break it down into these four questions. Does the program:

- Make participants more aware of their rights and responsibilities as a citizen?
- Inspire more participation in political practices and perhaps organizations?
- Lead participants to demand accountability and responsiveness from the state?
- Build horizontal relations of solidarity among participants around these political practices?

In what follows, we will measure the active citizenship produced through a civic engagement process in terms of these four criteria.

Research Design And Methodology

To answer the question of how WIL can be used to build active citizenship, we drew on data from one recent case of applied community-based research on changes to the social grants system in South Africa. Hence, we are using a case-study research design.[27] Further, it is largely a descriptive and exploratory case-study given the novel nature of the WIL approach, and the fact that the program is being implemented for the first time at UWC on a trial basis. We will explore the experiences of participants in the research project (the student researchers from UWC and the NGO partners who worked on the project) and reflect on the changes to consciousness and behavior of these respondents. The study thus follows a qualitative methodology informed by an interpretivist or social constructivist epistemology, and using participant observation, auto-ethnographic, and interview data collection methods.[28] While we are confident of the internal validity of our argument given the use of multiple methods to reach saturation and to triangulate the data, we present our findings as preliminary and subject to further testing as the evidence is drawn from a single case-study with a relatively small number of respondents.

The case itself is a 2019 collaboration between the Department of Political Studies at UWC in Cape Town and a human rights organization, the Black Sash. It was designed as a Work-Integrated Learning collaboration in that the students helped co-design and implement an applied research project with Black Sash staff. The findings of the project were used both by Black Sash in their subsequent advocacy work, and by the students in completing their master's theses. Thus, student theoretical learning in the University was completed by applied learning in the "workplace" as more abstract knowledge about citizen rights and accessing social protection met real world experiences. In this case, the workplace was among poor communities in the Western Cape where the impact of changes in social grant provision was researched, as well as the offices of Black Sash where the project was developed collaboratively. In this particular case then, the WIL workplace approached a form of community-based research, conducted with a pro-poor, rights-based advocacy organization, that provided fertile ground for something like community engagement.

Specifically, the research collaboration centered on researching changes to the payment of social grant recipients in South Africa. Around 17 million social grant payments are made every month in South Africa and reach roughly 11 million people, and roughly half the households in the country.[29] The major grants are the Child Support Grant for poor families, pensions to the elderly, and disability grants. Essentially, the pay points at which beneficiaries collected monthly stipends, run by the South African Social Security Agency (SASSA), were "decommissioned" or phased out. In place of this uniform national system set up for recipients of social grants, recipients now had to go either to the Post Office, various commercial retailers, or use cash machines or ATMs. Effectively, a bespoke national system for grant recipients was privatized, and the poor, elderly, and disabled were added to existing public queues.

As a human rights organization, Black Sash was concerned about the potential harm of this change to vulnerable recipients, especially the elderly who form a core constituency of the organization. Thus, the research project was designed to conduct in-depth and systematic research on the experience of elderly grant recipients from the decommissioning of pay points by the South African Social Services Agency (SASSA). To this end, studies were conducted exploring experiences of elderly grant recipients located near key Black Sash office sites in the Western Cape. The study was qualitative, as it intended to explore in detail the subjective and shared perceptions of grant recipients through interviews, focus group and participatory action research methods that collected various kinds of quantitative, qualitative, numerical, written, oral, and visual data. The study was implemented in Delft, Genadendal, Khayelitsha, and Robertson, and engaged approximately 60 respondents over three months between February, March, and June 2019.

At each site, researchers were to engage in a three-day process.

- Day 1 involved meeting with the grant recipients, as organized by the partner community-based organization of Black Sash. This day involved explaining the project, securing ethical clearance, and conducting "rivers of life" participatory activity to facilitate systematic reflection by each participant on their experiences of grant collection day.
- Day 2 involved the researchers travelling with selected recipients to collect their money, and interviewing, observing, and video documenting the process of the day.
- Between Day 1 and 3, researchers collated the data, produced visual products, and drafted a site-specific case for the Participedia website.[30]
- Day 3 (roughly a week after Day 1) involved a debrief, where the findings on the Participedia website are presented and workshopped, including a participatory "body mapping" exercise.

To collect data, researchers used three main instruments:

- An interview, focus group, and observation schedule to collect factual and perceptual data on the grant experience
- Two participatory techniques including a "river of life"[31] and "body mapping"[32] to enable participants systematic, personal, and collective reflection on the grant experience, including the affective dimensions of the experience
- Video documentary of the research process.

In addition, we went back to each site in July to further workshop knowledge of SASSA services and to map the areas to ascertain how far recipients had to travel. All activities were led by the students, with two different members of the Black Sash staff present in each site, and Professor Piper observing in three of the cases.

Ultimately, the research concluded that, as a result of privatizing payment points, the costs of transport and food, insecurity, administrative costs, and indignities endured by recipients increased—disproportionately impacting the bodies of elderly people. In short, where in the previous system the elderly were reasonably well treated with preferential access to bespoke pay points including administrative support for when there were problems with payment, in the new system they are required to queue for multiple hours, often without access to adequate seating, toilets, water, shelter, security and no onsite administrative support. In addition, decommissioning eliminated many rural pay points which forced recipients to travel further for their grants and to visit more distant regional SASSA offices to query problems on the accounts.[33]

On completion of the applied research project, we set out to reflect on the experience as an instance in which WIL, interpreted as a form of community-based research, could potentially build active citizenship among the research team of students and NGO fieldworkers. With this in mind, we identified the following research question for this chapter:

> How, if at all, did engaging in the Black Sash research project enhance active citizenship for the student and NGO researchers understood as (i) a greater consciousness of rights, (ii) learning new citizenship practices, (ii) demanding more accountability from the state and (iv) feeling greater solidarity with other participants.

Data was gathered from two sources: the two master's students and the five NGO workers. Data was gathered from the students through observation of fieldwork activities and autoethnographic reflection by the two master's students which involved the retrospective and selective analysis of key moments from an experience, whether negative or positive, as outlined by Ellis et al.[34] The process of autoethnographic analysis was done inductively, first by the two students individually, and then collectively by the students and Professor Piper. From this process, the key insight of the "personal as political" emerged. The observations were analyzed deductively using Gaventa and Barrett's fourfold conception of active citizenship. Data was gathered from the Black Sash staff via observations, semi-structured interviews, and from the project evaluation sheets completed by Black Sash staff during the original fieldwork. The semi-structured interviews were designed according to Gaventa and Barrett's typology, and analysis of all the staff data proceeded deductively on this basis.[35] In addition, some emergent themes were identified that are relevant to the research question on active citizenship.

On the one hand, as a single case-study with limited respondents, the external validity of the findings is limited. Therefore, we regard these results as preliminary and subject to further research to discern their wider relevance. On the other hand, we believe the study has strong internal validity due to saturation of evidence from multiple and triangulated methods. In addition, we assert that ethnographic reflection offers unique and privileged insight into the subjective experiences of participants—on a research question that is concerned precisely with subjective experiences. We took great care to emphasize the critical nature of the process of reflection, and to affirm that the integrity of the research process was the most important objective. Indeed, with ethnographic research the point is not objectivity so much as critical and honest reflection on experiences. It is clear from what follows that not all respondents experienced the project as profoundly as the two students, and several points of criticism are developed.

Findings And Analysis

We outline the findings of our research in using the categories of active citizenship identified above and add a category that emerged from the data-gathering: "from the personal to the political." This additional finding refers to the fact that, while both students and NGO workers were aware of issues of poverty and marginalization, when confronted by the life experiences of respondents it was made real to them in a way that inspired a desire to act. We demonstrate the general strengthening of a sense of active citizenship across all dimensions, but students and NGO workers took slightly different lessons from the experience. For the former, the experience was more of a revelation, personal and politicizing. For the latter, already largely politicized, it was more about how particular insights bolstered subsequent advocacy work.

Consciousness of rights

In general, both the students and the NGO workers reported a growing social consciousness as a result of the project, although more so for the students. The project itself was steeped in education about rights and how to enact them. As one Black Sash staff member notes:

> I found that people did not know very much about their rights and felt unable to get help because they were not sure of what they were entitled to. I felt personally responsible for making people aware of their rights even though this was not the main aim of the research. It seemed to me to now only was it my duty and obligation to inform people…

She also noted that, "despite a lack of knowledge around the rights and responsibilities for social grants, I found that respondents were eager to have their say and to be involved." Both researchers and workshop participants seemed eager to exercise their citizenship rights. One of the students observed:

> Prior to doing the research, my studies in political sciences and the South African public administration system had introduced me to the theoretical role of civil society and citizenry in South Africa. This study, however, has taught me about the social services provided to South African citizens. It has taught me about the processes involved in applying for state social services and, more specifically, the social grants system. The fact that there are thousands of South Africans who have access to, and make use of the social grants system, yet do not understand or aren't aware of the extent to which the state should be assisting them, however, is alarming. The research has highlighted the fact that citizens in rural areas are not as aware of their rights and responsibilities as those in or closer to the big cities. It has thus also taught me that my responsibility as a South African citizen is to help bridge this gap between those in rural and urban areas.

Gaining an understanding of rights and how to enact them is perhaps a core component of active and engaged citizenship. This means that you cannot act in accordance with your rights if you do not know what they are and, consequently, cannot demand accountability.

Greater participation

Regarding taking action around rights or engaging in political activity, most respondents reported that their experience conducting research reinforced their desire to act. One of the students reported that:

> Following my tenure as a student researcher on this project I joined the Rape Crisis Centre and participated in a workshop to become a community education officer. Additionally, I joined the NGO My Vote Counts as political systems researcher. The focus of the organization is to conduct research on democracy, electoral politics and corruption. It seeks to provide education and awareness on voter rights and citizen participation in democratic processes.

The other student also reported an impact on her career choice:

> The research has inspired me to not only participate in civil society, but to seek a job in [the nonprofit sector] on a full-time basis, on completion of my studies. The experiences learnt throughout this research process has (*sic.*) ensured that I have been able to find employment [with NGOs]. I can now use the theory learnt during my studies and the field experiences learnt during this study in my field of work as a researcher for an NGO. This research has encouraged me to further investigate the manner in which our state interacts with citizens. Because I am now aware of the harsh realities faced by so many South Africans, I can now contribute to the manner in which they are treated.

For the Sash staff members, the experience reinforced their sense of vocation. One stated that, "working on the ground and on [the] community level and seeing first-hand the struggles, inspires me to play my part in society or within advocacy campaigns", and another added that the research had given her "the resources and tools to properly assist the elderly with the social grants," adding that she "felt very responsible to help people with their SASSA since she was now aware of what their rights were and what the pertinent issues were for people who are grant recipients." For others more experienced working in the community, the project reinforced existing views rather than leading to new revelations. Hence, as one put it, "It was a good project but I am comfortable with these issues as I have spent my life working in these areas."

Demanding accountability

Participating in the project also deepened the researchers' readiness to demand responsiveness from the state. One of the students noted that the important role of advocacy groups in holding the state accountable:

> [The research] has led me to ask more questions about the effect of the decommissioning of the pay stations on the grant recipients, especially on those in rural areas. I now feel that the state needs to do more to ensure that grant recipients receive their grants as safely and effectively as possible. The research has presented the idea that if the state is not approached by civil society, South African citizens' rights are not taken care of. The role of [nonprofit advocacy groups] has been highlighted by this study, which is important in ensuring the state be held accountable for its actions.

For the NGO workers, the research had even stronger links to accountability work. Four of the workers reported that they cited the research in their work for Black Sash both in the public realm and in direct advocacy to the government. This was for advocacy work Black Sash initiated on this issue after the research was completed. As one worker states:

> I had many radio interviews and even one television interview as a direct consequence of this research. Part of the interview was requesting accountability and responsiveness from the state, especially to grant beneficiaries who are elderly, vulnerable, and have disabilities.

Another worker reported how, as a former government employee, she understands and has sympathy for both government and citizens struggling to access their rights. However, she added, "I feel like government has in some ways abandoned people," so people like herself who work for NGOs need to organize around ways to bring change. Finally, one shared that the insights she gained about the lack of access to administrative support after decommissioning inform her daily work, as she now "goes directly to the SASSA offices in Caledon to bring the concerns of the Genadendal community to them."

Relations of solidarity

Relations of solidarity is the idea that participation in society can bring about stronger horizontal social ties that foster greater resilience and facilitate collective action among communities. Both student researchers reported how they formed ties with many of the respondents and how these relationships endure. One of the students spoke of feeling like "I have an extended family in the respondents since they care as much about me as I do about them." She adds:

> For this research, we had developed a set of participatory research tools centered around expressing feelings and thoughts as art. These art forms ranged from drawing maps which visually represented a respondent's journey to collect grant money to drawing life size images of themselves where they could indicate where the emotional and physical pain was during that journey to collect grant money. Assisting respondents to create these artistic products was a very intense and involved process. Working so intently with people created an environment to become close with participants beyond the parameters of the research. The openness and kindness which I experienced from working

with some of the poorest and most disadvantaged has been unmatched. It was touching to me that people took time out to share with me intimate details of their life. It is this experience that has spurred me on to be more vocal about the injustices that I know exist. The relationship with the respondents has been maintained as these respondents sometimes message me to let me know how they are doing and sometimes to ask for assistance.

For the Sash staff members, a strong theme was that the research process led to greater connectedness with the participants and the wider communities in which the participants live. Two workers shared similar stories about how the research has helped build relations within the communities in which they work. In this regard, one stated that the research "helped to create a bond with the people of Genadendal" and helped "raise the visibility of Black Sash in the area." She noted that the participants in the workshops fondly recall creating the body map art and like to share these stories with her. Additionally, she recalls experiencing a feeling of freedom and connection being involved so closely in research that took place within communities. She reflected that the intensity of the days together doing the research workshops helped to create a feeling of togetherness which she believes made it easier for respondents to open up. In her subsequent visits to Genadendal, she notes that former respondents and others in the community show no reservations talking to her, and the conversation is intimate as if between friends as opposed to a conversation between an outsider and a member of the community.

From the personal to the political

The most salient outcome of the WIL program was the bridge between the personal and the political, especially for the students. While both student researchers were admittedly already interested in social issues and had some knowledge of them, it was not until their participation in fieldwork that they were confronted with realities of the social issues which they studied. Both student researchers, in their personal reflections, noted that personal connections had the most lingering effect on them, and illustrated this with specific instances.

There's no doubt this project was hard work. The students got up early, organized boxes full of paper and stationary materials, drove several hours, facilitated workshops in multiple languages, packed up and drove home again—for several days on end. Leading up to the fieldwork period, they had to liaise with Black Sash and community organizations in each of the four sites. We met regularly, both as a UWC team and with Black Sash, throughout the year of the project. It was also emotional work as we were confronted by hard stories from workshop participants. One comments:

> Since the end of the research one incident in particular has stayed with me. In conducting the research one of the activities we did was a "ride-along" where we followed participants on their journey to collect their social grant money. One of the women I was assigned to awoke at 6am in the morning to wash and get dressed and to make sure that she was early enough to walk to the ATM. She lived in a township outside of Robertson and would walk at least 45 mins from her home to the town center to join a queue of people at the ATM. I walked with her and stayed with her for almost three hours in line to finally get to the ATM to draw her money. We stood outside with no protection or chairs on a hot summer's day. When she eventually received her rather meager pension, she turned to me and said, "are you hungry?" and proceeded to buy a parcel of fish and chips and insisted on sharing her food with me. This was a woman who could not afford some of the bare necessities, who was old and tired from standing in the hot sun in a long line and her first reaction upon receiving her money was to take care of me. It was a profound moment which I have not forgotten.

The other student has a similarly vivid memory:

> Having to facilitate these workshops to people who were illiterate and to people who had never held a paint brush in their lives was both alarming and fulfilling. Alarming because I did not think that there would still be people today who could not read or write and fulfilling because I was part of the team who brought them their first painting opportunity and because I could see how much joy these exercises had brought to them. A participant had told me that they could not wait to take their art-work home to their grandchildren to show them their first art piece.

Indeed, a key theme in autoethnographic reflections was how the research brought abstract knowledge of social issues into harsh, tangible relief. Importantly, this confrontation with reality, a reality touched by real people's difficulties and emotions, proved a major inspiration for active citizenship.[36] In this regard, one of the students' states:

> For the study we had to travel to two rural and two historically poor urban areas. Until my participation in this study, I had not been to any of these areas. Our visits highlighted the harsh realities that so many South Africans face on a daily basis, realities my middle-class background had not exposed me to. It was a culture shock seeing the hardships of the poor in my country. Having to listen to how grant recipients in rural areas have to travel up to 70km just to receive their grants and do their monthly grocery shopping was hard, especially with minimal amounts recipients receive. I often had to remind myself that I was there to do research, as I found myself so immersed in their stories that I almost forgot why I was there.

Ultimately, the work was also rewarding and moved both students on a personal level. As one wrote in her reflections:

> The first area we visited was Delft, a vast urban area located outside Cape Town CBD. This area was a mostly lower-income area that had suffered under the policies of Apartheid spatial planning where large non-white communities were placed in tightly packed communities that were far from the resources and amenities of the city. This area was previously designated a "coloured" township. Coming to this area was emotionally charged because I was now face to face with the reality of how people lived in my city. My parents each came from a township of a similar type to Delft and had grown up poor during the height of Apartheid. Each were the first in their families to matriculate and to attend university, both at the University of the Western Cape (then designated as university for non-whites). As a second-generation university graduate of a now middle-class family, it was jarring to see in a very real way the disparities between my life and theirs.
>
> It was this initial reaction that made me realize that this research was not only going to be an academically rigorous one but also an emotionally challenging one. Feeling so personally connected to the people, lives and areas in which we were doing the research made me feel extra responsible for conducting research that would be beneficial.

The other added:

It brings me great fulfillment knowing that the outcomes of this research have brought about change in the manner in which the state treats grant recipients. This research has served as an eye-opener to the harsh realities faced by the poor in this country on a daily basis. I would not have been able to fully understand the plight of the poor had I not been part of this study. It has also encouraged me to question the motives of the state with regards to the decommissioning of the pay points.

Notably, confrontation with the reality of poverty and other forms of marginalization also impacted the Sash staff, although to a lesser extent. This is even more remarkable as these people work with these issues and communities all the time. For example, one Sash staff member reports that she found the workshops "more poignant because my parents are grant recipients. I have started asking them more questions and probing family members to find out if they had any problems with accessing the grant." Another stated that being exposed to the problems that the elderly face in accessing their grants made her want to be more involved. She has noticed that the COVID-19 lockdown has exacerbated these problems and has led people to be more confused as they do not understand what is happening with the social grants.

Conclusion

The findings from our case-study of the UWC-Black Sash research project reveal both personal and political transformations for the students and NGO staff members involved. Their responses affirm many dimensions of active citizenship identified by Gaventa and Barrett,[37] but add the notion of "the political as personal," where abstract knowledge is transformed into an imperative to act after connecting with people's experiences at a personal level. In addition, not only did the project support advocacy work by a nongovernmental organization, but the participating students now work in the human rights sector themselves and have a higher level of awareness and political consciousness regarding the rights and responsibilities of citizenship. The Black Sash staff members involved in the project also reported effects that affirmed active citizenship to varying degrees, reporting that the highly interactive, interpersonal, and immersive nature of the research project strengthened their relationship with, and status as a trusted partner in, the communities where they serve. While provisional and limited, our findings suggest that forms of community-based research or engagement conducted as part of a WIL program may enhance active citizenship skills among participants.

It is important to note what is being claimed here. WIL is broadly conceived as a form of learning for students that integrates theoretical knowledge in the classroom with practical knowledge in the workplace. Civic engagement, in contrast, is understood as actively participating in community decision-making activities. There is thus no inherent relationship between WIL and civic engagement in the abstract, nor necessarily in our master's program at UWC. Students could do a WIL master's conducting desk-top research for the Parliamentary Research Office on Middle East politics to support a parliamentary committee and then use the same data towards their thesis. However, as illustrated above, students on the WIL could also do applied research that involves community-based research or forms of community engagement that can cultivate active citizenship. To us, this seems like a potential stream that could be developed in WIL programs into the future.

While it is difficult to pin down exactly what conditions must be met to ensure that community-based research achieves the civic engagement goal of active citizenship, in our case the following five points seemed important. First, the students' pre-existent interest in the issues of social grants, poverty, and citizenship motivated them to persevere with the hard work involved in the study. Students were also favorably predisposed to the broad ideological and normative commitments of active citizenship. Second, the host organization is committed to human rights and dedicates itself to help poor South Africans find practical ways to access their social grants from the state. Not only do the ideological and normative commitments of Black Sash align with notions of active citizenship, but the organization's work includes citizenship building activities like conscientizing citizens about their rights. Third, students spent significant time with elderly and poor citizens, and thus were able to personally and directly understand previously abstract notions like "exclusion" or "poverty." Fourth, by collaboratively designing and implementing the project with Black Sash workers and conducting participatory exercises with respondents, social hierarchies and barriers between students, staff, and respondents were weakened. These shifts in power dynamics allowed for more equal, personal, and transformative relations to emerge. Fifth, access to financial and human resources to conduct research was necessary for the project to occur, and therefore investments from both the university and the NGO were required.

This one case-study may not be sufficient to determine the respective influence of these five factors on community-based research that builds active citizenship. We can confidently assert that a WIL approach alone is unlikely to achieve these outcomes. Rather, WIL provides a strategic opportunity to develop appropriate forms of community-based research or community-engagement projects able to build active citizenship. This case study bolsters our assertion that WIL is framed broadly enough in South African policy and practice to allow space for varying formations, some of which may end up resembling forms of civic engagement pedagogy utilized across the globe. This is because the WIL model combines research, collaboration, and learning into one process, while maintaining a productive blurring between theory and practice, research and advocacy, and the university and the workplace. The debate about the purpose of education exists across the globe, but education for work and professional development need not conflict with education for active citizenship. Programs can be designed to do both, and graduates of such programs will offer major benefits to societies in which they work and live. Indeed, we believe that our study shows the value to students, the university, and society of making the development of active citizens an explicit goal, or a specific track, within the wider WIL program.

Endnotes

1. Alison Rios Millett McCartney, "Teaching Civic Engagement: Debates, Definitions, Benefits, and Challenges," in *Teaching Civic Engagement: From Student to Active Citizen*, eds. Alison Rios Millett McCartney, Elizabeth A. Bennion, and Dick W. Simpson (Washington, DC: American Political Science Association, 2013), 14.

2. See https://participedia.net/case/5600

3. John Gaventa and Gregory Barrett, "So What Difference Does it Make? Mapping the Outcomes of Citizen Engagement," *IDS Working Papers* 347 (2010): 01–72.

4. McCartney, "Debates, Definitions."

5. Ibid.

6. Martin Wattenberg, *Is Voting for Young People?* (New York: Routledge, 2020).

7. McCartney, "Debates, Definitions."

8. Susan A. Ostrander, "Democracy, Civic Participation, and the University: A Comparative Study of Civic Engagement on Five Campuses," *Nonprofit and Voluntary Sector Quarterly* 33, no. 1 (2004): 74–93.

9. Constance Flanagan and Peter Levine, "Civic Engagement and the Transition to Adulthood," The Future of Children 20, no. 1 (2010): 159–179.

10. Tina Nabatchi, John Gastil, Matt Leighninger, and G. Michael Weiksner, eds., *Democracy in Motion: Evaluating the Practice and Impact of Deliberative Civic Engagement* (Oxford, UK: Oxford University Press, 2012).

11. J. Patrick Biddix, Patricia A. Somers, and Joseph L. Polman, "Protest Reconsidered: Identifying Democratic and Civic Engagement Learning Outcomes," *Innovative Higher Education* 34, no. 3 (2009): 133–147.

12. Martin Hall, "Institutional Culture of Mergers and Alliances in South Africa," in *Mergers and Alliances in Higher Education*, eds. Adrian Curaj, Luke Georghiou, Jennifer Casenga Harper and Eva Egron-Polak, 145–173, (Cham, Switzerland: Springer Nature, 2015).

13. Martin Lewis, Natasja Holtzhausen, and Susanne Taylor, "The Dilemma of Work-Integrated Learning (WIL) in South African Higher Education-the Case of Town and Regional Planning at the University of Johannesburg," *'Stads-en*

Streeksbeplanning', Town and Regional Planning 57 (2010): 25–35.

14. Lucky Albert Maseko, "A Review of Work-Integrated Learning in South African Mining Engineering Universities," *Journal of the Southern African Institute of Mining and Metallurgy* 118, no. 12 (2018): 1315–1323.

15. Ronel Blom, "A Policy Framework for Work-Integrated Learning," *The African Journal for Work-Based Learning* 2, no. 1 (2014): 1–12.

16. See https://www.gov.za/sites/default/files/gcis_document/201409/37229gon11.pdf.

17. See https://www.gov.za/sites/default/files/gcis_document/201409/37229gon11.pdf, 4.

18. Lewis et al., "Dilemma of Work-Integrated Learning (WIL)."

19. Ibid., 29.

20. Christine Winberg, Penelope Engel-Hills, James Garraway, and Cecilia Jacobs, "Work-Integrated Learning: Good Practice Guide–HE Monitor No. 12." *Pretoria: Council on Higher Education* (CHE), (2011), https://www.academia.edu/10020069/CHE_Winberg_C_Garraway_J_Engel_Hills_P_and_Jacobs_C_2011_Work_integrated_learning_Good_Practice_Guide_HE_Monitor_No_12_August_2011.

21. Winberg et al., "Good Practice Guide."

22. Stephen Billett, "Practice-Based Learning and Professional Education," in *Practice-Based Education*, eds. Joy Higgs, Ronald Barnett, Stephen Billett, Maggie Hutchings, and Franziska Trede, 101–112 (Rotterdam, Netherlands: SensePublishers, 2012).

23. Winberg et al., "Good Practice Guide," 6.

24. Ibid., 7.

25. Gaventa et al., "Mapping the Outcomes."

26. See https://www.ids.ac.uk/projects/development-research-centre-on-citizenship-participation-and-accountability/.

27. Robert Yin, *Case Study Research And Applications: Design And Methods*, 6th edition (London: Sage, 2018).

28. Carolyn Ellis, Tony E. Adams, and Arthur P. Bochner, "Autoethnography: an Overview," *Historical Social Research/Historische Sozialforschung* 36, no. 4 (2011): 273–290.

29. Laurence Piper, Sondré Bailey, and Robyn Pasensie, "'Like a Blow to my Body': The Negative Impact of the Decommissioning of SASSA Pay Points on the Bodies of Rural, Elderly Social Grant Recipients in the Western Cape." *SASSA Decommissioning Research Report for Black Sash,* Department of Political Studies, University of the Western Cape (2018), https://www.researchgate.net/publication/343761570_'Like_a_blow_to_my_body'_The_negative_impact_of_the_decommissioning_of_SASSA_pay_points_on_the_bodies_of_rural_elderly_social_grant_recipients_in_the_Western_Cape_SASSA_Decommissioning_Research_Report [accessed Sep 11 2020], 3

30. Participedia is "a global crowdsourcing platform for researchers, activists, practitioners, and anyone interested in public participation and democratic innovations". They funded the research. See https://participedia.net/case/5600.

31. Ziad Moussa, "Rivers of Life," in *Participatory Learning And Action: Community-Based Adaptation To Climate Change*, eds. Hannah Reid, Terry Cannon, Rachel Berger, Mozaharul Alam, and Angela Milligan, 183–86 (London: IIED, 2009).

32. Denise Gastaldo, Natalia Rivas-Quarneti & Lilian Magalhães, "Body-map Storytelling as a Health Research Methodology: Blurred Lines Creating Clear Pictures," *Forum Qualitative Sozialforschung/Forum: Qualitative Social Research* 19, no. 2 (2018): Art 3. http://dx.doi.org/10.17169/fqs-19.2.2858.

33. Piper et al., "Decommissioning of SASSA Pay Points."

34. Ellis et al., "Autoethnography," 276.

35. Gaventa et al., "Mapping the Outcomes."

36. A copy of the prompts used for these reflections is available on the companion website.

37. Gaventa et al., "Mapping the Outcomes."

17

Can Volunteering on 'Real World' Issues Influence Political Engagement among Young People? A UK Case Study

Mark Charlton and Alasdair Blair

De Montfort University

Political engagement among young people has been lower than other voting groups for several decades. In the United Kingdom, since 2010, the 18–24 age group has received considerable scrutiny in the wake of major political decisions and election outcomes. In light of low political engagement among young people, the government's Electoral Commission has encouraged universities to seek new ways to encourage more young people to vote. Volunteering, which is offered in some form by most UK universities, is recognized through various studies as a way of building social capital and creating civic engagement. This research presents a case study of whether a program of focused volunteering for university students can better enhance participants' political awareness by exposing them to people directly affected by political policies, in this case refugees and migrant communities.

KEYWORDS: Political Participation; Volunteering; Young People; Engagement; Voting.

Introduction

The issue of youth engagement in politics has come to the fore in recent years, notably with regard to levels of engagement in elections. In both the United States (US) and the United Kingdom (UK), young people have been credited with sending President Barack Obama to power in 2009[1] and creating a youth quake that shook up British politics with the election in 2015 of the controversial left wing Labour Party leader Jeremy Corbyn.[2] In both cases, despite the optimism that 18 to 24 year olds were finally getting involved in politics and taking their views to the ballot box, data indicates that the picture was not so clear cut. In the US, young voters only marginally avoided being the lowest turnout group, while Corbyn's much talked about 'youth quake' was far from youthful.[3] While in both cases the political discourse recognized the potential of engaging young people in democracy, research indicates that young people are increasingly less likely to engage in political affairs and vote in elections.[4]

Of the political science literature that has focused on civic and political engagement, a number of studies have analyzed the impact of voter education drives and student participation in political campaigns as methods of increasing voter turnout and political engagement among students. These studies tend, for the most part, to be based on the experience and initiatives of US-based scholars where there is a longer tradition of teaching civic engagement, of which voter education and voter mobilization have received particular interest.[5] Although these studies tend to report on initiatives undertaken at a particular class level to bring the subject of political science to life by bridging theory and practice, a number have also reported on broader campus-wide and multi-campus initiatives.[6] These include celebratory events in the form of festivals that aim to increase political engagement and establish a stronger sense of identity and purpose on campus.[7] Yet, there is less of an established body of literature outside of the US relating to voter education drives on university campuses and the integration of such activities into the teaching classroom. The UK is no exception to this rule. The teaching of academic subjects in the UK follows general principles set in subject benchmark statements written by academic experts and published by the Quality Assurance Agency (QAA) for Higher Education, whose role is to monitor standards and advise on the quality of UK higher education (HE). One impact of this is that UK degrees have less options outside of a specific academic discipline's requirements.[8] This background is important in the context of the wider issue of what should be in a university curriculum, as well as in the context of broader societal changes. The latter includes the move away from structured and often unionized employment, which by nature had a stronger focus on workers' education, to more irregular employment and an expansion in global HE.[9] In the UK there has been a significant expansion in HE in recent years, with undergraduate enrollments increasing from 518,090 in 2010–11 to 611,390 in 2019–20.[10] This expansion in student numbers has been influenced by government "widening participation" initiatives aimed at increasing participation from under-represented, disadvantaged students and removing barriers to accessing and succeeding at university. Since 2019–20, UK HE providers have also been required to publish access and participation plans which indicate how they will improve equality of access for underrepresented groups.[11] These under-represented groups are most likely to be young people from families of low incomes and minority ethnic groups and tend to represent sections of society least likely to vote.[12] The growth in students from under-represented backgrounds therefore presents new opportunities to revisit the public purpose of higher education, including growing politically engaged citizens and impacting areas of low democratic participation at a time when the relevance of higher education to society is frequently being questioned.[13]

Encouraging university students to participate in politics is itself not a novel concept; this has been a responsibility of universities almost since their inception. As far back as the 1820s, US President Thomas Jefferson advocated that a well-educated, informed electorate was essential to a healthy democracy and founded the University of Virginia on that principle. Jefferson's opinion is one that has been endorsed and developed by leading academics like Ernest Boyer and John Dewey, who have influenced teaching and learning methods for many decades. Dewey, like Jefferson, believed education should play a central role in building a strong democracy.[14] Boyer refers to the responsibility to democracy as higher education's "civic mandate."[15] Research also supports this position with findings from a number of studies showing that young people who become civically engaged during their time at university take that learned responsibility with them throughout their life and careers.[16] Universities are widely seen as institutions where students gain experiences and skills that lead to increased levels of political participation.[17] There is also often a societal expectation that the creation of politically engaged voters is expected as part of the core business of higher education, even if this expectation is not always acted upon.[18] Putnam has argued that education is the most powerful tool in growing political engagement.[19]

This chapter seeks to contribute to the literature on the teaching of civic engagement at a global level by reflecting on two projects which were independently undertaken to develop students' experiences of civic engagement at De Montfort University in the UK. De Montfort University is based in the City of Leicester, which at the time of the UK's last recorded census data in 2011 was one of the most ethnically diverse cities in the UK with a 49.5% non-white population.[20] The university's student population directly reflects the broad ethnic mix in the city of Leicester, with just over half of the student body coming from Black, Asian and Minority Ethnic (BAME) groups— who have been identified as less likely to vote. The first project was a political debating initiative that took place in the run-up to the 2017 General Election. This initiative had been designed in response to a request by the Electoral Commission, the UK's independent body to promote public confidence in the democratic process.[21] The second project was a volunteering initiative where students took part in volunteering with refugees.[22] A comparison of the two projects through survey responses and focus group outcomes sheds light on the impact of the two approaches in developing students' understanding of and engagement in politics. In doing so, the chapter adds to the ongoing debate on how to engage young people in politics and the way in which a scaffolded volunteering project can lead to students being more politically engaged.

In recent years there has been a general increase in the number of students participating in volunteering activities in the UK HE sector. This trend has benefited from a policy push with successive governments promoting the agenda through additional funding, accreditations and promotional campaigns.[23] Studies have pointed to the positive outcomes that volunteering brings to individuals and local communities.[24] This includes the positive benefits that volunteering brings to a student's personal development and future employment prospects.[25] But while volunteering can be viewed as having positive benefits for society and a student's education, research indicates that volunteering in and of itself does not lead to a stronger sense of civic purpose. As McCartney has noted, "volunteering can be a one-time event that does not necessarily connect to civic learning, require examining the ideas, structures or relationships that bring the volunteer to act, or include reflection."[26] Holdsworth and Quinn[27] point to concerns that have been raised in the US, that mandatory or pressurized involvement in volunteering activity has the potential to normalize students to social inequalities rather than stimulating political engagement.[28] Given the established viewpoints on the limitations attached to volunteering activity, is it then possible for volunteering to lead to students gaining a stronger understanding and awareness of their civic responsibility?

Universities, Civic Engagement, and Political Participation

Between 2011 and 2017, the UK electorate went to the polls at a national level on three occasions to vote in two general elections (2015 and 2017) and a referendum on membership of the European Union (2016). In each circumstance, the participation of young people aged 18–24 at the ballot box remained lower than that of other voting groups,[29] a situation that has been reflected in most elections in Europe and the US for several decades.[30] In an attempt to increase voter rates among young people, the UK Electoral Commission wrote to every UK university encouraging institutions to undertake initiatives to increase voter participation.[31] Back in 2002 the Electoral Commission identified that engagement among the young had to change, noting that "...unless this generation of young people becomes more civic-minded as they age, the nature of British democracy is likely to become increasingly passive."[32] Such a concern was similarly shared in the UK Government and Parliament, with an Advisory Group on Citizenship being established in 1997, "To provide advice on effective education for citizenship in schools—to include the nature and practices of participation in democracy; the duties, responsibilities and rights of individuals as citizens; and the value to individuals and society of community activity."[33] The final report that was published in September 1998 set out a framework for the introduction of citizenship education in schools.[34] This in turn led to the introduction of citizenship into the National Curriculum for England in September 2002. This meant that all school children aged between 11–16 in the state education sector in England had a statutory right to citizenship education. Yet, this attempt at developing democratic values has not proved to be as successful as was hoped for at the time. While research indicates that students who have taken citizenship education classes were more likely to vote in a previous general election than their counterparts, students who took these classes were also more skeptical with regard to the motivations of politicians.[35] This potentially highlights a lack of clarity with regard to the outcomes of the study, with the research also indicating that it was not possible to establish causality with regard to points such as the impact of teacher training.[36] This is, however, an issue that has been picked-up elsewhere with the House of Lords Select Committee on Citizenship and Civic Engagement commenting in 2018 that the state of citizenship education was poor.[37] This is despite data indicating that "consistent exposure" to citizenship education throughout secondary school can impact a young person's political knowledge and participation.[38] This is in keeping with other studies which emphasize that citizenship education can have positive lasting effects into adulthood.[39]

In writing to universities, the Electoral Commission was not prescriptive as to how they should increase engagement. It was also the case that this was not an entirely new endeavor for universities as many were already working on projects and campaigns to grow political engagement through the likes of registration drives, campus elections and debates.[40] However, the approach by the Electoral Commission was a public acknowledgment of the role that universities could play in grounding future graduates with the appropriate skills for civic life. By the end of the Electoral Commission's letter writing campaign to approximately 160 higher education providers, 76 universities responded with projects and voter drives to encourage the student cohort to register and cast their votes.

Such a public stance regarding the role of universities as civic educators is a more recent area of debate within the UK.[41] Indeed, of the political science literature focused on civic and political engagement, the majority of studies reporting on activities such as voter education drives and student participation in political campaigns, tend to be based on the experience and initiatives of scholars based in the US. While this might in part be a reflection of the fact that there is a longer tradition of teaching civic engagement in the US, it is also a broader reflection of the role that US universities and colleges have in being engaged with their local communities. One direct aspect of this is that there is a more established recognition in the US higher education system, from research-intensive universities to community colleges, of the importance of civic engagement activities structured around programs, civic engagement centers, or specific academic classes. And while there is far from a universal approach to these initiatives within the US, there is a general trend toward developing curricula that provide students with an understanding of, and engagement with, real-world issues through community engagement, including nonprofit organizations.

This contrasts significantly with the UK experience. This is in part influenced by the design of the UK HE system, whereby undergraduate students enroll in a degree program at the outset of their studies that tends to have little in the way of general education classes. The focus on studying a specific subject is reflected in the fact that the standard length for an undergraduate degree in England and Wales is three years, while in Scotland and Northern Ireland it is four years. This distinction is in part shaped by differences in the high school leaving age across the UK nations. The upshot of this is that there is less room for classes on electives like civic education because students tend to have less opportunities to choose classes outside of their own discipline. At a university level, it is also the case that university leaders, and the HE sector in general, have traditionally shown less interest in universities as both a voice for, and an actor engaged in, civic engagement. Where engagement with local communities has taken place, it tends to be typified by engaging with local community activities such as working with museums and galleries, engaging in discussions with local employers, and supporting access to higher education through widening participation initiatives. In this context, activities that increase political engagement or democratic behavior have not necessarily formed part of a university's core business. This is because challenges around improving teaching, student outcomes, and student satisfaction have typically been key areas of activity with university leaders focused on such factors to market themselves vis-à-vis their competitors.[42] In recent years, the most notable change in these discussions has been the intervention of the UPP Foundation, which is a private charity funded by the University Partnerships Programme (UPP) that is one of the UK's leading providers of student accommodation. In 2018-19 the UPP Foundation launched the Civic University Commission to gather evidence on what it means to be a civic university in the 21st century, which in turn led to the publication of a report in February 2019 that identified the need for universities to have a stronger civic focus by, among other factors, establishing a Civic University Agreement with other local civic partners. At the time of this writing, the outcome of these initiatives have still to materialize fully, with universities just starting to turn their attention to this issue after having dedicated the majority of their energies during 2020–21 responding to the COVID-19 pandemic.

Methods

To investigate these issues, we compare the views of a group of students who volunteered to help with a refugee project with those of a similarly sized group which took part in a series of political debates on campus. The research covered the experiences or impacts on #BeTheChange participants who took part in one or more of up to five events between Wednesday, May 3, 2017 and Friday, November 3, 2017. The refugee research covered the experiences or impacts on undergraduates who took part in volunteering with refugees at any time during their academic journey prior to April 2018. Students returning from a volunteering trip to Berlin in April 2018 also took part in a focus group to discuss their work, alongside German relief workers, with refugees, particularly from Syria, who were being resettled in the city. Both groups of students were self-selecting, and thereby not reflective of the whole of the university's student body. Similarly, a pre- and post-test survey was not undertaken to understand the overall change in students' views. While this inevitably attaches limitations to the implications of the findings, the participants were nonetheless asked to consider their views before and after the event, thereby providing some measure of change.

As far as the political debates were concerned, over a six-month period, starting in advance of the 2017 UK general election on Thursday, June 8th, a political engagement campaign called #BeTheChange was established. The title of the campaign was in reference to Mahatma Gandhi's famous quote: "You must be the change you wish to see in the world." The concept of the project was simple; that students and staff could gather together, listen to and debate prominent political issues. As outlined in table 1, each event had its own theme. Timings of the events were not uniform. The launch event was a 24-hour continuous cycle of debate, with hourly themes drawn from the key issues that were likely to form major campaign talking points in the forthcoming election, including immigration, health care and taxation. At that event, students participated based on subjects that they were interested in based on a timetable of activities that were published on the university's website. Other events spanned daytime formats, where students could participate as appropriate. At these events, academics with expertise in specific fields were invited to form panels, typically of five members, including a chair.[43]

Table 1. #BeTheChange Events					
Date	Length	Format	Location	Aims	Approximate attendees
Wednesday May 3 to Thursday May 4, 2017	24-hours	24-hour continuous activity to create a university manifesto.	Outdoors, central area of university campus.	Organic process of harnessing student voice to create a manifesto.	300
Friday May 26, 2017	11am to 3pm	3 x 1-hour debates of manifestos of the three main UK political parties.	Outdoors at Leicester Castle Business School.	To discuss critical issues in the run up to the general election.	50
Tuesday June 6, 2017	11am to 3pm	'The Final Countdown.' Two panel sessions, made up of five academics, and student audience.	Outdoors at Leicester Castle Business School.	To look closely at the final details of the three main political parties manifesto proposals.	50

Table 1. #BeTheChange Events					
Wednesday June 14, 2017	10:30am to 12:30pm	Panel of senior academics, British Embassy representatives and retired diplomats, student audience.	British Embassy, Berlin.	To discuss the impact of Brexit on Britain's future relationship with Europe.	250
Tuesday June 27, 2017	8am to 8pm	12 Hour Be The Change Research Festival on a variety of subjects and relationship with political policy.	Various locations across university campus.	To demonstrate how research relates to society, particularly in the context of political policy.	200
Friday November 3, 2017	12pm to 2pm	'Keep Universities for the Many' – A themed debate about how universities are funded. Panel of students and academics.	Courtroom, Leicester Castle Business School.	To gather opinion on how universities should be funded and gather ideas about how this might be best expressed to policy makers.	50

The selected panels had gender-balance and diversity representation. Students and staff were encouraged to participate via internal communications messages. The launch event promoted the idea that the university would create a manifesto of ideas that could be presented to the three main political parties in advance of the general election. It was felt this would empower students to feel they had a voice and were able to influence the political process. Staff from across all university departments were encouraged to promote the events to students, and also to participate in debates that were relevant to their chosen fields. Food and refreshments were served at regular intervals as another incentive to bring people together. The initial #BeTheChange events ran concurrently with voter registration drives on campus that had previously been launched via a central university communications campaign. Approximately 950 faculty, staff, and students attended the events, although the precise breakdown of attendees was not registered.

As far as the volunteering program was concerned, the university has a long-standing program for students that is widely promoted. The activities are open to everyone and students have the opportunity to choose the type of volunteering they wish to undertake and how long they spend on each project is at their discretion. Participants are encouraged to give a minimum of 12 hours to a project. They receive training, health and safety guidance and a Disclosure and Barring Service (DBS) check to ensure they are safe to work with vulnerable people and children. A variety of opportunities offered to students are often linked to courses. Examples include working with the homeless, activities in local schools, food distribution to the poor, work with refugees and supporting youth clubs. Many of these opportunities are also offered in an overseas context through the university's international student mobility program. Participants in either context were eligible to take part in the research.

To gain insight on the impact of these activities, a quantitative questionnaire was sent to all students who had registered participation in one or more #BeTheChange event and all those who had participated in refugee projects. The choice of using refugee volunteers as participants for the volunteering research was steered by the high-profile political nature of the subject: US President Donald Trump's "Build a Wall" rhetoric to keep out immigrants and the much debated immigration issue during the EU referendum, where the plight of refugees and responsibility to displaced people had received much media coverage in the UK. The data sought to provide a detailed picture of whether either project added any value to universities' initiatives to tackle the ongoing challenge of low voter turnout and which approach could be considered best. The qualitative survey was a key part of generating the data necessary to inform the main findings of this research.

The questionnaire was designed to capture how attitudes toward political engagement had changed by asking participants to reflect on their experiences (see sample survey). The majority of questions were multiple-choice answers, where the participant was required to give an answer chosen from a sliding scale of their experience. Questions reflected the various issues being investigated in a simple and understandable way for the participant, being mindful that some students may have limited political awareness. The questionnaire was distributed via the university's data-gathering software called MyGateway, which is regularly used to track student feedback at the university, and as such students were familiar with the instrument. The data generated was fed into a spreadsheet database enabling the findings to be viewed with ease. Students were incentivized to participate through the chance to win a £50 voucher to spend at a local shopping center. This incentive is typical of such surveys conducted at the university through MyGateway in order to increase response rates. A 10-day deadline was set to complete the questionnaire, with two reminder emails scheduled and sent at day five and day eight in order to pursue a maximum completion rate. Within the questionnaire there was an opportunity for further comments and an opportunity to volunteer for the focus groups.

Results

Be The Change Debate Survey Findings

Precisely 140 students responded to the #BeTheChange survey questionnaire, which was sent to approximately 3,000 students on the university's student volunteering database. Of the recipients, an estimated 400 students were eligible to participate in the survey, according to #BeTheChange attendance figures. The target cohort of 18–24 year-olds, which is widely recognized as the youth vote demographic, was applicable to 86% of responders. A further 10% were in the 25–35 bracket and the remaining 4% were over 35 years old. United Kingdom-based "home" students accounted for 86% of participants. The British Asian demographic formed the dominant group of participants at 78%, which was considerably higher than the proportion of British Asian students in the university in the 2016–17 academic year (23.7%).[44] The gender split was significantly uneven with 74% female compared to 26% male, whereas the gender split in the university was 52% female. Almost a third—29%—said that they had some sort of disability ranging from physical disability to learning difficulties like dyslexia, which was higher than the proportion of students with a declared disability at the time which was 17.4%.[45] While there was good representation from across all university divisions, there were three times as many students from Health and Life Sciences (61 = 43% of respondents) than Technology (18 = 13% of respondents). Elsewhere, 38 students were from Business and Law (27% of respondents) and 22 students from Arts, Design and Humanities (16% of respondents).

Of the participating students, the majority were not a member of a political party (103 = 74%), 62% (87 students) said they were a member of a club or society on or off campus, while 80% (112 students) said that they had previously signed a petition. The latter indicates a higher level of civic engagement than wider society, which was further confirmed by the fact that a majority of students (59%) indicated that they either always or almost always voted in elections, which is considerably higher than established voting patterns (figure 1).

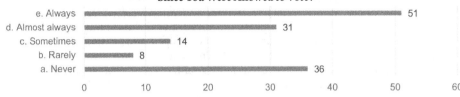

Figure 1. How Frequently Have You Voted in Local and National Elections Since You Were Allowed to Vote?

To gain an understanding of students' engagement with, and understanding of, contemporary events before and after the #BeTheChange events, participants were asked to comment on the extent to which they obtained information from social media, newspapers, radio and television news as research indicates that the changing habits of young people towards social media and away from more traditional sources such as newspapers is linked to a weakening in political participation.[46] Figures 2 and 3 provide students' responses about their engagement with media sources before and after the #BeTheChange events. Although social media remained the dominant

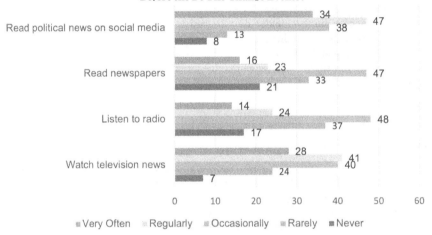

Figure 2. How Often Did You Undertake the Following Activities Before the Be The Change Events?

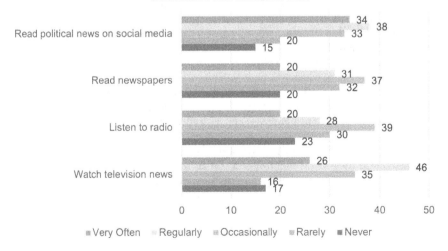

Figure 3. How Often Do You Now Undertake the Following Activities Since the Be The Change Events?

information channel where students got information (58% before and 51% after), there was a shift toward students gaining information from more traditional news channels. Students reported increased engagement with newspapers (28% before and 36% after), radio (27% before and 34% after) and television news (49% before and 51% after) with more students reporting that they very often or regularly accessed these sources after participating in #BeTheChange events. This trend reflects a self-reported shift toward information sources that are generally regarded as having a positive effect on political engagement.

To gain an understanding of students' active engagement in commenting on or sharing political content through online media, they were asked to indicate their levels of engagement over a number of social media platforms. Figures 4 and 5 highlight that while overall students rarely commented or shared political content on social media, there was nonetheless a positive shift towards more students engaging in an active way in political discussions. This was more marked with sharing political content on Facebook, where there was an increase from 19% of students sharing content before the #BeTheChange events to 24% after. While it is hard to draw firm conclusions from such data given the small sample size, the underlying trend was an increase in the number of students willing to comment on and share information related to political issues. A sense of political awakening was also reflected in focus group discussions, where comments included: "The seminars were very enlightening and I have paid attention because politics and finance play a crucial role in our daily lives. Politics plays a crucial role in our lives but most students trivialize the vital

Figure 4. How Often Did You Undertake the Following Activities
Before the Be The Change Events?

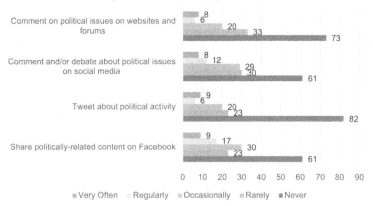

Figure 5. How Often Do You Now Undertake the Following Activities
Since the Be The Change Events?

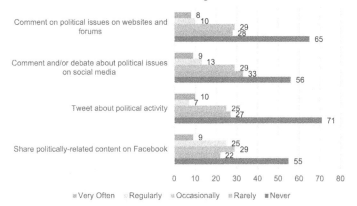

role of engaging in voting as if government policy or initiatives will not impact them in the future."

When asked, "How would you rate the impact of the Be the Change Events on your political participation?," more than a quarter of students regarded that #BeTheChange events were highly or extremely impactful on their political participation based on a Likert rating scale. This finding reflected the follow-up focus group discussions that were held with students, with comments such as, "I have realized to see things change for the better, I need to be a part of it and not just a passive observer. Times are changing and to make them change in a positive way, we need to step in and make a positive difference in some instances in our day to day lives." Finally, there was a 15% increase to 68% in the number of students volunteering on university outreach projects locally or overseas after #BeTheChange events. A potential conclusion from this, therefore, is to highlight that volunteering is not necessarily just a one off activity that students engage in, as is often depicted in the literature.

Refugee Project

From the pool of volunteers for the refugee project, 85 students responded to the survey questionnaire, which was sent to approximately 3,000 students on the university's student volunteering database, but specifically targeted those who had participated on the numerous strands of refugee volunteering opportunities offered by the university's public engagement team. Of the recipients, an estimated 200 students would be eligible to participate in the survey. The target cohort of 18–24 year-olds, which is widely recognized as the youth vote demographic, was applicable to 80% of responders, with the remainder aged 24 years or older. UK-based "'home'" students accounted for 64% of participants. BAME students formed 92% of the cohort. The gender split was again significantly uneven with 77% female versus 23% male. There was good representation from across all university divisions. Most came from Business and Law (41%), 31% from Health and Life Sciences, 16% from Technology, with Arts, Design and Humanities supplying the lowest number of respondents with 8%. Of the responding groups, 20% said they had never voted, while 37% said they always voted. Other responses were 22% almost always, 13% sometimes, 8% rarely. Almost a third of respondents (31%) said they were members of a political party, while 62% said they were members of a club or society.

Following participation, the refugee respondents said attention to political issues grew significantly with those regularly or always showing interest growing by 25%, the equivalent of 21 students in the group surveyed. The number of students discussing political issues with family and friends went up 8%, with the underlying trend being one of positive impact as highlighted in figure 6.

Figure 6. How Much Attention Did (Do) You Pay to Political Issues Before and After Volunteering with Refugees?

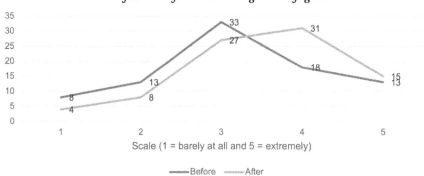

Scale (1 = barely at all and 5 = extremely)

When asked to compare the impact of the volunteering activities with refugees on a range of activities, figures 7 and 8 highlight that there was a general trend towards students having a higher level of engagement in activities that are associated with having a positive impact on political engagement after volunteering. In line with the #BeTheChange data, out of the 85 students who participated in the questionnaire, the number of students watching TV news regularly or very often increased from 52 to 53% (44 to 45 students). The number of students listening to radio news regularly or very often marginally fell from 34 to 33% (29 to 28 students). The number of students reading news via newspapers or newspaper websites regularly or very often increased from 31 to 34% (26 to 29 students). Use of social media to obtain political news increased from 61 to 65% (52 to 55 students) thereby maintaining its overall position as the most popular form of activity. Sharing of political content on Facebook grew from 20 to 22% (17 to 19 students). Tweeting about political activity also grew from 22 to 26% (19 to 22 students). Commenting or debating political issues on

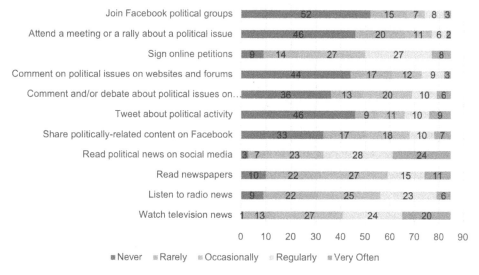

Figure 7. How Often Did You Undertake the Following Activities Before Volunteering with Refugees?

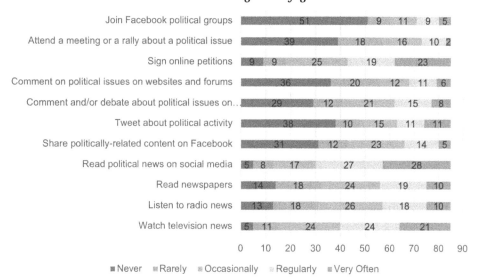

Figure 8. How Often Do You Now Undertake the Following Activities Since Volunteering with Refugees?

social media grew from 19 to 27% (16 to 23 students). Commenting or debating political issues on websites and forums grew from 14 to 20% (12 to 17 students), while signing online petitions increased from 41 to 49% (35 to 42 students). Attending a meeting or rally about a political issue went up from 9 to 14% (8 to 12 students). The number of students joining political groups on platforms such as Facebook grew from 13 to 16% (11 to 14 students). Those using Facebook as a platform for engaging in political content grew from 20 to 22% (17 to 19 students). Although these self-reported behavioral shifts are generally small, they point to increased engagement with political ideas and activities.

Elsewhere, figure 9 highlights that the students indicated a shift toward a more active level of discussion of political issues with their friends and family after volunteering. This data was supported by students' views in focus group discussions. One student commented, "The whole experience has broadened my view on refugees and migrants and gave me a much better understanding of asylum seekers and the difficult situations refugees and migrants face." A focus group made up of six third year BA students studying Business and Law subjects who had participated in a volunteering activity supporting Syrian refugees in Berlin, Germany, took part in a structured interview drawing on some of the outcomes of the surveys and reflecting on their experience. Comments included:

> **Student A**: "If they (other students) volunteered like we did, they would become more aware and actually want to have a say."
>
> **Student B**: "To those students not into politics, a vote is just a vote … I feel a lot more engaged in it (the refugee issue). I do want to know now about it and if there is any more for me to do to help."
>
> **Students C**: "I think the news only shows the first aid people provide to refugees. It never shows the extent to which integration is needed into society to have a normal life there. You won't see that on the news. Their social wellness, their mental health and all that care comes into consideration. For that to happen they need professional people as well as communities to help and that is not in the news. You only see the extreme and this (volunteering) has made me question things a lot more."

While it is hard to draw firm conclusions from a relatively small sample of respondents, the data nonetheless demonstrates a more active level of engagement after the students participated in the volunteering activity. These reflections are in line with the way in which students rated the impact of volunteering with refugees on their political participation. Moreover, figure 10 shows that almost a third (31%) of participants said volunteering with refugees was highly or extremely impactful on their political participation.

Figure 9. How Often Did (Do) You Discuss Political Issues with Your Family and Friends Before and After Volunteering with Refugees?

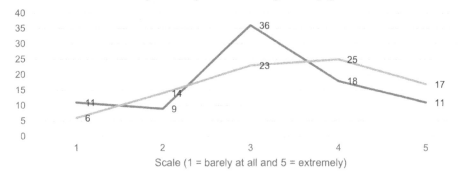

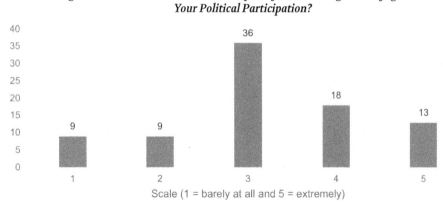

Figure 10. How Would You Rate the Impact of Volunteering with Refugees on Your Political Participation?

Discussion

This research gathered data from two sets of activities focused on two different types of broadly recognized modes of civic participation. Firstly, data was drawn from university activity designed to grow political participation through debating key issues and encouraging students to express their opinions or listen to the views of others in order to form their views and ultimately use this experience to participate in political activity, like voting. The second group took part in volunteering activities with refugees that included English classes and organizing sports sessions that assisted refugees settle into life in the city of Leicester. Such activities could be considered emotive, with students gaining an awareness of the challenges a marginalized group in society faces. This group's activity was designed to enrich their university experience, enhance their CV and give something back to society as part of a wider university volunteering program. This program included organizing community events that focused on arts and sports, as well as offering practical support to students volunteering with the Leicester Race Equality Centre to assist refugees learn employment skills, such as writing a CV, how to search for jobs through IT skills and to gain an understanding of what the job would involve. The latter is particularly important as a result of language and cultural difficulties, given that refugees often come from countries with different customs and practices relating to how a business is run.

In isolation, the results appear to support the premise that both methods of civic engagement have a positive role to play in growing political participation, with a quarter of all students who took part in either activity citing that the experience had significantly impacted their political participation. Elsewhere, there was a small, but nonetheless noticeable, impact in students very often or regularly either attending a meeting or rally about a political issue after participation. For #BeTheChange participants, there was an increase from 5 to 10% of students attending either a meeting or a rally about a political issue. For the volunteering project, there was a broadly similar increase from 9 to 14% of students either attending a meeting or a rally about a political issue. The outcome for #BeTheChange could be a result of experiencing the format of a political debate, which may have given these students confidence to attend other meetings. This is something that could be explored further.

The refugee project volunteers recorded significant outcomes in three areas. First, students paying strong attention to political issues grew by 25%. Second, there was a positive change in the way in which students found information about politics, with an increase in participation across all media outlets with the exception of radio news which only marginally declined by 1%. Third, there was an increase in the number of students recording that they signed online petitions in support of causes. Drawing out the themes of the changes, personal attention and interest were positive growth areas. Finding a voice—an issue explored in the small refugee project volunteers' focus group—grew. Particularly the idea that opinions on issues relating to the volunteering activity could be challenged or argued based on individual experiences. This was also reflected in social media use where material was being shared and commented on. In both cases, forms of expressing political participation grew, particularly through social media use and news consumption through various media. This was also reflected in the qualitative feedback from students. For example, in the #BeTheChange debates, comments from students included, "I have realized, to see things change for the better, I need to be a part of it and not just a passive observer," and "Politics plays a crucial role in our lives but most students trivialize the vital role of engaging in voting as if government policy or initiatives will not impact them in the future." Comments from students on the refugee volunteering project included, "The whole experience has broadened my view on refugees and migrants and gave me a much better understanding on asylum seekers and the difficult situations refugees and migrants face," and "If they (other students) volunteered like we did they would become more aware and actually want to have a say."

A notable outcome of the #BeTheChange political debate was that after the debates, the number of students volunteering for causes through the university's volunteer program went up by 15%. The motivation for this might link to students wanting to express political activism in their own way, which is consistent with earlier literature. The personal backgrounds of students are worthy of further exploration. Prior research documents lower voting rates among young people from Black, Asian, and Ethnic Minority backgrounds—which represent the majority of the university's students. People whose families are from poorer socio-economic groups also are recognized as having low-participation in elections. Future studies are needed to explore such patterns among university students.

Conclusion

The question posed by this chapter was, *Can volunteering on "real world" issues influence political engagement among young people?* From the data gathered in this study, there is evidence that shows a positive shift in attitudes toward politics and attention paid to political issues that seems to exceed more traditional attempts to engage young people in political participation. While the link between civic participation through volunteering or attending political meetings and debates like #BeTheChange and the growth of political participation is not a new idea, the role of how higher education helps to create a civically engaged electorate is under scrutiny. Some argue that this historic role has been eroded by the marketization of higher education and the focus of university leaders on enhancing student experiences and academic outcomes. This is a small-scale study of one university comparing two of its approaches to growing political engagement. Although the students who responded to the survey provide useful data for discussion, the outcomes should be understood in the context of the limitations of a single university case study. However, the data does provide interesting food for thought, particularly in the context of the wider UK HE sector where there has been an increase in the number of students from widening participation backgrounds—who are the least likely to vote—attending university. At the same time, attempts by the Electoral Commission in the UK have had limited success in growing voter engagement among young people through the use of marketing campaigns and voter registration drives. Students participating in both projects report growth of political awareness, voice, and activism. Whether this leads to the voting booth is unknown. In a university context, both projects were viewed by the participants, university staff and student representatives as an extremely positive opportunity to provide students with enhanced levels of civic competencies. Organizations external to the university also viewed the projects in a positive light, from the local council to local charities. At a global level, the university's work in this area also led to it being named by the UN in 2018 as the global hub for Sustainable Development Goal (SDG) 16 to promote peace, justice and strong institutions. Students who took part were self-selecting volunteers—encouraged only by internal promotion within the university—who sought a learning experience outside of the courses required to earn a degree. Attendance on neither project was incentivized with a reward nor contributed to their degree outcome. One immediate option for recognizing student contributions to civic engagement activities would be development of a civic engagement digital badge that could be used as a form of recognition that might positively contribute to raising overall engagement with, and understanding of, the importance of civic engagement education.[47]

While this research does not study why many young people do not vote, it adds to the debate among those in higher education tasked with growing political participation. There is no single defined approach to how universities grow political participation through their teaching, learning, research and extra-curricular activities. Some institutions, by the nature of the young people they attract, may already see high-levels of political engagement, because well educated, middle class young people are more likely to be politically engaged.[48] Other universities, whose intake may typically be from areas reflecting social challenges of high-deprivation or other recognized "widening participation" backgrounds of first-generation undergraduates, Black, Asian, Ethnic Minority and other recognized characteristics may face greater challenges to create a political voice within the cohort. Moreover, broader economic, environmental and political pressures will, among others, likely impact on political engagement in relation to the way in which they consider themselves able to change the status quo. This is an important consideration given the pressures that the present generation of young people have had to face, from the challenges of austerity and war, through to the erosion of the natural environment and the impact of the COVID-19 pandemic.[49] These factors will influence the approach university leaders might need to take to deliver activities that give young people the ability to understand, and get involved in, politics. As universities are regularly asked to encourage young people to become more politically active, identifying the best possible approaches and demonstrating impacts to improve democracy could be a valuable tool in demonstrating the value of higher education in the UK at a time when their role in society is under renewed scrutiny.[50]

Endnotes

1. Glenn L. Starks, "Barack Obama and the Youth Vote," in *How the Obama Presidency Changed the Political Landscape*, eds. Larry J. Walker, F. Erik Brooks and Ramon B. Goings (Santa Barbara: Praegar, 2017), 91.

2. James Sloam, Rakib Ehsan, and Matt Henn, "Youthquake: How and Why Young People Reshaped the Political Landscape in 2017," *Political Insight* (April 2018): 4–8.

3. In the 2015 and 2017 UK general election, the turnout for young voters aged 18–24 was between 40–50%, with the British Election Study concluding that 'there is no evidence of a dramatic change in the relationship between age and turnout between the 2015 and 2017 elections.'; Christopher Prosser, Edward A. Fieldhouse, Jane Green, Jonathan Mello and Geoffrey Evans, "Tremors But No Youthquake: Measuring Change in the Age and Turnout Gradients at the 2015 and 2017 British General Elections", *SSRN* (28 January 2018): 22, https://papers.ssrn.com/sol3/papers.cfm?abstract_id=3111839; Also see Chris Prosser, Ed Fieldhouse, Jane Green, Jon Mellon, and Geoff Evans, "The Myth of the 2017 'Youthquake' Election," *BBC News*, (29 January 2018), https://www.bbc.co.uk/news/uk-politics-42747342.

4. Martin P. Wattenberg, *Is Voting for Young People* 5th edition (Abingdon, UK: Routledge, 2020).

5. Elizabeth A. Bennion, "Civic Education and Citizen Engagement: Mobilizing Voters as a Required Field Experiment," *Journal of Political Science Education* 2, no. 2 (2006): 205–227.; Elizabeth A. Bennion and David W. Nickerson, "I Will Register and Vote if You Show Me How: A Field Experiment Testing Voter Registration in College Classrooms," *PS: Political Science & Politics* 49, no. 4 (2016): 867–871.

6. For example: Elizabeth A. Bennion and David W. Nickerson, "Decreasing Hurdles and Increasing Registration Rates for College Students: An Online Voter Registration Systems Field Experiment," *Political Behavior* (2021), https://doi.org/10.1007/s11109-020-09666-7.

7. Leigh Anne Howard and Brian D. Posler, "Reframing Political Message: Using a Festival to Reach Young Voters," *Journal of Political Science Education* 8, no. 4 (2012): 389–407.

8. For example: Quality Assurance Agency, *Subject Benchmark Statement: Politics and International Relations* (Gloucester, UK: Quality Assurance Agency for Higher Education, 2019), https://www.qaa.ac.uk/docs/qaa/subject-benchmark-statements/subject-benchmark-statement-politics-and-international-relations.pdf?sfvrsn=73e2cb81_5.

9. For example: Nick Bernards, *The Global Governance of Precarity: Primitive Accumulation and the Politics of Irregular Work* (Abingdon, UK: Routledge, 2018); Philip G. Altbach, Liz Reisberg, and Laura E. Rumbley, *Trends in Global Higher Education: Tracking an Academic Revolution* (Paris: UNESCO, 2010).

10. HESA, *Higher Education Student Statistics: UK, 2019/20,* (27 January 2021), https://www.hesa.ac.uk/news/27-01-2021/sb258-higher-education-student-statistics.

11. OFS, *Access and Participation Plans,* (2018), https://www.officeforstudents.org.uk/advice-and-guidance/promoting-equal-opportunities/access-and-participation-plans/.; Also see De Montfort University, *Access and Participation Plan 2020–21 to 2024–25* (Leicester, UK: De Montfort University, 2021), https://www.dmu.ac.uk/documents/university-governance/access-participation-plan-2020-2025.pdf.

12. Elise Uberoi and Neil Johnston, "Political Disengagement in the UK: Who is Disengaged?" *House of Commons Library Briefing Paper,* CBP-7501, (25 February 2021), https://commonslibrary.parliament.uk/research-briefings/cbp-7501/.

13. Ellen Hazelkorn, "Is the Public Good Role of Higher Education Under Attack," *International Higher Education* 91 (2017): 2–3.

14. John Dewey, *Democracy and Education: An Introduction to the Philosophy of Education* (New York: The Free Press, 2016).

15. Ernest L. Boyer, "The Scholarship of Engagement," *Journal of Public Service & Outreach* 1, no.1 (1996): 16.

16. For example: David E. Campbell, "What is Education's Impact on Civic and Social Engagement?" in *Measuring the Effects of Education on Health and Civic Engagement: Proceedings of the Copenhagen Symposium* (Paris: OECD Publishing, 2006), 25–126.; David Watson, Robert Hollister, Susan E. Stroud, and Elizabeth Babcock, *The Engaged University: International Perspectives on Civic Engagement* (London: Routledge, 2011).

17. For example: Adam J. Berinsky and Gabriel S. Lenz, "Education and Political Participation: Exploring the Causal Link," *Political Behavior* 33, no. 3 (2011): 357–373; Mikael Persson, "Education and Political Participation," *British Journal of Political Science* 45, no. 3 (2013): 689–703.

18. Andrew J. Perrin and Alanna Gillis, "How College Makes Citizens: Higher Education Experiences and Political Engagement," *Socius: Sociological Research for a Dynamic World* 5 (2019): 1–16.

19. Robert D. Putnam, "Bowling Alone: America's Declining Social Capital," *Journal of Democracy* 6, no.1 (1995): 65–78.

20. BBC, "Census 2011: Leicester 'Most Ethnically Diverse' in Region," *BBC,* (12 December 2012), https://www.bbc.co.uk/news/uk-england-leicestershire-20678326.

21. De Montfort University, *Be the Change Will Spark Student Debate,* (26 April 2017), https://www.dmu.ac.uk/about-dmu/news/2017/april/be-the-change-will-spark.aspx.

22. De Montfort University, *DMU Takes the World Lead on Refugee Support,* https://www.dmu.ac.uk/community/public-engagement/join-together.aspx.

23. Clare Holdsworth and Jocey Quinn, "Student Volunteering in English Higher Education," *Studies in Higher Education* 35, no. 1 (2010): 113–127.

24. Georgina Brewis and Clare Holdsworth, "University Support for Student Volunteering in England: Historical Development and Contemporary Value," *Journal of Academic Ethics* 9, no. 2 (2011): 165–176.

25. Clare Holdsworth, "Why Volunteer? Understanding Motivations for Student Volunteering," *British Journal of Educational Studies* 58, no. 4 (2010): 421–437.

26. Alison Rios Millett McCartney, "Introduction," in *Teaching Civic Engagement Across the Disciplines,* ed. Elizabeth C. Matto, Alison Rios Millett McCartney, Elizabeth A. Bennion and Dick Simpson (Washington DC: American Political Science Association, 2017): 5.

27. Holdsworth and Quinn.

28. For example: Sam Marullo and Bob Edwards, "From Charity to Justice: The Potential of University-Community Collaboration for Social Change," *American Behavioral Scientist* 43, no. 5 (2000): 895–912.

29. Gideon Skinner and Glenn Gottfried, "How Britain Voted in the 2016 EU Referendum," *Ipsos MORI,* September 5, 2016, https://www.ipsos.com/ipsos-mori/en-uk/how-britain-voted-2016-eu-referendum.; Gideon Skinner, "How Britain Voted in 2015," *Ipsos MORI,* https://www.ipsos.com/ipsos-mori/en-uk/how-britain-voted-2015.

30. International Institute for Democracy and Electoral Assistance, *Youth Voter Participation: Involving Today's Young in Tomorrow's Democracy* (IDEA, Stockholm, 1999), https://www.idea.int/publications/catalogue/youth-voter-participation-involving-todays-young-tomorrows-democracy.

31. Harriet Swain, "Roll Up! Universities Embark on Big Push to Boost Student Vote," *The Guardian,* (9 May 2017), https://www.theguardian.com/education/2017/may/09/universities-boost-student-vote-general-election.

32. The Electoral Commission, *Voter Engagement and Young People* (London: The Electoral Commission, 2002): 7, https://www.electoralcommission.org.uk/sites/default/files/electoral_commission_pdf_file/youngpplvoting_6597-6188_E_N_S_W_.pdf.

33. Bernard Crick, Advisory Group on Education for Citizenship and the Teaching of Democracy in Schools, *Education*

for Citizenship and the Teaching of Democracy in Schools. Final Report of the Advisory Group on Citizenship (London: Qualifications and Curriculum Authority,1998): 4, https://dera.ioe.ac.uk/4385/1/crickreport1998.pdf.

34. Ibid.

35. Ana Isabel Pontes, Matt Henn, and Mark D. Griffiths, "Youth Political (Dis)engagement and the Need for Citizenship Education: Encouraging Young People's Civic and Political Participation through the Curriculum," *Education, Citizenship and Social Justice* 14, no. 1 (2019): 11–13.

36. Ibid, 14.

37. House of Lords, *The Ties that Bind: Citizenship and Civic Engagement in the 21ˢᵗ Century.* House of Lords Select Committee on Citizenship and Civic Engagement, HL paper 118. 12 (London: House of Lords, 2018), https://publications. parliament.uk/pa/ld201719/ldselect/ldcitizen/118/118.pdf.

38. For example: Avril Keating, David Kerr, Thomas Benton, Ellie Mundy, and Joana Lopes, *Citizenship Education in England 2001–2010: Young People's Practices and Prospects for the Future: The Eighth and Final Report from Citizenship Education Longitudinal Study (CELS).* Research Report DFE-RR059. (London: Department of Education, 2010), https://assets. publishing.service.gov.uk/government/uploads/system/uploads/attachment_data/file/181797/DFE-RR059.pdf; Paul Whiteley, "Does Citizenship Education Work? Evidence from a Decade of Citizenship Education in Secondary Schools in England," *Parliamentary Affairs* 67, no. 3 (2014): 513–535; Jon Tonge, Andrew Mycock and Bob Jeffery, "Does Citizenship Education Make Young People Better-Engaged Citizens?" *Political Studies* 60, no. 3 (2012): 578–2012.

39. Michael X. Delli Carpini, "Age and History: Generations and Sociopolitical Change," in *Political Learning in Adulthood: A Sourcebook of Theory and Research*, ed. Roberta S. Sigel, 11–55 (Chicago, IL: University of Chicago Press, 1989); Daniel A. McFarland and Reuben J. Thomas, "Bowling Young: How Youth Voluntary Associations Influence Adult Political Participation," *American Sociological Review* 71, no. 3 (2006): 401–425; Avril Keating and Jan Germen Janmaat, "Education Through Citizenship at School: Do School Activities Have a Lasting Impact on Youth Political Engagement," *Parliamentary Affairs* 69, no. 2 (2016): 409–429.

40. Charlotte J. Snelling, "Young People and Electoral Registration in the UK: Examining Local Activities to Maximise Youth Registration," *Parliamentary Affairs* 69, no. 3 (2016): 663–685.

41. Notable exceptions include: John Annette, "'Active Learning for Active Citizenship': Democratic Citizenship and Lifelong Learning," *Education, Citizenship and Social Justice* 4, no. 2 (2009): 149–160.; Tonge, Mycock and Jeffery.

42. Roger Brown and Helen Carasso, *Everything for Sale? The Marketisation of UK Higher Education* (London: Routledge, 2013); Paul Temple, Claire Callender, Lyn Grove and Natasha Kersh, "Managing the Student Experience in English Higher Education: Differing Responses to Market Pressures," *London Review of Education* 14, no. 1 (2016): 33–46.

43. For example: De Montfort University, *DMU Launches First Be The Change Festival*, (23 June 2017), https://www.dmu.ac.uk/about-dmu/news/2017/june/dmu-launches-first-be-the-change-research-festival.aspx.

44. De Montfort University, *Access and Participation Plan 2020–21 to 2024–25* (Leicester: De Montfort University, 2021), 2, https://www.dmu.ac.uk/documents/university-governance/access-participation-plan-2020-2025.pdf.

45. Ibid, 6.

46. Wattenberg, 2020.

47. The idea of a digital badge is not a new one for the promotion of civic engagement. However, there appears to have been little take-up for this and the time might now be ripe to reconsider the adoption of a digital badge given their increasing prominence of use. See: Circle, *Civics, Digital Badges, and Alternative Assessments*, (27 March 2013), https://circle.tufts.edu/latest-research/civics-digital-badges-and-alternative-assessments.

48. Matt Henn and Nick Foard, "Social Differentiation in Young People's Political Participation: The Impact of Social and Educational Factors on Youth Political Engagement in Britain," *Journal of Youth Studies* 17, no. 3 (2014): 360–380.

49. For example: James Hart and Matt Henn, "Neoliberalism and the Unfolding Patterns of Young People's Political Engagement and Political Participation in Contemporary Britain," *Societies* 7, no. 4 (2017): 33.

50. Research ethics approval for this research was provided by De Montfort University.

A Call to Global Action

Introduction

Alison Rios Millett McCartney[1] and Elizabeth C. Matto[2]

1. Towson University; 2. Eagleton Institute of Politics, Rutgers University

This book has presented a sampling of how higher education institutions are working to advance civic engagement education inside and outside the classroom, across their campuses, and within their communities around the world. Dedicated educators have demonstrated innovative pathways to reclaiming the civic mission of our institutions as part of our societies' goals to continually rebuild and maintain our democracies and our rights. We are following Saltmarsh and Hartley's challenge 10 years ago to "reorient... the work from a vague emphasis on community involvement toward an agenda that seeks significant societal change [and] ...link[s] the pursuit of knowledge with the pursuit of a healthier society and a stronger, more robust democracy."[1] Still, there are problems, new developments, and structural barriers to the progress that this book and those before it have sought to overcome and signs that we are at a crossroads where we can decide to invest in a better future for all.

At a global level, one of the most notable developments has been a restriction in democratic freedoms as a result of the way that governments respond to major international disasters such as the global pandemic of coronavirus disease 2019 (COVID-19). Although a notable and understandable feature of the pandemic was the withdrawal of civil liberties through such public health measures as the enforcement of lockdowns, social distancing, the wearing of protective face masks, and travel bans, it also highlighted a broader trend towards intolerance, incivility, and censorship of viewpoints.[2] Some of this intolerance is related to long-standing religious differences which have at times been activated from simmering resentments and debates, while political intolerance, including a lack of listening to and respecting other peaceful viewpoints, has skyrocketed around the world, spurred by leaders with authoritarian tendencies.[3]

Domestically, as many authors throughout the book have noted, societies also face reckonings regarding ongoing racism, and ethnic and gender discrimination prevent these countries and their people from fulfilling their ideals of inclusive opportunities and respect for all members. If all of the people cannot fulfill their potential, then they cannot contribute their best to their societies and their own lives, needs which are crucial to achieving a peaceful and productive democracy. Civic engagement education is a vital means to address these and other problems because, when done properly, it provides a strong platform for all citizens to build the knowledge, skills, values, and sense of efficacy throughout their formative years that they need to become lifelong, participating members of well-functioning democratic communities.[4]

A misperception about civic engagement education is that it is too expensive to provide at a moment where countries are experiencing economic hardship.[5] *Teaching Civic Engagement: From Student to Active Citizen, Teaching Civic Engagement Across the Disciplines,* and now *Teaching Civic Engagement Globally* demonstrate how this is not the case at any level of education. Further, these books provide examples of how civic engagement education can work at all types of institutions, in all majors, with traditional and non-traditional age students, with students from a wide variety of socioeconomic backgrounds, and with students who hold varying political viewpoints. This book takes us a step further by also demonstrating that civic engagement education can work in many cultural and political contexts. It is appropriate at this juncture to discuss challenges and important considerations as we proceed on a path to even better outcomes for more people.

First, we need to expand the pedagogical tools for advancing civic engagement education. There is evidence that gamification, or using games to teach civic engagement skills and civic information literacy and inculcate civic engagement values, can be effective with secondary school and college students, especially those who start with the lowest levels of political knowledge and experiences.[6] Teaching technology is rapidly advancing. The COVID-19 pandemic prompted numerous adaptations to civic engagement education, even amidst contentious political times in many countries, as a few of the chapters in Section Two explore.

We are just beginning to learn about the effectiveness of these changes and whether or not outcomes include useful lessons for improving future civic engagement education.[7] We also can learn more about how to best construct and the impact of undergraduate research projects, such as the project featured in Chapter 16, on fostering skills, confidence, and student knowledge about their local, national, and global communities and the interactions between them, whether these projects are student-designed, faculty-designed, or part of an undergraduate research experience program.[8] Service-learning is a high-impact pedagogy for civic engagement education, as it puts students in the position of learning by working with and within communities and testing in person many of the theories, ideas, and concepts learned in the classroom. Plus, it provides students with an opportunity to explore their own and others' personal assumptions which may impact policies, processes, and institutions.[9] Finally, "community action learning," such as that discussed in Chapter 14, builds upon traditional classroom education by connecting participatory action research, project-based learning, and service-learning, meaning developing firsthand knowledge of community problems, practicing research, critical thinking, and presentation skills to dissect the sources of and potential solutions to these problems, exposing the value of this work, and inculcating the confidence to be an active participant and community problem-solver.[10] All of these tools can increase the likelihood of current and future civic engagement and leadership capacity.[11]

Second, we need to help students work on the skill of deliberation in civic engagement courses, activities, events, and programs.[12] As Longo, Manosevitch, and Shaffer explain, "[d]eliberative pedagogy integrates deliberative processes of working through issues with teaching, learning, and engagement—inside the classroom as well as in community settings."[13] It breaks from expert-driven models, or "sage on the stage" teaching, to invite students as full participants in a learning process of talking out ideas and perspectives that can become an inclusive basis for public action.[14] Beginning from a place of listening and respect, this pedagogy can help students build a sense of their roles in the "we" of our countries' futures, a value that is integral to democracy's success and is highlighted in the chapters in this section and elsewhere throughout the book. A diversity of voices equally heard in a context of respect and peaceful deliberation is a hallmark of democratic civic engagement. In order for that context to grow and flourish, we must create classroom cultures of empathy at all levels of education and help students to learn about and appreciate differences, communicate within and across cultures, and see all aspects of life from a variety of perspectives and experiences.[15] In Chapter 12, Webster offers a more inclusive model for global civic engagement that focuses upon communities' unique perspectives, histories, and narratives to enhance critical teaching and learning.

Deliberation has many facets, and there are many pathways to deliberative pedagogy. Practicing civility is a core part of deliberation. While civility can be misunderstood as political centrism or censorship, civility instead means politeness, respect, and responsiveness. Boatright (2019) adds that "it is entirely possible to be civil in discourse yet firmly committed to an ideological agenda... [and] civility can be an integral and effective part of articulating disagreements within the political status quo."[16] Easily accessible tools for deliberation include the National Student Issues Convention,[17] which can be adopted anywhere with cultural adaptations as needed. As the world is increasingly globalized, citizens need to practice civil deliberation to better understand the backgrounds, needs, and viewpoints of those in other countries with different cultures if we are to solve our common problems, and as we have repeatedly mentioned throughout this book, civic engagement education is incomplete without this global component.

In addition to deliberative pedagogy, simulations can help to build empathy and the ability to navigate through diverse and complex contexts regardless of where a student's institution is located and should also be prominent in the civic engagement education toolbox.[18] In fact, Chapter 8 highlights a simulation situated in Russia, suggesting the pedagogical possibilities of simulations even in less democratic contexts. New research into options such as "contemplative pedagogy," which uses mindfulness practices to enhance concentration and one's emotional capacity for thinking and the social context of learning could help educators to improve civic deliberation and students' sense of political efficacy.[19]

However, effective deliberation and building efficacy, as with other aspects of civic engagement education, face obstacles, such as the lack of inclusive atmospheres in some classrooms, co-curricular activities, and community situations, where women and people of color are not given the same opportunities to participate in actual situations. Chapter 1 by Ortbals et al. proposes techniques to counteract these potential influences, and Poloni-Staudinger and Strachan (2020) remind us that now is the best time for educators to confront this reality precisely because democratic structures, processes, and values are under threat. [20] This is the case in established, newly established, and less liberal democracies, while emerging democratic practices in authoritarian states are also under threat.[21]

Meanwhile, as access to college expands to more people, educators and administrators face a wider range of students' knowledge and skills when they enter college, which means that in addition to providing a welcoming community which supports diversity, we also must address what Beaumont (2013) terms the "democratic achievement gap." Some students come from the "political haves" situation, meaning higher socioeconomic status and homes which encouraged political participation through examples of politically engaged role models, while others enter college with lower political interest and experience with political engagement. Indeed, all colleges and universities are increasingly concerned about academic achievement gaps.[22] But as Strachan (2015) reminds us, fostering student learning and student success is complementary to civic engagement education in all types of institutions because civic engagement education simultaneously activates both academic success and citizenship.[23] Thus, we should consider civic engagement education as part of our institutions' plans for completion rates and success in public and private life after college. As Allen (2016) writes, "education itself—a practice of human development—has, intrinsic to the practice, important contributions to make to the cultivation of political and social equality, and to the emergence of fair economic orders."[24] She proposes that as we pursue these other educational goals, we "routinely leave out the civic," and when our educational plans lack the "civic," we are left without citizens with the "participatory readiness" that our societies need to address all types of issues.[25]

Third, critical thinking pedagogy is another important component of civic engagement education because it involves students learning the ability for and importance of questioning facts given to them, their own and others' perspectives and implicit biases, and fundamental assumptions that one may bring to any problem or discussion.[26] As such, critical thinking helps us to develop better policies, processes, and institutions for the benefit of all. Teacher-scholars have demonstrated that civic engagement education is neither political indoctrination nor an attempt to promote partisan viewpoints,[27] in part because doing so would be contrary to the very democratic principles, such as questioning, that civic engagement education promotes. Thus, critical thinking is a fundamental part of a citizen's ability to participate constructively in a democracy and a foundation of civic engagement education. In fact, critical thinking offers the populace an important tool for holding government accountable, and as Berthin shows in Chapter 9, pedagogical interventions can be a beneficial way of teaching young adults how to hold officials accountable.

To better pursue critical thinking, we must include information literacy in civic engagement education. Several recent articles have explored the significance of understanding where students get their information from and how they process and convey this information. Between the rise of social media as a dominant format, polarization and in some cases disenchantment with major news outlets, and the popularity of comedy talk-shows, we must consider whether the increase in cynicism and decrease in trust in government, particularly amongst youth, are consequences of a lack of a strong foundation in knowledge about government laws, processes, and institutions coupled with a lack of basic information literacy.[28] Further, we need to consider how gaps in access to rapidly evolving technology can exacerbate structural inequalities, citizen distrust and dissatisfaction, and discrimination, even as these technology-based options for citizen engagement with their leaders and government offices increase.[29] We also must ensure that our civic engagement education options do not fall into these gaps when extending such pedagogy across the globe.

As part of civic engagement information literacy, we need to push students to develop all types of data analysis skills, as they must be able to evaluate, for example, both the proposed outcomes of polling data and a leader's oratorical use of this data.[30] In addition, information is increasingly processed visually, starting with the advent of the television era but evolving rapidly with social media, and as such, we should push students to consider how visually-transmitted information communicates political and social messages as part of critical thinking skills needed for citizenship.[31]

As *Teaching Civic Engagement Across the Disciplines* (2017) extols, we must provide a space for effective civic engagement education in all majors. Chapter 6 even offers a model of how to include the arts in such instruction. All students should learn how they can bring the specific knowledge and skills from their disciplines to contribute to their communities. Within political science, there are calls to consider civic engagement education as a core part of the major as the discipline "rediscover[s] its roots in promoting civic and political involvement, bolstered by a vibrant scholarship of engagement."[32] Bernstein refers to this as a fundamental mission of the major, or a "citizenship imperative."[33] Next, we need to give more attention to thoughtfully designing, supporting, and enacting innovative practices throughout higher education, such as on-campus learning communities discussed by McTague (2017) and the placement of civic engagement in the university core curriculum proposed by Huerta and Jozwiak (2008). These practices can help us to reach more students and create a ladder of civic engagement education as is asserted in Section II so that the students who get one or more civic engagement learning experiences are not the lucky few.[34] We also cannot neglect the co-curricular realm, both in what types of civic engagement learning activities and events we support and our need to continually ensure that these are achieving their goals for students and their communities.[35]

To better understand the outcomes of these efforts, we also need resources to support research on longitudinal outcomes at all types of institutions. Battistoni (2019), Harriger et al (2017), and McCartney, Chaban, and Rice (2018) have started us on this path of longitudinal studies, but we also need more extensive studies and cross-institutional studies to better understand what aspects and tools of civic engagement education are and are not working in developing long-term civic engagement after college.[36] Good starts on this type of work are being pursued by programs such as Brandeis University's Educational Network for Active Civic Transformation (ENACT),[37] but we need programs which cover more countries and that can engage cross-national comparisons to develop high-quality scholarship of teaching and learning.

Finally, as discussed in the section I Introduction, in the two previous books, and in this last section of *Teaching Civic Engagement Globally*, we need to work in civic engagement activities with our primary and all types of secondary schools, with those who are training our teachers, and with those such as the Educating for Democracy project who are writing the materials and promoting reinvestment for civic education at these levels.[38] We should also consider the importance of educating at all levels as some countries have or are considering lowering their voting ages to age 16.[39] If we do not engage students at all levels and participate in the construction and content of civic engagement education at all levels, we are either forfeiting to others the opportunity to help to develop quality civic learning which must be built over time like all other skills and knowledge, or we are simply forfeiting our democracies' futures. This future depends on citizens who can work at local, national, and global levels[40] to confront our problems and build sustainable solutions to protect the rights of all and bring opportunities for peace, prosperity, and healthy, happy lives to people around the world.

In no small part, effective instruction in democratic citizenship is a function of educators' preparedness for teaching democratic citizenship. As Diana Owen and Isaac Riddle demonstrated in research published in *Teaching Civic Engagement Across the Disciplines*, high school students who are instructed by teachers who went through "We the People" professional development programs gained more political knowledge on a variety of subjects than those students whose teachers had not received such training.[41] Such training certainly does not end in secondary school. The work of Sarah Surak et al. has shown that faculty development programming at the college level is valuable for ensuring high-quality civic engagement education among university students, and we should increase our civic engagement education training of teachers at all levels.[42]

In Chapter 18 of this section, Benedikt Philipp Kleer and Johannes Diesing from the Department of Political Science at the Justus-Liebig-University Giessen extend this work in their study of a cohort of pre-service teachers in Germany. Recognizing the critical role that teachers of all disciplines play in the political socialization of young adults, Kleer and Diesing's research is focused upon the political knowledge, interest, and attitudes of teachers as they are preparing to teach primary and secondary students. Using a combination of survey research data and data gathered from focus groups, they find that levels of political knowledge and interest levels vary by teachers' subject matter and more alarmingly, that some teachers' survey results show support for authoritarian modes of government modes as well as tepid support for values such as gender equality and free elections. Kleer and Diesing's work underscores the critical role that preparing primary and secondary school teachers to teach democracy plays in the success of civic engagement education.

Of equal importance to high-quality teacher preparation is equity in providing civic engagement instruction. As indicated in the Introduction to Section I, gaps in educational opportunities undermine the health of democracies, and one of the biggest gaps certainly includes education in civic and political engagement. Niina Meriläinen from Tampere University in Finland demonstrates with her research that when civic education is not offered universally, not only do young people lose out on valuable instruction in democratic citizenship, but political discourse lacks the insights which they might provide. As she points out in her research, vocational secondary school students in Finland do not receive the sort of lessons in civic engagement that students who attend academic secondary schools receive. Meriläinen's qualitative research conducted with students enrolled in vocational school indicates that these students feel overlooked in their country's democracy. Although they find other ways to participate in agenda-setting, not only would the political process benefit from equitable political preparation of their younger generations, but democracy would be strengthened as the capacity for participation is widened.

A consistent theme throughout this text has been the possibilities for democracy when high-quality civic education is offered equitably. Without civic education, democracies suffer no matter how seemingly stable they are. Mauritius offers a cautionary tale. *The Washington Post* reports that the Economist Intelligence Unit ranked Mauritius among the 20 most democratic countries in the world in early 2021 but by March, the V-Dem Institute had placed it among the world's 10 most rapidly autocratizing countries.[43] This finding certainly echoes the vignette offered in Chapter 20 by Shantal Kaurooa and Sheetal Sheena Sookrajowa from the University of Mauritius. Their chapter explores challenges faced by educators and researchers who are seeking to strengthen or build stable foundations for democracy in countries with newer democratic systems such as Mauritius and calls for a shared commitment to provide this education for democracy not only in their country but in similarly situated countries globally. Sadly, their calls for concern have proven to be prescient, and as events unfold across the world, we see that their concerns are applicable to a wider range of countries than we would hope.

Our efforts at building and maintaining democracy worldwide thus have only just begun. As such, we end *Teaching Civic Engagement Globally* with a call to action by Dick Simpson from the University of Illinois at Chicago. In his chapter, Simpson uses his own experience in both government service and higher education to explain that we must work with government and private sector actors, across disciplines, and across borders if we are to make the connections, revamp our legislation, and gain the resources which we need for success in these endeavors.[44] His call to action ends with 12 points to guide us in our conversations at our own institutions and with our local, state, national, and international leaders.

Conclusion

To achieve its goals, civic engagement education must be versatile, regularly and widely offered to all, include both formal learning contexts and informal learning contexts, and be as inclusive as possible. In higher education, it must be available to all students in all disciplines at all types of institutions. Hurdles, some of which are inherent to the benefits and pitfalls of democracy, such as the anti-democratic social movements which have arisen around the world aided by social media and spurred by populist leaders, can seem discouraging.[45] Other challenges discussed throughout this book remain, such as systemic racism, ethnic and gender discrimination, inequalities, lack of information literacy and civility, and insufficient resources for all students and educators. This book seeks to show that teacher-scholars around the world are actively confronting these challenges within our societies as well as within our own classrooms and programs, as we know that there is still much work to be done. For if we do not expand and deepen our civic engagement education efforts, we risk losing our societies to the seemingly easy solutions posed by populists and authoritarianism.

As Battistoni and Longo exhort, "democratic-minded practitioners who care deeply about the civic engagement agenda must now focus on putting students at the center of their efforts."[46] They and others propose that we answer Harry Boyte's call for higher education to reclaim its "civic mandate."[47] Together with higher education organizations such as APSA, AAC&U, ECPR, and PSA, civic engagement organizations such as Campus Compact and the Kettering Foundation, and international organizations such as the United Nations, UNICEF, and UNESCO, to name a few, we can and should build a better, more comprehensive toolbox so that teacher-scholars of civic engagement education can fulfill this institutional mandate with a student-centered focus. These concluding chapters help us to navigate these challenges and construct pathways for our future conversations as we work to improve and advance civic engagement education around the world.

Endnotes

1. John Saltmarsh and Matthew Hartley, "To Serve a Larger Purpose," in *"To Serve a Larger Purpose:" Engagement for Democracy and the Transformation of Higher Education,* eds. John Saltmarsh and Matthew Hartley (Philadelphia, PA: Temple University Press, 2011): 1–13. Quote appears on p. 4.

2. The Economist Intelligence Unit, *Democracy Index 2020: In Sickness and in Health?* (London: The Economist Intelligence Unit, 2020): 14–25. https://www.eiu.com/n/campaigns/democracy-index-2020/.

3. The number of articles published on this point in the past six to ten years in particular is so great that it could almost be called countless. The sheer prevalence of this topic provides evidence that it is a common concern. More recently, examples across the world include: Debilynn Molineaux, "Intolerance is the Real Threat to our Democracy: Here's How We Can Fight It Together," *USA Today*, (30 August 2020), https://usatoday.com/story/opinion/2020/08/30/intolerance-not-our-opponents-true-enemy-democracy-column/5655944002/; Abdul Rehman, "Rise of Intolerance: Are We Moving Backwards?" *Modern Diplomacy*, (11 February 2021) https://moderndiplomacy.eu/2021/02/11/rise-of-intolerance-are-we-moving-backwards/; Mazhar Abbas, "Rising Culture of Political Intolerance," *The International News*, (18 June 2021), https://thenews.com.pk/print/851312-rising-culture-of-political-intolerance. See also the Pew Research Study on the topic of "cancel culture." Emily A. Vogels, Monica Anderson, Margaret Porteus, Chris Baronavski, Sara Atske, Colleen McClain, Brooke Auxier, Andrew Perrin, and Meera Ramshankar, "Americans and 'Cancel Culture': Where Some See Accountability, Others see Censorship, Punishment," Pew Research Center, (19 May 2021), https://pewresearch.org/internet/2021/05/19/americans-and-cancel-culture-where-some-see-accountability-others-see-censorship-punishment/.

4. Bobbi Gentry, "Bridging Adolescent Engagement and Adult Engagement: A Theory of Political Identity," in *Teaching Civic Engagement: From Student to Active Citizen*, eds. Alison Rios Millett McCartney, Elizabeth A. Bennion, and Dick Simpson (Washington, DC: American Political Science Association, 2013): 57–72; Matthew Woessner and April Kelly-Woessner, "Why College Students Drift Left: The Stability of Political Identity and Relative Malleability of Issue Positions among College Students," *PS: Political Science & Politics* 53, no. 4 (October 2020): 657–664.

5. Elissa Edmunds, Oreill Henry, and Emily Kovalesky, "Beyond Study Abroad: The Global Nature of Domestic Experiential Learning," *Diversity and Democracy* 22, no. 2/3 (Spring/Summer 2019): 37–39.

6. Dannagal G. Young, Matthew A. Baum, and Duncan Prettyman, "VMobilize: Gamifying Civic Learning and Political Engagement in a Classroom Context," *Journal of Political Science Education* 17, no. 1 (2021): 32–54; Patrick A. Stewart, Elaine Terrell, Alex M. Kareev, Blake Tylar Ellison, and Charini I. Uteaga, "'Gamifying' Online American National Government: Lessons Learned from the First Year of Developing 'Citizenship Quest,'" *Journal of Political Science Education* 16, no. 4 (2020): 508–525; Dominic D. Wells, "You All Made Dank Memes: Using Internet Memes to Promote Critical Thinking," *Journal of Political Science Education* 14, no. 2 (2018): 240–248; Francesca Vassallo, "Teaching Comparative Political Behavior in an Era of Digital Activism," *Journal of Political Science Education* 16, no. 3 (2020): 399–402.

7. Taiyi Sun, "Forced Experimentation: Teaching Civic Engagement Online During COVID-19," *PS: Political Science & Politics* 54, no. 1 (January 2021): 176–178. These two chapters foreshadowed many of the benefits and challenges to online formats for civic engagement learning, Reneé Bukovchik Van Vechten and Anita Chadha, "How Students Talk to Each Other: An Academic Social Networking Project," in McCartney, Bennion, and Simpson (2013): 167–188 and Gina Serignese Woodall and Tara M. Lennon, "Using Twitter to Promote Classroom and Civic Engagement," in *Teaching Civic Engagement Across the Disciplines*, eds. Elizabeth C. Matto, Alison Rios Millett McCartney, Elizabeth A. Bennion, and Dick Simpson (Washington, DC: American Political Science Association, 2017): 135–150. See also Heather K. Evans, "Encouraging Civic Participation through Twitter During (and After) the 2012 Election," in *Civic Education in the Twenty-First Century: A Multidimensional Inquiry*, eds. Michael T. Rogers and Donald M. Gooch (Lanham, MD: Lexington Books, 2015): 145–160.

8. Megan Becker, "Importing the Laboratory Model to the Social Sciences: Prospects for Improving Mentoring of Undergraduate Researchers," *Journal of Political Science Education* 16, no. 2 (2020): 212–224; Alison Rios Millett McCartney with Sivan Chaban, "Bringing the World Home: Effectively Connecting Civic Engagement and International Relations," in McCartney, Bennion, and Simpson (2013): 259–277; Alison Rios Millett McCartney, "Making the World Real: Using a Civic Engagement Course to Bring Home our Global Connections," *Journal of Political Science Education* 2, no. 1 (2006): 113–128.

9. Barbara Jacoby and Associates, *Civic Engagement in Higher Education: Concepts and* Practices (San Francisco: Jossey-Bass 2009); Christine M. Cress, David M. Donahue, and Associates, *Democratic Dilemmas of Teaching Service-Learning: Curricular Strategies for Success* (Sterling, VA: Stylus, 2011); Michelle Lorenzini, "From Active Service to Civic and Political Engagement: Fighting the Problems of Poverty," in McCartney, Bennion, and Simpson (2013): 119–136; Patrick McKinlay, "Political Hermeneutics as Pedagogy: Service-Learning, Political Reflection, and Action," in McCartney, Bennion, and Simpson (2013): 229–246; Laura Hosman and Ginger Jacobs, "From Active Learning to Taking Action: Incorporating Political Context into Project-Based, Interdisciplinary, International Service Learning Courses," *Journal of Political Science Education* 11, no.4 (October 2015): 404–421; Tara Kulkarni and Kimberly Coleman, "Service-Learning in an Environmental Engineering Classroom: Examples, Evaluation, and Recommendations," in Matto et al. (2017): 195–208; McCartney and Chaban, 2013.

10. See Shannon Jenkins, "Using Best Practices and Experience with Local Governments to Increase Political Engagement," in McCartney, Bennion, and Simpson (2013): 107–117; Dari E. Sylvester, "From Policy to Political Efficacy and Engagement: Using Government in Action to Promote Understanding of Public Policy," in McCartney, Bennion, and Simpson (2013): 137–152; Mahalley D. Allen, Sally A. Parker, and Teodora C. DeLorenzo, "Civic Engagement in the Community: Undergraduate Clinical Legal Education," in McCartney, Bennion, and Simpson (2013): 153–166; Susan Dicklitch, "Blending Cognitive, Affective, and Effective Learning in Civic Engagement Courses: The Case of Human Rights-Human Wrongs," in McCartney, Bennion, and Simpson (2013): 247–258; Brandon W. Lenoir, "Issue Advocacy: A Semester-Long Experiential Learning Project," *Journal of Political Science Education* 16, no. 3 (2020): 381–398.

11. Bennion and Laughlin provide an excellent overview of SoTL research regarding civic engagement pedagogy from 2005–2015 in the *Journal of Political Science Education* and is an important starting and reference point for anyone exploring this area. They include a summary of key articles and a table of submissions. Elizabeth A. Bennion and Xander E. Laughlin, "Best Practices in Civic Education: Lessons from the *Journal of Political Science Education*," *Journal of Political Science Education* 14, no. 2 (2018): 287–330.

12. The Kettering Foundation has published several studies on high-quality deliberation pedagogy and should be consulted by anyone seeking to better understand and use this pedagogical tool. Many of their works can be downloaded for free at www.kettering.org.

13. Nicholas V. Longo, Idit Manosevitch, and Timothy J. Shaffer, "Introduction," in Timothy J. Shaffer, Nicholas V. Longo, Idit Manosevitch, and Maxine S. Thomas, eds., *Deliberative Pedagogy: Teaching and Learning for Democratic Engagement* (East Lansing, MI: Michigan State University Press, 2017): xix–xii.

14. This book contains several useful chapters on why and how to foster deliberation across campus. Nicholas V. Longo and Timothy J. Shaffer, *Creating Space for Democracy: A Primer on Dialogue and Deliberation in Higher Education* (Sterling, VA: Stylus Publishing LLC, 2019). See also Nicholas V. Longo, "Deliberative Pedagogy in the Community: Connecting Deliberative Dialogue, Community Engagement, and Democratic Education," *Journal of Public Deliberation* 9, no. 2 (2013): Article 16.

15. Nancy Thomas and Margaret Brower, "Politics 365: Fostering Campus Climates for Student Political Learning and

Engagement," in Matto et al. (2017): 361–374; J. Cherie Strachan. "Deliberative Pedagogy's Feminist Potential: Teaching Our Students to Cultivate a More Inclusive Public Sphere," in Matto et al. (2017): 35–36; Chad Raymond, John Tawa, Gina Marie Tonini, and Sally Gomaa, "Using Experimental Research to Test Instructional Effectiveness: A Case Study," *Journal of Political Science Education* 14, no. 2 (2018): 167–176; Shane Nordyke, Marcheta Lee Wright, Michael Kuchinsky, and Ruth Ediger, "Track Three: Internationalizing the Curriculum I," *PS: Political Science & Politics* 40, no. 3 (2007): 577–578.

16. Robert G. Boatright, "Introduction: A Crisis of Civility?" in *A Crisis of Civility? Political Discourse and Its Discontents*, eds. Robert G. Boatright, Timothy J. Shaffer, Sarah Sobieraj, and Dannagal Goldthwaite Young (New York: Routledge, 2019): 1–5. Quotes appear on p. 3 and 5. This book has several excellent discussions across disciplines regarding civility, defining it, hindrances to it, and how we can pursue it.

17. Anthony Perry, "Practicing Politics: The National Student Issues Conventions," in McCartney, Bennion, and Simpson (2013): 189–202. See also Jean Johnson and Keith Melville, "The National Issues Forums: 'Choicework' as an Indispensable Civic Skill," in Boatright et al. (2019): 140–146. Perry's chapter explores an event for just college students, while Johnson and Melville include college students and a number of community stakeholders. Both are promising endeavors to practice and increase civil deliberation.

18. Monika Oberle, Johanna Leunig, and Sven Ivens, "What Do Students Learn from Political Simulation Games? A Mixed-Method Approach Exploring the Relation between Conceptual and Attitudinal Changes," *European Political Science* 19 (2020) 367–386; Tina M. Zappile, Danile J. Beers, and Chad Raymond, "Promoting Global Empathy and Engagement Through Real-Time Problem-Based Simulation," *International Studies Perspectives* 18, no. 2 (2017): 194–210; Bethany Blackstone and Elizabeth Oldmixon, "Simulating the Legislative Process with LegSim, *Journal of Political Science Education* 16, no. 4 (2020): 526–536; Jeffrey L. Bernstein, "Cultivating Civic Competence: Simulations and Skill-Building in an Introductory Government Class," *Journal of Political Science Education* 4, no. 1 (January 2008): 1–20.

19. Karen T. Liftin, "The Contemplative Pause: Insights for Teaching Politics in Turbulent Times," *Journal of Political Science Education* 16, no. 1 (2020): 57–66.

20. Lori Poloni-Staudinger and J. Cherie Strachan, "TLC Keynote: Democracy is More than a P-Value: Embracing Political Science's Civic Mission through Intersectional Engaged Learning," *PS: Political Science & Politics* 53, no. 3 (2020): 569–574.

21. See for example, Christopher F. Karpowitz, Tali Mendelberg, and Lee Shaker, "Gender Inequality in Deliberative Participation," *American Political Science Review* 106, no. 3 (2012): 533–54; Zhengxu Wang and Weina Dai, "Women's Participation in Rural China: Institutional, Socioeconomic, and Cultural Factors in Jiangsu County," *Governance* 26, no. 1 (January 2013): 91–118.

22. Elizabeth Beaumont, "Political Learning and Democratic Capacities: Some Challenges and Evidence of Promising Approaches," in McCartney, Bennion, and Simpson (2013): 41–55.

23. J. Cherie Strachan, "Student and Civic Engagement: Cultivating the Skills, Efficacy, and Identities that Increase Student Involvement in Learning and in Public Life," in *Handbook on Teaching and Learning in Political Science and International Relations*, eds. John Ishiyama, William J. Miller, and Eszter Simon, eds., (Cheltenham, UK: Edward Elgar Publishing Limited, 2015): 60–73.

24. Danielle Allen, *Education and Equality* (Chicago: University of Chicago Press, 2016): 3.

25. Ibid, 27–50.

26. Jeannie Grussendorf and Natalie C. Rogol, "Reflections on Critical Thinking: Lessons from a Quasi-Experimental Study," *Journal of Political Science Education* 14, no. 2 (2018): 151–166; Wells 2018.

27. Ryan L. Classen and J. Quin Monson, "Does Civic Education Matter? The Power of Long-Term Observation and the Experimental Method," *Journal of Political Science Education* 11, no. 4 (October 2015): 404–421.

28. See for example, Michael Baranowski, "The *Daily Show* vs. the *New York Times*: Comparing Their Effects on Student Political Knowledge and Engagement," *Journal of Political Science Education* 16, no. 3 (2020): 300–313; Meghann R. Dragseth, "Building Student Engagement Through Social Media," *Journal of Political Science Education* 16, no. 2 (2020): 243–256; Rebecca Glazier, "Satire and Efficacy in the Political Science Classroom," *PS: Political Science & Politics* 47, no. 4 (2014): 867–872; Alison Rios Millett McCartney, "The Rise of Populism and Teaching for Democracy: Our Professional Obligations," *European Political Science* 19 (2000): 236–245.

29. Hollie Russon Gilman, "Civic Tech for Urban Collaborative Governance," *PS: Political Science & Politics* 50, no. 3 (2017): 741–750; K. Sabeel Rahman, "From Civic Tech to Civic Capacity: The Case of Citizen Audits," *PS: Political Science & Politics* 50, no. 3 (2017): 751–757; Embracing Digital Democracy: A Call for Building an Online Civic Commons," *PS: Political Science & Politics* 50, no. 3 (2017): 758–763; Carolyn J. Lukensmeyer, "Civic Tech and Public Policy Decision Making," *PS: Political Science & Politics* 50, no. 3 (2017): 764–771.

30. Alexis Leanna Henshaw and Scott R. Meinke, "Data Analysis and Data Visualization as Active Learning in Political Science," *Journal of Political Science Education* 14, no. 4 (2018): 423–439; Sara A. Mehltretter Drury and Jeffrey P.

Mehltretter, "Engagement through the Oval Office: Presidential Rhetoric as Civic Education" in Rogers and Gooch 2015: 161–186.

31. See Hogan and Feeney, Chapter Six; Rasmus Karlsson, "Gallery Walk Seminar: Visualizing the Future of Political Ideologies," *Journal of Political Science Education* 16, no. 1 (2020): 91–100;

32. John Ishiyama, Marjike Breuning, Cameron G. Thies, Reneé Van Vechten, and Sherri L. Wallace, "Rethinking the Undergraduate Political Science Major," *PS: Political Science & Politics* 54, no. 2 (2021): 353–357. Quote appears on p. 354-355. See also Steven Rathgeb Smith and Meghan McConaughey, "The Political Science Major and Its Future: The Wahlke Report- Revisited," *PS: Political Science and Politics* 54, no. 2 (April 2021):358-362; Fletcher McClellan, "Curriculum Theory and the Undergraduate Political Science Major: Toward a Contingency Approach," *PS: Political Science and Politics* 54, no. 2 (2021): 368–372.

33. Jeffrey L. Bernstein, "Introduction: The Citizenship Imperative and the Political Science Research Methods Course," in *Teaching Research Methods in Political Science*, ed. Jeffrey L. Bernstein (Cheltenham, UK, Edward Elgar Publishing Limited: 2021): 1–11.

34. John McTague, "Politically Themed Residential Learning Communities as Incubators of Interest in Government and Politics," in Matto et al. (2017): 247-260; Juan Carlos Huerta, "Do Learning Communities Make a Difference?" *PS: Political Science & Politics* 37, no. 2 (2004): 291–296; Juan Carlos Huerta and Joseph Jozwiak, "Developing Civic Education in General Education Political Science," *Journal of Political Science Education* 4, no. 1 (January 2008): 42–60; Carolyn Forestiere, "Promoting Civic Agency Through Civic Engagement Activities: A Guide for Instructors New to Civic-Engagement Pedagogy," *Journal of Political Science Education* 11, no. 4 (October 2015): 455–471.

35. John Forren, "Partnering with Campus and Community to Promote Civic Engagement: Miami University's Citizenship and Democracy Week," in Matto et al. (2017): 209–214; J. Cherie Strachan and Elizabeth A. Bennion, "New Resources for Civic Engagement: The National Survey of Student Leaders, Campus Associational Life, and the Consortium for Inter-Campus SoTL Research," in Matto et al. (2017): 291–320; Thomas and Brower 2017; Elizabeth A. Bennion, "Moving Forward with Assessment: Important Tips and Resources," in Matto et al. (2017): 347–360; J. Cherie Strachan and Mary Scheuer Senter, "Student Organizations and Civic Education on Campus: The Greek System," in McCartney, Bennion, and Simpson (2013): 385–402; Claire Abernathy and Jennifer Forestal, "Civics Across Campus: Designing Effective Extracurricular Programming," *Journal of Political Science Education* 16, no. 1 (2020): 3–27.

36. Richard M. Battistoni, "Learning Politics by Doing Politics," paper presented at the Teaching and Learning Conference at APSA: Washington, DC, (31 August 2019); Katy J. Harrigerm Jill J. McMillan, Christy M. Buchanan, and Stephanie Gusler, "The Value of Longitudinal Assessment: The Impact of the Democracy Fellows Program," in *Deliberative Pedagogy: Teaching and Learning for Democratic Engagement*, eds. Timothy J. Shaffer, Nicholas V. Longo, Idit Manosevitch, and Maxine S. Thomas (East Lansing, MI: Michigan State University Press, 2017): 179–190; Alison Rios Millett McCartney, Mackenzie Rice, and Sivan Chaban "Does Civic Engagement Education Last? A Longitudinal Case Study," paper presented at the American Political Science Association Teaching and Learning Conference, Baltimore, MD, (2–4 February 2018).

37. Robert W. Glover, Daniel C. Lewis, Richard Meagher, and Katherine A. Owens, "Advocating for Engagement: Do Experiential Learning Courses Boost Civic Engagement," *Journal of Political Science Education*, forthcoming.

38. For examples, see Diana Owen, "The Influence of Civic Education as Electoral Engagement and Voting," in McCartney, Bennion, and Simpson (2013): 313–330; Betty O'Shaughnessy, "High School Students as Election Judges and Campaign Workers," in McCartney, Bennion, and Simpson (2013): 297–312; McCartney 2006; Michael T. Rogers, "The History of Civic Education in Political Science: The Story of a Discipline's Failure to Lead," in Matto et al. (2017): 73–96; David Menefee-Libey, "High School Civics Textbooks: What we Know Versus What We Teach in American Politics and Public Policy," *Journal of Political Science Education* 11, no. 4 (October 2015): 422–441; Educating for American Democracy (EAD), "Educating for American Democracy: Excellence in History and Civics for All Learners," *iCivics*, (2 March 2021), www.educatingforamericandemocracy.org.

39. Niall Guy Michelsen, *Votes at 16: Enfranchisement and the Renewal of American Democracy* (Lanham, MD: Lexington Books, 2020).

40. Note that we are not suggesting that there is some kind of "global citizenship" criteria conferred by an international government wherein some are included and others are excluded. Rather, we adhere to the concepts set forth by Luis Cabrera, which conceives of global citizenship as having a legal dimension based in international law but serves more as a guide for moral action by individuals, states, and international organizations. See Luis Cabrera, *The Practice of Global Citizenship* (Cambridge, UK: Cambridge University Press, 2010).

41. Diana Owen and G. Isaac W. Riddle, "Active Learning and the Acquisition of Political Knowledge in High School," in Matto et al. (2017): 103–121.

42. Sarah Surak, Christopher Jensen, Alison Rios Millett McCartney, and Alexander Pope, "Teaching Faculty to Teach Civic Engagement: Interdisciplinary Models to Facilitate Pedagogical Success," in Matto et al. (2017).

43. Louis Amédée Darga and Suhaylah Peeraullee, "Can Mauritians Save a Democracy in Trouble?" *Washington Post,*

The Monkey Cage, (25 June 2021): https://www.washingtonpost.com/politics/2021/06/25/can-mauritians-save-democracy-trouble/?utm_source=facebook&utm_medium=social&utm_campaign=wp_monkeycage&fbclid=IwAR2q_bg7LuBTEnvEHoSdoJo_Ursk-pXvv6WPEVodVVeNO5tb2Job7gf9wNY

44. See Dick Simpson, *The Good Fight: Life Lessons from a Chicago Progressive*, (Emmaus, PA: Golden Alley Press, 2017).

45. For discussions on this point and some interesting contrasts, see Daron Acemoglu and James A. Robinson, *The Narrow Corridor: States, Societies, and the Fate of Liberty* (New York: Penguin Press, 2019); K. Sabeel Rahman and Hollie Russman Gilman, *Civic Power: Rebuilding American Democracy in an Era of Crisis* (Cambridge, UK: Cambridge University Press, 2019).

46. Richard M. Battistoni and Nicholas V. Longo, "Putting Students at the Center of Civic Engagement," in Saltmarsh and Hartley, (2011): 199–216. Quote on p. 199.

47. Harry C. Boyte, Reinventing Citizenship as Public Work," in *Democracy's Education: Public Work, Citizenship, and the Future of Colleges and Universities*, ed. Harry C. Boyte (Nashville, TN: Vanderbilt University Press, 2015): 1–33.

18

How to Prepare Teachers to Teach Civic Engagement? Insights from a German University

B. Philipp Kleer & Johannes Diesing

Justus-Liebig-University Giessen

Schools and teachers are essential agents of political socialization, even in long-standing developed democracies. A teacher's task is to transfer factual knowledge and nurture support for fundamental political values and interest in politics upon which a democratic classroom relies. To create a democratic classroom, teachers need to be politically interested, knowledgeable, and supportive of fundamental political values. This chapter focuses on the importance of strengthening pre-service teachers' political knowledge, political interest, and support for fundamental political values while studying at universities. Our analysis shows that pre-service teachers differ in their political knowledge and political interest levels depending on their subjects. Furthermore, we show that some support authoritarian government modes and neglect general political values such as gender equality and free elections. For civic education, this result is highly problematic. Our results indicate the need for broader civic education at universities for future teachers.

KEYWORDS: Civic Education; Pre-Service Teachers; Democratic Values; Germany; Beutelsbacher Consensus

---

Introduction

Civic education is an essential facet of political socialization in a democratic system. Political socialization refers to how children and youth learn political values, norms, and behaviors and are influenced by socialization agents such as families, schools, or peers. Schools are essential for this process since attending school is mandatory, and most peer groups emerge in the context of schools. Studies of political support and political culture point out the importance of political socialization during childhood and youth.[1] Schwarzer and Zeglovits showed schools' crucial roles as agents of political information and knowledge in an Austrian youth election study.[2] Young citizens need to learn and understand the norms and values of democracy that guide political interaction within the "common rules" in order to get engaged and involved as democratic citizens.[3] Regrettably, the latest attacks from the far-right in Germany aim to diminish civic education's importance in schools and, particularly, teachers' role in civic education.[4]

Previous research on schoolchildren has shown that teachers have an essential role in nurturing schoolchildren's civic engagement. The way that teachers present civic and social issues matters more than other aspects of teachers' behaviors.[5] As Knowles showed, teachers' values impact how schoolchildren present civic and social issues.[6] Further, Campbell showed that an open classroom climate is positively linked to schoolchildren's knowledge about democratic procedures.[7] According to Hooghe and Dassenville, experiences of an open classroom and collaboration in group projects, in addition to specific civic studies classes, have positive effects on political knowledge.[8] Finally, Owen and Riddle showed that the construction of civic engagement courses matters at these levels, and foremost, an open democratic classroom climate supports nurturing civic engagement.[9] In sum, teachers need political knowledge, political interest, and support for political values to create and sustain a democratic classroom. The perception of teachers and classroom climate influences schoolchildren's engagement. It is necessary to empower pre-service teachers for civic education to strengthen young citizens' civic engagement in the future.

Depending on the level of development of democracy, civic education has different needs and challenges. Even in established democracies, civic education is an essential facet of engaging young citizens. Building upon the nearly 50-year consensus regarding civic education guidelines in Germany, we aim to highlight how crucial civic education is for pre-service teachers to prepare them for their professional roles as socialization agents.

We begin this chapter by introducing the German educational system's fundamental elements, reviewing the relevant literature on political socialization, and outlining our theoretical framework and research questions. Next, we describe the data set that we utilized for our study and the research design. Our survey data gathered from pre-service teachers allows us to analyze their political knowledge, political interest, and support for specific political values. Our analysis is complemented with information gathered at a focus group discussion with teaching staff from various schools. The purpose of the final section is to discuss possible findings on the importance and necessity of civic education for pre-service teachers at universities in established democracies.

Background

Recently, there has been growing interest and even conflict regarding civic education in German schools. The extreme right has focused on teachers who are "politically one-sided" and hold a liberal-democratic viewpoint. These teachers have been reported to websites hosted by the right-wing party *Alternative for Germany,* and teachers were publicly pilloried.[10]

Before exploring the literature on teachers' roles in political socialization and outlining our research questions, it is essential to provide background on the German educational system for teacher training and the particular background of civic education in Germany, the "Beutelsbacher Consensus." As we explain below, the most crucial element of the Beutelsbacher Consensus states that civic education is not only restricted to specific politics or social studies classes; it is instead a general aim of all subjects.

Historically, the states were exclusively responsible for higher education in Germany, which has led to differentiation at the state level.[11] State regulations differ regarding civic education in schools and the requirements for teacher training in the universities.[12] Our research case is a single university in the German state of Hesse, centrally located in Germany. The training of pre-service teachers on all subjects and school levels in Hesse includes two different stages (see figure 1). First, future teachers must study their specific subjects and additional teaching skills at a university or a university of applied sciences.[13] After the first state examination, pre-service teachers attend teacher training in schools as teaching staff members. Subsequently, pre-service teachers have to pass a second state examination before applying to be regular teaching staff. Pre-service teachers are students in both stages before they can officially apply for a teaching position at schools.

This chapter focuses on pre-service teachers in the first stage and their initial levels of political knowledge, political interest, and support for political values before they attend civic studies courses at universities in stage 1. Political science students might be more aware of the need for civic education as a cross-sectional task in schools because they chose to study and teach politics. This intrinsic motivation for politics could lead to higher levels of political interest and political

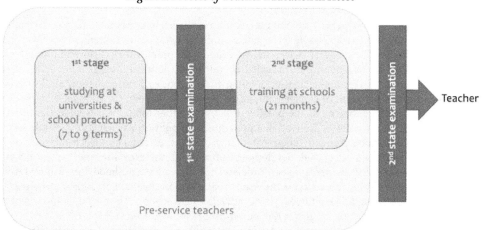

Figure 1. Process of Teacher Education in Hesse

knowledge. To compare the difference between politics and non-politics students, we divided the sample in our analysis.

Despite all of the differentiation resulting from the federal German education system, a set of principles has been the common ground for all civic education in Germany in the last 45 years. In 1976, Germany adopted the Beutelsbacher Consensus, a program that settled a dispute among experts about the foundations and aims of civic education in Germany.[14] Under the Beutelsbacher Consensus, civic education in schools is not restricted to the subject of politics or civic studies classes; it matters in all subjects. Overall, it aims to nurture schoolchildren's ability to analyze a societal or political conflict, their interests, and their capacity to act on their interests.[15]

These goals guide teachers and other practitioners in implementing civic education's general tasks in their teaching. The Beutelsbacher Consensus includes three principles:

1. Teachers should not overwhelm pupils;

2. Teachers should present matters which are controversial in society controversially in the classroom;

3. Teachers should nurture schoolchildren's ability to analyze a societal or political conflict, their own interests, and their capacity to act on their own interests.[16]

All three principles are logically intertwined, and the third principle follows logically from the first and second ones.[17] These principles focus on skills, and the third principle includes the ability to argue about political or societal issues. If teachers seek to nurture the democratic process of arguing, they should create a democratic classroom.

These required elements align with contemporary scholarship regarding civic engagement education, the need for a democratic culture in their classrooms, and educators' professional development, which enables them to create such a culture. To fulfill the aims of the Beutelsbacher Consensus and create a democratic classroom, teachers need to be politically interested and knowledgeable and support a democratic classroom's underlying political values.

Westheimer and Kahne introduced a more internationally known concept of citizenship.[18] They differentiate three groups of citizenship conceptions, (1) personally responsible citizens, (2) participatory citizens, and (3) justice-oriented citizens. Compared to Westheimer and Kahne's conceptions of citizenship, the Beutelsbacher Consensus aimed to create justice-oriented citizens who debate and question (established) systems. Furthermore, the Beutelsbacher Consensus puts weight on the individual's interests. It encourages pluralism since one should develop their interests within the larger political and social arena.

Political knowledge and political interest create an informed background to help people make political decisions and enable people to recognize and articulate political preferences.[19] Political knowledge refers to "the range of factual information about politics that is stored in long-term memory."[20] According to a definition provided by van Deth, political interest is the "degree to which politics arouses a citizen's curiosity."[21] Lupia and Philpot emphasize that political interest is a motivational component of engagement, and it represents a "citizen's willingness to pay attention to political phenomena at the possible expense of other topics."[22] It is widely acknowledged that political interest is a motivational prerequisite of political participation.[23] While some schoolchildren have not accumulated political interest at home, external political influences, such as schools, can positively affect their development of political interest.[24] In a study investigating the development of political interest in early adolescence and young adulthood, Russo and Stattin stated that the "impressionable years are the years of early adolescence, and possibly even before."[25] During early adolescence and childhood, young citizens attend schools. Thus, schools and teachers as socialization agents can have a major role in nurturing political interest.

In civic education, fundamental political values build the foundation of a democratic classroom. Fundamental political values restrict the possible output of the political system and restrict all areas of political interaction to the "common rules."[26] As for socialization agents, pre-service teachers need to support a system's underlying political values positively since they convey these rules and values to create a democratic classroom as teachers. This support's development is mainly based on political socialization processes and one's own experiences with the system.[27]

To date, several studies have investigated the civic education of pre-service teachers. Studies by Castro as well as Kickbusch examined the political knowledge, political interest, and political values of social studies pre-service teachers, and the effects of special teaching programs on the pre-service teachers' political interest levels and support for political values were evaluated. Among others, these studies show that social studies pre-service teachers hold differing understandings of or beliefs about citizenship when they enter the university, which affect their beliefs about civic education.[28] Pre-service teachers who support a conservative-based definition of citizenship focus on classroom rules, build a classroom community, and practice deliberate or cooperative exercises with students. Pre-service teachers who support an awareness-based definition of citizenship focus on individuals' awareness and ability to act in the community.[29] Journell also showed that pre-service teachers differ in their political knowledge levels: they score high on knowledge about governmental institutions and processes but low on parties, political actors, and recent domestic and foreign political issues.[30] In a study of German pre-service politics teachers' different dimensions of knowledge and professional role understanding, Weißeno, Weschenfelder, and Oberle showed that interest in politics is moderately positively correlated to political knowledge.[31]

Westheimer and Kahne examined the effect of two different teaching programs in the US.[32] Although the programs had a different focus (participatory-oriented citizenship vs. justice-oriented citizenship), they showed positive effects of the programs' intended directions: the program focusing on justice-oriented citizenship nurtured students' social critique and social activism, and the program focusing on participatory citizenship enhanced participants' capacities for and commitment to civic participation.[33] In another study, Lake et al. tested the effect of service-learning on pre-service teachers' pedagogical skills and enthusiasm.[34] Hands-on-activities, such as service-learning, had a positive effect and increased pre-service teachers' enthusiasm about the subject. Additionally, Duffin, Ziebarth-Bovill, and Krueger revealed positive effects of a program designed to enhance democratic norms, such as the process of democratic arguing, listening to different perspectives, or acceptance of democratic decisions (by majority rule), on pre-service teachers' support for democratic norms.[35] Fischer, Lange, and Oeftering showed that German politics pre-service teachers emphasize direct-democratic ideals and the acquisition of democratic competencies within their civic studies classes.[36]

In light of recent attacks in Germany and teachers' vital roles during young citizens' political socialization, the relevance of pre-service teachers' civic education needs to be explored and better understood. Much of the literature on democratic classrooms points out the positive influence of such pre-service training on developing political interest, political knowledge, and political values of politics teachers.[37] However, for the general task of civic education, a democratic classroom also matters in non-politics classes. By focusing on a German case, this chapter enhances the research on civic education in developed democracies. It offers a perspective, particularly for non-politics pre-service teachers, based on the background of longstanding civic education experiences operating under the Beutelsbacher Consensus.

The discussion of the Beutelsbacher Consensus, its prerequisites for its goals, and the prerequisites of sustaining a democratic classroom leads us to the following research questions regarding civic education at universities:

1. What are the levels of political knowledge, political interest, and support for political values of pre-service teachers before they attend civic studies courses at German universities?

2. To what extent do preconditions in levels of political knowledge, political interest, and support for political values differ between politics and non-politics pre-service teachers?

3. What problems and challenges do politics teachers highlight regarding the implementation of pre-service teachers' civic education at universities?

In the following section, we present the research design and method before presenting the twofold analysis results.

Research Design and Methods

This study uses quantitative analysis to gain insights into pre-service teachers' levels of political knowledge, political interest, and support for political values (research questions 1 and 2). Additionally, we used qualitative data to gain insights from current teaching staff from various schools to highlight the importance of pre-service teachers' civic education at universities and their challenges (research question 3). By discussing both results in the final section, we highlight the importance and necessity of civic education for pre-service teachers.

The quantitative data comes from a survey of pre-service teachers conducted by colleagues from Justus-Liebig-University Giessen in November 2016 (https://www.uni-giessen.de/fbz/zmi/projekte/emel).[38] The university is a medium-sized regional university with a broad focus on pre-service teachers' education in all school subjects and school levels in the German state of Hesse (https://www.uni-giessen.de/study/courses/teaching). The survey aimed at gaining first insights into political attitudes (e.g., free and fair elections, gender equality), civic engagement (e.g., in political parties, NGOs), media use (e.g., print/online, frequency), and trust in media of pre-service teachers. This chapter focuses on the data from this survey related to political interest, political knowledge, and support for political values.

The target population of this survey was a specific cohort of pre-service teachers at a German university. Pre-service teachers study two to three different subjects (e.g., math, languages, art, or even physical education). They choose between primary schools and different levels of secondary schools. Besides their specific school subjects, pre-service teachers in Hesse must study four basic sciences (*Grundwissenschaften*) (https://www.uni-giessen.de/study/courses/teaching).[39] The four basic sciences should provide pre-service teachers with essential knowledge and skills to fulfill their general tasks in their role as teachers. This category includes courses in educational science, psychology, sociology, and political science. In the basic science political science category, the courses focus on civic education in democratic societies regarding the Beutelsbacher Consensus. Pre-service teachers learn how to link democratic aspects of society to schools and their profession. They study basic science political science in their fifth or sixth term (second last academic year). The survey was conducted within the first weeks of the "Introduction to Civic Education" for pre-service teachers, which all pre-service teachers attend first in the basic science political science sequence.

The survey was administered to those in attendance in basic science (a population of 1209). Due to the moderate attendance regulations in the basic sciences, the response rate is 33%.[40] Overall, the sample consists of 399 completed surveys: 122 male, 244 female, four non-binary, and 29 without an answer on gender. Ninety-five percent of the sample are aged from 18 to 31 years (minimum: 17, maximum: 55). The sample includes 89 politics pre-service teachers and 310 non-politics pre-service teachers. The sample was not randomized and measures the initial levels of pre-service teachers' political knowledge, political interest, and support for political values. It does not evaluate or measure the impact of the actual program.

Notwithstanding this limitation, this survey's use helps us to understand the levels of political knowledge, political interest, and support for political values that pre-service teachers have when they start engaging in their professional roles and general tasks of civic education. As we argued before, in order to meet the criteria of the Beutelsbacher Consensus and provide a democratic classroom, pre-service teachers need political knowledge, political interest, and support for fundamental political values.

Pre-service teachers who chose to teach politics in their futures might be more aware of civic education as a general task in schools. This intrinsic motivation for politics could lead to higher levels of political interest and political knowledge for pre-service teachers who study politics (with any other subjects combined). Furthermore, politics pre-service teachers attended political science courses (4–5 modules, 11–14 courses) before the courses of civic education (basic science political science) start, so there is reason to expect higher political knowledge and political interest levels among these pre-service teachers. To compare the difference between politics and all other pre-service teachers, we divided the sample in our analysis (see figure 2). Pre-service teachers who study politics together with any other subject (e.g., math, art) are in the group of politics pre-service teachers. Pre-service teachers who study any other combination of subjects (e.g., Latin and math or art and music) without politics are non-politics pre-service teachers.

The survey included items measuring political interest, political knowledge, and political values. All variables are at least measured on an ordinal scale. Political interest was measured using a five-point scale from *not at all interested* to *very interested*. Regarding political knowledge, the survey included four items. The index of political knowledge combined two open and two single-choice questions on the survey.[41] Only participants who answered at least three questions were included in the index calculation. Wrong and *do not know* answers were coded as wrong.[42]

The survey included items on support for democracy in general, expert decisions, and a single leader. In studies of democratic support, it is well established to contrast support for democracy in general with statements on alternative (authoritarian) forms of government.[43] The theoretical framework holds that democratic citizens would positively evaluate the democratic form and eval-

Figure 2. Example of Sample Division

politics pre-service teachers			non-politics pre-service teachers		
Student 1 *Politics* *Math*	Student 2 *Art* *Politics*	Student 3 *German* *Politics*	Student 1 *Latin* *Math*	Student 2 *Art* *Music*	Student 3 *German* *French*
Student 4 *French* *English* *Politics*	Student 5 *Chemistry* *Politics* *Biology*	Student n *Politics* *English* *Spanish*	Student 4 *French* *English* *Spanish*	Student 5 *Chemistry* *Physics* *Biology*	Student n *Biology* *Spanish* *Math*

uate all alternative (authoritarian) modes of government negatively. Respondents evaluated the statements on an ordinal four-point scale from *very poor, rather poor, rather good,* to *very good.*

Furthermore, the survey included specific statements and political attitudes that build upon the fundamental political values within a liberal democracy. These items capture individual political value orientations and reference the general political values that an individual wants to see in the political system. These items capture the two distinct overall political values of freedom and equality within a liberal democracy.[44] The items include support for *civil rights, free elections, obedience to the government*, and *gender equality*. Respondents answered the items on a seven-point scale from *disagree completely* (lowest number) to *agree completely* (highest number).

We inspected the variables of interest for our analysis by comparing their distribution within the two relevant groups (politics and non-politics pre-service teachers). We then conducted tests of central tendency to check if the two groups differed significantly. We used unpaired t-tests for all variables on a (pseudo-)metric scale and Wilcoxon rank-sum tests for all variables on an ordinal scale. As argued earlier, differences in political knowledge, political interest, or support for political values might foster differences in teachers' attainment of civic education goals. We would expect those pre-service teachers who have low levels of political knowledge, political interest, or support for fundamental political values to have difficulties in providing a democratic classroom and, thereby, unable to meet the aim of the Beutelsbacher Consensus.

In addition to the survey data, we conducted a focus group discussion with current teaching staff from different schools in Hesse to get initial insights into their recommendations for pre-service teachers' civic education. We used the format of a focus group discussion to engage practitioners in the conversation about teachers' professionalism and why civic education is essential. In doing so, we wanted to counter some potential challenges that might come with such an approach. Focus groups are a valuable form of data collection when a phenomenon under investigation is socially constructed. It is also useful when the researcher wants to know how individuals think and act in social settings, especially when the research topic is sensitive.[45] Educational processes are, per se, socially constructed. Teachers and students engage in a social setting, the school. Research that touches on the professionalism of a given teacher might have sensitive implications for the participants. Focus groups allow participants to take over or own the interview space, which usually results in richer, deeper understandings of whatever is being studied.[46]

The focus group discussion included teaching staff of the subject of politics who teach in primary, secondary, or vocational schools. We chose to invite politics teachers because professional knowledge concerning civic education and its application is a sensitive topic (evaluation of teachers). Non-politics teachers themselves might not indicate their own shortcomings, but their politics peers might do so from observing their colleagues. The teachers varied in work experience (teachers' training, medium or long-term work experience, and nearly retiring teachers). Eleven politics teachers attended the discussion (7 female, 4 male). The focus group discussion was part of an advanced training day for politics teachers who registered voluntarily after a public call.[47]

The focus groups were structured as 30 minutes of discussion in groups of 3–4 persons and then 40 minutes of plenary discussion with all participants. We recorded only the plenary discussion, which was, to a limited extent, moderated. Additionally, the moderator took notes on certain points of interest. Before the small group discussions, we introduced the teachers to the survey mentioned above. In preparation for the plenary discussion, the groups considered and discussed four questions in small groups.[48]

We used the grounded theory methodology following Strauss and Corbin to analyze the focus group discussion's content.[49] After transcribing the audio recording, we started with an open coding to break down the data and delineate concepts in the raw data. We searched for occurrences in which recent teachers emphasized and problematized teachers' general roles in civic education. We then proceeded by axially coding to establish relationships between the concepts. The transcript of the group discussion is available upon request of the authors.

We recognize that this research design has methodological limitations. First, the project used a sample that only includes pre-service teachers of a specific cohort from a single university in

Germany. Generalizations are, therefore, not possible. However, the state of Hesse has the highest number of hours of civic education taught in secondary schools in Germany. Thus, this case can be seen as a vanguard in civic education. The problems and challenges we encountered in this research might be even more pressing in other German states or countries. Second, the group discussion was comparatively short and moderated only to a limited extent. The length of the group discussion may have influenced the depth of the observed conversation. Notwithstanding the limitations, this study enhances research on pre-service teachers and civic engagement education by focusing on a German case.

Pre-Service Teachers' Prior Political Knowledge, Interest, and Support

Our quantitative analysis centered around exploring the political interest, political knowledge, and support for political values of pre-service teachers and the differences between politics and non-politics pre-service teachers. As theorized, given teachers' roles as agents of political socialization, the overall aim of nurturing the development of democratic citizens as proposed in the Beutelsbacher Consensus, and the needs of a democratic classroom, teachers need political knowledge, political interest, and support for fundamental political values.

The figures below show bar plots of the distribution on each survey item of the split sample. Approximately 65% of politics pre-service teachers were medium interested or interested in politics, and 34.8% were very interested in politics (figure 3). Non-politics pre-service teachers showed only little interest: 3.6% were not at all interested in politics, 22.3% were only a little interested, and 51.5% showed medium interest in politics. Only 22.6% were interested or very interested in politics.

| *Figure 3. Political Interest, Frequencies (in Percentages)* | *Figure 4. Political Knowledge, Frequencies (in Percentages)* |

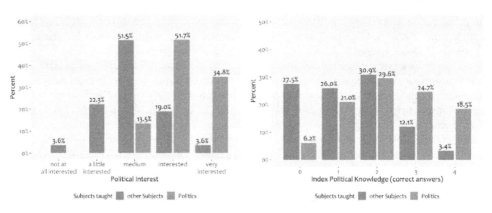

The level of political knowledge differs between pre-service teachers who will teach politics and those who will not teach politics (figure 4). The questions included basic knowledge of voting rights, the year of the constitution's entry into force, and the foreign minister's name, who was one of the most publicly known politicians in Germany. While 72.8% of the politics pre-service teachers answered two or more questions correctly, only 46% of non-politics pre-service teachers managed to do so. Up to 53.5% of non-politics pre-service teachers answered one or fewer questions correctly. Surprisingly, a quarter (27.2%) of the politics pre-service teachers answered one question correctly. This result shows the need to enhance basic contemporary political knowledge in pre-service teachers' education.

Table 1 shows the tests of central tendency between both groups on these survey items. In this use, significant tests only show essential data patterns; due to the sample selection, results cannot be generalized. On average, politics pre-service teachers revealed a higher interest than non-politics pre-service teachers, and they had higher political knowledge than non-politics pre-service teachers do. Both effect sizes are strong between the two groups.

Table 1. Political Interest and Political Knowledge, Comparison of Central Tendency			
Variable	Mean Difference	W-Value / t-value	Cohen's D
Political Interest	1.25***	3780.5	1.55
Political Knowledge	0.91***	-6.3374	0.80
*** p > 0.0001, **p < 0.01, * p < 0.05			

The frequency tables and the central tendency tests show that politics pre-service teachers began with higher levels of political knowledge and political interest. Both are a prerequisite for civic education as a general task. A teacher who is not interested in politics or does not have substantial political knowledge might be less focused on the general aim of civic education.

Regarding support for democratic values, a vast majority of respondents supported the statement that democracy is needed; however, this item's wording limits our complete understanding of this finding. As worded, the question does not specify if it is important for one to live in a democracy or important for all people worldwide (see survey instrument). None in both groups rated this statement as very poor; surprisingly, 2.2% of politics pre-service teachers and 0.3% of non-politics pre-service teachers rejected the necessity of democracy in a country (figure 5).

Furthermore, most in both groups clearly reject the authoritarian notion of a single leader. Around 98% of non-politics pre-service teachers and around 95% of politics pre-service teachers (figure 6) disagreed with the notion of preferring decision-making by a single leader over decision-making in parliament. A few pre-service teachers supported this statement, as 2.5% of non-politics and around 5% of politics pre-service teachers judged this governance mode as *good* or *very good*. This support is a problem: as latent socialization agents, teachers should reject this authoritarian notion. One cannot expect (pre-service) teachers who support this authoritarian notion to fulfill civic education's general pro-democracy task.

Another mode of governance which participants were asked to judge was expert decisions. Participants evaluated how poor or good it would be if experts made decisions about policy issues instead of governments. Although experts' inclusion (especially from science) is fundamental in a democratic decision process, elected representatives, not experts, should make final decisions. More than half of non-politics pre-service teachers supported expert decisions compared to around

Figure 5. "A Country Needs a Democratic System," Frequencies (in Percentages)

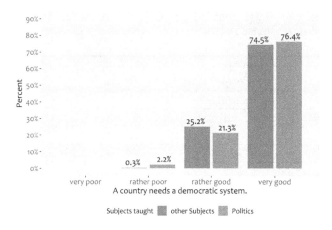

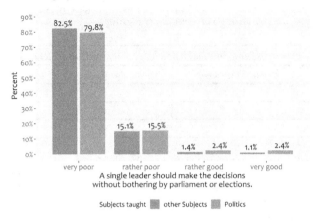

Figure 6. "A Single Leader Should Make the Decisions Without Bothering By Parliament or Elections," Frequencies (in Percentages)

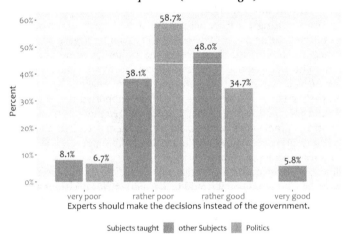

Figure 7. "Experts Should Make the Decisions Instead of the Government," Frequencies (in Percentages)

35% of politics pre-service teachers (*rather good* or *very good*) (figure 7).

Table 2 shows the tests of central tendency for the different governance modes. Pre-service teachers did not differ in support for democracy in general or a single leader–a clear authoritarian mode of government. On average, politics pre-service teachers favored the statement regarding expert decisions slightly less (table 2). However, the effect size is only medium.

Table 2. "Democracy in General", "Expert Decisions," "Single Leader," Comparison of Central Tendency			
Support of ...	Mean Difference	W-Value	Cohen's D
Democracy in General	0.00	13,074	-
Expert Decisions	-0.24**	9949	0.34
Single Leader	0.06	11,606	-
*** p > 0.0001, **p < 0.01, * p < 0.05			

This result is somewhat counterintuitive. Democratic decision-making depends on the process of arguments and the exchange of ideas. This process should hear from scientific experts, social groups, or other agencies. The Beutelsbacher Consensus underlines this component of democratic deliberation and decision-making as a core component of a well-functioning democratic system. Principles 2 and 3 support the idea that schoolchildren learn how to act on arguments and interests. Support for outsourcing political decisions to experts contradicts this principle and the general aim of civic education in schools.

The following figures (figures 8–12) show the distribution of statements regarding fundamental political values such as civic rights, free elections, or gender equality. As seen in figures 8 and 9, it is apparent that the dispersion on the items differs between politics and non-politics pre-service teachers. However, if we compare the total of the positive scale (codings 4 to 6), 93.2% of the politics pre-service teachers and 91.7% of non-politics pre-service teachers supported the idea of civil rights. Regarding free elections, the difference is somewhat higher: around 91% of politics pre-service teachers supported the statement compared to 86.1% of non-politics pre-service teachers. Surprisingly, a small but not insignificant group of persons in both groups disagreed completely or disagreed somewhat (coded 0 to 2) with the idea of free elections (politics: 5.7%, non-politics: 5.4%) and civil rights (politics: 1.1%, non-politics: 2.3%). Both items represent statements referring to fundamental political values of liberal democracy. Disagreeing with these statements is problematic for the task of teachers as political socialization agents in schools.

Figure 8. "Civil Rights Defend Citizens from State Oppression," Frequencies (in Percentages)

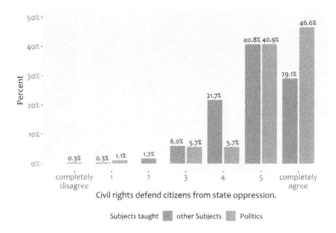

Figure 9. "Citizens Should Vote the Government in Free Elections," Frequencies (in Percentages)

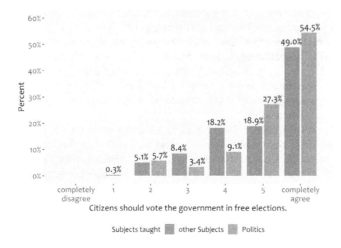

Figure 10. *"Citizens Should Obey Their Government," Frequencies (in Percentages)*

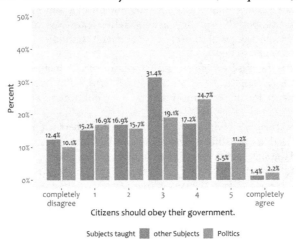

Figure 11. *"Women Should Have the Same Rights as Men," Frequencies (in Percentages)*

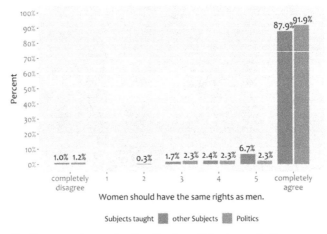

Additionally, figure 10 shows the distribution of the item *obedience towards the government*. Politics pre-service teachers supported this statement slightly more. Around 38% of politics pre-service teachers and a quarter of non-politics pre-service teachers supported this statement (4 to 6). Just 43% of politics pre-service teachers and 45% of non-politics pre-service teachers disagreed with this statement. The high support for this item is surprising. We might suspect that the pre-service teachers are not fully aware of the regulations regarding being a state official and misinterpret obedience in this item. If they do not, these results are problematic for civic education in schools: Civic education aims to nurture discussions and schoolchildren's ability to question authority while forming their own opinions. Schoolchildren need to learn how to question authorities before they decide to obey these authorities.

Both groups broadly supported the statements regarding gender equality (figure 11). Overall, the vast majority within both groups disagreed at least somewhat on the instrumental statement of gender equality (non-politics pre-service teachers: 88.9%, politics pre-service teachers: 86.2%, see figure 12). Just 11.5% of the politics pre-service teachers are indecisive (neither disagree nor agree, middle scale point) compared to 5.7% of non-politics pre-service teachers. About 5% of non-politics pre-service teachers and around 2% of politics pre-service teachers agree on the instrumental statement (figure 12). We see that, in both groups, pre-service teachers supported the general statement of gender equality strongly. However, if the statement is instrumental, support was lower and more dispersed in both groups.

Figure 12. "If Jobs are Scarce, Men Should Get Jobs Rather Than Women," Frequencies (in Percentages)

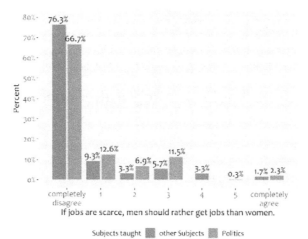

Table 3 shows the results of the unpaired t-tests between the two groups on each item. Politics pre-service teachers showed more support for the principles of civil rights and free elections. However, only the difference in civil rights is significant (effect size is medium). Additionally, we see that the mean support in both groups differed regarding *obedience towards the government*. Politics pre-service teachers were more in favor of this statement than non-politics pre-service teachers were. However, this effect is not significant.

Regarding gender equality, we see no difference between politics and non-politics pre-service teachers on the general item. The mean difference increases with the instrumental statement, but it is still insignificant. The two groups do not differ statistically; however, small groups of pre-service teachers in both groups disagreed on statements regarding free elections (politics: 5.7%, non-politics: 5.4%) and gender equality (politics: 1.3%, non-politics: 1.2%). For civic education, this result is highly problematic because those teachers might negatively influence students.

Table 3. "Civil Rights," "Free Elections," "Obedience to Government," "General Gender Equality," "Instrumental Gender Equality," Comparison of Central Tendency

Support of ...	Mean Difference	t-value	Cohen's D
Civil Rights	0.38**	-3.1229	0.38
Free Elections	0.24	-1.7453	-
Obedience to Government	0.26	-1.4418	-
General Gender Equality	0.03	-0.294	-
Instrumental Gender Equality	0.17	-1.0699	-
*** p > 0.0001, **p < 0.01, * p < 0.05			

Prior studies have noted the importance of a democratic classroom and teachers' unique roles to ensure this democratic space.[50] Overall, the results indicate that regarding political knowledge and political interest, non-politics pre-service teachers showed less political knowledge and less political interest compared to politics pre-service teachers. While this result may be expected, lower political knowledge levels and lower political interest among non-politics pre-service teachers might hinder civic education in German schools because civic education is not only part of the specific subject; it is also related to the classroom environment and all teachers' actual behavior.[51] We see high support for the fundamental values of a democracy (free elections, civil rights, and gender equality) in both groups.

According to the Beutelsbacher Consensus, the overall aim of civic education is that school-children should learn to act on their own opinions and interests in discussions on political or societal conflicts. For example, teachers who favor expert decisions—a majority of non-politics and just 35% of politics—might be less aware of civic education's general task (i.e., nurturing interest in political decision-making). They might not be interested in engaging schoolchildren in political discussions and nurturing their political interest and political judgment capacity.

What Do Teachers Emphasize Regarding Civic Education of Students?

Using the focus group discussion, we tried to learn more about practitioners' understandings in the field. The politics teachers we invited had first-hand experience with their non-political colleagues due to interaction in the same workplace. We expected them to be aware of shortcomings in the teaching of their colleagues. Specifically, we were interested in finding out how the problems we encountered in the survey results may present themselves in the everyday practice of teaching in school.

The group discussion was comparatively short and moderated only to a limited extent. The length of the group discussion may have influenced the depth of the observed conversation. In summary, the participants raised attention to three major topics:

1. lack of political knowledge and political interest among non-politics teachers;

2. challenges for non-politics teachers;

3. the capacity for political judgment by non-politics teachers.

First, the participants problematized the gap in political knowledge of pre-service teachers. They emphasized a general lack of trust in political institutions or actors and society overall among non-politics pre-service teachers.[52] They treated the lack of knowledge and interest of non-politics teachers as problematic for civic education awareness in schools.[53] On one hand, they highlighted that teachers are a representative subgroup of a society. Hence, support for fundamental values may be similarly distributed amongst the general population.[54] On the other hand, a single participant argued that teachers, as socialization agents, are a unique subgroup of the population. Hence, it is dramatic if even a small number of teachers neglect fundamental democratic values.[55] As theoretically argued, the participants highlighted teachers' specific roles and pointed out that teachers should support fundamental democratic values like gender equality.

Second, the focus group participants were aware that teaching civic education is a challenge for their colleagues who do not teach politics or civic studies classes. They identified a problematic lack of knowledge among their colleagues regarding political institutions and actors.[56] They experienced a tendency to deliver measurable results matching predefined subject objectives in their work as teachers. Other aspects of the educational process—like civic education in a biology class—tend to get lost within these processes.[57] Thus, non-politics teachers are less aware of their task of civic education. Based on their own educational experience at universities, they criticized the structure and content of civic education for pre-service teachers as rather vague and uninteresting, especially for non-politics pre-service teachers.[58] In their experience, their former study peers (non-politics pre-service teachers) evaluated the basic science political science as somewhat abstract and irrelevant. Their peers indicated a lack of specific and practical examples and instructions regarding linking civic education to their specific subjects (like biology or math).[59] A consequence might be that non-politics teachers and pre-service teachers are less aware of civic education's general task and have fewer tools to include civic education.

Third, they stressed the necessity of teaching political judgment capacity as a fundamental civic education task.[60] Teaching that focuses on the capacity of political judgment is based on the third and overall principle of the Beutelsbacher Consensus. Nonetheless, the participants did not mention a concise example of political judgment capacity and how it can be included in teaching. They mentioned vague ideas of how politics and non-politics teachers can implement the principle of the capacity of political judgment in classes.[61] However, they stressed the importance of pre-service teachers gaining hands-on experiences in civic education while studying at universities.[62]

Conclusion and Call for Action

This chapter aimed to explore the importance and necessity of civic education of pre-service teachers at universities by focusing attention on expectations of pre-service teachers to fulfill the general aims of the Beutelsbacher Consensus once they are in the classroom. Thus, we examined political knowledge, political interest, and support for political values amongst pre-service teachers and paid particular attention to differences between politics and non-politics pre-service teachers, as both are responsible for offering students civic education.

Furthermore, this chapter has examined what current teaching staff perceives as problematic in their peers' degree of knowledge and political interest. We also explained what the politics teachers who took part in the focus group emphasized as important in pre-service teachers' civic education. Despite its limited scope, this study offers insights into why pre-service teachers' civic education is still needed at universities and suggests that improvements are needed in non-politics teachers' civic education training to maintain our democracies. Teachers are essential socialization agents and mediators of political interest, political knowledge, and support for political values.

In a time of rising populism and continued attacks from the far right to diminish the importance of civic education in schools, not just in Germany but worldwide, civic education is a means of protecting democracies against these threats. Focusing on the civic education of pre-service teachers in Germany, our analysis showed that in training future teachers of all subjects, particular attention must be paid to increasing knowledge about political institutions, processes, and parties, arousing students' interest in political events, and fostering an awareness of the relevance of civic education across all subjects of teaching. With the Beutelsbacher Consensus, Germany is unique in its expectation that teachers of all disciplines participate in teaching democratic citizenship. Yet, as threats to democracies rise and memories of large-scale wars in which many fought against authoritarianism fade, it is critical that we fully appreciate all countries' levels of teacher preparedness for and disposition to teaching democracy. Teacher education is an oft-forgotten, but much-needed means to preserve peace, maintain democracy, and advance human rights at home and across the world.

Endnotes

1. Gabriel A. Almond and Sidney Verba, *The Civic Culture: Political Attitudes and Democracy in Five Nations* (Princeton, NJ: Princeton University Press, 1963); David Easton, *A Systems Analysis of Political Life* (New York, London, Sydney: John Wiley & Sons, Inc, 1965).

2. Steve Schwarzer and Eva Zeglovits, "The Role of Schools in Preparing 16- and 17-Year-Old Austrian First-Time Voters for the Election," in *Growing into Politics: Contexts and Timing of Political Socialisation*, ed. Simone Abendschön (Colchester, UK: ECPR Press, 2013).

3. Easton, *A Systems Analysis of Political Life*, 289; William A. Galston, "Political Knowledge, Political Engagement and Civic Education," *Annual Review of Political Science* 4, no. 1 (2001): 217–234.

4. In 2018, the right-wing party AfD launched websites in several states, on which schoolchildren and students can inform against teachers who are "politically one-sided" and act against a specific party. The AfD faction of the Saxonian parliament launched the website www.lehrersos.de initially. Right-wing groups launched similar websites in the US (https://www.professorwatchlist.org/) and the UK (https://tpointuk.co.uk/education-watch/).

5. Sevgi Bayram Özdemir, Hakan Stattin, and Metin Özdemir, "Youth's Initiations of Civic and Political Discussions in Class: Do Youth's Perceptions of Teachers' Behavior Matter and Why?" *Journal of Youth & Adolescence* 45, no. 11 (2016): 2233–2245.

6. Ryan T. Knowles, "Teaching Who You Are: Connecting Teachers' Civic Education Ideology to Instructional Strategies," *Theory and Research in Social Education* 46, no. 1 (2018): 68–109.

7. David E. Campbell, "Voice in the Classroom: How an Open Classroom Climate Fosters Political Engagement," *Political Behavior* 30, no. 4 (2008): 437–454; see also: Gema M. Garcìa-Albacete, "Promoting Political Interest in Schools: The Role of Civic Education," in *Growing into Politics: Contexts and Timing of Political Socialisation*, ed. Simone Abendschön (Colchester, UK: ECPR Press, 2013).

8. Marc Hooghe and Ruth Dassonneville, "The Effects of Civic Education on Political Knowledge: A Two Year Panel Survey Among Belgian Adolescents," *Educational Assessment, Evaluation and Accountability* 23, no. 4 (2011): 321–339.

9. Diana Owen and G. I. W. Riddle, "Active Learning and the Acquisition of Political Knowledge in High School" in *Teaching Civic Engagement Across the Disciplines*, eds. Elizabeth C. Matto, Alison R. M. McCartney, Elizabeth A. Bennion and Dick Simpson (Washington, DC: American Political Science Association, 2017).

10. Kate Connolly, "AfD Tells German Pupils to Denounce Teachers who Discuss Political Views," *The Guardian* (11 October 2018); Darrell Delamaide, "Germany's AfD Incites Schoolkids to Denounce Teachers," *Handelsblatt* (10 December 2018).

11. Otto Hüther and Georg Krücken, *Higher Education in Germany—Recent Developments in an International Perspective* (Higher Education Dynamics 49. Cham, Switzerland: Springer International Publishing, 2018), 14–15.

12. Mahir Gökbudak and Reinhold Hedtke, *Ranking Politische Bildung 2018. Politische Bildung an allgemeinbildenden Schulen der Sekundarstufe I im Bundesländervergleich* (Fakultät für Soziologie – Didaktik der Sozialwissenschaften, 2019).

13. The amount and content of the additional teaching skills varies widely between the 16 *Bundesländer*.

14. In 1976, the agreement on the "Beutelsbacher Consensus" solved a conflict of the tasks of civic education in Germany. During a conference of the *Landeszentrale für politische Bildung Baden-Württemberg*, various political didacts settled an academic dispute about the foundations and purpose of civic education in a minimal consensus to which every party in a polarized debate among scholars and practitioners could agree on.

15. Sybille Reinhardt, *Teaching Civics: A Manual for Secondary Education Teachers* (Opladen, Berlin, Toronto: Barbara Budrich Publishers, 2015), 30.

16. Reinhardt, *Teaching Civics*, 30.

17. Hans-Georg Wehling, "Konsens à la Beutelsbach? Nachlese zu einem Expertengespräch," in *Das Konsensproblem in der Politischen Bildung*, eds. Siegfried Schiele and Schneider Herbert (Stuttgart, Germany: Klett Verlag, 1977), 197–99.

18. Joel Westheimer and Joseph Kahne, "What Kind of Citizen? The Politics of Educating for Democracy," *American Educational Research Journal* 41, no. 2 (2004): 237–269.

19. Michael X. Delli Carpini, Leonie Huddy, and Robert Y. Shapiro, eds., *Rethinking Rationality* (Greenwich, CT: Jai Press, 1996); Henry Milner, *Civic Literacy: How Informed Citizens Make Democracy Work* (Hanover, NH: University Press of New England, 2002); Richard G. Niemi and Jane Junn, *Civic Education: What Makes Students Learn* (New Haven, CT: Yale University Press, 1998).

20. Delli Carpini, Huddy, and Shapiro, *Rethinking Rationality*, 10.

21. Jan W. van Deth, "Interest in Politics," in *Continuities in Political Action: A Longitudinal Study of Political Orientations in Three Western Democracies*, eds. M. Kent Jennings et al. (Berlin, Germany: De Gruyter, 1990), 278.

22. Arthur Lupia and Tasha S. Philpot, "Views from Inside the Net: How Websites Affect Young Adults' Political Interest," *The Journal of Politics* 67, no. 4 (2005): 1122.

23. Henry E. Brady, Sidney Verba, and Kay L. Schlozman, "Beyond SES: A Resource Model of Political Participation," *American Political Science Review* 89, no. 2 (1995); Delli Carpini, Huddy, and Shapiro, *Rethinking Rationality*; Jesper Strömbäck and Adam Shehata, "Media Malaise or a Virtuous Circle? Exploring the Causal Relationships Between News Media Exposure, Political News Attention and Political Interest," *European Journal of Political Research* 49, no. 5 (2010): 575–597; Sidney Verba, Kay Lehman Schlozman, and Henry E. Brady, *Voice and Equality: Civic Voluntarism in American Politics* (Cambridge, MA: Harvard University Press, 1995).

24. M. Kent Jennings, Laura Stoker, and Jake Bowers, "Politics Across Generations: Family Transmission Reexamined," *Journal of Politics* 71, no. 3 (2009): 782–799; Anja Neundorf, Kaat Smets, and Gema M. García-Albacete, "Homemade Citizens: The Development of Political Interest During Adolescence and Young Adulthood," *Acta Politica* 48, no. 1 (2013): 92–116.

25. Silvia Russo and Håkan Stattin, "Stability and Change in Youths' Political Interest," *Social Indicators Research* 132, no. 2 (2017): 654.

26. Easton, *A Systems Analysis of Political Life*, 289.

27. David Easton, "A Re-Assessment of the Concept of Political Support," *British Journal of Political Science* 5, no. 4 (1975): 445.

28. Antonio J. Castro, "What Makes a Citizen? Critical and Multicultural Citizenship and Preservice Teachers' Understanding of Citizenship Skills," *Theory & Research in Social Education* 41, no. 2 (2013): 219–246; Kenneth W. Kickbusch, "Civic Education and Preservice Educators: Extending the Boundaries of Discourse," *Theory & Research in Social Education* 15, no. 3 (1987): 173–188.

29. Castro, "What Makes a Citizen? Critical and Multicultural Citizenship and Preservice Teachers' Understanding of Citizenship Skills."

30. Wayne Journell, "What Preservice Social Studies Teachers (Don't) Know About Politics and Current Events—And Why It Matters," *Theory & Research in Social Education* 41, no. 3 (2013): 316–351.

31. Georg Weißeno, Eva Weschenfelder, and Monika Oberle, "Überzeugungen, Fachinteresse und professionelles Wissen von Studierenden des Lehramts Politik," in *Empirische Forschung in Gesellschaftswissenschaftlichen Fachdidaktiken: Ergebnisse Und Perspektiven,* eds. Georg Weißeno and Carla Schelle (Wiesbaden, Germany: Springer Fachmedien Wiesbaden, 2015).

32. Westheimer and Kahne, "What Kind of Citizen?"

33. Ibid.

34. Vickie E. Lake et al., "Reconceptualizing Teacher Education Programs: Applying Dewey's Theories to Service-Learning with Early Childhood Preservice Teachers," *Journal of Higher Education Outreach and Engagement* 19, no. 2 (2015): 93–116.

35. Diane L. Duffin, Jane Ziebarth-Bovill, and Rochelle H. Krueger, "Building Democratic Capacity in Preservice Teachers," *Delta Kappa Gamma Bulletin* 86, no. 1 (2019): 14–24.

36. Florian Fischer, Dirk Lange, and Tonio Oeftering, "Was ist Politische Bildung? Qualitative Forschung in der Politikdidaktik am Beispiel einer explorativen Studie zu den Vorstellungen von Lehramtsstudierenden über Politische Bildung," in *Perspektiven auf Politikunterricht heute: Vom Sozialwissenschaftlichen Sachunterricht bis zur Politiklehrerausbildung,* eds. Markus Gloe and Tonio Oeftering (Baden-Baden, Germany: Nomos Verlagsgesellschaft mbH & Co. KG, 2017).

37. Campbell, "Voice in the Classroom: How an Open Classroom Climate Fosters Political Engagement"; Owen and Riddle, "Active Learning and the Acquisition of Political Knowledge in High School"; Hooghe and Dassonneville, "The Effects of Civic Education on Political Knowledge."

38. The survey was conducted by Prof. Dr. Dorothée de Nève and Dr. Jutta Hergenhan (Justus-Liebig-University Giessen) in the project "Einstellungen-Medien-Engagement-Lehren" (EMEL). For project details see: https://www.uni-giessen.de/fbz/zmi/projekte/emel.

39. Since education falls exclusively under state regulation, the curriculum of teacher education at universities varies between the 16 *Bundesländer.*

40. Due to the study regulations, there is no attendance register in lectures and hence students do not have to attend lectures.

41. The index of political knowledge includes the following two open and two single choice questions: (1) In which year was the "Grundgesetz" implemented? (open) (2) What is the name of the recent (2016) foreign minister? (open) (3) What do you vote for with your first vote in federal elections? (single choice) (4) What do you vote for with your second vote in federal elections? (single choice)

42. Jeffrey J. Mondak, "Reconsidering the Measurement of Political Knowledge," *Political Analysis* 8, no. 1 (1999): 59.

43. See: Richard Rose, William Mishler, and Christian W. Haerpfer, *Democracy and Its Alternatives* (Baltimore, MD: The John Hopkins University Press, 1998); Pippa Norris, *Democratic Deficit. Critical Citizens Revisited* (New York: Cambridge University Press, 2011.)

44. Robert Dahl, *Polyarchy. Participation and Opposition* (New Haven, CT: Yale University Press, 1971).

45. Jennifer Cyr, *Focus Groups for the Social Science Researcher* (Cambridge, UK: Cambridge University Press, 2019), 19.

46. George Kamberelis and Greg Dimitriadis, *Focus Groups: From Structured Interviews to Collective Conversations* (Abingdon, UK: Routledge, 2013), 40.

47. In Hesse, teachers can enroll in additional training voluntarily and on these days they are exempt from teaching.

48. These four questions were: (1) "To what extent do you think there might be problems for future teachers in daily school life knowing the results of the survey?" (2) "As professionals, what would you emphasize in the civic education of future teachers at universities?" (3) "To what extent are the results problematic for the daily school tasks and tasks of civic education for teachers?" (4) "As professionals, what do you think future teachers, in particular, should learn at universities?"

49. Juliet Corbin and Anselm Strauss, *Basics of Qualitative Research: Techniques and Procedures for Developing Grounded Theory* (Thousand Oaks, CA: Sage Publications, 2008), 198.

50. Bayram Özdemir, Stattin, and Özdemir, "Youth's Initiations of Civic and Political Discussions in Class: Do Youth's Perceptions of Teachers' Behavior Matter and Why?"; Knowles, "Teaching Who You Are: Connecting Teachers' Civic Education Ideology to Instructional Strategies"; Campbell, "Voice in the Classroom: How an Open Classroom Climate Fosters Political Engagement"; Garcìa-Albacete, "Promoting Political Interest in Schools: The Role of Civic Education."

51. Erin Godfrey and Justina Grayman, "Teaching Citizens: The Role of Open Classroom Climate in Fostering Critical Consciousness Among Youth," *Journal of Youth and Adolescence* 43, no. 11 (2014): 1801–1817; Hooghe and Dassonneville, "The Effects of Civic Education on Political Knowledge"; Bayram Özdemir, Stattin and Özdemir, "Youth's Initiations of Civic and Political Discussions in Class: Do Youth's Perceptions of Teachers' Behavior Matter and Why?"; Lies Maurissen, Ellen Claes, and Carolyn Barber, "Deliberation in Citizenship Education: How the School Context Contributes to the Development of an Open Classroom Climate", *Social Psychology of Education* 21, no. 4 (2018): 951–972.

52. Focus Group, interview by Johannes Diesing, and Benedikt Philipp Kleer, (14 November 2019), Giessen, 271–273; 556–558.

53. Focus Group, 252–54.

54. Focus Group, 21–22; 266–267.

55. Focus Group, 591–94.

56. Focus Group, 633–34; Focus Group, 215–25.

57. Focus Group, 27–30; 316; 355–356.

58. Focus Group, 153–155; 295–296.

59. Focus Group, 641–45.

60. Focus Group, 278–280; 556–561.

61. Focus Group, 282–283; 634–643.

62. Focus Group, 643–46.

19 | "My Participation is Often Dismissed": How Vocational School Students Participate in Society

Niina Meriläinen

Tampere University, Finland

The precondition for a healthy democracy is the inclusion of its young people from various backgrounds in various forms of democratic participation. However, in democracies such as Finland, vocational secondary school students are not taught civic engagement and ways of becoming agenda-setters in society, as academic secondary school students are. In this research, students aged 16–26 years old from vocational secondary schools convey that they are not seen in the democratic development processes in Finland. Thus, their potential as participants in democratic processes is overlooked in society and by policymakers. This chapter argues that, while vocational secondary students are not given the civic engagement education that they need, they do act as agenda setters in numerous ways. The absence of civic education for these students continues to leave a gap in Finland's democracy. Its educational system fails to value and foster the democratic participation of all young people.

KEYWORDS: Youth Participation; Vocational Schools; Civic Engagement Education.

Introduction

The precondition for the democratic development of a society is the participation of youth from various backgrounds in democratic processes such as grassroots actions and policymaking. In particular, if leaders and citizens desire to achieve the goal of establishing and maintaining equal, inclusive, and sustainable societies, the active participation and empowerment of all youth is an essential requirement for lasting, legitimate change. However, all young people may not be empowered, taught, or traditionally seen as participants in societal and political change processes. Additionally, officials and politicians may overlook the value and expertise of young people from vocational studies backgrounds. Moreover, research that focuses on youth participation may only take into account the political participation that is tied to institutions, such as voting, official legislative processes, and youth councils.

Finland, as an established, stable, and prosperous democracy, is a suitable case study to explore the dichotomy between what types and how much civic engagement education academic secondary school students and vocational secondary school students are offered. Overall, civic participation is taught and encouraged in Finnish society. Yet, in academic secondary schools, which traditionally lead to university spots, civic engagement education and related topics are largely integrated into the basic curriculum, whereas in vocational secondary schools, which do not traditionally lead to university spots and direct youth immediately into the workforce, these topics are often only in selective studies categories. These course categories are not mandatory, so encouragement and education for active social participation can be missing altogether in their schooling. Thus, in Finland, young people are divided in terms of how much—if any—civic education they receive in adolescence based on where they have been tracked in their secondary education.

There has been little research on the views of young people from different secondary educational backgrounds regarding their political participation and the students' understanding of the nature of participation. Specifically, we do not know how vocational secondary school students frame participation and how, if at all, they themselves act as participants in less formal ways and how they act as agenda setters in society. By agenda setting I refer to actors, such as young people, who can influence discussions and raise issues salient to them in offline and online debates from grassroots to policy levels, with the aim(s) of influencing society. Agenda setting is the process where actors, including youth, use framing to create their understanding of issues, actors, events, and such political concepts as participation. This framing then impacts their views on participation and how they think that they can best influence and participate in society and even if they think that they should or can participate.

It is important to understand how young vocational school students understand participation because it is only then that we can formulate an understanding as to how the young people participate and by which means, rather than focusing on those traditional means of participation that adults view as relevant. The formal and traditional means of participation include such activities as law-drafting and participating in youth councils, whereas less formal means of participation might include social media discussions and activism, offline grassroot activism, and consumer behavior.[1]

This chapter presents some research focused on the participation of youth vocational school students and highlights the need for further research on this group. I asked this group: what, if anything, it means to them to participate and whether they see themselves as agenda setters in society. From these results, I argue that, if democracies are to be equitable and truly inclusive, we must recognize, develop, and support the value of participation of young people from all backgrounds. Only by also fostering civic participation of vocational secondary students at the same level as secondary academic students can we encourage and expect lifelong civic participation, fully representative democratic governments, and stable, inclusive societies.

The plan of this chapter is to first review the significance of developing participatory models and education for youth in vocational settings. Then, I provide an overview of the methodology and parameters of the research and the conduct of the workshops. The next section outlines the actual workshop process, explaining how responses were collected. Fourth, I present some qualitative results from the youth studied and combine their responses to form an understanding of their frames for participation and their potential roles in social, political, and economic agenda setting.

The Importance of Youth Participation

Although the wider discussion on societal views on youth participation is beyond the scope of this chapter, we may note that youth participation is a central principle in Finnish legislation, in the UN's Agenda 2030, which guarantees the rights for all youth to participate in politics and society.[2] Also, Article 10 of the European Convention on Human Rights states, "everyone has the right to freedom of expression. This right shall include freedom to hold opinions and to receive and impart information and ideas without interference by public authority and regardless of frontiers."[3] In addition, the UN's Convention on the Rights of the Child guarantees the right of children to participate.[4] Moreover, the EU Youth Strategy 2019–2027 focuses on engaging, enabling, and strengthening the participation of EU's young people in policies and society at various levels.[5]

Key, powerful actors' understandings are framed in selective ways.[6] Frames create and influence political, social, and economic institutions and change processes. In practice, this means that the gatekeeper's understandings or narratives are traditionally the salient ones.[7] For example, such gatekeeper-designed frames regarding participation may privilege the views of young people in traditional youth councils versus those who participate in climate change protests and civil rights movements elsewhere. Or, these frames may fail to acknowledge or incorporate the participation of young people from non-political studies backgrounds, such as is the case with students from vocational schools.[8] An example of this exclusion is the Youth Barometer 2018 study in Finland which only focused on measuring interests and participation as voting in elections or being tied to institutions such as youth councils or political parties and processes.[9] In limiting participation to these categories, one may incorrectly conclude that young vocational school students are non-participants, uninterested, and silent. Youth are often studied for their participation,[10] but the use of only traditional categories for participation may "pit" the two groups of students against each other.

Previous studies, such as Checkoway and Gutiérrez (2006),[11] have shown that including young people in youth parliament and institutionally-tied mechanisms of participation can advance active citizenship and integration into society and societal decision-making structures and processes.[12] Other studies such as Walsh, Black, and Prosser (2018), for example, focus on youth who can be described as agenda setters, with the emphasis on class distinctions, such as belonging to middle-to-upper class backgrounds.[13] Studies like these tend to create a power relationship between young people from and at different socio-economic backgrounds, which then fosters the notion that participation, agenda-setting abilities, and change agency is tied to existing participatory structures which are mostly accessible to wealthier youth who are viewed as "valuable" participants. Gretschel and Kiilakoski (2012) say that demonstrations are youth-driven ways to participate in society and are a way to make one's voice heard.[14] Andersson (2018) claims that youth do not have influence in the legislative processes because "...decision makers decide what they think young people want."[15] Also Walgrave and Van Aelst (2016) highlight the power of the political elite to influence or update policies, which can easily lead to excluding vocational school students.[16] Indeed, reasons for encouraging youth participation can vary from being a means to satisfy the (economic) interests of decision makers, preparation for 'real' political participation in the future such as voting, and promoting the right—i.e., approved—behavior based on the interest of decision makers, to viewing participation as a democratic and political right. Thus, the identity of who defines 'participation' is important.

Pietilä, Varsaluoma, and Väänänen (2019) use the concept of "societal participation" to refer to participation of an individual or a group in the processes of the society, such as voting or participating in decision making, or engaging in political discussions.[17] However, Piškur et al. (2014) assert that (social) participation has not been explicitly defined.[18] Some argue that societal participation must have intersectional views. Hästbacka, Nygård, and Nyqvist (2016) say that the complex concept of societal participation can mean various things and is highly related to the context of the research and participation.[19] The authors continue to state that the term "societal" can be connected with other dimensions of one's life, such as political participation or employment. Some authors press the connection between societal and political participation. For instance Ekman and Amnå (2012) highlight the multidimensionality of both concepts.[20] Meriläinen, Pietilä, and Varsaluoma (2018) examine youth participation in societal issues in the context of a wider human rights perspective of exclusivity and accessibility, as well as in the realms of digital services.[21] Moreover, Merilainen and Piispa (2020) researched the participation of vocational school students and found many ways in which young people participate in climate change actions by using formats outside of the institutional forms such as law-drafting and voting.[22] Students' participation in demonstrations and the usage of social media are part of self-determined means to use one's voice and to execute democratic participation regarding climate change.

Still further, Cahill and Dadvand (2018) argue that we should acknowledge that not everyone has equal access to the discourses that allow them to take up certain positions because some may adopt more dominant roles, while others may be relegated to subservient positions within the social space.[23] This can manifest in interpersonal relationships as well as within institutional practices and structures. Ten Brummelaar et al. (2018) found various narratives that illustrate how young people have limited possibilities for 'meaningful' participation in decision-making and their participation does not always seem meaningful or really impact a decision concerning them.[24]

In other cases, the lack of civic engagement training of vocational students has a clear impact. For example, those who have a legal education and can speak the legal language have an advantage because of their knowledge of legal language, concepts, and mechanisms.[25] Actors such as civil servants, those in the economic sector, and researchers have more powerful positions in the law-drafting process than other actors because of their knowledge and experience.[26] Cahill and Dadvand argue that participation may or may not produce social good, since it may replicate the patterns of inequality or the status quo, or even deepen discourses which categorize, segregate, and stigmatize those who do not attend university.[27]

Finally, evaluation of political participation of vocational secondary school students is largely missing from international literature on youth political engagement. A recent study by Meriläinen and Piispa (2020) is a step to bridge the gap by showing that vocational school students do indeed participate in the society as agenda setters and are interested in political issues such as climate change and human & LGBTQI rights, while some studies tend to paint the picture that vocational school students are not interested.[28] The authors did show that Finnish vocational school students are not silent, but in to some degree believe that their participation is not valued, seen, or heard in the society. These researchers explored the participation of vocational school students and found many ways in which young people participate in climate change actions outside the traditional ways tied to institutions, though young vocational school students felt that their participation was not seen or taken seriously. This topic was not previously studied among vocational school students. Climate activism studies in particular can be almost inclusively done among so-called youth activists and among those who are titled as youth activists. Mirroring the results from Meriläinen and Piispa, in a recent youth survey done in a medium-size city in Finland, 74% of the respondents said that they act more environmentally friendly in society, but adults do not take their forms of climate participation into account.[29]

Overall, as Kallio and Häkli (2013) argue, youth participation can increase if practical means to do so are provided to them.[30] Their forms of participation need to be seen, as they may not be heard or included in traditional legislative processes,[31] and we need ways to measure these forms both before age 18 and afterwards. We also need to acknowledge that, as Head (2011) argues "[the final] argument in favor of enhanced youth participation centres on the developmental benefits which are claimed to emerge from the experience of young people being engaged in various forms of social participation. These benefits may be at the individual or the wider social levels."[32] Being heard and the hope that this voice gives them helps young people to learn that they can be constructive members in society as we build solutions to problems such as climate change, racism, and other human rights issues.[33] Young people who are not active in traditional ways may be regarded as non-active or gated from participation, despite perhaps being active elsewhere in other issue arenas such as hobbies, social media, or local demonstrations.[34] In some cases, young people are not empowered as they do not have the information needed to participate, while others may simply not be interested.[35] Or, some young people may be disregarded because their views do not fit into current political agendas.[36] Also, Fridkin, Kenney, and Crittenden (2006) claim that "minority youth lag behind Anglos in terms of their opportunities to practice democratic skills and their understanding of politics" to which they add "minority students hold more negative attitudes about politics and are less attached to the political system."[37] Indeed, distributions of power, position, and resources permit some youth to become gatekeepers, while others remain gated and have a less influential position in decision making processes.[38] In this line, Feldman (2000) states that power relations and narratives influence legislative processes, which may result in silencing, excluding and othering groups such as minorities, and disregarding their views.[39] These concerns are all tied to the issue of real participation and who in fact participates.

Methodology and Workshop Design

Vocational training and education is designed both for young people without upper secondary qualifications and for adults already in the workforce. Traditionally young people apply, and if accepted, enroll in vocational school or high school education after elementary school. Some young people complete a joint degree where they study in vocational school and also complete the matriculation examination from high school. This study focused on youth, which, according to the Finnish Youth Act, refers to people under 29 years old, though this sample only includes those aged 16–26 years old. The dataset consists of 185 vocational school students who provided qualitative responses gathered from questionnaires and written workshop works obtained in 23 workshops held at vocational schools in five municipalities in western Finland between 2018–2020. The workshops were held in classes which focused on various fields of study to reach as diverse of a group of students as possible. This research was conducted with students in their own language (Finnish) and gathered where young people were easily approachable as research partners—the schools.

Workshops were chosen as a process to gather information because they can be conducted in more open and free learning atmospheres and surroundings versus traditional classroom teaching settings, which may also increase their utility as a teaching method for civic engagement. Workshops have also been shown as a useful teaching method to engage with young people and get their viewpoints directly from them.[40] If researchers seek to gain insights from young people, they should listen to people in their own surroundings and go where those people are. Echoing the findings of Lapadat et al. (2020), when young people are given clear tasks but also the option of movement to be creative in an engaging context, workshops are a useful method, but they call for careful planning.[41] When workshops are designed, multiple factors must be addressed. For example, Lapadat et al. and Cahill and Dadvand have observed that power relations between young people and adults exist.[42]

Moreover, these researchers raise the need to allow young people anonymity, the importance of understanding ethical issues such as various disabilities, differences in language skills, and differences in accessing information in dealing with young people, and their time constraints. Also, anonymity allows young participants to express their opinions freely, especially if the purpose is to gather information from young people. As Lapadat et al. say, research that involves youth may involve additional time, communication, support, and attentiveness to the power differentials.[43] Further, the youths' motivations in participating in the workshops may differ from adults and academic researchers, and it is important to acknowledge both groups' priorities. These may be, for example, researchers' time restrictions and need to gather data quickly, or young people's need to simply get a mark of attendance from the workshops.

The vocational school research was designed, carried out, and analyzed by the author alone. The author consulted teachers at the vocational schools throughout the design process in case questions arose. Also, during the workshops, if any impediments arose, the workshop plan was altered to fit the goals of the researcher and the needs of the students. A clear example of this adaptation was a behavioral issue—bullying—which arose in two workshops where students bullied each other before the workshops in other classes. The bullying was addressed head on by the researcher in front of the group and one-on-one with the young students involved to ensure that no more bullying occurred. Finally, one can also say that the vocational school students acted as consultants by evaluating the workshops.

The following steps were taken to set up the cooperation between the researcher, vocational school students, and vocational school teachers. First, preliminary discussions occurred in person between the researcher and the vocational school about the possibility of conducting the research, the purposes of the research, the operative plan of the research, and the expected outcomes. After these meetings, the university where the author was working compiled the research permit between the City of Tampere and the vocational school. Next, oral agreements and email discussions finalized agreements between the researcher and the vocational teachers regarding the parameters of cooperation, design, and conduct of the research. For the sake of the youths' anonymity, the names of the participating municipalities are not stated here per those agreements and the permit. In the age of social media, there is a possibility that the students could be identified through coordinating identifiers like field of study and municipalities named in the answers, and thus no identifying information was gathered, even though this information may have bolstered the research. Finally, the timetables for the workshops depended on the time slot in the curriculum in each municipality.

In these workshops, the young vocational students participated in discussions of various issues. The workshops were designed to fit the existing curriculum, were integrated into multiple study subjects, and were between 2–3 ½ hours long. The issues were chosen by the researcher to focus on the topic of the research project she was working on at the university. The research focused on the participation of vocational school students in the society. However, the discussions were in no way limited to those topics, as the students were free to bring about notions from other areas as well. Discussion was based on open communication and free expression. The data collected included written workshop documents and post-workshop questionnaires which were distributed during the class in a Word document. They were sent back to the researcher via email either by the students or by the teacher as a Word document (see questionnaire). The results were then divided into four narrative categories, with presentation of select direct quotes below to illustrate the findings.

Narrative research has previously been utilized in traditional communication and organizational as well as multidisciplinary human rights and power relations research.[44] This research framework maintains that different frames, and thus understandings, by various actors have to be communicated for change to happen.[45] Framing is a mandatory and essential aspect of any social context, such as discussions, including policymaking, and every actor uses it.[46] In this case, I sought to reveal how young vocational school students frame, and thus understand, their participation, how they view themselves as agenda setters in society (or not), and what barriers they see which may limit or block their political and social participation.

This research does have limitations. First, it was not designed as a comparative experiment. Thus, there is no comparison in the data with academic secondary school students or with vocational secondary school students in other countries. Second, no quantitative data was gathered, as this was exploratory research to determine if larger studies are warranted. The only requirements for participation were enrollment in one of the selected Finnish vocational schools and being part of the 16–26 age group. Third, no identifying information from the students was collected, as explained above, so differences based on different gender identities, those who are in the older youth group versus the younger youth group, or the groups at various locations cannot be ascertained. Fourth, there was no quantification of the coding of the qualitative data (example: how many times a certain word or phrase appeared) due to language translation issues. Nonetheless, it is hoped that the lessons learned from this study will spark further research and changes in vocational secondary education around the world which include increased civic engagement education.

Workshop Process And Data Collection

During the researcher-led workshops, the students discussed and answered qualitative questions on topics such as, but not limited to: their lives, hopes, dreams, their areas of study, their views on social and political participation, law, and climate change. Each student was given a laptop to use by the vocational school, which is common practice in Finland, or desktop computers were made available. Also, once the workshops started, students were welcomed to use other devices, such as cell phones if they had them, to find information, initiate discussion on the topics of the workshop, or provide written data to the researcher. The written works and the questionnaires could be returned to the researcher during the workshops on paper, printed on the school's devices and returned to the researcher, or sent to the researcher's work email address. If the data was emailed, the researcher added the data to the collection site on the university's internal server and completely deleted the email.

There were two periods of data gathering April 2018–May 2019 and October 2019–March 2020. In the first set, which included 17 workshops of 90 total students, the topics that we discussed included participation, equality, bullying, sustainable development, a happy life, and legislative processes under the larger umbrella of human rights. After discussing the themes in a free-flowing manner, the students prepared and wrote short presentations on the topic(s) of their choosing in a style of their choosing and presented them to the class. In the second set, which included six workshops of 95 total students, the main topics were participation, influencing society, climate change, and youth views on what constitutes a good life. There were fewer workshops than planned in the second data set due to the coronavirus pandemic.

The workshops started in the students' regularly assigned classrooms. The vocational class teacher introduced the researcher, and then the researcher started the workshop by presenting the project, its design, and its purpose. First, the researcher led the discussion to get it started. The discussions continued first in one big group with all the students and then the students broke into small groups. The students could choose a small group of two to five people or do individual assignments to discuss with the researcher. After this beginning, students were free to use the other facilities of the vocational school, such as cafes and hallways. Some used the classroom, while others took advantage of other places on the school grounds. Students had the formal right to decline to participate in the study individually or in the smaller groups. They were free to ask questions at any time during the study from the researcher.

Given the purpose of the project to understand their definitions and their frames, students were not provided with an adult-derived definition of participation. To ensure equal possibilities to participate online and offline, participatory methods were created to help those with various disabilities or language barriers or anxiety in group situations. Help was provided by first identifying the need for help, and in one case, a student acted as an interpreter between another student and the researcher because the young person could not speak Finnish or English but was willing to speak in her native language. To offer help and to diffuse these situations, the students were free to leave the workshop if they wished and were free to complete the workshop work at home.

Students were given various options to participate. The students could also use pen and paper if they felt uncomfortable using computers or laptops. The researcher offered to help with writing either by using paper or a computer. Also, if anyone felt that they did not or could not write, the researcher interviewed or simply talked with the young person/persons and made notes. Students were not forced to do group assignments or to speak out if they felt pressure or anxiety speaking out loud. The students had the possibility to work alone, do written assignments and leave the workshop if they felt uncomfortable.

The Results

The resulting qualitative data was coded and analyzed to develop a picture of how youth vocational secondary school students understand or frame participation, how they see themselves–if at all–as participants, and what barriers they perceive to participation. Through this content analysis, five categories or narratives emerged:[47]

- Narrative 1: Participation as understood by youth vocational secondary school students.
- Narrative 2: How young people from vocation schools participate.
- Narrative 3: How they feel that participation is viewed by decision makers.
- Narrative 4: How vocational school students view participation in legislative processes.
- Narrative 5: How young people name obstacles in their participation.

This research method has previously been utilized in various studies relating to human rights, youth participation, and power relations research.[48] Based on the results, the workshops were useful in creating discussions between young people but also between young people and the researcher, and sufficient data was acquired to make some conclusions, discussed below. Overall, the youth had varying understandings of participation and how youth could participate to address issues such as climate change and racism. Only a handful of participants were interested in institutionally-tied types of participation, such as legislative processes.

Narrative 1: Participation as understood by youth vocational secondary school students

Based on the data, the students had several frames of participation which they used to create their understanding of participation. For them participation is about "being part of something" and "having an influence." One student said that "participation is about the feeling of being part of something bigger, and also the feeling of being able to influence it [without defining "it"]." Similarly, another said that participation is having one's voice heard:

> "There are many good ways to get your opinion out, but then the content needs to be thought-provoking and have an emotional impact in order to change people's attitudes."

Interestingly, based on the students' answers, for them participation was not simply "having an impact." Rather, it was a combination of taking actions, being connected, making personal choices, belonging, sharing opinions, and having an impact. Moreover, participation included areas of life such as relationships, studying, work, and hobbies as well belonging to an NGO and influencing (something) through those organizations. This example is telling:

> "I could have influence by joining some youth influencer organization and share my opinion via that."

Also, some students had thought-provoking ideas regarding participation.

> "The experience of participation arises when you are involved in something that has effects beyond yourself, such as people or the environment. The opposite of this is the feeling of incompetence, it is a common curse in societies that have lost their lives, that individuals feel separated from the group and loneliness and consequently helplessness take them over."

Narrative 2: How young people from vocation schools participate

This narrative illustrates how young people framed their own participation in society, whether they did participate, and where, if at all. Based on the data, the students did participate in societal issues such as fighting against climate change and for human rights issues. They participated in various ways, mainly through personal choices, for example, by engaging in discussions about climate change with friends, classmates, and family members, discussing the untold negative effects of electric cars on social media, engaging in recycling and responsible consumption, reducing their use of plastics and waste packaging, buying from flea markets, eating sustainable foods, and being part of student organizations, which are common in Finland. These organizations focus on students' wellbeing and education but also on societal and political debates. Some students felt that their field of study made them more prone to participate and did not feel that anyone was silencing or "gating" them.

When asked if the youth could detail any experiences of participation, the students mention, for example, taking part in LGBTQI Pride demonstrations or signing petitions for human rights, peace, or advancing a cause. Moreover, for some the reality was not an either or situation but rather one where they "cannot" participate or "don't know" about participation or ways to participate:

> "My chances of influencing society at the moment are quite slim. Only by

voting can there be some effect, because again boomers do not want to listen to or believe the youth about what would be best for the society, for example, on equality and protection of nature and the climate."

"I don't really feel that I have an impact on society, at least not yet, maybe when I'm older and when my name counts for more."

Some youth were skeptical and not interested in social and political participation.

"There may certainly be opportunities to participate, but I have no interest in influencing or participating."

"I guess there are those possibilities but I will not use them."

"Not participating is just great, [I] don't have to take a stance on anything."

Overall, what emerged was that vocational school students have several understandings of what participation is, and they frame it in various ways. They participate by taking everyday actions online and offline, also as consumers; they are concerned with issues such as climate change, electric cars, racism, and bullying; and they take part in demonstrations. Moreover, their concerns causally flow through their personal lives to studies and future employment. They are active in discussions at school, speak with friends online and in social media, disseminate information, and sign petitions, and they have casual means of participation that are akin to bandwagoning. For them, this is social and/or political participation.

Narrative 3: How they feel that participation is viewed by decision makers

Similarly, the actions of decision makers were mentioned as an important factor in the students' participation. Some students said that decision makers do not care about young vocational school students, whereas others simply wished for respect when they participate:

"Participation makes a person feel that they are part of something, for example, an organization or just one's schoolmates. Appreciation and respect within one's own community is part of participation."

However, some of the students felt powerless and even apathetic because they saw that their participation was not appreciated or seen as credible by the decision makers. Also many young people said that they do not have "word power."

"It's hard for a small person to get their voices heard. Small everyday actions are the ones where you play your main part in changing things."

"I'm not interested in influencing society, because I don't believe I have enough strength to influence things and it is useless to use up energy for such issues which I get nothing out of."

Narrative 4: How vocational school students view participation in legislative processes

Although some young people did see themselves as influencing society and participating in social and political issues in various ways, traditional legislative processes were more unfamiliar to the students. Though the students could name various laws and detail their content in relation to their lives, the world, and their future professions, many saw no reason to change them. The laws that the youth discussed were tied to their own lives or area of study and the future profession for which they were studying. Many of the students regarded the current laws they knew about as "functional," but some argued that they should be taught more at vocational schools. According to the students, the most taught laws connected to their fields of study, human rights, and labor rights.

> "In my opinion there is no need to change the laws because they are functional."

> "I feel that the laws related to my field of study are functional and I don't feel that they need to be changed. However I do feel that there needs to be improvements in teaching about them and how they are highlighted. It would have been nice to learn more about them during the first year [of studies]."

> "I have not yet encountered a law that would not be functional. Only shortages in actualization of laws."

However some students, with a few skeptical exceptions, did say that laws have already been modified and need to be even further modified to improve working conditions and equality in society, for example, as well as to tighten up the penal code with regard to environmental laws or to combat climate change. Some students were afraid of the improvement of women's rights, and some students stated that issues such as bullying and human rights violations towards the LGBTQI need to be addressed better in legislation.

> "Yes legislation should be modified so that everyone should have some kind of position, for example, in how to act in cases of bullying or in some other situations."

> "ICT [information and communication technology]-sector....in many laws, the politicians can be very far behind."

> "Improving equality is challenging because it affects almost everything we do, but it is not impossible."

Many students said that the way they have become familiar with the laws was through studies, work, and other aspects of their own lives. One student became familiar with marriage law through a family member and a reality TV-personality. This example shows how young people get information from non-traditional ways and how they tie the information gained from celebrities to their own lives, also related to laws and legislation.

> "[Kim Kardashian] wondered if it would be worthwhile for her to change her last name after her wedding or to take a combination last name and how those names would work. I have also come across other laws."

When asked if they would be interested in being part of the legislative process, the majority of the students said they were not. However, others did say that they are interested in being part of the legislative processes either alone or with a larger group in order to change laws. Some students said that they would like to be involved in discussions with decision makers, the police, and other actors involved in legislation to hear "why they decided the way that they did."

The responses below show some of the students expressing a desire to be involved in legislative processes:

> "I would always like to be involved in the consultation processes that address the facilities I have designed or projects that I have been involved in. I would

like to be present in a concrete manner or have a conversation with someone who is involved in the [the law drafting] process."

"I would be interested in giving ideas based on my experiences to a member of the parliament or independently [to someone]."

"I would be interested to take part through an organization. I could hear various points of views from the other members of the organization... and I could widen my own viewpoint in this way. From the organization I could also get my own kind of assurance... Thru an organization, issues would be taken into consideration more easily than hearing about it from the mouth of only one person."

"If there would be a possibility, I could participate independently."

One student had a strong vision of who should be listened to in legislative processes:

"Marginalized, lonely and those rejected by society as well as those who many believe belong to the lower class [should be consulted during the law-drafting processes] because they often have real experiences and views regarding this world and its legislation, and when it has not worked or treated people as people. Those are actors who truly have that grassroots understanding of issues!"

Narrative 5: How young people name obstacles in their participation

Relating to the focus of the research, the data shows that young people said that they can participate in society in various ways. However, they felt that they are not listened to in society and that "old people" and "boomers" do not want young people to participate. Also, some said they do not care whether they are listened to or not. Interestingly, some said that they are scared to take part as agenda setters and are afraid of being bullied by friends, other young people, and adults—basically anyone who sees their participation online and offline. They said they do have possibilities to participate but still feel invisible, lacking the power to be active and visible. Most notably, many youths felt that their participation does not matter since they are seen as the "silent" ones.

Even when young people said that they participated, some felt apathy, believing they would not be listened to by gatekeepers or other adults. This points to a lack of empowerment and also perhaps to the effects of negative experiences, such as bullying, and is highlighted in this remark: "You are the first one who has shown any interest in what I think about things," while another said, "I don't know how to say it in a smart way," showing that some of the students framed themselves as gated actors. One student said that it makes them sick that gatekeepers such as President Trump and other "grown-ups are bullying Greta [Thunberg]," which in turn makes participation less appealing and contributes to an understanding that participation is scary and results in being bullied by the central gatekeepers—boomers.

"If the issue is important, then it would be nice to be making decisions... however societal discussion and decision making feel distant."

"Comes the feeling, that I guess I sit silently."

"It does not feel good to be silenced. Society silences."

"I don't really feel that I have an impact on society, at least not yet, maybe when I'm older and when there is more power in [my] name."

Moreover, based on their answers, they strongly felt that they are not "smart" or knowledgeable enough to participate:

> "I could not create a rational/sane law, so I will leave that to smarter [people]."

> "A lot should be done but you cannot do everything so you get the feeling I am completely useless."

On the other side, some students were very clear they did not want to be part of the legislative processes and have no interest in laws because the subject was "boring."

> "[Regarding legislative processes,] I'm not interested because I feel that the subject is boring."

Based on the results, young vocational school students participate in society as agenda setters. They are interested in profound societal and political topics such as climate change, racism, human rights, and their and others well-being. However, at the same time, those acting as agenda setters fear bullying, and silencing in society hinders participation. They also fear that adults will bully them if they become agenda setters. At the same time, not all students cared to participate and they were uninterested in issues outside their own living spaces.

Based on these narratives, young vocational school students had various understandings of what participation was, how they participate, and what motivated them but also who should be listened to in the society—including young vocational school students.

Conclusion

The study suggests that young people in vocational secondary schools need to be educated, inspired, empowered, and seen as legitimate actors in grassroots and legislative/policy making processes to create better and more sustainable social, political, and economic policies. Their non-traditional forms of participation must be recognized in society, and vocational students must be respected as equal, active participants. Additionally, leaders and gatekeepers may overlook the possible hidden expertise and not recognize the value of the participation of these young people, and they should take a long-term view of these youths' voices rather than stay tied to their own frameworks and political agendas. Several students knew about and showed specific knowledge of various laws and spoke about how to apply the laws to their own lives, for example, their interests and future professions. Yet, officials and policymakers may be disregarding young people who do have knowledge that is in fact relevant to the democratic political process.

At the worst, this situation creates apathy, ignores the benefits of the development of long-term and inclusive citizen participation, and fosters a gap between young people by creating somewhat artificial distinctions between active and less-active youth, thus gatekeeper and gated youth. It speaks more to the assumed credibility and decision-making power of the gatekeepers and their perceived unwillingness to listen to those young people who have traditionally been invisible and inactive in the eyes of policy makers. This positioning could be amplified in years to come and create a wider gap between those who attended vocational secondary schools and others who attended academic secondary schools, perpetuating class and workforce distinctions which may divide rather than unite society. Further research is needed beyond this preliminary study to explore this gap in the civic engagement education literature throughout different countries if we are indeed to build stable, healthy democracies. In the meantime, leaders and educators can act now to recognize this gap and improve civic engagement education opportunities for all secondary school students, regardless of the type of institution. If all of these students really are to be equal participants in our societies, then we must start by giving them equal support, tools, voices, and experiences to contribute to our democracies.

The empirical data collecting was part of the ALL-YOUTH Research project. The project is funded by the Strategic Research Council (SRC) at the Academy of Finland decisions 312689 and 326604. The analysis and writing process was supported by a personal research grant from The Helsingin Sanomat Foundation, Finland.

Endnotes

1. Joanna Kidman and Vincent O'Malley, "Questioning the Canon: Colonial History, Counter-memory and Youth Activism," *Memory Studies* 13, no. 4 (2020): 537–550; Niina Meriläinen and Mikko Piispa, "'Antaa Isojen Herrojen Ja Rouvien Päättää'—Lasten Ja Nuorten Oikeudet Ja Osallisuus Ilmastonmuutoksen Ajassa," in *Maapallon Tulevaisuus Ja Lapsen Oikeudet*, eds. E. ja Tuukkanen Pekkarinen, T. Lapsiasiavaltuutetun toimiston julkaisuja (2020) 124–136; Niina Meriläinen, Iikka Pietilä, and Jari Varsaluoma, "Digital Services and Youth Participation in Processes of Social Change: World Café Workshops in Finland," presented at the ECPR General Conference (2018).

2. Agenda 2030, "The Sustainable Development Goals," https://www.un.org/sustainabledevelopment/sustainable-development-goals/; Finnish legislation: *Youth Act*, Section 24; *Local Government Act*, Section 26; *General Upper Secondary Schools Act* (High School Act); *Vocational Education and Training Act*, Section 106.

3. *EU Charter of Fundamental Rights*, Article 10 of the *European Convention on Human Rights*, https://fra.europa.eu/en/eu-charter/article/11-freedom-expression-and-information.

4. *Convention on the Rights of the Child*, https://www.ohchr.org/EN/ProfessionalInterest/Pages/CRC.aspx

5. The EU Youth Strategy 2019–2027, https://eur-lex.europa.eu/legal-content/EN/TXT/PDF/?uri=OJ:C:2018:456:FULL&from=EN.

6. Niina Meriläinen, "Understanding the Framing of Issues in Multi-actor Arenas: Power Relations in the Human Rights Debate," PhD diss., (University of Jyväskylä, 2014); Niina Meriläinen, "Narratives of Human Trafficking in International Issue Arenas with Implications for Policy Formation," in *International Handbook of Human Trafficking: A Multi-disciplinary and Applied Approach*, eds. Rochelle Dalla and Donna Sabella (London: Taylor & Francis, 2019): 103–132.

7. Kidman and O'Malley, 2020; Meriläinen and Piispa, 2020; Niina Meriläinen, Heta-Elena Heiskanen, and Jukka Viljanen, "Participation of Young People in Legislative Processes: A Case Study of the General Upper Secondary Schools Act in Finland–A School Bullying Narrative," *The Journal of Legislative Studies* (2020): 1–32, https://doi.org/10.1080/13572334.2020.1826095.

8. Meriläinen and Piispa, 2020.

9. State Youth Council and Finnish Youth Research Society, "Youth Barometer 2018: Influence On the Edge of Europe," (2019), https://tietoanuorista.fi/en/publications/youth-barometer-2018-never-before-have-young-people-been-this-interested-in-politics/.

10. Thomas Akiva, Kai S. Cortina, and Charles Smith, "Involving youth in program decision-making: How common and what might it do for youth?," *Journal of Youth and Adolescence* 43, no. 11 (2014): 1844–1860.

11. Barry Checkoway and Lorraine M. Gutierrez, "Youth Participation and Community Change: An Introduction," *Journal Of Community Practice* 14, no. 1–2 (2006): 1–9.

12. Sratos Patrikios and Mark Shephard, "Representative and Useful? An Empirical Assessment of the Representative Nature and Impact of the Scottish Youth Parliament," *The Journal of Legislative Studies* 20, no. 2 (2014): 236–254; Ariadne Vromen and Philippa Collin, "Everyday Youth Participation? Contrasting Views from Australian Policymakers and Young People," *Young* 18, no. 1 (2010): 97–112.

13. Lucas Walsh, Rosalyn Black, and Howard Prosser, "Young People's Perceptions of Power and Influence as a Basis for Understanding Contemporary Citizenship," *Journal of Youth Studies* 21, no. 2 (2018): 218–234.

14. Anu Gretschel and Tomi Kiilakoski, *Demokratiaoppitunti. Lasten Ja Nuorten Kunta 2010-Luvun Alussa* (Helsinki: Nuorisotutkimusseura, 2012).

15. Erik Andersson, "Young People's Political Participation: A Public Pedagogy Challenge at the Municipal Level," *Young* 26, no. 2 (2018), 183.

16. Stefaan Walgrave and Peter Van Aelst, "Political Agenda Setting and the Mass Media," in *Oxford Research Encyclopedia of Politics*, ed. William R. Thomas (Oxford, UK: Oxford University Press, 2016).

17. Iikka Pietilä, Jari Varsaluoma, and Kaisa Väänänen, "Understanding the Digital and Non-digital Participation by the Gaming Youth," presented at Human-Computer Interaction International Conference (2019).

18. Barbara Piškur, Ramon Daniëls, Marian Jongmans, Marjolijn Ketelaar, Rob Smeets, Meghan Norton, and Anna Beurskens, "Participation and Social Participation: Are They Distinct Concepts?," *Clinical Rehabilitation*, 28, no. 3 (2014): 211–220.

19. Elisabeth Hästbacka, Mikael Nygård, and Fredrica Nyqvist, "Barriers and Facilitators to Societal Participation of People with Disabilities: A Scoping Review of Studies Concerning European Countries," *Alter* 10, no. 3 (2016): 201–220.

20. Joakim Ekman and Erik Amnå, "Political Participation and Civic Engagement: Towards a New Typology." *Human Affairs*," 22, no. 3 (2012): 283–300.

21. Meriläinen, Pietilä, and Varsaluoma, 2018.

22. Meriläinen and Piispa, 2020.

23. Helen Cahill and Babak Dadvand, "Re-Conceptualising Youth Participation: A Framework to Inform Action," *Children and Youth Services Review* 95, no. 1 (2018): 243–253.

24. Mijntje D.C. ten Brummelaar, Annemiek T. Harder, Margrite E. Kalverboer, Wendy J. Post, and Erik J. Knorth, "Participation of Youth in Decision-Making Procedures During Residential Care: A Narrative Review," *Child & Family Social Work* 23, no. 1 (2017): 33–44.

25. Meghan M. Burke, Linda Sandman, Beatrize Perez, and Meghann O'Leary, "The Phenomenon of Legislative Advocacy Among Parents of Children with Disabilities," *Journal of Research in Special Educational Needs* 18, no. 1 (2018): 50–58; Stratos and Shephard, 2014.

26. Riitta Ahtonen and Anssi Keinänen, "Sidosryhmien Vaikuttaminen Lainvalmisteluun—Empiirinen Analyysi Valiokuntakuulemisesta," (2012): 1–26; Juho Vesa and Anu Kantola, "Kuka Pääsee Mukaan? Miten Järjestöjen Ääni Kuuluu Lakien Valmistelussa," (2016).

27. Cahill and Dadvand, 2018.

28. Meriläinen and Piispa, 2020.

29. Youth Survey in Mikkeli, 2020.

30. Kirsi Pauliina Kallio and Jouni Häkli, "Children and Young People's Politics in Everyday Life," *Space and Polity* 17, no. 1 (2013): 1–16.

31. Kidman and O'Malley, 2020.

32. Brian Head, "Why Not Ask Them? Mapping and Promoting Youth Participation," *Children And Youth Services Review* 33, no. 4 (2011): 544.

33. Maria Ojala, "Hope and Climate Change: The Importance of Hope for Environmental Engagement Among Young People," *Environmental Education Research* 18, no. 5 (2012): 625-642; Adam Corner, Olga Roberts, Sybille Chiari, Sonja Völler, Elisabeth S. Mayrhuber, Sylvia Mandl, and Kate Monson, "How Do Young People Engage With Climate Change? The Role of Knowledge, Values, Message Framing, and Trusted Communicators," *Wires Climate Change* 6, no. 5 (2015): 523–534.

34. Meriläinen and Piispa, 2020.

35. Pietilä, Varsaluoma, and Väänänen, 2019; Meriläinen and Piispa, 2020.

36. Kidman and O'Malley, 2020.

37. Kim Fridkin, Patrick J. Kenney, and Jack Crittenden, "On the Margins of Democratic Life: The Impact of Race and Ethnicity on the Political Engagement of Young People," *American Politics Research* 34, no. 5 (2006): 615.

38. Lance W. Bennett, Kirsten Foot, and Michael Xenos "Narratives And Network Organization: A Comparison of Fair Trade Systems in Two Nations," *Journal of Communication* 61, no. 2 (2011): 219–245.

39. Alice Feldman, "Othering Knowledge and Unknowing Law: Oppositional Narratives in the Struggle for American Indian Religious Freedom," *Social & Legal Studies* 9, no. 4 (2000): 557–582.

40. Meriläinen and Piispa, 2020; Susanna Ågren, Iikka Pietilä, and Tiina Rättilä, "Palkkatyökeskeisen Ajattelun Esiintyminen Ammattiin Opiskelevien Työelämäasenteissa" in *Hyvää Työtä! Nuorisobarometri 2019 Valtion Nuorisoneuvosto*, eds. Lotta Haikkola and Sami Myllyniemi, 157–178 (Helsinki: Nuorisotutkimusseura, Nuorisotutkimusverkosto & Opetus Ja Kulttuuriministeriö, 2020).

41. Laura Lapadat, Anusha Balram, Joanna Cheek, Eugenia Canas, Andrea Paquette, and Erin E Michalak, "Engaging Youth in the Bipolar Youth Action Project: Community-Based Participatory Research," *Journal of Participatory Medicine*, 12, no. 3 (2020), e19475.

42. Cahill and Dadvand, 2018; Lapadat et al., 2020.

43. Lapadat et al., 2020.

44. Alan Hudson, "NGOs' Transnational Advocacy Networks: From 'Legitimacy' To 'Political Responsibility'?," *Global Networks* 1, no. 4 (2001): 331–352; Gerald M Steinberg, "The Politics Of NGOs, Human Rights and the Arab-Israel Conflict," *Israel Studies* 16, no. 2 (2011): 24–54; Manuel Castells, *Communication Power* (New York: Oxford University Press, 2009); Erin Michelle Kamler, "Negotiating Narratives of Human Trafficking: NGOs, Communication and the Power of Culture," *Journal of Intercultural Communication Research* 42, no. 1 (2013): 73-90; Meriläinen, 2019; Meriläinen, Heiskanen, and Viljanen, 2020; Clifford Bob, *The Global Right Wing and the Clash of World Politics* (Cambridge, UK: Cambridge University Press, 2012); Kurt Lewin, "Frontiers in Group Dynamics: II. Channels of Group Life; Social Planning and Action Research," *Human Relations* 1, no. 2 (1947), 143–153.

45. Andrew Pettigrew, *The Politics Of Organizational Decision-Making* (London: Routledge, 2014;) Harold Lasswell, "The Structure and Function of Communication in Society," *The Communication of Ideas* 37, no. 1 (1948): 136–139.

46. Meriläinen, 2019.

47. The direct quotations presented in this chapter come from the participants in the vocational school workshops and the questionnaires that the students answered. All of the questionnaires were completed anonymously, and no identifying information was collected. Individual students cannot be identified from the citations used in this chapter. The answers have been translated to English from their original Finnish by the researcher. The research ethics guidelines of The Finnish National Board on Research Integrity (TENK) were followed in collecting and processing the material. Also, a research permit to complete the research was acquired by the administrator of the research project from the City of Tampere, Finland. The author of this chapter was told orally that the research permit had been acquired. This was deemed sufficient enough by the employer of the researcher, Tampere University, Finland.

48. Kamler, 2013; Meriläinen, 2019; Niina Meriläinen and Marita Vos, "Framing Issues in the Public Debate: The Case of Human Rights," *Corporate Communications, An International Journal* 18, no. 1 (2013): 119–134; Niina Meriläinen and Marita Vos, "Public Discourse on Human Trafficking in International Issue Arenas," *Societies* 5, no. 1 (2015): 14–42; Meriläinen, Heiskanen, and Viljanen, 2020.

20 | Challenges of Civic Education in Non-Western Countries: A Vignette from Mauritius

Shantal Kaurooa and Sheetal Sheena Sookrajowa

University of Mauritius

This chapter explores the importance of civic education in both primary and secondary school curriculum in Mauritius. Civic education is not prioritized as a subject in Mauritius. In the interest of upholding the country's democratic ideals, it is critical to educate youngsters to be engaged citizens throughout all of their schooling. Such education is especially important in newer democratic states such as Mauritius. The vignette we offer in this chapter explores the challenges faced by educators and researchers who are seeking to strengthen or build stable foundations for democracy in countries such as Mauritius and encourages a shared commitment to providing a democratic education not only in Mauritius but in similarly situated countries globally.

KEYWORDS: Civic Education; Youth; Political Socialization; Primary Secondary School Curriculum.

Introduction

As Brennan writes, civic education builds a virtuous and knowledgeable civic culture supported by active committed citizens. Without this foundation, a country is static.[1] Many established democracies have become more reflective on ways to build youth civic participation as a means of ensuring a stable, and democratic future. Scholars and educators agree that this path to building youth participation should occur both inside and outside of the classroom, as institutions of education at all levels are the incubators and custodians of active citizens for the future and current success of democracies around the world.

In less developed states, however, some of the tools to build and foster civic education may be minimal or absent entirely. An absence of political knowledge and skills leads to a lack of efficacy and declines in youth voting, which will then impact future political and civic engagement in these countries.[2] In the case of Mauritius, civic education has not been prioritized in the school curriculum and remains a neglected subject, hindering the political socialization of young Mauritians. As Tovmasyan and Thoma advocate, "the ultimate goal of civic education is to prepare generations for the essential principles and values of democracy embodied with a high sense of responsibility and active engagement in issues the society, community, or state face in their everyday life."[3]

This chapter explores challenges faced by educators and researchers who are seeking to strengthen or build stable foundations for democracy in countries with newer democratic systems and calls for a shared commitment to provide this education for democracy not only in Mauritius but in similarly situated countries globally.

Challenges

As this book and previous APSA books on civic engagement explain, civic education is a formative learning experience focused on democratic principles which frames democratic competence, meaning the necessary knowledge, skills, beliefs, values, attitudes, and dispositions for rational human action to enhance decision making and responsibility in the democratization of society.[4] Hess and Torney demonstrate that children can develop political experience as early as elementary school. By the end of primary education, they show that children can expand their political efficacy more clearly by cultivating informal methods for political engagement.[5] Before the age of 10, Piaget explains that children see class rules and body of laws as autocratic, but at 10-years-old they start to discover democracy by respecting and observing rules as a means of promoting an ethical community.[6] Lee Ehman affirmed that early to mid-adolescence (11–17 years-old) is a period when students can engage in political thought with abstractions. Henceforward, we can see that adolescence brings a remarkable watershed of political idealism fed by utopianism, where teenagers search for ideologies for an ethical society. The National Assessment for Educational Progress (NAEP) showed that from 1969 to 1976 in the United States, students between the ages of 13 and 17 had noteworthy changes in their political attitudes.[7]

In the case of Mauritius, such a change was witnessed during the 1970s when student movements made a great impact on society. Mauritius gained its independence from the United Kingdom in 1968, and leaders quickly established a democratic government with a substantial welfare state which included free education. Universal adult suffrage was granted in Mauritius in 1956 when both men and women could vote at the age of 21, and in 1976 the voting age was reduced to age 18.

As the new Mauritius was established in the 1970s and 1980s, leaders recognized that the youth must be educated about the new government and political system in order to build and stabilize the multi-ethnic country. Thus, secondary school social studies textbooks in the 1980s had a complete unit titled, "How is our society governed?" with sub-topics such as "our constitution," "general elections," and one for each branch of government. The text even included a case study of how the government functions to enhance informed awareness of what happens in governance and how it happens.[8] In the 1980s and 1990s, though led primarily by only two governing families, Mauritius had become a largely stable and prosperous country, reaching the *high human development* category of the United Nations Development Program's Human Development Index in 1996.[9]

The economic development of Mauritius has been termed the "Mauritius Miracle." The economy is fueled by exports of sugar and textiles, tourism, and financial services, and the country has a diverse set of export and import partners. The average gross domestic product per capita totaled US $22,870 before the coronavirus pandemic, placing it at 85th in the world, which is striking for a population of just over 1.3 million people. Literacy is high at 91% of the population, and while overall pre-pandemic unemployment was low at 6.65%, youth unemployment (24 years old and under) totaled 21.8% in 2017. Poverty is not unusually high in Mauritius, at 10.3%. This economic success after independence has helped to support democratic governance, even though leadership has been largely controlled by two families.[10]

Mauritius has no indigenous population. Instead, its people are the ancestors of those brought by British, French, and Dutch colonial powers to the island. The resulting population includes those with backgrounds from Hindu and Muslim Indians, Chinese, and various African countries, in addition to the European colonial groups. The country has not included questions on ethnicity in its census since 1972, and thus such demographic or identity data do not exist. The dominant language is Creole, though English, spoken by a small percent of the population, is the official language of the government. Almost one-half of the population considers Hindu their religion; one-quarter adhere to Roman Catholicism; and about 17% are Muslims.[11] In this multi-ethnic context, preserving the common foundational values of Mauritian democracy is of great importance.[12] According to the National Curriculum Framework under the Mauritius Institute of Examination, the subject of social studies is supposed to nurture informed and engaged citizenship and to enhance harmony and unity in society.[13]

However, there are concerns that more recent leaders are dismantling the educational supports for Mauritian democracy. In 2013, new secondary school social studies textbooks were issued, but the previous extensive sections on democracy and governance were eliminated. Starting in 2005, education became compulsory up to age 16 with the introduction of mandatory 11-year schooling.[14] To strengthen its education system as a knowledge hub empowering versatile youth, the Government Program of 2015–2019 included a launch of the Nine-Year Continuous Basic Education Reform (NYS).[15] This reform brought forth new versions of the textbook that grouped social studies knowledge into three main areas—history, geography, and sociology.

The history section helps students to learn about past events, examine different values such as social justice, and challenge viewpoints of diverse groups in society. History helps them to associate with their ancestors and preserve their own culture and heritage which fosters a sense of patriotism, hopefully promoting national unity. The geography section explores the interaction of human beings within the physical environment and how changes in this environment affect their lives. The goal is to help students better understand the consequences of people's interactions in their surroundings and the ways that they can improve resources and institutions. The third section—sociology—examines current issues and the way of life in Mauritius' changing society. Students are exposed to influential societal forces and are educated to confront the challenges of social reality. This section purports to emphasize ways to develop active citizenship so that young people can make better decisions concerning the country.[16]

Yet, while the 2015 reform acknowledges the importance of citizenship education in primary school education (grades 1 to 6) and includes "Values and Citizenship" as a single subject which is integrated across all subjects, the same learning area is omitted from grade 7 and above.[17] The new secondary social studies textbook's section on sociology mostly covers law and order issues, with a mere six pages for a section titled, "Developing Responsible Citizenship." Significant explanations of the government and the constitution and how they work are absent. Though updates were certainly needed from the 1980s text, crucial basic information on democracy and the vibrant section on how governance works in practice have been eliminated.

Recent interviews with former government ministers and members of parliament reveal their concerns about the future of the country when education about government is diminished in secondary schools.[18] One minister stated that citizenship education (his preferred term) needs to be properly conceived as an interactive process relating topical issues such as the death penalty or legalization of cannabis to governance. He proposed active learning formats, such as debates in any language which students want, and research projects constructed as opportunities for students to speak up and interview people. He raised the examples of Singapore and Scandinavian countries as taking more than 40 years to build the kind of citizenship that they have and to which Mauritians should aspire, meaning disciplined, responsible, and productive citizens who participate regularly in democratic governance.

Another former minister stated that, above all, civic education should be student-centered and not exam-based. He also highlighted that students should learn about the parliament, the constitution, and basic political processes from the beginning of their education and build this knowledge at different stages. Both former ministers also emphasized that the government should support the kind of citizens that Mauritius wants for its future and, as such, the students who are Mauritius's future must understand our democratic system, their human rights, the importance of voting, and law and order issues.

In contrast, a senior educator believed that learning the basics of the political system at an early stage is sufficient since pupils are already overloaded with dozens of subjects in secondary school. One of the social studies teachers stated that they saw politics as a vicious circle, noting some negative images of our politicians, and proposed that the introduction of civic education would be a waste of time. This dichotomy between the views of this small sample of ministers and educators is by no means conclusive, but it does highlight some potential rifts in seeking to advance civic engagement education in Mauritius.

Informal interviews with a small sample of Mauritius students reveal some possible consequences of the lack of civic education.[19] A quasi-structured survey was given in December 2017 to 200 secondary school and college students, which included 38.5% males and 61.5% females. While more research is needed to clarify results, one theme was clear—a large majority did not understand even basic components of the government and how it works. These students have experienced the new curriculum, and the results suggest that the lack of civic education is impacting their ability to engage as knowledgeable and active citizens.

Educating for Mauritian Democracy: An Example of Needs for the Future

Mauritius is at a crossroads in its political future. The generation which built its independence is retiring, and the newest generation has not received a comprehensive education in politics and citizenship. This lack of knowledge about how their government works is certain to have negative consequences for the democracy that previous generations sought to establish after centuries of colonial rule. Youth comprise just over one-third of the population, and if their civic education is neglected, this situation could be dangerous for democracy.[20]

Further, researchers face other challenges in collecting and evaluating accurate data about youth participation because key data, such as voting participation by age group, is not gathered by the government. Much political participation data is not gathered by ethnicity as government leaders in the early days of Mauritian democracy were concerned that requiring reporting by ethnicity could exacerbate existing ethnic tensions. Yet, data by age group in measurable areas such as voting could help policymakers, educators, and researchers discern where gaps in political participation exist for all groups. This information also could point to interventions in the educational system, especially the secondary education years that lead directly into voting and adulthood, which could support the future of democracy in Mauritius and in other countries with a colonial history and fairly new democratic governments. Finally, while relative economic prosperity in the past 50 years has helped to stabilize Mauritian democracy, the economic impacts of the pandemic on crucial sectors, such as tourism, demonstrate that this factor cannot be taken for granted as a structure to support democracy.

Overall, this chapter points to the role of education in the future of post-colonial democracies. Whether in multi-ethnic or homogenous contexts, poor or more developed economies, post-colonial democracies need to invest in quality, comprehensive civic engagement education and research at all levels, especially as the generations which fought to establish these democracies pass on governing to a new group. This next generation must have the tools to face increasing complexities and challenges to democracy at all levels of government.

Endnotes

1. Jason Brennan, *The Ethics of Voting* (Princeton, NJ: Princeton University Press, 2012).

2. Richard Pratte, *The Civic Imperative: Examining the Need for Civic Education. Advances in Contemporary Educational Thought Series, Volume 3.* (New York: Teachers College Press, 1988).

3. Tigran Tovmasyan and Marcie Taylor Thoma, "The Impact of Civic Education on Schools, Students, and Communities," in *Final Analytical Report* (Armenia: Caucuses Resource Research Centers, 2008). https://www.crrc.am/hosting/file/_static_content.

4. Alison Rios Millett McCartney, Elizabeth A. Bennion, and Dick Simpson, eds. *Teaching Civic Engagement: From Student to Active Citizen* (Washington, DC: American Political Science Association, 2013); Elizabeth Matto, Alison Rios Millett McCartney, Elizabeth A. Bennion, and Dick Simpson, eds. *Teaching Civic Engagement Across the Disciplines* (Washington, DC, American Political Science Association, 2017); Margaret Branson and Charles Quigley, *The Role of Civic Education. 1st ed* (2002).

5. Robert Hess and Judith Torney, *The Development of Political Attitudes in Children* (Chicago: Aldine, 1967).

6. Jean Piaget, *The Moral Judgement of the Child* (Glencoe, IL: Free Press, 1948).

7. Lee H. Ehman, "The American School in the Political Socialization Process," *Review of Educational Research* 50, no.1 (1980).

8. Mauritius Institute of Education, *Social Studies* (MIE & Edition de l'ocean indien, 1980).

9. Thomas Hylland Eriksen and Ramola Ramtohul, "Introduction," in *The Mauritian Paradox: Fifty Years of Development, Diversity, and Democracy,* eds. Thomas Hylland Eriksen and Ramola Ramtohul (Baltimore, MD: University of Mauritius Press, 2018).

10. CIA, "Mauritius," *CIA World Factbook.* https://www.cia.gov/the-world-factbook/countries/mauritius/.

11. See: Embassy of the Republic of Mauritius, "General Information about Mauritius," Washington, DC. https://mauritius-washington.govmu.org/Pages/Mauritius%20-%20Washington/General-Information-about-the-Republic-of-Mauritius.aspx; CIA, "Mauritius."

12. Marie Hyleen Sandra Mariaye, "The Role of the School in Providing Moral Education in a Multicultural Society: The Case of Mauritius," (University of South Africa, PhD dissertation, 2006).

13. Mauritius Institute of Education, "Syllabus Forms I, II, and III," Government of Mauritius, (2011).

14. Ministry of Education, Culture & Human Resources, *Education Human Resources Strategy Plan 2008–2020* (Port Louis: Government of Mauritius, 2009).

15. Mauritius Institute of Education, *National Curriculum Framework: Nine Year Continuous Basic Education* (Port Louis: Government of Mauritius, 2016).

16. Mauritius Institute of Education, *The National Curriculum Framework: Secondary* (Government of Mauritius, 2009).

17. Mauritius Institute of Education, *National Curriculum Framework: Nine Year Continuous Basic Education* (Port Louis: Government of Mauritius, 2016).

18. The authors conducted eight interviews which included two former government ministers, one former member of parliament, one former adviser of a minister, one senior educator at the college level, one former college Rector, and two social studies teachers. Sample questions included: Is today's generation interested in politics? Should the Ministry of Education implement civic education as a subject in the secondary curriculum? How effective school would be to channel political orientations of students through civic education? While the university does not have an American-style institutional review board, a transcript of the interviews was provided to the book editors, and the interviewees were told that their comments would otherwise be kept anonymous.

19. Again, the university lacks a review board. The questions and answers were provided to the book editors for review.

20. CIA, "Mauritius."

21

A Global Advance in Civic Engagement

Dick Simpson

University of Illinois at Chicago

Democracy around the globe is under attack which is why we need to increase the teaching of civic engagement. Additionally, civic engagement can be taught even in non-democratic countries using different techniques. A further goal is to create global citizens who think beyond their own community and nation. But to be able to teach civic engagement globally we need to have a new commitment, apply new methods, and obtain greater funding. We will need support at the international level as well. Based upon the experiences detailed in this book, we have created a joint agenda for change in order to better teach civic engagement globally.

KEYWORDS: Agenda for Change; Global Citizen; Democracy; Non-Democratic Countries; Nation.

Introduction

The last decade of the 20th century was marked by a major advance in creating more democracy in countries around the world. The beginning of the 21st century, though, has brought a backsliding of democracy with populism and authoritarianism on the rise in both developed and developing countries. In the United States (US), the Donald Trump era brought an insurrection in the US Capitol. In the United Kingdom (UK), Brexit undid decades of developing a European Union. Some former Soviet Union countries fell back into autocratic ways. China cracked down on Hong Kong. Indonesia had a military coup. The Arab Spring mostly failed to achieve more democracy in the Middle East. And so it has gone around the globe.

As Freedom House observed:

> These withering blows marked the 15th consecutive year of decline in global freedom. The countries experiencing deterioration outnumbered those with improvements by the largest margin recorded since the negative trend began in 2006. The long democratic recession is deepening... Nearly 75 percent of the world's population lived in a country that faced deterioration last year.[1]

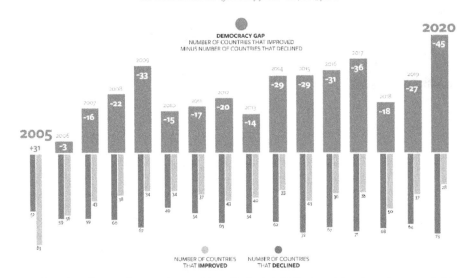

Figure 1. A Growing Democracy Gap: 15 Years of Decline
Countries with aggregate score declines in *Freedom in the World* have outnumbered those with gains every year for the past 15 years.

Source: *Freedom in the World 2021,* Freedom House; For past editions of *Freedom in the World* and more information on the report methodology, visit freedomhouse.org.

The 15-year decline in democracy and the global increase in authoritarian tendencies needs to be countered, as Lynn Pasquerella has written in the foreword of this book, by "renewed global leadership and solidarity among democratic states." She further urges that colleges and universities demonstrate "the value of civic education in safeguarding democracy and countering authoritarianism." As the report on "The Role of Education in Taming Authoritarian Attitudes" from Georgetown University argues, "higher education is the cornerstone of successful democracies not easily shaken by authoritarian threats."[2]

As Steven Smith wrote in the preface to this book, "Given the volatility and unpredictability of different country politics, active citizenship becomes increasingly important for the future of democracy and good governance. Citizens participating in their communities through the electoral process and civil society organizations are critical to the building of social capital and effective public policies. This active citizenship requires comprehensive and informed civic education through elementary and secondary schools and higher education institutions." Thus, the development of civic engagement globally using techniques appropriate and effective in each country is essential.

As the authors in this book have written repeatedly, it is necessary to educate every generation about democracy and to provide them the skills and values of democracy. We do this to maintain democracy because democratic citizens are not just born—they learn to become citizens through education and engaged participation in the democratic process. In this book we focus especially on how colleges and universities can be active in reversing rising challenges to democracy and the low participation across the world. If we fail in our mission, our countries face backsliding into the authoritarianism and disregard for human rights once again.[3]

Dmitry Lanko from his work in Russia adds that "Teaching civic engagement in international relations involves helping students to develop the skill to think beyond oneself, one's community, and even one's country."[4] Creating global citizens requires us to help students engage meaningfully with other people, places, and events. Thus, our authors work on establishing a global classroom and developing innovative new experimental methods which enlarge students' development as both national and global citizens in ways that can be duplicated in different circumstances. The purpose of this book has been to provide "a set of evidence-based best practices in how to foster civic knowledge, skills, and dispositions" which can guide the development of these different courses and education programs.[5]

There is an especially great need for civic engagement education globally now. Even where democracies exist, such as in the US and Europe, there is a need for reforming undemocratic features like the Electoral College and the US Senate's use of the filibuster. A recent survey by the Pew Research Center found that "roughly two-thirds of adults in France and the US, as well as about half in the United Kingdom, believe their political systems need major changes or need to be completely reformed." As many as two-thirds of Americans believe "most politicians are corrupt.... And those who say most politicians are corrupt are much more likely to think their political systems need serious reform."[6] The Pew Center further found that trust in government across most Western democracies surveyed was only about 50% and only the same percentage think that "ordinary people, can do a lot to influence the government."[7]

Given the growth of autocracies, populism, and the lack of trust in government even in established democracies, the task of strengthening democracy around the world is especially crucial in the coming decade following the COVID-19 global pandemic. The pandemic, and the economic recession which it caused, demonstrated the failure of governments around the world to safeguard and protect their citizens. Central to the task of rebuilding, reforming, and strengthening our countries is increasing civic engagement by youth—especially high school and college students. In many countries, they lack civic knowledge, skills, and motivation. Our task is to change that condition.

Any program of teaching for democracy must be done across disciplines, across universities, and across the globe. It will require a concerted effort, but it will take different forms in different countries. It will also take "scaffolding learning or successively building upon students' civic knowledge, skills, and attitudes throughout their schooling."[8] It can't be done by a single faculty member or accomplished in a single course. But as the assessment of the courses and programs around the world represented in this book demonstrates, major gains can be made when they are done intentionally.

Call to Action

One of Lenin's books is entitled: *What is to be done?*[9] That question confronts us today. There is overwhelming evidence that democracy is in trouble in different countries around the world. And whether or not a country is currently democratic, there is a need to provide civic education. Educators have been particularly concerned to develop a "toolbox" of effective instructional techniques for teaching citizenship.[10]

As the chapters in this book illustrate, there is a growing effort in all parts of the world to increase civic engagement. These experiments allow us to share insights and best practices on an ever-expanding basis. Civic education efforts have progressed from just a few courses in selected disciplines like political science, urban planning, or social work to coursework across the disciplines and campus-wide. Efforts to teach civic engagement are expanding across universities and through multi-university efforts like Model United Nations or the National Student Issues Convention in the US. We even have reached the stage where explicit collaboration across countries is also possible. New technologies like Skype and Zoom make this collaboration easier as several chapters in this book illustrate.

The level of civic participation depends upon many different factors beyond the classroom, such as appeals by candidates, political parties, and social movements. But civic engagement education can make a critical contribution to building civic society. While there are different challenges in our local communities and countries, civic engagement efforts in our universities and community colleges are beginning to have real and measurable effects as demonstrated in the reports in our book.

To use my own campus, the University of Illinois at Chicago (UIC), as an example, we have increased student voter registration by several hundred percent over the last decade since we began concerted planned civic engagement efforts across the university. Our rate of student voter registration grew from 58% to 71%, and student voting grew from 41% to 55% between 2012–2016. They increased again to 20,629 registered voters and 67% student voting in 2020. Comparable data from many campuses in the US prove that teaching civic engagement and providing curricular and co-curricular civic engagement opportunities make concrete differences in civic outcomes.[11] As several chapters in this text demonstrate, the positive benefits of embedding civic engagement education into higher education also can be seen on campuses across the globe.

This book is unique because it documents the focused civic engagement efforts in different countries—from so-called developed democracies to autocratic countries and failed democracies that have slid back towards autocracy. Civic engagement efforts and experiments over the last decade have made it possible to undertake successful civic engagement education in autocratic countries like China and Russia, more conservative countries like Singapore, and developing countries like Belize and Guatemala. It is also possible for college students in one country to engage successfully in experiences in other countries through study abroad programs and joint distance learning classes. Students then bring those new-found experiences, commitments, and understandings back with them to their home countries and communities.

In the US, efforts to promote civic engagement of college students have increased since the publication of *Educating for Democracy* in 2007[12] and *A Crucible Moment* in 2012.[13] Civic engagement efforts have been further documented by the previous books in this series of *Teaching Civic Engagement* that the American Political Science Association initiated in 2013.[14] *Teaching Civic Engagement Globally* joins that literature in documenting the advances in civic engagement and offering new ideas to teachers around the world to help them to implement civic engagement programs that best fit their local and national situations. It shows how civic engagement education can happen in any country's community colleges, high schools, four-year liberal arts colleges, technical schools, and research universities. We expect that the publication of ideas on future teaching civic engagement globally will lead to an expansion in journal articles and books so that future students can benefit and so the dismal decline of democracies can be reversed.

However, for now, there are still major gaps in civic engagement education globally. For instance, the low level of teaching civic engagement in vocational schools and community colleges, as opposed to what is available at traditional high schools and colleges, is acute. In the US, many individual community colleges and professors have promoted service-learning and are moving to civic engagement. Some national organizations like The Citizens Campaign are launching experiments in civic engagement education at community colleges.[15] But these community college programs are still only beginning to be developed. Similarly, almost no civic engagement education is provided at vocational schools around the world. This situation needs to change if we are to spread education for democracy to the youth and future citizen-leaders.

Another example of efforts to significantly expand civic engagement education at the elementary to high school level is CIVIX Now, a "national cross-partisan coalition of over 100 organizations focused on improving our nation's K-12 in and out-of-school civic education."[16] One of CIVIX Now's projects is to encourage states to adopt formal civic engagement education courses in elementary and high schools as a requirement of graduation. This legislation is an attempt to close the gap between states with little civic education and states with better programs as a way to secure additional funding from the federal government to make civic education a priority as STEM (Science, Technology, Engineering, and Math) education is currently. There are, of course, significant gaps between the level of civic engagement in different countries. These parallel a major difference between states in the US which require civic engagement education courses to graduate high school and those that do not.

This example illustrates that our challenge is not simply a matter of developing and sharing pedagogy. A political effort is also required to get government sponsorship and resources for the effort.

What is Happening in Civic Engagement Education Today?

One of the primary purposes of this book has been to survey teaching civic engagement projects which are happening around the world. We wanted to highlight the teaching of global and international affairs in a way to move beyond simply knowing facts like the location of a country on a map or simple information like a country's governmental form and structure.

There is a major effort underway to teach in different countries the knowledge, skills, and motivation to be effective citizen participants. Of course, this is done differently in established democracies, autocracies, developing democracies, and failed democracies. Different methods are required to build and employ social capital effectively under different regimes. Yet our overall goal must be to support and reform governments so as to involve citizens positively in their communities, societies, and governance. In this book we seek to catalogue some of the myriad ways in which civic engagement is taught. Whatever our circumstances, we can learn from these experiments and adapt them to our classes, colleges, and universities.

Since there is no global index or encyclopedia of civic engagement, we began the basic task of describing the state of affairs in our world today as we move into the post-pandemic era. This is particularly important as we begin the task of rebuilding our economies, societies, and governments after the pandemic and the economic recession that it caused. Simply documenting successful efforts helps others to adopt best practices rather than having to reinvent the wheel.

The advantage of this approach is that it also allows us to describe interventions which may be effective in diverse countries and to suggest improvements that may make those interventions more successful. It adds to our toolbox and widens the lens with which we view civic engagement education.

In addition, we undertake at this stage of development an objective evaluation of various efforts to teach civic engagement using both quantitative and qualitative methods. We judge and measure the degree to which these interventions from classes, workshops, community campaigns, and creative techniques help to create better citizens and improve communities and societies more broadly. It is not enough to report what we have done; we also need to provide an assessment of the successes and weaknesses of different techniques.

From this accounting, it becomes immediately clear that no single intervention, workshop, class, or project by itself can help students to become the most effective citizens and leaders possible. Even in universities that take teaching civic engagement as one of their primary missions, a single intervention cannot accomplish this task. We not only map the effect of each technique, but where multiple interventions are used, report their overall success. In general, we find that no one class or exercise is sufficient, but efforts across disciplines and across the entire university or college are the most effective in improving concrete outcomes like higher levels of voting and participation.

In section I, we appreciate the differences in such countries as the UK, China, Brazil, Singapore, and the United States in their history and in their degree of openness to civic engagement. The authors demonstrate that the techniques which work in any one country must be responsive to different cultures and societies and modified accordingly. Yet, there are useful lessons from each to be applied to others.

Each country has a slightly different history of teaching democracy. For instance, as Craig discusses in chapter 5, in the UK, Oxford and Cambridge originally had an elitist and paternalistic approach to training the elite who ran the country and British empire. Today, there is broader citizenship education for all citizens. There is a near universal need for civic engagement education advocates and new methods in all countries.

This section focuses upon our role as educators in fostering civic engagement among all our students in different countries. We define this civic engagement education as "an evidence-based pedagogy which includes a wide range of activities ... that develop knowledge about the community, its systems, and its problems, seek constructive solutions to these problems...build skills to enable students to pursue these solutions...[and] to build a sense of efficacy that one's voice and actions matter."[17]

Section II records the wide range of civic engagement pedagogy and begins to assess the successes and challenges of each approach. We learn how students in different countries perceive civic engagement differently and how diverse classroom techniques can enhance their knowledge and skills. Finally, we consider how civic engagement education can teach agency, create a sense of efficacy, and empower our students.

In Section III, we learn about the need to develop educational institutions as opposed to only pursuing individual classroom interventions. New concepts like Work-Integrated Learning and new techniques like the use of theater in Brazil and critical study abroad within communities in The Gambia and Senegal are explored. This section expands civic engagement education for all students through both curricular and co-curricular programs.

Finally, in Section IV we develop a call to global action and an agenda for change for the decade ahead. We consider not only the development of individual students through teaching civic engagement, but also how we teach teachers and change curricula. Our agenda for change ranges from changing our own pedagogy to developing future books and journal articles on critical civic engagement efforts around the world to changing national laws and international norms.

This is only a beginning map of the possibilities for creating a new generation of more active citizens able to reshape the globe into a more democratic and humane world.

Priority and Funding

Perhaps one of the most troubling findings in our book is that there is little recognition and inadequate funding for civic engagement education. However, new campaigns are beginning to increase awareness of the need and importance of civic engagement education. Efforts are underway to increase the funding. For instance, the Civics Secures Democracy Act has been introduced in the US House of Representatives to provide major new funding for civic engagement education on the model by which STEM education has been funded over the last decade in the US.

Some countries provide civic engagement education as part of the regular high school curriculum and fund it accordingly, but most do not. There is no doubt that there is a need to make civic engagement education a priority and to provide adequate funding. This is missing in most countries, today. **Thus, the highest priority on our action agenda is to gain greater recognition of the need for civic engagement education and sufficient funding to provide it to all students.**

An additional goal of this book is to provide a pedagogical "toolbox" from experiments around the world and examples of "best practices" under different social and political conditions. As educators, administrators, and public officials, we need to know what works and what does not. We also need better assessments of these efforts. As was made evident during the COVID-19 global pandemic, we need "evidence based" policies and techniques to address public health emergencies. This is true of civic engagement education as well.

That is why the commitment of national educational organizations like the American Political Science Association and American Association of Colleges and Universities is so essential. This is true for disciplinary and educational organizations in all countries.

The next steps in improving civic engagement in most countries is the passage of legislation at the national level to adopt the goal of civic engagement education more broadly and implement "best practices" at the university and high school levels. In all countries, there needs to be more attention to developing and implementing quality civic engagement education for all students. Reaching this goal requires legislation and funding at the national and/or local levels.

Training and Rewarding the Teaching of Civic Engagement

Over the last decade or so there has been a gradual recognition of the importance of teaching civic engagement, especially in response to the increase in authoritarianism and the decrease in democracy around the world. However, while we know much more about "best practices" and exciting experiments than we did a decade ago, there is still the need to train faculty to succeed in this work and to provide the resources they need to be effective. So, one priority is to develop the materials and "trainers" to provide faculty the tools they need. However, when faculty do undertake this work, it is usually not well rewarded. Faculty in many colleges are promoted based upon publications they produce or the number of classes they teach. Almost no one is promoted because they have successfully taught civic engagement. The promotion and tenure standards will have to change around the world if more faculty across disciplines are to take the extra time and effort that teaching civic engagement requires. Even more so, teaching civic engagement globally to create more global citizens in the 21st century is underdeveloped and under-rewarded. At a minimum, it needs to be counted positively as teaching or service in promotion, tenure, and salary raise decisions.

A New International Commitment

One example of the slowly developing international commitment to civic engagement is that the current UN Youth Declaration adopted in 2018 declares that youth will:

> Become active global citizens supporting our peers across their spectrum of needs, from ending poverty in all dimensions, supporting women and girls, to quests for public office and other leadership positions in service of the community. We also proactively demand space for youth in all public fora.

The youth declaration further calls upon governments to back educational efforts:

> States to ensure access to quality and culturally-relevant education for all, reaching even the most vulnerable communities, providing the materials and knowledge to cultivate independent learners.

> States to integrate Agenda 2030 into all facets of their education curricula, considering informal, nonformal, experiential, service-based and interdisciplinary education as emphasized elements of the learning experience.

> **States to consciously design their education systems to enhance global citizenship** by fostering inclusivity, developing leadership, and encouraging innovation and creativity in youth. (emphasis added)[18]

Despite such declarations, international agencies like the United Nations and the World Bank have yet to promote civic engagement education in any meaningful way. If we are to create new global citizens in the next generation, we need an international commitment to do so.

Critical Civic Engagement

As Nicole Webster and other authors in this text make clear, uncritical civic engagement measured by simple performance data like the rate of student voter registration, voting, or service-learning activities is insufficient. This is especially so for global civic engagement where too often actions are considered without regard to structural injustices, "while a critical approach examines the efforts while exploring structural injustices" in the hope of transforming the students into critically aware global citizens and inspiring sustainable community improvements abroad.[19]

So, this book aspires not only to multiply the global civic engagement opportunities at universities and other educational levels by providing a menu of possible techniques, workshops, and class alternatives. In addition, this text seeks to foster more international cooperative efforts as well as provide faculty and administrators with an appreciation of more critical civic engagement education occurring globally. Hopefully, we can move from surface contact and feel-good experiences to widen student horizons with civic engagement learning activities, creating genuine personal transformations and community enrichment.

As the pandemic and economic recession have taught us, the 21st century will be filled with challenges like climate change, institutional racism, sexism, and economic injustice. These challenges cannot be solved by local actions alone. They can be ameliorated only by a global approach. If we are to enlarge democracy, increase citizen empowerment, and oppose populism, we must help our students to become global citizens and leaders.

One Size Doesn't Fit All

What this survey of civic engagement around the globe shows is the diversity in what is being accomplished and the clear limits of what is possible now. What can be done in less liberal societies like China and Singapore is quite different from what is possible in more liberal societies like Australia and European countries. Even the definition of what civic engagement can be differs in different places. In Singapore it is to "educate citizens of the world...and encourage an ethic of service."[20] In more liberal countries, the definition of civic engagement includes citizen participation in politics and government, if not protests and challenges to government policies and programs. In liberal countries, civic engagement might include challenging social norms such as institutional racism, climate change, and inequality. In less liberal societies, there is a high priority "on social stability and the need to avoid anything that might destabilize the country" and student civic engagement is expected to focus on "civic society," voluntarism, and consultation."[21] While they can push norms and laws in the name of civic engagement, students also must adhere to them and stay within existing societal and governmental boundaries.

Thus, the social and political context of each country, university, or educational system provides a different beginning point, different barriers, different opportunities, and different possibilities. Yet, American and European universities would still benefit from adopting some of the core curriculum from Yale-NUS in Singapore, while other countries could benefit from some of the American experiments in political science and across the disciplines documented in previous APSA books on teaching civic engagement.

Our goal should be to advance civic engagement education across disciplines, across countries and across the world. We should celebrate and support these efforts in every country. We should borrow techniques and ideas without the false belief that we are creating one plan, one curriculum, or one standard of what civic engagement means. States which have the most similar social, economic, and political circumstances should collaborate as to what works best in their circumstances, but we can all borrow ideas from each other. We can benefit from achievements in other countries as we push our own countries to provide more resources and more latitude in encouraging civic engagement by all citizens and in teaching civic engagement to our youth.

One lesson that the Singapore example provides is the need to promote civic ties and engagement not just within, but across countries. Some study abroad programs and simulations like Model UN achieve this goal. With new technologies like Skype and Zoom, it is possible to engage students in other countries in conversations and debates in ways that were not possible on a large scale before. One of the best ways forward is to increase the number of international students on all of our campuses while at the same time finding better ways to incorporate them into student and community life. This allows local students to learn from the perspectives, traditions, and cultures of students from abroad and international students to learn from living and studying in another country. While we have some programs for international students like teaching them the language in the country where they are studying and brief campus orientation programs, we have paid too little attention to the ways in which the next generations might better use these experiences to become citizens of the world. We need to facilitate more students obtaining international contacts and experiences.

We use slogans of global cooperation and understanding, but our civic engagement education agenda rarely has a global perspective. We are pleased if we are able to help our students meet with local officials to promote a policy proposal or if more of them register and vote in national elections. But as many of the chapters in this book indicate, there are deeper possibilities of global civic learning such as critical study abroad programs with a civic engagement focus. There are opportunities to turn our campuses into incubators for global citizens. Previous decades have brought the invention of programs like the Peace Corps in the US to send former college students around the globe on missions of peace. What will be the equivalent of the Peace Corps in the post-pandemic era? We have yet to invent and advocate for such programs today. The challenges of our time demand that we do so now.

A New Era of Civic Engagement

So civic engagement has entered a new phase—global, diverse, and inventive. A beginning agenda for teaching civic engagement globally must include:

1. Better recognition and greater funding at the national and university levels for critical civic engagement education.

2. New laws mandating minimum levels of civic engagement education for all students.

3. Requiring civic engagement education at elementary and high school levels.

4. Increased civic engagement education at community colleges and vocational education programs as well as at four-year colleges and universities.

5. Developing model civic learning programs in countries around the world including both less liberal and more liberal countries from autocracies to mature democracies.

6. Developing civic engagement activities which create genuine personal transformations and community enrichment rather than activities which train students only for passive citizenship.

7. Adding to the scholarship on teaching civic engagement globally by promoting the publication of research on civic education in refereed journals and university press books.

8. Adopting civic engagement education as a core function of national and international educational associations such as AAC&U and APSA.

9. Making teaching civic engagement a meaningful component of promotion, merit, and tenure decisions for faculty.

10. Increasing the number of international students on our campuses and providing better opportunities for them to share their insights with domestic students.

11. Developing large national programs to encourage the creation of global citizen leaders through programs like study abroad and expanded Peace Corps programs, perhaps under the auspices of the United Nations.

12. Adopting a new United Nations Declaration or an Amendment to the 2018 UN Youth Declaration which focuses on building youth world citizenship and the need for critical civic engagement education worldwide.

There is much work to be done to provide civic engagement education globally. Much of it can be done in our own classrooms or locally at our own educational institutions. But some of it will require new national and international commitments and resources. For this we will need not to just preach the gospel of civic engagement education but undertake civic actions ourselves. As in past times, it is likely that our students will lead the way in demanding a better and fuller education so that they will have the tools to participate effectively in shaping the future.

Endnotes

1. Sara Repucci and Amy Slipowitz, "Democracy Under Siege," Freedom House (2021), http://freedomhouse.org/report/freedom-world/ 2021/democracy-under-siege.

2. Center for Education and the Workforce, "The Role of Education in Taming Authoritarian Attitudes," https://cew.georgetown.edu/cew-reports/authoritarianism.

3. Alasdair Blair and Alison Rios Millett McCartney, Introduction, Section I in this volume.

4. Dmitry Lanko, "Teaching Group-Oriented Foreign Police Analysis for Civic Engagement," Chapter 8 in this volume.

5. Elizabeth C. Matto and Taiyi Sun, Introduction, Section II in this volume.

6. Richard Wike et. al., "Many in US, Western Europe Say Their Political System Needs Reform," *The Pew Research Center*, (31 March 2021), https://www.pewresearch.org/global/2021/03/31/many-in-us-western-europe-say-their-political-system-needs-major-reform/.

7. Ibid.

8. Matto and Sun, Introduction, Section II.

9. Lenin's *Collected Works*, Volume 5 (Moscow, Russia: Foreign Languages Publishing House, 1961), 347–530.

10. Matto and Sun, Introduction, Section II.

11. The data on both student registration at UIC and nationally is available at The National Study of Learning, Voting, and Engagement (NSLVE) at https://idhe.tufts.edu/nslve.

12. Anne Colby, Elizabeth Beaumont, Thomas Ehrlich, Josh Corngold, *Educating for Democracy* (San Francisco, CA: Jossey-Bass, 2007).

13. The National Task Force on Civic Learning and Democratic Engagement, *A Crucible Moment* (Washington, DC: American Association of Colleges and Universities, 2012).

14. McCartney, et. al., *Teaching Civic Engagement: From Student to Citizen* (Washington, DC: American Political Science Association, 2013). See also *Teaching Civic Engagement Across the Disciplines* (Washington, DC: American Political Science Association, 2017).

15. See https://thecitizenscampaign.org/ for more information on this effort.

16. See https://www.civxnow.org/.

17. Blair and McCartney, Introduction, Section I.

18. United Nations, "Youth Declaration," (2018), https://www.un.org/en/67th-un-dpingo-conference/page/youth-declaration.

19. Nicole Webster, "Re-centering the Ecosystem of Global Civic Engagement: A Collaborative Center Approach," Chapter 12 in this volume.

20. Catherine Shea Sanger and Wei Lit Yew, Chapter 4 in this volume.

21. Ibid.

Bibliography

AAC&U (Association of American Colleges and Universities). "General Education for a Global Century." Accessed October 23, 2020. https://www.aacu.org/sites/default/files/files/Global/LuceGlobalLearningProposal.pdf.

AAC&U (Association of American Colleges and Universities). "Civic Learning in the Major by Design." *AACU*, 2017. https://www.aacu.org/peerreview/2017/Fall.

Abbas, Mazhar. "Rising Culture of Political Intolerance." *The International News*, June 18, 2021. https://thenews.com.pk/print/851312-rising-culture-of-political-intolerance.

ABC. "Corte Orçamentário Atinge Desenvolvimento e Soberania Nacionais." *ABC*, April 1, 2019. http://www.abc.org.br/2019/04/01/corte-orcamentario-atinge-desenvolvimento-e-soberania-nacionais/?fbclid=IwAR1O-wzgMpUrCDGb-dGnnCSbdX_1jeOBkm9OrCxxZAkVbk1XWWpLeshg5Zo.

Abernathy, Claire, and Jennifer Forestal. "Civics Across Campus: Designing Effective Extracurricular Programming." *Journal of Political Science Education* 16, no. 1 (2020): 3–27.

Abrahams, Jessica, and Nicola Ingram. "The Chameleon Habitus: Exploring Local Students' Negotiations of Multiple Fields." *Sociological Research* 18, no. 4 (2013).

Acemoglu, Daron, and James A. Robinson. *The Narrow Corridor: States, Societies, and the Fate of Liberty*. New York: Penguin Press, 2019.

Achen, Christoper H., and Larry M. Bartels. *Democracy for Realists: Why Elections Do Not Produce Responsive Government*. Princeton, NJ: Princeton University Press, 2016.

Adler, Richard P. and Judy Goggin. "What Do We Mean by "Civic Engagement"?" *Journal of Transformative Education* 3, no. 3 (2005): 236–253.

Advisory Committee on Citizenship. *Education for Citizenship and the Teaching of Democracy in Schools*. London: Qualifications and Curriculum Authority, 1998.

Agarwal, Shikhar. "Coping: With Reality, With Myself, With the End of the World." *The Octant*, February 14, 2020. Accessed June 8, 2021. https://theoctant.org/edition/issue/opinion/coping-with-reality-with-myself-with-the-end-of-the-world/.

Agenda 2030. "The Sustainable Development Goals." *United Nations*. https://www.un.org/sustainabledevelopment/sustainable-development-goals/.

Ågren, Susanna, Iikka Pietilä and Tiina Rättilä. "Palkkatyökeskeisen Ajattelun Esiintyminen Ammattiin Opiskelevien Työelämäasenteissa," in *Hyvää Työtä! Nuorisobarometri 2019. Valtion Nuorisoneuvosto*, ed. Lotta Haikkola and Sami Myllyniemi, 157–178. Helsinki, Finland: Nuorisotutkimusseura, Nuorisotutkimusverkosto & opetus- ja kulttuuriministeriö, 2020.

Ahmad, Iftikhar. *Citizenship Education in the United States*. London: Routledge, 2017.

Ahtonen, Riitta, and Anssi Keinänen. "Sidosryhmien Vaikuttaminen Lainvalmisteluun—Empiirinen Analyysi Valiokuntakuulemisesta." (2012): 1–26

Ai, Huy Luu, and Tulsi Yogesh. "What the Petition Against Dr Guruswamy Revealed About 'Foreign Influence' in Singapore." *RICE*, November 17, 2019. Accessed June 8, 2021. https://www.ricemedia.co/current-affairs-commentary-menaka-guruswamy-foreign-influence-377a-singapore/.

Ainley, John, Wolfram Schulz, and Tim Friedman. "ICCS 2009 Encyclopedia: Approaches to Civic and Citizenship Education Around the World." *The International Civic and Citizenship Education Study* 125 (2013).

Ajaps, Sandra O., and Adaobiagu N. Obiagu. "Increasing Civic Engagement Through Civic Education: A Critical Consciousness Theory Perspective." *Journal of Culture and Values in Education* 4, no. 1 (2020).

Akiva, Thomas, Kai S. Cortina, and Charles Smith. "Involving Youth in Program Decision-making: How Common and What Might it do for Youth?" *Journal of Youth and Adolescence* 43 (2014): 1844–1860.

Aktas, Fatih, Kate Pitts, Jessica C. Richards, and Iveta Silova. "Institutionalizing Global Citizenship: A Critical Analysis of Higher Education Programs and Curricula." *Journal of Studies in International Education* 21 (2017): 65–80. https://doi.org/10.1177/1028315316669815.

Alexander, M. Jacqui, and Chandra T. Mohanty. *Feminist Genealogies, Colonial Legacies, Democratic Futures*. New York: Routledge, 1997.

Alhamad, Laila. "Formal and Informal Venues of Engagement," in *Political Participation in the Middle East*, ed. Ellen Lust-Okar and Saloua Zerhouini. Boulder, CO: Lynne Rienner, 2008.

Alizada, Nazifa, Rowan Cole, Lisa Gastaldi, Sandra Grahn, Sebastian Hellmeier, Palina Kolvani, Jean Lachapelle, Anna

Lührmann, Seraphine F. Maerz, Shreeya Pillai, and Staffan I. Lindberg. *Autocratization Turns Viral. Democracy Report 2021.* University of Gothenburg, Sweden: V-Dem Institute, 2021.

Allen, Danielle. *Education and Equality.* Chicago: University of Chicago Press, 2016.

Allen, Mahalley D., Sally A. Parker, and Teodora C. DeLorenzo. "Civic Engagement in the Community: Undergraduate Clinical Legal Education," in *Teaching Civic Engagement: From Student to Active Citizen*, eds. Alison Rios Millett McCartney, Elizabeth A. Bennion, and Dick Simpson, 153–166. Washington, DC: American Political Science Association, 2013.

Almond, Gabriel A., and Sidney Verba. *The Civic Culture: Political Attitudes and Democracy in Five Nations.* Princeton, NJ: Princeton University Press, 1963.

Altbach, Philip G., Maria Yudkevich, and Laura E. Rumbley. "Academic Inbreeding: Local Challenge, Global Problem." *Asia Pacific Education Review* 16, no. 3 (2015): 317–330.

Alvarez, Sonia E. "Advocating Feminism: The Latin American Feminist NGO Boom." *International Feminist Journal of Politics* 1 (1999): 181–209.

Aly, Shereen. "Citizenship Education: A Critical Content Analysis of the Egyptian Citizenship Education Textbooks after the Revolution," in *Education during the Time of the Revolution in Egypt: Dialectics of Education in Conflict*, ed. Nagwa Megahed. Rotterdam, Netherlands: Sense Publishers, 2017.

American Association of Colleges and Universities. "Diversity, Equity, and Student Success." *AACU*, 2020. https://www.aacu.org/diversity-equity-and-student-success.

American Political Science Association. "About APSA." *APSA*, 2020. https://www.apsanet.org/ABOUT/About-APSA.

American Political Science Association. "APSA Resources on Systemic Racism & Social Justice." *APSA*, 2020. https://www.apsanet.org/RESOURCES/APSA-Resources-for-Addressing-Systemic-Racism-Social-Justice.

American Political Science Association. "APSA Statement on the Essential Role of Social Scientific Inquiry in Maintaining a Free, Participatory, Civil, and Law-Governed Society." *APSA*, 2020. https://www.apsanet.org/APSA Statement on the Essential Role of Social Scientific Inquiry in Maintaining a Free, Participatory, Civil, and Law-Governed Society.

American Political Science Association. "APSA Task Force on Civic Education in the 21st Century: Expanded Articulation Statement: A Call for Reactions and Contributions." *PS: Political Science & Politics* 31, no. 3 (1998): 636–638.

American Political Science Association. *Goals for Political Science: Report of the Committee for the Advancement of Teaching.* New York: William Sloane Associates, 1951.

American Political Science Association. *The Teaching of Government: Report to the American Political Science Association by the Committee on Instruction.* New York: Macmillan, 1916.

Anderson, Derek, Don Barr and Christina Labaij. "Repetitive Microteaching: Learning to Teach Elementary Social Studies." *Journal of Social Studies Education Research* 3, no. 2 (2012): 21–44.

Anderson, Lisa. "'…To Save Us All': Lessons from the American University in Cairo, a Community of Learning in Revolutionary Times," in *American Universities Abroad: The Leadership of Independent Transnational Higher Education Institutions*, eds. Ted Purinton and Jennifer Skaggs, 27–40. New York; Cairo: American University in Cairo Press, 2017.

Andersson, Erik. "Young People's Political Participation: A Public Pedagogy Challenge at the Municipal Level." *Young* 26 (2018): 179–195, p.183.

ANDIFES. "Entidades Científicas e Acadêmicas Publicam Nota sobre Severo Corte do Orçamento."*ANDIFES*, 2019. http://www.andifes.org.br/entidades-cientificas-e-academicas-publicam-nota-sobre-severo-corte-orcamento/?fbclid=IwAR0S n8SbzRKOqHiboyqbSAhlDu106bKal1JRODACy8WoyzIn3jbCJLmHA9I.

Andreadis, Ioannis and Theodore Chadjipadelis. "Differences in Voting Behavior." *Proceedings of the 20th IPSA World Congress.* Fukuoka, Japan, 2006.

Ang, Hwee Min. "3 Arrested Over Protest Against Transphobia Outside MOE Building." *CNA*, January 26, 2021. https://www.channelnewsasia.com/news/singapore/moe-transphobia-protest-3-arrested-student-hormone-therapy-14045320.

Ang, Hwee Min. "Yale-NUS Course: Schools Should Not be Misused for Partisan Politics, Says Ong Ye Kung." *CNA*, October 7, 2019. https://www.channelnewsasia.com/news/singapore/yale-nus-course-schools-should-not-be-misused-for-partisan-11975994.

Ang, Prisca. "Yale-NUS Talk by Lawyer Who Helped Strike Down India's Gay Sex Law Carries Low Risk of Contempt of Court Here: Shanmugam." *The Straits Times*, November 11, 2019. Accessed June 8, 2021. https://www.straitstimes.com/singapore/no-significant-risk-of-sub-judice-with-yale-nus-talk-on-indias-section-377-law-despite.

Angelo, Claudio. "Brazil's Government Freezes Nearly Half of its Science Spending." *Nature*, April 8, 2019. https://www.nature.com/articles/d41586-019-01079-9?fbclid=IwAR0--ZTviI9uU0GY1s6SHYFsBiWrqPGp-ZhzlQ667896HC6G-gx1d0Q5Kxc.

Annette, John. "'Active Learning for Active Citizenship': Democratic Citizenship and Lifelong Learning." *Education, Citizenship and Social Justice* 4, no. 2 (2009): 149–160.

Annette, John. "Character, Civic Renewal and Service Learning for Democratic Citizenship in Higher Education." *British Journal of Educational Studies* 53, no. 3 (2005): 326–340.

APM Research Lab Staff. "APM Survey: Americans' Views on Government Funding and Aid for Public Colleges and Universities." *American Public Media*, February 25, 2019. https://www.apmresearchlab.org/highered.

Apple, Michael W. *Ideology and Curriculum*. New York: Routledge, 2019.

Asal, Victor. "Playing Games with International Relations." *International Studies Perspectives* 6, no. 3 (2005): 359–373. https://doi.org/10.1111/j.1528-3577.2005.00213.x.

Asal, Victor, Inga Miller, and Charmaine N. Willis. "System, State, or Individual: Gaming Levels of Analysis in International Relations." *International Studies Perspectives* 21, no. 1 (2020): 97–107. https://doi.org/10.1093/isp/ekz018.

Asghar, Mandy, and Nick Rowe. "Reciprocity and Critical Reflection as the Key to Social Justice in Service Learning: A Case Study." *Innovations in Education and Teaching International* 54, no. 2 (2017): 117–125.

Asimeng-Boahene, Lewis. "Creating Strategies to Deal with Problems of Teaching Controversial Issues in Social Studies Education in African Schools." *Intercultural Education* 18, no. 3 (2007): 231–242.

Atlas Brasil. *Atlas do Desenvolvimento Humano no Brasil*, 2020. http://www.atlasbrasil.org.br/. Accessed April 18, 2021.

Auh, Yoonil, and Heejung Raina Sim. "Global Justice and Education for Global Citizenship: Considerations for Education Policy-planning Process." *Asian Journal of Political Science* 26 (2018): 221–37. doi: 10.1080/02185377.2018.1481440.

Avid, Williams Robert. "Increasing Youth Participation in Accountability Mechanisms." Birmingham, UK: GSDRC, University of Birmingham, 2015.

Axelrod, Robert. *The Evolution of Cooperation*. New York: Basic Books, 1984.

Bacon, Edwin. "Teaching Applied Politics: From Employability to Political Imaginary." *Politics* 38, no. 1 (2018): 94–108.

Bacon, Michael, and James Sloam. "John Dewey and the Democratic Role of Higher Education in England." *Journal of Political Science Education* 6, no. 4 (2010): 336–352.

Baer, Hester. "Redoing Feminism: Digital Activism, Body Politics, and Neoliberalism." *Feminist Media Studies* 16 (2016): 17–34. doi: 10.1080/14680777.2015.1093070.

Baez-Camargo, Claudia. *Harnessing the Power of Communities against Corruption: A Framework for Contextualizing Social Accountability-U4 Brief*. Bergen: Norway, Michelsen Institute, 2018.

Baildon, Mark, Jasmine B-Y. Sim, and Agnes Paculdar. "A Tale of Two Countries: Comparing Civic Education in the Philippines and Singapore." *Compare: A Journal of Comparative and International Education* 46, no. 1 (2016): 93–115. DOI: 10.1080/03057925.2014.940848.

Baiocchi, Gianpaolo, Patrick Heller, and Marcelo Silva. *Bootstrapping Democracy: Transforming Local Governance and Civil Society in Brazil*. Stanford, CA: Stanford University Press, 2011.

Baksh-Soodeen, Rawwida, and Wendy Harcourt, ed. *The Oxford Handbook of Transnational Feminist Movements*. USA: Oxford University Press, 2015.

Banks, James A. "Failed Citizenship and Transformative Civic Education." *Educational Researcher* 46, no. 7 (2017): 366–377.

Banks, Nicola, David Hulme, and Michael Edwards. "NGOs, States, and Donors Revisited: Still Too Close for Comfort?" *World Development* 66 (2015): 706–18.

Baquero, Marcello. "Cultura Política Participativa e Desconsolidação Democrática: Reflexões Sobre o Brasil Contemporâneo." *São Paulo em Perspectiva* 15, no. 4 (2001): 98–104.

Baquero, Marcello. *Cultura(s) Política(s) e Democracia no Século XXI na América Latina*. Porto Alegre: Editora UFRGS, 2011.

Baranowski, Michael. "The *Daily Show* vs. the *New York Times*: Comparing Their Effects on Student Political Knowledge and Engagement." *Journal of Political Science Education* 16, no. 3 (2020): 300–313.

Barber, Brian K. "Youth Experience in the Palestinian Intifada: A Case Study in Intensity, Complexity, Paradox, and Competence." In *Roots of Civic Identity: International Perspectives on Community Service and Activism in Youth* (1999): 178–204.

Barker, Ernest. *Education for Citizenship*. London: University of London Institute for Education, 1936.

Barnes, Sarah. "England's Civic Universities and the Triumph of the Oxbridge Ideal." *History of Education Quarterly* 36, no. 3 (1996): 271–305.

Barnett, Ronald. *Higher Education: A Critical Business*. Bristol, PA: The Society for Research into Higher Education and Open

University Press, 1997.

Barrett, Katherine, and Richard Greene. "Civic Education: A Key to Trust in Government," in *Teaching Civic Engagement Across the Disciplines,* eds. Elizabeth Matto, Alison Rios Millett McCartney, Elizabeth A. Bennion, and Dick Simpson, 65–72. Washington DC: American Political Science Association, 2017.

Bartels, Larry M. "Ethnic Antagonism Erodes Republicans' Commitment to Democracy." *Proceedings of the National Academy of Sciences of the United States of America* 117, no. 37 (2020): 22752–22759. https://www.pnas.org/content/pnas/117/37/22752.full.pdf.

Barthes, Roland. *Elements of Semiology.* New York: Hill and Wang, 1968.

Bartling, Izzy. "Arizona Professor Talks About Community Activism at US-Mexico Border." *The Daily Orange,* October 1, 2019. Accessed September 6, 2020. http://dailyorange.com/2019/10/arizona-professor-talks-community-activism-u-s-mexico-border/.

Bates, David. "'Making Politics Matter': Political Education in a 'Knowledge-Exchange' Context." *European Political Science* 11, no. 2 (2012): 164–174.

Batista, Jose R. M. "Os Estereótipos e o Efeito do Contato Virtual no Preconceito contra Negros e Nordestinos." *Tese de Doutorado UFPB/CCHLA,* 2014. https://repositorio.ufpb.br/jspui/bitstream/tede/7561/2/arquivototal.pdf.

Battistoni, Richard M. "Learning Politics by Doing Politics." Paper presented at the Teaching and Learning Conference at APSA: Washington, DC, August 31, 2019.

Battistoni, Richard M., and Nicholas V. Longo. "Putting Students at the Center of Civic Engagement," in *Engagement for Democracy and the Transformation of Higher Education,* eds. John Saltmarsh and Matthew Hartley, 199–216. Philadelphia, PA: Temple University Press, 2011.

Bayram Özdemir, Sevgi, Hakan Stattin, and Metin Özdemir. "Youth's Initiations of Civic and Political Discussions in Class: Do Youth's Perceptions of Teachers' Behavior Matter and Why?" *Journal of Youth & Adolescence* 45, no. 11 (2016): 2233–45.

BBC. "Census. 2012. 2011: Leicester 'Most Ethnically Diverse' in Region." *BBC,* December 12, 2012. https://www.bbc.co.uk/news/uk-england-leicestershire-20678326.

BBC. "EU Referendum: The Result in Maps and Charts." *BBC News,* June 8, 2021. https://bbc.com/news/uk-politics-36616028.

BBC. "Hong Kong Activist Joshua Wong Barred from Entering Thailand." *BBC,* October 5, 2016. https://www.bbc.com/news/world-asia-china-37558908.

Beaumont, Elizabeth. "Political Learning and Democratic Capacities: Some Challenges and Evidence of Promising Approaches," in *Teaching Civic Engagement: From Student to Active Citizen,* eds. Alison Rios Millett McCartney, Elizabeth A. Bennion, and Dick Simpson, 41–55. Washington, DC: American Political Science Association Press, 2013.

Beaumont, Elizabeth, Anne Colby, Thomas Ehrlich, and Judith Torney-Purta. "Promoting Political Competence and Engagement in College Students: An Empirical Study." *Journal of Political Science Education* 2, no. 3 (2006): 249–270. doi: 10.1080/15512160600840467.

Beaven, Brad, and John Griffiths. "Creating the Exemplary Citizen: The Changing Notion of Citizenship in Britain 1870–1939." *Contemporary British History* 22, no. 2 (2008): 203–225.

Becker, Harold S. "Scenarios: A Tool of Growing Importance to Policy Analysis in Government and Industry." *Technological Forecasting and Social Change* 23, no. 2 (1983): 95–120.

Becker, Megan. "Importing the Laboratory Model to the Social Sciences: Prospects for Improving Mentoring of Undergraduate Researchers." *Journal of Political Science Education* 16, no. 2 (2020): 212–224.

Bell, Avril. "'Cultural Vandalism' and Pākehā Politics of Guilt and Responsibility," in *Tangata Tangata: The Changing Ethnic Contours of New Zealand,* ed. Paul Spoonley, David G. Pearson, and Cluny Macpherson, 89–107. Southbank, Victoria: Thomson Press, 2004.

Bell, Daniel A. "A Communitarian Critique of Authoritarianism." *Society* 32, no. 5 (1995): 38–43.

Benenson, Jodi, Barbara Pickering, Andrea M. Weare, and Anthony M. Starke, Jr. "Focused Engagement: Lessons Learned from a Study Assessing Campus Climates for Political Learning and Engagement in Democracy." *Journal of Community Engagement & Higher Education* 11, no. 3 (2019): 58–68.

Bennett, Lance W., Kirsten Foot and Michael Xenos. "Narratives and Network Organization: A Comparison of Fair Trade Systems in Two Nations." *Journal of Communication* 61 (2011): 219–245.

Bennion, Elizabeth A. "Assessing Civic and Political Engagement Activities: A Toolkit," in *Teaching Civic Engagement: From Student to Active Citizen,* eds. Alison Rios Millett McCartney, Elizabeth A. Bennion, and Dick Simpson, 407–422. Washington, DC: American Political Science Association, 2013.

Bennion, Elizabeth A. "Civic Education and Citizen Engagement: Mobilizing Voters as a Required Field Experiment." *Journal of Political Science Education* 2, no. 2 (2006): 205–227.

Bennion, Elizabeth A. "Moving Assessment Forward: Teaching Civic Engagement and Beyond," in *Teaching Civic Engagement: From Student to Active Citizen*, eds. Alison Rios Millett McCartney, Elizabeth A. Bennion, and Dick Simpson. Washington, DC: American Political Science Association, 2013.

Bennion, Elizabeth A. "Moving Forward with Assessment: Important Tips and Resources," in *Teaching Civic Engagement Across the Disciplines*, eds. Elizabeth C. Matto, Alison Rios Millett McCartney, Elizabeth A. Bennion, and Dick Simpson. Washington, DC: American Political Science Association, 2017.

Bennion, Elizabeth A., and David W. Nickerson. "Decreasing Hurdles and Increasing Registration Rates for College Students: An Online Voter Registration Systems Field Experiment." *Political Behavior* (2021). https://doi.org/10.1007/s11109-020-09666-7.

Bennion, Elizabeth A., and David W. Nickerson. "I Will Register and Vote if You Show Me How: A Field Experiment Testing Voter Registration in College Classrooms." *PS Political Science & Politics* 49, no. 4 (2016): 867–871.

Bennion, Elizabeth A., and Xander E. Laughlin. "Best Practices in Civic Education: Lessons from the Journal of Political Science Education." *Journal of Political Science Education* 14, no. 3 (2018): 287–330.

Benzécri, Jean Paul et al. *L'Analyse des Données. Tome 1: La Taxinomie. Tome 2: Analyse des Correspondances.* Paris: Dunod, 1973.

Berinsky, Adam J., and Gabriel S. Lenz. "Education and Political Participation: Exploring the Causal Link." *Political Behavior* 33, no. 3 (2011): 357–373.

Bernstein, Jeffrey L. "Cultivating Civic Competence: Simulation and Skill-Building in an Introductory Government Class." *Journal of Political Science Education* 4, no. 1 (2008): 1–20. https://doi.org/10.1080/15512160701815996.

Bernstein, Jeffrey L. "Introduction: The Citizenship Imperative and the Political Science Research Methods Course," in *Teaching Research Methods in Political Science*, ed. Jeffrey L. Bernstein, 1–11. Cheltenham, UK, Edward Elgar Publishing Limited, 2021.

Berthin, Gerardo and Gilbert-Roberts, Terri-Ann. "Explaining Youth Policy Participation in Latin America and the Caribbean Through Social Auditing Processes." *Revista Olhares Amazonicos, Boa Vista* 6, no. 2 (2018): 1186–1221.

Berthin, Gerardo. *A Practical Guide to Social Audit as a Participatory Tool to Strengthen Democratic Governance, Transparency, and Accountability.* Panama: UNDP Regional Centre for Latin America and the Caribbean, 2011.

Berthin, Gerardo. *Exploring the Dynamics of Youth Political Participation in Local Governments in Latin America.* Panama: UNDP Regional Centre for Latin America and the Caribbean, 2013.

Berthin, Gerardo. "Why Youth are a Key Investment for Accountability and Public Integrity?" *Blog 4democraticgovernence*, October 20, 2018.

Berthin, Gerardo. "Youth Political Participation in Local Governments: Initial Evidence from Latin America." *Social Economic Studies* 63, no. 3 & 4 (2014):107–142.

Bertin, Joan, Marjorie Heins, Cary Nelson, and Henry Reichman. "An Open Letter from the AAUP to the Yale Community." *American Association of University Professors*, 2012. https://www.aaup.org/news/2012/open-letter-aaup-yale-community.

Biddix, J. Patrick, Patricia A. Somers, and Joseph L. Polman. "Protest Reconsidered: Identifying Democratic and Civic Engagement Learning Outcomes." *Innovative Higher Education* 34, no. 3 (2009): 133–147.

Biesta, Gert. "What Kind of Citizenship for European Higher Education? Beyond the Competent Active Citizen." *European Educational Research Journal* 8, no. 2 (2009).

Billett, Stephen. "Practice-Based Learning and Professional Education," in *Practice-Based Education*, eds. Joy Higgs, Ronald Barnett, Stephen Billett, Maggie Hutchings, and Franziska Trede, 101–112. Rotterdam, Netherlands: SensePublishers, 2012.

Billings, Meredith S., and Dawn Geronimo Terkla. "The Impact of the Campus Culture on Students' Civic Activities, Values, and Beliefs." *New Directions for Institutional Research* 162 (2014): 43–53. doi: 10.1002/ir.2007.

Bissio, Roberto. "Civil Society and the MDGs." *UNDP Development Policy Journal* 3 (2003): 151–160.

Biswas, Bidisha, and Agnieszka Paczynka. "Teaching Theory, Writing Policy: Integrating Lessons from the Foggy Bottom into the Classroom." *PS: Political Science & Politics* 48, no. 1 (2014): 157–161. https://doi.org/10.1017/S104909651400170X.

Blackstone, Bethany, and Elizabeth Oldmixon. "Simulating the Legislative Process with LegSim." *Journal of Political Science Education* 16, no. 4 (2020): 526–536.

Blair, Alasdair. "Making and Remaking the Political: Lessons from The US Experience of Civic and Political Engagement in The Teaching Of Political Science." *Politics* 37, no. 4 (2017): 486–499.

Blair, Alasdair, and Steven Curtis. *International Politics: An Introductory Guide.* Edinburgh, UK: Edinburgh University Press,

2009.

Blair, Alasdair, Steven Griggs, and Eleanor Mackillop. "Engaging Students as Co-Producers: A Critical Reflection on The Policy Commission Model." *Politics* 38, no. 4 (2018): 514–530.

Blake, Stanley E. *The Vigorous Core of Our Nationality: Race and Regional Identity in Northeastern Brazil.* University of Pittsburgh Press, 2011.

Blom, Ronel. "A Policy Framework for Work-integrated Learning." *The African Journal for Work-Based Learning* 2, no. 1 (2014): 1–12.

Blunkett, David and Matthew Taylor. "Active Citizenship and Labour," in *Active Citizenship: What Could it Achieve and How?* eds. Bernard Crick and Andrew Lockyer, 26–38. Edinburgh, UK: University of Edinburgh Press, 2010.

Boal, Augusto. *A Estética do Oprimido.* Rio de Janeiro, Brazil: Editora Garamond, 2009.

Boal, Augusto. *STOP: C'est Magique!* Rio de Janeiro, Brazil: Civilização Brasileira, 1980.

Boatright, Robert G. "Introduction: A Crisis of Civility?" in *A Crisis of Civility? Political Discourse and Its Discontents*, eds. Robert G. Boatright, Timothy J. Shaffer, Sarah Sobieraj, and Dannagal Goldthwaite Young, 1–5. New York: Routledge, 2019.

Bocken, Inigo. "Learning from Casanus: The Power of Images." *Humboldt Kosmos* 86, no. 1 (2005).

Bogdanor, Vernon. "Oxford and The Mandarin Culture: The Past That Is Gone." *Oxford Review of Education* 32, no. 1 (2006): 147–165.

Bolen, Mell, ed. *A Guide to Outcomes Assessment in Education Abroad.* Carlisle, PA: Forum on Education Abroad, 2007.

Bondi, Liz. "Empathy and Identification: Conceptual Resources for Feminist Fieldwork." *ACME: An International Journal for Critical Geographies* 2 (2003): 64–76. https://www.acme-journal.org/index.php/acme/article/view/708.

Boucher, David, and Andrew Vincent. *British Idealism: A Guide of the Perplexed.* London. Continuum, 2012.

Boyer, Ernest L. "The Scholarship of Engagement." *Journal of Public Service and Outreach* 1, no. 1 (1996): 11–20.

Boylan, Brandon M., Mary F. Ehrlander, and Troy J. Bouffard. "A Multimethod and Interdisciplinary Approach to Educating Postsecondary Students on Arctic Challenges and Governance." *Journal of Political Science Education* (2019). https://doi.org/10.1080/15512169.2019.1628766.

Boyte, Harry C. "Reinventing Citizenship as Public Work," in *Democracy's Education: Public Work, Citizenship, and the Future of Colleges and Universities*, ed. Harry C. Boyte, 1–33. Nashville, TN: Vanderbilt University Press, 2015.

Brady, Henry E., Sidney Verba, and Kay L. Schlozman. "Beyond SES: A Resource Model of Political Participation." *American Political Science Review* 89, no. 2 (1995): 271–94.

Brasil. "Plano Nacional de Educação (PNE) 2014-2024." *PNE Em Movimento*, 2014. http://pne.mec.gov.br/18-planos-subnacionais-de-educacao/543-plano-nacional-de-educacao-lei-n-13-005-2014.

Brasil. "Resolução nº 7, de 18 de Dezembro de 2018." *Imprensa Nacional*, December 19, 2018. https://www.in.gov.br/materia/-/asset_publisher/KujrwoTZC2Mb/content/id/55877808.

Brazil. "Constitution of the Federative Republic of Brazil." *Presidência da República*, 1988. Accessed April 18, 2021. http://www.planalto.gov.br/ccivil_03/constituicao/constituicaocompilado.htm.

Brazil. "Decree Nº 9.235, of 15 December 2017." *Presidência da República*, 2017. Accessed April 18, 2021. http://www.planalto.gov.br/ccivil_03/_Ato2015-2018/2017/Decreto/D9235.htm,

Brechenmacher, Saskia. *Civil Society Under Assault: Repression and Responses in Russia, Egypt, and Ethiopia* 18. Massachusetts: Carnegie Endowment for International Peace, 2017.

Brennan, Jason. *The Ethics of Voting.* Princeton, NJ: Princeton University Press, 2012.

Brennan, Tom. *Political Education and Democracy.* Cambridge, UK: Cambridge University Press, 1981.

Brewis, Georgina, and Clare Holdsworth. "University Support for Student Volunteering in England: Historical Development and Contemporary Value." *Journal of Academic Ethics* 9, no. 2 (2011): 165–176.

Bristow, Steve, and Vicky Randall. *Politics in the Polytechnics.* London: Political Studies Association and Centre for the Study of Public Policy, University of Strathclyde, 1981.

Brooks, Margaret. "Drawing: The Social Construction of Knowledge." *Australian Journal of Early Childhood* 29, no. 2 (2004).

Brown, Roger, and Helen Carasso. *Everything for Sale? The Marketisation of UK Higher Education.* London: Routledge, 2013.

Brunkert, Lennart, Stefan Kruse, and Christian Welzel. "A Tale of Culture-bound Regime Evolution: The Centennial Democratic Trend and its Recent Reversal." *Democratization* 26, no. 3 (2019): 422–443.

Brux, Jacqueline M., and Blake Fry. "Multicultural Students in Study Abroad: Their Interests, Their Issues, and Their Constraints." *Journal of Studies in International Education* 14, no. 5 (2010): 508–527.

Buarque de Holanda, Sérgio. *Raízes do Brasil*. Rio de Janeiro, Brazil: José Olympio, 1969.

Burgo, Clara. "Service-learning for Students of Spanish: Promoting Civic Engagement and Social Justice Through an Exchange Tutoring Service." *Revista de Linguistica y Lenguas Aplicadas* 11 (2016): 11–18.

Burke, Edmund. "Speech to the Electors of Bristol at the Conclusion of the Poll," in *The Works of the Right Honourable Edmund Burke, in Twelve Volumes*, ed. J. C. Nimmo, 2nd ed. London, 1780.

Burke, Meghan M., Linda Sandman, Beatrize Perez, Meghann O'Leary. "The Phenomenon of Legislative Advocacy Among Parents of Children with Disabilities." *Journal of Research in Special Educational Needs* 18 (2018): 50–58.

Butin, Dan. "Introduction," in *The Engaged Campus: Certificates, Minors, and Majors as the New Community Engagement*, eds. Dan W. Butin and Scott Seider, 1–14. New York: Palgrave Macmillan, 2012.

Butler-Kisber, Lynn, and Tiiu Poldma. "The Power of Visual Approaches in Qualitative Inquiry: The Use of Collage Making and Concept Mapping in Experiential Research." *Journal of Research Practice* 6, no. 1 (2010).

Cabrera, Luis. *The Practice of Global Citizenship*. Cambridge, UK: Cambridge University Press, 2010.

Cahill, Helen, and Babak Dadvand. "Re-conceptualising Youth Participation: A Framework to Inform Action." *Children and Youth Services Review* 95 (2018): 243–253.

Caleiro, Antonio. "Educação e Desenvolvimento: Que Tipo de Relação Existe?" in *I Encontro Luso-Angolano em Economia, Sociologia e Desenvolvimento Rural*. Portugal: University of Évora, 2008.

Campbell, David E. "Voice in the Classroom: How an Open Classroom Climate Fosters Political Engagement." *Political Behavior* 30, no. 4 (2008): 437–54.

Campbell, David E. "What is Education's Impact on Civic and Social Engagement?" in *Measuring the Effects of Education on Health and Civic Engagement: Proceedings of the Copenhagen Symposium*, 25–126. Paris: OECD Publishing, 2006.

Campbell, David E. *Why We Vote: How Schools and Communities Shape Our Civic Life*. Princeton University Press, 2006.

Campus Compact. "Campus Compact Overview." *Campus Compact*, 2020. https://compact.org/who-we-are/.

CAPE. "Issue 1: Importance of Context." *Community for Advocacy and Political Education (CAPE)*, March 20, 2019. Accessed June 8, 2021. https://cape.commons.yale-nus.edu.sg/2019/03/18/issue-1-importance-of-context/.

Cardone, Rebecca. "Empathetic British Feminists at the Crossroads of Colonialism and Self-determination." *International Journal of Sociology and Social Policy* 39 (2019): 84–97. doi: 10.1108/IJSSP-04-2018-0058.

Carothers, Thomas. "Is Democracy the Problem." *The American Interest*, January 16, 2019. https://www.the-american-interest.com/2019/01/16/is-democracy-the-problem/.

Carothers, Thomas and Andrew O'Donohue. "Democracies Divided: The Global Challenge of Political Polarization." *Brookings Institution*, September 24, 2019. https://www.brookings.edu/book/democracies-divided/.

Carothers, Thomas and de Gramont Diane. *Aiding Governance in Developing Countries: Progress Amid Uncertainties*. Washington, DC: Carnegie Endowment for International Peace, 2011.

Carpenter, Charli. "What to Read on Gender and Foreign Policy." *Foreign Affairs*, December 22, 2009. https://www.foreignaffairs.com/articles/2009-12-22/what-read-gender-and-foreign-policy.

Carr, Wilfred, and Anthony Harnett. "Civic Education, Democracy and the English Political Tradition," in *Beyond Communitarianism: Citizenship, Politics and Education*, eds. Jack Demaine and Harold Entwistle, 64–82. Basingstoke, Hampshire: Macmillan Press, 1996.

Caruana, Viv. "Re-thinking Global Citizenship in Higher Education: From Cosmopolitanism and International Mobility to Cosmopolitanisation, Resilience and Resilient Thinking." *Higher Education Quarterly* 68, no. 1 (2014): 85–104.

Carvalho, Igor. "Confusão em Dados sobre Corte nas Universidades Federais é Proposital, diz Professor." *Brasil de Fato*, May 14, 2019. https://www.brasildefato.com.br/2019/05/14/confusao-em-dados-sobre-corte-nas-universidades-federais-e-proposital-diz-professor/.

Castells, Manuel. *Communication Power*. New York: Oxford University Press, 2009.

Castro, Antonio J. "What Makes a Citizen? Critical and Multicultural Citizenship and Preservice Teachers' Understanding of Citizenship Skills." *Theory & Research in Social Education* 41, no. 2 (2013): 219–46.

Center for Assessment and Research Studies. *The Political Engagement Project Survey Fall 2017 & Spring 2019 Report*. Harrisonburg, VA: James Madison University, 2019.

Center for Education and the Workforce. "The Role of Education in Taming Authoritarian Attitudes." *Georgetown University Center for Education and the Workforce*, n.d. https://cew.georgetown.edu/cew-reports/authoritarianism.

Center for Systemic Peace. "Polity5 Regime Narratives 2018." *Center for Systemic Peace*, 2020. https://www.systemicpeace.org/p5creports.html.

Central Statistics Office. "Population and Migration Estimates." *An Phríomh-Oifig Staidrimh,* August 20, 2020. https://www.cso.ie/en/releasesandpublications/er/pme/populationandmigrationestimatesapril2020/.

Chadjipadelis, Thedore. "Parties, Candidates, Issues: The Effect of Crisis. Correspondence Analysis and Related Methods." *CARME 2015.* Napoli, Italy, 2015.

Chadjipadelis, Theodore. "What Really Happened: Party Competition in the January and September 2015 Parliamentary Elections." *European Quarterly of Political Attitudes and Mentalities* 6, no. 2 (2017): 8–39.

Chalari, Athanasia and Panagiota, Serifi. "The 'Crisis Generation': The Effect of the Greek Crisis on Youth Identity Formation." *GreeSE papers* 123. London: Hellenic Observatory, European Institute, 2018.

Chan, Anita. *China's Workers under Assault: The Exploitation of Labor in a Globalizing Economy.* Armonk, NY: Sharpe, 2001.

Chan, Chitat, and Melanie Sage. "A Narrative Review of Digital Storytelling for Social Work Practice." *Journal of Social Work Practice* 107, no. 1 (2019).

Cheang, Bryan, and Donovan Choy. *Liberalism Unveiled: Forging a New Third Way in Singapore.* Singapore: World Scientific Publishing, 2021.

Checkoway, Barry, and Lorraine M. Gutierrez. "Youth Participation and Community Change: An Introduction." *Journal of Community Practice* 14 (2006): 1–9.

Chen, Feng. "Between the State and Labour: The Conflict of Chinese Trade Unions' Double Identity in Market Reform." China Quarterly 176 (2003): 1006–28.

Cheng, Yi'En. "Liberal Arts Educated Citizen: Experimentation, Subjectification and Ambiguous Contours of Youth Citizenship." *Area* 51, no. 4 (2019): 618–626.

Chien, Chin-Lung. "Beyond Authoritarian Personality: The Culture-Inclusive Theory of Chinese Authoritarian Orientation." *Frontiers in Psychology* 7 (2016): 924.

Cho, Alexander, Byrne, Jasmina and Pelter, Zoë. *Digital Civic Engagement by Young People: Rapid Analysis.* New York, NY: UNICEF, 2020.

Chong, Terence. "Civil Society in Singapore: Popular Discourses and Concepts." *Sojourn: Journal of Social Issues in Southeast Asia* 20, no. 2 (2005): 273–301.

Chowdhury, Faiz Ahmed. "Geo-Politics, Democratization and External Influence: The Bangladesh Case." *Institute of Governance Studies, BRAC University,* 2013. http://dspace.bracu.ac.bd/xmlui/handle/10361/11662.

Chua, Beng Huat. *Communitarian Ideology and Democracy in Singapore.* London: Routledge, 1997.

Chua, Beng Huat. *Liberalism Disavowed: Communitarianism and State Capitalism in Singapore.* Singapore: NUS Press, 2017.

Chua, Lynette J. *Mobilizing Gay Singapore: Rights and Resistance in an Authoritarian State.* Singapore: NUS Press, 2014.

Chua, Beng Huat. "Not Depoliticized but Ideologically Successful: The Public Housing Programme in Singapore." *International Journal of Urban and Regional Research* 15, no. 1 (1991): 24–41.

Chua, Beng Huat. "The Relative Autonomies of State and Civil Society in Singapore," in *State-Society Relations in Singapore*, eds. Gillian Koh and Giok Ling Ooi, 62–76. Singapore: Institute of Policy Studies, 2000.

CIA. "Mauritius." *CIA World Factbook.* Accessed May 10, 2021. https://www.cia.gov/the-world-factbook/countries/mauritius/.

Cichowski, Rachel. "Sustaining Democracy: A Study of Authoritarianism and Personalism in Irish Political Culture." *Center for the Study of Democracy Working Paper Series* 40 (2000): 1–23.

CIRCLE. *Civics, Digital Badges, and Alternative Assessments*, March 27, 2013. https://circle.tufts.edu/latest-research/civics-digital-badges-and-alternative-assessments.

CIRCLE. "Half of Youth Voted in 2020, An 11-Point Increase From 2016." *Center for Information and Research on Civic Learning and Engagement*, April 29, 2021. https://circle.tufts.edu/index.php/latest-research/half-youth-voted-2020-11-pointincrease-2016/.

CIRCLE (Center for Information and Research on Civic Learning and Engagement). "Election Night 2018: Historically High Youth Turnout, Support for Democrats." *CIRCLE*, November 7, 2018. https://circle.tufts.edu/latest-research/election-night-2018-historically-high-youth-turnout-support-democrats.

Clark, John, ed. *Globalizing Civic Engagement: Civil Society and Transnational Action.* London: Earthscan Publications, 2003.

Classen, Ryan L., and J. Quin Monson. "Does Civic Education Matter? The Power of Long-Term Observation and the Experimental Method." *Journal of Political Science Education* 11, no. 4 (2015): 404–421.

Clauset, Aaron, Samuel Arbesman, and Daniel B. Larremore. "Systemic Inequality and Hierarchy in Faculty Hiring Networks." *Science Advances* 1, no. 1 (2015): 1–6.

Clayton, Patti. H., Robert G. Bringle, Bryanne Senor, Jenny Huq, and Mary Morrison. "Differentiating and Assessing Relationships in Service-Learning and Civic Engagement: Exploitative, Transactional, or Transformational." *Michigan Journal of Community Service Learning* 16, no. 2 (2010): 5–21.

Clement, Rachel, et al. "Youth Civic Engagement & Leadership: A Review of Literature from Academia & Practice." Unpublished Manuscript, April 21, 2014.

Clemons, Randy S., and Mark K. McBeth. *Public Policy Praxis: A Case Approach to Understanding Policy and Analysis*, 4th edition. New York: Routledge, 2020.

Cleuren, Herwing and Silva, Patrício. *Widening Democracy: Citizens and Participatory Schemes in Brazil and Chile*. Netherlands: Koninklijke, 2009.

Colby, Anne, Elizabeth Beaumont, Thomas Ehrlich, and John Corngold. *Educating for Democracy Preparing Undergraduates for Responsible Political Engagement*. San Francisco, CA: Jossey-Bass, 2007.

Coles, Romand. *Visionary Pragmatism: Radical and Ecological Democracy in Neoliberal Times*. Durham, NC: Duke University Press, 2016.

Collini, Stefan, Donald Winch, and John Burrow. *That Noble Science of Politics: A Study in Nineteenth-Century Intellectual History*. Cambridge, UK: Cambridge University Press, 1983.

Commission of the European Communities. *Towards a European Research Area. Communication from the Commission to the Council, the European Parliament, the Economic and Social Committee and the Committee of the Regions, COM*. Brussels: Commission of the European Communities, 2000.

Committee on the Expansion of the University Sector (CEUS). *Report of the Committee on the Expansion of the University Sector: Greater Choice, More Room to Excel Final Report*. Committee Chairman Lui Tuck Yew. Singapore: Higher Education Division, Ministry of Education, 2008.

Committee on Higher Education. *Report of the Committee Appointed by the Prime Minister Under the Chairmanship of Lord Robbins*. London: Her Majesty's Stationery Office, 1963.

Connolly, Kate. "AfD Tells German Pupils to Denounce Teachers Who Discuss Political Views." *The Guardian*, October 11, 2018. https://www.theguardian.com/world/2018/oct/11/afd-tells-german-pupils-to-denounce-teachers-who-discuss-political-views.

Conway, Janet M. "Troubling Transnational Feminism (s): Theorising Activist Praxis." *Feminist Theory* 18 (2017): 205–27. doi: 10.1177/1464700117700536.

Cook, Karen. "Social Capital and Inequality: The Significance of Social Connections," in *Handbook of the Social Psychology of Inequality*, eds. Jane McLeod, Edward Lawler, and Michael Schwalbe. Dordrecht, Netherlands: Springer, 2014.

Coonrod, John. "Participatory Local Democracy: Key to Community-led Rural Development." *Development* 58 (2015): 333–340.

Coppedge, Michael, John Gerring, Adam Glynn, Carl Henrik Knutsen, Staffan I. Lindberg, Daniel Pemstein, Brigitte Seim, Svend-Erik Skaaning, and Jan Teorell. *Varieties of Democracy: Measuring Two Centuries of Political Change*. Cambridge, UK: Cambridge University Press, 2020.

Corbin, Juliet M., and Anselm L. Strauss. *Basics of Qualitative Research: Techniques and Procedures for Developing Grounded Theory* 3rd edition. Los Angeles, CA: Sage Publications, 2008.

Corcoran, Katie E. "Emotion, Religion, and Civic Engagement: A Multilevel Analysis of US Congregations." *Sociology of Religion* 81, no. 1 (2020): 20–44.

Cordell, Diane. *Using Images to Teach Critical Thinking Skills*. Santa Barbra, CA: ABC-CLIO, 2016.

Corner, Adam, Olga Roberts, Sybille Chiari, Sonja Völler, Elisabeth S. Mayrhuber, Sylvia Mandl and Kate Monson. "How do Young People Engage with Climate Change? The Role of Knowledge, Values, Message Framing, and Trusted Communicators." *Wires Climate Change* 6 (2015): 523–534.

Corrales, Javier. "The Authoritarian Resurgence: Autocratic Legalism in Venezuela." *Journal of Democracy* 26, no. 2 (2015): 37–51.

Coughlan, Sean. "Only 1% of UK University Professors are Black." *BBC News*, January 19, 2021. https://www.bbc.co.uk/news/education-55723120.

Craig, John. "The Emergence of Politics As A Taught Discipline At Universities In The United Kingdom." *British Journal of Politics and International Relations* 22, no. 2 (2020): 145–163.

Craig, John, and Sarah Hale. "Implementing Problem-Based Learning in Politics." *European Political Science* 7, no. 2 (2008): 165–174.

Crawford, Pat, and Brett Burquist, eds. *Community Engagement Abroad: Perspectives and Practices on Service, Engagement, and Learning Overseas*. East Lansing, MI: State University Press, 2020.

Cress, Christine M., Cathy Burack, Dwight E. Giles, Julie Elkins and Margaret C. Stevens. *A Promising Connection: Increasing College Access and Success through Civic Engagement*. Boston, MA: Campus Compact, 2010.

Cress, Christine M., David M. Donahue, and Associates. *Democratic Dilemmas of Teaching Service-Learning: Curricular Strategies for Success*. Sterling, VA: Stylus, 2011.

Crick, Bernard. "Advisory Group on Education for Citizenship and the Teaching of Democracy in Schools," in *Education for Citizenship and the Teaching of Democracy in Schools: Final report of the Advisory Group on Citizenship*. London: Qualifications and Curriculum Authority, 1998. https://dera.ioe.ac.uk/4385/1/crickreport1998.pdf.

Crick, Bernard. "The Introducing of Politics," in *The Teaching of Politics*, ed. D.B. Heater, 1–21. London: Metheun Educational, 1969.

Crick, Bernard, and Alex Porter eds. *Political Education and Political Literacy*. London: Longman, 1978.

Crigler N., Ann, Thomas Goodnight, Stephen Armstrong, and Ramesh Aditi. "Collaborative Civic Engagement: A Multidisciplinary Approach to Teaching Democracy with Elementary and University Students," in *Teaching Civic Engagement Across the Disciplines*, eds. Elizabeth C. Matto, Alison Rios Millett McCartney, Elizabeth A. Bennion and Dick Simpson, 261. Washington, DC: American Political Science Association, 2017.

Croke, Kevin, Guy Grossman, Horacio A. Larreguy, and John Marshall. "Deliberate Disengagement: How Education Decreases Political Participation in Electoral Authoritarian Regimes." *American Political Science Review* 110, no. 3 (2016): 579–600.

Csaky, Zselyke. "Nations in Transit 2020: Dropping the Democratic Facade." *Freedom House*, 2020. https://freedomhouse.org/report/nations-transit/2020/dropping-democratic-facade#Facade..

Curley, Stephanie L., Jeong-eun Rhee, Binava Subhedi, and Sharon Subreenduth. "Activism as/in/for Global Citizenship: Putting Un-Learning to Work towards Educating the Future," in *The Palgrave Handbook of Global Citizenship and Education*, eds. Ian Davies, Li-Ching Ho, Dina Kiwan, Carla L. Peck, Andrew Peterson, Edda Sant and Yusef Waghid, 589–606. London: Palgrave Macmillan, 2018.

Curriculum Committee of Yale-NUS College. *Yale-NUS College: A New Community of Learning*. Singapore: Yale-NUS College, 2013.

Curtis, Steven, and Alasdair Blair. "The Scholarship of Engagement for Politics," in *The Scholarship of Engagement for Politics: Placement Learning, Citizenship and Employability*, eds. Steven Curtis and Alasdair Blair, 3–20. Birmingham: C-SAP, 2010.

Cyr, Jennifer. *Focus Groups for the Social Science Researcher*. Cambridge, UK: Cambridge University Press, 2019.

da Silva Cordeiro Moita, Filomena Maria Gonçalves, and Fernando Cézar Bezerra de Andrade. "Ensino-pesquisa-extensão: Um Exercício de Indissociabilidade na Pós-graduação." *Revista Brasileira de Educação* 14, no. 41 (2009): 269–280.

da Silva, José Graziano, Mauro Eduardo Del Grossi, and Caio Galvão de França, eds. "The Fome Zero (Zero Hunger) Program: The Brazilian Experience." *Brasília: Ministry of Agrarian Development*, 2011. Accessed April 18, 2021. http://www.fao.org/docrep/016/i3023e/i3023e.pdf.Dahl, Robert. *Polyarchy. Participation and Opposition*. New Haven, CT: Yale University Press, 1971.

Dahlgren, Peter. *Young Citizens and New Media: Learning for Democratic Participation*. New York: Routledge, 2007.

Dahlum, Sirianne, and Carl Henrik Knutsen. "Democracy by Demand? Reinvestigating the Effect of Self-Expression Values on Political Regime Type." *British Journal of Political Science* 47, no. 2 (2017): 437–461.

Dahrendorf, Ralph. *A History of the London School of Economics and Political Science 1895–1995*. Oxford, UK: Oxford University Press, 1995.

Dal Bó, Pedro Foster, Andrew Putterman Louis. "Institutions and Behavior: Experimental Evidence on the Effects of Democracy." *American Economic Review* 100, no. 5 (2010): 2205–2229.

Dalton, Russell J., and Nhu-Ngoc T. Ong. "Authority Orientations and Democratic Attitudes: A Test of the 'Asian Values' Hypothesis." *Japanese Journal of Political Science* 6, no. 2 (2005): 211–231.

Danziger, Marie. "Policy Analysis Postmodernized: Some Political and Pedagogical Ramifications." *Policy Studies Journal* 23, no. 3 (1995): 435–450. https://doi.org/10.1111/j.1541-0072.1995.tb00522.x.

Darga, Louis Amédée and Suhaylah Peeraullee. "Can Mauritians Save a Democracy in Trouble?" *Washington Post, Monkey Cage*, June 25, 2021. https://www.washingtonpost.com/politics/2021/06/25/can-mauritians-save-democracy-trouble/?utm_source=facebook&utm_medium=social&utm_campaign=wp_monkeycage&fbclid=IwAR2q_bg7LuBTEnvEHoSdoJo_Ursk-pXvv6WPEVodVVeNO5tb2Job7gf9wNY.

Davies, Ian. "What has Happened in the Teaching of Politics in Schools in England in the Last Three Decades, and Why?"

Oxford Review of Education 25, no. 1/2 (1999): 125–140.

Davies, Ian, and John Issitt. "Reflections on Citizenship Education in Australia, Canada And England." *Comparative Education* 41, no. 4 (2005): 389–410.

Davies, Jonathan S. "Active Citizenship: Navigating the Conservative Heartlands of The New Labour Project." *Policy & Politics* 40, no. 1 (2012): 3–19.

Davis, Lucy, and Qi Siang Ng. "Why Yale-NUS Must Divest." *The Octant*, April 7, 2017. Accessed June 8, 2021. https://theoctant.org/edition/issue/opinion/yale-nus-must-divest.

Dawson, Richard E. and Kenneth Prewitt. *Political Socialization.* Boston, MA: Little, Brown & Co., 1969.

De Mesquita, Bruce Bueno, and George W. Downs. "Development and Democracy." *Foreign Affairs* (2005): 77–86.

De Montfort University. *Access and Participation Plan 2020–21 to 2024–25.* Leicester: De Montfort University, 2021. https://www.dmu.ac.uk/documents/university-governance/access-participation-plan-2020-2025.pdf.

De Montfort University. "Be the Change Will Spark Student Debate." *DMU*, April 26, 2017. https://www.dmu.ac.uk/about-dmu/news/2017/april/be-the-change-will-spark.aspx.

De Montfort University. "DMU Launches First Be The Change Festival." *DMU*, June 23, 2017. https://www.dmu.ac.uk/about-dmu/news/2017/june/dmu-launches-first-be-the-change-research-festival.aspx.

De Montfort University. "DMU Takes the World Lead on Refugee Support." *DMU*, n.d. https://www.dmu.ac.uk/community/public-engagement/join-together.aspx.

De Wit, Hans. "Internationalization of Higher Education: Nine Microconcepts." *International Higher Education* 64 (2011): 6–7.

Dean, Jon. "Drawing what Homelessness Looks Like: Using Creative Visual Methods as a Tool of Critical Pedagogy." *Sociological Research Online* 20, no. 1 (2015).

Dehler, Gorden M., Ann Welsh and Marianne Lewis. "Critical Pedagogy in the "New Paradigm": Raising Complicated Understanding in Management Learning," in *Essential Readings in Management Learning*, eds. Christopher Grey and Elena Antonacopoulou. London: Sage, 2004.

DeLaet, Debra L. "A Pedagogy of Civic Engagement for the Undergraduate Political Science Classroom." *Journal of Political Science Education* 12, no. 1 (2010).

Delamaide, Darrell. "Dictatorship 101." *Handelsblatt*, October 12, 2018. https://www.handelsblatt.com/23583610.html.

Delgado, R., & Stefancic, J. *Critical Race Theory: An Introduction.* NYU Press, 1995.

Della Coletta, Ricardo, and Danielle Brant. "Bolsonaro Nega Praticar Censura, mas Defende Valores Cristãos na Cultura." *Folha de São Paulo*, 2019. https://www1.folha.uol.com.br/ilustrada/2019/10/bolsonaro-nega-praticar-censura-mas-defende-valores-cristaos-na-cultura.shtml.

Delli Carpini, Michael X. "Age and History: Generations and Sociopolitical Change," in *Political Learning in Adulthood: A Sourcebook of Theory and Research*, ed. Roberta S. Sigel, 11–55. Chicago, IL: University of Chicago Press, 1989.

Delli Carpini, Michael X., Leonie Huddy, and Robert Y. Shapiro, ed. *Rethinking Rationality.* Greenwich: Jai Press, 1996.

Department of Education and Skills. *National Strategy for Higher Education to 2030.* Dublin: Department of Education and Skills, 2011.

DeRocher, Patricia. *Transnational Testimonios: The Politics of Collective Knowledge Production. Decolonizing Feminisms.* Seattle, WA: University of Washington Press, 2018.

Deslandes, Paul R. *Oxbridge Men: British Masculinity and the Undergraduate Experience, 1850–1920.* Bloomington, IN: Indiana University Press, 2005.

DeVereaux, Constance. "Fostering Civic Engagement Through the Arts: A Blueprint," in *Teaching Civic Engagement Across the Disciplines*, eds. Elizabeth C. Matto, Alison Rios Millett McCartney, Elizabeth A. Bennion, and Dick Simpson. Washington, DC: American Political Science Association, 2017.

Devereux, Erik A., and Dan Durning. "Going Global? International Activities by U.S. Schools of Public Policy and Management to Transform Public Affairs Education." *Journal of Public Affairs Education* 7, no. 4 (2001): 241–260. https://doi.org/10.1080/15236803.2001.12023521.

Dewey, John. *Democracy and Education: An Introduction to the Philosophy of Education.* New York: The Free Press, 1916.

Dewey, John. "The Need of an Industrial Education in an Industrial Society." *Manual Training and Vocational Education* 17 (1916).

Di Giovanni, Janine. "The First Draft of History: Why the Decline of Foreign Reporting Makes for Worse Foreign Policy." *Foreign Policy*, January 15, 2021. https://foreignpolicy.com/2021/01/15/history-foreign-correspondents-media-press-journalism-war-reporting-photography/.

Dickinson, Kesicia A., Jasmine C. Jackson, and Princess H. Williams. "Jackson State University: Challenging Minds and Cultivating the Political Science Pipeline." *PS: Political Science & Politics* 53, no. 1 (2020): 148–151.

Dicklitch, Susan. "Blending Cognitive, Affective, Effective Learning in Civic Engagement Courses: The Case of Human Rights-Human Wrongs," in *Teaching Civic Engagement: From Student to Active Citizen,* eds. Alison Rios Millett McCartney, Elizabeth A. Bennion, and Dick Simpson, 247–258. Washington, DC: American Political Science Association, 2013.

Dimock, Michael and Richard Wike. "America is Exceptional in the Nature of its Political Divide." *Pew Research Center,* November 13, 2020. https://www.pewresearch.org/fact-tank/2020/11/13/america-is-exceptional-in-the-nature-of-its-political-divide/.

do Mar Pereira, Maria. "Struggling Within and Beyond the Performative University: Articulating Activism and Work in an 'Academia Without Walls'." *Women's Studies International Forum* 54 (2016): 100–110.

Doherty, Carroll, Jocelyn Kiley, and Bridget Johnson. "Elections in America: Concerns over Security, Divisions Over Expanding Access to Voting." Washington, DC: Pew Research Center, 2018.

Doherty, Carroll, Jocelyn Kiley, and Bridget Johnson. "Little Partisan Agreement on the Pressing Problems Facing the US" Washington, DC: Pew Research Center, 2018.

Donnelly, Paul F., and John Hogan. "Engaging Students in the Classroom: 'How Can I Know What I Think Until I See What I Draw?'" *European Political Science* 12, no. 3 (2013).

Dorio, Jason N. "The Revolution as a Critical Pedagogical Workshop: Perceptions of University Students Reimagining Participatory Citizenship(s) in Egypt," in *Education During the Time of the Revolution in Egypt: Dialectics of Education in Conflict*, ed. Nagwa Megahed. Rotterdam, Netherlands: Sense Publishers, 2017.

Dragseth, Meghann R. "Building Student Engagement Through Social Media." *Journal of Political Science Education* 16, no. 2 (2020): 243–256.

Du Plessis, Joy, and Irfan Muzaffar. "Professional Learning Communities in the Teachers' College: A Resource for Teacher Educations." *EQUIP1* 45 (2010): 26.

Dudley, Robert, and Alan Gitelson. "Civic Education, Civic Engagement, and Youth Civic Development." *PS: Political Science & Politics* 36, no. 2 (2003): 263–67.

Duffin, Diane L., Jane Ziebarth-Bovill, and Rochelle H. Krueger. "Building Democratic Capacity in Preservice Teachers." *Delta Kappa Gamma Bulletin* 86, no. 1 (2019): 14–24.

Durkheim, Emile. *Education and Sociology.* New York: Free Press, 1956.

Duverger, Maurice. *Political Parties: Their Organization and Activity in the Modern State.* New York: John Wiley, 1954.

Easton, David. "A Re-Assessment of the Concept of Political Support." *British Journal of Political Science* 5, no. 4 (1975): 435–57.

Easton, David. *A Systems Analysis of Political Life.* New York, London, Sydney: John Wiley & Sons, Inc., 1965.

Easton, David and Robert D. Hess. "The Child's Political World." *Midwest Journal of Political Science* 6 (1962): 229–246.

Eckersley, Robyn. "Responsibility for Climate Change as a Structural Injustice," in *The Oxford Handbook of Environmental Political Theory*, eds. Teena Gabrielson, Cheryl Hall, John M. Meyer and David Schlosberg. Oxford University Press, 2016.

The Economist. "Global Democracy has a Very Bad Year." *The Economist,* February 2, 2021. Accessed March 9, 2020. https://www.economist.com/graphic-detail/2021/02/02/global-democracy-has-a-very-bad-year.

The Economist. "Vaccine Nationalism Means that Poor Countries Will Be Left Behind." *The Economist,* January 28, 2021. https://www.economist.com/graphic-detail/2021/01/28/vaccine-nationalism-means-that-poor-countries-will-be-left-behind.

The Economist Intelligence Unit. *Democracy Index 2020: In Sickness and in Health?* London: The Economist Intelligence Unit, 2020. https://www.eiu.com/n/campaigns/democracy-index-2020/.

The Economist Intelligence Unit. "Safe Cities Index 2019." *The Economist,* 2020. https://safecities.economist.com/safe-cities-index-2019/.

Edmunds, Elissa, Oreill Henry, and Emily Kovalesky. "Beyond Study Abroad: The Global Nature of Domestic Experiential Learning." *Diversity and Democracy* 22, no. 2–3 (2019): 37–39.

Educating for American Democracy (EAD). "Educating for American Democracy: Excellence in History and Civics for All Learners." *iCivics*, March 2, 2021. www.educatingforamericandemocracy.org.

Ehman, Lee H. "The American School in the Political Socialization Process." *Review of Educational Research* 50, no. 1 (1980).

Ekman, Joakim, and Erik Amnå. "Political Participation and Civic Engagement: Towards a New Typology." *Human Affairs* 22

(2012): 283–300.

El Ashmawi, Yvonne Pilar, Ma Eugenia Hernandez Sanchez, and Judith Flores Carmona. "Testimonialista Pedagogues: Testimonio Pedagogy in Critical Multicultural Education." International Journal of Multicultural Education 20 (2018): 67–85. doi: 0.18251/ijme.v20i1.1524.

The Electoral Commission. *Voter Engagement and Young People.* London: The Electoral Commission, 2002. https://www. electoralcommission.org.uk/sites/default/files/electoral_commission_pdf_file/youngpplvoting6597-6188ENSW.pdf.

Elenes, Alejandra C. "Nepantla, Spiritual Activism, New Tribalism: Chicana Feminist Transformative Pedagogies and Social Justice Education." *Journal of Latino- Latin American Studies* (JOLLAS) 5 (2013): 132–41.

Ellis, Carolyn, Tony E. Adams, and Arthur P. Bochner. "Autoethnography: An Overview." *Historical Social Research/Historische Sozialforschung* 36, no. 4 (2011): 273–290.

Elster, Jon. *Deliberative Democracy.* Cambridge, UK: Cambridge University Press, 1998.

Embassy of the Republic of Mauritius. "General Information about Mauritius." Accessed May 14, 2021. govmu.org.

Emert, Holly, and Diane Pearson. "Expanding the Vision of International Education: Collaboration, Assessment, and Intercultural Development." *New Directions for Community Colleges* 138 (2007): 67–75.

Engel, Arthur. "Political Education in Oxford 1823-1914." *History of Education Quarterly* 20, no. 3 (1980): 257–280.

Engler, Mark and Paul Engler. *This is an Uprising: How Nonviolent Revolt is Shaping the Twenty-First Century.* New York: Nation Books, 2017.

Entwistle, Harold. *Political Education in a Democracy.* London: Routledge and Keegan Paul, 1971.

Eriksen, Thomas Hylland, and Ramola Ramtohul. "Introduction," in Eriksen and Ramtohul, *The Mauritian Paradox: Fifty Years of Development, Diversity, and Democracy*, eds. Thomas Hylland Eriksen and Ramola Ramtohul. Baltimore, MD. University of Mauritius Press, 2018.

Esen, Berk, and Sebnem Gumuscu. "Rising Competitive Authoritarianism in Turkey." *Third World Quarterly* 37, no. 9 (2016): 1581–1606.

Espín, Oliva M., and Andrea L. Dottolo. "A Transnational Feminist Perspective on the Psychology of Migration," in *Transnational Psychology of Women: Expanding International and Intersectional Approaches, Psychology of women*, ed. L. H. Collins, S. Machizawa, and J. K. Rice, 121–39. Washington, DC: American Psychological Association, 2019. doi: 10.1037/0000148-006.

Espinosa, Lorelle L., Jonathan M. Turk, Morgan Taylor, and Hollie M. Chessman. *Race and Ethnicity in Higher Education: A Status Report.* Washington, DC: American Council on Education, 2019.

European Union. "EU Charter of Fundamental Rights, Article 10 of the European Convention on Human Rights." *Fundamental Rights Agency.* https://fra.europa.eu/en/eu-charter/article/11-freedom-expression-and-information.

European Union. "The EU Youth Strategy 2019–2027." *Official Journal of the European Union* 61, 2018. https://eur-lex.europa. eu/legal-content/EN/TXT/PDF/?uri=OJ:C:2018:456:FULL&from=EN.

European Union Agency for Fundamental Rights. "Survey on Minorities and Discrimination in EU (2016)." *Brussels: EUAFR,* April 17, 2017. https://fra.europa.eu/en/publications-and-resources/data-and-maps/%20survey-data-explorer-second-eu-minorities-discrimination-survey?mdq1=theme&mdq2=974.

European University Association. *Universities as the Motor for the Construction of a Europe of Knowledge. Input to the Barcelona Summit.* Brussels: EUA, 2002.

Evans, Heather K. "Encouraging Civic Participation through Twitter During (and After) the 2012 Election," in *Civic Education in the Twenty-First Century: A Multidimensional Inquiry*, eds. Michael T. Rogers and Donald M. Gooch, 145–160. Lanham, MD: Lexington Books, 2015.

Falcón, Sylvanna M. "Transnational Feminism as a Paradigm for Decolonizing the Practice of Research: Identifying Feminist Principles and Methodology Criteria for US-Based Scholars." *Frontiers: A Journal of Women Studies* 37 (2016): 174–94. Accessed September 9, 2020. doi:10.5250/fronjwomestud.37.1.0174.

Faoro, Raymundo. *Os Donos do Poder.* Rio de Janeiro: Globo, 1975.

Farrell, David M. *Electoral Systems: A Comparative Introduction.* London and New York: Palgrave, 2001.

Faulks, Keith. "Education of Citizenship in England's Secondary Schools: A Critique of Current Principle and Practice." *Journal of Education Policy* 21, no. 1 (2006): 59–74.

Feaver, Peter, and Christopher Gelpi. *Choosing Your Battles: American Civil-Military Relations and the Use of Force.* Princeton, NJ: Princeton University Press, 2004.

Feeney, Sharon. *Institutional Quality Review in Higher Education in the Republic of Ireland and Northern Ireland: A Comparison of*

Two Approaches. Doctoral thesis, Sheffield: University of Sheffield, 2014.

Feeney, Sharon, and Conor Horan. "The Bologna Process and the European Qualifications Framework: A Routines Approach to Understanding the Emergence of Educational Policy Harmonisation – From Abstract Ideas to Policy Implementation," in *Policy Paradigm in Theory and Practice: Discourses, Ideas and Anomalies in Public Policy Dynamics*, eds. John Hogan and Michael Howlett. Basingstoke, UK: Palgrave, 2015.

Feeney, Sharon, and John Hogan. "Using Drawings to Understand Perceptions of Civic Engagement Across Disciplines: 'Seeing is Understanding.'" *Politics* 39, no. 2 (2019).

Feeney, Sharon, and John Hogan. "Using Drawings to Understand Undergraduates' Perceptions of Civic Engagement Across Countries - Ireland and Egypt," in *Teaching Civic Engagement Globally*, eds. Elizabeth C. Matto, Alison Rios Millett McCartney, Elizabeth A. Bennion, Dawn Michele Whitehead, Taiyi Sun, and Alasdair Blair. Washington DC: American Political Science Association, 2021.

Feeney, Sharon, John Hogan and Paul F. Donnelly. "What Stick Figures Tell Us about Irish Politics: Creating a Critical and Collaborative Learning Space." *Teaching in Higher Education* 20, no. 3 (2015).

Fehling, Maya, Brett Nelson, and Sridhar Venkatapuram. "Limitations of the Millennium Development Goals: A Literature Review." *Global Public Health: An International Journal for Research, Policy and Practice* 8, no. 10 (2013): 1109–1122.

Feldman, Alice. "Othering Knowledge and Unknowing Law: Oppositional Narratives in the Struggle for American Indian Religious Freedom." *Social & Legal Studies* 9 (2000): 557–582.

FEMNET (African Women's Development and Communication Network). 2020. Accessed September 9, 2020. https://femnet. org/.

Ferguson, Ron and William Dickens, ed. *Urban Problems and Community Development.* Washington, DC: Brookings, 1999.

Ferman, Barbara. "Youth Civic Engagement in Practice: The Youth VOICES Program." *The Good Society* 14, no. 3 (2005): 45–50.

Fernandes, Leela. *Transnational Feminism in the United States: Knowledge, Ethics, Power.* New York: NYU Press, 2013. doi: 10.18574/9780814762998.

Ferrari, Walacy. "Brasil tem Recorde de Ausências, Votos Brancos e Nulos em Eleições Municipais em 2020." *UOL*, November 16, 2020. https://aventurasnahistoria.uol.com.br/noticias/historia-hoje/brasil-tem-recorde-de-ausencias-votos-brancos-e-nulos-em-eleicoes-municipais-em-2020.phtml.

Ferree, Myra Marx, and Aili Mari Tripp, eds. *Global Feminism: Transnational Women's Activism, Organizing, and Human Rights.* New York: NYU Press, 2006.

Fesnic, Florin N. "Can Civic Education Make a Difference for Democracy? Hungary and Poland Compared." *Political Studies* 64, no. 4 (2016): 966–978. doi: 10.1111/1467-9248.12215.

Fewsmith, Joseph. *The Logic and Limits of Political Reform in China.* Cambridge: Cambridge University Press, 2013.

Finley, Ashley. "Defining and Developing Civic-Minded Institutions." Association of American Colleges & Universities" *Diversity & Democracy* 22, no. 4 (2020). https://www.aacu.org/diversitydemocracy/2020/summer/finley.

Fischer, Florian, Dirk Lange, and Tonio Oeftering. "Was ist Politische Bildung? Qualitative Forschung in der Politikdidaktik am Beispiel einer Explorativen Studie zu den Vorstellungen von Lehramtsstudierenden über Politische Bildung," in *Perspektiven auf Politikunterricht Heute: Vom Wozialwissenschaftlichen Sachunterricht bis zur Politiklehrerausbildung*, eds. Markus Gloe and Tonio Oeftering, 256–82. Baden-Baden, Germany: Nomos Verlagsgesellschaft mbH & Co. KG, 2017.

Flanagan, Constance, and Peter Levine. "Civic Engagement and the Transition to Adulthood." *The Future of Children* 20, no. 1 (2010).

Flick, Uwe. "Triangulation in Data Collection," in *The Sage Handbook of Qualitative Data Collection*, ed. Uwe Flick. London: SAGE, 2018.

Flores-Macías, Gustavo A., and Jessica Zarkin. "The Militarization of Law Enforcement: Evidence from Latin America." *Perspectives on Politics* (2019): 1–20. doi:10.1017/S1537592719003906.

Floridia, Antonio. *From Participation to Deliberation: A Critical Genealogy of Deliberative Democracy.* ECPR Press, 2007.

Foa, Roberto Stefan, Andrew Klassen, Daniella Wenger, Alex Rand, and Michael Slade. "Youth and Satisfaction with Democracy: Reversing the Democratic Disconnect?" Cambridge, UK: Centre for the Future of Democracy, 2020.

Foa, Robeto Stefan, Andrew Klassen, Michael Slade, Alex Rand, and Rosie Collins. "The Global Satisfaction with Democracy Report 2020." Cambridge, UK: Centre for the Future of Democracy, 2020. https://cam.ac.uk/system/files/report/2020_003.pdf.

Foa, Roberto Stefan and Yascha Mounk. "The Danger of Deconsolidation: The Democratic Disconnect." *Journal of Democracy* 27, no. 3 (2016): 5–17. doi: 10.1353/jod.2016.0049. https://bennettinstitute.cam.ac.uk/media/uploads/files/Youth_and_

Satisfaction_with_Democracy_lite.pdf.

Forestiere, Carolyn. "Promoting Civic Agency Through Civic Engagement Activities: A Guide for Instructors New to Civic-Engagement Pedagogy." *Journal of Political Science Education* 11, no. 4 (2015): 455–471.

Forren, John. "Partnering with Campus and Community to Promote Civic Engagement: Miami University's Citizenship and Democracy Week," in *Teaching Civic Engagement Across the Disciplines*, eds. Elizabeth C. Matto, Alison Rios Millett McCartney, Elizabeth A. Bennion, and Dick Simpson, 209–214. Washington, DC: American Political Science Association, 2017.

Fowler, Adam. "Civic Agency," in *International Encyclopedia of Civil Society*, eds. Helmut K. Anheier, Stefan Toepler and Regina List. New York: Springer, 2010.

Fox, Jonathan and Aceron, Joy. *Doing Accountability Differently: A Proposal for the Vertical Integration of Civil Society Monitoring and Advocacy*. Bergen, Norway: U4 Anti-Corruption Resource Centre/Chr. Michelsen Institute, 2016.

Fox, Jonathan, and Halloran, Brendan, eds. *Connecting the Dots for Accountability: Civil Society Policy Monitoring and Advocacy Strategies*, report from international workshop, June 18–20, 2015 in Washington, DC. London: Transparency and Accountability Initiative, School of International Service-American University, International Budget Partnership, Government Watch, SIM Lab, 2016.

Fox, Madeline., Kavitha Mediratta, Jessica Ruglis, Brett Stoudt, S. Shah, and Michelle Fine. "Critical Youth Engagement: Participatory Action Research and Organizing." *Handbook of Research on Civic Engagement in Youth* (2010): 621–649.

Franks, Benjamin. "The Direct Action Ethic From 59 Upwards." *Anarchist Studies* 11 (2003): 13–41.

Fraser, Elizabeth. "Citizenship Education: Anti-political Culture and Political Education in Britain." *Political Studies* 48, no. 1 (2000): 88–103.

Freedom House. "Brazil." *Freedom in the World*, 2020. https://freedomhouse.org/country/brazil/freedom-world/2020.

Freedom House. "Countries and Territories." *Freedom House*, 2021. https://freedomhouse.org/countries/freedom-world/scores.

Freedom House. "Egypt: Freedom in the World 2020." *Freedom House*, 2021. https://freedomhouse.org/country/egypt/freedom-world/2020.

Freedom House. "Freedom on the Net 2020 Country Report." *Freedom House*, 2020. https://freedomhouse.org/country/singapore/freedom-net/2020.

Freedom House. "Freedom in the World 2019: Democracy in Retreat." *Freedom House*, 2019. https://freedomhouse.org/report/freedom-world/2019/democracy-retreat.

Freedom House. "Freedom in the World 2021: Democracy Under Siege." https://freedomhouse.org/report/freedom-world/2021/democracy-under-siege.

Freire, Paulo. *Pedagogia da Esperança: Um Reencontro com a Pedagogia do Oprimido*. São Paulo, Brazil: Paz e Terra, 1992.

Freire, Paulo. *Pedagogia do Oprimido*. Rio de Janeiro, Brazil: Editora Paz e Terra, 1987.

Freire, Paulo. *The Politics of Education: Culture, Power and Liberation*. Westport, CT: Bergin & Garvey, 1985.

Frey, William H. "Turnout in 2020 Election Spiked Among Both Democratic and Republican Voting Groups, New Census Data Shows." Washington, DC: Brookings Institution, May 5, 2021. https://brookings.edu/research/turnout-in-2020-spiked-among-both-democratic-and-republican-voting-groups-new census-data-shows/.

Freyre, Gilberto. *Casa-grande & Senzala* 25th ed. Rio de Janeiro, Brazil: José Olympio, 1986.

Fridkin, Kim, Patrick J. Kenney and Jack Crittenden. "On the Margins of Democratic Life: The Impact of Race and Ethnicity on the Political Engagement of Young People." *American Politics Research* 34 (2006): 605–626, p. 615.

Frye, Timothy M. "Capture or Exchange? Business Lobbying in Russia." *Europe-Asia Studies* 54, no. 7 (2002): 1017–1036.

Fu, Diana and Greg Distelhorst. "Grassroots Participation and Repression Under Hu Jintao and Xi Jinping." *The China Journal* 79 (2017).

Fu, Hualing and Richard Cullen. "Weiquan (Rights Protection) Lawyering in an Authoritarian State: Building a Culture of Public-Interest Lawyering." *China Journal* 59 (2008): 111–27.

Fukuda-Parr, Sakiko. "From the Millennium Development Goals to the Sustainable Development Goals: Shifts in Purpose, Concept, and Politics of Global Goal Setting for Development." *Gender & Development* 24, no. 1 (2016): 43–52.

Fukuyama, Francis. *The End of History and the Last Man*. London: Hamish Hamilton, 1992.

Gallagher, Mary E. "China: the Limits of Civil Society in a Late Leninist State," in *Civil Society and Political Change in Asia*, ed. Muthiah Alagappa. Stanford, CA: Stanford University Press, 2004.

Gallagher, Mary Elizabeth. "China's Workers Movement and the End of the Rapid-Growth Era." *Daedalus* 143, no. 2 (2014):

81–95.

Gallagher, Mary Elizabeth. *Contagious Capitalism: Globalization and the Politics of Labor in China.* Princeton, NJ: Princeton University Press, 2005.

Galston, William A. "Civic Education and Political Participation." *PS: Political Science and Politics* 37, no. 2 (2004): 263–266.

Galston, William A. "Political Knowledge, Political Engagement and Civic Education." *Annual Review of Political Science* 4, no. 1 (2001): 217–34.

Galvão, Thiago G. "ODS 11: Tornar as Cidades e os Assentamentos Humanos Inclusivos, Seguros, Resilientes e Sustentáveis," in *Os Objetivos de Desenvolvimento Sustentável e as Relações Internacionais,* ed. Henrique Zeferino Menezes, 209–234. João Pessoa, Brazil: Editora Universidade Federal da Paraíba (EDUFPB), 2019.

Galvão, Thiago G., and Guilherme Almeida Monteiro. "ODS 6: Assegurar a Disponibilidade e Gestão Sustentável da Água e Saneamento para Todas e Todos," in *Os Objetivos de Desenvolvimento Sustentável e as Relações Internacionais,* ed. Henrique Zeferino. UFB, 2019.

Ganz, Marshall. "Leading Change: Leadership, Organization, and Social Movements." *Handbook of Leadership Theory and Practice* 19 (2010): 1–10.

Ganz, Marshall. "Public Narrative, Collective Action, and Power," in *Accountability Through Public Opinion: From Inertia to Public Action,* eds. Sina Odugbemi and Taeku Lee, 273–89. Washington DC: The World Bank, 2011.

Ganz, Marshall. "Public Narrative: Self & Us & Now." *Marshallganz usmblogs,* 2013. http://marshallganz.usmblogs.com/files/2012/08/Public-Narrative-Worksheet-Fall-2013-.pdf.

Ganz, Marshall. "Why David Sometimes Wins: Strategic Capacity in Social Movements," in *The Psychology of Leadership: New Perspectives and Research,* 209–238. Mahwah: Lawrence Erlbaum Associates, 2005.

García, N. A., & Longo, N. V. "Going Global: Re-Framing Service-Learning in an Interconnected World." *Journal of Higher Education Outreach and Engagement* 17, no. 2 (2013): 111–136.

Garcia, Ruben. S., Cita Cook, and Jenice L. View. "Universidad Sin Fronteras: Transgressing Intellectual Borders and Redefining Learning," in *The Cambridge Handbook of Service Learning and Community Engagement,* eds. Corey Dolgon, Tina D. Mitchell, and Timothy K. Eatman. Cambridge, UK: Cambridge University Press, 2017.

Garcìa-Albacete, Gema M. "Promoting Political Interest in Schools: The Role of Civic Education," in *Growing into Politics. Contexts and Timing of Political Socialisation,* ed. Simone Abendschön, 91–114. Colchester: ECPR Press, 2013.

Gastaldo, Denise, Natalia Rivas-Quarneti & Lilian Magalhães. "Body-map Storytelling as a Health Research Methodology: Blurred Lines Creating Clear Pictures." *Forum Qualitative Sozialforschung/Forum: Qualitative Social Research* 19, no 2 (2018): 3. http://dx.doi.org/10.17169/fqs-19.2.2858.

Gastil, John. "Embracing Digital Democracy: A Call for Building an Online Civic Commons." *PS: Political Science & Politics* 50, no. 3 (2017): 758–763.

Gauntlett, David. *Creative Explorations: New Approaches to Identities and Audiences.* London: Routledge, 2007.

Gaventa, John, and Gregory Barrett. "So What Difference does it Make? Mapping the Outcomes of Citizen Engagement." *IDS Working Papers* 347 (2010): 1–72.

Gentry, Bobbi. "Bridging Adolescent Engagement and Adult Engagement: A Theory of Political Identity," in *Teaching Civic Engagement: From Student to Active Citizen,* eds. Alison Rios Millett McCartney, Elizabeth A. Bennion, and Dick Simpson, 57–72. Washington, DC: American Political Science Association, 2013.

George, Cherian. *Freedom from the Press: Journalism and State Power in Singapore.* Singapore: NUS Press, 2012.

George, Cherian. "Remaking an Untenable Media System: Why SPH's Proposed Overhaul is Not Enough." *Academia SG,* May 7, 2021. https://www.academia.sg/academic-views/media-system.

Gerber, Brian. "Three Ways R3's Stand Out From the Crowd." *The Evolution,* August 15, 2016. https://evolllution.com/managing-institution/higher_ed_business/three-ways-r3s-stand-out-from-the-crowd/.

Gerdes, Karen E., Elizabeth A. Segal, Kelly F. Jackson, and Jennifer L. Mullins. "Teaching Empathy: A Framework Rooted in Social Cognitive Neuroscience and Social Justice." *Journal of Social Work Education* 47 (2011): 109–31.

Gernhardt, Ariane, Hartmut Rubeling, and Heidi Keller. "Cultural Perspectives on Children's Tadpole Drawings: At the Interface Between Representation and Production." *Frontiers in Psychology* 6, no. 1 (2015).

Gerring, John. *Case Study Research: Principles and Practices.* Cambridge, UK: Cambridge University Press, 2007.

Gert, Biesta. *Learning Democracy in School and Society, Education, Lifelong Learning and the Politics of Citizenship.* University of Stirling UK: Sense Publishers, 2011.

Gert, Biesta, and Robert Lawy. "From Teaching Citizenship to Learning Democracy: Overcoming Individualism in Research,

Policy and Practice." *Cambridge Journal of Education* 36, no. 1 (2006): 63–79. doi: 10.1080/03057640500490981.

Gilman, Hollie Russon. "Civic Tech for Urban Collaborative Governance." *PS: Political Science & Politics* 50, no. 3 (2017): 741–750.

Ginwright, Shawn, and Julio Cammarota. "New Terrain in Youth Development: The Promise of a Social Justice Approach." *Social Justice* 29, no. 4 (2002): 82–95.

Giroux, Henry A. *Pedagogy and the Politics of Hope: Theory, Culture, and Schooling.* Boulder, CO: Westview Press, 1997.

Glazier, Rebecca A. "Running Simulations Without Ruining Your Life: Simple Ways to Incorporate Active Learning into Your Teaching." *Journal of Political Science Education* 7, no. 4 (2011): 375–393. https://doi.org/10.1080/15512169.2011.615188.

Glazier, Rebecca A. "Satire and Efficacy in the Political Science Classroom." *PS: Political Science & Politics* 47, no. 4 (2014): 867–872.

Globo. "Jair Bolsonaro é Eleito Presidente com 57,8 Milhões de Votos." *Eleições 2018,* October 29, 2018. https://g1.globo.com/politica/eleicoes/2018/apuracao/presidente.ghtml.

Glover, Robert W., Daniel C. Lewis, Richard Meagher, and Katherine A. Owens. "Advocating for Engagement: Do Experiential Learning Courses Boost Civic Engagement." *Journal of Political Science Education,* forthcoming.

Godfrey, Erin, and Justina Grayman. "Teaching Citizens: The Role of Open Classroom Climate in Fostering Critical Consciousness Among Youth." *Journal of Youth & Adolescence* 43, no. 11 (2014): 1801–17.

Goetz, Anne M. "The New Competition in Multilateral Norm-Setting: Transnational Feminists & the Illiberal Backlash." *Daedalus* 149 (2020): 160–79. Accessed September 2, 2020. https://www.amacad.org/publication/transnational-feminists-illiberal-backlash.

Goh, Choon Kang. "Singapore Does Not Need a 'Colour Revolution'." *The Straits Times,* September 21, 2019. Accessed June 8, 2021. https://www.straitstimes.com/opinion/singapore-does-not-need-a-colour-revolution.

Gökbudak, Mahir, and Reinhold Hedtke. *Ranking Politische Bildung 2018. Politische Bildung an allgemeinbildenden Schulen der Sekundarstufe I im Bundesländervergleich.* Universität Bielefeld: Fakultät für Soziologie – Didaktik der Sozialwissenschaften, 2019.

Gold, Thomas B. "The Resurgence of Civil Society in China." *Journal of Democracy* 1, no. 1 (1990): 18–31.

Goldberg, Abraham, Dena A. Pastor, and Carah Ong Whaley. *Assessing the Effectiveness of a Campus-Wide Census 2020 Education Initiative* (forthcoming).

Golub, Stephen, and Ahmadou Mbaye. "National Trade Policies and Smuggling in Africa: The Case of Gambia and Senegal." *World Development* 37, no. 3 (2009): 595–606.

Gordon, Peter, and John White. *Philosophers as Educational Reformers: The Influence of Idealism on British Educational Thought and Practice.* London: Routledge and Kegan Paul, 1979.

Gorham, Eric. "Service Learning and Political Knowledge." *Journal of Political Science Education* 1, no. 3 (2005): 345–365.

Grant, Wyn. *The Development of a Discipline. The History of the Political Studies Association.* Chichester, West Sussex, UK: Wiley-Blackwell, 2010.

Green, Adrienne. "The Re-Politicization of America's Colleges." *The Atlantic,* February 12, 2016. https://www.theatlantic.com/education/archive/2016/02/freshman-survey/462429/.

Green, Duncan. "Promoting Active Citizenship: What Have We Learned from 10 Case Studies of Oxfam's Work?" *Oxfam International* (2014).

Greenacre, Michael. *Correspondence Analysis in Practice.* Boca Raton: Chapman and Hall/CRC, 2007.

Greenhalgh, Susan. "Fresh Winds in Beijing: Chinese Feminists Speak Out on the One-child Policy and Women's Lives." *Signs: Journal of Women in Culture and Society* 26, no. 3 (2001): 847–88.

Gretschel, Anu, and Tomi Kiilakoski. *Demokratiaoppitunti. Lasten ja Nuorten Kunta 2010-luvun Alussa.* Helsinki: Nuorisotutkimusseura, 2012.

Grussendorf, Jeannie, and Natalie C. Rogol. "Reflections on Critical Thinking: Lessons from a Quasi-Experimental Study." *Journal of Political Science Education* 14, no. 2 (2018): 151–166.

Gutiérrez, R., J. Auerbach, and R. Bhandar. "Expanding US Study Abroad Capacity: Findings From an IEE-forum Survey," in *Institute of International Education Study Abroad White Paper Series, 6.* New York, NY: Institute of International Education, 2009.

Habashy, Noel. "If I Had More of a Relationship With Them, it Would be Good: Community Members' Perspectives of Community-Engaged Education Abroad Programs in Costa Rica." PhD diss. Pennsylvania State University, 2019.

Hadow, W.H. *Citizenship.* Oxford, UK: Clarendon Press, 1923.

Hall, B. Welling. "Teaching Students about Congress and Civic Engagement." *PS: Political Science & Politics* 44, no. 4 (2011): 871–81. http://doi.org/10.1017/S1049096511001508.

Hall, Emese. "The Ethics of 'Using' Children's Drawings in Research," in *Visual Methods with Children and Young People. Studies in Childhood and Youth*, eds. Eve Stirling and Dylan Yamada-Rice. London: Palgrave Macmillan, 2015.

Hall, Emese. ""My Brain Printed it Out!" Drawing, Communication, and Young Children: A Discussion." Paper presented at the *British Educational Research Association Annual Conference*. Edinburgh, 2008.

Hall, Martin. "Institutional Culture of Mergers and Alliances in South Africa," in *Mergers and Alliances in Higher Education*, eds. Adrian Curaj, Luke Georghiou, Jennifer Casenga Harper and Eva Egron-Polak, 145–173. Cham, Netherlands: Springer Nature, 2015.

Hall, Matthew, David Marsh & Emma Vines. "A Changing Democracy: Contemporary Challenges to The British Political Tradition." *Policy Studies* 39, no. 4 (2018): 365–382.

Halliday, Fred. "Hidden from International Relations: Women and the International Arena." *Millenium: Journal of International Studies* 17, no. 3 (1988): 419–428. https://doi.org/10.1177%2F03058298880170030701.

Hammond, Christopher D., and Avril Keating. "Global Citizens or Global Workers? Comparing University Programmes for Global Citizenship Education in Japan and the UK." *Compare: A Journal of Comparative and International Education* 48, no. 6 (2018): 915–934.

Han, Kirsten. "On Accusations and Gaslighting." *Kirsten Han*, September 25, 2019. https://www.kirstenhan.com/blog/2019/9/26/on-accusations-and-gaslighting.

Hanson, A. H. "III. Politics as a University Discipline." *Universities Quarterly* 8, no. 1 (1953): 34–43.

Hansson, Eva, and Meredith L. Weiss, ed. *Political Participation in Asia: Defining and Deploying Political Space*. New York: Routledge, 2017.

Hargreaves David H. *The Challenge for the Comprehensive School: Culture, Curriculum and Community*. London: Routledge, 1982.

Harrigern, Katy J., Jill J. McMillan, Christy M. Buchanan, and Stephanie Gusler. "The Value of Longitudinal Assessment: The Impact of the Democracy Fellows Program," in *Deliberative Pedagogy: Teaching and Learning for Democratic Engagement*, eds. Timothy J. Shaffer, Nicholas V. Longo, Idit Manosevitch, and Maxine S. Thomas, 179–190. East Lansing, MI: Michigan State University Press, 2017.

Hart, James, and Matt Henn. "Neoliberalism and the Unfolding Patterns of Young People's Political Engagement and Political Participation in Contemporary Britain." *Societies* 7, no. 4 (2017): 33.

Hart, Jeffrey. "Three Approaches to the Measurement of Power in International Relations." *International Organization* 30, no. 2 (1976): 289–305. https://doi.org/10.1017/S0020818300018282.

Harward, Brian M., and Daniel M. Shea. "Higher Education and the Multiple Modes of Engagement," in *Teaching Civic Engagement: From Student to Active Citizen,* eds. Alison Rios Millett McCartney, Elizabeth A. Bennion, and Dick Simpson, 21–40. Washington, DC: American Political Science Association Press, 2013.

Haski-Leventhal, Debbie, Ed Metz, Edward Hogg, Barbara Ibrahim, David H. Smith, and Lili Wang. "Volunteering in Three Life Stages," in *The Palgrave Handbook of Volunteering*, eds. David H. Smith, Robert A. Stebbins and Jurgen Grotz. Palgrave: Civic Participation and Nonprofit Associations Basingstoke, 2016.

Hassid, Jonathan. "China's Contentious Journalists: Reconceptualizing the Media." *Problems of Post-communism* 55, no. 4 (2008): 52–61.

Hästbacka, Elisabeth, Mikael Nygård, and Fredrica Nyqvist. "Barriers and Facilitators to Societal Participation of People with Disabilities: A Scoping Review of Studies Concerning European Countries." *Alter* 10 (2016): 201–220.

Hawkins, Bryan. "Children's Drawing, Self-expression, Identity and Imagination." *International Journal of Art & Design Education* 21, no. 3 (2002).

Hayes, Kecia. "Critical Service-Learning and the Black Freedom Movement," in *Critical Service-Learning as Revolutionary Pedagogy: A Project of Student Agency in Action*, eds. Brad J. Porfilio and Heather Hickman, 47–70. Charlotte, NC: Information Age Publishing, 2011.

Hazelkorn, Ellen. "Is the Public Good Role of Higher Education Under Attack." *International Higher Education* 91 (2017): 2–3.

Head, Brian. "Why Not Ask Them? Mapping and Promoting Youth Participation." *Children and Youth Services Review* 33 (2011): 541–547, p. 544.

Healey, Shawn. "Essential School Supports for Civic Learning," in *Teaching Civic Engagement Across the Disciplines,* eds. Elizabeth C. Matto, Alison Rios Millett McCartney, Elizabeth A. Bennion, and Dick Simpson, 123–134. Washington DC: American Political Science Association, 2017.

Hemmings, Clare. "Affective Solidarity: Feminist Reflexivity and Political Transformation." *Feminist Theory* 13 (2012): 147–61.

Heng, Janice. "Yale-NUS Rejects Call on Envoy to Quit Post." *The Straits Times*, February 6, 2016. https://www.straitstimes.com/singapore/yale-nus-rejects-call-on-envoy-to-quit-post.

Henn, Matt, and Nick Foard. "Social Differentiation in Young People's Political Participation: The Impact of Social and Educational Factors on Youth Political Engagement in Britain." *Journal of Youth Studies* 17, no. 3 (2014): 360–380.

Henshaw, Alexis Leanna, and Scott R. Meinke. "Data Analysis and Data Visualization as Active Learning in Political Science." *Journal of Political Science Education* 14, no. 4 (2018): 423–439.

Heron, John, and Peter Reason. "A Participatory Inquiry Paradigm." *Qualitative Inquiry* 3, no. 3 (1997).

Hersh, Eitan. *How to Move Beyond Political Hobbyism, Take Action, and Make Real World Change.* New York: Scribner, 2020. Accessed September 23, 2020. https://thehill.com/opinion/campaign/520277-another-political-gender-gap-emerges.

HESA. *Higher Education Student Statistics: UK, 2019/20,* January 27, 2021. https://www.hesa.ac.uk/news/27-01-2021/sb258-higher-education-student-statistics.

Hess, Robert and Judith, Torney. "The Development of Political Attitudes in Children," in *Political Socialization*, ed. Edwards S. Greenberg. New York: Routledge, 1967.

Ho, Li-Ching. "Conceptions of Global Citizenship Education in East and Southeast Asia," in *The Palgrave Handbook of Global Citizenship and Education*, eds. Ian Davies, Li Ching Ho, Dina Kiwan, Carla L. Peck, Andrew Peterson, Edda Sant and Yusef Waghid, 83–95. London: Palgrave Macmillan, 2018.

Ho, Li-Ching, Jasmine B-Y. Sim, and Theresa Alviar-Martin. "Interrogating Differentiated Citizenship Education: Students' Perceptions of Democracy, Rights and Governance in Two Singapore Schools." *Education, Citizenship and Social Justice* 6, no. 3 (2011): 265–276.

Ho, Li-Ching, and Keith C. Barton. "Preparation for Civil Society: A Necessary Element of Curriculum for Social Justice." *Theory & Research in Social Education* 48, no. 4 (2020): 471–491.

Ho, Li-Ching, and Tricia Seow. "Teaching Controversial Issues in Geography: Climate Change Education in Singaporean Schools." *Theory & Research in Social Education* 43, no. 3 (2015): 314–344. doi: 10.1080/00933104.2015.1064842.

Holbein, John B., and D. Sunshine Hillygus. *Making Young Voters: Converting Civic Attitudes Into Civic Action.* Cambridge, UK: Cambridge University Press, 2020.

Holden, Philip. "A Building with One Side Missing: Liberal Arts and Illiberal Modernities in Singapore." *Sojourn: Journal of Social Issues in Southeast Asia* 33, no. 1 (2018): 1–28.

Holdsworth, Clare. "Why Volunteer? Understanding Motivations for Student Volunteering." *British Journal of Educational Studies* 58, no. 4 (2010): 421–437.

Holdsworth, Clare, and Jocey Quinn. "Student Volunteering in English Higher Education." *Studies in Higher Education* 35, no. 1 (2010): 113–127.

Hooghe, Marc, and Ruth Dassonneville. "The Effects of Civic Education on Political Knowledge: A Two Year Panel Survey among Belgian Adolescents." *Educational Assessment, Evaluation and Accountability* 23, no. 4 (2011): 321–39.

hooks, bell. *Black Looks: Race and Representation.* New York: Routledge, 1992.

hooks, bell. *Teaching to Transgress: Education as the Practice of Freedom.* New York: Routledge, 1994.

Hoon, Geoff. "Towards European Citizenship," in *Beyond Communitarianism: Citizenship, Politics and Education*, eds. Jack Demaine and Harold Entwistle, 131–140. Basingstoke, UK: Macmillan Press, 1996.

Horowitz, Donald L. "Electoral Systems: A Primer for Decision Makers." *Journal of Democracy* 14, no. 4 (2003): 115–127.

Hosman, Laura, and Ginger Jacobs. "From Active Learning to Taking Action: Incorporating Political Context Into Project-Based, Interdisciplinary, International Service Learning Courses." *Journal of Political Science Education* 14, no. 4 (2018): 473–490.

Hougua, Ben Ahmed, El Amine Rachid, and Siyouri Hind. "The Authoritarian Spectrum Through the Prism of Individualism/Collectivism: Lessons for Political Socialization in Moroccan Society." *Contemporary Arab Affairs* 11, no. 3 (2018): 47–68.

House of Lords Select Committee on Citizenship and Civic Engagement. *The Ties that Bind: Citizenship and Civic Engagement in the 21st Century.* Report of Session 2017–19, HL Paper 118. London: House of Lords, 2018.

Howard, Brian M., and Daniel M. Shea. "Higher Education and the Multiple Modes of Engagement," in *Teaching Civic Engagement: From Student to Active Citizen*, eds. Alison Rios Millett McCartney, Elizabeth A. Bennion, and Dick Simpson, 21–40. Washington DC: American Political Science Association, 2013.

Howard, Leigh Anne, and Brian D. Posler. "Reframing Political Message: Using a Festival to Reach Young Voters." *Journal of Political Science Education* 8, no. 4 (2012): 389–407.

Huang, Jianli. "Positioning the Student Political Activism of Singapore: Articulation, Contestation and Omission." *Inter-Asia Cultural Studies* 7, no. 3 (2006): 403–430.

Hubback, E.M. "Methods of Training for Citizenship," in *Training for Citizenship*, eds. Sir Ernest Simon and Eva M. Hubback, 17–48. Oxford, UK: Oxford University Press, 1935.

Hudson, Alan. "NGOs' Transnational Advocacy Networks: From 'Legitimacy' to 'Political Responsibility'?" *Global Networks* 1 (2001): 331–352.

Huerta, Juan Carlos. "Do Learning Communities Make a Difference?" *PS: Political Science & Politics* 37, no. 2 (2004): 291–296.

Huerta, Juan Carlos, and Joseph Jozwiak. "Developing Civic Education in General Education Political Science." *Journal of Political Science Education* 4, no. 1 (2008): 42–60.

Human Rights Watch. "'Kill the Chicken to Scare the Monkeys': Suppression of Free Expression and Assembly in Singapore." *Human Rights Watch*, December 12, 2017. Accessed June 8, 2021. https://www.hrw.org/report/2017/12/12/kill-chicken-scare-monkeys/suppression-free-expression-and-assembly-singapore.

Hung, Cheng-Yu. "Educators as Transformative Intellectuals: Taiwanese Teacher Activism during the National Curriculum Controversy." *Curriculum Inquiry* 48, no. 2 (2018): 167–183.

Hutchings, Sharon, and Andrea Lyons-Lewis. "Reflections on our Critical Service Learning Provision. Is It Critical or Are We Social Justice Dreamers?" in *Public Sociology as Educational Practice: Challenges, Dialogues and Counterpublics*, ed. Eurig Scandrett, 299–314. Bristol, UK: Bristol University Press, 2020.

Hüther, Otto, and Georg Krücken. *Higher Education in Germany—Recent Developments in an International Perspective.* Higher Education Dynamics 49. Cham, Netherlands: Springer International Publishing, 2018.

Hyman, Herbert H. *Political Socialization. A Study in the Psychology of Political Behavior.* Glencoe, IL: Free Press, 1959.

Iau, Jean. "Louis Ng Public Assembly Investigation: Dos and Don'ts under the Public Order Act." *The Straits Times*, March 3, 2021. https://www.straitstimes.com/singapore/louis-ng-public-assembly-investigation-dos-and-donts-under-the-public-order-act.

IEA. "International Civic and Citizenship Education Study." *International Association for the Evaluation of Educational Achievement*, 2021. https://www.iea.nl/studies/iea/iccs.

Independente. "Deputada Questiona Despreparo de Ricardo Velez, Ministro da Educação, em Comissão na Câmara." *YouTube*, March 28, 2019. https://www.youtube.com/watch?v=ngFoaSWUegg&fbclid=IwAR3iK8bvIPCPFeeJeJ_lLQ8uM1BJEb7mnotGZ4cqmJGdquIbaPJkOERgTqs.

Ingram, Nicola. "Within School and Beyond the Gate: The Complexities of Being Educationally Successful and Working Class." *Sociology* 45, no. 2 (2011).

Innovations in Civic Participation (ICP). *Youth Civic Participation in Action: Meeting Community and Youth Development Needs Worldwide.* Washington, DC: ICP, October 2010.

Institute for International Education. *Open Doors.* 2019.

Institute for International Education. *Open Doors.* 2020.

International Institute for Democracy and Electoral Assistance. *Youth Voter Participation: Involving Today's Young in Tomorrow's Democracy.* Stockholm: IDEA, 1999. https://www.idea.int/publications/catalogue/youth-voter-participation-involving-todays-young-tomorrows-democracy.

International Monetary Fund. "World Economic Outlook Database." *World Economic and Financial Surveys*, October 2020. https://www.imf.org/en/Publications/WEO/weo-database/2020/October/weo-report

Investe São Paulo. "99% das Pesquisas São Feitas Pelas Universidades Públicas." February 20, 2019. https://www.investe.sp.gov.br/noticia/99-das-pesquisas-sao-feitas-pelas-universidades-publicas/?fbclid=IwAR1BDR-Hi2pQV8nyvvwlP4VVmnvZS6Ya3nKNHmRxtINrv22bI2N3tsFYQk4.

Ipsos MORI. "Fake News, Filter Bubbles and Post-truth Are Other People's Problems." *IPSOS*, September 6, 2018. https://www.ipsos.com/ipsos-mori/en-uk/fake-news-filter-bubbles-and-post-truth-are-other-peoples-problems.

Ipsos MORI. "Perceptions Are Not Reality: Things the World Gets Wrong." *IPSOS*, October 29, 2014. https://www.ipsos.com/ipsos-mori/en-uk/perceptions-are-not-reality-things-world-gets-wrong.

Jack, Andrew, and Jamie Smyth. "Coronavirus: Universities Face a Harsh Lesson." *Financial Times*, April 21, 2020. https://www.ft.com/content/0ae1c300-7fee-11ea-82f6-150830b3b99a.

Jacobs, Lawrence R., and Robert Y. Shapiro. *Politicians Don't Pander: Political Manipulation and the Loss of Democratic Responsiveness.* Chicago: University of Chicago Press, 2000.

Jacoby, Barbara, ed. *Civic Engagement in Higher Education: Concepts and Practices.* San Francisco, CA: Jossey-Bass, 2009.

Jacoby, Barbara, and Elizabeth Hollander. "Securing the Future of Civic Engagement in Higher Education," in *Civic Engagement in Higher Education: Concepts and Practices*, ed. Barbara Jacoby and Associates, 227–248. San Francisco, CA: Jossey-Bass, 2009.

James Madison Center for Civic Engagement. *Political Learning and Democratic Engagement at JMU: A Campus Climate Study.* Harrisonburg, VA: James Madison University, 2019.

Jamieson, Kathleen Hall. "Reconceptualizing Public Engagement by Land-Grant University Scientists." Proceedings of the *National Academy of Sciences* 117 (2020): 2734–6. doi: 10.1073/pnas.1922395117.

Janzen, Melanie D. "Where is the (Postmodern) Child in Early Childhood Education Research?" *Early Years* 28, no. 3 (2008).

Janzen, Monica, and Catherine Ford. "Scaffolding Civic Engagement Projects: A Study into the Effectiveness of Supported Small-Scale, Interrelated, Student-Designed Projects." *Transformative Dialogues: Teaching and Learning Journal Winter 2020* 13, no. 3 (2020). https://journals.kpu.ca/index.php/td/index.

Jary, David, and Martin Parker. "The New Higher Education - Dilemmas and Directions of the Post-Dearing University," in *The New Higher Education: Issues and Directions for the Post-Dearing University*, eds. David Jary and Martin Parker, 3–16. Stoke-on-Trent, UK: Staffordshire University Press, 1998.

Jenkins, Shannon. "Using Best Practices and Experience with Local Governments to Increase Political Engagement," in *Teaching Civic Engagement: From Student to Active Citizen*, eds. Alison Rios Millett McCartney, Elizabeth A. Bennion, and Dick Simpson, 107–117. Washington, DC: American Political Science Association, 2013.

Jennings, M. K., Laura Stoker, and Jake Bowers. "Politics Across Generations: Family Transmission Reexamined." *Journal of Politics* 71, no. 3 (2009): 782–99.

Jervis, Robert L. "Realism, Game Theory and Cooperation." *World Politics* 40, no. 3 (1988): 317–349. https://doi.org/10.2307/2010216.

Johnson, Jean, and Keith Melville, "The National Issues Forums: 'Choicework' as an Indispensable Civic Skill," in *A Crisis of Civility? Political Discourse and Its Discontents*, eds. Robert G. Boatright, Timothy J. Shaffer, Sarah Sobieraj, and Dannagal Goldthwaite Young, 160–146. New York: Routledge, 2019.

Johnson, Laura R, and Julie S Johnson-Pynn. "Cultivating Compassion and Youth Action around the Globe: A Preliminary Report on Jane Goodall's Roots & Shoots Program." *Journal of Youth Development* 2, no. 2 (2007): 26–41.

Johnson, Michael. *Corruption, Contention and Reform.* New York: Cambridge University Press, 2013.

Jones, Christopher and Richard Anthony Baker. *Report on the Uncivil, Hate and Bias Incidents on Campus Survey.* Washington, DC: The LEAD Fund, 2019. https://www.aaaed.org/images/aaaed/LEAD_Fund/LEAD-Fund-Report-UHBIOC-Report.pdf.

Jones, David R. *The Origins of Civic Universities: Manchester, Leeds and Liverpool.* London: Routledge, 1988.

Jones, Sir Henry. "The Education of the Citizen," in *Essays and Literature and Education*, ed. Sir Henry Jones, 225–281. London: Hodder and Stoughton, 1947.

Journell, Wayne. "What Preservice Social Studies Teachers (Don't) Know About Politics and Current Events - And Why It Matters." *Theory & Research in Social Education* 41, no. 3 (2013): 316–51.

Kahne, Joseph, and Ellen Middaugh. "Democracy for Some: The Civic Opportunity Gap in High School." *CIRCLE Working Paper 59.* Boston: Center for Information and Research on Civic Learning and Engagement, 2008. https://files.eric.ed.gov/fulltext/ED503646.pdf.

Kahne, Joseph, and Joel Westheimer. "In the Service of What? The Politics of Service Learning." *Service-learning for Youth Empowerment and Social Change* (1999): 25–42.

Kaldor, Mary, and Sonia Marcoux. "La Sécurité Humaine: Un Concept Pertinent?" *Politique* étrangère 71, no. 4 (2006): 901–914. https://www.jstor.org/stable/42716375.

Kallio, Kirsi Pauliina, and Jouni Häkli. "Children and Young People's Politics in Everyday Life." *Space and Polity* 17 (2013): 1–16.

Kamberelis, George, and Greg Dimitriadis. *Focus Groups: From Structured Interviews to Collective Conversations.* Abingdon, UK: Routledge, 2013.

Kamler, Erin Michelle. "Negotiating Narratives of Human Trafficking: NGOs, Communication and the Power of Culture." *Journal of Intercultural Communication Research* 42 (2013): 73–90.

Kanyakumari, D., and Priya Kulasagaran. "Crowd Forces Its Way through Locked UM Gates." *The Star*, October 27, 2014. https://www.thestar.com.my/News/Nation/2014/10/27/anwar-ibrahim-talk-universiti-malaya-crowd-build-up.

Kaplan, Caren and Inderpal Grewal. "Transnational Feminist Cultural Studies: Beyond the Marxism/Poststructuralism/ Feminism Divides," in *Between Women and Nation: Nationalism, Transnational Feminisms, and the State*, eds. Caren

Kaplan, Norma Alarcón and Minoo Moallem, 349–63. Durham, NC and London: Duke University Press, 1999.

Karapistolis, Dimitris. *Software Method of Data Analysis MAD*, 2010. http://www.pylimad.gr/.

Karasik, Ron. "Community Partners' Perspectives and the Faculty Role in Community-Based Learning." *Journal of Experiential Education* 43, no. 2 (2020): 113–135.

Karlsson, Rasmus. "Gallery Walk Seminar: Visualizing the Future of Political Ideologies." *Journal of Political Science Education* 16, no. 1 (2020): 91–100.

Karpowitz, Christopher F., Tali Mendelberg, and Lee Shaker. "Gender Inequality in Deliberative Participation." *American Political Science Review* 106, no. 3 (2012): 533–54.

Keating, Avril, David Kerr, Thomas Benton, Ellie Mundy and Joana Lopes. *Citizenship Education in England 2001–2010: Young People's Practices and Prospects for the Future: The Eighth and Final Report from Citizenship Education Longitudinal Study (CELS)*. Research Report DFE-RR059. London: Department of Education, 2010. https://assets.publishing.service.gov. uk/government/uploads/system/uploads/attachment_data/file/181797/DFE-RR059.pdf.

Keating, Avril, Debora Hinderliter Ortloff, and Stavroula Philippou. "Citizenship Education Curricula: The Changes and Challenges Presented By Global And European Integration." *Journal of Curriculum Studies* 41, no. 2 (2009): 145–158.

Keating, Avril, and Jan Germen Janmaat. "Education Through Citizenship at School: Do School Activities Have a Lasting Impact on Youth Political Engagement." *Parliamentary Affairs* 69, no. 2 (2016): 409–429.

Kelly, Jemina. "How Hate Became a Driving Force in Elections." *Financial Times*, October 15, 2020. https://www.ft.com/content/018e1286-3641-4921-b7b0-927081ec7fc6.

Kickbusch, Kenneth W. "Civic Education and Preservice Educators: Extending the Boundaries of Discourse." *Theory & Research in Social Education* 15, no. 3 (1987): 173–88.

Kidman, Joanna, and Vincent O'Malley. "Questioning the Canon: Colonial History, Counter-memory and Youth Activism." *Memory Studies* 13 (2020): 537–550.

Kiernan, Anabelle. "Teaching Frameworks for Participation – Can We? Should We?" *European Political Science* 11, no. 2 (2012): 186–195.

Kisby, Ben. "New Labour and Citizenship Education." *Parliamentary Affairs* 60, no. 1 (2007): 84–101.

Knowles, Ryan T. "Teaching Who You Are: Connecting Teachers' Civic Education Ideology to Instructional Strategies." *Theory and Research in Social Education* 46, no. 1 (2018): 68–109.

Koesel, Karrie. *Religion and Authoritarianism: Cooperation, Conflict, and the Consequences*. Cambridge, UK: Cambridge University Press, 2014.

Koh, Tai Ann. "Civil or Civic Society? The Singapore Idea." *The Business Times*, May, 31, 1998.

Korolczuk, Elżbieta. "Explaining Mass Protests Against Abortion Ban in Poland: The Power of Connective Action." *Zoon Politikon* 7 (2016): 91–113.

Krasner, Stephen D. *Sovereignty: Organized Hypocrisy*. Princeton, NJ: Princeton University Press, 1999.

Krasnyak, Olga. *National Styles in Science, Diplomacy, and Science Diplomacy*. Leiden and Boston: Brill, 2019.

Kuh, George. *High-impact Educational Practices: What They Are, Who has Access to Them, and Why They Matter*. Washington, DC: Association of American Colleges and Universities, 2008.

Kuhar, Roman and David Paternotte. *Anti-Gender Campaigns in Europe: Mobilizing Against Equality*. Lanham, MD: Roman and Littlefield, 2017.

Kuhn, Berthold. *Civil Society in China: A Snapshot of Discourses, Legislation, and Social Realities*. Berlin: Dialogue of Civilizations Research Institute, 2019.

Kuhns, Katherine. *Globalization of Knowledge and Its Impact on Higher Education Reform in Transitioning States: The Case of Russia*. PhD diss., School of Education and the Committee on Graduate Studies, Stanford University, 2011. https://purl. stanford.edu/rc358bn5948.

Kulkarni, Tara and Kimberly Coleman. "Service-Learning in an Environmental Engineering Classroom: Examples, Evaluation, and Recommendations," in *Teaching Civic Engagement Across the Disciplines*, eds. Elizabeth C. Matto, Alison Rios Millett McCartney, Elizabeth A. Bennion, and Dick Simpson, 195–208. Washington, DC: American Political Science Association, 2017.

Kulke, Christine. "Politische Sozialisation und Geschlechterdifferenz," in *Neues Handbuch der Sozialisationsforschung*, ed. Hurrelmann,Klaus and Dieter Ulich, 595–613. Weinheim: Beltz, 1991.

Kumar, Rohit. "The Importance of Being a Good Political Science Teacher in Modi's India." *The Wire*, December 1, 2019. https://thewire.in/education/the-importance-of-being-a-good-political-science-teacher-in-modis-india.

Kurohi, Rei. "Parliament: Institutions Should Not Expose Students to Risk of Breaking the Law, Says Ong Ye Kung." *The Straits Times*, October 8, 2019. Accessed June 8, 2021. https://www.straitstimes.com/politics/institutions-should-not-expose-students-to-risk-of-breaking-the-law-ong-ye-kung.

Kurohi, Rei. "Singapore GE2020: Hwa Chong Defends Advice to Students to Not Discuss Election on Social Media." *The Straits Times*, July 4, 2020. Accessed June 8, 2021. https://www.straitstimes.com/politics/singapore-ge2020-hwa-chong-defends-advice-to-students-to-not-discuss-election-on-social.

Kyriacopoulos, Konstantine. "Research on Civic Engagement and Youth," in *Encyclopedia of Diversity in Education*, ed. James A. Banks, 383–385. Thousand Oaks, CA: SAGE Publications, 2012.

Laird, Thomas F. Nelson, and Mark E. Engberg. "Establishing Differences Between Diversity Requirements and Other Courses with Varying Degrees of Diversity Inclusivity." *The Journal of General Education* 60 (2011): 117–37. doi: 10.5325/jgeneeduc.60.2.0117.

Lake, Vickie E., Christian Winterbottom, Elizabeth A. Ethridge, and Loreen Kelly. "Reconceptualizing Teacher Education Programs: Applying Dewey's Theories to Service-Learning With Early Childhood Preservice Teachers." *Journal of Higher Education Outreach and Engagement* 19, no. 1 (2015): 93–116.

Lantis, Jeffrey S. "Ethics and Foreign Policy: Structured Debates for the International Studies Classroom." *International Studies Perspectives* 5, no. 2 (2004): 117–33. https://doi.org/10.1111/j.1528-3577.2004.00162.x.

Lapadat, Laura, Anusha Balram, Joanna Cheek, Eugenia Canas, Andrea Paquette and Erin E Michalak. "Engaging Youth in the Bipolar Youth Action Project: Community-Based Participatory Research." *Journal of Participatory Medicine* 12 (2020): e19475.

Lasswell, Harold. "The Structure and Function of Communication in Society." *The Communication of Ideas* 37 (1948): 136–139.

Latinobarómetro. "Análisis de Datos. *Latinobarómetro*, 2018. https://www.latinobarometro.org/latOnline.jsp.

Law Info China. "Law of the People's Republic of China on the Administration of Activities of Overseas Non-Governmental Organizations within the Territory of China." *Standing Committee of the National People's Congress of China* 44 (2017). http://www.lawinfochina.com/display.aspx?lib=law&id=21963.

Lawson, Edward. "TRENDS: Police Militarization and the Use of Lethal Force." *Political Research Quarterly* 72 (2019): 177–89. https://doi.org/10.1177/1065912918784209.

Lee, Ching Kwan. *Against the Law: Labor Protests in China's Rustbelt and Sunbelt*. Berkeley, CA: University of California Press, 2007.

Lee, Choonib. "Black Panther Women in the Third World." Paper presented at the American Historical Association Session 119, January 3, 2019. Accessed September 8, 2020. New York, NY. https://aha.confex.com/aha/2015/webprogram/Paper16629.html.

Lee, Joseph. *Ireland, 1912–1985*. Cambridge, UK: Cambridge University Press, 1989.

Lee, Shaun, and Zachary Loh. "Breaking Out of Capitalist Realism: Minority Political Perspectives in Yale-NUS." *The Octant*, September 24, 2020. Accessed June 8, 2021. https://theoctant.org/edition/issue/allposts/opinion/breaking-out-of-capitalist-realism-minority-political-perspectives-in-yale-nus/.

Leeman, Jennifer, and Lisa Rabin. "Critical Perspectives for the Literature Classroom." *Hispania* 90 (2007).

Lenin, Vladimir. *Lenin Collected Works*. Moscow: Foreign Languages Publishing House, 1961.

Lenoir, Brandon W. "Issue Advocacy: A Semester-Long Experiential Learning Project." *Journal of Political Science Education* 16, no. 3 (2020): 381–398.

Lerner, Gerda. *The Creation of Patriarchy*. New York: Oxford University Press, 1987.

Levin, Brian, and Lisa Nakashima. "Report to the Nation: Illustrated Almanac – Decade Summary: Hate and Extremism with Updated 2019 FBI, U.S. City, Canada, & Europe Data." San Bernardino, CA: Center for the Study of Hate and Extremism, California State University, San Bernardino, 2019. https://csusb.edu/site/default/files/Almanac%2012%202019_0.pdf.

Levitsky, Steven, and Lucan A Way. *Competitive Authoritarianism: Hybrid Regimes After the Cold War*. New York: Cambridge University Press, 2010.

Lewis, Ann, and Geoff Lindsay. "Emerging Issues," in *Researching Children's Perspectives*, ed. Ann Lewis and Geoff Lindsay. Buckingham, UK: Open University Press, 2000.

Lewis, Martin, Natasja Holtzhausen, and Susanne Taylor. "The Dilemma of Work-Integrated Learning (WIL) in South African Higher Education-The Case of Town and Regional Planning at the University of Johannesburg." *Stads-en Streeksbeplanning, Town and Regional Planning* 57 (2010): 25–35.

Li, Zhou, Nancy Regina Gómez Arrieta, and Risa Whitson. "Empathy through Imaginative Reconstruction: Navigating

Difference in Feminist Transnational Research in China and Peru." *Gender, Place & Culture* 27 (2020): 587–607. doi: 10.1080/0966369X.2019.1639630.

Liew, Kai Khiun, Natalie Pang, and Brenda Chan. "New Media and New Politics with Old Cemeteries and Disused Railways: Advocacy Goes Digital in Singapore." *Asian Journal of Communication* 23, no. 6 (2013): 605–619.

Liftin, Karen T. "The Contemplative Pause: Insights for Teaching Politics in Turbulent Times." *Journal of Political Science Education* 16, no. 1 (2020): 57–66.

Liik, Kadri. "The Last of the Offended: Russia's First Post-Putin Diplomats." *Policy Brief of the European Council on Foreign Relations*, November 19, 2019. https://ecfr.eu/publication/the_last_of_the_offended_russias_first_post_putin_diplomats/.

Lijphart, Arend. *Patterns of Democracy*. New Haven, CT: Yale University Press, 1999.

Lim, Leonel, Michael Tan, and Eisuke Saito. "Culturally Relevant Pedagogy: Developing Principles of Description and Analysis." *Teaching and Teacher Education: An International Journal of Research and Studies* 77, no. 1 (2019): 43–52.

Lindley-French, Julian. "The Revolution in Security Affairs: Hard and Soft Security Dynamics in the 21st Century," in *Soft Security Threats and Europe*, eds. Anne Aldis and Graeme P. Herd, 1–16. London and New York: Routledge, 2005.

Lipman, Maria. "At the Turning Point to Repression: Why There are More and More "Undesirable Elements" in Russia." *Russian Politics & Law* 54, no. 4 (2016): 341–350.

LiRen Rural Library. "Liren Rural Library's Open Letter on the Suspension of Operations." *China Development Brief,* 2014. http://www.chinadevelopmentbrief.org.cn/news-16604.html.

Littenberg-Tobias, Joshua, and Alison K. Cohen. "Diverging Paths: Understanding Racial Differences in Civic Engagement Among White, African American, and Latina/o Adolescents Using Structural Equation Modeling." *American Journal of Community Psychology* 57, no. 1–2 (2016): 102–117.

Liu, Sida. "The Changing Roles of Lawyers in China: State Bureaucrats, Market Brokers, and Political Activists," in *The New Legal Realism: Studying Law Globally*, eds. Heinz Klug and Sally Engle Merry, 180–98. Cambridge, UK: Cambridge University Press, 2016.

Loeb, Ketty. "A Grim Outlook for China's Civil Society in the Wake of the 19th Party Congress." *Asia Pacific Bulletin* 402 (2017).

Longo, Nicholas V. "Deliberative Pedagogy in the Community: Connecting Deliberative Dialogue, Community Engagement, and Democratic Education." *Journal of Public Deliberation* 9, no. 2 (2013): Article 16.

Longo, Nicholas V., Idit Manosevitch, and Timothy J. Shaffer. "Introduction," in *Deliberative Pedagogy: Teaching and Learning for Democratic Engagement*, ed. Timothy J. Shaffer, Nicholas V. Longo, Idit Manosevitch, and Maxine S. Thomas, xix-xii. East Lansing, MI: Michigan State University Press.

Longo, Nicholas V., and Timothy J. Shaffer. *Creating Space for Democracy: A Primer on Dialogue and Deliberation in Higher Education*. Sterling, VA: Stylus Publishing LLC, 2019.

Lorenzini, Michelle. "From Active Service to Civic and Political Engagement: Fighting the Problem of Poverty," in *Teaching Civic Engagement: From Student to Active Citizen,* eds. Alison Rios Millett McCartney, Elizabeth A. Bennion, and Dick Simpson, 119–135. Washington, DC: American Political Science Association Press, 2013.

Lowe, Philip D. and Michael Worboys. "The Teaching of Social Studies of Science and Technology in British Polytechnics." *Social Studies of Science* 5, no. 2 (1975): 177–192.

Luger, Jason. "Singaporean 'Spaces of Hope?' Activist Geographies in the City-state." *City* 20, no. 2 (2016): 186–203.

Lukensmeyer, Carolyn J. "Civic Tech and Public Policy Decision Making." *PS: Political Science & Politics* 50, no. 3 (2017): 764–771.

Lupia, Arthur, and Tasha S. Philpot. "Views from Inside the Net: How Websites Affect Young Adults' Political Interest." *The Journal of Politics* 67, no. 4 (2005): 1122–42.

Ma, Deyong, and Feng Yang. "Authoritarian Orientations and Political Trust in East Asian Societies." *East Asia* 31 (2014): 323–341.

Mahmud, Aqil Haziq. "Shanmugam Warns of Foreign Interference in Singapore; Questions Agenda, Funding of The Online Citizen." *CNA*, March 20, 2021. https://www.channelnewsasia.com/news/singapore/the-online-citizen-toc-foreign-interference-singapore-shanmugam-11940004.

Mak, Asher. "How 4 Millennial Greenfluencers Advocate Sustainable Living Using Social Media." *Zula*, January 15, 2020. Accessed June 8, 2021. https://zula.sg/millennial-greenfluencers/.

Mäkinen, Sirke. "Geopolitics Teaching and Worldviews: Making the Future Generation in Russia." *Geopolitics* 19, no. 1 (2014): 86–108. https://doi.org/10.1080/14650045.2013.847430.

Mäkinen, Sirke. "In Search of the Status of an Educational Great Power? Analysis of Russia's Educational Diplomacy

Discourse." *Problems of Post-Communism* 63 (2016): 183–196. https://doi.org/10.1080/10758216.2016.1172489.

Mansbridge, Jane. "Why Do We Need Government? The Role of Civic Education in the Face of the Free-Rider Problem," in *Teaching Civic Engagement Across the Disciplines,* eds. Elizabeth C. Matto, Alison Rios Millett McCartney, Elizabeth A. Bennion, and Dick Simpson, 11–20. Washington DC: American Political Science Association, 2017.

Marangudakis, Manusos and Theodore Chadjipadelis. *The Greek Crisis and its Cultural Origins.* New York: Palgrave-Macmillan, 2019.

Marber, Peter, and Daniel Araya, ed. *The Evolution of Liberal Arts in the Global Age.* New York: Routledge, 2017.

Marcus, Jon. "Most Americans Don't Realize State Funding for Higher Ed Fell by Billions." *PBS NewsHour Public Broadcasting Corporation*, February 26, 2019. https://pbs.newshour.org/education/amwricans-dont-realize-state-funding-for-higher-ed-fell-by-billions.

Mariaye, Marie Hyleen Sandra. "The Role of the School in Providing Moral Education in a Multicultural Society: The Case of Mauritius." PhD diss, 2006.

Martin, Roger, and Sally Osberg. *Getting Beyond Better: How Social Entrepreneurship Works.* Boston, MA: Harvard Business Review Press, 2015.

Martin, Stephanie, and Eleanor Weisman. "Aligning Civic Engagement with the Strategic Goals of an Institution: Focus on Allegheny College." *Journal of College and Character* 13, no. 1 (2012): 1–8. doi:10.1515/jcc-2012-1843.

Marullo, Sam, and Bob Edwards. "From Charity to Justice: The Potential of University-Community Collaboration for Social Change." *American Behavioral Scientist* 43, no. 5 (2000): 895–912.

Maseko, Lucky Albert. "A Review of Work-integrated Learning in South African Mining Engineering Universities." *Journal of the Southern African Institute of Mining and Metallurgy* 118, no. 12 (2018): 1315–1323.

Matthews, Julie, and Ravinder Sidu. "Desperately Seeking the Global Subject: International Education, Citizenship, and Cosmopolitanism." *Globalisation, Societies, and Education* 3 (2005): 49–66.

Matto, Elizabeth C., Alison Rios Millett McCartney, Elizabeth A. Bennion, and Dick Simpson, eds. *Teaching Civic Engagement Across the Disciplines*. Washington, DC: American Political Science Association, 2017.

Matto, Elizabeth C., and Mary McHugh. "Civic Engagement Centers and Institutes:Promising Routes for Teaching Lessons in Citizenship to Students of All Disciplines," in *Teaching Civic Engagement Across the Disciplines*, eds. Elizabeth C. Matto, Alison Rios Millett McCartney, Elizabeth A. Bennion, and Dick Simpson. Washington, DC: American Political Science Association, 2017.

Maurissen, Lies. "Political Efficacy and Interest as Mediators of Expected Political Participation Among Belgian Adolescents." *Applied Developmental Science* 24, no. 4 (2020): 339–353. https://doi.org/10.1080/10888691.2018.1507744.

Maurissen, Lies, Ellen Claes, and Carolyn Barber. "Deliberation in Citizenship Education: How the School Context Contributes to the Development of an Open Classroom Climate." *Social Psychology of Education* 21, no. 4 (2018): 951–72.

Mauritius Institute of Education. "The National Curriculum Framework." *Mauritius Institute of Education, Social Studies, MIE & Edition de l'ocean indien*, 1980.

Mauritius Institute of Education. "National Curriculum Framework: Nine Year Continuous Basic Education." *MIE*, 2016.

Mayhew, Matthew J, and Sonia D. Fernandez. "Pedagogical Practices That Contribute to Social Justice Outcomes." Review of Higher Education 31 (2007): 55–80.

McAvoy, Paula and Diana Hess. "Classroom Deliberation in an Era of Political Polarization." *Curriculum Inquiry* 43, no. 1 (2013): 14–47.

McCartney, Alison Rios Millett. "Introduction," in *Teaching Civic Engagement Across the Disciplines*, eds. Elizabeth C. Matto, Alison Rios Millett McCartney, Elizabeth A. Bennion and Dick Simpson. Washington DC: American Political Science Association, 2017.

McCartney, Alison Rios Millett. "Making the World Real: Using a Civic Engagement Course to Bring Home Our Global Connections.*" Journal of Political Science Education* 2, no. 1 (2006): 113–128.

McCartney, Alison Rios Millett. "The Rise of Populism and Teaching for Democracy: Our Professional Obligations." *European Political Science* 19 (2020): 236–245.

McCartney, Allison Rios Millett. "Teaching Civic Engagement: Debates, Definitions, Benefits, and Challenges," in *Teaching Civic Engagement: From Student to Active Citizen*, eds. Alison Rios Millett McCartney, Elizabeth A. Bennion, and Dick Simpson. Washington, DC: American Political Science Association, 2013.

McCartney, Alison Rios Millett. "'Teachnology' and Civic Engagement in the Year of COVID-19 Instruction," in *RAISE the Vote*. Washington, DC: American Political Science Association, 2020. https://connect.apsanet.org/raisethevote/2020/09/17/technology-and-civic-engagement-in-the-year-of-covid-19-instruction/.

McCartney, Alison Rios Millett, Elizabeth A. Bennion, and Dick Simpson, eds. *Teaching Civic Engagement: From Student to Active Citizen.* Washington DC: American Political Science Association, 2013.

McCartney, Alison Rios Millett, Mackenzie Rice, and Sivan Chaban. "Does Civic Engagement Education Last? A Longitudinal Case Study." Paper presented at the American Political Science Association Teaching and Learning Conference, Baltimore, MD, 2–4 February 2018.

McCartney, Alison Rios Millett, and Sivan Chaban. "Bringing the World Home: Effectively Connecting Civic Engagement and International Relations," in *Teaching Civic Engagement: From Student to Active Citizen*, eds. Alison Rios Millett McCartney, Elizabeth A. Bennion, and Dick Simpson. Washington, DC: American Political Science Association, 2013.

McClellan, Fletcher. "Curriculum Theory and the Undergraduate Political Science Major: Toward a Contingency Approach." *PS: Political Science & Politics* 54, no. 2 (2021): 368–372.

McCowan, Tristan. "Opening Spaces for Citizenship in Higher Education: Three Initiatives In English Universities." *Studies in Higher Education* 37, no. 1 (2012): 51–67.

McCulloch, Gary. *Philosophers and Kings: Education for Leadership in Modern England.* Cambridge, UK: Cambridge University Press, 1991.

McDonald, Michael. "Voter Turnout Demographics 2020." *The Election Project.* Gainesville, FL: University of Florida, 2020. https://electproject.org/home/voter-turnout/demographics.

McDonald, Michael K. "Internships, Service-Learning, and Study Abroad: Helping Students Integrate Civic Engagement Learning across Multiple Experiences," in *Teaching Civic Engagement: From Student to Active Citizen,* eds. Alison Rios Millett McCartney, Elizabeth A. Bennion, and Dick Simpson, 369–83. Washington, DC: American Political Science Association Press, 2013.

McFarland, Daniel A., and Reuben J. Thomas. "Bowling Young: How Youth Voluntary Associations Influence Adult Political Participation." *American Sociological Review* 71, no. 3 (2006): 401–425.

McFaul, Michael. "Ukraine Imports Democracy: External Influences on the Orange Revolution." *International Security* 32, no. 2 (2007): 45–83.

McHugh, Mary and Russell Mayer. "The Different Types of Experiential Learning Offered in a Political Science Department: A Comparison of Four Courses," in *Teaching Civic Engagement: From Student to Active Citizen,* eds. Alison Rios Millett McCartney, Elizabeth A. Bennion, and Dick Simpson. Washington, DC: American Political Science Association Press, 353–67.

McKelvey, Tara, ed. *One of the Guys: Women as Aggressors and Torturers.* New York: Basic Books, 2007.

McKinlay, Patrick. "Political Hermeneutics as Pedagogy: Service-Learning, Political Reflection, and Action," in *Teaching Civic Engagement: From Student to Active Citizen*, eds. Alison Rios Millett McCartney, Elizabeth A. Bennion, and Dick Simpson, 229–246. Washington, DC: American Political Science Association, 2013.

McMillan, Janice, and Timothy Stanton. "Learning Service" in International Contexts: Partnership-Based Service-Learning and Research in Cape Town, South Africa." *Michigan Journal of Community Service Learning* 21, no. 1 (2014): 64–78.

McTague, John. "Politically Themed Residential Learning Communities as Incubators of Interest in Government and Politics," in *Teaching Civic Engagement Across the Disciplines*, eds. Elizabeth C. Matto, Alison Rios Millett McCartney, Elizabeth A. Bennion, and Dick Simpson. Washington, DC: American Political Science Association, 2017.

Means, Gordon Paul. "Soft Authoritarianism in Malaysia and Singapore." *Journal of Democracy* 7, no. 4 (1996): 103–117.

MEC Brasil. "Plano Nacional de Extensão Universitária." *Fórum de Pró-Reitores de Extensão das Universidades Públicas Brasileiras e SESu,* 2001. Accessed April 18, 2021. http://www.uemg.br/downloads/plano_nacional_de_extensao_universitaria.pdf.

Mehltretter Drury, Sara A., and Jeffrey P. Mehltretter. "Engagement through the Oval Office: Presidential Rhetoric as Civic Education," in *Civic Education in the Twenty-First Century: A Multidimensional Inquiry,* eds. Michael T. Rogers and Donald M. Gooch, 161–186. Lanham, MD: Lexington Books, 2015.

Melo, Itamar. "O que é a Associação Mães & Pais pela Democracia, que se Contrapõe ao Escola Sem Partido." *GZH,* August 8, 2019. https://gauchazh.clicrbs.com.br/educacao-e-emprego/noticia/2019/08/o-que-e-a-associacao-maes-pais-pela-democracia-que-se-contrapoe-ao-escola-sem-partido-cjz2ruu3600ip01qm2fhyx4vb.html.

Melo, Veriene. "Emancipatory Education and Youth Engagement in Brazil: A Case Study Bridging the Theory and Practice of Education for Social Transformation." *Education Sciences* 9, no. 1 (2019): 1–14.

Mendes borges, Aleida Cristina. "Youth Agency in Civic Education: Contemporary Perspectives from Cabo Verde." *Societies* 10, no. 3 (2020): 53.

Menefee-Libey, David. "High School Civics Textbooks: What We Know Versus What We Teach in American Politics and Public Policy." *Journal of Political Science Education* 11, no. 4 (2015): 422–441.

Meriläinen, Niina. "Narratives of Human Trafficking in International Issue Arenas with Implications for Policy Formation," in *International Handbook of Human Trafficking: A Multi-disciplinary and Applied Approach,* eds. Rochelle Dalla and Donna Sabella, 103–132. London: Taylor & Francis 2019.

Meriläinen, Niina. *Understanding the Framing of Issues in Multi-actor Arenas: Power Relations in the Human Rights Debate* No. 238. University of Jyväskylä. 2014.

Meriläinen, Niina, Heta-Elena Heiskanen and Jukka Viljanen. "Participation of Young People in Legislative Processes: A Case Study of the General Upper Secondary Schools Act in Finland–A School Bullying Narrative." *The Journal of Legislative Studies* (2020): 1–32.

Meriläinen, Niina, Iikka Pietilä, and Jari Varsaluoma. "Digital Services and Youth Participation in Processes of Social Change: World Café Workshops in Finland." ECPR General Conference (2018).

Meriläinen, Niina, and Marita Vos. "Framing Issues in the Public Debate: The Case of Human Rights." *Corporate Communications, an International Journal* 18 (2013): 119–134.

Meriläinen, Niina, and Marita Vos. "Public Discourse on Human Trafficking in International Issue Arenas." *Societies* 5 (2015): 14–42.

Meriläinen, Niina, and Mikko Piispa. "Antaa Isojen Herrojen ja Rouvien Päättää" - Lasten ja Nuorten Oikeudet ja Osallisuus Ilmastonmuutoksen Ajassa," in *Maapallon Tulevaisuus ja Lapsen Oikeudet*, ed. Pekkarinen, E. ja Tuukkanen, T. Lapsiasiavaltuutetun toimiston julkaisuja 4 (2020): 124–136.

Merriman, Brian, and Suzanne Guerin. "Using Children's Drawings as Data in Child-centred Research." *The Irish Journal of Psychology* 27, no. 1 (2006).

Mertha, Andrew. *China's Water Warriors: Citizen Action and Policy Change*. Ithaca, NY: Cornell University Press, 2008.

Meyer, Alan. D. "Visual Data in Organizational Research." *Organization Science* 2, no. 2 (1991).

Michelsen, Niall Guy. *Votes at 16: Enfranchisement and the Renewal of American Democracy*. Lanham, MD: Lexington Books, 2020.

Mies, Maria. *The Lace Makers of Narsapur. Indian Housewives Produce for the World Market*. London: Zed Press, 1982.

Milner, Henry. *Civic Literacy: How Informed Citizens Make Democracy Work*. Hanover: University Press of New England, 2002.

Ministry of Education, Culture & Human Resources. "Education Human Resources Strategy Plan 2008–2020." *Government of Mauritius*, 2009.

Mirpuri, Ashok Kumar. "Singapore's Ambassador to the US Responds to Criticism of 'Fake News' Law." *The Diplomat*, July 16, 2020. https://thediplomat.com/2020/07/singapores-ambassador-to-the-us-responds-to-criticism-of-fake-news-law/.

Mirra, Nicole, et al. "Educating for a Critical Democracy: Civic Participation Reimagined in the Council of Youth Research." *Democracy and Education* 21, no. 1 (2013): 1–10.

Misco, Thomas. "'We Do Not Talk about These Things': the Promises and Challenges of Reflective Thinking and Controversial Issue Discussions in a Chinese High School." *Intercultural Education* 24, no. 5 (2013): 401–416. doi: 10.1080/14675986.2013.842663.

Mitchell, Tania D. "Traditional vs. Critical Service-Learning: Engaging the Literature to Differentiate Two Models." *Michigan Journal of Community Service Learning* 14, no. 2 (2008): 50–65.

Moallem, Mahnaz. "The Impact of Synchronous and Asynchronous Communication Tools on Learner Self-regulation, Social Presence, Immediacy, Intimacy and Satisfaction in Collaborative Online Learning." *The Online Journal of Distance Education and e-Learning* 3, no. 3 (2015): 55–77.

Moberly, Sir Walter. *The Crisis in the University*. London: SCM Press, 1949.

MOE (Ministry of Education of the People's Republic of China). "The New Version of the Compulsory Education Curriculum Plan and Curriculum Standards will be Announced Next Year." *Sohu Education Express*, 2020. https://www.sohu.com/a/428398162_105067.

MOE (Ministry of Education of the People's Republic of China). "Notice of the Ministry of Education on Printing and Distributing the 'Basic Education Curriculum Reform Outline (Trial)." *MOE*, 2001. http://www.moe.gov.cn/srcsite/A26/jcj_kcjcgh/200106/t20010608_167343.html.

Mohamed Nasir, Kamaludeen, and Bryan S. Turner. "Governing as Gardening: Reflections on Soft Authoritarianism in Singapore." *Citizenship Studies* 17, no. 3–4 (2013): 339–352.

Mohanty, Chandra Talpade. *Feminism Without Borders: Decolonizing Theory, Practicing Solidarity*. Durham, NC: Duke University Press, 2003.

Mohanty, Chandra Talpade, Ann Russo, and Lourdes Torres, eds. *Third World Women and the Politics of Feminism*. Bloomington, IN: Indiana University Press, 1991.

Molineaux, Debilynn. "Intolerance is the Real Threat to Our Democracy: Here's How We Can Fight It Together." *USA Today*, August 30, 2020. https://usatoday.com/story/opinion/2020/08/30/intolerance-not-our-opponents-true-enemy-democracy-column/5655944002/.

Monchinski, Tony. *Critical Pedagogy and the Everyday Classroom*. New York: Springer, 2008.

Mondak, Jeffery J. "Reconsidering the Measurement of Political Knowledge." *Political Analysis* 8, no. 1 (1999): 57–82.

Moore, Martin. *Shrinking World: The Decline of International Reporting in the British Press*. London: Media Standards Trust, 2010. http://mediastandardstrust.org/wp-content/uploads/downloads/2010/10/Shrinking-World-The-decline-of-international-reporting.pdf.

Moravcsik, Andrew. "Taking Preferences Seriously: A Liberal Theory of International Politics." *International Organization* 51, no. 4 (1997): 524. https://doi.org/10.1162/002081897550447.

Morgenbesser, Lee. "The Autocratic Mandate: Elections, Legitimacy and Regime Stability in Singapore." *The Pacific Review* 30, no. 2 (2017): 205–231.

Morgenbesser, Lee. "The Menu of Autocratic Innovation." *Democratization* 27, no. 6 (2020): 1053–1072.

Moro, Giovanni. *Citizens in Europe: Civic Activism and the Community Democratic Experiment*. New York: Springer, 2012.

Morozov, Viatcheslav. *Russia's Postcolonial Identity: A Subaltern Empire in a Eurocentric World*. London: Palgrave Macmillan, 2015.

Morris, Paul, and Anthony Sweeting. "Education and Politics: The Case of Hong Kong from an Historical Perspective." *Oxford Review of Education* 17, no. 3 (1991): 249–267.

Moura, Fernanda, and Salles, Diogo da Costa. "O Escola sem Partido e o ódio aos Professores que Formam Crianças (Des) viadas." *Revista Periódicus* 9, no. 1 (2018): 136–160.

Moura, Mariluce. "Universidades Públicas Respondem por mais de 95% da Produção Científica do Brasil." *Cência na Rua*, April 11, 2019. http://ciencianarua.net/universidades-publicas-respondem-por-mais-de-95-da-producao-cientifica-do-br asil/?fbclid=IwAR0rFPYP85uHZPH7LPDXZ_igAxTpXDe4WTFLSSwPKEjIm9viDvc3Lu3_ON0.

Mouritsen, Per, and Astrid Jaeger. *Designing Civic Education for Diverse Societies: Models, Tradeoffs, and Outcomes*. Brussels, Belgium: Migration Policy Institute Europe, 2018.

Moussa, Ziad. "Rivers of Life," in *Participatory Learning And Action: Community-Based Adaptation To Climate Change*, ed. Hannah Reid, Terry Cannon, Rachel Berger, Mozaharul Alam, and Angela Milligan, 183–86. London: IIED, 2009.

Mulford, Matthew, and Jeffery Berejikian. "Behavioral Decision Theory and the Gains Debate in International Politics." *Political Studies* 50, no. 2 (2002): 209–229. https://doi.org/10.1111%2F1467-9248.00367.

Müller, Martin. "Education and the Formation of Geopolitical Subjects." *International Political Sociology* 5, no. 1 (2011): 1–17. https://doi.org/10.1111/j.1749-5687.2011.00117.x.

Munro, Carissa, and Kyrya. Monica. *Values Education for Public Integrity: What Works and What Doesn't*. Berg, Norway: U4 Anti-Corruption Resources Centre/ Michelsen Institute, 2020.

Murphy, Richard J. Judith Scott-Clayton, and Gillian Wyness. "Lessons from the End of Free College in England." *Evidence Speaks Reports* 2, no. 13 (2017). https://www.brookings.edu/wp-content/uploads/2017/04/es_20170427_scott-clayton_evidence_speaks.pdf.

Musil, Caryn McTighe. "Excerpts From A Crucible Moment and Civic Prompts," in *Teaching Civic Engagement Across the Disciplines*, eds. Elizabeth C. Matto, Alison Rios Millett McCartney, Elizabeth A. Bennion and Dick Simpson, 55–64. Washington DC: American Political Science Association, 2017.

Mutz, Diana C. *Hearing the Other Side: Deliberative versus Participatory Democracy*. Cambridge, UK: Cambridge University Press, 2012. doi: 10.1017/CBO9780511617201.

Mwawashe, Kenyatta. "Youth as Drivers of Accountability: Conducting a Youth Social Audit," in *Young Citizens: Youth and Participatory Governance in Africa*, 181–186. London: England, International Institute for Environment and Development, 2011.

Nabatchi, Tina, John Gastil, Matt Leighninger, and G. Michael Weiksner, eds. *Democracy in Motion: Evaluating the Practice and Impact of Deliberative Civic Engagement*. Oxford, UK: Oxford University Press, 2012.

Nadelman, Racheld, Le, Ha and Sah, Anjali. "How Does the World Bank Build Citizen Engagement Commitments into Project Design? Results from Pilot Assessments in Mozambique, Myanmar, Nigeria, and Pakistan." *IDS Working Paper* 525 (2019).

National Center for Education Statistics. "Annual Report: Undergraduate Enrollment." *NCES*, 2021. https://nces.ed.gov/programs/coe/indicator/cha.

National Center for Education Statistics. "Characteristics of Postsecondary Faculty." *NCES*, May, 2020. https://nces.ed.gov/

programs/coe/indicator/csc.

National Forum for Engagement and Participation, ed. "Service Learning in Teacher Training - Promotion of Engagement at the Interface of University and School." German Association for Public and Private Welfare eV. Berlin, 2013.

The National Task Force on Civic Learning and Democratic Engagement. *A Crucible Moment: College Learning and Democracy's Future.* Washington, DC: Association of American College and Universities, 2012. https://www.aacu.org/sites/default/files/files/crucible/Crucible_508F.pdf

NCES, USDE (National Center for Education Statistics, U.S. Department of Education). "Graduation Rates." *NCES, USDE,* 2019. http://nces.ed.gov/fastfacts/display.asp?id=40.

Neumann, Iver B., and Erik F. Øverland. "International Relations and Policy Planning: The Method of Perspectivist Scenario Building." *International Studies Perspectives* 5, no. 3 (2004): 258–77. https://doi.org/10.1111/j.1528-3577.2004.00173.x.

Neundorf, Anja, Kaat Smets, and Gema M. García-Albacete. "Homemade Citizens: The Development of Political Interest During Adolescence and Young Adulthood." *Acta Politica* 48, no. 1 (2013): 92–116.

New Naratif. "Subhas Nair, Renaissance Man." *New Naratif,* May 5, 2021. https://newnaratif.com/podcast/subhas-nair-renaissance-man/.

New, Jake. "Get Ready for More Protests." *Inside Higher Ed,* February 11, 2016. https://www.insidehighered.com/news/2016/02/11/survey-finds-nearly-1-10-freshmen-plan-participating-campus-protests.

Newhouse, John. "Diplomacy, Inc.: The Influence of Lobbies on U.S. Foreign Policy." *Foreign Affairs* 88, no. 3 (2009): 73–92. https://www.jstor.org/stable/20699564.

Nicoll, K., Fejes, A., Olson, M., Dahlstedt, M. and Biesta, G. "Opening Discourses of Citizenship Education: a Theorization with Foucault." *Journal of Education Policy* 28, no. 6 (2013): 828–846. doi: 10.1080/02680939.2013.823519.

Nie, Norman H., Jane Junn., and Kenneth Stehlik-Barry. *Education and Democratic Citizenship in America.* Chicago: University of Chicago Press, 1996.

Niemi, Richard G., and Jane Junn. *Civic Education: What Makes Students Learn.* New Haven, CT: Yale University Press, 1998.

Nietzel, Michael T. "Five Reasons 2020 will be the Year of the Student Protest." *Forbes,* July 10, 2020. https://www.forbes.com/sites/michaeltnietzel/2020/07/10/five-reasons-2020-is-the-year-of-the-student-protest/?sh=13005ee373ce.

Nodia, Ghia. "External Influence and Democratization: The Revenge of Geopolitics." *Journal of Democracy* 25, no. 4 (2014): 139–150.

Noori, Neema. "Academic Freedom and the Liberal Arts in the Middle East: Can the US Model Be Replicated?" in *The Evolution of Liberal Arts in the Global Age,* ed. Peter Marber and Daniel Araya, 141–149. New York: Routledge 2017.

Nordmeyer, Kristjane, Nicole Bedera, and Trisha Teig. "Ending White Saviorism in Study Abroad." *Contexts* 15, no. 4 (2016): 78–79.

Nordyke, Shane, Marcheta Lee Wright, Michael Kuchinsky, and Ruth Ediger. "Track Three: Internationalizing the Curriculum I." *PS: Political Science & Politics* 40, no. 3 (2007): 577–578.

Norris, Pippa. *Democratic Deficit. Critical Citizens Revisited.* New York: Cambridge University Press, 2011.

Norris, Pippa. "What Maximises Productivity and Impact in Political Science Research?" *European Political Science* 20, no. 1 (2021): 34–57.

North Central College. "Strategic Plan." *NCC,* 2020. https://www.northcentralcollege.edu/northcentral-college-strategic-plan.

NPR/Ipsos. "Public Poll Findings and Methodology." *Ipsos,* 2020. https://www.ipsos.com/sites/default/files/ct/news/documents/2020-12/topline_npr_misinformation_poll_123020.pdf.

Nye Jr., Joseph S. "Bridging the Gap Between Theory and Policy." *Political Psychology* 29, no. 4 (2008): 593–603. https://doi.org/10.1111/j.1467-9221.2008.00651.x.

O'Brien, J. Kevin and Lianjiang Li. *Rightful Resistance in Rural China.* Cambridge, UK: Cambridge University Press, 2006.

O'Brien, J. Kevin and Rachel E. Stern. "Studying Contention in Contemporary China," in *Popular Protest in China,* ed. Kevin J. O'Brien. Cambridge, MA: Harvard University Press, 2008.

O'Brien, J. Kevin and Lianjiang Li. "Suing the Local State: Administrative Litigation in Rural China." *China Journal* 51 (2004): 75–96.

O'Shaughnessy, Betty. "High School Students as Election Judges and Campaign Workers: Does the Experience Stick?" in *Teaching Civic Engagement: From Student to Active Citizen,* eds. Alison Rios Millett McCartney, Elizabeth A. Bennion, and Dick Simpson, 297–312. Washington, DC: American Political Science Association, 2013.

Oberle, Monika, Johanna Leunig, and Sven Ivens. "What Do Students Learn from Political Simulation Games? A Mixed-Method Approach Exploring the Relation Between Conceptual and Attitudinal Changes." *European Political Science* 19

(2020): 367–386.

OFS. *Access and Participation Plans*, 2018. https://www.officeforstudents.org.uk/advice-and-guidance/promoting-equal-opportunities/access-and-participation-plans/.

Oh, Cheol H., and Robert F. Rich. "Explaining Use of Information in Public Policymaking." *Knowledge and Policy* 9 (1996): 3–35.

Oh, Jennifer S. "Strong State and Strong Civil Society in Contemporary South Korea: Challenges to Democratic Governance." *Asian Survey* 52, no. 3 (2012): 528–549.

Ojala, Maria. "Hope and Climate Change: The Importance of Hope for Environmental Engagement Among Young People." *Environmental Education Research* 18 (2012): 625–642

Okech, Awino, and Dinah Musindarwez. "Building Transnational Feminist Alliances: Reflections on the Post-2015 Development Agenda." *Contexto Internacional* 41 (2019): 255–73. doi: 10.1590/s0102-8529.2019410200002.

Oliver, Steven, and Kai Ostwald. "Explaining Elections in Singapore: Dominant Party Resilience and Valence Politics." *Journal of East Asian Studies* 18, no. 2 (2018): 129–156.

Ong, Aihwa. *Spirits of Resistance and Capitalist Discipline: Factory Women in Malaysia (Suny Series in the Anthropology of Work.* State University of New York Press, 1987.

Organization for Economic Cooperation. *Benchmarking Higher Education System Performance: Conceptual Framework and Data, Enhancing Higher Education System Performance.* Paris: OECD, 2017. https://www.oecd.org/education/skills-beyond-school/Benchmarking%20Report.pdf.

Organization for Economic Co-operation and Development (OECD). "Education for Integrity: Teaching on Anti-Corruption, Values and the Rule of Law." Paris, France: OECD, 2018.

Oros, Andrew L. "Let's Debate: Active Learning Encourages Student Participation and Critical Thinking." *Journal of Political Science Education* 3, no. 3 (2007): 293–311.

Orr, Catherine M. "Activism," in *Rethinking Women's and Gender Studies*, ed. Catherine M. Orr, Ann Braithwait, and Diane Lichtenstein. New York: Routledge, 2012.

Ortbals, Candice D., and Meg E. Rincker. "Fieldwork, Identities, and Intersectionality: Negotiating Gender, Race, Class, Religion, Nationality, and Age in the Research Field Abroad: Editors' Introduction." *PS: Political Science & Politics* 42 (2009): 287–90. doi:10.1017/S104909650909057X.

Ortmann, Stephan. "Political Change and Civil Society Coalitions in Singapore." *Government and Opposition* 50, no. 1 (2015): 119–139.

Ostergaard, Clemens. "Citizens, Groups, and Nascent Civil Society in China: Towards an Understanding of the 1989 Student Demonstrations." *China Information* 4 (1989): 28–41.

Ostrander, Susan A. "Democracy, Civic Participation, and the University: A Comparative Study of Civic Engagement on Five Campuses." *Nonprofit and Voluntary Sector Quarterly* 33, no. 1 (2004): 74–93.

Oswald, Hans. "East German Adolescents' Attitudes Towards West German Democracy," in *Images of Germany: Perceptions and Conceptions*, eds. P.M. Daly, H.W. Frischkopf, T.E. Goldsmith-Reber, & H. Richter, 121–134. Berlin, Germany: Peter Lang, 2000.

ÓTuathail, Gearóid, and John Agnew. "Geopolitics and Discourse: Practical Geopolitics Reasoning in American Foreign Policy." *Political Geography* 11, no. 2 (1992): 190–204. https://doi.org/10.1016/0962-6298(92)90048-X.

Owen, Diana. "The Influence of Civic Education on Electoral Engagement and Voting," in *Teaching Civic Engagement: From Student to Active Citizen*, eds. Alison Rios Millett McCartney, Elizabeth A. Bennion, and Dick Simpson, 313–330. Washington, DC: American Political Science Association, 2013.

Owen, Diana, and Isaac Riddle. "Active Learning and the Acquisition of Political Knowledge in High School," in *Teaching Civic Engagement Across the Disciplines*, eds. Elizabeth C. Matto, Alison Rios Millett McCartney, Elizabeth A. Bennion, and Dick Simpson, 103–122. Washington, DC: American Political Science Association, 2017.

Owusu-Agyeman, Yaw, and Magda Fourie-Malherbe. "Students as Partners in the Promotion of Civic Engagement in Higher Education." *Studies in Higher Education* (2019): 1–15.

Page, Margaret L., and Hugo Gaggiotti. "A Visual Enquiry into Ethics and Change." *Qualitative Research in Organizations and Management* 7, no. 1 (2012).

Painter, David L., and Courtney Howell. "Community Engagement in the Liberal Arts: How Service Hours and Reflections Influence Course Value." *Journal of Experiential Education* 43, no. 4 (2020): 416–430.

Pakseresht, Louise. "What do the Sustainable Development Goals Say About... Science and Innovation?" *The Royal Society* [blog], 2015. Accessed April 18, 2021. http://blogs.royalsociety.org/in-verba/2015/11/19/what-do-the-sustainable-development-goals-say-about-science-and-innovation/.

Panagiotidou, Georgia and Theodore Chadjipadelis. "First-time Voter in Greece: Views and Attitudes of Youth on Europe and Democracy," in *Data Analysis and Rationality in a Complex World*, eds. Chadjipadelis, Theodore et al. New York: Springer International Publishing, 2019.

Papadimitriou, Giannis and Giannoula Florou. "Contribution of the Euclidean and Chi-square Metrics to Determining the Most Ideal Clustering in Ascending Hierarchy (in Greek)," in *Annals in Honor of Professor I. Liakis*, 546–581. University of Macedonia: Thessaloniki, 1996.

Parisi, Laura, and Lynn Thornton. "Connecting the Local with the Global: Transnational Feminism and Civic Engagement." *Feminist Teacher* 22 (2012): 214–32.

Parker, Lee D. "Photo-elicitation: An Ethno-historical Accounting and Management Research Prospect." *Accounting Auditing & Accountability Journal* 22, no. 8 (2009).

Parsons, Talcott. "An Outline of the Social System," in *Theories of the Society*, eds. Talcott Parsons, et al. Englewood Cliffs, NJ: Prentice-Hall, 1971.

Partnoy, Alicia, and Raquel Partnoy. *The Little School: Tales of Disappearance & Survival*. Translated by Lois Edwards Athey and Sandra Braunstein. 2nd edition. San Francisco, CA: Cleis Press, 1998.

Pasquerella, Lynn. "Liberal Education and Threats to Democracy." *Liberal Education*. https://www.aacu.org/liberaleducation/2020/fall/president.

Pateman, Carole. "Political Culture, Political Structure and Political Change." *British Journal of Political Science* 1, no. 3 (1971): 291–305.

Patil, Vrushali. "From Patriarchy to Intersectionality: A Transnational Feminist Assessment of How Far We've Really Come." *Signs: Journal of Women in Culture and Society* 38 (2013): 847–67.

Patnode, Rene. *Cosmopolitan Universals and the Chinese University: Authoritarian Education and Its Impact on Global Perspectives*. PhD diss., UC San Diego, 2017.

Patrikios, Sratos, and Mark Shephard. "Representative and Useful? An Empirical Assessment of the Representative Nature and Impact of the Scottish Youth Parliament." *The Journal of Legislative Studies* 20 (2014): 236–254;

Pavlović, Zoran, and Bojan Todosijević. "Global Cultural Zones the Empirical Way: Value Structure of Cultural Zones and their Relationship with Democracy and the Communist Past." *Quality & Quantity* 54, no. 2 (2020): 603–622.

Peake, Linda, and Karen De Souza. "Feminist Academic and Activist Praxis in Service of the Transnational," in *Critical Transnational Feminist Praxis*, eds. Amanda Lock Swarr and Richa Nagar, 105–23. Albany, NY: SUNY Press, 2010.

Pearce, Katy E, Deen Freelon, and Sarah Kendzior. "The Effect of the Internet on Civic Engagement Under Authoritarianism: The Case of Azerbaijan." *First Monday* (2014).

Pei, Minxin. "Citizens v. Manandarins: Administrative Litigation in China." *The China Quarterly* 152 (1997).

Percheron, Annick. *La Socialisation Politique*. Paris: PFNSP, 1985.

Percheron, Annick. *Les 10-16 Ans et la Politique*. Paris: PFNSP, 1978.

Percheron, Annick. *L'Univers Politique des Enfants*. Paris: PFNSP, 1974.

Pereznieto, Paola and Hamilton Harding, James. "Youth and International Development Policy: The Case for Investing in Young People." *Overseas Development Institute (ODI) Project Briefing* no. 80 (2013).

Perrin, Andrew J., and Alanna Gillis. "How College Makes Citizens: Higher Education Experiences and Political Engagement." *Socius: Sociological Research for a Dynamic World* 5 (2019): 1–16.

Perry, Anthony. "Practicing Politics: The National Student Issues Conventions," in *Teaching Civic Engagement: From Student to Active Citizen*, eds. Alison Rios Millett McCartney, Elizabeth A. Bennion, and Dick Simpson 189–202. Washington, DC: American Political Science Association Press, 2013.

Perry, Elizabeth J. "Educated Acquiescence: How Academia Sustains Authoritarianism in China." *Theory and Society* 49, no. 1 (2020): 1–22.

Perry, Martin, Lily Kong, and Brenda S. A. Yeoh. *Singapore: A Developmental City State*. New York: Wiley, 1997.

Persson, Mikael. "Education and Political Participation." *British Journal of Political Science* 45, no. 3 (2013): 689-703.

Petersen, Karen Lund. "Terrorism: When Risk Meets Security." *Alternatives: Global, Local, Political* 33, no. 2 (2008): 173–190. https://doi.org/10.1177%2F030437540803300204.

Peterson, Andrew. *Civic Republicanism and Civic Education: The Education of Citizens*. New York: Palgrave Macmillan, 2011.

Peterson, Marshalita Sims. "Public Deliberation and Practical Application of Civic Engagement Through a "Train the

Trainer" Process at a Historically Black College." *The Journal of Negro Education* 83, no. 1 (2014): 77–92.

Pettigrew, Andrew. *The Politics of Organizational Decision-making.* Routledge, 2014.

Piaget, Jean. *The Moral Judgement of the Child.* Glencoe, IL: Free Press, 1948: 65–76.

Pietilä, Iikka, Jari Varsaluoma and Kaisa Väänänen. "Understanding the Digital and Non-digital Participation by the Gaming Youth," in *Lecture Notes in Computer Science vol 11747.* Paper presented at Human-Computer Interaction – INTERACT 2019, ed. Lamas D., Loizides F., Nacke L., Petrie H., Winckler M., Zaphiris P, 453-471. Paphos, Cyprus: Springer, Cham, 2019.

Pils, Eva. *China's Human Rights Lawyers: Advocacy and Resistance.* New York: Routledge, 2014.

Piper, Laurence, Sondré Bailey, and Robyn Pasensie. "'Like a Blow to my Body': The Negative Impact of the Decommissioning of SASSA Pay Points on the Bodies of Rural, Elderly Social Grant Recipients in the Western Cape," in *SASSA Decommissioning Research Report for Black Sash.* Department of Political Studies, University of the Western Cape, 2018. https://www.researchgate.net/publication/343761570_'Like_a_blow_to_my_body'_The_negative_impact_of_the_decommissioning_of_SASSA_pay_points_on_the_bodies_of_rural_elderly_social_grant_recipients_in_the_Western_Cape_SASSA_Decommissioning_Research_Report.

Piškur, Barbara, Ramon Daniëls, Marian Jongmans, Marjolijn Ketelaar, Rob Smeets, Meghan Norton and Anna Beurskens. "Participation and Social Participation: Are they Distinct Concepts?" *Clinical Rehabilitation* 28 (2014): 211-220.

Pitkin, Hanna F. *The Concept of Representation.* Berkeley, CA: University of California Press, 1967.

Plum Consulting. *Research into Recent Dynamics of the Press Sector in the UK and Globally.* Report undertaken for the UK Government Department for Digital, Culture, Media and Sport, May, 2020. https://assets.publishing.service.gov.uk/government/uploads/system/uploads/attachment_data/file/924325/Plum_DCMS_press_sector_dynamics_-_Final_Report_v4.pdf.

PND. "Russia's Crackdown on NGOs Includes Some Unexpected Targets." *Philanthropy News Digest,* 2015. https://philanthropynewsdigest.org/news/russia-s-crackdown-on-ngos-includes-some-unexpected-targets.

PNUD. "Desenvolvimento Humano nas Macrorregiões Brasileiras." *Brasília: PNUD; IPEA; FJP,* 2016. Accessed April 18, 2021. https://1drv.ms/b/s!AuwEBHxVU0YSgbNZGjK6AIgz1ijfmQ?e=VjZxyR,

Polizzi, Gianfranco. "Information Literacy in the Digital Age: Why Critical Digital Literacy Matters for Democracy," in *Informed Societies: Why Information Literacy Matters for Citizenship, Participation and Democracy,* ed. Stéphanie Goldstein, 1–23. London: Facet Publishing, 2020.

Polletta, Francesca. "'Free Spaces' in Collective Action." *Theory and Society* 28, no. 1 (1999): 1–38.

Poloni-Staudinger, Lori M., and J. Cherie Strachan. "TLC Keynote: Democracy is More Important Than a P-Value: Embracing Political Science's Civic Mission through Intersectional Engaged Learning." *PS: Political Science & Politics* 53 no. 3 (2020): 569–74.

Pompa, Lori. "Service-Learning as Crucible: Reflections on Immersion, Context, Power, and Transformation." *Michigan Journal of Community Service Learning* 9, no. 1 (2002): 67–76.

Pontes, Ana Isabel, Matt Henn and Mark D. Griffiths. "Youth Political (Dis)engagement and the Need for Citizenship Education: Encouraging Young People's Civic and Political Participation through the Curriculum." *Education, Citizenship and Social Justice* 14, no. 1 (2019): 11–13.

Prado, Débora, Ana Mauad, and Cairo Junqueira. "Covid-19 e os Limites da Federação." *O Globo,* 2021. Accessed April 18, 2021. https://oglobo.globo.com/opiniao/a-covid-19-os-limites-da-federacao-24854517,

Prague Communiqué. *Towards the European Higher Education Area.* Communiqué of the Meeting of European Ministers in Charge of Higher Education. Prague: 2001.

Pratte, Richard. *The Civic Imperative: Examining the Need for Civic Education. Advances in Contemporary Educational Thought Series, Volume 3.* 1234 Amsterdam Ave., New York, NY: Teachers College Press, 10027, 1988.

Programa de las Naciones Unidas (PNUD). *Guatemala: ¿Un país de Oportunidades para la Juventud? Informe Nacional de Desarrollo Humano 2011/2012.* Guatemala City: Guatemala, 2012.

Project Pericles. "Advocate. Empower. Inspire." *Project Pericles,* 2020. https://www.projectpericles.org/.

Prosser, Christopher, Ed Fieldhouse, Jane Green, Jon Mellon, and Geoff Evans. "The Myth of the 2017 'Youthquake' Election." *BBC News,* January 29, 2018. https://www.bbc.co.uk/news/uk-politics-42747342.

Prosser, Christopher, Edward A. Fieldhouse, Jane Green, Jonathan Mello and Geoffrey Evans. *Tremors But No Youthquake: Measuring Change in the Age and Turnout Gradients at the 2015 and 2017 British General Elections,* January 28, 2018. https://papers.ssrn.com/sol3/papers.cfm?abstract_id=3111839.

Pülzl, Helga, and Doris Wydra. "The Evaluation of the Implementation of Sustainability Norms: An Expertise for Experts or Citizens?" in *Creating a Sustainable Social Ecology Using Technology-driven Solutions*, ed. Elias. G. Carayannis, 32–45. Hershey: IGI Global, 2013. https://doi.org/10.4018/978-1-4666-3613-2.ch003.

Puplick, Christopher J. "Lowering Australia's Voting Age." *Politics* 6, no. 2 (1971): 188–200.

Purinton, Ted, and Jennifer Skaggs, ed. *American Universities Abroad: The Leadership of Independent Transnational Higher Education Institutions*. New York; Cairo: American University in Cairo Press, 2017.

Purinton, Ted, and Jennifer Skaggs. "Leadership for the Liberal Arts: Lessons from American Universities Abroad." *Liberal Education* 104, no. 3 (2018): 20–25.

Putnam, Robert. *Comunidade e Democracia*. Rio de Janeiro: FGV, 1993.

Putnam, Robert D. "Bowling Alone: America's Declining Social Capital", *Journal of Democracy* 6, no. 1 (1995): 65–78.

Putman, Robert, Leonardi, Robert, and Nanetti, Rafaella. *Making Democracy Work: Civic Traditions in Modern Italy*. Princeton, NJ: Princeton University Press, 1993.

Quality Assurance Agency. *Subject Benchmark Statement: Politics and International Relations*. 4th Edition. Gloucester, Gloucester: Quality Assurance Agency, 2019.

Quigley, Charles N, and N Hoar. "Civitas: An International Civic Education Exchange Program." *Spons Agency* 129 (1999).

Quillinan, Bernie, Eileen McEvoy, Ann MacPhail, and Ciara Dempsey. "Lessons Learned from a Community Engagement Initiative within Irish Higher Education." *Irish Educational Studies* 27, no. 1 (2018).

Rahman, K. Sabeel. "From Civic Tech to Civic Capacity: The Case of Citizen Audits." *PS: Political Science & Politics* 50, no. 3 (2017): 751–757.

Rahman, K. Sabeel and Hollie Russman Gilman. *Civic Power: Rebuilding American Democracy in an Era of Crisis*. Cambridge, UK: Cambridge University Press, 2019.

Rainsford, Emily. "Young People and Brexit: Not All That We Think." United Kingdom: Political Studies Association, 2019. https://www.psa.ac.uk/psa/news/young-people-and-brexit-not-all-we-think.

Ramaley, Judith A. "The Changing Role of Higher Education: Learning to Deal with Wicked Problems." *Higher Education* 18, no. 3 (2014): 7–22.

Ramaley, Judith A. "Thriving in the 21st Century by Tackling Wicked Problems." *Higher Education* 8, no. 2 (2013): 23–27.

Rankin, Susan, and Robert Reason. "Transformational Tapestry Model: A Comprehensive Approach to Transforming Campus Climate." *Journal of Diversity in Higher Education* 1, no. 4 (2008): 262–274.

Raymond, Chad, John Tawa, Gina Marie Tonini, and Sally Gomaa. "Using Experimental Research to Test Instructional Effectiveness: A Case Study." *Journal of Political Science Education* 14, no. 2 (2018): 167–176.

Reason, Robert D., and Kevin Hemer."Civic Learning and Engagement: A Review of the Literature on Civic Learning, Assessment, and Instruments." *Research Institute for Studies in Education (RISE) Iowa State University*, 2015. https://www.aacu.org/sites/default/files/files/qc/CivicLearningLiteratureReviewRev1-26-15.pdf.

Redden, Elizabeth. "Canceled Course Renews Academic Freedom Concerns." *Inside Higher Ed*, October 1, 2019. https://www.insidehighered.com/news/2019/10/01/cancellation-course-dissent-yale-nus-campus-singapore-prompted-academic-freedom.

Redden, Elizabeth. "China Exerts More Control Over Foreign Universities." *Inside Higher Ed*, November 20, 2017. https://www.insidehighered.com/quicktakes/2017/11/20/china-exerts-more-control-over-foreign-universities.

Redden, Elizabeth. "The Middlemen of Study Abroad." *Inside Higher Ed* 20 (2007).

Redden, Elizabeth. "Whose Yale College?" *Inside Higher Ed*, March 28, 2012. https://www.insidehighered.com/news/2012/03/28/yale-faculty-raise-governance-questions-about-decision-open-branch-singapore.

Rehman, Abdul. "Rise of Intolerance: Are We Moving Backwards?" *Modern Diplomacy*, February 11, 2021. https://moderndiplomacy.eu/2021/02/11/rise-of-intolerance-are-we-moving-backwards/.

Reichert Frank. "Who is the Engaged Citizen? Correlates of Secondary School Students' Concepts of Good Citizenship." *Educational Research and Evaluation* 22, no. 5–6 (2016): 305–332. doi: 10.1080/13803611.2016.1245148.

Reichert, Frank, and Judith Torney-Purta. "A Cross-National Comparison of Teachers' Beliefs About the Aims of Civic Education in 12 Countries: A Person-Centered Analysis." *Teaching and Teacher Education* 77 (2019): 112–125.

Reinders, Heinz. "Service Learning – Theoretical Considerations and Empirical Studies on Learning through Engagement." *Beltz Juventa, Weinheim / Basel*, 2016.

Reinders, Robert C. "Toynbee Hall and the American Settlement Movement." *Social Services Review* 56, no. 1 (1982): 39–54.

Reinhardt, Sybille. *Teaching Civics: A Manual for Secondary Education Teachers*. Opladen, Berlin, Toronto: Barbara Budrich

Publishers, 2015.

Reisinger, William L. "2x2 Games of Commitment in World Politics." *International Studies Quarterly* 33, no. 1 (1989): 111–118. https://doi.org/10.2307/2600496.

Reporters Without Borders. "Singapore: An Alternative Way to Curtail Press Freedom." *Reporters Without Borders*, 2021. https://rsf.org/en/singapore.

Repucci, Sara, and Amy Slipowitz. "Democracy Under Siege." *Freedom House*, 2021. http://freedom house.org/report/freedom-world/ 2021/democracy-under-siege.

Reuters Staff. "Egypt Population Reaches 100 Million People: Statistics Agency." *Reuters*, February 11, 2020. https://www.reuters.com/article/us-egypt-population-idUSKBN2051MS.

Reynolds, Andrew. *The Architecture of Democracy*. Oxford: Oxford University Press, 2002.

Richter, Melvin. *The Politics of Conscience: T.H. Green and His Age*. London: Weidenfeld and Nicolson, 1964.

Ridley, Pauline, and Angela Rogers. *Drawing to Learn: Arts & Humanities*. Brighton: University of Brighton, 2010.

Rimmerman, Craig. "Service-Learning Lessons," in *Service-Learning in the Liberal Arts: How and Why It Works*, ed. Craig A. Rimmerman 187–190. Lanham, MD: Lexington Publishers, 2011.

Rincker, Meg, Marisa Henderson, Renato Vidigal, and Daniel Delgado. "Evaluating the Representation and Responsiveness of the United Nations Commission on the Status of Women (CSW) to Diverse Women Populations Worldwide." *Frontiers in Sociology* 4 (2019). doi: 10.3389/fsoc.2019.00041.

Ritchie, D.G. "The Teaching of Political Science at Oxford." *Annals of the American Academy of Political and Social Science* 2, no. 1 (1891): 85–95.

Rittel, H. W., & Webber, M. M. "Dilemmas in a General Theory of Planning. *Policy Sciences* 4, no. 2 (1973): 155–169.

Rizvi, Fazal. "Towards Cosmopolitan Learning." *Discourse: Studies in the Cultural Politics of Education* 30, no. 3 (2009): 253–268.

Robson, W.A. *The University Teaching of Social Sciences: Political Science*. Paris: UNESCO, 1954.

Rockquemore, Kerry Ann and Harwell Schaffer, Regan. "Toward a Theory of Engagement: A Cognitive Mapping of Service-Learning Experiences." *Michigan Journal of Community Service Learning* 7, no. 1 (2000): 14–25.

Rodan, Garry. *Participation without Democracy: Containing Conflict in Southeast Asia*. Ithaca, NY: Cornell University Press, 2018.

Rodino-Colocino, Michelle. "Me Too, #MeToo: Countering Cruelty with Empathy." *Communication and Critical/Cultural Studies* 15 (2018): 96–100. doi: 10.1080/14791420.2018.1435083.

Rogers, Michael T. "The History of Civic Education in Political Science: The Story of a Discipline's Failure to Lead," in *Teaching Civic Engagement Across the Disciplines,* eds. Elizabeth C. Matto, Alison Rios Millet McCartney, Elizabeth A. Bennion, and Dick Simpson, 73–96. Washington DC: APSA, 2017.

Rogers, Michael T., and Donald M. Gooch, ed. *Civic Education in the Twenty-First Century: A Multidimensional Inquiry*. Lanham, MD: Lexington Books, 2015.

Romanova, Tatiana A., and Nikolay N. Gudalov. "Role-Play Simulation of Negotiations Between the EU and the Eurasian Economic Union: Teaching While Enhancing a Transnational Dialogue." *Journal of Contemporary European Research* 15, no. 4 (2019): 410–424. https://doi.org/10.30950/jcer.v15i4.1093.

Rose, Gillian. *Visual Methodologies: An Introduction to the Interpretation of Visual Materials*. London: Sage, 2008.

Rose, Richard, William Mishler, and Christian W. Haerpfer. *Democracy and Its Alternatives*. Baltimore: The John Hopkins University Press, 1998.

Roser, Max. "Democracy." *Our World in Data*, 2019. https://ourworldindata.org/democracy#share-of-world-population-living-in-democracies.

Roshanravan, Shireen. "Staying Home While Studying Abroad: Anti-Imperial Praxis for Globalizing Feminist Visions." *Journal of Feminist Scholarship* 2 (2018): 1–23. https://digitalcommons.uri.edu/jfs/ vol2/iss2/7.

Ross, Dorothy. *The Origins of American Social Science*. Cambridge, UK: Cambridge University Press, 1991.

Roth, Benita. "Second Wave Black Feminism in the African Diaspora: News from New Scholarship." *Agenda: Empowering Women for Gender Equity* 17 (2003): 46–58. Accessed September 9, 2020. http://www.jstor.org/stable/4548095.

Roth, Kenneth. "The Dangerous Rise of Populism: Global Attacks on Human Rights Values." *World Report 2017 Human Rights Watch,* 2018. https://hrw.org/world-report/2017/country-chapters/global-4.

Rudolph, Christopher. "Sovereignty and Territorial Borders in a Global Age." *International Studies Review* 7, no. 1 (2005): 1–20.

Russo, Silvia, and Håkan Stattin. "Stability and Change in Youths' Political Interest." *Social Indicators Research* 132, no. 2 (2017): 643–58.

Saine, Abdoulaye. "The Military and Human Rights in The Gambia 1994-1999." *Journal of Third World Studies* 19, no. 2 (2002): 167–187.

Saldaña, Paulo. "Weintraub Escolhe Gestores não Ligados à Educação para Secretarias do MEC." April 10, 2019. https:// www1.folha.uol.com.br/educacao/2019/04/weintraub-escolhe-gestores-nao-ligados-a-educacao-para-secretarias-do-mec.shtml?fbclid=IwAR3LBLWME5CHZThOzlfC66XfQZvaXnh-nuTveKHGUvB_CSbpKfEwQnEhzo8.

Saltmarsh, John, and Matthew Hartley. "To Serve a Larger Purpose," in *"To Serve a Larger Purpose:" Engagement for Democracy and the Transformation of Higher Education,* eds. John Saltmarsh and Matthew Hartley, 1–13. Philadelphia, PA: Temple University Press, 2011.

Sanctum, Flavio. "Estética do Oprimido de Augusto Boal Uma Odisseia pelos Sentidos." Master's Dissertation presented to the Post-Graduate Program on Science of Art at the Federal Fluminense University, 2011.

Sanders, Martha Atwood, Tracy Van Oss, and Signian McGeary. "Analyzing Reflections in Service Learning to Promote Personal Growth and Community Self-Efficacy." *Journal of Experiential Education* 39, no. 1 (2016): 73–88.

Sanger, Catherine Shea, and Nancy W. Gleason, ed. *Diversity and Inclusion in Global Higher Education: Lessons from Across Asia.* Singapore: Springer Singapore, 2020.

Santos, Boaventura de Sousa. *A Universidade no Século XXI.* São Paulo: Corte, 2004.

Santos, Michelly. "UFPB Ingressa na Elite para Desenvolvimento Sustentável da ONU." *Ascom/UFPB*, 2020. Accessed April 18, 2021. https://www.ufpb.br/ufpb/contents/noticias/ufpb-ingressa-na-elite-para-desenvolvimento-sustentavel-da-onu.

Sarkissian, Ani. "Religion and Civic Engagement in Muslim Countries." *Journal for the Scientific Study of Religion* 51, no. 4 (2012): 607–622.

Sassen, Saskia. *Globalization and Its Discontents.* New York: New Press. 1998.

Saul, Stephanie. "N.Y.U. Professor is Barred by United Arab Emirates." *New York Times*, March 16, 2015. https://www.nytimes.com/2015/03/17/nyregion/nyu-professor-is-barred-from-the-united-arab-emirates.html.

Schaffer, Timothy J. "Supporting the 'Archstone of Democracy': Cooperative Extension's Experiment with Deliberative Group Discussion." *Journal of Extension* 55 (2017). https://www.joe.org/joe/2017october/a1.php.

Schattle, Hans. *The Practices of Global Citizenship.* Lanham, MD: Rowman & Littlefield, 2008.

Schiff, Jennifer, and Carol Burton. "'Wicked Problems' in General Education: The Challenges of Diversity, Civic Engagement, and Civil Discourse." *The Journal of General Education* 68, no. 1–2 (2020): 85–103.

Schlozman, Kay L., Henry E. Brady, and Sidney Verba. *Unequal and Unrepresented: Political Inequality and the People's Voice in the New Gilded Age.* Princeton, NJ: Princeton University Press, 2018.

Schmitter, Philippe C. "Still the Century of Corporatism?" *The Review of Politics* 36, no. 1 (1974): 85–131.

Schodt, David. "Using Cases to Teach Analytical Skills," in *The New International Studies Classroom: Active Teaching, Active Learning,* eds. Jeffrey S. Lantis, Lynn M. Luzma, John Boehrer. Boulder, CO: Lynne Rienner, 2000.

Scholars' Choice. "Scholar's Experiences Details - Mightier than the Sword." *Scholars' Choice*, July 12, 2019. Accessed June 8, 2021. https://www.scholarschoice.com.sg/experience/293/mightier_than_the_sword.

Schulz, Sam and Deborah Agnew. "Moving toward Decoloniality in Short-Term Study abroad under New Colombo: Constructing Global Citizenship." *British Journal of Sociology of Education*, 2020. doi: 10.1080/01425692.2020.1822152\.

Schwarcz, Lilia Moritz. *Sobre O Autoritarismo Brasileiro.* São Paulo: Companhia Das Letras, 2019.

Schwarzer, Steve, and Eva Zeglovits. "The Role of Schools in Preparing 16- and 17-year-old Austrian First-Time Voters for the Election," in *Growing into Politics. Contexts and Timing of Political Socialisation,* ed. Simone Abendschön, 73–90. Colchester: ECPR Press, 2013.

SEED for Social Innovation. "2017 SEED Fellow Revisit Survey Report." *The SEED Foundation,* 2020.

SEED for Social Innovation. "Observations and Analysis of Social Force Participation Under COVID-19, a Research Report." *The Seed Foundation,* 2020.

SEED for Social Innovation. "SEED 2018 Annual Report." *The SEED Foundation,* 2018. https://static1.squarespace.com/static/57bc83d737c5819f22ed1f08/t/5c48e9d2b91c91570023e8ae/1548282328529/2018+Annual+Report+Web.pdf.

SEED for Social Innovation. "SEED 2019 Annual Report." *The SEED Foundation,* 2019. https://static1.squarespace.com/static/57bc83d737c5819f22ed1f08/t/60538d0a03064b3485dd16fb/1616088332145/2019+SEED+Foundation+Annual+Report.pdf.

Seeley, J.R. *Lectures and Essays.* London: Macmillan, 1870.

Seidman, Sarah. "Feminism and Revolution: Angela Davis in Cuba." Paper presented at the American Historical Association Session 119, January 3, 1998. Accessed September 7, 2020. New York, NY. https://aha.confex.com/aha/2015/webprogram/

Paper16621.html.

Seligson, Mitchell A., and John A. Booth. "Political Culture and Regime Type: Evidence from Nicaragua and Costa Rica." *The Journal of Politics* 55, no. 3 (1993): 777–792.

Sen, Amartya. *Development as Freedom.* Oxford: Oxford University Press, 1999.

Shanahan, Michael J., Jeylan T. Mortimer, and Helga Kruger. "Adolescence and Adult Work in the Twenty-First Century." *Journal of Research on Adolescence* 12, no. 1 (2002): 99–120.

Sharbaugh, Patrick E, and Dang Nguyen. "Make Lulz, Not War: How Online Remix and Meme Culture are Empowering Civic Engagement in the Socialist Republic of Vietnam." *Asiascape: Digital Asia* 1, no. 3 (2014): 133–168.

Shattock, Michael. *Making Policy in British Higher Education 1945–2011.* Maidenhead, UK: McGraw Hill/Open University Press, 2012.

Shaw, Carolyn M. "Using Role-Play Scenarios in the IR Classroom: An Examination of Exercises on Peacekeeping Operations and Foreign Policy Decision Making." *International Studies Perspectives* 5, no. 1 (2004): 1–22. https://doi.org/10.1111/j.1528-3577.2004.00151.x.

Shellman, Stephen M., and Kürşad Turan. "Do Simulations Enhance Student Learning? An Empirical Evaluation of an IR Simulations." *Journal of Political Science Education* 2, no. 1 (2006): 19–32. https://doi.org/10.1080/15512160500484168.

Shelly, Bryan. "Bonding, Bridging, and Boundary Breaking: The Civic Lessons of High School Activities." *Journal of Political Science Education* 7, no. 3 (2011): 95–311. doi: 10.1080/15512169.2011.590079.

Shen, Yifei. *Feminism in China: An Analysis of Advocates, Debates, and Strategies.* Shanghai: Friedrich Eberto Stiftung, 2016.

Shepard, Daniel D. *How Young People Influence Policy: A Literature Review.* England, Oxfam, 2017.

Sherman, Paul. "Preparing Social Workers for Global Gaze: Locating Global Citizenship Within Social Work Curricula." *Social Work Education* 35, no. 6 (2016): 632–642.

Shermer, Michael. *Why People Believe Weird Things: Pseudoscience, Superstition, and Other Confusions of Our Time.* New York, NY: Freeman, 2002.

Sherrod, Lonnie R., Judith Torney-Purta, and Constance A. Flanagan. "Introduction," in *Handbook of Research on Civic Engagement in Youth,* eds. Lonnie R. Sherrod, Judith Torney-Purta, and Constance A. Flanagan, 1–20. Hoboken, NJ: John Wiley and Sons Inc, 2010.

Shumer, Robert, Carolina Lam, and Bonnie Laabs. "Ensuring Good Character and Civic Education: Connecting through Service Learning." *Asia Pacific Journal of Education* 32, no. 4 (2012): 430–440.

Sierra, Horacio. "Higher Education Lacks Diversity." *Baltimore Sun,* May 2, 2021. https://www.baltimoresun.com/opinion/op-ed/bs-ed-op-0502-academia-ivory-tower-race-20210430-nrzxi3sa75af3bwhyyyxnavvqi-story.html.

Sigmon, Robert L. "Serving to Learn, Learning to Serve - Linking Service with Learning." *Council for Independent Colleges Report,* 1994.

Silova, Iveta, and Elmina Kazimzade. "The Civics Education Applications in Post-Soviet Context." *Academica.edu.* http://www.academia.edu/download/35812646/Civic_education_in_AZ.doc.

Silver, Harold and John Brennan. *A Liberal Vocationalism.* London: Methuen, 1988.

Sim, Cheryl. "Co-Curricular Activities in Schools." *National Library Board EResources,* 2014. https://eresources.nlb.gov.sg/infopedia/articles/SIP_2014-11-08_124430.html.

Sim, Jasmine B-Y., and Murray Print. "Citizenship Education in Singapore: Controlling or Empowering Teacher Understanding and Practice?" *Oxford Review of Education* 35, no. 6 (2009): 705–723. doi: 10.1080/03054980903141549.

Sim, Jasmine B-Y., Shuyi Chua, and Malathy Krishnasamy. ""Riding the Citizenship Wagon": Citizenship Conceptions of Social Studies Teachers in Singapore." *Teaching and Teacher Education* 63 (2017): 92–102.

Sim, Stuart. *Addicted to Profit: Reclaiming Our Lives from the Free Market.* Edinburg, UK: Edinburg University Press, 2012.

Simeone, James, James Sikora, and Deborah Halperin. "Unscripted Learning: Cultivating Engaged Catalysts," in *Teaching Civic Engagement Across the Disciplines,* eds. Elizabeth C. Matto, Alison Rios Millett McCartney, Elizabeth A. Bennion, and Dick Simpson, 273–289. Washington DC: American Political Science Association, 2017.

Simon, E.D. "The Case for Training for Citizenship in Democratic States," in *Training for Citizenship,* eds. Sir Ernest Simon and Eva M. Hubback, 7–16. Oxford, UK: Oxford University Press, 1935.

Simon, Karla W. *Civil Society in China: The Legal Framework from Ancient Times to the "New Reform Era."* Oxford, UK: Oxford University Press, 2013.

Simpson, Archie W., and Bernd Kaussler. "IR Teaching Reloaded: Using Silms and Simulations in the Teaching of International Relations." *International Studies Perspectives* 10, no. 4 (2009): 413–427. https://doi.org/10.1111/j.1528-

3585.2009.00386.x.

Simpson, Dick. *The Good Fight: Life Lessons from a Chicago Progressive*. Emmaus, PA: Golden Alley Press, 2017.

Simpson, Dick. "Teaching Civic Engagement Today," in *Teaching Civic Engagement Across the Disciplines*, eds. Elizabeth C. Matto, Alison Rios Millett McCartney, Elizabeth A. Bennion, and Dick Simpson, 375–390. Washington DC: American Political Science Association, 2017.

Sinclair-Chapman, Valeria. "Leveraging Diversity in Political Science for Institutional and Disciplinary Change." *PS: Political Science & Politics* 48, no. 3 (2015): 454–458.

Singh, Bilveer. *Understanding Singapore Politics*. Hackensack, New Jersey: World Scientific, 2017.

Sintomer, Yves, Carsten Herzberg, Giovanni Allegretti, and Anja Röcke. *Learning from the South: Participatory Budgeting Worldwide – an Invitation to Global Cooperation*. Bonn: GIZ, 2010.

Siver, Christi, and Claire Haeg. "Incorporating and Assessing Methods Across the Political Science Curriculum," in *Teaching Research Methods in Political Science*, ed. Jeffrey L. Bernstein, 177–193. Cheltenham, UK: Edward Elgar Publishing Limited, 2021.

Skinner, Gideon. "How Britain Voted in 2015." *Ipsos MORI*. https://www.ipsos.com/ipsos-mori/en-uk/how-britain-voted-2015.

Skinner, Gideon, and Glenn Gottfried. "How Britain Voted in the 2016 EU Referendum." *Ipsos MORI*, September 5, 2016. https://www.ipsos.com/ipsos-mori/en-uk/how-britain-voted-2016-eu-referendum.

Skocpol, Theda. *Diminished Democracy, From Membership to Management in American Civic Life*. Cambridge, MA: Harvard University Press, 2003.

Sloam, James, Rakib Ehsan and Matt Henn. "'Youthquake': How and Why Young People Reshaped the Political Landscape in 2017." *Political Insight* April (2018): 4–8.

Slutskaya, Natalia, Alex Simpson, and Jason Hughes. "Butchers, Quakers and Bankrupts: Lessons from Photo-elicitation." *Qualitative Research in Organizations and Management* 7, no. 1 (2012).

Smith, Dan. *The State of the World Atlas*. Oxford, UK: Myriad, 2020.

Smith, Graham, Roger Ottewill, Esther Jubb, Elizabeth Sperling and Matthew Wyman. "Teaching Citizenship in Higher Education." *European Political Science* 7, no. 2 (2008): 135–143.

Smith, Kathryn M. "Female Voice and Feminist Text: Testimonio as A Form of Resistance in Latin America." *Florida Atlantic Comparative Studies Journal* 12 (2010): 21–37.

Smith, Steven Rathgeb, and Meghan McConaughey. "The Political Science Major and Its Future: The Wahlke Report-Revisited." *PS: Political Science & Politics* 54, no. 2 (2021): 358–362.

Snelling, Charlotte J. "Young People and Electoral Registration in the UK: Examining Local Activities to Maximise Youth Registration." *Parliamentary Affairs* 69, no. 3 (2016): 663–685.

Snyder, Glenn H. "'Prisoner's Dilemma' and 'Chicken' Models in International Politics." *International Studies Quarterly* 15, no. 1 (1971): 66–103. https://doi.org/10.2307/3013593.

Snyder, R. Claire. "Should Political Science Have a Civic Mission? An Overview of the Historical Evidence." *PS: Political Science & Politics* 34, no. 2 (2001): 301–305.

Sofer, Reba N. *Ethics and Society in England: The Revolution in the Social Sciences 1870–1914*. Berkeley, CA: University of California Press, 1978.

Solt, Frederick. "The Social Origins of Authoritarianism." *Political Research Quarterly* 65, no. 4 (2012): 703–713.

Soon, Minh. "Dissent And Sensibility: Yale-NUS and Anti Establishmentarianism." *The Octant*, 2020. Accessed June 8, 2021. https://theoctant.org/edition/issue/news/dissent-and-sensibility-yale-nus-and-anti-establishmentarianism/.

SOUL. "Ihumātao." *Save Our Unique Landscape*, 2020. Accessed August 27, 2020. https://www.protectihumatao.com/.

Speck, K. "Effects of Service Learning in Germany." State of Research, Carl von Ossietzky University Oldenburg, 2012.

Sperling, Valerie. "Women's Organizations: Institutionalized Interest Groups or Vulnerable Dissidents?" in *Russian Civil Society: A Critical Assessment*, eds. Alfred Evans, Lisa McIntosh-Sundstrom, and Laura Henry, 161–177. Armonk, NY: M.E. Sharpe, 2006.

Spiess, Robin. "Female Genital Mutilation: A Cut, Unseen." *Southeast Asia Globe*, June 7, 2019. https://southeastasiaglobe.com/singapore-female-genital-mutilation/.

Staeheli, Lynn, and Caroline R Nagel. "Whose Awakening is It? Youth and the Geopolitics of Civic Engagement in the 'Arab Awakening'." *European Urban and Regional Studies* 20, no. 1 (2013): 115–119.

Stallivieri, Luciane. "El Sistema de Educación Superior de Brasil: Características, Tendencias y Perspectivas." *Red de Revistas*

Científicas de América Latina y el Caribe, España y Portugal 34 (2007): 48–61.

Stammers, Neil, Helga Dittmar, and Janet Henney. "Teaching and Learning Politics: A Survey of Practices and Change in UK Universities." *Political Studies* 47, no. 1 (1999): 114–126.

Stapleton, Julia. "Citizenship Versus Patriotism in Twentieth-Century England." *The Historical Journal* 48, no. 1 (2005): 151–178.

Starks, Glenn L. "Barack Obama and the Youth Vote," in *How the Obama Presidency Changed the Political Landscape,* eds. Larry J. Walker, F. Erik Brooks, and Ramon B. Goings, 90–108. Santa Barbara, CA: Praeger, 2017.

State Youth Council. "Youth Barometer 2018: Influence on the Edge of Europe." *State Youth Council,* 2018. https://tietoanuorista.fi/en/publications/youth-barometer-2018-never-before-have-young-people-been-this-interested-in-politics/.

Stein, Michael B. "Major Factors in the Emergence of Political Science as a Discipline in Western Democracies: A Comparative Analysis of the United States, Britain, France, and Germany," in *Regime and Discipline: Democracy and the Development of Political Science*, eds. David Easton, John G. Gunnell, and Michael B. Stein, 169–196. Ann Arbor, MI: University of Michigan Press, 1995.

Steinberg, Gerald M. "The Politics of NGOs, Human Rights and the Arab-Israel Conflict." *Israel Studies* 16 (2011): 24–54.

Steinhardt, Christoph H. and Fengshi Wu. "In the Name of the Public: Environmental Protest and the Changing Landscape of Popular Contention in China." *China Journal* 75 (2016): 61–82.

Stewart, Patrick A., Elaine Terrell, Alex M. Kareev, Blake Tylar Ellison, and Charini I. Uteaga. "'Gamifying' Online American National Government: Lessons Learned from the First Year of Developing 'Citizenship Quest.'" *Journal of Political Science Education* 16, no. 4 (2020): 508–525.

Stewart, Trae, and Nicole Webster, ed. *Exploring Cultural Dynamics and Tensions Within Service Learning*. IAP, 2011.

Stewart, W.A.C. *Higher Education in Postwar Britain*. Basingstoke, UK: Macmillan, 1989.

Stockemer, Daniel. "Does Democracy Lead to Good Governance? The Question Applied to Africa and Latin America." *Global Change, Peace & Security* 21, no. 2 (2009): 241–255.

Stoecker, Randy, Amy Hilgendorf, and Elizabeth A. Tryon, eds. *The Unheard Voices: Community Organizations and Service Learning*. Philadelphia, PA: Temple University Press, 2009.

Stolarchuk, Jewel. "Yale-NUS Students Protest School's Decision-making Methods; Demand More Student Representation." *The Independent*, March 11, 2018. Accessed June 8, 2021. https://theindependent.sg/yale-nus-students-protest-schools-decision-making-methods-demand-more-student-representation/.

Stone, Diane. "Non-Governmental Policy Transfer: The Strategies of Independent Policy Institutes." *Governance* 13, no. 1 (2000): 45–70. https://doi.org/10.1111/0952-1895.00123.

Strachan, J. Cherie. "Deliberative Pedagogy's Feminist Potential: Teaching Our Students to Cultivate a More Inclusive Public Sphere," in *Teaching Civic Engagement Across the Disciplines,* eds. Elizabeth C. Matto, Alison Rios Millett McCartney, Elizabeth A. Bennion, and Dick Simpson, 35–36. Washington, DC: American Political Science Association, 2017.

Strachan, J. Cherie. "Student and Civic Engagement: Cultivating the Skills, Efficacy, and Identities that Increase Student Involvement in Learning and in Public Life," in *Handbook on Teaching and Learning in Political Science and International Relations,* eds. John Ishiyama, William J. Miller, and Eszter Simon, 60–73. Cheltenham, UK: Edward Elgar Publishing Limited, 2015.

Strachan, J. Cherie, and Elizabeth A. Bennion. "New Resources for Civic Engagement: The National Survey of Student Leaders, Campus Associational Life, and the Consortium for Inter-Campus SoTL Research," in *Teaching Civic Engagement Across the Disciplines*, eds. Elizabeth C. Matto, Alison Rios Millett McCartney, Elizabeth A. Bennion, and Dick Simpson. Washington, DC: American Political Science Association, 2017.

Strachan, J. Cherie, Lori M. Poloni-Staudinger, Shannon Jenkins, and Candice D. Ortbals. *Why Don't Women Rule the World?* Washington, DC: SAGE-CQ Press, 2019.

Strachan, J. Cherie, and Mary Scheuer Senter. "Student Organizations and Civic Education on Campus: The Greek System," in *Teaching Civic Engagement: From Student to Active Citizen*, eds. Alison Rios Millett McCartney, Elizabeth A. Bennion, and Dick Simpson 385–402. Washington, DC: American Political Science Association Press, 2013.

Strömbäck, Jesper, and Adam Shehata. "Media Malaise or a Virtuous Circle? Exploring the Causal Relationships Between News Media Exposure, Political News Attention and Political Interest." *European Journal of Political Research* 49, no. 5 (2010): 575–97.

Sun, Taiyi. "Civic Transformation in the Wake of the Wenchuan Earthquake: State, Society, and the Individual." *Made in China* 3, no. 1 (2018): 66–70.

Sun, Taiyi. "Deliberate Differentiation for Outsourcing Responsibilities: The Logic of China's Behavior Toward Civil Society

Organizations." *The China Quarterly* 240 (2019): 880–905.

Sun, Taiyi. "Forced Experimentation: Teaching Civic Engagement Online Amid COVID-19." *PS: Political Science & Politics* 54, no. 1 (2020): 176–178.

Sun, Taiyi and Quansheng Zhao. "The Delegated Censorship: The Dynamic, Decentralized, and Multi-Layered Information Control Regime in China." *Politics and Society* (2021).

Surak, Sarah, Christopher Jensen, Alison Rios Millett McCartney, and Alexander Pope. "Teaching Faculty to Teach Civic Engagement: Interdisciplinary Models to Facilitate Pedagogical Success," in *Teaching Civic Engagement Across the Disciplines*, eds. Elizabeth C. Matto, Alison Rios Millett McCartney, Elizabeth A. Bennion, and Dick Simpson, 231–246. Washington DC: American Political Science Association, 2017.

Svolik, Milan W. *The Politics of Authoritarian Rule.* Cambridge University Press, 2012.

Swain, Harriet. "Roll Up! Universities Embark on Big Push to Boost Student Vote." *The Guardian*, May 9, 2017. https://www.theguardian.com/education/2017/may/09/universities-boost-student-vote-general-election.

Sylvest, C. "Interrogating the Subject: Errol Morris's The Fog of War," in *Classics of International Relations: Essays in Criticism and Appreciation*, eds. H. Bliddal, C. Sylvest and P. Wilson. Abingdon, UK: Routledge, 2013.

Sylvester, Dari E. "From Policy to Political Efficacy and Engagement: Using Government in Action to Promote Understanding of Public Policy," in *Teaching Civic Engagement: From Student to Active Citizen*, eds. Alison Rios Millett McCartney, Elizabeth A. Bennion, and Dick Simpson, 137–152. Washington, DC: American Political Science Association, 2013.

Taft, Jessica K., Sandi Kawecka Nenga, ed. *Youth Engagement: The Civic-Political Lives of Children and Youth.* Bingley, UK: Emerald Group Publishing Limited, 2013.

Tan, Audrey. "Activists Plan to Compile 'Climate Scorecard' for GE." *The Straits Times*, January 15, 2020. https://www.straitstimes.com/singapore/environment/activists-plan-to-compile-climate-scorecard-for-ge.

Tan, Audrey. "Young Activists Planning 'Green Dot' Gathering on Sept 21." *The Straits Times*, August 13, 2019. https://www.straitstimes.com/singapore/environment/young-activists-planning-green-dot-gathering-on-sept-21.

Tan, Charlene. "Thinking Critically about Liberal Arts Education: Yale-NUS College in Singapore," in *The Evolution of Liberal Arts in the Global Age*, eds. Peter Marber and Daniel Araya, 127–140. New York: Routledge, 2017.

Tan, Kenneth Paul. "Service Learning Outside the US: Initial Experiences in Singapore's Higher Education." *PS: Political Science & Politics* 42, no. 3 (2009): 549–557.

Tan, Kenneth Paul, and Andrew Sze-Sian. "Civic Society and the New Economy in Patriarchal Singapore: Emasculating the Political, Feminizing the Public." *Crossroads* 15, no. 2 (2001): 95–122.

Tan, Natalie Christian. "Here's How the Conversation around Religion and LGBTQ Needs to Change This Year." *RICE*, January 14, 2019. https://www.ricemedia.co/current-affairs-commentary-singapore-conversation-lgbtq-change-2019/.

Tan, Netina. "Manipulating Electoral Laws in Singapore." *Electoral Studies* 32, no. 4 (2013): 632–643.

Tan, Netina. "Singapore: Challenges of 'Good Governance' Without Liberal Democracy," in *Governance and Democracy in the Asia-Pacific*, eds. Stephen McCarthy and Mark R. Thompson, 48–73. London; New York: Routledge, 2020.

Tan, Soo Jiuan, and Siok Kuan Tambyah. "Civic Engagement and Wellbeing in Singapore: The Impact of Generalized Trust, Personal Values, and Religiosity." *Current Politics and Economics of South, Southeastern, and Central Asia* 26, no. 2 (2017): 125–150.

Tan, Tai Yong. "Oral History Interview with Tan Tai Yong, President of Yale-NUS College." Transcript of interview by Jaime Koh. *National Archives Singapore*, October 19, 2016. https://www.nas.gov.sg/archivesonline/oral_history_interviews/interview/E000844.

Tan, Tai Yong. "Yale-NUS College Graduation 2019 Speech." *Yale-NUS College President's Office,* May 13, 2019. https://president.yale-nus.edu.sg/speeches-essays/speech/graduation-2019/.

Tang, Louisa. "Activist Jolovan Wham Chooses 22 days' Jail Over Fine for Holding Illegal Public Assembly on MRT Train." Today, February 15, 2021. Accessed June 8, 2021. https://www.todayonline.com/singapore/activist-jolovan-wham-chooses-22-days-jail-over-fine-holding-illegal-public-assembly-mrt.

Tang, Wenfang. *Populist Authoritarianism: Chinese Political Culture and Regime Sustainability.* Oxford, UK: Oxford University Press, 2016.

Tanscheit, Talita, and Thamy Pogrebinschi. "Moving Backwards: What Happened to Citizen Participation in Brazil?" *Open Democracy*, 2017. Accessed April 18, 2021. https://www.opendemocracy.net/en/democraciaabierta/moving-backwards-what-happened-to-citizen-part/,

Tarrant, Michael. "The Added Value of Study Abroad Fostering a Global Citizenry." *Journal of Studies in International*

Education 18, no. 2 (2010): 141–161.

Taskforce on Active Citizenship. *Report of the Taskforce on Active Citizenship.* Dublin, 2007.

Tee, Zhuo. "Millennial Activism: Daryl Yang Fights for LGBT Issues and More." *The Straits Times*, April 14, 2019. https://www.straitstimes.com/lifestyle/millennial-activism-daryl-yang-fights-for-lgbt-issues-and-more.

Tee, Zhuo. "Millennial Activism: Student Group Calls on NUS to Divest from Fossil Fuels." *The Straits Times*, April 14, 2019. https://www.straitstimes.com/lifestyle/millennial-activism-student-group-calls-on-nus-to-divest-from-fossil-fuels.

Temple, Paul, Claire Callender, Lyn Grove and Natasha Kersh. "Managing the Student Experience in English Higher Education: Differing Responses to Market Pressures." *London Review of Education* 14, no. 1 (2016): 33–46.

ten Brummelaar, Mijntje D.C., Annemiek T Harder, Margrite E Kalverboer,Wendy J Post and Erik J Knorth. "Participation of Youth in Decision-Making Procedures During Residential Care: A Narrative Review." *Child & Family Social Work* 23 (2017): 33–44.

Teresi, Holly and Melissa R. Michelson. "Wired to Mobilize: The Effect of Social Networking Messages on Voter Turnout." *The Social Science Journal* 52, no. 2 (2015): 195–204. doi: 10.1016/j.soscij.2014.09.004.

Thayer-Bacon, Barbara J. "A Pragmatist and Feminist Relational (E)pistemology." *European Journal of Pragmatism and American Philosophy* 2 (2010): 1–22. doi: 10.4000/ejpap.948.

Thomas, Glyn V. and Richard P. Jolley. "Drawing Conclusions: A Re-examination of Empirical and Conceptual Bases for Psychological Evaluation of Children from their Drawings." *British Journal of Clinical Psychology* 37, no. 2 (1984).

Thomas, Nancy L. "The College and University as Citizen," in *Civic Responsibility and Higher Education,* eds. Thomas Ehrlich. Phoenix, AZ: American Council on Education/Oryx Press, 2000.

Thomas, Nancy, and Margaret Brower. "Conceptualizing and Assessing Campus Climates for Political Learning and Engagement in Democracy." *Journal of College and Character* 19, no. 4 (2018): 247–263. doi: 10.1080/2194587X.2018.1517651.

Thomas, Nancy, and Margaret Brower. "Politics 365: Fostering Campus Climates for Student Political Learning and Engagement," in *Teaching Civic Engagement Across the Disciplines,* eds. Elizabeth C. Matto, Alison Rios Millett McCartney, Elizabeth A. Bennion, and Dick Simpson. Washington, DC: American Political Science Association, 2017.

Thomas, Nancy, and Margaret Bower. "The Politically Engaged Classroom," in *Teaching Civic Engagement Across the Disciplines,* eds. Elizabeth C. Matto, Alison Rios Millett McCartney, Elizabeth A. Bennion, and Dick Simpson. Washington, DC: American Political Science Association, 2017.

Thomas, Nancy, and Margaret Brower. "Promising Practices to Facilitate Politically Robust Campus Climates." *Change: The Magazine of Higher Learning* 50, no. 6 (2018): 24–29. doi: 10.1080/00091383.2018.1540818.

Thomas, Nancy, Margaret Brower, Ishara Casellas Connors, Adam Gismondi, and Kyle Upchurch. *Election Imperatives Version 2.0: Ten Recommendations to Increase College Student Voting and Improve Political Learning and Engagement.* Medford, MA: Institute for Democracy and Higher Education, 2019. https://idhe.tufts.edu/sites/default/files/ElectionImperatives-v2.pdf.

Tight, Malcolm. "How Many Universities are There in the United Kingdom? How Many Should There Be?" *Higher Education* 62, no. 5 (2011): 649–663.

Tilly, Charles. *Durable Inequality.* Berkeley and Los Angeles, CA: University of California Press, 1998.

Tinkler, Alan, Barri Tinkler, Ethan Hausman, and Gabe Tufo-Strouse. "Key Elements of Effective Service-Learning Partnerships from the Perspective of Community Partners." *Partnerships: A Journal of Service-Learning and Civic Engagement* 5, no. 2 (2014): 137–152.

Togeby, Lise. "The Gender Gap in Foreign Policy Attitudes." *Journal of Peace Research* 31, no. 4 (1994): 375–392. https://doi.org/10.1177%2F0022343394031004002.

Tolstrup, Jakob. "When Can External Actors Influence Democratization? Leverage, Linkages, and Gatekeeper Elites." *Democratization* 20, no. 4 (2013): 716–742.

Tong, Rosemarie. *Feminist Thought: A More Comprehensive Introduction*, 2nd edition. Boulder, CO: Westview Press, 2009.

Tonge, Jon, Andrew Mycock and Bob Jeffery. "Does Citizenship Education Make Young People Better-Engaged Citizens?" *Political Studies* 60, no. 3 (2012): 578–2012.

Tormos-Aponte, Fernando, and Mayra Velez-Serrano. "Broadening the Pathway for Graduate Students in Political Science." *PS: Political Science & Politics* 53, no. 1 (2020): 145–146.

Torney-Purta, Judith. *Citizenship and Education in Twenty-Eight Countries: Civic Knowledge and Engagement at Age Fourteen.* Amsterdam, The Netherlands: IEA Secreatariat, Herengracht 487, 1017 BT, 2001.

Torney-Purta, Judith. "Patterns in the Civic Knowledge, Engagement, and Attitudes of European Adolescents: The IEA Civic

Education Study." *European Journal of Education* 37, no. 2 (2002): 129–141.

Torney-Purta, Judith, Carolyn H. Barber, and Britt Wilkenfeld. "Latino Adolescents' Civic Development in the United States: Research Results from the IEA Civic Education Study." *Journal of Youth and Adolescence* 36, no. 2 (2007): 111–125.

Torney-Purta, Judith, Julio C. Cabrera, Katrina Crotts Roohr, Ou Lydia Liu, and Joseph A. Rios. *Assessing Civic Competency and Engagement in Higher Education: Research Background, Frameworks, and Directions for Next-Generation Assessment. (Research Report No. RR-15-34).* Princeton, NJ: Educational Testing Service, 2015. doi: 10.1002/ets2.12081.

Toscano, Michael. "Honoring the Past, Securing the Present." *Academic Questions* 28, no. 1 (2015): 106–110. https://doi. org/10.1007/s12129-015-9480-5.

Tovmasyan, Tigran, and Marcie Taylor Thoma. "The Impact of Civic Education on Schools, Students, and Communities." *Final Analytical Report*, 2008. https://www.crrc.am/hosting/file/_static_content.

Treviño, Ernesto, Consuelo Béjares, Cristóbal Villalobos, and Eloísa Naranjo. "Influence of Teachers and Schools on Students' Civic Outcomes in Latin America." *The Journal of Educational Research* 110, no. 6 (2017): 604–618.

Trueb, Bettina. "Teaching Students to Write for Real Life: Policy Paper Writing in the Classroom." *PS: Political Science & Politics* 46, no. 1 (2013): 137–141. https://doi.org/10.1017/S1049096512001333.

Tsou, Tang. *The Cultural Revolution and Post-Mao Reforms: A Historical Perspective.* Chicago: The University of Chicago Press, 1986.

Tuck, Eve, and Marcia McKenzie. *Place in Research: Theory, Methodology, and Methods.* New York, NY: Routledge, 2015.

Tymoczko, Maria. *Translation, Resistance, Activism.* University of Massachusetts Press, 2010.

Uberoi, Elise, and Neil Johnston. "Political Disengagement in the UK: Who is Disengaged?" *House of Commons Library Briefing Paper*, CBP-7501, February 25, 2021. https://commonslibrary.parliament.uk/research-briefings/cbp-7501/.

UCLG. *Turin Communique on Localizing the Post-2015 Development Agenda.* 2014. Accessed April 18, 2021. http://www.uclg.org/sites/default/files/turin_communique_localizing_13_oct.pdf.

UFPB. "Plano de Desenvolvimento Institucional UFPB: 2019–2023." 2019. Accessed April 18, 2021. http://www.proplan.ufpb.br/proplan/contents/documentos/pdi/pdi_2019-2023_posconsuni-1.pdf.

UFPB. "Resolução Nº 07/2002: Aprova o Estatuto da Universidade Federal da Paraíba." *ACI/UFPB*, 2002. Accessed April 18, 2021. https://www.ufpb.br/aci/contents/documentos/documentos-ufpb/estatuto-da-ufpb.pdf/view,

UNDP. *Desenvolvimento Humano nas Macrorregiões Brasileiras.* Brasília: PNUD; IPEA; FJP, 2016. https://1drv.ms/b/s!AuwEBH xVUoYSgbNZGjK6AIgz1ijfmQ?e=VjZxyR.

UNDP. "The Next Frontier: Human Development and the Anthropocene." *Human Development Report*, 2020. Accessed April 18, 2021. http://hdr.undp.org/sites/default/files/hdr2020.pdf,

UNGA. "A/RES/57/254 United Nations Decade of Education for Sustainable Development," *United Nations*, 2003. Accessed April 18, 2021. https://undocs.org/en/A/RES/57/254,

United Nations. "Convention on the Rights of the Child." *Office of the High Commissioner*, September 2, 1990. https://www.ohchr.org/EN/ProfessionalInterest/Pages/CRC.aspx.

United Nations. *Millennium Development Goals.* Geneva: United Nations, 2000. https://www.un.org/millenniumgoals/.

United Nations. *Sustainable Development Goals.* Geneva: United Nations, 2015. https://sdgs.un.org/#goal_section.

United Nations. *The Sustainable Development Goals Report 2020.* Geneva: United Nations, 2021. https://unstats.un.org/sdgs/report/2020/.

United Nations. *Youth and the 2030 Agenda for Sustainable Development: World Youth Report.* New York: NY, United Nations/UNDESA, 2018.

United Nations. *Youth Civic Engagement: World Youth Report.* New York: NY, United Nations/UNDESA, 2016.

United Nations Children's Fund (UNICEF). *Making Social Audit Work for Vietnam: Key Findings and Lessons Learned from a Pilot of Four Social Audit Tools.* London: England, ODI, 2011.

United Nations Development Programme (UNDP). *Guatemala Independent Country Programme Evaluation (ICPE).* New York, NY: UNDP/IEO, 2019.

United Nations Development Programme (UNDP). "Local Governance and Accountability and Transparency: Exploring Opportunities for a Post 2015 Agenda," in *Report on the Fourth Meeting of the Anti-Corruption Community of Practice in Latin America and the Caribbean.* Panama: UNDP Regional Center, 2014.

United Nations Educational, Scientific and Cultural Organization (UNESCO) and Child and Family Research Centre. "Understanding Youth Civic Engagement: Debates, Discourses and Lessons from Practice." Galway: Ireland, National University of Ireland, 2012.

United States Agency for International Development (USAID). *Guatemala: Country Development Cooperation Strategy (2012-2016)*. Guatemala: USAID, 2012.

United States Agency for International Development (USAID). *Youth in Development Policy: Realizing the Demographic Opportunity*. Washington, DC: USAID, October 2012.

United States Agency for International Development (USAID). *Youth Engagement in Development: Effective Approaches and Action-Oriented Recommendations for The Field*. Washington, DC, USAID, 2014.

University of Cambridge. "Democracy: Millennials Are the Most Disillusioned Generation 'in Living Memory' – Global Study." *EurekAlert!*, October 19, 2020. https://eurekalert.org/pub/releases/2020-10/uoc-dma101620.php.

University of Southern California's Race and Equity Center. "About Us." *USC*, 2020. https://race.usc.edu/about-us/.

Vaccaro, Annemarie. "Campus Microclimates for LGBT Faculty, Staff, and Students: An Exploration of the Intersections of Social Identity and Campus Roles." *Journal of Student Affairs Research and Practice* 49, no. 4 (2012): 429–446.

Vala, Carsten T. "Protestant Christianity and Civil Society in Authoritarian China: The Impact of Official Churches and Unregistered Urban Churches on Civil Society Development in the 2000s." *China Perspectives* 3 (2012): 43.

Valladares, Massiel. "Beyond the Bubble." *Beyond the Bubble*, 2020. Accessed October 10, 2020. https://massi98v.wixsite.com/beyondthebubble.

Valoy, Patricia. "Transnational Feminism: Why Feminist Activism Needs to Think Globally." *Everyday Feminism*, January 28, 2015. Accessed August 30, 2020. https://everydayfeminism.com/2015/01/why-we-need-transnational-feminism/.

van Deth, Jan W. "Interest in Politics," in *Continuities in Political Action: A Longitudinal Study of Political Orientations in Three Western Democracies*, eds. M. K. Jennings, Jan W. van Deth, Samuel H. Barnes, Dieter Fuchs, Felix Heunks, Ronald Inglehart, Max Kaase, Hans-Dieter Klingemann and Jacques J. A. Thomassen, 275–312. Berlin: De Gruyter, 1990.

Vande Berg, Michael. "Intervening in the Learning of U.S. Students Abroad." *Journal of Studies in International Education* 11, no. 4 (2007): 392–399.

Vande Berg, Michael, R. Michael Paige, and Kris Hemming Lou. *Student Learning Abroad: What Our Students are Learning, What They're Not, and What We Can Do About It*. Sterling, VA: Stylus Publishing, 2012.

Vandemoortele, Jan. "If Not the Millennium Development Goals, Then What?" *Third World Quarterly* 32, no. 1 (2011): 9–25.

VanVechten, Renée Bukovchik and Anita Chadha. "How Students Talk to Each Other: An Academic Social Networking Project," in *Teaching Civic Engagement: From Student to Active Citizen*, eds. Alison Rios Millett McCartney, Elizabeth A. Bennion, and Dick Simpson 167–187. Washington, DC: American Political Science Association Press, 2013.

Vassallo, Francesca. "Teaching Comparative Political Behavior in an Era of Digital Activism." *Journal of Political Science Education* 16, no. 3 (2020): 399–402.

Vavrus, Frances, Matthew Thomas, and Lesley Barlett. *Ensuring Quality by Attending to Inquiry: Learner-Centered Pedagogy in Sub-Saharan Africa*. Addis Ababa, Ethiopia: UNESCO-IICBA, 2011.

Ventura do Monte, Elizete. "UFPB em Números 2012-2019." *João Pessoa: EDUFPB*, 2020. Accessed April 18, 2021.

Verba, Sydney, Kay Lehman Schlozman, and Henry Brady. *Voice and Equality, Civic Voluntarism in American Politics*. Cambridge, MA: Harvard University Press, 1995.

Vercellotti, Tim and Elizabeth Matto. "The Kitchen-Table Connection: The Effects of Political Discussion on Youth Knowledge and Efficacy." *CIRCLE Working Paper #72*, 2010. Accessed August 26, 2020. https://files.eric.ed.gov/fulltext/ED512248.pdf.

Verjee, Begum. "Critical Race Feminism: A Transformative Vision for Service-Learning Engagement." *Journal of Community Engagement and Scholarship* 5, no. 1 (2012): 7.

Vernon, Keith. "Engagement, Estrangement or Divorce? The New Universities and Their Communities In The 1960s." *Contemporary British History* 31 no. 4 (2017): 501-523.

Vesa, Juho, and Anu Kantola. "Kuka Pääsee Mukaan? Miten Järjestöjen ääni Kuuluu Lakien Valmistelussa." (2016).

Vetter, Delaney. "'They Don't Let Me Finish My Sentences:' Conservative Students Share Their Experiences on a Liberal Campus." *The Beacon*, April 17, 2019. Accessed June 8, 2021. https://www.upbeacon.com/article/2019/04/conservatives-on-campus.

Villasenor, John. "Views Among College Students Regarding the First Amendment: Results from a New Survey." *Brookings Institution*, September 18, 2017. https://www.brookings.edu/blog/fixgov/2017/09/18/views-among-college-students-regarding-the-first-amendment-results-from-a-new-survey/.

Vincent, Andrew, and Raymond Plant. *Philosophy, Politics and Citizenship: The Life and Thought of the British Idealists*. Oxford, UK: Basil Blackwell, 1984.

Vogels, Emily A., Monica Anderson, Margaret Porteus, Chris Baronavski, Sara Atske, Colleen McClain, Brooke Auxier, Andrew Perrin, and Meera Ramshankar. "Americans and 'Cancel Culture:' Where Some See Accountability, Others See Censorship, Punishment." *Pew Research Center*, May 19, 2021. https://www.pewresearch.org/internet/2021/05/19/americans-and-cancel-culture-where-some-see-calls-for-accountability-others-see-censorship-punishment/.

Vormann, Boris, and Michael D. Weinman, eds. *The Emergence of Illiberalism: Understanding a Global Phenomenon.* London: Routledge, 2020.

Vorrath, Judith. "Post-Conflict Democratization: Pitfalls of External Influence." *CSS Analyses in Security Policy* 79 (2010).

Vromen, Ariadne, and Philippa Collin, "Everyday Youth Participation? Contrasting Views from Australian Policymakers and Young People." *Young* 18 (2010): 97–112.

Waitangi Tribunal Report. *He Whakaputanga me te Tiriti: the Declaration and the Treaty.* Wai 1040, 2014.

Walgrave, Stefaan, and Peter Van Aelst. "Political Agenda Setting and the Mass Media," in *Oxford Research Encyclopedia of Politics.* Oxford, UK: Oxford University Press, 2016.

Walker, Tim. "Education is Political': Neutrality in the Classroom Shortchanges Students." *National Education Association*, December 11, 2018. https://www.nea.org/advocating-for-change/new-from-nea/educationpolitical-neutrality-classroom-shortchanges-students.

Walsh, Lucas, Rosalyn Black, and Howard Prosser. "Young People's Perceptions of Power and Influence as a Basis for Understanding Contemporary Citizenship." *Journal of Youth Studies* 21 (2018): 218–234.

Wampler, Brian. "Expanding Accountability through Participatory Institutions: Mayors, Citizens, and Budgeting in Three Brazilian Municipalities." *Latin American Politics and Society* 46, no. 2 (2004): 73–99.

Wang, Zhengxu, and Weina Dai. "Women's Participation in Rural China: Institutional, Socioeconomic, and Cultural Factors in Jiangsu County." *Governance* 26, no. 1 (2013): 91–118.

Warren, Samantha. "Photography and Voice in Critical Qualitative Management Research." *Accounting, Auditing and Accountability Journal* 18, no. 6 (2009).

Watson, David. *Managing Civic and Community Engagement.* Maidenhead: Open University Press, 1987.

Watson, David, Robert Hollister, Susan E. Stroud and Elizabeth Babcock. *The Engaged University: International Perspectives on Civic Engagement.* London: Routledge, 2011.

Wattenberg, Martin P. *Is Voting for Young People* 5th edition. Abingdon, UK: Routledge, 2020.

Weber, Max. "Politics as a Vocation." in *From Max Weber: Essays in Sociology*, eds. H. H. Gerth and C. Wright Mills. London: Routledge, 1991.

Wedig, Timothy. "Getting the Most from Classroom Simulations: Strategies for Maximizing Learning Outcomes." *PS: Political Science & Politics* 43, no. 3 (2010): 547–555. https://doi.org/10.1017/S104909651000079X.

Wehling, Hans-Georg. "Konsens à la Beutelsbach? Nachlese zu einem Expertengespräch," in *Das Konsensproblem in der politischen Bildung*, eds. Siegfried Schiele and Schneider Herbert, 173–84. Stuttgart: Klett Verlag, 1977.

Weißeno, Georg, Eva Weschenfelder, and Monika Oberle. "Überzeugungen, Fachinteresse und Professionelles Wissen von Studierenden des Lehramts Politik," in *Empirische Forschung in Gesellschaftswissenschaftlichen Fachdidaktiken: Ergebnisse und Perspektiven*, eds. Georg Weißeno and Carla Schelle, 139–54. Wiesbaden: Springer Fachmedien Wiesbaden, 2015.

Weimer, David L., and Aidan R. Vining. *Policy Analysis: Concepts and Practice,* 6th edition. New York: Routledge, 2017.

Weinberg, James, and Matthew Flinders. "Learning for Democracy: The Politics and Practice of Citizenship Education." *British Educational Research Journal* 44, no. 4 (2018): 573–592.

Weiss, Meredith L. "Intellectual Containment: The Muting of Students in Semidemocratic Southeast Asia." *Critical Asian Studies* 41, no. 4 (2009): 499–522.

Weiss, Meredith L. *The Roots of Resilience: Party Machines and Grassroots Politics in Southeast Asia.* Ithaca, NY: Cornell University Press, 2020.

Welch, Marshall. "Identifying and Teaching Civic Engagement Skills through Service Learning," in *Higher Education and Civic Engagement: International Perspectives*, eds. Iain Mac Labhrainn and Lorraine McIlrath. Hampshire, UK: Ashgate, 2007.

Welch, Penny. "Thinking about Teaching Politics." *Politics* 20, no. 2 (2000): 99–104.

Wells, Dominic D. "You All Made Dank Memes: Using Internet Memes to Promote Critical Thinking." *Journal of Political Science Education* 14, no. 4 (2018): 240–248.

Westheimer, Joel. "Civic Education and the Rise of Populist Nationalism." *Peabody Journal of Education* 94, no. 1 (2019): 4–16.

Westheimer, Joel and Joseph Kahne. "Educating the 'Good' Citizen: Political Choices and Pedagogical Tools." *PS: Political*

Science & Politics 37, no. 2 (2004): 241–47.

Westheimer, Joel, and Joseph Kahne. "What Kind of Citizen? The Politics of Educating for Democracy." *American Educational Research Journal* 41, no. 2 (2004): 237–69.

Wetterberg, Anna, Brinkerhoff, Derick W. and. Hertz, Jana C. ed. *Governance and Service Delivery Practical Applications of Social Accountability Across Sectors.* Research Triangle Park, NC: RTI International, 2016.

Whiteley, Paul. "Does Citizenship Education Work? Evidence from a Decade of Citizenship Education in Secondary Schools in England." *Parliamentary Affairs* 67, no. 3 (2014): 513–535.

WHO. "Depression and Other Common Mental Disorders Global Health Estimates." *World Health Organization,* 2017. https://apps.who.int/iris/bitstream/handle/10665/254610/WHO-MSD-MER-2017.2-eng. pdf;jsessionid=EB34AFA4AF067816FE69C784A4A75D85?sequence=1.

Wike, Richard, Laura Silver, Shannon Schumacher, and Aidan Connaughton. "Many in U.S., Western Europe Say Their Political System Needs Reform." *The Pew Research Center*, March 31, 2021. https://www.pewresearch.org/global/2021/03/31/many-in-us-western-europe-say-their-political-system-needs-major-reform/.

Wilke, Richard, Laura Silver and Alexandra Castillo. "Many Across the Globe Are Dissatisfied With How Democracy Is Working." Washington DC: Pew Research Center, 2017. https://pewresearch.org/2019/04/29/many-across-the-globe-are-dissatisfied-with-how-democracy-is-working/.

Willoughby-Herard, Tiffany. "Conferencing is Not a Luxury and Neither is the Scholarly Life of Our Future Colleagues." *PS: Political Science & Politics* 53, no. 1 (2020): 146–8.

Wilson, Brent, and Marjorie Wilson. "Pictorial Composition and Narrative Structure: Themes and the Creation of Meaning in the Drawings of Egyptian and Japanese Children." *Visual Arts Research* 13, no. 2 (1987).

Winberg, Christine, Penelope Engel-Hills, James Garraway, and Cecilia Jacobs. *Work-integrated Learning: Good Practice Guide–HE Monitor No. 12.* Pretoria: Council on Higher Education (CHE), 2011. https://www.academia.edu/10020069/CHE_Winberg_C_Garraway_J_Engel_Hills_P_and_Jacobs_C_2011_Work_integrated_learning_Good_Practice_Guide_HE_Monitor_No_12_August_2011.

Wittmann, Barbara, "Drawing Cure: Children's Drawings as a Psychoanalytic Instrument." *Configurations* 18, no. 3 (2010).

Woessner, Matthew and April Kelly-Woessner. "Why College Students Drift Left: The Stability of Political Identity and Relative Malleability of Issue Positions among College Students." *PS: Political Science & Politics* 53, no. 4 (2020): 657–664.

Wokler, Robert. "The Professoriate of Political Thought in England Since 1914: A Tale of Three Chairs," in *The History of Political Thought in National Context*, eds. Dario Castiglione and Iain Hampsher-Monk, 134–158. Cambridge, UK: Cambridge University Press, 2001.

Wolflink, Alena. "Learning to Globalise: Socrates, US Education Abroad, and the Boundaries of Citizenship." *Globalisation, Societies and Education* 16, no. 1 (2018): 106–119.

Woodall, Gina Serignese, and Tara M. Lennon. "Using Twitter to Promote Classroom and Civic Engagement," in *Teaching Civic Engagement Across the Disciplines*, eds. Elizabeth C. Matto, Alison Rios Millett McCartney, Elizabeth A. Bennion, and Dick Simpson, 135–150. Washington, DC: American Political Science Association, 2017.

World Bank. "GDP per Capita (Current US$)." Accessed April 18, 2021. https://data.worldbank.org/indicator/NY.GDP.PCAP.CD.

World Bank. "World Bank Country and Lending Groups." *The World Bank*, 2021. https://datahelpdesk.worldbank.org/knowledgebase/articles/906519-world-bank-country-and-lending-groups.

World Economic Forum. *These Are the World's Most Fragile States in 2019.* https://www.weforum.org/agenda/2019/04/most-fragile-states-in-2019-yemen/.

World Population Review. *Human Trafficking by State, 2020.* Accessed October 12, 2020. Retrieved from: https://worldpopulationreview.com/state-rankings/human-trafficking-statistics-by-state.

Wright, Suzanne. "Graphic-narrative Play: Young Children's Authoring through Drawing and Telling," *International Journal of Education and the Arts* 8, no. 8 (2007).

Xie, Yihui. "Making Change with the Social Impact Fellowship." *The Octant*, November 19, 2019. https://theoctant.org/edition/issue/allposts/features/making-change-with-the-social-impact-fellowship/.

Ximenes, Salomão, and Fernanda Vick. "A Extinção Judicial do Escola sem Partido." *Le Monde Diplomatique Brasil*, July 1, 2020. https://diplomatique.org.br/a-extincao-judicial-do-escola-sem-partido/.

Xinhuanet. "'行动者联盟2019公益盛典'举行 ('Action League 2019 Charity Ceremony' was held')." *Xinhua News*, 2019. http://www.xinhuanet.com/gongyi/2019-12/09/c_1210388394.htm.

Yale-NUS College. *Creating a New Community of Learning: Year in Review 2014.* Singapore: Yale-NUS College, 2014.

Yale-NUS College. "Intergroup Dialogue." *Yale-NUS College Student Life.* Accessed June 8, 2021. https://studentlife.yale-nus.

edu.sg/intercultural-engagement/intergroup-dialogue/.

Yan, Xiaojun. "Engineering Stability: Authoritarian Political Control Over University Students in Post-Deng China." *The China Quarterly* (2014): 493–513.

Yang, Daryl. "How to Make a Difference to the World: Yale-NUS Students Learn All about Social Impact Work." *Yale-NUS College Newsroom*, July 10, 2018. Accessed June 8, 2021. https://www.yale-nus.edu.sg/newsroom/10-july-2018-how-to-make-a-difference-to-the-world-yale-nus-students-learn-all-about-social-impact-work/.

Yang, Gloria. "Racism Today Versus Racism After 9/11." *Berkeley Political Review*, October 30, 2017. https://bpr.berkeley.edu/2017/10/30/racism-today-versus-racism-after-911/.

Ye, Yinjiao, Ping Xu, and Mingxin Zhang. "Social Media, Public Discourse and Civic Engagement in Modern China." *Telematics and Informatics* 34, no. 3 (2017): 705–714.

Yep, Kathleen S., and Tania D. Mitchell. "Decolonizing Community Engagement: Reimagining Service Learning through an Ethnic Studies Lens," in *The Cambridge Handbook of Service Learning and Community Engagement,* 294–303. Cambridge University Press, 2017. https://doi.org/10.1017/9781316650011.028.

Yew, Wei Lit. "Matrix of Free Spaces in China: Mobilizing Citizens and the Law through Digital and Organizational Spaces." *International Journal of Communication* 13 (2019): 3341–3360.

Yin, Robert. *Case Study Research And Applications: Design And Methods* 6th edition. London: Sage, 2018.

Yip, Jia Qi. "Posters, Town Halls, Angry Opinion Articles: Dissent and Disagreement at Yale-NUS." *The Octant*, March 18, 2019. Accessed June 8, 2021. https://theoctant.org/edition/issue/news/posters-town-halls-angry-opinion-articles-dissent-and-disagreement-at-yale-nus/.

Yip, Jie Ying. "Frustrated At College Administration, Yale-NUS Students Stage Sit-In Protest." *The Octant*, March 15, 2018. Accessed June 8, 2021. https://theoctant.org/edition/ix-6/news/frustrated-college-administration-yale-nus-students-stage-sit-protest/.

Young, Dannagal G., Matthew A. Baum, and Duncan Prettyman. "VMobilize: Gamifying Civic Learning and Political Engagement in a Classroom Context." *Journal of Political Science Education* 17, no. 1 (2021): 32–54.

Young, Iris Marion. *Responsibility for Justice.* Oxford and New York: Oxford University Press, 2011.

Youniss, James, Susan Bales, Verona Christmas-Beat, Marcelo Diversi, Millbrey Mclaughlin, and Rainer Silbereisen. "Youth Civic Engagement in the Twenty-First Century." *Journal of Research on Adolescence* 12, no. 1: 121–148.

Youth Power Learning. *Promising Practices in Engaging Youth in Peace and Security: Summary of Key Interventions and Examples.* Washington, DC: USAID/PEPFAR/Youth Power Learning, 2016.

Yuen, Samson. "Friend or Foe? The Diminishing Space of China's Civil Society." *China Perspectives* 3 (2015): 51–56.

Yuen, Sin. "MHA Says Foreign Sponsors Not Allowed for Pink Dot, or Other Events, at Speakers' Corner." *The Straits Times*, June 7, 2016. https://www.straitstimes.com/singapore/mha-says-foreign-sponsors-not-allowed-for-pink-dot-or-other-events-at-speakers-corner.

Yuen, Timothy Wai Wa, and Yan Wing Leung. "Political Education: Controversial Issues, Neutrality of Teachers and Merits of Team Teaching." *Citizenship, Social and Economics Education* 8, no. 2–3 (2009): 99–114. doi: 10.2304/csee.2010.8.2.99.

Zaller, John. *The Nature and Origins of Mass Opinion.* Cambridge: Cambridge University Press, 1992.

Zamboni, Yves. "Participatory Budgeting and Local Governance: An Evidence-based Evaluation of Participatory Budgeting Experiences in Brazil." Working Paper, Bristol University, 2007.

Zappile, Tina M., Daniel J. Beers, and Chad Raymond. "Promoting Global Empathy and Engagement through Real-Time Problem-Based Simulations." *International Studies Perspectives* 18 (2017): 194.

Ziai, Aram. "Postcolonial Perspectives on 'Development.'" *Peripherie* 120 (2010): 399–426.

Zohar, Danah. *Rewiring the Corporate Brain: Using the New Science to Rethink How We Structure and Lead Organizations.* San Francisco, CA: Berrett-Koehler Publishers, 1997.

Zuboff, Shoshana. *In the Age of the Smart Machine: The Future of Work and Power.* New York, NY: Basic Books, 1988.

About the Authors

Mariana Pimenta Oliveira Baccarini

Mariana Baccarini is a professor at the Federal University of Paraíba, based at the Department of International Relations. Mariana holds a PhD in political science from UFMG (2014). She is a teacher in the Undergraduate Course in International Relations and in the Post-Graduate Course in Political Science and International Relations. She has experience in the field of political science, working mainly on the following topics: international institutions, institutional change, feminism. She is the Coordinator of Interna-só-na-mente Political Theater Group, and is a mother of two.

Sondré Bailey

Sondré Bailey currently works as a researcher for an NGO called Gender Dynamix. She has worked in the NGO sphere for the past five years, advocating for basic human rights. She has completed her BAdmin degree, majoring in political studies and public administration, as well as her honors degree in political studies. She is also in the process of completing her MAdmin in political studies. In her free time, she enjoys many outdoor activities, exploring as much of South Africa as she can.

Emily Beausoleil

As a political theorist, Emily Beausoleil explores the conditions, challenges, and possibilities of democratic engagement in diverse societies, with a particular attention to the capacity for 'voice' and listening in conditions of inequality. Connecting affect, democratic theory, neuroscience, and the performing arts, her work responds to compelling calls to find new models for coalition and community by asking how we realize these ideals in concrete terms. She is editor-in-chief for *Democratic Theory Journal*, Distinguished Global Associate of the Sydney Democracy Network, and associate investigator for the current Australian Research Centre grant 'Democratic Resilience: The Public Sphere and Extremist Attacks.' Current community collaborations include co-design of a nationwide anti-racism program Tauiwi Tautoko and creation of a UNESCO-funded project to support youth-led dialogue post-March 15th Christchurch attacks. Her work has been published in *Political Theory, Contemporary Political Theory, Constellations, Conflict Resolution Quarterly*, and *Ethics & Global Politics*, as well as various books.

Elizabeth A. Bennion

Dr. Elizabeth Bennion is Chancellor's Professor of Political Science and American Democracy Project Director at Indiana University South Bend. A nationally recognized expert on civic education and engagement, Professor Bennion has won numerous local, state, and national awards for her teaching, research, and service. With over 80 publications, 200 invited presentations, and 600 media appearances, Bennion is committed to sharing her research and teaching beyond the classroom. Bennion is Director of Voter Services for the local League of Women Voters, president of the Indiana Debate Commission, and host of WNIT Public Television's weekly program *Politically Speaking*. A frequent speaker at community events, academic conferences, and college campuses, Bennion is cofounder of APSA's Civic Engagement Section, co-PI for several national surveys and field experiments, and coeditor of two previous books on teaching civic engagement: *Teaching Civic Engagement: From Student to Active Citizen* (2013) and *Teaching Civic Engagement Across the Disciplines* (2017).

Gerardo Berthin

Mr. Gerardo Berthin is currently the director for Latin America and Caribbean Programs at Freedom House in Washington, DC. Prior to joining Freedom House, he worked as a Senior Adviser on Democratic Governance at Tetra Tech, one of the largest consulting firms in the United States. From 2009–2014, Mr. Berthin served as the Governance and Decentralization Policy Adviser at the UNDP Service Center for Latin America and the Caribbean in Panama. Gerardo Berthin is a political scientist with work experience in in 40 countries in Africa, Latin America, the Caribbean, and Central and Eastern Europe. Mr. Berthin holds two master's Degrees: one in political science from the University of Chicago, and the other in Latin American Studies from Georgetown University. In addition, he has a certificate from Harvard University's JFK School of Government for Leaders in Development to Manage Political and Economic Reform.

Alasdair Blair

Alasdair Blair is Associate Pro Vice-Chancellor Academic and Jean Monnet Professor of International Relations at De Montfort University. He is a is a National Teaching Fellow, a principal fellow of the Higher Education Academy, a fellow of the Chartered Management Institute, a fellow of the Royal Historical Society, and a Certified Management and Business Educator. He has been editor of *European Political Science* since 2015 and served as reviews editor of European Foreign Affairs Review from 2002–2016. He also served as Honorary Treasurer of the UK Political Studies Association from 2015–2018. Alasdair's research interests include higher education, civic engagement, and European integration/international relations. His current projects include the 3rd edition of *The European Union since 1945* (Routledge, 2022) and a 2nd edition of *International Politics* (Edinburgh University Press, 2022).

Theodore Chadjipadelis

Theodore Chadjipadelis is a professor of applied statistics and the director of the Laboratory of Applied Political Research since 2001. He has taught undergraduate and postgraduate courses on methodology, electoral geography, decisions theory, teaching and learning statistics and social sciences at the Aristotle University and the Hellenic Open University. His research interests cover the fields of applied statistics, educational systems, teaching and learning statistics and social sciences, public opinion, political, social and electoral behavior, and urban and regional planning. He has published more than 150 papers and books. He has participated in more than 100 conferences, in many of them as member of the scientific and/or organizing committee. He served in many positions in the University and in public administration. He is head of the Committee for Control of Public Surveys, vice president of the Greek Data Analysis Society and director of the Observatory for Democracy in the Balkans.

Mark Charlton

Mark Charlton is Associate Director of Public Engagement at De Montfort University and the university lead for United Nations Academic Impact Hub for SDG 16. He is passionate about civic engagement education and learning-linked volunteering and all the other ways we describe students sharing their skills and knowledge beyond the campus. As a PhD scholar he is researching the impacts of civic engagement on students' political participation. Mark's broader research interests include the examination of policies that encourage public good in higher education and university strategies for tackling social exclusion in local communities. He has presented his work at international conferences, including the ECPR General Conference and the APSA TLC.

Suzanne M. Chod

Dr. Suzanne Chod is a professor of political science and coordinator of the Gender and Sexuality Studies Program at North Central College in Naperville, IL. Dr. Chod teaches classes in American political institutions, parties, campaigns, and elections, as well as courses focused on women in American politics and research methods. While her early conference and published work was in the area of Congress, specifically the House of Representatives, her current research examines pedagogy, the use of technology in college classrooms to foster civic engagement, and how to increase political efficacy of young people. Dr. Chod also contributes public-facing scholarship with op-eds and a monthly blog.

John Craig

John Craig (PhD, University of Leeds) is professor of politics and dean of Leeds School of Social Sciences at Leeds Beckett University in Yorkshire, England. He is a Trustee of the Political Studies Association (PSA) and co-chair of the PSA's Teaching and Learning Network. In 2009 he was awarded a National Teaching Fellowship. He is a member of the editorial board for the *Journal of Political Science Education* and is currently researching the development of political science as a taught discipline.

Johannes Diesing

Johannes Diesing studied political science and philosophy at the University of Rostock and has a PhD in political sciences from the University of Rostock. He is currently working as a postdoctoral researcher at the Professorship for Germany's Political and Social System/Comparing Political Systems at Justus-Liebig University of Giessen.

Sharon Feeney

Dr. Sharon Feeney is Head of Learning Development, Technological University, Dublin. She is a Chartered Director, and is a board member of the Higher Education Authority (in the role of deputy chair from 2016–2020) and is chair of the Audit and Risk Committee (2016–2021). She is also a board member of the National Forum for the Enhancement of Teaching and Learning in Higher Education (2019–2024) and is a member of their Finance Committee (as an expert in governance). She is an organizational psychologist by profession and her research interests focus on higher education policy at the institutional, national, and international levels. She is involved in research projects that focus on learning and teaching methods in higher education (particularly the use of student generated drawings), and higher education policy.

Abraham Goldberg

Abraham Goldberg is the inaugural executive director of the James Madison Center for Civic Engagement, a nonpartisan academic entity at James Madison University with a mission to educate and inspire people to address public issues and cultivate a just and inclusive democracy. He is also an associate professor of political science. Prior to arriving at JMU in 2017, he was the director of the Office of Service-Learning and Community Engagement at the University of South Carolina Upstate. Abe recently coauthored a chapter in *Democracy, Civic Engagement, and Citizenship in Higher Education: Reclaiming Our Civic Purpose* with JMU President Jonathan Alger. He has also written extensively about how the built environment of urban places and the accessibility of community amenities contributes to the social connectivity, health, and happiness of residents, as found in *Social Science and Medicine, Urban Design and Planning, Urban Affairs Review*, and *Journal of Urbanism*.

John Hogan

John Hogan is a Senior Research Fellow and Lecturer at the College of Business, Technological University Dublin, Ireland. Widely published, he has edited several volumes, including *Policy Paradigms in Theory and Practice* (Palgrave Macmillan, 2015) with Michael Howlett and *Policy Analysis in Ireland* (Policy Press, 2021). He is coauthor of *Regulating Lobbying: A Global Comparison* (Manchester University Press, 2010; 2019). He has served on the boards of a number of Policy Studies Organization journals. A former chair of the Midwest Political Science Association's Comparative Policy Section, he has mainly researched the nature of policy change and global lobbying regulations. He has advised the Irish government, and several other European governments, on matter to do with lobbying regulation and governmental transparency and accountability.

Shantal Kaurooa

Shantal Kaurooa received a bachelor's degree in political science with specialization in public administration from the University of Mauritius. She is currently pursuing her Master of Public Policy and Administration at the same institution. Her research project focuses on the importance of civic education in the school curriculum in the interest of upholding her country's democratic ideals since civic education is not prioritized as a subject in Mauritius. She has presented her work in the UOM Research Week. Shantal is a strong believer in "writing to learn" and wants to explore new horizons in her researching career. As such, she is passionate about research studies in social sciences, politics, democracy and policy making and hopes to enroll in MPhil/PhD studies in the future.

B. Philipp Kleer

B. Philipp Kleer is a doctoral research associate in the department of political science (chair of empirical research methods) at Justus-Liebig-University Giessen. Previously, he studied political science at the University of Vienna (MA) and Social Sciences at the University of Cologne (BSc). His research and teaching focus on political support, political attitudes/value orientations, political socialization processes, and quantitative methods.

Dmitry Lanko

Dmitry A. Lanko, PhD (comparative politics), is associate professor at the Department of European Studies, School of International Relations, St. Petersburg State University, Russia. He is currently program co-chair of the Cross-Border Double Degree Master's program in international relations, jointly implemented by the St. Petersburg State University, the Tampere University, Finland, and the Petrozavodsk State University, Russia. He is also a research fellow at the Centre for Modernization Studies of the European University in St. Petersburg. For multiple years, he has been with the Joint Russian-Finnish Commission on the Utilization of Frontier Waters, and with the Joint Russian-Estonian Commission on the Protection and Sustainable Utilization of Trans-Boundary Waters. His research interests focus on Russian foreign policy, nexus between modernization and international relations in Europe, environmental cooperation and political science pedagogy.

Debora Lopreite

Debora Lopreite holds a PhD in public policy from Carleton University, Ottawa, Canada and a MA and BA in political science from the University of Buenos Aires. Currently Debora is a professor at the University of Buenos Aires. She has published several articles in peer-reviewed journals about gender policy in Latin America. Her current research projects focus on the Argentinean gender regime changes—particularly on violence and abortion—and women in cabinets in Latin America.

Elizabeth C. Matto

Elizabeth C. Matto is an associate research professor at the Eagleton Institute of Politics at Rutgers University and the director of the Institute's Center for Youth Political Participation (CYPP). She earned her doctorate in American politics at George Washington University and, prior to her work at Eagleton, taught a variety of courses at Princeton University, Temple University, and George Washington University. As director of CYPP, Matto leads research as well as educational and public service efforts designed to encourage and support the political learning of high school and college students and civic action among young adults. In 2016, she was the recipient of the Craig L. Brians Award for Excellence in Undergraduate Research & Mentorship by the American Political Science Association.

Alison Rios Millett McCartney

Alison Rios Millett McCartney (PhD, University of Virginia) is professor of political science and faculty director of the Towson University Honors College in Towson, Maryland, USA. Coeditor of *Teaching Civic Engagement Across the Disciplines* (2017) and *Teaching Civic Engagement: From Student to Active Citizen* (2013) and cofounder of the International Service-Learning Network, she has published widely and conducted many presentations and webinars on civic engagement education. Dr. McCartney received the P20 Partnership Award from Campus Compact Mid-Atlantic, the University of Maryland Board of Regents Faculty Award for Mentoring, the TU Presidential BTU community engagement award, the TU Outstanding Service-Learning Faculty award, and the APSA Political Science Education Section Distinguished Service award. She is a member of the *Journal of Political Science Education* editorial board, the Steering Committee of the AAC&U American Democracy Project, the Maryland Collegiate Honors Council Executive Board, is co-creator of the Towson University-Baltimore County Model United Nations conference, a free civic engagement and global learning program for local youth, and serves as a consultant on civic engagement pedagogy.

Henrique Zeferino de Menezes

Henrique Menezes is a senior lecturer at the Department of International Relations and the Postgraduate Program in Political Science and International Relations at the Federal University of Paraíba, Brazil. He is the coordinator of the university's Center of Public Policies and Sustainable Development (NPDS). He finished his PhD in political science at the State University of Campinas, Brazil. His research focuses on the international political economy and international cooperation. He has published some research articles in recognized academic journals, and recently published two books in Brazil on the US international political economy and intellectual property and development.

Niina Meriläinen

Niina Meriläinen (PhD) works as a researcher at Tampere University (Finland) in the Department of Social Sciences. Currently her research is funded by Helsingin Sanomat Foundation. Niina specializes in critical multidisciplinary research on agenda setting/vetting, framing, narratives, power relations and human rights. During her career of over 10 years, Niina has worked in numerous national and international research projects as well as a researcher in Finland and in Germany. She has been part of various national and international research funding application processes. Her critical research focused on various human rights areas and societal & political participation of vocational school students and user-based design of digital interactive technologies, just to name a few. At the center of all Niina's theoretical and empirical research are power relations in societal and political decision-making and participation.

Xaman Minillo

Xaman Minillo is an assistant professor at the Department of International Relations at the Federal University of Paraíba. Before that she worked at the Japan International Cooperation Agency (JICA) monitoring and evaluating international development cooperation projects. Xaman is a mentor in the female mentorship program Alma Mater/Alumna. She is also a member of the MulheRIs collective, working towards promoting gender equality in Brazilian IR academia. Currently she is working on her PhD at the University of Bristol researching Zimbabwean LGBTIQ activisms as a route to enacting citizenship. Her research interests are in sexual citizenship, African LGBTIQ activisms, politics of the Global South, and development. Xaman is a cancer survivor seeking to enjoy a healthy and happy life.

William Muck

William Muck is professor of political science, chair of the Political Science Department, and coordinator of the Global Studies program at North Central College. He teaches a variety of courses on international politics and foreign policy. His scholarship focuses on international security, the practice of military intervention, and the pedagogy of promoting civic engagement. He has been active in presenting research at various international studies conferences around the world. In 2018, Bill was named a Ruge Fellow by North Central College for his contributions to teaching and learning on campus. He is coauthor of the book, *Technology and Civic Engagement in the College Classroom* as well as other articles on international security and higher education pedagogy. You can also listen to Bill on his weekly podcast, *The Politics Lab*.

Carah Ong Whaley

Dr. Carah Ong Whaley is associate director of the James Madison Center for Civic Engagement at James Madison University where she works in partnership with students, faculty, staff and community partners to embed civic learning and democratic engagement across campus through curricular and cocurricular programming. Carah currently serves as the vice chair of the Civic Engagement Section of the American Political Science Association. Carah has developed innovative pedagogy, melding scholarship and experiential learning to teach courses on civic engagement, campaigns and elections, and state and local politics. At the heart of her research interests is a desire to understand and illuminate how the interactions of political actors and institutions structure public access and participation in policy- and decision-making processes. Recent research and publications include *American Government: Roots and Reform* (chapters on Political Parties, Campaigns, Elections and Voting, and The Media).

Candice D. Ortbals

Candice D. Ortbals is professor of political science and University Scholar at Abilene Christian University. Her publications pertain to gender and terrorism, gender and politics in Spain, and qualitative methods. She has coauthored *Why Don't Women Rule the World? Understanding Women's Civic and Political Choices* (2019) and *Gender and Political Violence: Women Changing the Politics of Terrorism* (2018). She has been the newsletter editor, president-elect, and president of the Women's Caucus of the Midwest Political Science Association. She also served as president for the National Women's Caucus of Political Science. She has taught at the University of Seville, and she was winner of the Carrie Chapman Catt Prize for Research on Women and Politics. She also has received numerous grants from the government of Spain to study women in regional and local government.

Georgia Panagiotidou

Dr. Georgia Panagiotidou is a political scientist specializing in applied political analysis and research. She teaches as a lecturer on contract in the Department of Political Science of the Aristotle University of Thessaloniki as well as in the postgraduate program "Governance and Regional Development." Her research interests and activities are focused on the analysis of political, electoral behavior and political competition, quantitative and qualitative methodology in social sciences, data analysis, development of voting prediction models, political marketing, and civic education. She has participated in research of the laboratory of applied political analysis, focusing on the political behavior of young people, attitudes, and political behavior of the electorate. She has participated in international scientific conferences as, journals and collective volumes. In the past she has worked as a technical consultant of local government for European programs, and as business analyst and revenue manager for ELLINAIR SA airline.

Robyn Pasensie

Robyn Pasensie is a postgraduate student in the Political Studies Department at the University of the Western Cape. Her focus areas are race and political violence with a special interest in community work and social justice.

Lynn Pasquerella

Lynn Pasquerella was appointed president of the Association of American Colleges and Universities in 2016, after serving as the eighteenth president of Mount Holyoke College. She has held positions as provost at the University of Hartford and Vice Provost for Academic Affairs and Dean of the Graduate School at the University of Rhode Island. A philosopher whose work has combined teaching and scholarship with local and global engagement, Pasquerella has written extensively on medical ethics, metaphysics, public policy, and the philosophy of law. She is president of the Phi Beta Kappa Society and the host of Northeast Public Radio's *The Academic Minute*. A recipient of Mary Baldwin University's Sullivan Award for outstanding service to humanity, Pasquerella serves as a member of the advisory board of the Newman's Own Foundation and sits on the boards of the Lingnan Foundation and the National Humanities Alliance, as well as George Washington University Hospital's ethics committee. Named by *Diverse Issue* as one of higher education's top 35 leaders, Pasquerella is a graduate of Quinebaug Valley Community College, Mount Holyoke College, and Brown University. Pasquerella has also received honorary doctorates from Elizabethtown College, Bishop's University, the University of South Florida, the University of Hartford, and the University of Rhode Island.

Dena A. Pastor

Dena A. Pastor is a professor of graduate psychology and associate director of assessment operations at James Madison University. She provides assessment consultation to the James Madison Center for Civic Engagement and has provided several presentations, workshops, and webinars on the topic of civic engagement assessment. She teaches courses in multilevel modeling, categorical data analysis, and data management and her research applies statistical and psychometric techniques to the modeling and measurement of college student learning and development.

Laurence Piper

Laurence Piper is a political scientist at the University of the Western Cape interested in urban governance, democracy, and informality in South Africa and comparatively. His latest book is *Democracy Disconnected: Participation and Governance in a City of the South* (Routledge, 2019), with Dr. Fiona Anciano. He is the previous president of the South African Association of Political Studies (SAAPS) 2016–8.

Lori M. Poloni-Staudinger

Lori M. Poloni-Staudinger (PhD, Indiana University, 2005) is interim dean in the College of Social and Behavioral Sciences at Northern Arizona University and a professor in the department of Politics and International Affairs. She previously served as department chair and most recently as associate dean for research, personnel, and graduate programs. Her research and publications focus on social movements, political contention and political institutions, mainly in Western Europe. The author of five books and dozens of articles, book chapters and reports, her recent work is situated in two strains of inquiry, gender and political violence and gender and political ambition. She has most recently published *Why Don't Women Rule the World: Understanding Women's Civic and Political Choices* and *American Difference: A Guide to American Politics from a Comparative Perspective* both with CQ-Sage Press as well as *Gender and Political Violence: Women Changing the Politics of Terrorism* with Springer Press. She was a Distinguished Fulbright Fellow at the Diplomatic Academy in Vienna, Austria and has served as a consultant for the Organization for Security and Co-operation in Europe. She also taught at University of the Basque Country in San Sebastian, Spain. She served as treasurer, vice president, and president of the Women's Caucus for the Midwest Political Science Association. Lori is a Kettering Foundation Fellow and also serves as vice president of a school board and president of a 2000-member nonprofit board in Flagstaff, Arizona.

Catherine Shea Sanger

Dr. Catherine Shea Sanger is Director of the Centre for Teaching and Learning and Senior Lecturer in Global Affairs at Yale-NUS College. She is co-editor of *Diversity and Inclusion in Global Higher Education: Lessons from Across Asia* (Palgrave, 2020), and has published in the *Chronicle of Higher Education*, *Times Higher Education*, and *Faculty Focus*. In 2021, Dr. Sanger founded Intentional Higher Education, which offers faculty development, research, and consulting services to higher education institutions and professionals. She holds a PhD in International Affairs from the University of Virginia and a BA from Wellesley College.

Aminata Sillah

Dr. Aminata Sillah is an assistant professor of political science in the Department of Political Science at Towson University. Her current research focuses on urban government and politics, international development, public administration, community development and civic engagement.

Dick Simpson

Dick Simpson has uniquely combined a distinguished academic career with public service in government. He is a former Chicago alderman and candidate for US Congress. He has published widely, been an outstanding teacher, and affected public policy. He began his academic career at the University of Illinois at Chicago in 1967 where he has taught for more than 50 years. At UIC he received the highest awards given for teaching and the American Political Science Association (APSA) and Pi Sigma Alpha National Award for Outstanding Teaching. He is a former Department Head from 2006–2012 and currently professor of political science. He has published more than 25 books and over 200 journal, magazine, and newspaper articles and op-eds. He has served on a dozen transition teams for government officials and is a frequent media commentator.

Steven Rathgeb Smith

Steven Rathgeb Smith is the executive director of the American Political Science Association and adjunct professor at the McCourt School of Public Policy at Georgetown University. Previously, he taught at several universities including the University of Washington where he was the Nancy Bell Evans Professor at the Evans School of Public Policy and Governance and director of the Nancy Bell

Evans Center for Nonprofits & Philanthropy. He is a past president of the Association for Research on Nonprofit Organizations and Voluntary Action and formerly editor of the association's journal, *Nonprofit and Voluntary Sector Quarterly*. He is the author of several books including most recently, *The Changing Dynamic of Government–Nonprofit Relationships: Advancing the Field(s)* (with Kirsten A. Gronbjerg), Cambridge University Press, 2021.

Sheetal Sheena Sookrajowa

Sheetal Sheena Sookrajowa is a lecturer in political science in the Department of History and Political Science at the University of Mauritius. Her main research interests are ethnicity, political parties, elections, voting behavior, migration, and public policy.

J. Cherie Strachan

J. Cherie Strachan is professor of political science and author of the recent Sage-CQ textbook, *Why Don't Women Rule the World*, as well as over 30 reviewed and invited articles and book chapters. Her applied research addresses partisan polarization, political civility, and engagement pedagogy—especially opportunities for student learning in deliberative forums and in campus student organizations. She currently serves as the review editor for the *Journal of Political Science Education* and is the cofounder and codirector of the Consortium for Inter-Campus SoTL Research (CISR), which facilitates multi-campus data collection to assess campus civic engagement initiatives. She can be reached at strachanjc@vcu.edu.

Taiyi Sun

Dr. Taiyi Sun is an assistant professor of political science at Christopher Newport University. His research interests include Chinese politics, disaster politics, civil society, civic engagement, international political economy, and Sino-US relations. His work has appeared in *PS: Political Science & Politics*, *Politics and Society*, the *China Quarterly*, *China Information*, *Journal of Chinese Political Science*, *Made in China*, *Japan Studies*, Routledge, and Australia National University Press. Taiyi is the US new media coordinator of the Global Forum of Chinese Political Scientists and is the executive editor of its main publication, *Global China* (海外看世界). As a member of Phi Beta Kappa, he received his BA in politics & government and business administration from Ripon College in Ripon, Wisconsin, and MA in international affairs from American University School of International Service, Washington DC, and PhD in political science from Boston University.

Claire Timperley

Claire Timperley is a lecturer in political science at Te Herenga Waka—Victoria University of Wellington, New Zealand. Her teaching and research interests include feminist political theory, gender politics, critical pedagogy, and the politics of Aotearoa New Zealand. Her articles have appeared in *Politics, Groups and Identities*, *Contemporary Political Theory*, *International Studies Perspectives* and *PS: Political Science & Politics*. Her coedited book *Government and Politics in Aotearoa New Zealand* was published by Oxford University Press in 2021.

Celia Valiente

Celia Valiente is professor of sociology at the Universidad Carlos III de Madrid, Spain. Her main research interests are the women's movement and gender equality policies in Spain from a comparative perspective. Her research has been published by: *British Journal of Sociology*; *European Journal of Political Research*; *European Political Science Review*; *Gender & Society*; *International Journal of the History of Sport*; *International Review for the Sociology of Sport*; *Politics & Gender*; *Research in Social Movements, Conflicts and Change*; *Social Movement Studies*; *Social Science Research*; *South European Society & Politics*; *Sport in Society*, and *Women's Studies International Forum*.

Nicole Webster

Nicole Webster is an associate professor at the Pennsylvania State University with over 15 years of academic research and teaching experience in both formal and nonformal sectors across the African and Caribbean diasporas. Her research primarily focuses on understanding the impact of civic engagement experiences on the economic, social, and personal development of youth and young adults in historically marginalized communities. Primarily using community-based research approaches, she offers a way to redress the underrepresentation of Black youth who are disproportionately underrepresented in the literature of youth civic engagement. Her body of scholarship can be found in various peer reviewed journals, practitioner outlets, and edited books which focus on youth development and community engagement. Dr. Webster also works with global ministries of education, agriculture, and youth and sports, with the objective of creating and evaluating public engagement and civic programs that aim to increase the positive engagement of youth in society.

Dawn Michele Whitehead

Dawn Michele Whitehead is the vice president of the Office of Global Citizenship for Campus, Community, and Careers at the Association of American Colleges and Universities (AAC&U), the leading national association dedicated to advancing the vitality and public standing of liberal education by making quality and equity the foundations for excellence in undergraduate education in service to democracy. Whitehead has written and presented nationally and internationally on global learning, community-based learning, experiential learning, and civic engagement. Prior to joining AAC&U, she served as the Director of Curriculum Internationalization at Indiana University-Purdue University Indianapolis (IUPUI) and was the faculty director for global service-learning programs. Whitehead earned her PhD from Indiana University, Bloomington.

Donn C. Worgs

Dr. Donn Worgs is a professor of political science at Towson University where he is also the director of African and African American studies and a cofounder of the Empowering Communities Project which seeks to help build the capacity of community-based organizations. He teaches and writes about a range of topics related to African American politics and community development.

Wei Lit Yew

Wei Lit Yew is a lecturer in the Department of Government and International Studies at Hong Kong Baptist University. Prior to this, he was a postdoctoral fellow at Yale-NUS College in Singapore. Based disciplinarily in comparative politics and environmental studies, his research has focused on the politics of development and environmental activism, and more broadly on civil society dynamics in China and Southeast Asia. Yew obtained a PhD in Asian and International Studies from City University of Hong Kong. He received his MSc in Comparative Politics (Asia) from the London School of Economics and his BIT from Multimedia University (Malaysia).

CPSIA information can be obtained
at www.ICGtesting.com
Printed in the USA
BVHW011139071021
618447BV00010B/123